D1224928

Also by Shirley O. Corriher

*CookWise: The Hows and Whys of Successful Cooking
with over 230 Great-Tasting Recipes*

BakeWise

*The Hows and Whys of Successful Baking
with over 200 Magnificent Recipes*

Shirley O. Corriher

SCRIBNER
New York London Toronto Sydney

SCRIBNER
A Division of Simon & Schuster, Inc.
1230 Avenue of the Americas
New York, NY 10020

Copyright © 2008 by Confident Cooking, Inc.
Photographs by AKELstudio, Inc.

First Scribner hardcover edition October 2008

SCRIBNER and design are registered trademarks of The Gale Group, Inc.,
used under license by Simon & Schuster, Inc., the publisher of this work.

For information about special discounts for bulk purchases,
please contact Simon & Schuster Special Sales:
1-800-456-6798 or business@simonandschuster.com

DESIGNED BY ERICH HOBBING

Text set in Sabon

Manufactured in the United States of America

10 9 8 7 6 5 4 3 2 1

Library of Congress Control Number: 2008032681

ISBN-13: 978-1-4165-6078-4
ISBN-10: 1-4165-6078-5

BakeWise is dedicated to

Chef Marty Thompson

and
the young chefs like him who study and work so hard
and
generously share their talents with us

My Gratitude and Thanks

Many talented cooks contributed to *BakeWise*.

Chef Marty Thompson diligently tested recipes for both *CookWise* and *BakeWise*. In spite of running his own very demanding cleaning service and catering business, and later attending a culinary academy, Marty would get up at 5 a.m. or work until very late to test my recipes with exacting precision.

Young as he was, Marty loved cooking and read every food book that he could get his hands on for years before he had the opportunity to become an outstanding student in an Atlanta culinary academy. One of his teachers would address questions to the class prefaced by, "Does anyone other than Mr. Thompson know . . . ?" Marty did not live long enough to complete his chef's training, but he will always be a young culinary hero and, to me, Chef Marty Thompson.

My husband, Arch, worked night and day on *BakeWise*. Even though sometimes I wasn't doing something the way he thought that I should, he always came through for me. A master of computer databases, Arch can retrieve information that no one else can find. And, most of all, he put up with me through the agonies and triumphs of working on a book. In his way, when I needed it the most, he was tender and supportive.

My friend Gena Berry is a food expert extraordinaire! And master organizer of food projects of any size. She manages the Taste of the NFL—the big dinner for about 3,500 the night before the Super Bowl. Gena managed both the final recipe testing and the food preparation for the photographs for *BakeWise*. Gena and Virginia Willis, author of *Bon Appétit, Y'all*, directed my DVD with cooking lessons (available at kitchensecretsrevealed.com). Through thick and thin, Gena jumped right in to help solve whatever problems I faced.

Maggie, Maggie Green! This book wouldn't be here without Maggie, my excellent line editor. Not only is Maggie a master of clear, direct writing—even with Shirley's molecules—but Maggie always knew what we should do and stayed calm through my frantic calls, Arch's frantic calls, and probably frantic calls from my editor, Beth Wareham.

BakeWise was blessed to have the incredible talent of a great young photographer, Alex Koloskov, a true genius with light. I was awed by his work and thrilled to get him for the photography for *BakeWise*.

BakeWise has truly been a team effort. Beth Wareham at Scribner has fought for the very best for *BakeWise* and I am so grateful. My agent, Judith Weber, has been in there pitching, making sure that I had what I needed for the book.

Thanks to the many talented experts at Scribner who contributed to *BakeWise*—Whitney Frick, Associate Editor; Rex Bonomelli, Art Director; Brian Belfiglio, Director of Publicity; my publicist, Kate Bittman; and my copyeditor, Suzanne Fass. What a good job she did. Alexandra Nickerson created a wonderful index.

Thanks to my friend Delores Custer, who got Lynn Miller, food stylist and former pastry chef, to do the styling for *BakeWise*. I really appreciate Lynn's talents and her cheerful, positive personality through the long hours. You have only to look at the pictures to see what an outstanding job she did.

I had taught many of these recipes or I had tested them for articles. I had a heroic team of home-front testers who came to my rescue over and over again. I got great suggestions for things that should be included in the recipe directions from my daughter, Terry Infantino. My son-in-law, Carmelo Infantino, was the delicate-job expert (doing such things as the intricate work of cutting the snowflake cookies). My daughter-in-law, opera singer Beth McCool, with much help from four-year-old Daniel, many times managed emergency testing of a recipe in spite of the demands of very young Kevin.

Then the recipes went to Gena's team of experts. I am so grateful to these outstanding bakers for all of their work both testing recipes and preparing dishes for the photography, many times under frantic time demands. Some, like Doris Koplin, have their own cookbook (Doris's is *The Quick Cook*), and both Doris and Barb Pires have operated baking businesses. Gil Kulers, *The Atlanta Journal-Constitution* wine columnist, makes my Tunnel of Fudge Cake frequently and prepared two versions. I am truly grateful to these experienced bakers: Alison Berry, Sue Clontz, Tamie Cook, Samantha Enzmann, Jerry Johnson, Shirley Lawrence, Julie Opraseuth, Vanessa Parker, Debbie Peterson, Robert Schiffli, Judy Sellner, and Paula Skinner. Special thanks to Robert Schiffli for juggling mixers and food processors, getting us in and out of places for testing and the photography.

My thanks to Mary Taylor, who taught me so much about ovens and baking, and arranged for Arch and me to spend a day in a major oven manufacturer's test kitchen.

Special thanks to my science buddies:

Dr. Harold McGee, author of *On Food and Cooking*, for his major support—everything from looking after Arch and me when I got my titanium knee to the great fun of making presentations with him.

Dr. Sara Risch, international flavor chemist, who is a reliable source of information and a joy to have as a co-speaker on programs.

Dr. Rob Shewfelt, fruit and vegetable expert, and Dr. Carl Hosney, starch expert, always came to my rescue when I had questions.

Finally, my thanks and gratitude to many others who are named specifically in the text or recipes and to those who have been inadvertently omitted.

Contents

BAKEWISE

Introduction

My goal in *BakeWise* is to give you tools—information that you can use to make not just successful baked goods, but outstanding baked goods.

And in *BakeWise*, I strive to give you the information that you need to get the product that *you want*. Many times in cooking there is not a right or a wrong but simply a difference. For example, some people like fudgy brownies, some want cakey brownies, some want a crust on brownies, others want minimum crust. My goal is to explain what ingredient or technique produces these characteristics—reduce the flour in the brownie recipe to make it fudgy, beat vigorously with a mixer after you add the eggs to the batter for more crust.

I come from a science background (I was a research chemist for the Vanderbilt Medical School). I think it is fascinating that many times master bakers' directions follow almost exactly what the science texts say. For example, Chef Roland Mesnier, the White House executive pastry chef for twenty-five years—his directions for beating the egg-sugar mixture for a génoise are "right on" what the science texts' directions are for making the most stable foam.

Chef Roland cautions that reducing the speed when you are whipping the eggs is vital, because lengthy whipping at high speed produces large air bubbles, which will rise to the surface and pop during baking and produce a heavy cake. It is the same principle as overleavening a shortened cake. Roland's beating times are 5 minutes on high and 12 minutes on medium, until the foam is completely cool, thick, and shiny. Science texts say beating on high produces larger bubbles, medium speed is ideal for a stable foam, and that, as beating time is extended, the stability of the foam increases.

Pastry chef Paul Prosperi at The Culinary Institute of America gives students a clear example of why they should use medium speed and lengthy beating for a génoise. In *Baking Boot Camp,* Darra Goldstein describes Chef Paul showing the students how to observe the foam during beating. When beating on high, eventually the foam falls, and the same happens when beating on low. But when beating on medium, the foam remains high regardless of the beating time.

Other things that I get excited about are finding something that is really helpful—like how to read the label on baking powder to tell when it will release bubbles in baking (immediately after it is stirred into the batter or dough, after a few minutes, or in the hot oven). I definitely don't want a baking powder that makes 100% of the bubbles instantly. If I am doing several things at once and am slow getting the cake in the oven, or if I get interrupted by a phone call, I may lose most of my leavening.

I could never remember long chemical names, so I make a list of the acids that I want in a baking powder before I go to the store. I use the guidelines on page 47, which shows when each acid releases a specific percentage of bubbles for eight different acids used in baking powder. And I see that I want a baking powder that contains one or more of the following acids: monocalcium phosphate, sodium acid pyrophosphate, or sodium aluminum phosphate. Most of these release bubbles at all three stages.

MEASUREMENTS

Weights in the recipes in *BakeWise* are either averages from my actual weighing or are from the USDA National Nutrient Database for Standard Reference, which is online at www.nal.usda.gov/fnic/foodcomp/search. This database contains nutrient information on foods, and also their weights. The recipes were tested using standard cups, tablespoons, and teaspoons. In many places, I have given metric measures derived by calculation. The recipes have not been tested using metric measures.

HOW TO USE *BAKEWISE*

You can go to any chapter. For example, if you are making cookies, you can just go to the cookie chapter, you don't have to read other chapters first. You may see discussions of ingredients like flour in several different chapters. This is because, for different baked goods, you need to pay attention to different characteristics of flour.

EQUIPMENT: MIXER

I used a KitchenAid counter mixer and a KitchenAid hand mixer for putting together most recipes. I love the strength of the KitchenAid hand mixer and have found that I can use it many times when you would ordinarily need the counter mixer.

WHY I USE A BAKING STONE: BASIC PROBLEMS IN BAKING

In baking you have a constant battle going on. You need to get the batter or dough hot and rising before the heat from the top of the oven forms a crust on the baked good, holding it down. You want heat from the bottom and you want the baked good away from the hot top of the oven. But you don't want to burn the bottom. How can you do all of this? First, we need to take a look at how ovens work.

HOW OVENS WORK

Basic Operation

There are many types of home and commercial ovens, both gas and electric. Although the details are different, they all have some common properties.

Most ovens consist of an insulated enclosure with one or more heat sources. The oven is preheated to the desired temperature, and then the food to be baked is placed in it. The control unit turns the heat sources in the oven on and off according to the selected settings.

Temperature Settings

In the first place, realize that when you set the dial on your oven at 350°F/177°C, the manufacturer, in an effort to take into consideration that you just put a cold pan of batter into the oven, may have designed the oven to go to a slightly higher temperature. So, when you set your dial at 350°F/177°C, your oven may be designed to go to 360°F/182°C or 365°F/185°C in an effort to balance the cooler batter so that the oven, including the cooler pan of batter, does reach 350°F/177°C.

Oven Temperature Fluctuates

Also, when you set an oven at a given temperature—say, 350°F/177°C—it does not stay at that exact temperature. It goes up and down around that temperature (see graph below). When the oven reaches a certain temperature above the set point of 350°F/177°C—say, 370°F/188°C—the heating units cut off and then, when the oven cools down to a certain temperature below the set point of

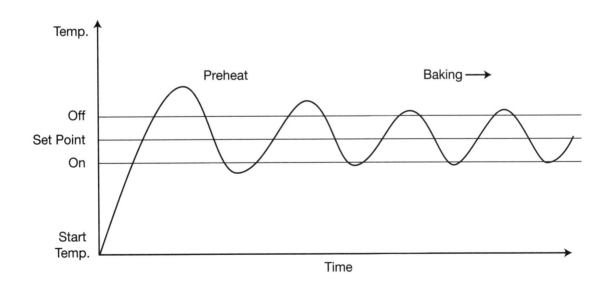

350°F/177°C—say, 330°F/166°C—the heating units come back on. So the oven is not at exactly 350°F/177°C the whole time, but fluctuates somewhere around that temperature. These temperature swings may be at least 15 to 20°F (8 to 11°C) above and below the set temperature, and can be greater for older ovens. The figure on page 3 indicates how oven temperatures swing above and below a set temperature.

This figure shows the approximate temperature variations in an oven during the preheat time and the baking time. A value is set for the desired baking temperature (the "Set Point" as shown by a horizontal line). When the heat sources in the oven are turned on to preheat, the temperature increases from the starting value and rises to a point where the control unit turns the heat off. The temperature in the oven continues to increase before it starts to fall, as shown in the figure, and it also falls below the set point before it rises again. The timing of the oscillations and amount of overshoot and undershoot of the desired baking temperature depend on the design and construction of the oven and its control unit. If the oven is empty or has a very light load, the peaks and valleys will be much sharper than those shown in the figure.

Fast Preheat

Modern ovens are designed to preheat FAST! Heating units in different locations in the oven come on full power until the oven reaches the set temperature. Any food in the oven can be burned to a crisp.

In times past, to get heat from the bottom and a cold top of the oven, you could put the batter or dough to be baked in a cold oven, turn the oven on, and be assured of heat from the bottom for a good rise and that the top of the batter or dough would not crust until the top of the oven got hot.

However, modern ovens can have heating units at different locations in the oven, not just in the bottom. And, some modern ovens are designed to preheat FAST! Every heating unit in the oven comes on full power until the oven reaches the set temperature. Any food in the oven can be burned to a crisp. So this method is out.

A Baking Stone to the Rescue

A baking stone placed on a lower shelf and well preheated can give you fast, even heat from the bottom and let you keep your baked good away from the hot top of the oven.

A baking stone placed on a lower shelf and well preheated can give you fast, even heat from the bottom and let you keep your baked good away from the hot top of the oven. I have not used a baking stone in my cookie recipes because they don't have to rise much and the baking time is short.

I have a large (about 14 x 16 inches/36 x 41 cm) baking stone that is about ³⁄₄ inch (2 cm) thick. I place the stone on a shelf in the lower third of the oven, about 5 inches (13 cm) from the oven floor. I preheat the oven for 30 to 45 minutes to ensure that the stone is hot. Then, when I place my pan of batter or dough on the hot stone, I get instant, even heat to start my baked good rising fast. And since my shelf is low in the oven, I have some distance from the hot top of the oven. With the very even heat of the stone, I don't have to worry about burning on the bottom.

A baking stone, especially a thicker one (¾ inch/2 cm), holds its temperature so in spite of the oven temperature going up and down a little, the stone stays right there on the set temperature.

Steam in the Oven

Back to our basic problem in baking—how to keep the top from crusting before the baked good fully rises. For yeast doughs and baked goods like cream puffs (pâte à choux), a moisture-filled oven can help keep the top of the baked good moist and expanding.

Ideally, if the oven is full of steam when you place a loaf of bread or pâte à choux dough in, the moisture will condense on the cooler dough and keep it moist for a while.

Not many home ovens have a steam option, but you can make a good steamer with a heavy, ovenproof pan (never, never use heatproof glass—it will break) and a few stones. Peter Nyberg, an outstanding sourdough baker, taught me how to do this.

Place a few clean small rocks (about 1 to 2 inches/2.5 to 5 cm each—you can buy these at a gardening store) in a pan with 2-inch (5-cm) sides and place the pan on the floor of the oven near the front of the stove. You are going to pour about 1½ cups (355 ml) of boiling water over the pre-heated rocks before you put the bread in the oven. This steam will condense on the dough to keep it moist and allow a good "oven rise."

For the boiling water, place a saucepan with about 2 cups (473 ml) of water on a burner and bring to a low boil. Wear oven mitts and be *very careful* to have your arms and face out of the way when you pour the boiling water over the hot stones. A great billow of super-hot steam blasts up from the pan and can cause severe burns.

Opening the Oven Door

When you open the oven door, the temperature drops dramatically. I was shocked to realize how great this drop is. Even if you only open the door long enough to touch the top of the cake or quickly insert and remove a toothpick to test for doneness (about 30 seconds), the temperature drop can be 150°F/66°C or more. You can see that if you frequently open the oven door, it can take "forever" for the cake to get done.

Even though you have a well-preheated oven, if you open the oven door, walk across the kitchen, pick up the pan of batter, walk back across the kitchen, place the pan in the oven, and close the oven door (the time that the oven was open can be over 1 minute) the drop in the oven temperature can be 175°F/79°C. Recovery time can be several minutes.

Opening the oven door, for whatever reason, may cause burning. When the temperature drops so far below the set temperature, the heating units have to come on to get the oven back up to temperature.

Just being aware of how ovens work can make you a more careful, better baker—one who limits oven door opening.

Bakeware

Mary Taylor, now retired from a major oven manufacturer, is a true oven expert who taught me much about ovens. Mary cautioned that many baking problems come from differences in bakeware. A dark pan is going to absorb more heat than a lighter one and can easily burn baked goods.

A heavier pan made of a metal that distributes heat well, such as aluminum, can give you excellent baked goods.

INGREDIENTS THAT I USE

Flour

I use a number of different types of flour that have different characteristics and different weights for a given volume. In the ingredient lists, I specify the type of flour, the weight in both ounces and grams, the volume, and how I measured the volume. Weighing is the most accurate way to follow a recipe, but many home cooks do not have a scale. In measuring volume, there can be more than a 2-tablespoon (0.5-oz/14-g) difference per cup in different measuring methods (dipping the cup into the flour and leveling it against the inside of the bag versus spooning the flour into a cup and leveling it with a straightedge). So how you measure the flour does matter.

I find that many cooks will not read this Introduction or the headnote on a recipe that explains how the ingredients were measured. They do, however, read the ingredient line, so that is where I put which measuring technique was used.

Sugar

Sugar in the ingredient lists is regular granulated sugar unless otherwise specified. Superfine, light brown, dark brown, and confectioners' sugar are called for in some recipes, and are listed as such in the ingredient list.

Butter

Unsalted butter is used in most of the baking recipes. If a type of butter is not specified, it is unsalted.

Eggs

Grade A large eggs, which were kept refrigerated, are used throughout this book. Many recipes give directions for warming eggs by allowing them to stand in hot water.

Starches

Tapioca Starch/Tapioca Flour

Asian markets are the best place to buy this starch. You can get a 1-pound (454-g) bag for under $2.00. It may be labeled tapioca starch or tapioca flour. It is a root starch that freezes and thaws beautifully, and remains crystal-clear hot or cold, making it ideal for many fruit pies.

It does not thicken firm enough to be cut cleanly, but rather makes a crystal-clear thick coating. You can add a small amount of cornstarch to get a firmer product, but for clarity when cold, you need to use primarily tapioca starch with a small amount of cornstarch. Cornstarch-thickened cherry pies can be yucky cloudy-looking when cold.

Potato Starch

Most supermarkets carry potato starch, but rather than with the cornstarch or flour it is found with the kosher ingredients, where the matzo meal is located. Potato starch swells to huge granules—much larger than any other starch. This starch can hold water for a moister cake, but it can dramatically change the texture. Using a small amount, such as substituting it for 10% of the flour in a pound cake, would loosen the very tight pound cake texture just a breath and not really be detectable. But in a regular cake, it can produce a very coarse texture. Sand cakes with a very coarse, open texture are made with a larger amount of potato starch.

Potato starch is a potent thickener. It takes only 2¼ teaspoons (0.3 oz/8 g) to thicken 1 cup (237 ml) liquid, while it takes 2 tablespoons (0.5 oz/14 g) flour or 1 tablespoon plus 1 teaspoon (0.35 oz/9 g) cornstarch to thicken the same cup of liquid.

Salt

My favorite salt is sea salt. For baked goods, the texture needs to be fine. I do have a salt grinder and use it to grind sea salt. A sea salt like Maldon that is in the form of delicate flakes is ideal for baking. You can substitute sea salt tablespoon for tablespoon with regular granular table salt. You need 1½ tablespoons Morton kosher salt (blue box) to get the same weight of salt as 1 tablespoon granular table salt. And you need 2 tablespoons of Diamond Crystal kosher (red and white box) salt to get the same weight of salt as 1 tablespoon granular table salt.

Milk

Milk is whole milk unless otherwise indicated.

CHAPTER ONE

Cakes, Luscious Cakes! Muffins, Quick Breads, and More

Priceless Knowledge in This Chapter

How to create your own perfect cakes

How to spot cakes that won't work and how to fix them

How to make cakes, muffins, and quick breads more moist

Even if you have never baked, how to ice a cake as spotlessly smooth as glass and looking as if it came from an elegant professional bakery

How to read the label on baking powder and know whether it will produce bubbles only immediately, after a few minutes, only in the hot oven, or at all three times

Recipes Include

Southern cakes like the super-moist Dinner-on-the-Grounds Coconut Cake, bourbon-soaked Lane Cake, and Serious Rum Cake

Elegant cakes like the French Cake aux Fruits and the Deep, Dark Chocolate Cake with Ganache and Chocolate Ruffles

Spectacular cakes like Improved Tunnel of Fudge Cake and a breathtaking chocolate sculpture, Bali's Alabaster Chocolate Tower

Favorites like Shirley Corriher's "Touch-of-Grace" Southern Biscuits (see photograph insert), Shirley's Crazy Cake, and Golden Brown Puffed Cheesy Rice Spoon Bread

The Recipes

Baked creations leavened with baking powder and baking soda—chemically leavened baked goods—may sound scientific, but here are luscious, moist cakes; ethereal, fluffy biscuits; and deep, dark chocolate cakes. Lose yourself in soft, moist, fall-apart-tender morsels of cake with unbelievably creamy icing.

Yeast doughs can't contain much sugar. More than one tablespoon of sugar per cup of flour will wreck gluten (see page 485). And, only a few yeast doughs, like brioche, contain much butter.

Steam/egg-leavened cakes like génoise, chiffon cakes, and angel food cakes can contain only so much fat. On the other hand, biscuits, scones, shortened cakes, muffins, and quick breads leavened by baking soda and baking powder can be rich and wonderful.

Baked goods leavened by chemical leaveners like baking soda and baking powder are rich and luscious—absolutely delicious.

Baked goods leavened with baking powder and baking soda run from doughs like biscuits and scones, to regular batters like cakes, muffins, and quick breads, all the way to thinner batters like spoon bread.

The French and Italians have their beautiful egg-leavened tortes like feather-light genoise. My beloved moist layer cakes with gooey icing are more a part of British and American culinary heritage.

The Recipe

Our grandmothers had a repertoire of cakes that they cooked from memory. These may have been learned from years of standing at their mother's side. However, modern cake making is a far cry from a dash of this and a pinch of that. It is no longer a matter of "try this, and if it doesn't work, try something else." Most cake experts like Rose Beranbaum, Bruce Healy, Nick Malgieri, Susan Purdy, or Carole Walter, to name a few, do not just guess at the amounts of ingredients to go in a cake. They start a cake by doing the math—checking to see if the recipe is balanced.

BALANCING THE RECIPE

The primary four ingredients of cakes—flour, sugar, fat (butter, shortening, or oil), and eggs—are in balance in a successful cake.

Flour and eggs contain the proteins that set to hold the cake. They are the structural elements; however, they can dry the cake. When some of the proteins in flour form gluten, they absorb water, which removes some moisture from the cake. Egg whites are incredible drying agents.

The four main cake ingredients—flour, sugar, fat, and eggs—are in balance in a successful cake.

Sugar and fat, on the other hand, make the cake tender and moist but they can wreck the structure. Fat coats flour proteins to prevent their joining to form gluten, and too much sugar prevents proteins from setting, so that the cake ends up being pudding.

For a successful cake, the structural elements (flour and eggs) have to be balanced with the structure wreckers (sugar and fat). If you have too much flour and/or eggs, the cake will be dry. If you have too much sugar and/or fat, the cake will not set. The perfect balance of the four main ingredients creates a moist, tender cake.

PERFECT BALANCE—*QUATRE QUARTS*—THE POUND CAKE

As far as structure is concerned, the classic pound cake is the perfect balance of ingredients. In *The Art of the Cake*, Bruce Healy explains that *quatre quarts* means four quarters, or four equal weights. The classic pound cake contains a pound of each of the primary ingredients: flour, sugar, fat, and eggs, which makes a huge cake.

THE "MODERN" POUND CAKE

The only problem is that a classic pound cake is dry and minimally sweet—not necessarily delicious. Many master bakers today make small changes to improve pure or classic pound cakes. For example, Bruce Healy substitutes an egg yolk and potato starch for 10% of the flour for a moister, more tender cake. For additional moisture, Rose Levy Beranbaum adds a little milk and leavening, while Susan Purdy adds 1 teaspoon baking powder and beats the yolks and whites separately.

For the most part, pound cake recipes in cookbooks today resemble classic pound cake recipes only in their lack of, or limited, leavening.

The Great American Pound Cake

My daughter-in-law's mother, Bonnie, is of Moravian descent, and makes those wonderful paper-thin spice cookies. Bonnie is an outstanding baker and her pound cake is said to be "the best." My stepdaughter's friend's mother, Frances, is said to make the best pound cake anywhere. John Egerton, in his book *Southern Food*, gives a great Southern pound cake recipe. And then, Sylvia Hocking, of *Sylvia's Cakes & Breads*, says, "This is undoubtedly one of the most popular cakes that ever came out of my shop! I have shipped them all over the United States and got nothing but rave reports."

Now, my fascinating discovery is that these four great cakes are all essentially the same recipe! They all have 3 cups flour, about 3 cups sugar, 1½ to 1¾ cups fat, 5 or 6 eggs, a little leavening (under a teaspoon), 2 to 3 teaspoons flavoring, and 1 cup liquid. Each has a different liquid: Bonnie's has sour cream, Frances's uses buttermilk, John's has heavy cream, and Sylvia's has milk. With the sour cream, Bonnie also uses ⅓ cup whole milk to compensate for the fact that cream or sour cream has a high fat content and therefore less liquid for creating steam than does milk or buttermilk.

So, Happy, Happy, Happy! I had a great pound cake recipe—THE Great American Pound

Cake. People all over the country had proclaimed this cake to be the best! Bonnie and Frances prepared their cakes in a large 12-cup (2.8-L) Bundt pan, John's cake is in a 10-inch (25-cm) tube pan, and Sylvia's directions say prepare it in a 10-inch (25-cm) tube pan or two 9 x 5 x 3-inch (23 x 13 x 8-cm) loaf pans.

I did "the math" on the cake (see page 33 for details about "The Math") to see if the weights of the ingredients were in balance. To do this, I fit the weights of the ingredients into the baker's formulas. (All of this will be covered in the following section. If you like, you may read ahead to understand baker's formulas, page 29). I have only given you "the math" in a few places, but the necessary ingredient weights are in many recipes so that you can do the calculations if you like.

If you look at "The Math" for The Great American Pound Cake (page 33), you will see that this recipe is not in balance and predicted not to work. It has too much sugar and too much fat to be a technically successful cake. So it's not technically perfect. But thousands of people can't be wrong!

Undeterred by the scientific prediction of failure, I charged ahead making the cake. I decided to make the cake with sour cream, and I wanted to do the two large loaves. Joyously, I prepared the pound cake perfectly, beating air into the butter, beating air into the sugar-butter mixture, and beating in one egg at a time—all the techniques for a great cake. It was to bake at 325°F/163°C for an hour for loaves to an hour and a half for the Bundt or tube pan.

I couldn't wait for the timer to ring. At the sound of the bell, I rushed to the oven. I was devastated! Both loaves were not only flat; they were sunken in the middle—really "sad." How could this be? This was THE Great American Pound Cake that everyone raved over.

With determination, I prepared the cake again—this time with whole milk and in the loaf pans. The same results—now, four sad cakes went into the freezer. Once again, I made the cake—this time with buttermilk, and instead of the loaf pans, I used a large Bundt pan. The finished cake was a little dipped in the middle, but almost level, and of course, when I turned the cake out of the pan, the cake was perfect! I brushed it with a melted apple jelly glaze and it was truly a work of art.

I made the cake again—this time with sour cream and in a 10-inch (25-cm) tube pan. It was beautiful! Remember the statue of *The Thinker*—remember "the math" that predicted failure. It's no wonder that the loaf pound cakes were sunken in the center and had not domed. The recipe is low on flour and eggs in relation to sugar and fat; it doesn't have enough protein to provide structure. But when the cake is baked in a Bundt pan or tube pan, since the cake is completely in the pan, you can get away with less structure.

Happy, Happy, Happy! I had a great pound cake recipe—THE Great American Pound Cake. People all over the country had proclaimed this cake to be the best!

Since the recipe is low on flour and eggs in relation to sugar and fat, the cake batter doesn't have enough protein to provide structure to create a nice domed top. In a Bundt pan or tube pan, since the cake does not have to rise above the pan, you can get away with less structure. Also, you invert the cake, so the slightly sunken top is now hidden. No one knows that it didn't look perfect! And the cake tastes wonderful!

"A SAD CAKE IS A HAPPY CAKE"

Once again, I made the cake. I divided the batter in half. I filled one loaf pan with the batter just as I mixed it. To the other half of the batter, I stirred in ½ cup (2.2 oz/62 g) flour and an egg—the proteins that were missing for sound structure. I baked them side by side. The first loaf was sunken, just as it had been before. But the loaf with the additional flour and egg domed nicely!

Now, the proof of the pudding is in the eating. When we tasted both loaves, the sad, sunken loaf was by far more moist and the taste was much better than the domed loaf. I told my next-door neighbor and her mother, Dodgie Shaffer, how good the sad cake tasted. My neighbor's mother said, "You know, my mother (Mary Walden) had a saying that 'a sad cake is a happy cake.'"

So, the moral of all of this is, "Make cakes like this Great American Pound Cake in a Bundt or tube pan." They can't fail. So what if they come out level or a little sunken on top—who cares? You're turning them upside down. No one will ever know!

So that you can see the changes that I made, I have included the original recipe for The Great American Pound Cake; but do not bake it, go on to Shirley's Even Greater American Pound Cake (page 22) where I incorporated all of the improvements (page 18). And then, I learned about adding whipped cream—not whipping cream, but cream that is whipped until soft peaks form (see page 19 for more). So, that improvement is in Shirley's Even Greater Pound Cake, too.

"Make it in a Bundt or tube pan." Delicious cakes that have too much sugar and fat to have a good structure will be perfect in a tube or Bundt pan. Because you invert the cake, no one ever knows that the original top wasn't perfectly domed.

The Great American Pound Cake

A delicious cake that won the hearts of America. This recipe is here to make certain points. You may not want to bake it, but for actual baking skip down to Shirley's Even Greater American Pound Cake, page 22.

What This Recipe Shows

An excess of sugar and butter makes this cake wonderfully moist.

The cake should be baked in a 12-cup (2.8-L) Bundt or a 10-inch (25-cm) tube pan, which does not require as much protein to provide structure to look perfect as a loaf cake does.

The flavoring is blended with the fat, because the fat is a great flavor carrier and distributes the flavorings well.

There will be holes in the cake if the leavening is not evenly distributed, so it is important to beat the flour and leavening and any dry ingredients together well with a fork or hand beater.

Nonstick cooking spray with flour
1 cup (8 oz/227 g) unsalted butter, cut in
    2-tablespoon (1-oz/28-g) pieces
    [6.4 oz/181 g fat]*
1/2 cup (3.4 oz/96 g) shortening [3.4 oz/96 g
    fat]*
3 cups (21 oz/595 g) sugar
1 teaspoon (5 ml) pure vanilla extract
1 teaspoon (5 ml) pure almond extract
1/2 teaspoon (2.5 ml) pure lemon extract
5 large eggs (8.75 oz/248 g)
3 cups (13.2 oz/374 g) spooned and leveled
    bleached all-purpose flour

1 teaspoon (5 g) baking powder
1 teaspoon (6 g) salt
1 cup (237 ml) heavy cream [2.9 oz/83 g fat;
    5.2 oz/147 g water]*
1/3 cup (79 ml) buttermilk or whole milk (see
    Note)
Soaking Solution for Pound Cake (recipe
    follows)
Shiny Glaze for Pound Cake (page 18),
    optional
Icing for Pound Cake (page 18), optional

*The weights in square brackets are for doing "The Math," page 33.

Note: The Great American Pound Cake original recipe calls for 1 cup (237 ml) of buttermilk or milk. You can substitute sour cream or heavy cream for the milk, but if you do be sure to add ⅓ cup (80 ml) of extra milk or buttermilk due to the higher fat content of the cream or sour cream.

1. Arrange a shelf in the lower third of the oven, place a baking stone on it, and preheat the oven to 350°F/177°C.

2. Spray a 10-inch (25-cm) tube pan or a 12-cup (2.8-L) Bundt pan generously with nonstick cooking spray with flour.

3. With a mixer on medium speed, beat the butter to soften. Add the shortening and beat until the mixture is light and pale in color, about 3 minutes. Add the sugar and continue to beat (cream) until very light, scraping down the sides and the bottom of the bowl at least once. While creaming, feel the bowl. If it does not feel cool, place in the freezer for 5 minutes and then continue creaming.

4. Beat in the vanilla, almond, and lemon extracts. On the lowest speed, beat in the eggs, one at a time.

5. In a medium bowl, with a fork or hand mixer, beat together the flour, baking powder, and salt for at least 30 seconds.

6. On the lowest speed, blend one-third of the flour mixture into the butter mixture. Alternate adding cream, and then flour, until all of both are incorporated. Scrape down the sides and across the bottom of the bowl at least once with a large flexible spatula. Blend in the buttermilk just to incorporate.

7. Pour the batter into the prepared pan. Drop the pan onto the counter from a height of about 4 inches (10 cm) to knock out bubbles. Smooth the batter with a spatula.

8. Place the cake on the baking stone and bake until the cake springs back when lightly touched, or a toothpick inserted in the middle comes out clean but moist, about 1 hour. Ideally, the cake should not pull away from the sides until it has just come out of the oven. Place the cake in the pan on a rack to cool.

9. With a meat fork, punch holes in the cake and begin to slowly pour the Soaking Solution on the cake. Allow it to soak in, then pour again. Repeat until all of the soaking solution is absorbed. Allow to stand for about 10 minutes, and then shake the pan to loosen the cake all around. Allow the cake to stand in the pan for another hour to cool. Make sure that the cake is loosened from the pan by jarring it against the counter. Invert the cake onto the serving platter to finish cooling.

10. While the cake is still warm, brush and rebrush several times with the Shiny Glaze if you are using it. This cake improves upon standing for 2 or 3 days, well wrapped (see page 150) and refrigerated. If using icing, drizzle on the icing just before serving, not solidly but with drools that run down the side.

Soaking Solution for Pound Cake

2 cups (473 ml) water
2 cups (14 oz/397 g) sugar

1 tablespoon (15 ml) pure vanilla extract
1 teaspoon (5 ml) pure almond extract

In a heavy saucepan over medium heat, stir together the water and sugar and heat just until the sugar dissolves. Remove from the heat and stir in the flavorings.

Shiny Glaze for Pound Cake

1/4 cup (59 ml) apple or red currant jelly, melted, or 1/4 cup (59 ml) apricot or peach preserves or orange marmalade, melted and strained

1 tablespoon (15 ml) light corn syrup
1 teaspoon (5 ml) Grand Marnier liqueur

Stir together the melted jelly, corn syrup, and Grand Marnier. Brush the glaze onto the warm cake with a pastry brush until the glaze is absorbed. Rebrush several times.

Icing for Pound Cake

1 cup (4 oz/120 g) confectioners' sugar
2 to 3 tablespoons (30 to 45 ml) heavy cream

1/4 teaspoon (1.25 ml) pure vanilla extract

In a 2-cup (473 ml) measuring cup with a spout (so that you can pour a drizzle easily), stir together the sugar, cream, and vanilla. You want the consistency thick but pourable. Add more sugar or cream as needed. Drizzle on the icing, not solidly but with drools that run down the side.

SHIRLEY'S IMPROVED AMERICAN POUND CAKE

I can never leave well enough alone. I love really moist cakes. So I set out to make The Great American Pound Cake more moist. First, I decided to go with Bruce Healy's tip of substituting potato starch for 10% of the flour. The swollen granules of potato starch are larger than other starch granules. The cake still has pound-cake texture, but not quite as tight. Potato starch is available in most grocery stores, but it is not located with the flour or starch. It is probably sold with the matzo meal and other kosher ingredients.

Another great secret to cake moisture is to substitute oil for part of the fat. When the two flour proteins, glutenin and gliadin, join to form gluten, they grab water. This means that moisture is removed from the batter. We need a little bit of gluten to keep the cake from being crumbly, but if we can reduce the amount of gluten formed, the cake will be moister. Oil is perfect for this job. Fats grease flour proteins and prevent their joining to form gluten. Oil is much better at greasing the flour proteins than either butter or shortening (see page 70). Oil is definitely the ingredient of choice for moist cakes and muffins.

Substituting oil for part of the butter improves a cake's moisture. Oil greases flour proteins better than either butter or shortening to prevent gluten from forming and tying up water.

A STARTLING NEW INGREDIENT, "WHIPPED CREAM," CHANGES EVERYTHING

I had developed my Great American Pound Cake with all of the improvements that I just went over. But, wonder of wonder, something so great came along that I had to stop everything and include it too. My even more improved cake became Shirley's Even Greater American Pound Cake (page 22).

But first, let me tell you more about this amazing secret weapon for magnificent cakes. Heather Hurlbert, a wonderfully creative young chef, is the Executive Pastry Chef at the Cherokee Town Club in Atlanta, Georgia. Chef Heather makes many beautiful desserts, but when I took a bite of this pound cake, bright lights exploded in my head! This was the best pound cake that I had ever had! It turned my whole world upside down.

Chef Heather generously shares with us her recipe, Chef Heather Hurlbert's Magnificent Moist Whipped Cream Pound Cake. Of course it makes sense—why not whip the cream? You are introducing more air for a slightly lighter cake, and the texture of whipped cream introduces a softness and a moistness to a cake. And whipped cream has an incredible taste and texture with an airy silky smoothness, different from the same cream before whipping.

Actually, whipped cream in cakes has been around for a while. There is a cake recipe in the 1975 edition of *The Joy of Cooking* that uses whipped cream. And now that I was looking for whipped cream, I found others. I never noticed, possibly because I had not eaten the results and didn't realize how wonderful whipped cream in a cake can be.

Chef Heather Hurlbert's Magnificent Moist Whipped Cream Pound Cake

MAKES ONE LARGE 12-CUP (2.8-L) BUNDT CAKE, OR 24 SMALL FLUTED CAKES

This sensationally moist, wonderfully flavorful cake may instantly be your favorite pound cake. I love this cake plain—no blueberries. I just love the taste of the cake itself. I have the luxury of a stand mixer and a hand mixer so I can mix the cake in the stand mixer and have my hand mixer available to whip the cream. If you are using a hand mixer for everything, just rinse the beaters after Step 5 and chill them along with a mixing bowl for whipping the cream.

What This Recipe Shows

Using a little whipped cream in a cake lightens the texture, adds moisture, and produces a wonderful flavor.

Since fat is a great flavor carrier, adding flavoring to the butter-sugar mixture enhances its distribution.

I normally use nonstick cooking spray for Bundt pans, but Chef Heather prefers to grease well with butter and then sprinkle with flour and shake it around and dump out the excess. I think whatever you prefer is fine.

---

2 tablespoons each butter and flour to prepare the pan or pans

2 cups (16 oz/454 g) unsalted butter, cut in 2-tablespoon (1-oz/28-g) pieces

2¾ cups (19.3 oz/546 g) sugar

1 tablespoon (15 ml) pure vanilla extract

6 large eggs (10.5 oz/298 g), room temperature

2¾ cups (12.1 oz/343 g) spooned and leveled bleached all-purpose flour

½ cup (118 ml) heavy cream

2 cups (8 oz/227 g) fresh or frozen and thawed blueberries, optional

1. Generously butter a 12-cup (2.8-L) Bundt pan or 24 fluted brioche tins. Add 2 tablespoons (0.5 oz/14 g) flour and rotate the pan to coat. Dump out any excess.

2. Arrange a shelf in the lower third of the oven, place a baking stone on it, and preheat the oven to 350°F/177°C.

3. With a mixer on medium speed, beat the butter to soften. Add the sugar and continue to beat (cream) until very light and fluffy, scraping down the sides and the bottom of the bowl at least once. While creaming, feel the bowl; if it does not feel cool, place in the freezer for 5 minutes and then continue creaming.

4. Beat in the vanilla. On the lowest speed, beat in the eggs one at a time.

5. Add the flour in several batches, and mix just until blended well.

6. Place a medium bowl with the beaters and the heavy cream in the freezer to chill for 5 minutes. Then with the cold bowl and cold beaters, whip the cream until soft peaks form when the beater is lifted. Whip just a little beyond the soft peak stage.

7. Stir about one-quarter of the whipped cream into the batter. Then gently fold the rest of the whipped cream into the batter. If using, fold in the blueberries. Pour the batter into the prepared pan.

8. Place the cake in the oven on the stone and bake until a toothpick inserted near the center comes out moist but without crumbs, 50 to 60 minutes for the Bundt pan, about 20 minutes for small tins. Place the cake in the pan on a rack to cool for 10 minutes. Loosen the cake from the pan by jarring it against the counter. Invert the cake onto the serving platter to finish cooling.

OTHER APPLICATIONS FOR A REMARKABLE INGREDIENT

Once I learned how wonderful whipped cream was as an ingredient, I went wild. I tried it first in my Shirley's Even Greater American Pound Cake (page 22). Also, I instantly made my Magnificent Moist Golden Cake (page 37) with whipped cream. In both cakes, it was sensational! The texture was like velvet. The softness that it gives a cake is remarkable.

I moved on to Sweet Pears and Crunchy, Roasted Walnut Muffins and French Cake aux Fruits (pages 133 and 139). There is a whole world of cakes and other baked goods that may be improved by folding in ½ cup (118 ml) heavy cream whipped to soft peaks.

Shirley's Even Greater American Pound Cake

MAKES ONE 12-CUP (2.8-L) BUNDT CAKE OR ONE 10-INCH (25-CM) TUBE CAKE

An improved, really moist version of the delicious cake that is beloved all across America. With my improvements, the cake is sweet enough without pouring a soaking solution over it.

What This Recipe Shows

An excess of sugar and butter makes this cake moist, but without enough protein structure for a domed top.

The cake should be baked in a Bundt or tube pan, which does not require the cake to have as much protein to provide structure to look good as a loaf cake does.

Replacing some of the butter with oil makes this cake extra moist.

The flavoring is blended with the fat, because fat is a great flavor carrier and distributes the flavoring well.

Adding two egg yolks adds emulsifiers for an excellent texture and increased moisture.

Replacing some of the flour with potato starch adds moisture, and the large granules produce excellent texture—still tight like a pound cake, but not super tight.

There will be holes in the cake if the leavening is not evenly distributed, so it is important to beat the flour, leavening, and other dry ingredients together well with a fork or hand beater.

Whipping the cream makes a big difference. Heavy cream, whipped until soft peaks form when the beater is lifted, gives the cake a soft texture and adds moisture and wonderful taste.

Nonstick cooking spray with flour

¾ cup (6 oz/170 g) unsalted butter, cut in 2-tablespoon (1-oz/28-g) pieces [4.8 oz/136 g fat]*

½ cup (3.4 oz/96 g) shortening [3.4 oz/96 g fat]*

3 cups (21 oz/595 g) sugar

1 tablespoon (15 ml) pure vanilla extract

¼ teaspoon (1.25 ml) pure almond extract

⅓ cup (79 ml) (2.4 oz/70 g) canola oil

2 large egg yolks (1.3 oz/37 g)

5 large eggs (8.75 oz/248 g)

2⅔ cups (11.7 oz/332 g) spooned and leveled bleached all-purpose flour

¼ cup (1.6 oz/45 g) potato starch (in the kosher ingredient section)

1 teaspoon (5 g) baking powder

1 teaspoon (6 g) salt

¼ cup (59 ml) buttermilk

½ cup (118 ml) heavy cream

Cream Glaze (recipe follows), optional

Pound Cake Icing (page 24), optional

*The weights in square brackets are for doing "The Math," page 29.

1. Arrange a shelf in the lower third of the oven, place a baking stone on it, and preheat the oven to 350°F/177°C.

2. Spray a 10-inch (25-cm) tube pan or a 12-cup (2.8-L) Bundt pan generously with nonstick cooking spray with flour.

3. With a mixer on medium speed, beat the butter to soften. Add the shortening and beat until the mixture is light and pale in color, about 3 minutes. Add the sugar and continue to beat (cream) until very light, scraping down the sides and across the bottom of the bowl at least once. While creaming, feel the bowl; if it does not feel cool, place in the freezer for 5 minutes and then continue creaming.

4. Beat in the vanilla and almond extracts. Beat in the oil a little at a time until incorporated. On the lowest speed, with a minimum of beating, blend in the yolks, then the whole eggs, one at a time.

5. In a medium bowl, with a fork or hand mixer, beat together the flour, potato starch, baking powder, and salt for a full 30 seconds, until very well blended.

6. On the lowest speed, blend one-third of the flour mixture into the butter mixture. Alternate adding buttermilk, then the flour mixture, until all of both are incorporated, scraping down the sides and across the bottom at least once.

7. Place a bowl, beaters, and the heavy cream in the freezer to chill for 5 minutes. Whip the cream until soft peaks form when the beater is lifted. Whip just a little beyond the soft peak stage. Stir about one-quarter of the whipped cream into the batter to lighten. Then gently fold the rest of the whipped cream into the batter.

8. Pour the batter into the prepared pan. From a height of about 4 inches (10 cm), drop the pan onto the counter to knock out bubbles. Smooth the batter with a spatula.

9. Place the cake in the oven on the stone and bake until the cake springs back when touched, or a toothpick inserted in the middle comes out clean but moist, about 1 hour. (My baking usually takes about 1 hour and 5 minutes to 1 hour and 10 minutes.) Ideally, the cake should not pull away from the sides until it has just come out of the oven. Place the cake in the pan on a rack to cool for 10 minutes. Loosen the cake from the pan by jarring it against the counter. Invert the cake onto the serving platter to finish cooling.

10. While the cake is hot, if desired, brush and rebrush several times with the Cream Glaze. This cake improves upon standing for two or three days, well wrapped (see page 150) and refrigerated. When ready to serve, if desired, drizzle on Pound Cake Icing.

Cream Glaze for Pound Cake

$\frac{1}{3}$ cup (79 ml) heavy cream
$\frac{3}{4}$ cup (5.3 oz/150 g) sugar

2 tablespoons (30 ml) light corn syrup

In a small saucepan over medium heat, heat the cream, sugar, and corn syrup until the sugar is dissolved. Brush and rebrush onto the warm cake until the glaze is absorbed.

Pound Cake Icing

1 cup (4 oz/120 g) confectioners' sugar
2 to 3 tablespoons (30 to 45 ml) heavy cream

$\frac{1}{4}$ teaspoon (1.25 ml) pure vanilla extract

In a 2-cup (473-ml) measuring cup with a spout (so that you can pour a drizzle easily), stir together the sugar, cream, and vanilla. You want the consistency thick, but just barely pourable. Add more sugar or cream as needed. Drizzle the icing over the top of the cake, not solidly but with drools that run down the side.

Take-Your-Breath-Away Lemon Pound Cake

MAKES ONE 12-CUP (2.8-L) BUNDT CAKE OR ONE 10-INCH (25-CM) TUBE CAKE

Here is a lemon version of Shirley's Even Greater American Pound Cake (page 22) based on a recipe by Maida Heatter, the generous, loving great lady of desserts. In her Best Damn Lemon Cake, she has more nerve than I can muster. She uses a whole 1-ounce (30-ml) bottle of lemon extract for only 1½ cups (6.6 oz/187 g) of flour! Plus, she uses the zest of 3 lemons and ⅓ cup (79 ml) of lemon juice! Now that's courage. It's an incredible cake and inspired me to do this one.

What This Recipe Shows

An excess of sugar and butter makes this cake moist, but without enough protein structure for a domed top.

The cake should be baked in a Bundt or tube pan, which does not require the cake to have as much protein to provide structure to look good as a loaf cake does.

Replacing some of the butter with oil makes this cake extra moist.

The flavoring is blended with the fat, which is a great flavor carrier and distributes the flavoring well.

Adding two egg yolks adds emulsifiers for an excellent texture and increased moisture.

There will be holes in the cake if the leavening is not evenly distributed, so, it is important to beat the flour and leavening and other dry ingredients together well with a fork or hand beater.

Some ground almonds are added for both texture and subtle flavor undertones.

Whipping the cream makes a big difference. Heavy cream, whipped until soft peaks form when the beater is lifted, gives the cake a soft texture and adds moisture and wonderful taste.

Nonstick cooking spray with flour
¾ cup (6 oz/170 g) unsalted butter, cut in
    2-tablespoon (1-oz/28-g) pieces
½ cup (3.4 oz/96 g) shortening
3 cups (21 oz/595 g) sugar
⅓ cup (79 ml) canola oil
2 tablespoons (30 ml) pure lemon extract
Zest (grated peel) of 4 large lemons
3 tablespoons (45 ml) lemon juice
2 large egg yolks (1.3 oz/37 g)

5 large eggs (8.75 oz/248 g)
2⅔ cups (11.7 oz/332 g) spooned and leveled
    bleached all-purpose flour
½ cup (1.8 oz/52 g) finely ground blanched
    almonds
1 teaspoon (5 g) baking powder
1 teaspoon (6 g) salt
½ cup (118 ml) heavy cream
Lemon Glaze (recipe follows), optional
Pound Cake Icing (page 24), optional

1. Arrange a shelf in the lower third of the oven, place a baking stone on it, and preheat the oven to 350°F/177°C.

2. Spray a 10-inch (25-cm) tube pan or a 12-cup (2.8-L) Bundt pan with nonstick cooking spray with flour.

3. With a mixer on medium speed, beat the butter to soften. Add the shortening and beat until the mixture is light and pale in color, about 3 minutes. Add the sugar and continue to beat (cream) until very light, scraping down the sides and the bottom of the bowl at least once. While creaming, feel the bowl; if it does not feel cool, place in the freezer for 5 minutes and then continue creaming. Beat in the oil, lemon extract, lemon zest, and lemon juice.

4. On the lowest speed, with a minimum of beating, blend in the yolks and then the whole eggs, one at a time.

5. In a medium bowl, with a fork or hand mixer, beat together the flour, ground almonds, baking powder, and salt for a full 30 seconds.

6. On the lowest speed, blend the flour mixture into the butter mixture in three additions. Scrape down the sides and all the way to the bottom at least once.

7. Place a bowl, beaters, and the cream in the freezer to chill for 5 minutes. Whip the cream until soft peaks form when the beater is lifted. Whip just past this soft peak stage. Stir about one-quarter of the whipped cream into the batter to lighten. Then gently fold the rest of the whipped cream into the batter.

8. Pour the batter into the prepared pan. Drop the pan onto the counter from a height of about 4 inches (10 cm) to knock out bubbles. Smooth the batter with a spatula.

9. Place the cake in the oven on the stone and bake until the cake springs back when touched, or a toothpick inserted in the middle comes out clean but moist, about 1 hour. Ideally, the cake should not pull away from the sides until it has just come out of the oven. Place the cake in the pan on a rack to cool. Allow to stand in the pan for 10 to 20 minutes. Make sure that the cake is loosened from the pan by jarring it against the counter. Invert the cake onto the serving platter to finish cooling.

10. While the cake is hot, if desired, brush and rebrush several times with the Lemon Glaze. This cake improves upon standing for two or three days, well wrapped (see page 150) and refrigerated. When ready to serve, if desired, drizzle on Pound Cake Icing.

Lemon Glaze

⅓ cup (79 ml) lemon juice   ½ cup (3.5 oz/99 g) sugar

Stir the lemon juice and sugar together until the sugar is completely dissolved. If the sugar will not dissolve, heat briefly until dissolved. Brush on the hot cake. Brush and rebrush until the glaze is absorbed.

Serious Rum Cake

MAKES ONE 12-CUP (2.8-L) BUNDT CAKE OR ONE 10-INCH (25-CM) TUBE CAKE

This marvelous rum version of The Great American Pound Cake is truly memorable. Using a good-quality rum makes all the difference. Myers's is my favorite.

What This Recipe Shows

An excess of sugar and butter makes this cake moist, but without enough protein structure for a domed top.

The cake should be baked in a Bundt or tube pan, which does not require the cake to have as much protein to provide structure to look good as a loaf cake does.

Replacing some of the butter with oil makes this cake extra moist.

The flavoring is blended with the fat, which is a great flavor carrier and distributes the flavoring well.

Adding two egg yolks adds emulsifiers for an excellent texture and increased moisture.

There will be holes in the cake if the leavening is not evenly distributed, so it is important to beat the flour and leavening and other dry ingredients together well with a fork or hand beater.

Some ground almonds are added for both texture and subtle flavor undertones.

Whipping the cream makes a big difference. Heavy cream, whipped until soft peaks form when the beater is lifted, gives the cake a soft texture and adds moisture and wonderful taste.

Nonstick cooking spray with flour
3/4 cup (6 oz/170 g) unsalted butter, cut in
    2-tablespoon (1-oz/28-g) pieces
1/2 cup (3.4 oz/95 g) shortening
2 3/4 cups (19.3 oz/546 g) sugar
1/3 cup (79 ml) canola oil
1 teaspoon (5 ml) pure vanilla extract
1/4 cup (59 ml) dark rum, preferably Myers's
1 tablespoon (15 ml) orange zest (grated peel)
2 large egg yolks (1.3 oz/37 g)
4 large eggs (7 oz/198 g)

2 1/2 cups (11 oz/312 g) spooned and leveled
    bleached all-purpose flour
1 teaspoon (5 g) baking powder
1 teaspoon (6 g) salt
1/2 cup (1.8 oz/52 g) finely ground blanched
    almonds
1/2 cup (118 ml) buttermilk
1/2 cup (118 ml) heavy cream
Serious Rum Cake Glaze (recipe follows)
Serious Rum Cake Icing (recipe follows),
    optional

1. Arrange a shelf in the lower third of the oven, place a baking stone on it, and preheat the oven to 350°F/177°C.

2. Spray a 10-inch (25-cm) tube pan or a 12-cup (2.8-L) Bundt pan generously with nonstick cooking spray with flour.

3. With a mixer on medium speed, beat the butter to soften. Add the shortening and beat until the mixture is light and pale in color, about 3 minutes. Add the sugar and continue to beat (cream) until very light, scraping down the sides and the bottom of the bowl at least once. While creaming, feel the bowl; if it does not feel cool, place in the freezer for 5 minutes and then continue creaming.

4. Beat in the oil, the vanilla, rum, and orange zest.

5. On the lowest speed, blend in the egg yolks and then the whole eggs, one at a time.

6. In a medium bowl, with a fork or hand mixer, beat together the flour, baking powder, salt, and ground almonds for a full 30 seconds.

7. On the lowest speed, blend one-third of the flour mixture into the butter mixture. Alternate adding buttermilk, and then flour, until all of both are incorporated. Scrape down the sides and across the bottom at least once.

8. Place a bowl, beaters, and the cream in the freezer to chill for 5 minutes. Whip the cream until soft peaks form when the beater is lifted. Beat just a little beyond this soft peak stage. Stir about one-quarter of the whipped cream into the batter to lighten. Then gently fold the rest of the whipped cream into the batter.

9. Pour the batter into the prepared pan. Drop the pan onto the counter from a height of about 4 inches (10 cm) to knock out bubbles. Smooth the batter with a spatula.

10. Place the cake in the oven on the stone and bake until the cake springs back when touched, or a toothpick inserted in the middle comes out clean but moist, about 45 minutes to 1 hour. Ideally,

the cake should not pull away from the sides until it has just come out of the oven. Place the cake in the pan on a rack to cool. Allow the cake to stand for about 20 minutes. Shake the pan to loosen the cake all around. Make sure that the cake is loosened from the pan by jarring it against the counter. Invert the cake onto the serving platter to finish cooling.

11. For a shiny surface, while the cake is hot, brush and rebrush several times with the Serious Rum Cake Glaze. This cake improves upon standing for two or three days, well wrapped (page 150) and refrigerated. When ready to serve, if desired, drizzle on Serious Rum Cake Icing.

Serious Rum Cake Glaze

⅓ cup (79 ml) pineapple preserves
1 tablespoon (15 ml) light corn syrup

1 tablespoon (15 ml) dark rum, preferably
  Myers's

In a small saucepan, heat the preserves over very low heat just to melt. Strain through a medium strainer, catching the thin liquid that drips through into a small bowl. Stir the corn syrup and rum into the liquid. Brush on the warm cake. Brush and rebrush until the glaze is absorbed.

Serious Rum Cake Icing

1 cup (4 oz/120 g) confectioners' sugar
1 to 2 tablespoons (15 to 30 ml) heavy cream

1 teaspoon (5 ml) dark rum, preferably
  Myers's

In a 2-cup (473-ml) measuring cup with a spout (so that you can pour a drizzle easily), stir together the sugar, cream, and rum. You want the consistency very thick but just barely pourable. Add more sugar or cream as needed. Drizzle the icing over the top of the cake, not solidly, but with drools that run down the side.

BAKER'S FORMULAS ("THE MATH")

In a successful cake, the four main ingredients—flour, sugar, fat, and eggs—are in balance. Professional bakers have worked out three mathematical formulas to balance the ingredients. Years ago, when cakes were primarily pound cakes, or first cousins to pound cakes, the first formula was: the weight of the sugar should be equal to the weight of the flour. That makes sense—one structure breaker and one structure maker in perfect balance.

The second formula was: the weight of the eggs should be equal to or greater than the weight of the fat. The toughening effect of the eggs is balanced by the tenderizing effect of the fat. Perfect: now we have all the ingredients balanced. Why do we need a third formula? The third formula was: the weight of the liquid (which includes the weight of the eggs and any other liquid) should equal the weight of the sugar (or flour, since they are the same). You must have enough liquid to dissolve the sugar without using up the liquid that is needed for the starch in the flour to swell.

These are known as the formulas for regular shortened cakes (also known as lean cakes) and are summarized below.

FORMULAS FOR REGULAR SHORTENED CAKES (LEAN CAKES)
1. The weight of the sugar should be equal to or less than the weight of the flour.
   weight of sugar = or < weight of flour
2. The weight of the eggs should be equal to or greater than the weight of the fat.
   weight of eggs = or > weight of fat
3. The total weight of the liquid (eggs and any other liquid) should equal the weight of the sugar.
   weight of liquid including eggs = weight of sugar

"High-Ratio" Cakes

Fortunately, ingredients have improved and we now have cake flour, which is ground much finer and bleached by chlorination. Fat adheres to chlorinated starch, producing a better-combined batter. We can get a more uniform dispersion of the fat and the air bubbles.

Another improvement is that some modern fats like Crisco, or even extra virgin olive oil, contain emulsifiers that can hold the fat and liquids of the batter together much better. This means that batters can now hold both more fat and more liquid. In a regular cake, the weight of the fat ran 35 to 50% of the weight of the flour. Now, using fat with emulsifiers, the weight of the fat runs 40 to 70% of the weight of the flour.

Fat adheres to chlorinated starch, producing a better-combined batter— more uniform dispersion of the fat and the air bubbles.

With these superior ingredients, bakers can make cakes moister and sweeter. The emulsifiers allow more liquid and with more liquid you can have more sugar. Remember, there has to be enough liquid to dissolve the sugar without taking liquid away from the starch. In regular shortened cakes, also called lean cakes, the weight of the sugar equaled the weight of the flour or the limit was (as baker's percentages go—page 32) 100% sugar based on flour.

So new formulas evolved with these great ingredients. This time, instead of the weight of the sugar equaling the weight of the flour, the formula is: the weight of the sugar equals or exceeds the weight of the flour. In modern cakes using cake flour, the weight of the sugar is frequently 125% the weight of the flour. The weight of the sugar can be as high as 140% the weight of the flour, or in a chocolate cake, even up to 180%.

The second formula is: the weight of the eggs should exceed the weight of the fat. With more fat, it is important that the cake have enough structural ingredients (proteins) to set the cake. Some bakers figure that ideally the weight of the eggs should be 110% the weight of the fat. There is margin for less, but minimally you need equal weights of eggs and fat.

Now, since we can have more liquid, the third formula has changed to: the weight of the liquid (including eggs) should equal or exceed the weight of the sugar. Practically, the weight of the sugar should not exceed 90 to 95% of the weight of the liquid. Lean cakes, or cakes with nonemulsified shortening, usually contain equal weights of eggs and milk (liquid), while cakes with emulsified shortening can get as high as 165% milk to eggs.

Cakes with the weight of the sugar equal to or greater than the weight of the flour are known as "high-ratio" cakes, and the formulas are summarized below.

FORMULAS FOR "HIGH-RATIO" CAKES

1. The weight of the sugar should be equal to or greater than the weight of the flour.

   weight of sugar = or > weight of flour
2. The weight of the eggs should be greater than the weight of the fat.

   weight of eggs > weight of fat
3. The weight of the liquid (eggs and milk) should be equal to or greater than the weight of the sugar.

   weight of liquid including eggs = or > weight of sugar

These formulas are not ironclad, but if variations get too great, you will have noticeable changes from a balanced cake. When the sugar is increased by 25%, volume increases and the texture is more tender, but the crumb is coarser and less uniform. When the sugar is decreased by 25%, volume is reduced and there is finer grain, but tougher and tighter texture. A 25% increase in fat produces no larger grain but a slight reduction in volume and a slightly greasy mouthfeel. A 25% increase in liquid produces a cake with reduced volume, but a tighter fine grain and a moist, tender crumb. In a cake with 25% reduction in the liquid, the grain becomes coarse and less uniform, the texture is still fairly tight and the cake is dry, but the volume is increased.

Notice that all these formulas deal with weights, not volume. For example, one cup of sugar weighs about 7 oz (198 g) and one cup of flour (depending on the type of flour and on the way the cup is filled) weighs 4 to 5 oz (113 to 142 g). Cake flour spooned into a cup and leveled is about 4 oz (113 g); measured the same way, bleached all-purpose flour like Gold Medal weighs about 4.4 oz (125 g). It is a big help to make a chart of the weights of common cake ingredients to refer to when creating a cake recipe (see page 495).

Variations in Ingredients

I take into account significant variations in composition of ingredients. For example, butter is only 81% fat, so I would get misleading results assuming that all of the butter is fat. I round this off to 80% for easier calculations.

There can be significant differences in heavy cream. My grocery store carton indicates that it is 33% fat, so 1 cup is 2.6 oz fat and 5.4 oz water.

BAKER'S PERCENTAGES

Baker's percentages are used by professional bakers to designate the amounts of the various ingredients in a recipe. They may be used, for example, to compare the amount of fat to the amount of flour. The flour weight is set at 100%. The baker's percentage guide for fat in a cake is that the weight of the fat should run 30 to 70% the weight of the flour. These are ballpark estimates and vary a little from one technical book to another. Some books say 40 to 60%.

Baker's percentage guides for sugar vary, depending upon whether the cake is a lean cake (regular shortened cake) or a high-ratio cake. With a high-ratio cake that uses cake flour and a fat with emulsifiers or egg yolks, the weight of the sugar can be up to 145% of the weight of the flour. The finely ground cake flour absorbs more liquid, and the emulsifiers bind liquid and fat better, allowing more liquid to be used. Since a cake needs enough liquid to dissolve all of the sugar, more liquid permits more sugar.

But for a lean cake (regular shortened cake), with all-purpose flour and no extra emulsifiers, the weight of the sugar should not run over 100% the weight of the flour.

USING "THE MATH" TO SPOT BAD RECIPES

You can check a cake recipe to make sure that it falls in the range of workable recipes by checking the weights of the ingredients. Using "the math" you can predict a lot about the cake's outcome. If the math indicates a recipe with an excessive amount of flour and/or eggs (proteins), the cake will have a strong structure but may be dry. If the recipe has an excess of sugar and fat, like The Great American Pound Cake, it may be lacking in structure, but it may be moist and delicious.

The example for The Great American Pound Cake recipe (page 16) indicates exactly how the cake came out.

DIFFERENT CRITERIA FOR DIFFERENT CAKES

The goal for layer cakes is to produce a level layer, while loaf cakes can be domed, or like the pound cake, if they are sunken they can be inverted. The formulas and percentages apply beautifully to level cakes. So I can use the formulas to create a moist basic layer that can be cut into three layers, which can be made into many fine cakes. Loaf cakes will be covered on page 137.

USING FORMULAS TO CREATE A MOIST BASIC CAKE

Initially, I wanted to make this cake with self-rising flour because the leavening is evenly distributed, producing an even-textured cake with no holes. I made cake after cake, but I could not get the sweet, moist layer that I wanted without cake flour. The combination of the emulsifiers (in the egg yolks) and the cake flour permit the batter to hold more liquid, which enables the use of more sugar to produce the sweet, moist layer that I wanted. So if I want a level cake, cake flour is a necessity.

I want to make a single 9 x 2-inch (23 x 5-cm) round moist layer that I can slice horizontally into

"The Math" for The Great American Pound Cake (page 16)

I am only going to include "the math" for a cake in a few places. So if you are not interested, simply bake these wonderful cakes and enjoy them. For those who want to do the math, in many recipes the major ingredient weights are given so that you may do the math yourself.

INGREDIENT	WEIGHTS IN THE RECIPE
Flour	(13.2 oz/374 g)
Sugar	(21 oz/595 g)
Eggs	(8.75 oz/248 g)
Fat (butter + shortening + cream)	(6.4 oz/181 g) + (3.4 oz/96 g) + (2.9 oz/83 g) = (12.7 oz/360 g)
Liquid (which includes eggs)	(5.2 oz/147 g) + (2.5 oz/71 g) + (8.75 oz/248 g) = (16.4 oz/466 g)

Applying Baker's Formulas

The weight of the sugar should be equal to the weight of the flour in a lean cake. In a high-ratio cake, the weight of the sugar can be greater than the weight of the flour. If cake flour were used, this cake would be halfway to high-ratio. If we added several egg yolks, it *would* be a high-ratio cake.

Actually, as it is, this cake is a lean cake, and the weight of the sugar should be equal to the weight of the flour. (For simplification only ounces are used in the calculations below.)

21 oz sugar is not = 13.2 oz flour   Not OK

The weight of the eggs should be equal to or greater than the weight of the fat.

8.75 oz eggs is not = or > 12.7 oz fat   Not OK

The weight of the liquid should be greater than the weight of the sugar.

16.4 oz liquid is not > 21 oz sugar   Not OK

Checking the math for The Great American Pound Cake indicates that the cake will fail. When I made The Great American Pound Cake in loaf pans, the results were just as the formulas had predicted—sad, sunken cakes. They had too much sugar and too much fat for good structure, but they were delicious. I found a solution by using a Bundt pan. Since the cake is inverted, no one knows that the original top was slightly sunken. This can be done with loaf pans, too. Slice the top so that it is level and invert the cake. You can decorate or glaze the top, which used to be the bottom.

three layers. I know from experience that this will require about 7 oz (for simplicity I am limiting my calculations to ounces only) cake flour. Using the weights from the table on page 495, this is about 1½ cups (4.9 x 1.5 = 7.3 oz) if you scoop the cup into the flour, and then press the cup against the side of the bag to level. It is about 1¾ cups (1.75 x 4.1 oz = 7.1 oz) if you spoon the flour into the cup and carefully scrape across the top to level. A cup of cake flour measured by spooning and leveling weighs 4.1 oz.

Flour (cake flour): 1¾ cups = 7.1 oz, about 7 oz

To compensate for measuring errors and for simplicity, I am going to round this off to 7 oz.

To get my amount of sugar using percentage estimates, in a high-ratio cake the weight of the sugar can go as high as 140% the weight of the flour:

Sugar at 140% x 7 = 9.8 oz

The weight of sugar is 7 oz/cup, this equals 1.4 cups, or between 1⅓ and 1½ cups. If I want to avoid using 1⅓ + 1 or 2 tablespoons, I will have to go with too little (1⅓ cups) or a little too much (1½ cups). I ended up going with 1½ cups (10.5 oz) sugar.

To find my amount of fat, I use the percentage estimates, which can run 30 to 70%. I want to go with the higher amount:

Fat at 70% x 7 = 4.9 oz

I want to make the layer really moist, so I substitute oil (canola or vegetable) for some of the butter because oil coats flour proteins better than butter. Coating the flour proteins prevents their forming gluten, which ties up water, thus leaving more water in the batter to make a moister cake. I need to arrive at a combination of butter and oil for the fat total to be close to or a little over 4.9 g:

4 tablespoons (2 oz) unsalted butter = 1.6 oz fat
+ ⅓ cup canola oil = 2.4 oz fat
+½ cup heavy cream = 1.3 oz fat

Fat total = 5.3 oz

The weight of the eggs should be greater than the weight of the fat:

2 large eggs = 3.50 oz
+ 3 large egg yolks = 1.95 oz

Total eggs = 5.45 oz

5.45 oz eggs > 5.3 oz fat

The weight of the liquid should be greater than the weight of the sugar. This ensures that there is enough liquid to dissolve the sugar and have some additional liquid to allow the starch to swell.

Liquid at 100% weight of sugar needs to be above 10.5 oz
10.5 - 5.4 eggs = 5.1 oz liquid
½ cup heavy cream has about 2.6 oz water-type liquid

So I still need at least 2.5 oz liquid. This could be ⅓ cup (79 ml) milk or buttermilk. I love buttermilk in cakes. And since I learned how wonderful whipped cream is, I love that, too. For the creaming (see page 120) or two-stage (see page 126) methods, I can use buttermilk and whipped cream. The texture of the cake with whipped cream is pure velvet. With the dissolved-sugar method, buttermilk works well, but it does curdle when you heat it to dissolve the sugar. So I can dissolve my sugar in ⅓ cup water (2.6 oz) and add ½ cup (118 ml) whipped cream later. I can easily get away with ½ cup whipped cream because it is only about 60% water-type liquid.

Now, I have my basic ingredient amounts.

I need to add leavening. One teaspoon baking powder per cup of flour would be 1¾ teaspoons (8 g).

I really want the flavor of the whipped cream to come through, so I will limit flavorings to vanilla and salt. Here are my first estimates for ingredients:

1¾ cups (7.1 oz/201 g) spooned and leveled cake flour
1½ cups (10.5 oz/298 g) sugar
4 tablespoons (2 oz/57 g) unsalted butter [1.6 oz/45 g fat]
⅓ cup (79 ml/2.4 oz/70 g) canola oil
3 large egg yolks (1.95 oz/55 g)
2 large eggs (3.5 oz/99 g)
⅓ cup buttermilk (79ml/2.8 oz/80 g)
½ cup heavy cream (118 ml, 4.23 oz/120 g) [1.3 oz fat/2.6 oz water]
1¾ teaspoons (8 g) baking powder
2 teaspoons (10 ml) pure vanilla extract
½ teaspoon (3 g) salt

I can now write my recipe and test it. This is similar to but slightly larger than the cake that I created for *CookWise*. In that cake, I used more butter but I didn't have the whipped cream. They are both wonderfully sweet and moist.

One time when I was on the TV show *Sara Moulton Live,* we made the *CookWise* cake—just this single bare layer. We had sliced a piece for each of us, held it on a napkin, waved *bon appétit,* and ended the show eating our cake. Sara is so much fun. We stood there giggling and talking and slicing off and eating more cake. Before we realized it, we had eaten half of the cake. It had been a while since I made this cake, and I had forgotten how really good it is.

Cake mixing methods are covered on pages 119 to 135. I have given three versions of this Magnificent Moist Golden Cake—the traditional creaming method (page 124), the two-stage method (page 126), and a method that is not widely known called the "dissolved-sugar" method, which follows.

My initial instinct was to use the recipe with the creaming method first because that is the one that most people know. But in considering how many little things can go wrong in the creaming method, I decided to go with the dissolved-sugar method instead. I really like this method the best of all. Putting a cake together in this manner may seem unusual, but I think that you will like it and you will love the results. You can read more about this Dissolved-Sugar Method on page 37.

Magnificent Moist Golden Cake
(Dissolved-Sugar Method)

Makes one 9 x 2-inch (23 x 5-cm) round layer

This is a wonderfully moist, sweet cake that I developed because I can't stand dry cakes. It makes a single thick layer that can be sliced horizontally into three layers and used as the base for many different cakes. Having moist, sweet layers can dramatically improve any cake creation. This is a level, perfectly shaped cake.

What This Recipe Shows

A balanced recipe (balanced weights of tenderizing and toughening ingredients) creates a successful cake.

Adding the flavorings to the fat, which is an excellent flavor carrier, distributes the flavors well.

Because of the high sugar content, this cake gets brown on top but, since you invert it, this is not a problem.

Using a little whipped cream in a cake adds moisture, and produces a velvet-soft texture and a wonderful taste.

Nonstick cooking spray with flour

1¾ cups (7.1 oz/201 g) spooned and leveled cake flour (NO SUBSTITUTE—the cake will be sunken in the center and simply will not work correctly if other flour is used, see page 60)

1¾ teaspoons (8 g) baking powder

1½ cups (10.5 oz/298 g) sugar

⅓ cup (79 ml) water

4 tablespoons (2.4 oz/57 g) unsalted butter, cut in 1-tablespoon (0.5-oz/14-g) pieces

2 teaspoons (10 ml) pure vanilla extract

½ teaspoon (3 g) salt

⅓ cup (79 ml) canola oil

3 large egg yolks (1.95 oz/55 g)

2 large eggs (3.5 oz/99 g)

½ cup (118 ml) heavy cream

1. Arrange a shelf in the lower third of the oven, place a baking stone on it, and preheat the oven to 350°F/177°C.

2. Spray a 9 x 2-inch (23 x 5-cm) round cake pan with nonstick cooking spray with flour and line the bottom with a parchment circle. (I very lightly spray the top of the parchment, too.)

3. Beat flour and baking powder for a full 30 seconds at medium speed on the mixer, and then pour the flour mixture into a large bowl and set aside. Don't wash the mixer bowl. Add the sugar to the bowl and place it back on the mixer.

4. Heat the water to a simmer in the microwave, or on the stove, and add it to the mixer bowl. Beat a few seconds to dissolve the sugar, and then beat in the butter, vanilla, and salt. Add the oil and mix on medium to blend.

5. Sprinkle one-third of the flour mixture over the sugar mixture. Blend in on low with a minimum amount of beating. Continue adding the flour until all is incorporated.

6. By hand, stir in the egg yolks one at a time, and then stir in the whole eggs one at a time.

7. Place a bowl, beaters, and the heavy cream in the freezer to chill for 5 minutes. Whip the cream until soft peaks form when the beater is lifted. Whip just a little beyond this soft peak stage. Stir about one-quarter of the whipped cream into the batter to lighten. Then gently fold the rest of the whipped cream into the batter.

8. Pour the batter into the prepared pan. Drop the pan onto the counter from a height of about 4 inches (10 cm) to knock out bubbles. Place the cake in the oven on the stone and bake until the center springs back when touched, or a toothpick inserted in the center comes out clean but moist, about 40 minutes. Ideally, the cake should not pull away from the sides until it has just come out of the oven. The center temperature should be about 209°F/98°C if you check by inserting an instant-read thermometer.

9. Place the cake in the pan on a rack to cool for about 10 minutes, then shake the pan to loosen the cake all around. Spray the cooling rack with nonstick cooking spray and invert the cake onto the rack to finish cooling.

CAKES USING THE MAGNIFICENT MOIST GOLDEN CAKE LAYERS

You can make many cakes using these moist layers. I have included several cakes, but let your mind go wild and you can come up with cake after cake. You will get moist, sweet layers using any of the mixing methods that you like—Dissolved-Sugar Method (page 37), Creaming Method (page 124), or Two-Stage Method (page 126).

Methods of Slicing Cakes into Layers

Make sure that the cake is completely cool before slicing. In fact, it will slice better chilled. You may want to wrap it well and chill in the freezer for about 30 minutes or in the refrigerator for 1 hour.

With a Long Knife

Using two toothpicks, mark the cake height in thirds. Repeat at three more equally spaced places around the edge of the cake. (Pretend as if the cake is a clock face. At 12, 3, 6, and 9 on a clock, use two toothpicks to mark the cake layer in thirds.)

Using the toothpicks as guides, with a long serrated knife, moving the knife in a sawing motion, slice off a layer by slicing horizontally through the cake. Again, using the toothpicks as guides, slice the remaining two-thirds of the cake in half horizontally, making three layers.

With Dental Tape

As above, use two toothpicks to mark the cake height in thirds. Repeat at three more equally spaced places around the edge of the cake. (Pretend as if the cake is a clock face. At 12, 3, 6, and 9 on a clock, use two toothpicks to mark the cake layer in thirds.)

Pull off a piece of dental tape or floss long enough to go around the cake with about 8 inches (20 cm) to spare. Loop the dental tape or floss around the cake, resting on the top row of toothpicks. Cross over the ends of the tape. Now, with the tape crossed, the end from the right side of the cake in your left hand and the end from the left side of the cake in your right hand, gently pull. The tape will cut through the cake. You now have the top layer cut. Gently slip a cardboard cake circle or two large spatulas into the cut and lift the upper section of cake from its bottom. To cut the middle and bottom layers apart, loop the tape around the cake again—this time resting on the lower row of toothpicks. Cross over the ends of the tape as before and cut the layers apart.

With a Cake Leveler

A cake leveler is a specialty piece of equipment available from pastry suppliers such as Wilton Industries and others (see Sources, page 507). There are at least two main types. One has a spring frame, uses a wire to cut, and is relatively inexpensive. A more expensive professional type uses one or two blades in a rigid frame.

Following directions, set the wire or blade at the desired height and make the cut. For three equal layers, cut first at one-third of the cake height and then cut the remaining two-thirds in half.

Dinner-on-the-Grounds Coconut Cake

MAKES ONE 9-INCH (23-CM) 3-LAYER ROUND CAKE

Here is an incredibly moist—almost soggy—Southern coconut cake. I was trying to make a cake like the wonderful coconut cakes of my youth—my favorite at dinner-on-the-grounds events. I have tried and tried to make the cake that I remembered so well, but not until I tasted Betty McCool's coconut cake did I find it. Betty is a musician and a wonderful home cook who makes incredible desserts. Her Coconut Soaking Solution and Icing are fabulous! This was the Dinner-on-the-Grounds Coconut Cake that I remembered. I used my Magnificent Moist Golden Cake layers and Betty's Soaking Solution and Icing.

What This Recipe Shows

Cut cake layer surfaces are turned up for the bottom and middle layers to encourage the soaking of icing into the layers.

---

1 recipe Magnificent Moist Golden Cake
    (page 37, 124, or 126), baked, cooled,
    and sliced into 3 layers (see page 39)

Betty McCool's Ole Time Coconut Soaking
    Solution (recipe follows), warm
1 package (6 oz/170 g) frozen grated coconut
Betty McCool's Coconut Icing (recipe follows)

1. Place a cake layer cut side up on a serving platter, serving dish, or cardboard cake circle. Spoon one-third of the Coconut Soaking Solution over the bottom layer, then place next layer on and spoon on another third. Place top layer on cut side down and spoon all remaining soaking solution on the cake.

2. Sprinkle the coconut over top layer that you have already poured soaking solution on. Now pour on the icing, allowing it to drip down the sides of the cake.

3. Refrigerate at least 2 hours before serving. Best if refrigerated overnight, covered with a plastic or glass cake dome. Serve cold.

Betty McCool's Ole Time Coconut Soaking Solution

1 cup (237 ml) whole milk
1 cup (7 oz/198 g) sugar

1 package (6 oz/170 g) frozen grated coconut

In a medium saucepan, stir the milk, sugar, and coconut together. Bring to a boil over medium heat. Let cool slightly. Can be used hot or warm.

Betty McCool's Coconut Icing

1 cup (7 oz/198 g) sugar
3 tablespoons (45 ml) water
$\frac{1}{4}$ teaspoon (1 g) cream of tartar

$1\frac{1}{2}$ teaspoons (7.5 ml) pure vanilla extract
$\frac{1}{3}$ cup (79 ml) light corn syrup
3 large egg whites (3 oz/85 g)

Place all the ingredients in the top of a double boiler over simmering water. Beat with a hand beater until icing thickens, about 8 minutes. Allow to cool 5 minutes before pouring on the cake.

Chocolate-Walnut Frosted Golden Layer Cake

MAKES ONE 9-INCH (23-CM) 3-LAYER ROUND CAKE

I designed this cake using the Magnificent Moist Golden Cake layers for moist layers with chocolate icing and walnuts. This wonderfully well-behaved icing is not very sweet, so I wanted to use a sweet soaking solution on the layers. If you are using a really sweet chocolate icing, omit the soaking solution.

What This Recipe Shows

Cut cake layer surfaces are turned up for the bottom and middle layers to encourage the soaking solution to soak into the layers.

Roasting enhances the flavor of nuts.

---

3 cups (10.5 oz/300 g) walnut pieces

1 tablespoon (0.5 oz/15 g) butter

$\frac{1}{4}$ teaspoon (1.5 g) salt

Wax paper

1 recipe Magnificent Moist Golden Cake
(choose any version on pages 37, 124, or
126), baked, cooled, and sliced into 3
layers (see page 39)

Golden Layers Soaking Solution (recipe
follows)

1 recipe Luscious, Creamy Chocolate Icing
(page 143)

1. Arrange a shelf in the lower third of the oven, place a baking stone on it, and preheat the oven to 350°F/177°C.

2. Spread the nuts out on a baking sheet, place in the oven on the stone, and roast 10 minutes. While nuts are hot, stir in the butter and salt. When cool, coarsely chop and set aside.

3. To keep the serving platter clean, cut a 10-inch (25-cm) long piece of waxed paper, cut it in half lengthwise, then cut each half lengthwise in half again. Now you have four 3 x 10-inch (8 x 25-cm) strips. Lay the strips in a square on the serving platter with their outside edge touching the outer edge of the platter. Place a cake layer, cut side up, on the platter, partially on the strips. (These strips can be pulled away later, keeping the platter clean while you ice the cake.) Drizzle 3 to 4 tablespoons (45 to 60 ml) of the soaking solution over the layer. Ice the prepared bottom layer with about $\frac{1}{4}$-inch (0.6-cm) thickness of the icing, making the icing just a little thicker around the outer edge. Sprinkle with about $\frac{1}{2}$ cup (1.7 oz/50 g) of the roasted walnuts.

4. Place the middle layer on top of the iced bottom layer, cut side up. Drizzle evenly with 3 to 4 tablespoons (45 to 60 ml) of the soaking solution. Ice with about $\frac{1}{4}$-inch (0.6-cm) thickness of the icing, making the icing just a little thicker around the outer edge. Sprinkle with about $\frac{1}{2}$ cup (1.7 oz/50 g) of the walnuts.

5. Place the last layer on top of the iced middle layer with the cut side down. Using a long metal spatula, ice the top and sides with the remaining icing. Press the remaining 2 cups (7 oz/200 g) roasted walnuts into the icing around the sides of the cake. Remove the waxed paper by pulling each strip out.

Golden Layers Soaking Solution

1 cup (7 oz/198 g) sugar

1 cup (237 ml) hot water

2 tablespoons (30 ml) Frangelico, rum, or
walnut liqueur, optional

1 teaspoon (5 ml) pure vanilla extract

Stir the sugar into the water to dissolve. Then stir in the liqueur, and if using, the vanilla.

Shirley's Boston Cream Pie

Makes one 9-inch (23-cm) 3-layer round cake

You have probably already discovered that Boston cream pie is a cake and not a pie. *The Boston Globe* reprinted the original Parker House recipe a few years ago, stating that "Boston cream pie was invented by Monsieur Sanzian, a French pastry chef hired in 1855 by the former Parker House (now the Omni Parker House)." Executive chef Joseph Ribas, who has been with the hotel for twenty-seven years, says Sanzian invented it "because he was topping an English cream cake with chocolate." The original cake was a two-layered sponge cake with rum-flavored custard and chocolate icing. I make no attempt at adhering to the original in any way. I have flavored my Magnificent Moist Golden Cake with rum and split it into three layers. Then, I have not one but two layers of vanilla pastry cream filling and a ganache icing.

1 recipe Magnificent Moist Golden Cake (choose version on page 37, 124, or 126) prepared with 3 tablespoons (45 ml) Myers's rum added when you add the vanilla

1½ recipes Pastry Cream (*Crème Pâtissière*, page 330), cooled
1 recipe Velvety Ganache Glaze (page 98)

1. When the cake has cooled, slice it horizontally into three layers (see page 39).

2. Place one cake layer, cut side up, on a serving platter, on the serving dish, or on a cardboard cake circle. Spread half of the pastry cream on the cake. Gently place the middle layer on top of the Pastry Cream. Press down just enough so that the Pastry Cream layer spreads out to be even with the cake layers. Spread this second layer with the remaining Pastry Cream and place the last layer on top, cut side down. Again press down just enough so that the Pastry Cream spreads out to be even with the cake layers. Gently cover the cake with plastic wrap and refrigerate overnight or for several hours.

3. When you are ready to ice the cake, prepare the ganache. Follow the Double-Icing Technique (see page 141) and divide the ganache in half. When the ganache cools to 90°F/32°C, ice the cake with one half. Refrigerate for 30 minutes to set the icing. Heat the second half of the ganache and strain it into a measuring cup with a spout. Pour the ganache on the cake and tilt to spread. Do not use a spatula to spread the ganache. Cover and refrigerate. Cut with a serrated knife.

Shirley's Not-the-Traditional Lane Cake

MAKES ONE 9-INCH (23-CM) 3-LAYER ROUND CAKE

Traditional Lane cake is made with white cake layers, a great nutty, raisiny filling and fluffy white icing. The filling may have a touch of sherry. As a child, I loved the filling and the icing, but the cake layers were frequently dry and not that tasty.

So this moist, flavorful cake bears only a little resemblance to the traditional Lane Cake. I used my Magnificent Moist Golden Cake for moist cake layers and, since anything worth doing is worth overdoing, I sprinkled the layers with a bourbon soaking solution. I tried dry sherry first, but it was wimpy and the flavor was lost. Bourbon is perfect! It contributes great flavors without any hint of alcohol.

What This Recipe Shows

Bourbon adds more flavor to the cake than dry sherry.

Using moist, golden cake layers makes a moister cake than dry, white layers.

---

1 recipe Magnificent Moist Golden Cake
  (choose any version on page 37, 124,
  or 126)

Lane Cake Soaking Solution (recipe follows)
1 recipe Lane Cake Filling (page 45)
1 recipe Italian Meringue (page 187),
  prepared just before icing the cake

1. Prepare the Magnificent Moist Golden Cake as directed. When the cake has cooled, slice it horizontally into 3 layers (see page 39). Place one layer on a serving platter, cut side up.

2. Spoon or sprinkle about 4 tablespoons (60 ml) of the soaking solution evenly over the bottom layer. Cover with half of the filling. Place the middle layer on top. Spoon or sprinkle about 4 tablespoons (60 ml) of the soaking solution evenly over the layer. Top with the remaining filling. Cover with the top layer, cut side down, and sprinkle it with about 4 tablespoons (60 ml) of the soaking solution.

3. Tightly wrap the cake, first with Saran Wrap, which is an outstanding barrier, around the sides and fold down over the top. Then wrap with plastic cling wrap to hold the Saran on securely. Refrigerate tightly wrapped, overnight or for a day or two.

4. With the prepared the Italian Meringue, ice the cake. Create swirls and peaks with the back of a wet serving spoon. For a dramatic effect, you can use a small blowtorch to darken the tips of the peaks.

Lane Cake Soaking Solution

1 cup (7 oz/198 g) sugar
1 cup (237 ml) hot water

¼ cup (59 ml) quality bourbon, such as
  Maker's Mark, or Tennessee whiskey,
  such as Jack Daniel's

Stir the sugar into the water to dissolve. Stir in the bourbon.

Lane Cake Filling

What This Recipe Shows

Soda breaks down cell walls and softens the dates.

Roasting enhances the flavor of nuts.

½ teaspoon (2.5 g) baking soda
1 cup (6.3 oz/178 g) chopped dates
1 cup (237 ml) boiling water
1 cup (3.5 oz/99 g) pecans
1 cup plus 1 tablespoon (8.5 oz/241 g)
  unsalted butter, divided
¼ teaspoon (1.5 g) salt

8 large egg yolks (5.2 oz/147 g)
1 cup (7 oz/198 g) sugar
1 teaspoon (5 ml) pure vanilla extract
¼ cup (59 ml) quality bourbon, such as
  Maker's Mark, or Tennessee whiskey,
  such as Jack Daniel's

1. While the cake is baking, sprinkle the baking soda over the dates, then cover with the boiling water and allow to stand at least 30 minutes.

2. Arrange a shelf in the lower third of the oven, place a baking stone on it, and preheat the oven to 350°F/177°C.

3. Spread the pecans out on a baking sheet, place in the oven on the stone, and roast 10 minutes. While nuts are hot, stir in 1 tablespoon (0.5 oz/14 g) of the butter and the salt. When cool, coarsely chop and set aside.

4. Combine the egg yolks, sugar, and the remaining 1 cup (8 oz/227 g) butter in a double boiler. Cook, stirring until it thickens, about 15 minutes. Remove from the heat, and stir in vanilla and bourbon.

5. Drain the dates well. Stir the dates and pecans into the cooked egg mixture.

6. Spread the filling between the layers as described on page 44.

Chemical Leaveners

TYPICAL CHEMICAL LEAVENERS

To most cooks, chemical leaveners mean baking powder or baking soda, and, indeed, these are the primary chemical leaveners used in home cooking.

Baking soda (sodium bicarbonate), when used alone, breaks down when heated to form carbon dioxide gas and sodium carbonate (washing soda), which has an unpleasant soapy taste and is moderately alkaline. However, if baking soda is combined with an acid, carbon dioxide gas is produced much faster and only a small amount of a milder-tasting salt is left behind. Baking soda works beautifully with foods that contain mild acids like chocolate, honey, molasses, citrus juice, sour cream, buttermilk, and brown sugar, to name a few.

Baking powder contains both baking soda and the exact amount of a powdered acid to use up all the soda. In 1 teaspoon (5 g) of baking powder there is only ¼ teaspoon (1 g) baking soda, so soda has four times the leavening power of baking powder. Baking powder also contains cornstarch to separate these two ingredients and to keep both ingredients dry by absorbing moisture.

Baking powders can be fast-acting, slow-acting, or double-acting, depending on the acid or acids that they contain. Fast-acting baking powders contain an acidic ingredient (like cream of tartar, tartaric acid, or monocalcium phosphate) that dissolves rapidly in cold water. If the baking powder has an acidic ingredient that does not dissolve easily (like sodium aluminum sulfate or anhydrous monocalcium phosphate), it does not start producing gas until the batter is hot—this is a slow-acting baking powder.

> Baking soda has four times the leavening power of the same weight of baking powder.

Double-acting baking powders contain an acid that dissolves rapidly in water and an acid that does not dissolve until the batter reaches a higher temperature in the hot oven. Encapsulation of a single acidic ingredient is also used to make some baking powders double-acting.

Most widely distributed grocery store brands of baking powder, such as Rumford, Calumet, and Clabber Girl, are double-acting. Rumford and Clabber Girl are both made by Hulman & Company, with Rumford being an all-phosphate baking powder (containing no aluminum). It is faster acting than most double-acting powders. You need to move fast and get cakes made with Rumford into the oven promptly since most of the bubbles are released shortly after mixing. Baking powders made with sodium aluminum sulfate have most of their action delayed until the batter is hot in the oven.

On page 47 is a table of reaction times of some leavening acids. You can check the label on your baking powder for one of these ingredients to help determine when most of the bubbles will be produced. Many baking powders use more than one acid to give more than one time of bubble production.

HOW LEAVENERS WORK

Baking soda and baking powder do not create new bubbles in a batter or dough; the carbon dioxide that they release only enlarges bubbles that already exist in the batter or dough. This means that

Reaction Times of Leavening Acids During Cake Making

Leavening Acid	% Carbon Dioxide Released		
		10–15 min	
	2 min Mixing	Bench Action	During Baking
Monocalcium phosphate (MCP)	60	0	40
Anhydrous monocalcium phosphate (AMCP)	15	35	50
Sodium acid pyrophosphate (SAPP)	28	8	64
Sodium aluminum phosphate (SALP)	22	9	69
Sodium aluminum sulfate (SAS)	0	0	100
Dicalcium phosphate-dihydrate (DCP)	0	0	100
Monopotassium tartrate (cream of tartar)	70	very little	30
Glucono-delta-lactone (GDL)	25	40	35

Source: LaBaw, G.D., "Chemical Leavening Agents and Their Use in Bakery Products." *Baker's Digest* 56(1), 16 (1982).

bubbles created during mixing are a vital part of leavening, too. Also, in chemically leavened baked goods, in addition to the carbon dioxide from baking powder and baking soda, we have steam from liquids (including eggs) that inflates bubbles in the batter or dough. In a hot oven, just as carbon dioxide from the chemical leaveners expands air bubbles, the steam generated from the liquid and/or the eggs inflates bubbles in the batter or dough, too. Neither chemical leaveners nor steam create a single new bubble. They only enlarge bubbles that already exist in the dough.

In the "Touch-of-Grace" Biscuits (page 152), a wet dough (that produces an abundance of steam) is the magic ingredient that makes these biscuits unbelievably light and moist.

This means that creating fine bubbles in the batter during the mixing is a crucial part of leavening. On pages 119 through 135, we will go into different mixing methods and how effective they are at incorporating fine bubbles in the batter.

> Carbon dioxide (from the chemical leaveners) and steam (from liquids in the dough) enlarge bubbles that already exist in the batter or dough. They do not create a single new bubble.

BUYING, USING, AND STORING CHEMICAL LEAVENERS

Just as milk and other perishable grocery items are dated with an expiration date, so are chemical leaveners. I always look at the dates on several cans of the brand that I want and select the one with the latest expiration date.

Careful measuring of chemical leaveners is vital. Since an amount as small as $\frac{1}{4}$ teaspoon (1 g) of baking soda controls a whole cup of flour, using accurate measuring spoons and leveling the spoon is important.

To store, close the lid tightly, and store chemical leaveners in a dry place to keep them potent. You can check the potency of baking powder by stirring ¼ teaspoon (1 g) in ½ cup (118 ml) of very hot water. If the baking powder is good, you instantly see a mass of fine bubbles.

You can check baking soda in a similar manner but add ¼ teaspoon (1.25 ml) white vinegar to the water before you add the soda. You should get fine bubbles instantly with fresh baking soda.

MAKING YOUR OWN BAKING POWDER

You can make your own fast-acting baking powder by mixing baking soda with cream of tartar and cornstarch. A workable formula is: 1 tablespoon (14 g) baking soda with 2 tablespoons (18 g) cream of tartar and 1½ tablespoons (11 g) cornstarch.

THE BIG PICTURE

Of all the chemical leavening information included here, the two most important and ever-present problems that a cook faces are:

How much chemical leavener to use?
and
How to evenly distribute the leaveners throughout the batter or dough?

The two most frequent problems in using chemical leaveners are: using the correct amount of leavener and evenly distributing the leaveners throughout the batter.

With too much leavening, the bubbles get too big, run into each other, float to the top and *POP*, producing heavy, fallen cakes, quick breads, and muffins.

Amount of Leavener

If a cake falls or does not rise well, you might think that that you did not use enough leavening. More frequently, however, the problem is just the opposite. When a recipe contains too much baking powder or soda, the bubbles get too big, run into each other, float to the top, and *POP*—there goes your leavening! Your cake or muffins will be very heavy or fall completely. This is a widespread problem. Even in "good" cookbooks there are many recipes that contain excessive amounts of leavening agents. Unfortunately, this leads to heavy cakes, quick breads, and muffins.

Often the problem is with the quantity of baking soda. Each teaspoon of baking powder contains only ¼ teaspoon (1 g) baking soda. Baking soda is strong stuff! It should be used carefully and cautiously.

Guidelines for ideal quantities of leavening are:

For each cup of all-purpose flour (4.4 oz/125 g) in a recipe use no more than:

1 to 1¼ teaspoons (5 to 6 g) baking powder
or
¼ teaspoon (1 g) baking soda

Many baking recipes call for both baking powder and baking soda. This may seem redundant since they are both essentially baking soda, but there can be reasons to use both. Baking powder is very reliable. It never leaves a soapy aftertaste because it contains exactly the right amount of acid for the amount of soda, and most baking powder is double-acting, meaning it releases carbon dioxide both immediately in the batter and later in the hot oven. But if a recipe contains a considerable amount of an acidic ingredient such as yogurt or sour cream, a little soda may be added in order to neutralize some of the acidity. However, I am a strong believer in creating more acidic batters and doughs (which makes the proteins set faster, see page 64). I tend to avoid soda altogether or use it in very small amounts.

For example, ½ teaspoon (2 g) baking soda will neutralize 1 cup (237 ml) of a mildly acidic ingredient like buttermilk or sour cream. If you have a recipe with 3 cups (13.2 oz/374 g) of flour that also contains 1 cup (8.5 oz/241 g) of sour cream, in addition to 2 teaspoons (9 g) baking powder, you could use ¼ teaspoon (1 g) of soda, which will neutralize only ½ cup (4.2 oz/119 g) of the sour cream, still leaving ½ cup of sour cream to maintain a slightly acidic batter. You will now have the equivalent of 3 teaspoons (14 g) baking powder—correct leavening for 3 cups (13.2 oz/374 g) of flour.

Variations in Guidelines of Leavening Quantities

These are guidelines; there can be variations in the correct amount of baking powder to use. You may need to make adjustments for your own cooking conditions.

When you change pan size from the original recipe, the amount of baking powder should be altered. If switching to a very large pan, in which the batter will not be as deep and will have a much larger surface area, the leavener can easily expand and rise, so you will need less baking powder; if switching to a smaller pan with deeper batter, you will need more baking powder.

Rose Levy Beranbaum in *The Cake Bible* gives the exact amounts of baking powder for 6 to 18-inch (15 to 46-cm) round pans. For example, for white or yellow cakes, she recommends: 1½ teaspoons (7 g) baking powder for 6 to 8-inch (15 to 20-cm) pans, 1⅓ teaspoons (6 g) for 9 to 10-inch (23 to 25-cm), 1⅛ teaspoons (5 g) for 11 to 14-inch (28 to 36-cm), 1 teaspoon (5 g) for 15 to 17-inch (38 to 43-cm), and ⅞ teaspoon (4 g) for an 18-inch (46-cm) pan.

Slightly more leavening can be used if the recipe calls for a lot of heavy ingredients like chopped fruits and nuts. You can initially try about 20% more leavening. If the volume increases, fine. If the volume decreases, cut back on the leavening.

SPOTTING AND REPAIRING OVERLEAVENED RECIPES

Most frequently, over-
leavening is from the
baking soda. Many
cooks do not realize
the leavening strength
of baking soda.

By applying leavening quantity guidelines, you can spot and repair overleavened recipes. Look at the amount of flour, and then check the amounts of both the baking powder and baking soda. Apply the guidelines: 1 teaspoon (5 g) baking powder per 1 cup (4.4 oz/124 g) of flour, or ¼ teaspoon (1 g) baking soda per cup of flour. If you have the right amount of leavening for the amount of flour, the recipe is properly leavened. Most frequently, the error is with the baking soda. Many cooks do not realize the strength of baking soda.

Another "tip off" that the recipe may be overleavened is the pan. With cakes, many times an overleavened recipe is baked in a Bundt or tube pan. Major cake errors are not as obvious when the cake is made in this type of pan. On page 16 you will find a pound cake recipe that makes a sunken, miserable-looking loaf cake but makes a lovely Bundt cake! It doesn't matter if the top of the pound cake in a Bundt or tube pan is slightly sunken, you're going to turn it upside down. No one will ever know!

Many cake errors are
not obvious when the
cake is made in a
Bundt or tube pan.

High-Altitude Baking

At high altitudes, with less air pressure on baked goods, two major things happen: liquids evaporate more easily, and gas bubbles in baked goods rise to the top and pop more readily.

With the loss of liquid other ingredients become more concentrated. With greater sugar concentrations, a baked good can have trouble setting and may not set at all. The slower the baked good sets, the more moisture it loses and the worse the problem gets. You can have a soggy mess. Some experienced high-altitude bakers substitute extra-large eggs for the large eggs in recipes. This provides a little more liquid and more protein to set faster. Some reduce the amount of sugar. Some increase the oven temperature. The severity of the problem depends on the altitude. Some bakers use all three techniques.

With the loss of gas bubbles, leavening is lost and the product becomes heavy. Bakers sometimes reduce the amount of leavener—baking powder. For an altitude of 7,000 feet (Denver is only 5,280 feet in altitude), USDA recommends a reduction of ¼ teaspoon per teaspoon baking powder in the recipe. *Baking Science and Technology* recommends a reduction of about ½ teaspoon per teaspoon. The Agricultural Extension Services in states with high-altitude areas offer suggestions on solving baking problems. You can see this is a complicated problem.

Cookbook author Susan Purdy has an excellent book on high-altitude baking, *Pie in the Sky*. She bakes all kinds of baked goods at sea level, 3,000, 5,000, 7,000, and 10,000 feet, and tells you what changes she makes at each altitude to get a successful product.

Improving an Overleavened Recipe

Overleavened batters and doughs result in a finished product that can be quite heavy. These cakes are greatly improved by adjusting the leavening. Here is an example of an overleavened recipe, Pop Corriher's Original Applesauce Cake, and how I adjusted the leavening.

Pop Corriher's Original Applesauce Cake

MAKES ONE 12-CUP (2.8-L) BUNDT CAKE OR ONE 10-INCH (25-CM) TUBE CAKE

This recipe produces a heavy (overleavened), dry cake. My husband, Arch, insists that Pop's cake was not dry! Maybe we don't have the real recipe! For a great version, see Shirley's Version (page 54).

What This Recipe Shows

In spite of having a large amount of butter, this cake is dry.

Per "The Math" (page 29), the weight of the sugar is about equal to the weight of the flour—it does not exceed it like most high-ratio cakes—and this, in good part, accounts for the dryness.

The only liquid comes from the applesauce and butter. This also may contribute to dryness.

Nonstick cooking spray

1 cup (8 oz/227 g) unsalted butter

2 cups (16.8 oz/476 g) dark brown sugar, packed

2 large eggs (3.5 oz/99 g)

3½ cups (15.4 oz/437 g) spooned and leveled bleached all-purpose flour

2 teaspoons (9 g) baking soda

2 teaspoons (4 g) ground cloves

2 teaspoons (4 g) ground cinnamon

2 teaspoons (4 g) ground allspice

2 cups chunky applesauce (17.2 oz/488 g), see Note

1 pound (16 oz/454 g) *seeded* raisins (see A Raisin Is a Raisin?, page 53)

Note: Applesauce is 82 to 88% water, and my favorite chunky applesauce contains 12% sugar (2 oz) and 82% water (14 oz).

1. Arrange a shelf in the lower third of the oven, place a baking stone on it, and preheat the oven to 325°F/163°C.

2. Spray a Bundt pan heavily with nonstick cooking spray, or spray a tube pan with nonstick cooking spray, line the bottom of the pan with parchment, and spray the top of the parchment lightly.

3. In a mixer, beat the butter on medium speed until light, about 2 minutes. Add sugar in three batches, and beat in after each addition. Beat until light and fluffy. On low speed, beat in the eggs one at a time until just blended.

4. In a large bowl, with a fork or hand mixer, stir together the flour, soda, cloves, cinnamon, and allspice. Stir the flour mixture into the butter mixture. Stir in the applesauce, then the raisins. Pour into the prepared pan.

5. Place in the oven on the baking stone and bake until the center springs back when touched, or a toothpick inserted in the center comes out clean but moist, about 1 hour and 20 minutes. If you check the center temperature with an instant-read thermometer, it should be about 209°F/98°C.

6. Place the cake in the pan on a rack to cool. Allow to stand in the pan 10 to 20 minutes. Make sure that the cake is loosened from the pan by jarring it against the counter. Invert the cake onto a serving platter to finish cooling. This cake improves upon standing for two or three days, well wrapped (see page 150) and refrigerated. (At Christmas, Pop soaked the cake with rum or bourbon.)

CHANGES THAT I MADE TO POP'S APPLESAUCE CAKE, AND WHY

Leavening

First, I checked the leavening: 2 teaspoons (9 g) of baking soda is enough to leaven 8 cups (35 oz/998 g) of flour! Since I have 3½ cups (15.4 oz/437 g) of flour, I will reduce the soda to 1 teaspoon (5 g).

Dryness

As it is, this cake is dry. To add moisture, I am going to increase the sugar from 2 cups to 2½ cups. And I am going to substitute oil for some of the butter. Oil greases flour proteins better and reduces gluten formation, and thus reduces the water absorbed, leaving more moisture in the cake.

These changes greatly improved the cake, but if I felt more improvement was needed, I could add ¼ cup (59 ml) freshly squeezed orange juice.

Roasted Nuts

Either roasted pecans or roasted walnuts greatly improve the flavor and texture of the cake. So I also added roasted nuts.

A Raisin Is a Raisin?

Golden raisins and regular raisins I knew about, but I thought that was it as far as raisins were concerned. Then I ran into Pop Corriher's applesauce cake. Pop Corriher, my husband's father, had an apple orchard. At ninety, Pop milked a cow every day just so he could have fresh cream on his strawberries. The recipe for Pop's applesauce cake calls for "seeded" raisins. I thought that was an older terminology for "seedless" raisins. Seeded, seedless, what's the difference? As it turns out, there is quite a difference because raisins (dried grapes) can be made from a number of varieties of grapes.

The unique, sweet Muscat grape produces raisins with flavors that are ideal for meat or fish dishes, cereals, desserts, or candies. So the Muscat, a large, sweet grape with seeds, was for many years the grape used to make raisins in the United States, Europe, and Australia. For easy use, the seeds needed to be removed, thus producing "seeded" raisins. When the seeds are removed, the raisins are smushed and, since Muscat grapes are very juicy and sweet, seeded raisins are sold in solid, gooey blocks. As a boy, my husband separated the raisins from the gooey block and coated them with flour for Pop's cake.

These seeded raisins are very different from our modern seedless raisins. When Scottish immigrant William Thompson grew a grape variety, Lady deCoverly, that is a seedless, thin-skinned, sweet grape, it was an ideal raisin grape—the grape "born" to be a raisin. Today, 95 percent of California raisins are made from Thompson seedless grapes grown in the San Joaquin Valley. These grapes did not have to be split and seeded, just dried—no gooey blocks nowadays.

In baking, seeded Muscat raisins are wetter and sweeter than Thompson seedless grape raisins. In the past, in the fall, we were able to get both seeded and unseeded Muscat raisins from Sun-Maid in California. When you can't get seeded raisins, you can soak seedless raisins briefly in hot sugar water (2 cups hot water with 1 cup sugar for each pound of raisins) to more closely simulate the sweeter seeded raisins.

Shirley's Version of Pop Corriher's Applesauce Cake

MAKES ONE 12-CUP (2.8-L) BUNDT CAKE OR ONE 10-INCH (25-CM) TUBE CAKE

This delicious cake is now moist, but still has the intense spice seasoning of the original (page 51). I was stunned to see 2 teaspoons of cloves! That is an enormous amount of cloves, especially in addition to other spices. My husband, Arch, and I ate a slice right after I baked the cake and we thought it was too heavily spiced. The next day we were going to his daughter Lisa's house. We really didn't like the cake that much, so we saved about two slices and took the rest of the cake to Lisa.

Two days later, we had a small piece of the cake. It was wonderful! The spices had mellowed and the cake was marvelous. We ate every crumb. Lisa had said that neither her husband nor her children would touch the cake, and it was a huge cake. So we called to tell her that we would take half of it back. She had already eaten the whole cake by herself! I had to make another cake for us.

We learned the hard way that cakes can completely change after a day or two in the refrigerator. Be sure to allow time for this cake to stand for a day or two before serving.

What This Recipe Shows

Substituting oil, which is more effective at preventing gluten formation, for some of the butter makes cakes moister.

Using egg yolks instead of whole eggs enhances moisture and texture in cakes.

A cake, well wrapped, in the refrigerator can change greatly after mellowing for a day or two.

---

2 cups (7 oz/198 g) pecan or walnut pieces

¾ cup plus 2 tablespoons (7 oz/198 g) unsalted butter, divided

¾ teaspoon (4.5 g) salt, divided

Nonstick cooking spray

2½ cups (21 oz/595 g) dark brown sugar, packed

4 large egg yolks (2.6 oz/74 g)

2 large eggs (3.5 oz/99 g)

½ cup (118 ml) canola oil

3½ cups (15.4 oz/437 g) spooned and leveled bleached all-purpose flour

1 teaspoon (5 g) baking soda

2 teaspoons (4 g) ground cloves

2 teaspoons (4 g) ground cinnamon

2 teaspoons (4 g) ground allspice

2 cups (17.2 oz/488 g) chunky applesauce

1 pound (454 g) raisins—*seeded* raisins if available, or soak regular seedless raisins in 2 cups (473 ml) hot water with 1 cup (7 oz/198 g) sugar for one hour, then drain well

1. Arrange a shelf in the lower third of the oven, place a baking stone on it, and preheat the oven to 350°F/177°C.

2. Spread the nuts out on a baking sheet, place in the oven on the stone, and roast for 10 minutes. While the nuts are hot, stir in 2 tablespoons (1 oz/28 g) butter and ¼ teaspoon (1.5 g) salt. When cool, coarsely chop and set aside.

3. Reduce the oven temperature to 325°F/163°C. Spray a Bundt pan heavily with nonstick cooking spray or spray a tube pan with nonstick cooking spray, line the bottom of the pan with parchment, and spray the top of the parchment lightly.

4. In a mixer, beat the ¾ cup (6 oz/170 g) butter on medium speed until light. Add the sugar in three batches, beating after each addition. Beat until light and fluffy. On low speed, beat in the egg yolks. Continue on low speed to beat in the eggs, one at a time until just blended. Beat in the oil.

5. In a large bowl, with a fork or a hand mixer, beat together well the flour, soda, remaining ½ teaspoon (3 g) salt, the cloves, cinnamon, and allspice. On the lowest speed, beat the flour mixture into the butter mixture until blended. Stir in the applesauce and roasted nuts. Drain the raisins, pat them dry with a paper towel, and stir them into the batter. Pour the batter into the prepared pan.

6. Place the pan in the oven on the stone and bake until the center springs back when touched, or a toothpick inserted in the center comes out clean but moist, about 1 hour and 20 minutes. The center temperature should be about 209°F/98°C.

7. Place the cake in the pan on a rack to cool. Allow to stand in the pan 10 to 20 minutes. Make sure that the cake is loosened from the pan by jarring it against the counter. Invert the cake onto a serving platter to finish cooling. This cake improves upon standing for two or three days, well wrapped (see page 150) and refrigerated.

MORE EXAMPLES OF OVERLEAVENED RECIPES

Overleavened cake recipes are everywhere. Here are some examples from various cookbooks. I will list only the ingredients, with weights given for flour and leavener. Flour and leaveners are in capital letters. Next, I point out the overleavening and explain what I would do to correct the leavening to make a lighter cake.

Remember the leavening guidelines: 1 to 1¼ teaspoons (5 to 6 g) baking powder per cup of flour in the recipe or ¼ teaspoon (1 g) baking soda per cup of flour in the recipe.

OVERLEAVENED CAKE RECIPE #1: RHUBARB CAKE
2 cups fresh rhubarb, finely chopped
1¼ cups sugar
2 CUPS (8.8 oz/249 g) FLOUR
1¼ TEASPOONS (6 g) BAKING SODA

½ teaspoon salt
1 teaspoon cinnamon
1 teaspoon nutmeg
1 teaspoon vanilla
1 cup chopped walnuts
3 eggs
½ cup oil

The recipe contains 2 cups (8.8 oz/249 g) of flour, but with 1¼ teaspoons (6 g) of baking soda, we have enough leavening for 5 cups (22 oz/623 g) of flour. These two 9-inch layers of cake will fall and be very dense. The thought was probably that the soda would neutralize the acidity of the rhubarb, which it will. But it is also making an excess of carbon dioxide, which expands the bubbles in the batter too much, causes them to run into each other, float to the top, and POP. Reducing the baking soda to ½ teaspoon (2 g) will reduce acidity in the batter, leaven it correctly, and make the cake layers much lighter.

Overleavened Cake Recipe #2: Layered Apple Cake
2 CUPS (8.8 oz/249 g) SELF-RISING FLOUR
2 cups sugar
2 TEASPOONS (9 g) BAKING SODA
2 teaspoons cinnamon
1¼ cups Wesson oil
4 eggs
3 cups grated baking apples

This recipe is inconceivably overleavened! The writer did not appear to understand that self-rising flour *already* contains the proper amount of leavening. The recipe needs no additional leavening at all with this flour. The recipe, as written, has enough leavening for 10 cups (44 oz/1,246 g) of flour yet it has only 2 cups (8.8 oz/249 g)! With bleached all-purpose (not self-rising) flour, I would use only 2 teaspoons (9 g) of baking powder rather than ½ teaspoon (2 g) baking soda in order to keep the batter acidic (acidic batters set better, see page 64).

Overleavened Cake Recipe #3: Apple, Walnut, Honey Cake
3 large eggs
½ cup canola oil
½ cup honey
2 teaspoons vanilla
2 CUPS (8.8 oz/249 g) FLOUR
1½ cups sugar
1 TEASPOON (5 g) BAKING POWDER

1 TEASPOON (5 g) BAKING SODA
2 teaspoons ground cinnamon
3 cups (about 3 medium) peeled, cored, and thinly sliced apples
2 cups walnuts, coarsely chopped

In the headnote for this cake, the author honestly admits that this is a very dense cake and that it was included in the book because of its good taste. With 1 teaspoon (5 g) of baking powder and 1 teaspoon (5 g) baking soda, there is enough leavening for 5 cups (22 oz/623 g) of flour, while the recipe contains 2 cups (8.8 oz/249 g). I would select self-rising flour and use no additional leavening in this recipe to simplify leavening and mixing.

"FIXING" OVERLEAVENED RECIPES

In the above examples of overleavened recipes, I gave my choice of the correct leaveners available. When selecting a leavener, you have a number of options. In some cakes with a high sugar content that you want to be incredibly moist, like my Magnificent Moist Golden Cake (pages 37, 124, and 126), using cake flour is absolutely necessary (see page 60). In this case, you have a choice between baking powder and baking soda. My choice is baking powder unless the batter is extremely acidic—in which case, I would use baking powder as the primary leavener and add a minimum of baking soda to leave the batter acidic (see page 64).

In cakes that contain fruit or other sources of moisture, or in cakes that you do not want to be very sweet, you can use baking powder, baking soda, self-rising flour (which already contains leavening), or some combination. Some great advantages of self-rising flours are that they are usually slightly lower in protein than all-purpose flour and the leavening is evenly distributed, producing a smooth-textured cake.

Not only is the leavening evenly distributed, but commercial flour companies have more leaveners available to them than home cooks and they have complete control over the time that bubbles are produced. I have used self-rising flours both from large nationally distributed mills and from White Lily, a small, quality miller, and found them to do an excellent job of leavening (see page 58).

So in many recipes, my choice for leavening is self-rising flour, which also simplifies the recipe, getting rid of one or two ingredients—baking powder and baking soda. This is a personal choice. Some bakers object to using self-rising flour (read page 63 for more details).

DISTRIBUTION OF LEAVENING

Another big challenge in cake making is achieving even distribution of the leavener in the batter. If the leavener is unevenly distributed, the cake will have holes here and there, along with areas that are tightly compressed.

Many cooks think that an uneven texture is caused by the mixing method. For example, many think that you will get an uneven texture using the "muffin" method—combining all of the

It is the uniform distribution of the leavener that produces even-textured cakes, not the choice of mixing method.

dry ingredients, combining all the wet ingredients, and then stirring the two together. This is not necessarily true. You can get a perfectly smooth cake using the "muffin" method if you use self-rising flour. It is usually the uniform distribution of the leavener that produces even-textured cakes, not the choice of mixing method.

GETTING EVEN DISTRIBUTION OF LEAVENERS

The following methods for distribution are frequently advised in recipes.

Sifting for Even Distribution of Leaveners

You may think that sifting would evenly distribute the leavening. Unfortunately it doesn't. My husband suggested that I take a dark powder (so that I could see it) whose consistency was similar to baking powder, measure it onto flour as I would baking powder, then sift and observe its distribution. I watched as I sifted. Much to my dismay, I saw many dark patches. The patches get covered with the next layer of sifted ingredients, but they are there. I smeared through the sifted flour with the back of a spoon and, although a lot of the sifted flour was a mixed-color mixture, I could still see white streaks—areas where there was no dark powder.

This was in no way an accurate measure of distribution. When you sift two more times, you visibly have a pretty even blend. However, I know that the distribution can be far from perfect. I have experienced cakes that have ingredients that were sifted two or three times, yet they have an uneven texture (not terrible, but a few holes). In summary, you are going to have to sift three times or more for even distribution of leavener to create a cake with a uniform texture, and even then the cake may not be perfect.

In a recipe that instructs "sifting," you can get a more even blend of ingredients by beating them together for thirty seconds with the mixer, a fork, or a whisk.

Not being able to get the cake texture perfectly even drove my friend Rose Levy Beranbaum crazy. "It [sifting] does not do an adequate job of mixing dry ingredients; this is better accomplished with a mixer or even by stirring with a fork." In her recipes, she beats all of the dry ingredients together with the mixer for a full thirty seconds (which is quite long when you time it). She already has her sugar and flour blended, so she can't use the creaming method. She uses the Two-Stage or Flour/Batter Method (see pages 126 and 128), which she prefers.

Self-Rising Flours for Even Distribution of Leaveners

Self-rising flours are a perfectly uniform blend of leaveners and lower-protein flour. Commercial companies have many more leaveners at their disposal than home cooks and these companies can control all phases of the leavening. However, even though some flours like White Lily self-rising are mildly chlorinated and low in protein, there are cases in which only cake flour will produce a perfect cake.

One example is my Magnificent Moist Golden Cake (pages 37, 124, and 126). Also, self-rising flour is not suitable for very large layers that require less leavening. You can use self-rising flour and reduce the leavening of the mixture by blending in some plain flour. (See page 63.)

Dissolving in Liquid for Even Distribution of Leaveners

Bakers frequently dissolve salt in a liquid so that it will be evenly distributed throughout the batter. But baking powder can start to lose a part of its leavening with this technique.

Chemical Leaveners At a Glance

Problem	What to Do
How much leavener is correct?	Use 1 teaspoon (5 g) baking powder or $\frac{1}{4}$ teaspoon (1 g) baking soda per cup of flour (4.4 oz/124 g). Or use self-rising flour and eliminate all additional leavening.
Do I use baking soda or baking powder?	Baking soda releases bubbles immediately and must have an acidic ingredient in the batter.
	Baking powder has the exact amount of acids to neutralize all of the soda, leaving no soapy taste.
	Baking powder is usually double-acting, meaning it works in two phases: when cold and when heated.
Which baking powder to use?	Read the name of the acids on the label. Check chart on page 47. Make sure you use an acid that has a considerable amount of its action during baking.
What is best way to evenly distribute leavener?	Beating baking powder and flour together with a mixer, or beating well with a fork, is more effective than sifting.
How can you check for leavener activity?	Stir a small portion of leavener into a glass of hot water that contains a few drops of vinegar. You should have a profusion of fine bubbles.

Other Ingredients in Cakes and
Other Chemically Leavened Baked Goods

FLOUR

There are many different kinds of flour, which I will cover with their pros and cons regarding cake making. First let's take a look at what flour does in cakes.

Flour's Role in Cakes

Flour and eggs provide the proteins to set and hold a cake. As you will see in sections to follow, you can really understand the role of flour or eggs when you make a flourless cake (page 66) or an eggless cake (page 82). You can make either flourless or eggless cakes, but this places the whole job of setting the cake on one ingredient instead of the customary two.

Different Types of Flour

Here is a look at different types of flour, and the pros and cons of using specific flours in chemically leavened baked goods.

All-Purpose Flour

Many bakers would never think of using anything other than cake flour for cakes. But there are differences of opinion, and some bakers prefer a low- to moderate-protein all-purpose flour. Cake flour does have a definite taste. Some bakers even object to the fine texture that you get with cake flour and want the coarser texture of bleached all-purpose. All bread flours and most unbleached all-purpose flours have a higher protein content, meaning that more gluten can be developed creating potentially tougher baked goods. However, in spite of this, one pastry expert, Bruce Healy, prefers Gold Medal unbleached flour (page 62).

Cake Flour

Cake flour is different from all-purpose flour in a number of ways. You will get a different texture and taste in a cake using cake flour.

Cake flour is very finely ground, with a silky-smooth texture that produces a fine-textured cake. Because it is finely ground and has increased surface area, cake flour can absorb more liquid than plain bleached flours. More liquid in cakes means that use of more sugar is possible. You must have enough liquid to dissolve the sugar without taking liquid from the starch, which needs liquid to swell.

Cake flour is a low-protein flour (about 8 grams protein per cup, about 7 to 8%) and will not produce as much tough gluten as regular all-purpose flour. When used appropriately, it can produce very tender products.

Cake flour is chlorinated, which means that it is bleached with chlorine gas and deliberately left slightly acidic. Chlorination gives cake flour several advantages over non-chlorinated flour:

The acidity causes cakes to set slightly sooner (page 64), producing cakes with a finer texture.

Chlorination enhances the starch's ability to absorb water and swell.

Fat sticks to chlorinated starch but not to starch from the same wheat that has not been chlorinated. Since all the air bubbles are in the fat, this means a more even distribution of the bubbles, producing a finer texture.

The amount of chlorination influences taste. White Lily, a Southern low-protein, fine-textured flour, is slightly chlorinated and does not have the slightly sharp taste that cake flour does.

Chlorination makes a significant difference. The texture and taste of the cake will be different from one made with non-chlorinated flour. Cake flour in the United States is chlorinated; however, this is not true in many countries. Cake flour in Japan is not chlorinated. Chlorinated flour in the United Kingdom is available only as "self-raising"—that is, self-rising with baking powder (leaveners) already added. This creates problems for large cake layers in wedding cakes, which need less leavening. Rose Levy Beranbaum had this problem when adapting *The Cake Bible* for an edition in the United Kingdom. Nick Malgieri, author of *Nick Malgieri's Perfect Pastry,* offered Rose a solution: use the leavened chlorinated flour (for fine texture) and add a small amount of plain unleavened all-purpose flour to correct for the excess of leaveners.

The taste of cake flour is not the only thing that influences a baker's choice of flour. I wanted to use self-rising flour in my basic cake because the leavening is evenly distributed, producing an even-textured cake—no holes. But my primary goal was to achieve a moist, sweet layer.

I thought that White Lily self-rising flour, which is ideal for biscuits, would be perfect. It works beautifully in many cakes, giving you the fine texture and many of the advantages of cake flour. And it is both self-rising and lightly chlorinated. However, I tried and tried and could not get the amount of sugar and liquid that I wanted in the recipe and not have a slightly sunken center in the baked cake. I could get the perfect shape—a level top—by adding a little more flour, but I lost some of the sweetness and the moisture. Because the White Lily didn't absorb as much liquid as the cake flour, I was unable to get my extremely sweet, moist cake without a slightly sunken center. So I ultimately decided to use cake flour.

Bleached and Unbleached Flours

National-brand bleached all-purpose flour dependably has an intermediate protein content (11 to 12%) and is preferable to an unknown local-brand all-purpose flour, which may be quite high in protein. Most brands of flour use a higher-protein flour in their unbleached.

Most millers put a higher-protein flour in their unbleached types.

So, since higher protein means more tough gluten, when baking tender cakes, muffins, and quick breads, you should use bleached all-purpose flour if you don't use cake flour. Most unbleached flours and bread flours have high protein contents and should be avoided for cakes but coveted for yeast doughs. I have always firmly believed this.

But then there is the taste. I took a baking workshop from Didier Rosada, the chef who has trained our Baking Team USA, which won bread-baking competitions against French and Italian bakers several times. It's hard to believe, but the Americans baked better baguettes than the French! For these magnificent baguettes, Didier insisted on using unbleached all-purpose flour from hard red winter wheat, which has a reasonably high carotenoid content. Didier said that because of the taste, he wanted this flour rather than the higher-protein bread flour that most bakers preferred. And, indeed, Didier's baguettes do taste better than anyone else's. For more information, see page 431.

And then there is Bruce Healy, a great French-trained pastry chef. Bruce is a perfectionist and intent on knowing why things happen. (He also has a PhD in physics from Yale.) Bruce insists on using unbleached Gold Medal all-purpose flour for cakes. I yelled and screamed that that was all wrong, and he yelled and screamed back that all I had to do was taste cakes made from cake flour and cakes made from his unbleached flour. I do realize that most of Bruce's cakes are French génoise, and these cakes are steam leavened, not chemically leavened, but he swears that he also likes the unbleached for *quatre quarts* (pound cakes). To reduce the protein count, he does substitute potato starch for 10% of his flour. Well, to each his own. The longer I cook, the more open-minded I get.

Millers try to produce flour that gives their customers outstanding baked goods. For this reason, millers make most brands of unbleached flour higher in protein than the bleached. They know that most of the people buying the unbleached flour are using it to make yeast bread, and a higher-protein flour will give them lighter bread. People using the bleached flour are probably making muffins and quick breads, which are more tender with a lower-protein flour.

However, all that being said, Bruce swore that Gold Medal bleached and unbleached had the same protein content. I couldn't test chemically, but I tested both using the water-absorption test (see page 468) and Bruce was absolutely correct. If they weren't the same, they were very close.

In some cakes, Bruce substitutes potato starch for part of the flour, which would lower the protein content of the mix. Also, potato starch granules are extremely large, so potato starch is a great absorber of liquid. This enables his flour–potato starch mixture to absorb almost as much liquid as cake flour. Of all the starches, potato starch is the most potent thickener, so it takes a smaller amount to thicken than any other starch.

So this mixture would give you the water-absorption advantage of cake flour. Plus, potato starch makes baked goods that taste great. Its disadvantage is texture. The potato starch granules swell to be very large (over 100 times their original size, while cornstarch swells to only 20 times original size). In a tight-textured cake like a pound cake, a slight loosening of the texture is not noticeable, but in a regular cake, potato starch can produce a coarse texture. (Sand cakes are cakes with a coarse texture containing a large amount of potato starch.)

Potato starch granules are a great absorber of liquid, so Bruce's flour–potato starch mixture can absorb almost as much liquid as cake flour.

We have conventional training telling us to use bleached all-purpose flour or cake flour. Cake expert Rose Levy Beranbaum says use cake flour only, and cake expert Bruce Healy swears by Gold Medal unbleached all-purpose flour. And then there is White Lily, which is similar to the silky fine texture of cake flour with a better taste and is available as self-rising—most cake flour in the United States is not self-rising. White Lily flours are available in grocery stores in Southern states, and by mail order (see Sources, page 510).

Which flour should you use? I used to think that I knew, but at this point, I don't know. Perhaps this is a matter of personal opinion. You should try cake flour, White Lily self-rising, bleached and unbleached all-purpose, and decide for yourself. The texture and taste of the baked goods will differ. I use cake flour for my Magnificent Moist Golden Cake (pages 37, 124, and 126), and White Lily self-rising flour for my biscuits, muffins, scones, and in a number of cakes.

Self-Rising Flour

Self-rising flours are a perfectly uniform blend of leaveners and flour. This eliminates the problem of uneven mixing of the leavener with the flour resulting in an uneven texture. Also, millers can control every phase of leavening throughout the mixing and baking since they have more leavening acids available to them than home cooks do. For example, they can slow the first phase of the leavening— the gas that is produced when liquid is added. This means that if you have a phone call and take five minutes to get the cake in the oven, you will not lose all of this part of the leavening.

I hate sifting, and know that it does not do a good job of blending leaveners and flour (see page 58). Beating with a mixer or even with a fork blends them more evenly. I love to use self-rising flour for its perfect distribution of leaveners. Beranbaum doesn't use it; her point is that self-rising flour contains the equivalent of 1½ teaspoons (7 g) baking powder per cup, which is slightly too much leavening in some specific situations (such as making large cake layers).

Different millers have different blends of leaveners. It has been my experience that many millers' blends of self-rising flour are excellent. One of the old, small milling companies, White Lily, has worked on their leavening blend since 1920, so I know that I can trust it to be better than any combination I can make. I also know that it is an ideal blend for biscuits.

Corby Kummer, food writer and coffee expert, is a great purist who wants everything made from scratch. I challenged him to make biscuits comparing White Lily self-rising flour with his favorite leavening (baking powder and/or soda or his own blend of soda and cream of tartar). It was amazing how much better-tasting, lighter, and higher the biscuits made with self-rising flour were. Even Corby admitted that, in this case, self-rising produced a better biscuit than the ones made with his own leavener.

Understanding Flour's Role: Flourless Cakes

Flourless cakes are easier to make successfully than eggless cakes because all-purpose flour contains only about 10% protein, so when you omit the flour, you are not giving up very much of your protein structure. The particles that flour usually provides can be supplied by ground nuts (even peanut butter), as we see in the cookies on page 383, or by cocoa particles in either cocoa powder or chocolate. There are many flourless cakes containing finely ground nuts or cocoa powder, or both.

Eggs, on the other hand, are essentially just protein and water with a little fat. So eggs contribute plenty of protein to set and hold the cake if the conditions are right.

ACIDITY

Acidity pops up in all kinds of places in cooking. If something is too acidic, it will not brown (page 404). On the other hand, if the reddish-blue compounds (anthocyanins) in food are not kept acidic, they turn blue. You may have seen red cabbage turn blue, or you may have seen blue halos around cherries in muffins.

I never thought about acidity in cakes until I ran into problems with flourless and eggless cakes. The egg and flour proteins in cakes set faster if they are acidic.

Eggs especially need an acidic batter. They simply won't set if conditions are not acidic enough. Without acidic conditions, you can get pudding instead of cake. When you have both flour and eggs in a cake, you have plenty of proteins, and different proteins that set over a range of acidity, so acidity doesn't matter quite as much. But in the case of flourless or eggless cakes, the role of acidity becomes more important. I experienced this in a big way in developing the recipe for my "Flourless" Luscious, Decadent Chocolate Torte (page 66). When I inadvertently reduced the acidity of the batter by substituting heavy cream for the melted butter, I got pudding!

> Proteins (egg and flour proteins in cakes) set faster if they are acidic. Sometimes, without acidic conditions, proteins won't set. You can get pudding instead of cake.

Chocolate Flourless Cakes

There are many wonderful "flourless" chocolate cakes that take advantage of the fact that the cocoa particles in chocolate act as flour. In fact, any chocolate with sugar (bittersweet/semisweet) contains three of our four major cake ingredients: the cocoa particles act as "flour," the cocoa butter is the fat, and the finely ground sugar particles are the sugar.

All that we need to complete a cake made with chocolate are the eggs. The "Flourless" Luscious, Decadent Chocolate Cake illustrates this very well. This is not a chemically leavened cake, but is a clear illustration of the cocoa particles in chocolate acting as flour.

In testing flourless chocolate recipes, I found that most use butter and possibly sugar with the chocolate and eggs. I tested a number of traditional recipes, but they were all dry, which was not a surprise because the recipes contain so

> In chocolate, you have three of the four major cake ingredients: there is sugar, cocoa particles acts as flour, and cocoa butter is fat.

many eggs. Egg whites dry things out (see page 81). I knew that I had to do something. I can't stand dry cakes. I love the taste of cream, so I thought I would try using cream instead of butter. The cream made the cake moister—too moist: it was pudding. I was stunned! What happened? All that I did was to substitute ½ cup (118 ml) heavy cream for melted butter and my cake went from bone dry to pudding!

The first thing that I thought of was acidity. The batter needs to be acidic for the eggs to set well. The acidity of the semisweet chocolate had been enough. Why did the addition of ½ cup (118 ml) of cream take that acidity away?

Oops! That is exactly what happened. Dairy products like the heavy cream contain buffers, compounds that grab hydrogen ions (the acidic part of acids). These buffers tie up the hydrogen ions and keep them from making the batter any more acidic.

Even when you add additional acidic ingredients, the cream, milk, or buttermilk can absorb acidity so the batter stays at about the same acidity. In some cases, with the acidity eliminated or greatly reduced, the proteins will not set firmly and you get pudding or a gummy cake.

> Dairy products like heavy cream or milk contain buffers, compounds that grab hydrogen ions (the acidic part of acids), tie them up, and keep them from making the batter any more acidic.

My flourless chocolate cake set firmly with melted butter. Butter is over 80% fat, with 18 to 19% water, so there is only a small amount of "dairy products" in the butter. Cream, however, contains a much higher percentage of dairy products and enough of these buffering compounds to reduce the acidity of the batter just enough to prevent firm setting of the egg proteins.

So I compromised. I tested the cake with ¼ cup (2 oz/56 g) butter and only ⅓ cup (79 ml) heavy cream. It set beautifully and was no longer pudding, and it was much softer and moister than the cake made with butter. This was just what I wanted—a little interference with the firm, dry setting of the egg proteins, but not enough to change from a cake to a pudding.

I kept playing with the recipe by adding a little acidity from cream of tartar, and tried to see how much I could reduce the eggs. When I got down to four eggs, it took an hour to cook and again the cake was on the border between cake and pudding. My granddaughter loved it; she wanted to take the whole cake to school. I decided that I would need one or two more eggs to push it securely into the cake category.

My editor at the time, Harriet Bell, said that she improved her flourless chocolate cakes by straining the beaten eggs. This removes more goopy stuff than you might think; the chalazae (the white strings in every egg) are removed. These are actually shock cords that hold the yolk in the center and keep it from banging against the inside of the shell.

I incorporated all of this and came up with the great flourless chocolate torte below. For another flourless cake, see Chocolate Pecan Torte with a Hint of Bourbon, page 237.

"Flourless" Luscious, Decadent Chocolate Torte

MAKES ONE 9-INCH (23-CM) ROUND TORTE

A chocolate lover's delight! You can garnish this cake simply with a sprinkling of confectioners' sugar. This torte is beautiful iced with Shiny Ganache Glaze (page 97), Velvety Ganache Glaze (page 98), or Satin-Smooth Ganache Glaze (page 99). I love to serve it with sweetened whipped cream or vanilla ice cream.

What This Recipe Shows

Strain the eggs for a smoother batter and cake.

Many flourless chocolate tortes contain melted butter, not cream. When I substituted cream for the melted butter, I got a pudding instead of cake. The cream contained dairy buffers that reduced the acidity of the batter to a point that the eggs would not set firmly. I found that if I added cream of tartar (a little more acidity), 1/3 cup (79 ml) cream interfered with the setting just enough to give me a moister cake—still cake, but not as firm and dry as with butter.

Originally, I had used heavy cream—not whipped. Then I switched to my beloved whipped cream.

Nonstick cooking spray
6 large eggs (10.5 oz/298 g)
1 cup (7 oz/198 g) sugar
16 ounces (454 g) semisweet chocolate
1 teaspoon (3 g) cream of tartar

1 teaspoon (5 ml) pure vanilla extract
1/8 teaspoon (pinch) salt
1/4 cup (2 oz/56 g) butter, melted
1/3 cup (79 ml) heavy cream

1. Arrange a shelf in the lower third of the oven, place a baking stone on it, and preheat the oven to 375°F/191°C.

2. Spray a 9 x 2-inch (23 x 5-cm) round cake pan with nonstick cooking spray and line with a parchment circle. (I very lightly spray the top of the parchment, too.)

3. Place 6 eggs (4 for the whole eggs and 2 for yolks) in a bowl of hot water to warm them to room temperature or slightly above. Separate 2 of the eggs. In a medium mixing bowl, stir the 4 whole eggs and the 2 yolks until the yolks and whites are well blended. Strain the eggs and discard the goopy mess left in the strainer. Add the sugar and beat on medium speed for 10 minutes.

4. Place the chocolate in a large glass bowl and microwave with frequent stirring to melt; 50% power for 2 minutes usually works.

5. Add the cream of tartar, vanilla, salt, and butter to the beaten egg mixture and beat for a few seconds to blend.

6. Pour a little of the melted chocolate into the egg mixture and gently fold together by hand with a large spoon or spatula. Fold in more and more chocolate until all is added.

7. In a cold bowl with cold beaters, whip the cream until soft peaks form when the beater is lifted. Beat a little beyond this soft peak stage. Stir about one-quarter of the whipped cream into the batter to lighten. Then fold the rest of the whipped cream into the batter. Pour the batter into the prepared pan.

8. In a medium saucepan, bring about 3 cups (708 ml) of water to a boil. To make a water bath, place the cake pan in a larger pan and place in the oven on the stone. Carefully pour the boiling water into the larger pan until it comes about 1½ inches (3.8 cm) up the side of the cake pan. Close the oven door and bake uncovered in the water bath for about 45 minutes. Make sure that the torte is sufficiently done; a toothpick inserted into the torte should come out clean and the torte should be firm to the touch.

9. Allow to cool in the pan on a rack for 1 hour. When completely cooled, wrap well with plastic wrap and refrigerate for 4 hours.

10. To remove from the pan, run a thin knife around the edge of the cake. Heat the bottom over a burner on the stove for about 10 seconds and then invert onto an 8-inch (20-cm) cake cardboard if decorating with icing, or onto a serving platter if sprinkling with confectioners' sugar. Sprinkle with confectioners' sugar or ice according to directions (see page 141) with Shiny Ganache Glaze (page 97), Velvety Ganache Glaze (page 98), or Satin-Smooth Ganache Glaze (page 99).

Acidic Ingredients

Which ingredients are acidic and which are not? Cake flour is acidic, about pH 5, which helps cakes set (see page 64). However, in an eggless cake, you need all the protein that you can get and cake flour is low in protein. Shirley's Crazy Cake (page 83) simply uses vinegar to ensure acidity.

In chocolate cakes, it is helpful to use natural cocoa powder, which is acidic, instead of Dutch process, which is alkaline.

Acidity of Some Cake Ingredients

The chart below shows acidity of a number of typical ingredients. Acidity is measured in a unit called pH. The lower the pH, the more acidic a substance is. Neutral is pH 7, so ingredients below pH 7 are acidic, and those above are alkaline.

Ingredient	pH	Ingredient	pH
Eggs	8.5–9.5	Cornstarch	4.0–7.0
Egg whites	7.0–9.0	Cocoa powder:	
Egg yolks	6.4	Natural	5.0–5.9
Butter	6.1–6.4	Dutch process:	
Milk	6.2–7.3	lightly processed	6.0–6.6
Cream	6.5	strongly processed	6.7–7.1
Buttermilk	4.5	very strong	7.8–8.2
Molasses	5.0–5.5	Bread	5.3–5.8
Honey	3.9	Wheat flour	6.0–6.3
Corn syrup	5.0	Chocolate cake	7.2–7.6
Sugar	5.0–6.0	Devil's food cake	7.5–8.0
Yeast	3.0–3.5	Pound cake	6.6–7.1
Vinegar	2.0–3.4	Yellow layer cake	6.7–7.1
Limes	1.9	White layer cake	7.1–7.4
Lemons	2.1	Angel food cake	5.2–5.6
Apples	3.1	Sponge cake	7.3–7.6
Raisins	3.8–4.0	Biscuits	7.1–7.3
Apple cider	2.9–3.3		

FATS

Different Roles of Fats

In the delicate balance of ingredients in shortened (butter) cakes, fats and sugars are the tenderizers. They soften and moderate the firm structure made by the proteins in the flour, eggs, and milk.

In shortened cakes, fats perform three crucial roles: they make the cake light and delicate by holding the tiny air bubbles that the gases from baking powder or baking soda can expand; they make the cake melt-in-your-mouth tender by coating the flour proteins so that they cannot form gluten; and they carry rich flavors and essential nutrients. Solid fats such as butter and Crisco do a better job of holding air bubbles to aid in leavening, while liquid fats such as canola oil and vegetable oil do a better job as tenderizers because they coat flour proteins so well.

Commercially available shortenings with emulsifiers, such as Crisco, make high-ratio cakes (cakes that contain more liquid) possible. The emulsifiers allow the fat to hold onto more liquid, which, in turn, permits the use of more sugar in the cake batter. (There must be enough liquid to dissolve all the sugar and also allow the starch to swell.) This produces a sweeter, moister cake. (Read more about high-ratio cakes, page 31.)

> In cakes, fats perform three crucial roles: they contribute to leavening, tenderize, and carry flavors.

Fats in Leavening

Solid fats, which hold air bubbles well, include butter, shortening, margarines, spreads, and solid animal fats. Animal fats, which can have a slightly meaty flavor, are used primarily in savory pastries, steamed Christmas puddings, and mincemeat baked goods.

Baking powder and baking soda do not make a single new bubble. Their gases simply enlarge the bubbles that already exist in the batter. With most solid fats, these vital bubbles must be beaten in during the creaming or mixing of the cake. However, shortening such as Crisco has an advantage over other solid fats in that it already contains millions of fine bubbles to aid in leavening.

Unprocessed solid shortening has a glassy, unappetizing appearance. For a more appealing snow-white appearance, manufacturers bubble nitrogen, a nonreactive gas, into the shortening. Shortenings are, by volume, about 12% fine nitrogen bubbles. This means that shortenings will make a lighter cake because they already contain all these bubbles ready to be enlarged. Also, many shortenings have emulsifiers such as mono- and diglycerides that aid in better distribution of the fat in the batter. Better distribution of fat means better distribution of the air bubbles for a better-textured cake. Shortenings with emulsifiers extend freshness, increase volume, and enhance eating quality.

Shortening has an ideal texture to beat for increased volume and aeration. Even at warm room temperature, there is no danger that shortening will melt and lose its air-holding ability. Butter from the refrigerator must warm slightly to be beaten, and it can melt if the room is too warm. And, of course, butter

> The bubble-holding capacity of solid fats is a vital part of leavening because baking powder and baking soda do not make new bubbles but only enlarge bubbles that already exist in the batter.

does not contain the 12% of volume in fine bubbles that shortening has. Nevertheless, there is nothing like the taste of real butter, so butter is normally the fat of choice of fine cake bakers. I must say, however, I have been amazed at the good taste of cookies made with butter-flavored shortening. Crisco now offers a trans fat–free shortening.

Margarines have all the disadvantages of butter without its flavor advantage. Spreads, with their high water content, gums, starches, and major differences from brand to brand, will behave in unpredictable ways and do not contribute much to taste.

Fats as Tenderizers

Oil coats flour proteins better than a solid fat and prevents their absorbing liquid from the batter to make gluten. This leaves more moisture in the batter. Cakes made with oil can be not only tender but also very moist. When it is formed, gluten ties up water. So less gluten means more liquid free for a moister cake. This is why in cake after cake in this book I have used both butter and oil. Butter gives you great taste and aeration, and oil gives you tenderness and moisture. When you want a baked good that is really moist, think of oil. Every time that I bite into a horribly dry muffin, I think, "They should have used oil."

I love the Carrot Cake made with oil in the 1975 edition of *The Joy of Cooking*.

Golden, Moist Carrot Cake

MAKES ONE 8-INCH (20-CM) 4-LAYER ROUND CAKE

Moist and wonderful! Spices and orange zest make this a little zippier than some carrot cakes. I love the flavors that develop when combining the brown sugar with carrots.

What This Recipe Shows

Oil makes a wonderfully moist cake.

Roasting enhances the flavor of nuts.

Self-rising flour produces an even texture (in the cake part, not with regard to the nuts).

---

2 cups (7 oz/198 g) pecan or walnut pieces

2 tablespoons (1 oz/28 g) butter

3/4 teaspoon (4.5 g) salt, divided

Nonstick cooking spray

2 1/3 cups (10.2 oz/291 g) spooned and leveled self-rising flour

1 teaspoon (2 g) ground cinnamon

1/2 teaspoon (1 g) nutmeg (freshly grated, if possible)

1/2 teaspoon (1 g) allspice, optional

1 tablespoon orange zest (grated peel)

3 large eggs (5.25 oz/149 g)

2 large egg yolks (1.3 oz/37 g)

2 cups (15.4 oz/437 g) light brown sugar, packed

1 cup (237 ml) canola oil

1 teaspoon (5 ml) pure vanilla extract

1/4 cup (59 ml) fresh orange juice

3 cups (11.6 oz/329 g) peeled and very finely grated carrots, about 6 carrots (I like to process in the food processor until very finely chopped)

Carrot Cake Cream Cheese Icing (recipe follows)

1. Arrange a shelf in the lower third of the oven, place a baking stone on it, and preheat the oven to 350°F/177°C.

2. Spread the nuts out on a baking sheet, place in the oven on the stone, and roast 10 minutes. While nuts are hot, stir in the butter and 1/4 teaspoon (1.5 g) salt. When cool, coarsely chop and set aside.

3. Spray two 8 x 2-inch (20 x 5-cm) round cake pans (you need the 2-inch/5-cm high pans) with nonstick cooking spray and line with a parchment circle. (I very lightly spray the top of the parchment, too.)

4. In a large mixing bowl, beat together well the flour, remaining ½ teaspoon (3 g) salt, the cinnamon, nutmeg, allspice, and orange zest.

5. In another bowl, stir together the whole eggs, egg yolks, and brown sugar. Stir in the oil, vanilla, and orange juice. Make a hole in the center of the flour mixture and stir the egg mixture in a little at a time by hand. Stir in the carrots and the roasted nuts.

6. Pour the batter into the prepared pans. Spoon the batter from one pan to the other until the batter is divided equally. Drop the pans, one at a time, onto the counter from a height of 4 inches (10 cm) to knock out large bubbles.

7. Place both pans in the oven on the stone. Bake until the center springs back when touched, about 30 to 35 minutes. Ideally, the cake should not pull away from the sides until it has just come out of the oven. The center temperature should be about 209°F/98°C if you check by inserting an instant-read thermometer.

8. Place both layers of the cake in the pan on a rack to cool for 10 minutes, then shake the pan to loosen the cake all around. Spray a cooling rack with nonstick cooking spray. Place the rack sprayed side down on top of the cake, invert, and lift off the pans. Allow to finish cooling. When completely cool, slice each layer in half horizontally, creating four layers.

9. Ice with Carrot Cake Cream Cheese Icing. Divide the icing in half. Save one half to ice the top and sides, and divide one half into thirds for the layers. Place one layer cut side up on a serving dish and spread with one third of the divided icing. Place another layer on top of the icing, cut side up, and spread it with another third. Place the third layer on, cut side up on top of the second layer, and spread with the remaining icing. Place the top layer on, cut side down. Ice the top and sides with the reserved icing.

Carrot Cake Cream Cheese Icing

½ cup (4 oz/113 g) unsalted butter, cut in 2-tablespoon (1-oz/28-g) pieces
Two 8-ounce packages (454 g) cream cheese

4 cups (16 oz/454 g) confectioners' sugar
1 teaspoon (5 ml) pure vanilla extract
1 tablespoon (15 ml) Grand Marnier liqueur

In a large mixing bowl, beat the butter until soft. Add the cream cheese and beat until blended and smooth. Blend in the sugar, vanilla, and Grand Marnier. Refrigerate until ready to use.

SUGAR

Sugar's Many Roles in Cakes

Our most familiar sugar, table sugar or granulated sugar, is a double sugar (sucrose) made of glucose and fructose joined together. It may be an ordinary household item, but it plays amazing roles in cooking. Sugar is used to preserve the shape of fruits and vegetables (page 310). It is the reason that, after cooking all day, Boston baked beans still retain their shape. And in desserts, sugar can keep fruit in perfect shape.

In the balance of cake ingredients, sugar and fat are the tenderizers and moisturizers of the cake. When combining with flour proteins, sugar prevents them from joining each other to make tough gluten. One flour protein, glutenin, combines with sugar to form a soluble protein-sugar compound, and gliadin, the other gluten-forming protein, combines with sugar in the same manner. Sugar is a great tenderizer in pie crusts and cookies, and it plays the same role in cakes. Since sugar can substitute for fat as a tenderizer, it is an important ingredient in reduced-fat baked goods (page 79).

Some of the other characteristics of sugar (sucrose) that contribute to cakes are:

Moisture-holding ability—Sugar is hygroscopic; it has the ability to attract and hold water. By absorbing water, sugar helps baked goods stay moist, and it limits the swelling of starch to contribute to the texture.

Contribution to texture—Sucrose's ability to absorb and hold water affects the texture of cakes, muffins, and quick breads by limiting the amount of water that is available to allow the starch to swell. This creates a finer texture and crumb in cakes but may be more clearly visible in cookies. The high amount of sugar creates crispness by preventing the starch from swelling, and by melting and then recrystallizing. The cracked surface on gingersnaps is a clear example of this (see page 394).

Controlling microbial activity—In yeast breads, microbial activity breaks sucrose and starch down into simple sugars to provide food for yeast as well as to enhance browning.

Browning—Under nonacidic conditions, sugar can be a contributor to browning.

Adding bulk—Sucrose provides a considerable portion of the bulk in batters or doughs.

Complex flavor influence—Sugar has complex indirect influences on flavor. Researchers at the University of Nottingham can analyze the gases present in the nasal cavity. Test subjects chewed gum with mint and sugar until the flavor was gone. But there was still mint detected in their nasal cavities. When they were given sugar, the mint flavor returned. A friend from the UK said that, as children, when their gum ran out of flavor, they rolled it in the family sugar dish and it was like new! As little as $\frac{1}{2}$ teaspoon (2 g) of sugar in a dish can make an amazing taste difference.

Sugar in Action

If you have too much flour or eggs, a cake can be dry; too much fat or sugar, and the cake may not set. The wonderful Improved Tunnel of Fudge Cake (below) is a perfect example of what sugar can do to a cake's structure. There is so much sugar in this cake that the center does not set with regular cooking time and temperature. (Technically, this cake should go with the egg- and steam-leavened cakes in the next chapter, but it is the perfect example of what an excess of sugar can do. I couldn't resist putting it in now.)

Improved Tunnel of Fudge Cake

MAKES ONE 12-CUP (2.8-L) BUNDT CAKE

You can go crazy over this cake. My husband and I ate a whole cake in 3 days! Tunnel of Fudge Cake was THE chocolate cake of the 1960s. It "made" the Bundt pan. The recipe was on the label of Pillsbury's fudge icing after it won an award in the 1966 Pillsbury Bake-Off. When Pillsbury stopped making the icing, angry home cooks bombarded them: "You can't do this. The Tunnel of Fudge is my signature cake." So Pillsbury had to publish a recipe for the famous cake using ingredients available to home cooks. I found that this recipe had many problems, so I revamped it considerably. *The New York Times* (Dec. 28, 2004) featured my cake on the front page of the Science section, where I explained each change that I made and why. I substituted 2 yolks for 1 of the eggs and substituted oil for part of the butter to make the cake moister. I also substituted dark brown sugar for some of the sugar to give the cake even fudgier flavors. The roasted nuts are really important. Without them, the cake seems ordinary, but with them, it's fantastic.

What This Recipe Shows

Brown sugar makes chocolate taste fudgy.

With this extreme amount of sugar the cake does not fully cook, thus creating the "tunnel of fudge" in the center.

The roasted nuts make this cake. Don't leave them out.

2½ cups (8.7 oz/250 g) walnut pieces or mixed walnuts and pecans

1¼ cups plus 2 tablespoons (11 oz/311 g) unsalted butter, cut in 2-tablespoon (1-oz/28-g) pieces, divided

¾ teaspoon (4.5 g) salt, divided

Nonstick cooking spray

1 cup (7 oz/198 g) granulated sugar

¾ cup (6.3 oz/178 g) dark brown sugar, packed

1 teaspoon (5 ml) pure vanilla extract

⅓ cup (79 ml) canola oil

2 large egg yolks (1.3 oz/37 g)

2 cups (8 oz/240 g) confectioners' sugar

¾ cup (2.1 oz/61g) natural cocoa powder (my favorites are Ghirardelli and Scharffen Berger)

4 large eggs (7 oz/198 g)

2¼ cups (9.9 oz/281 g) spooned and leveled bleached all-purpose flour

Confectioners' sugar, to garnish, or Rum Drizzle (recipe follows), optional

1. Arrange a shelf in the lower third of the oven, place a baking stone on it, and preheat the oven to 350°F/177°C.

2. On a large baking sheet, roast the nuts for 10 minutes. Pour into a bowl, add 2 tablespoons (1 oz/28 g) of the butter and ¼ teaspoon (1.5 g) of the salt, and toss well. When cool, coarsely chop and set aside.

3. Spray a 12-cup (2.8-L) Bundt pan generously with nonstick cooking spray.

4. With a mixer, beat the remaining 1¼ cups (10 oz/283 g) butter to soften and get to the fluffy stage. Add the granulated sugar, then the brown sugar, and continue to beat until light and airy. While beating, feel the bowl; if it does not feel cool, place in the freezer for 5 minutes, and then continue beating.

5. Beat in the remaining ½ teaspoon (3 g) salt and the vanilla. Blend in the oil and egg yolks.

6. By hand, stir in the confectioners' sugar, then the cocoa powder.

7. By hand, one at a time, stir the eggs into the batter, with minimum stirring just to blend them into the batter well.

8. In a large mixing bowl, stir together the flour and roasted chopped nuts. Fold the flour-nut mixture into the batter and pour into the prepared pan. (Atlanta wine expert Gil Kulers, who makes this cake frequently, heats the empty pan for about 5 minutes just before he pours in the batter. This ensures that he gets a good ¾ inch [2 cm] of well-set cake to hold the fudge center.)

9. Bake for 45 minutes. You can't use the toothpick test for doneness because this cake has so much sugar that the center is not going to set, but remains a "tunnel of fudge" in the center. You are totally dependent on the correct oven temperature of 350°F/177°C and the 45-minute cooking time.

10. When you remove the cake from the oven, you can't see it but it will have a runny fudge core with an air pocket above the fudge. This air pocket is not desirable and will become a hole under the fudge when the cake is chilled. To minimize this air pocket, about 20 minutes after you take the cake out of the oven, while still in the pan, press the inside and outside edges of the cake bottom down all the way around. This will press the whole bottom down and reduce the air pocket. Leave the cake in the pan until completely cooled. I cool the cake in the pan on a rack for 2 to 3 hours. This is very important. With a thin knife, loosen the cake around the edges. Place a platter on top of the pan and invert.

11. Cool completely. Sprinkle with confectioners' sugar (my favorite) or drizzle with Rum Drizzle to garnish. I love this cake at room temperature or cold. At room temperature, the fudge is runny. When cold, the fudge center becomes firm, like a piece of fudge with nuts.

Rum Drizzle

1 cup (4 oz/120 g) confectioners' sugar
1 teaspoon (5 ml) pure vanilla extract

$^{1}/_{2}$ teaspoon (2.5 ml) rum or brandy
About 2 tablespoons (30 ml) heavy cream

Stir together the sugar, vanilla, and rum. Add the cream to get to a consistency that will give you a thick drizzle.

Different Sugars

In addition to table sugar, cooks have many other sweeteners available—both natural and artificial. Alternative nutritive sweeteners include honey, corn syrup (glucose), maple syrup, rice malt syrup, molasses, turbinado sugar, Sucanat, and Rapadura, to name a few. Some of these, such as turbinado, Sucanat, and Rapadura, are still sucrose with minerals from molasses. All of these have calories, cause tooth decay, and elevate blood glucose levels. There are also many nonnutritive alternative sweeteners (see page 79). Different sugars have different characteristics in cooking. Here is a look at a few of our more widely used nutritive sweeteners.

Honey

Honey, which is 42% fructose, absorbs water from the atmosphere and makes cakes and muffins good keepers. Under the same conditions, baked goods made with honey stay moist longer than those made with sugar. Brown sugar contains some fructose too, and baked goods made with it retain moisture as well. Realize that this means that products like cookies made with honey or brown sugar will not remain crisp; they will soften as they absorb moisture from the air.

Brown Sugar

There are two commercial methods of making brown sugar. In one, the brown sugar is separated out during the refining of white sugar and is further processed without removing all of the molasses. In the other method, molasses is added to completely refined white sugar. The term that processors use is that the sugar is "painted." I would guess that the molasses is sprayed on in some manner.

Possibly a reason for these two methods is that molasses processed from sugar beets smells so bad that it can't be used for human food. I imagine that refined sugar made from sugar beets has to be "painted" with sugarcane molasses to make brown sugar.

You can't tell by a quick glance at a single brown sugar which process was used, but if you have brown sugars made by each of the processes side by side, you can see a difference. It you rub the "painted" brown sugar between your thumb and forefinger, you can actually rub off the molasses.

The same company may use both methods to produce brown sugar. I had a call from Jan Hazard, who was then editor of *Ladies' Home Journal*. She explained that she had two boxes of a name-brand brown sugar with exactly the same labels, but they were different. How did this happen? I explained that the same company may have many processing plants and may use both of the processing methods.

Syrups

All syrups offer an advantage in that the sugar is already dissolved. The dissolved-sugar method of mixing a cake is described on page 134. This method is not widely known, but it is my favorite. It produces a tender crust and crumb, excellent aeration, and fine texture.

Syrups can be thick, and so, with the addition of egg whites, can hold air bubbles to help with aeration. Corn syrup (glucose) also gives additional flavor, which aids in reduced-fat baking.

Corn syrup browns at lower temperatures than other sugars. Depending upon the specific situation, this enhanced browning may be an advantage or a disadvantage.

Nonnutritive Alternative Sweeteners

Nonnutritive alternative sweeteners do not have calories, cause tooth decay, or elevate blood glucose levels. Some of these sweeteners—sugar alcohols (polyols) like xylitol, sorbitol, mannitol, malitol, lactitol, isomalt, and hydrogenated starch—are primarily used in the commercial production of candies, chewing gum, jams and jellies, and frozen desserts. There are also naturally occurring super-sweeteners like stevia, the thaumatins, and glycyrrhizin, many but not all of which have some licorice or bitter flavor. I have had some that are very pleasant tasting.

I have limited the rest of this section to nonnutritive, artificial (man-made) sweeteners. Some of these are the sweeteners readily available to and most used by consumers and include saccharin (Sweet 'n Low), cyclamates, acesulfame K (Sunett), aspartame (Equal), alitame, and sucralose (Splenda).

Saccharin (Sweet 'n Low), which is 300 to 600 times sweeter than sucrose and has a slightly bitter, metallic aftertaste, was discovered in 1878 and has been in wide use since 1900. It can tolerate baking temperatures. Saccharin is approved in more than ninety countries. Epidemiological studies have not shown any relationship between ingestion of saccharin and increased risk of cancer in humans.

In 1977, one study indicated that rats given the equivalent of the amount of saccharin in 800 to 1,000 cans of soda per day did have an increased risk of bladder cancer. Considering that outrageously large amount, and the fact that rat bladders are physiologically unique and different from human bladders, saccharin is allowed to be sold in the United States with a warning label: "This product contains saccharin which has been determined to cause cancer in laboratory animals." Numerous scientific groups, health groups, and regulators support the removal of this warning, which is still under review.

Cyclamates, which are 30 times sweeter than sucrose, were discovered in 1937. They can tolerate baking temperatures. Cyclamates are valued for their synergism (a situation where two substances combined have a greater total effect than the sum of their individual effects). Saccharin with cyclamates produces a sweetener with a better taste than saccharin alone. Cyclamates are approved for food use in more than fifty countries and were approved in the United States until 1970, when a faulty study indicated they may cause cancer in rats. Many studies since then have found cyclamates not to be carcinogenic. Petitions have been filed to remove the ban, which is still effective only in the United States.

Acesulfame K (Sunett) is 200 times sweeter than sugar and has a clean, sweet taste. It can tolerate baking temperatures and is not subject to microbial breakdown. It forms synergistic blends with many other sweeteners. It is approved in twenty-five countries and more than ninety studies indicate that acesulfame K is neither carcinogenic nor mutagenic. In the United States, it has been approved for use in tabletop sweeteners, chewing gum, nondairy creamers, puddings, gelatin, instant coffee and teas, dry-mix beverages, and soft drinks.

Aspartame (Equal) is between 160 and 220 times sweeter than sugar and has a clean taste with no bitter or metallic aftertaste. It is also a flavor enhancer with acidic fruit flavors. It breaks down at normal baking temperatures and is no longer sweet.

Aspartame is one of the most widely reviewed and studied food additives. On the basis of many clinical studies, scientists from national and international organizations have concluded that aspartame and its decomposition products are safe for human consumption. It is approved in more than ninety countries and is the most widely used artificial sweetener available in the marketplace today. Aspartame is approved in the United States as a general-purpose sweetener, but is not effective in baking.

People with phenylketonuria (PKU), a rare hereditary condition in which the amino acid phenylalanine is not properly metabolized, have to avoid phenylalanine in all foods, aspartame included.

Alitame is 2,000 times sweeter than sugar. Like aspartame, it is made from large amino acids. Unlike aspartame, it can survive baking temperatures. It is approved for use in Australia, New Zealand, Mexico, and Canada. A petition for food-additive status has been filed in the United States, but it is still under review.

Sucralose (Splenda), the only artificial sweetener made from sucrose, is between 400 and 800 times sweeter than sucrose. It does not break down with heat and may be used in cooking and baking. More than 100 animal and human studies show that sucralose is noncarcinogenic and nonmutagenic. When consumed, it goes through the body untouched and is excreted unchanged. It was approved in 1999 as a general-purpose sweetener and can be used in all food and beverage products. It does not elevate blood glucose or cause cavities.

Artificial Sweeteners in Cooking

Artificial sweeteners have the advantages of few or no calories, they do not raise blood glucose levels, and they do not cause cavities. Unfortunately, all that artificial sweeteners do is sweeten. On the other hand, sugar (sucrose) is much more than just a sweetener in cooking.

Some of the things that sucrose contributes to cooking and baking that most artificial sweeteners do not are:

Browning—With heat and acidic ingredients, some sucrose breaks down into fructose and glucose to provide browning for everything from toast to meat. This browning from the Maillard reactions is not just a brown color formation, but is also a major flavor enhancement with all the wonderful flavors of caramel.

Tenderizing—In any baked good containing wheat flour, sugar is a major tenderizer. Sucrose combines with the flour proteins to prevent their joining to make tough gluten. Sugar is the great tenderizer in pie crusts, cookies, cakes, and muffins. Sugar can substitute for fat as a tenderizer, making it an important ingredient in reduced-fat baked goods.

Leavening—In cakes, muffins, and quick breads, sugar is a major contributor to the leavening by helping incorporate fine air bubbles into the batter in the creaming step.

Back on page 73, I went into detail about other things that sugar (sucrose) does in baking. I am going to simply list these again here: sugar holds moisture, contributes to texture, supports microbial activity that aids in browning and supplying food for yeast in yeast doughs, adds bulk, and has complex indirect influences on flavor.

So how can you use artificial sweeteners in cooking or baking? In beverages, sauces, mousses, and puddings there are few problems. You can enhance browning in everything from turkeys to cookies by adding a teaspoon of corn syrup, a natural sweetener. The microbial activity of sugar is vital in yeast breads and there is not enough sugar in breads to make a dietary difference. Only in sweet yeast breads would a partial substitution of artificial sweeteners be practical.

In baking, the only successes that I have had using artificial sweeteners were with partial substitutions. Sugar just does too much for many baked goods to work without it. Using Splenda Sugar Blend or Splenda Brown Sugar Blend, which are made of part Splenda and part sugar, I have made excellent muffins using recipes that have a good quantity of fruit and nuts to act as bulk (see Ruth Fowler's Beautiful Morning Glory Muffins, recipe below).

Ruth Fowler's Beautiful Morning Glory Muffins

MAKES 18 MEDIUM (2¾ X 1⅛-INCH/7 X 2.8-CM) MUFFINS

Ruth Fowler, an outstanding home baker in Atlanta, shared her recipe for these moist, delicious muffins with my sister, Joyce Hutcheson, and now generously shares the recipe with us. Because Splenda does not promote browning, I would ordinarily add a teaspoon of corn syrup for good color, but these muffins contain cinnamon, apple, raisins, and nuts that all contribute to good color.

What This Recipe Shows

Apples, raisins, nuts, and coconut add bulk to the muffins to replace the bulk that sugar usually provides.

Coconut holds moisture to fill the moisture-holding role of sugar.

Cinnamon, apple, raisins, and nuts all contribute good color, so I did not need to add a teaspoon of corn syrup for browning.

---

1 cup (3.5 oz/99 g) pecans
1 tablespoon (0.5 oz/14 g) butter
¾ teaspoon (4.5 g) salt, divided
2 cups (8.8 oz/249 g) spooned and leveled
    bleached all-purpose flour
2 teaspoons (0.3 oz/9 g) baking powder
2 teaspoons (4 g) ground cinnamon
1 cup (8 oz/227 g) Splenda Brown Sugar
    Blend, packed
3 large eggs (5.25 oz/149 g)

1 cup (237 ml) canola oil
2 teaspoons (10 ml) pure vanilla extract
1 medium-large ripe Fuji or Golden Delicious
    apple, peeled, cored, and cut into chunks
2 medium carrots, peeled and cut into
    chunks, or about 20 baby carrots
½ cup (2.6 oz/73 g) golden raisins
½ cup (1.6 oz/45 g) frozen grated coconut
Nonstick cooking spray with flour

1. Arrange a shelf in the lower third of the oven, place a baking stone on it, and preheat the oven to 350°F/177°C.

2. Spread the nuts out on a baking sheet, place in the oven on the stone, and roast 10 minutes. While nuts are hot, stir in the butter and ¼ teaspoon (1.5 g) of the salt. When cool, coarsely chop and set aside.

3. Turn oven up to 400°F/204°C.

4. In a large bowl, with a hand mixer or by hand with a fork, beat together the flour, baking powder, the remaining $\frac{1}{2}$ teaspoon (3 g) salt, the cinnamon, and Splenda Brown Sugar Blend for 30 full seconds.

5. In another bowl, stir together the eggs, oil, and vanilla.

6. Put the apple and carrots into a food processor with the steel blade. Chop with quick on/offs until the pieces are about the size of rice. Stir this chopped fruit mixture into the flour mixture and immediately stir in the egg mixture. Stir in the raisins, roasted chopped pecans, and coconut.

7. Spray two 6-cup medium ($2\frac{3}{4}$ x $1\frac{1}{8}$-inch/7 x 2.8-cm) muffin pans with nonstick cooking spray. (See Muffin Pan Sizes, page 132. If you make muffins in a pan that is a different size than the recipe indicates, you will need to adjust baking time, and the yield will be different.)

8. Spoon the batter into the prepared muffin tins to the top of the cups because these do not rise much. Place in the oven on the hot stone and bake until a toothpick inserted in the center comes out clean, about 18 minutes. Cool in the muffin tins on a wire rack for 5 minutes. Jar the edges of the pans to loosen the muffins, and then gently shake the muffins out onto a rack. Serve warm.

EGGS

Eggs in Cakes

As always, eggs are not just eggs—whites are an incredible drying and leavening agent, and yolks are nature's great emulsifiers that provide a creamy texture.

Do not limit yourself to using whole eggs. If cakes or muffins are dry, cut an egg white from the recipe. Use two yolks instead of the whole egg, and add a little more sugar and fat. Many high-ratio cakes require extra emulsifiers to handle the large amounts of sugar and liquid. You will see many cake recipes that contain yolks alone. On the other hand, if you have a cake that's a soggy mess, you may need to add an egg white to dry the cake a little.

Egg whites are excellent leavening agents, too. Frequently, some whites are beaten and folded into the batter during mixing. A cake can become a soufflé, and if you use all beaten whites in a cake, it will fall like a soufflé. When egg whites are beaten, they are denatured and, so to speak, partially "cooked." They are no longer the strong contributors to structure that raw eggs are. You must have enough raw egg, milk, and flour proteins left to cook, and set the batter, or the cake will fall. It is true that meringues and angel food cakes are all beaten egg whites; however, they are foam cakes—essentially fat free, very high in sugar, and basically a cooked egg-white foam. Read more about angel food cakes on page 217.

> If you beat all of the whites in a cake, it will fall like a soufflé. Beaten egg whites are denatured and partially set. They do not contribute to the structure of a cake like unbeaten whites do.

Eggless Cakes

Eggs are one of the four basic cake ingredients. Eggs and flour supply the protein to set and hold the cake. Without this protein, cakes can be total mush. How can you make an eggless cake?

If we are working without eggs, the job of setting and holding the cake together falls entirely on the flour. We need to optimize the flour's ability to form gluten and to set. To form gluten to hold a cake together, we need to use a high-protein all-purpose flour like King Arthur Unbleached, and we need to mix the cake in a way that allows the water to reach the flour and form gluten before the fat reaches the flour and greases the flour proteins so that they can't join to make gluten.

Also, we need to be sure that the batter is acidic, which will help the proteins to set (coagulate or cook) faster. And we need to be sure to have a little salt present to strengthen the gluten.

Now, all of this sounds like a tall order. But good home cooks before us have already figured this out. A simple cake, Crazy Cake (also known as Wacky Cake), has been handed down since the 1940s and is a perfect example of all of these technical points. Thank goodness for our grandmothers in the kitchen! This cake possibly came from the days of rationing eggs during World War II.

About Crazy Cake

This beloved, easy eggless chocolate cake has been passed down for at least two generations and is mixed in a number of different ways. One method mixes all the liquids together and pours the mixture into each of the holes made in the flour. What is important is that water gets to the flour to create gluten before the oil does or the cake may be too tender to hold together. I think that the traditional technique below ensures that water gets to the flour to hold the cake together.

To make Shirley's Crazy Cake (recipe follows) stir the flour, cocoa, sugar, baking powder, and salt together well in an 8 x 8 x 2-inch (20 x 20 x 5-cm) pan. You can see how well mixed it is by how well the cocoa is distributed in the flour. Then, you hollow out two small holes and one large hole in the flour mixture. Vanilla goes into one small hole, vinegar into the other small hole, and oil into the larger hole. The oil will overflow, but don't worry about it. Now you pour a cup of water over the top and stir to mix the batter together smoothly.

When you add the water, the oil floats, which allows the water to get to the flour and form gluten when you stir. The acidity from the vinegar helps flour proteins to coagulate and set the cake nicely. A PhD in food science could not have done better!

In the Crazy Cake recipes, there is some variation in the ingredients. The cocoa powder runs from 3 tablespoons to 5 tablespoons (15 to 25 g), and the oil runs from 5 tablespoons to 8 tablespoons (75 to 120 ml). I elected to go with the greater amount of cocoa powder for more chocolate flavor and the greater amount of oil for a very tender and moist cake. Cold water or weak coffee is the option for the liquid. I personally like water. The traditional version has 1 teaspoon (4 g) baking soda, which is too much for good leavening, so I switched to baking powder to keep the batter more acidic and went with 1½ teaspoons (7 g). This same version also had 1 tablespoon (15 ml) vinegar, which does give you too much aftertaste. I found that the cake still sets nicely with just 1 teaspoon (5 ml) of vinegar and tastes much better.

Serious Stuff Gingerbread (page 84) is another successful eggless cake. Molasses and brown sugar contribute acidity to help set the flour proteins, and unbleached flour ensures that there are enough proteins to hold the gingerbread together.

Shirley's Crazy Cake

MAKES ONE 8 X 8 X 2-INCH (20 X 20 X 5-CM) SQUARE CAKE

A super easy, moist, tender, eggless chocolate cake—fabulous with vanilla ice cream or whipped cream.

What This Recipe Shows

Without any eggs, this is a very moist cake.

Gluten from the flour is the only thing holding this cake together, so it is important to stir to get some water into the flour to make gluten. If the cake is too crumbly, use unbleached or bread flour.

Vinegar is added to ensure an acidic batter so that the proteins will set (coagulate) to hold the cake together.

Dutch process cocoa needs to be avoided because its alkalinity may interfere with the setting of the cake.

1$\frac{1}{2}$ cups (6.6 oz/187 g) spooned and leveled unbleached all-purpose flour
1 cup (7 oz/198 g) sugar
$\frac{1}{3}$ cup (1 oz/28 g) natural cocoa powder (*not* Dutch process)
1$\frac{1}{2}$ teaspoons (7 g) baking powder
$\frac{1}{2}$ teaspoon (3 g) salt

1 teaspoon (5 ml) apple cider vinegar
2 teaspoons (10 ml) pure vanilla extract
$\frac{1}{2}$ cup (118 ml) canola oil
1 cup (237 ml) cold water or weak coffee
Simple Cream Cheese Icing (recipe follows), or Italian Meringue (page 187), optional

1. Arrange a shelf in the lower third of the oven, place a baking stone on it, and preheat the oven to 350°F/177°C.

2. In an 8 x 8 x 2-inch (20 x 20 x 5-cm) nonstick pan, stir together to blend the flour, sugar, cocoa powder, baking powder, and salt. Poke 2 small holes and 1 large hole in the dry ingredients with the handle of a wooden spoon. Spoon the vinegar into one small hole, and the vanilla into the other small hole. Pour the oil into the large hole. If it overflows, it is okay. Pour the cold water over the top and stir well to blend all of the ingredients together until smooth. Don't hesitate to stir. You want to develop some gluten to hold the cake together.

3. Place the pan in the oven on the baking stone and bake until a toothpick inserted in the center comes out moist, about 30 minutes. Place the cake on a rack to cool in the pan. You can garnish by sprinkling with confectioners' sugar, or ice with a simple frosting like the Simple Cream Cheese Icing or Italian Meringue. The Simple Cream Cheese Icing below is a smaller amount and simpler than the cream cheese icing with the carrot cake (page 72). Serve from the pan.

Simple Cream Cheese Icing

One 8-ounce package (227 g) cream cheese
½ cup (2 oz/56 g) confectioners' sugar

2 to 4 tablespoons (30 to 60 ml) heavy cream
1 teaspoon (5 ml) pure vanilla extract

Beat the cream cheese and sugar until soft. Beat in 2 tablespoons (30 ml) of the cream, then the vanilla. Add more cream to get a spreadable consistency. Spread on completely cooled cake.

Serious Stuff Gingerbread

MAKES ONE 8 X 8 X 2-INCH (20 X 20 X 5-CM) SQUARE CAKE

This is an eggless, intensely flavorful and moist gingerbread.

What This Recipe Shows

Molasses and brown sugar contribute to the acidity of the batter, which helps set the proteins.

Using a moderately high-protein flour, like unbleached all-purpose, contributes extra protein for a good set.

Ginger, cinnamon, and allspice, along with the molasses and brown sugar, produce intense flavors.

1¾ cups (7.7 oz/218 g) spooned and leveled unbleached all-purpose flour

½ teaspoon (2 g) baking soda

½ teaspoon (3 g) salt

2 teaspoons (3 g) ground ginger

1 teaspoon (2 g) ground cinnamon

1 teaspoon (2 g) ground allspice

½ cup (4.2 oz/119 g) dark brown sugar, packed

½ teaspoon (2.5 ml) apple cider vinegar

1 teaspoon (5 ml) pure vanilla extract

⅓ cup (79 ml) canola oil

⅔ cup (156 ml) cold water

½ cup (118 ml) unsulfured molasses (such as Grandma's brand)

1. Arrange a shelf in the lower third of the oven, place a baking stone on it, and preheat the oven to 350°F/177°C.

2. In an 8 x 8 x 2-inch (20 x 20 x 5-cm) nonstick pan, stir together to blend the flour, baking soda, salt, ginger, cinnamon, allspice, and sugar. Poke 3 medium holes in the ingredients with the handle of a wooden spoon. Spoon the vinegar into one hole, and the vanilla into another hole. Pour oil into the last hole. It is okay if it overflows. Pour the cold water over the top and stir in well. Add the molasses and stir all of the ingredients together until smooth.

3. Place the pan in the oven on the baking stone and bake until a toothpick inserted in the center comes out clean, about 30 minutes. Place the pan on a rack to cool. Serve from the pan.

CHOCOLATE

Chocolate is a vital ingredient in many baked goods, especially cakes and icings. In *Theobroma cacao*, the name of the tropical cacao bean tree, *Theobroma* translates as "food of the gods." Chocolate is just that to many.

What Is Chocolate?

Chocolate is a mixture of finely ground cocoa and sugar particles in a rich fat, cocoa butter. This fat, cocoa butter, has a sharp melting point, which just happens to be right at body temperature (98.6°F/37°C). You bite into hard, firm pieces of chocolate and then, seconds later, your whole mouth is filled with a luscious, thick liquid, sensuous aromas, and the sublime taste of real chocolate. This melting in your mouth is a sensual experience beyond taste alone.

Cocoa butter's sharp melting point is at body temperature. You bite into hard, firm pieces of chocolate and then, seconds later, your whole mouth is filled with a luscious, thick liquid, sensuous aromas, and the sublime taste of real chocolate.

From the Jungle to the Wrapper

Ripe cacao (the plant that cocoa comes from is the cacao plant) pods are removed from the trees, the pods are split, and the pulp and beans are removed and wrapped in banana leaves to ferment. The sugary pulp decomposes, heating the beans. Many chemical changes take place that affect flavor, aroma, and color—the rich cocoa aromas develop, and the beans change from purple to chocolate brown. After fermentation, the beans are dried on bamboo mats or wooden floors, with frequent turning.

These dried beans are shipped to the manufacturing plants, where they are cleaned, sorted, and roasted. Not only does the variety of the cacao tree influence flavor, but fermentation and roasting also have major influences on the flavor of a chocolate. The same beans roasted in different ways can have very different flavors.

Roasting develops flavor and aroma and also loosens the bean shells so that they can be removed more easily. The beans are then lightly crushed and the husks are blown away (a process called "winnowing"). After removing the husks and the germ, the 82% of the bean remaining, the cotyledon, is now in dark chips called "nibs." When the nibs are crushed, this mixture of unrefined cocoa particles in cocoa butter is called "chocolate liquor" or "chocolate mass."

Different roasting will produce different flavors from the same cacao beans.

For dark, semisweet, and bittersweet chocolates, nibs and sugar are ground until the cocoa and sugar particles range in size from 25 microns (0.001 inch) to 75 microns. This paste of cocoa butter and fine cocoa particles from the nibs and fine sugar particles is kneaded ("conched") for up to 72 hours to further smooth and blend all particles, creating the creaminess of fine chocolates.

Types of Chocolate

To make baking chocolate and candy bars, chocolate liquor is further processed with sugar and tiny amounts of other things like lecithin, dairy products, and so on. Chocolates can vary in the amount of cocoa particles, amount of cocoa butter, amount of sugar, and additives (emulsifiers, dairy products, flavorings like vanilla or vanillin).

Unsweetened Chocolate (Baking Chocolate)

In refining, the cocoa particles are ground very fine and smooth, and an emulsifier like lecithin may be added along with vanilla or vanillin, but no sugar. When it is tempered and cooled, it is baking chocolate in the United States in the familiar 8-ounce packages of 1-ounce squares.

For cooks, an important relationship to remember is that to get the same amount of cocoa particles that you have in unsweetened chocolate, you will need about twice as much regular semisweet or bittersweet chocolate (because they contained 50 to 55% chocolate liquor, not 100% like unsweetened). I know that, in comparing brownie recipes, I saw a recipe with twice as much chocolate as the usual recipe with unsweetened chocolate. I thought, "Wow! these brownies must really be chocolaty!" Then I realized that the high-chocolate recipe was using bittersweet chocolate, not unsweetened, so that the actual amount of cocoa particles in both recipes was almost exactly the same.

Dark, Bittersweet, and Semisweet

Bittersweet does not necessarily mean that the chocolate has less sugar than semisweet. The amount of sugar varies from company to company. One company's bittersweet may have more sugar than another company's semisweet. By Federal regulation, this chocolate must contain a minimum 35% chocolate liquor. (See the table FDA Standards of Identity on page 91.) Until the past few years, top American and European brands contained 50 to 55% chocolate liquor, with the rest of the blend being sugar. This is the chocolate that we have been accustomed to eating and using in cooking.

High-Percentage Chocolate

Alice Medrich's 2003 book *Bittersweet* explains all about the new chocolates that are sometimes called high-percentage chocolates. They contain 60% or 70%, or even more, chocolate liquor. These chocolates contain a lot more cocoa particles and a little more cocoa butter than the regular semisweet and bittersweet chocolates that have been on the market for years. The older chocolates with 50 to 55% chocolate liquor contained 20 to 22% cocoa particles; now the chocolates with 60 to 70% chocolate liquor contain 28 to 30% cocoa particles. This makes a big difference in the amounts of liquids that we must use to blend these chocolates with other ingredients in recipes (see page 94 for more details).

Couverture

This is quality chocolate that contains a larger amount of cocoa butter than regular semisweet or bittersweet chocolate. It is more free flowing when melted and it is perfect for coating candy centers. It can also be used to make chocolate ice sculptures (see below for more information).

Couverture chocolates have no relation to high-percentage chocolate, which contains a lot more cocoa particles and a little more cocoa butter. Couverture chocolates, on the other hand, can have the same amount of cocoa particles as regular semisweet or bittersweet chocolate, but they contain a lot more cocoa butter.

Chocolate Sculpture Formed in Ice

You can make amazing chocolate sculptures with ice. Fill a container (like a Starbucks plastic cup) with ice cubes, pour thin (couverture) melted chocolate over the ice so that it drains between the cubes, then allow the chocolate to harden in the refrigerator. Finally, run cool water over to melt the ice. You end up with a fascinating sculpture with holes where the ice had been!

Delores Custer told me about one of her food-styling students, Anurag Bali, from New Delhi, who made a white chocolate tower in this manner. He placed two perfect strawberries on top of the tower. It was quite impressive.

Using this technique, you can make amazing sculptures. Heather Hurlbert, executive pastry chef at the Cherokee Town Club in Atlanta, had learned this technique in Europe and she does fascinating sculptures. She uses a large, shallow container about 16 inches (41 cm) in diameter and about 6 inches (15 cm) deep. She drizzles white chocolate to different depths so that when the chocolate is inverted it looks like a coral reef. It is a spectacular display.

"THIN" CHOCOLATE

If you are using dark (semisweet/bittersweet) chocolate, you can make a real showpiece, but you should temper the chocolate first (see page 104). The chocolate hardens almost instantly when it touches the ice, so you need the melted chocolate to be thin to run quickly between the ice cubes. If you can find couverture (see above), that is the best chocolate to use.

Even with couverture, you need to add some melted cocoa butter to thin the chocolate. Cocoa butter is available from Sweet Celebrations, Inc. (see Sources, page 508).

WHITE CHOCOLATE

If you are using white chocolate, check to see what type of fat it contains. I look for cocoa butter. Unfortunately, Ghirardelli classic white chips contain palm kernel oil, which will not blend with cocoa butter. On the other hand, Ghirardelli slabs containing cocoa butter are available in about half-pound (227 g) chunks at Trader Joe's at a very reasonable price.

For your first attempt, I suggest something small like the recipe below. If you use a clear plastic cup you can see how deep the chocolate goes down before it sets.

Use large ice cubes for your first venture and make the sculpture in sections. Fill the cup only one-quarter full with ice cubes, pour chocolate over that section, then add another layer of ice cubes and pour more chocolate. Continue in this manner to the top of the cup. If you work in layers like this, you can get the chocolate to the bottom. For detailed directions, see Bali's Alabaster Chocolate Tower (recipe follows).

Bali's Alabaster Chocolate Tower

MAKES ONE 8-INCH (20-CM) SCULPTURE

This is my simplified version of Bali's Tower, a dramatic, holey, snow-white, modern-art-looking sculpture of chocolate in a moat of brilliant red Strawberry-Chambord Sauce, topped with two perfect strawberries and sprigs of mint. When I tested this recipe I couldn't find couverture, so this recipe uses white chocolate containing cocoa butter.

3 ounces (85 g) cocoa butter, finely chopped

12 ounces (340 g) white chocolate containing cocoa butter, cut in 1-inch (2.5-cm) pieces

Ice cubes to fill the cup (small to medium cubes are best)

Strawberry-Chambord Sauce (recipe follows)

2 whole perfect strawberries, rinsed and stemmed

2 sprigs fresh mint leaves

1. In a 4-cup (1-L) glass measuring cup with a spout, melt the cocoa butter in the microwave on 50% power using bursts of 30 seconds. Stir after each burst.

2. In a food processor, with quick on/offs, process the white chocolate until finely chopped. Stir the white chocolate into the melted cocoa butter and microwave on 30% power in 30-second bursts, stirring, until about two-thirds of the chocolate is melted.

3. Cut a circle out of Release foil the size of the bottom of a 12-ounce (355-ml) clear plastic cup (my cup is about 5 inches [13 cm] tall and 3½ inches [9 cm] in diameter at the top) and place in the cup with the nonstick side up. Place ice cubes in the cup to about one-quarter of the way up.

4. Stir the melted chocolate. If it is not completely melted, microwave on 30% power for 30 seconds and stir well. If the chocolate is still not melted, continue to microwave on 30% power in 30-second bursts, stirring well each time.

5. Pour the melted chocolate into the cup, down the cracks and only up to near the top of the ice. Hopefully, the chocolate will cover the bottom of the cup. Add ice cubes to halfway up the cup and pour chocolate over the cubes until they are almost covered. Add more ice cubes to bring them to three-quarters of the way up the cup. Pour on more chocolate. Finally, fill the cup almost full with ice cubes and pour on more chocolate to level. Place the cup in the refrigerator for about 30 minutes to set the chocolate firmly.

6. Remove the cup from the refrigerator and run cool water in and drain. Continue running cool water in and draining until most of the ice is melted. Set the tower on a couple of paper towels to completely drain and dry.

7. Place the tower on the serving plate and spoon Strawberry-Chambord Sauce on the plate around the bottom of the tower. Place 2 perfect strawberries on top with the sprigs of mint to garnish.

Strawberry-Chambord Sauce

MAKES ABOUT ⅔ CUP (158 ML)

One 10-ounce package (283-g) frozen strawberries

1 tablespoon (7 g) cornstarch

1 tablespoon (15 ml) Chambord, Grand Marnier, or other raspberry or orange liqueur

Let the strawberries thaw in a strainer, catching the liquid in a medium saucepan. When the strawberries have thawed, stir the cornstarch into the juice and heat over medium heat, stirring constantly, until the juice thickens. Stir in the liqueur and gently fold in the strawberries.

Milk Chocolate

In addition to sugar, this chocolate contains cream or dairy products. You can see from the following table of FDA Standards of Identity that milk chocolate is required to have a minimum of 10% chocolate liquor. You will find that the flavors in milk chocolates vary greatly—some creamy, some more caramelly.

White Chocolate and White Confectionery Coating

White chocolate, which until 2002 was not allowed to be called "chocolate" in the United States because it contains no chocolate liquor (see table below), consists of cocoa butter, sugar, dairy products, and flavorings. Some brand names are Alpine White and Narcissus. The better brands contain cocoa butter, but others (called white confectionery coatings) are made with partially hydrogenated soy, palm, palm kernel, or cottonseed oil.

Almond bark and many other white coatings do not even contain cocoa butter. They are made with palm kernel oil (lauric acid type) and are flavored to taste something like chocolate. They contain neither cocoa particles nor cocoa butter. Wilton calls their brand like this "candy melts" and they come in white or a number of other colors.

Other FDA Standards require a minimum 20% cocoa butter and a maximum of 55% sucrose (sugar) for the blend to be labeled white chocolate.

Different Forms

These different types of chocolate are available in various forms. For example, you can get semisweet chocolate in 10-pound (4.5-kg) slabs, bars, or as chocolate chips, mini chips, or chunks. With the slabs or bars, you need to chop the chocolate for even melting. So an advantage of the chips is that you do not have to chop them to melt. Alice Medrich feels that you get a better quality of chocolate when you use the slabs or bars.

Care of Chocolate

Chocolate does require tender loving care. It can suffer from improper storage conditions. Too moist or too warm and a gray coating will appear on chocolate. This coating is called bloom—and there are actually two kinds of bloom. As you may suspect, one is caused by moisture and the other by warmth.

U.S. FDA Standards of Identity for Cocoa-Derived Products

Product	% Chocolate Liquor
Chocolate Liquor	100
Bittersweet and Semisweet	35
Sweet (like German's)	10 to 35
Milk	10 (min)
White	0

Sugar Bloom

If chocolate is not tightly wrapped, moisture from the atmosphere condenses on the surface when the temperature lowers. This moisture dissolves some sugar from the chocolate. When the air warms again, the moisture evaporates, leaving behind a gray film of very fine sugar called "sugar bloom."

Fat Bloom

Chocolate contains a complex mixture of fats. If chocolate is held for six months or more at a temperature in the high 70s Fahrenheit (mid-20s Celsius), tiny amounts of some fats in the cocoa butter melt and float to the surface of the chocolate forming a gray film, "fat bloom." In appearance, fat bloom and sugar bloom look alike, but there is a slightly oily feel to the fat bloom.

Using Chocolate That Has Bloom

Bloom may be unattractive but it does not affect the taste. You can certainly eat chocolate that has bloomed and you can use it in many recipes. It will "seize" (see page 93) if you try to melt it by itself, but it works beautifully if you melt it with enough liquid to prevent seizing.

Working with Chocolate

Working with chocolate can be startling! When you are melting chocolate, you can have glistening, thick, oozing chocolate, and then suddenly, just a few degrees hotter, you have dark, grainy lumps in pale, golden oil.

Equally startling, your shiny, flowing, melted chocolate can suddenly become a dull, solid, grainy mass. Overheating and moisture cause these two most common problems with chocolate.

Melting and Overheating

Chocolate is a complex mixture of particles and fats. When heated, the fats soften, melt, and become more fluid as heating continues. Cocoa butter melts in the low-90s Fahrenheit (low-30s Celsius), which is not very hot—it literally melts in your mouth. When you heat chocolate, the cocoa butter crystals melt and the chocolate becomes fluid, but if you get the chocolate too hot, it can separate into burned, blackened cocoa particles and pale golden liquid. You can use the cocoa butter as hand cream but that is about it! Like Humpty Dumpty, this is irreversible. Your chocolate is gone.

Chocolate can separate irreversibly into burned, blackened cocoa particles and pale golden liquid when overheated.

When French pastry expert Bruce Healy asked me, "How hot is too hot?" I thought that this was an easy question—somewhere around 120°F/49°C. It seems that a lot of things say, "Don't heat over 120°F." But Bruce pointed out that in Valhrona tempering directions, they advise heating above 131°F/55°C. I thought we could just look it up in Bernard Minifie's *Chocolate, Cocoa, and Confectionery,* the technical chocolate bible. Bruce had already looked. It wasn't there.

We both scoured every source we could imagine. It seemed like such a simple question, "At what temperature does chocolate separate into cocoa particles and melted cocoa butter?"

I finally reached Dr. Paul Dimick, chocolate expert emeritus at Penn State University. He explained that cocoa butter, like most natural products, is a complex mixture of fats. It contains small amounts of fats that do not melt until at high temperatures—over 200°F/93°C.

Cocoa beans from different locations are very different since the plants adapt to the climate of their surroundings. In a room at moderate temperature, say at 70°F/21°C, cocoa butter from Malaysian beans that grew near the equator would be quite firm, while cocoa butter from Brazilian beans that grow in a much colder mountain climate would be quite soft.

Stir chocolate constantly while melting to keep the temperature even and to prevent separation.

Dr. Dimick says that one of the major factors causing separation when heating is inadequate stirring. With constant stirring, you can exceed chocolate's normal separation temperature by a little without ill effects. This separation temperature for dark chocolate is over 130°F/54°C (the exact temperature depends on the cocoa bean from which chocolate was made), and for lighter chocolates, it is 115°F/46°C, which is not very hot.

Ideally, to melt chocolate, chop it into small pieces or process it a few seconds in the food processor. These fine pieces melt faster and more evenly than large lumps. Stir the chocolate constantly while melting to keep the temperature even throughout.

Stirring at 15-second intervals while melting chocolate in the microwave is vital because when some chocolates melt in the microwave they hold their form even though they have melted.

Many recipes suggest melting chocolate in a double boiler. However, I really don't like to use a double boiler; there is too much risk that a little steam will get to the chocolate and cause "seizing" (see below).

Chocolate can be safely melted in many different ways—on very low heat, over or in hot, not simmering water (avoid steam), or in the microwave at 50%

power for semisweet, 30% power for milk or white chocolate, stirring every 15 seconds. Heat and stir until the chocolate is just melted.

To melt large quantities of chocolate, you can use everything from the pilot light in a gas oven with the heat off, to a heating pad or a plant-warming pad. You just need to make sure that your heat is not too high.

Moisture—Seizing

Chocolate's "seizing" (becoming a solid, grainy mass) is a sudden, totally unreal happening. It is as if a witch put an evil spell over your beautiful velvety brown liquid. Actually, this "evil spell" is caused by moisture. The tiniest bit of moisture, even steam, can cause flowing, shiny melted chocolate to become a solid, dull, grainy mass.

Dr. Richard Schwartz at Wilbur Chocolates explains this phenomenon using a sugar bowl as an example. If you pour a cup of boiling water into a sugar bowl, it dissolves all the sugar—no lumps. But, if you dip a spoon that you just used to stir your coffee into the sugar bowl, you get little grainy lumps of sugar. The small amount of moisture from your spoon caused the dry sugar particles to glue together. This is exactly what happens when you get a little moisture on melted chocolate: the fine, dry sugar and cocoa particles glue together to change melted chocolate into a solid, grainy mass.

The tiniest bit of moisture, even steam, can cause flowing, shiny, melted chocolate to become a solid, dull mass.

What can you do when chocolate seizes? Is there anything that you can do to retrieve it? Yes and no. Apply the sugar bowl example: add more water so that all the cocoa particles get wet, and they will no longer stick together. Work a tablespoon of warm water into the grainy mess by breaking up the solid and pressing the mess with the back of the spoon. When this liquid is incorporated, work another tablespoon of warm water in until you have a smooth, shiny chocolate again. This slightly watered-down chocolate is fine for many uses—icing, fillings, etc.—but will not work for enrobing candy where you need a hard, shiny finished product.

Preventing Seizing: The Recipe—Enough Water-Type Liquid

Cooks have to check their recipes and make sure that there is enough water-type liquid in the recipe to prevent seizing.

In recipes containing water-type liquid (this can be the water in butter, milk, heavy cream, eggs, etc.) and chocolate, there is going to be a certain amount of water-type liquid that the recipe must contain to prevent seizing. (An amount that is enough to wet all the cocoa particles.) See pages 86–88 for chocolate liquor, high-percentage chocolates, etc.

With the regular 55 to 60% chocolates (bittersweet and semisweet that contain 55 to 60% chocolate liquor), the minimum amount of water-type liquid needed to prevent seizing is 1 tablespoon (15 ml) per 2 ounces (57 g) of chocolate. High-percentage (60 to 70%) chocolates, which contain more cocoa particles, require more liquid—1½ tablespoons (22 ml) water-type liquid per 2 ounces (57 g) of chocolate. Unsweetened chocolate requires 2 tablespoons (30 ml) of water-type liquid for 2 ounces (57 g) of chocolate. Any recipe with less liquid may cause the chocolate to seize.

Unfortunately, there are many chocolate truffle recipes that call for adding a small amount of liqueur to melted chocolate. The recipe usually says something like "the chocolate will thicken." Thicken nothing! This is seizing.

Since high-percentage chocolates require more liquid, recipes that worked beautifully with regular chocolates (containing 55 to 60% chocolate liquor) may not work with the high-percentage chocolates (containing 60 to 70% chocolate liquor), which have many more cocoa particles that have to be wet. So you may well have a recipe that you have made for years with regular chocolate that is a disaster with high-percentage chocolates.

Add Melted Chocolate to Other Ingredients

To prevent seizing, you must also avoid any situation where you have a small amount of liquid with chocolate, for example, when combining melted chocolate and the other ingredients in the recipe. If you pour liquid into chocolate, you can have that dreaded situation of a lot of chocolate and a little water-type liquid. Cooks should add the melted chocolate to the other ingredients with stirring to ensure that there is always plenty of water to wet all of the cocoa particles.

> With regular bittersweet and semisweet chocolates that contain about 55% chocolate liquor, you need 1 tablespoon (15 ml) of water-type liquid for each 2 ounces (57 g) of chocolate to prevent seizing. High-percentage chocolates (about 70% chocolate liquor) require 1½ tablespoons (22 ml) water-type liquid per 2 ounces (57 g) chocolate to prevent seizing. And, unsweetened chocolate requires 2 tablespoons (30 ml) of water-type liquid per 2 ounces (57 g) of chocolate to prevent seizing.

One of the few situations where you can get away with adding liquid to chocolate is in a food processor, with the processor running, when you add hot cream to the finely chopped chocolate, but Alice Medrich cautions that the cream must be added in less than 15 seconds.

Watching the voluptuous, flowing, melted chocolate turn instantly into a grainy rock is a startling, terrifying experience. It is not something that you forget. The two lessons that I have learned from seizing are: Lesson one, never even think of combining melted chocolate with an ingredient unless there are enough water-type liquid ingredients to wet all the chocolate particles.

Lesson two, always add melted chocolate to other ingredients. If you add a liquid to melted chocolate, you risk having the terrible situation of a lot of chocolate with too little liquid. Even if this lasts for a just few seconds, tiny seized particles of chocolate can appear. And these tiny particles remain even when the rest of the chocolate is smooth, flowing, and melted.

> The fail-safe way to combine chocolate with other recipe ingredients is to melt the chocolate with any liquid or butter in the recipe, making sure that you have enough water-type liquid to prevent seizing.

The fail-safe way to combine chocolate with other recipe ingredients is to melt the chocolate with any liquid or butter in the recipe. As long as you have the amount of water-type liquid necessary to prevent seizing you will be okay.

Experienced dessert cooks write their recipes in just this way—melting the chocolate with liquid from the recipe. Maida Heatter melts chocolate and butter together in her Palm Beach Brownies; Alice Medrich melts chocolate, butter, and corn syrup together for her glassy smooth chocolate icing; Ortrud Carstens's ganache (*Fine Cooking,* April–May 1994) melts the chocolate with hot cream.

It is much safer to stir melted chocolate into other ingredients than to stir liquid into melted chocolate. For a second, you have a lot of chocolate and only a little liquid and seizing will begin. You can end up with fine particles that you cannot get rid of.

> To avoid tiny seized dots of chocolate, which can make a dish grainy, add melted chocolate to other liquids, not a liquid to melted chocolate.

Ganache

Classic ganache is a creamy mixture of chocolate and heavy cream—good stuff!

Pastry chef Sherry Yard, in her book *The Secrets of Baking,* does a beautiful job of explaining the three types of ganache. There are:

Medium ganache, containing equal *weights* of bittersweet or semisweet chocolate and heavy cream—8 ounces (227 g) chocolate to 8 ounces (227 g) heavy cream;

Soft ganache, made with two parts by *weight* heavy cream to one part by *weight* of chocolate—16 ounces (454 g) heavy cream to 8 ounces (227 g) chocolate; and

Firm ganache, made with two parts by *weight* of chocolate for each one part by *weight* heavy cream—16 ounces (454 g) chocolate to 8 ounces (227 g) heavy cream.

Soft ganache can be chilled and whipped like whipped cream to create fabulous chocolate mousses, like Simple Chocolate Mousse, page 96. You can make "chocolate whipped cream" mousses with soft bittersweet, semisweet, or white chocolate ganache. Soft ganache mousses make an excellent cake filling and a component of impressive desserts, or can be used to make chocolate sauces.

Both medium and firm ganache can be used as icings for cakes (Shiny Ganache Glaze, page 97; Velvety Ganache Glaze, page 98; Satin-Smooth Ganache Glaze, page 99), and for chocolate truffles (see Famous Smoothest-Ever Truffles, page 103).

Firm ganache can even be turned into a torte with the addition of eggs. Sherry Yard has a wonderful recipe for Baked Whiskey Tortes using a firm ganache in *The Secrets of Baking.*

Simple Chocolate Mousse

MAKES SIX ½-CUP (120-ML) SERVINGS

What could be easier? Melt chocolate in heavy cream, chill overnight, and whip. *Voilà*, chocolate mousse!

What This Recipe Shows

Adding finely chopped chocolate to hot cream avoids the situation where you have a lot of chocolate and a little liquid, so you do not risk seizing.

Cold fat droplets stick together around air bubbles to stabilize whipped cream, so it is vital to have the cream cold before whipping.

---

2 cups (473 ml) heavy cream
1 cup (7 oz/198 g) sugar

1⅓ cups (8 oz/227 g) semisweet chocolate, finely chopped

1. In a heavy saucepan, heat the cream until you see steam. Remove from the heat and stir in the sugar. Stirring slowly, dump in the chocolate all at once. Stir slowly until all of the chocolate is melted and sugar is dissolved.

2. Allow the chocolate cream to cool for about 30 minutes, then pour into a medium bowl, cover tightly, and refrigerate for at least 4 hours or overnight. The cream must be thoroughly chilled.

3. Whip with a hand mixer or in a stand mixer on medium-high speed until soft peaks form when the beater is lifted. Carefully, continue whipping until you get a moderately firm peak consistency—perfect for a mousse.

4. Divide among six individual serving dishes. Keep refrigerated until serving. You can garnish with a swirl of whipped cream.

Different Ganaches

I used to think that these ganache formulas were bible and you had to use them exactly. This is not true. It's your dish. If the you think the ganache is difficult to use as runny as it is, change it. In my Shiny Ganache Glaze (below), I make a glaze that is halfway between a medium ganache and a firm ganache. I find that it is a little easier to work with at this consistency (at about 90°F/32°C, of course).

Now, this is icing. With my Southern sweet tooth, I would like it a little sweeter. So I added a little sugar to my Shiny Ganache Glaze. If you don't like things so sweet, just leave the sugar out.

Shiny Ganache Glaze

MAKES ABOUT 1⅔ CUPS (394 ML) OF ICING

With this glaze you can make a professional-looking perfect satiny-smooth cake with a beautiful deep sheen. The Double-Icing Technique (see page 141) allows even a beginner to make a gorgeous cake. I added some sugar, which will smooth out the taste of the chocolate. This is not necessary if you are using a very high–quality chocolate.

What This Recipe Shows

Corn syrup gives this glaze its deep glossy sheen. See page 99 for more details.

Adding the grated chocolate to the cream helps prevent "seizing" (page 93).

This is not as thin as a medium ganache (page 95) or as thick as a firm ganache. The texture makes the glaze not as runny and a little easier to work with than a medium ganache.

---

16 ounces (454 g) semisweet chocolate, cut
    into pieces
1½ cups (355 ml) heavy cream

½ cup (3.5 oz/99 g) sugar
2 tablespoons (30 ml) corn syrup

1. Place the chocolate in a food processor with the steel blade and finely chop.

2. In a large heavy saucepan, carefully bring the cream and sugar to a boil. Watch constantly. Let simmer for 1 minute. Pour the hot cream mixture into a medium mixing bowl that has a wide surface. Stir in the corn syrup. Let cool about 30 seconds. All at once, pour the chopped chocolate over the entire surface. Jar or barely shake the bowl to get the chocolate to settle. Allow to stand about 30 seconds. Start stirring in the middle, blending the melted chocolate and cream together. Try not to incorporate air. Stir slowly until all the chocolate is melted and blended. Use immediately, or refrigerate and reheat to thin.

Ganaches Made with Butter

Cream is essentially fat and water, with a small amount of dairy products, so butter, which is also fat and water but with an even smaller amount of dairy products, is an easy substitute for cream in a ganache (see Velvety Ganache Glaze, below).

Velvety Ganache Glaze

MAKES 1⅔ CUPS (394 ML)

This is a butter-and-water ganache patterned after Alice Medrich's wonderful Sarah Bernhardt Chocolate Glaze. It is the perfect glaze for cakes that are refrigerated because it stays beautiful when chilled.

What This Recipe Shows

Cream is essentially fat and water, with a small amount of dairy products, so butter, which is also fat and water but with an even smaller amount of dairy products, is an easy substitute for cream in a ganache.

Corn syrup in this recipe produces a deep velvet glow instead of the more glossy sheen that you get with corn syrup in my cream ganache like the Shiny Ganache Glaze, page 97.

---

8 ounces (227 g) semisweet chocolate, cut into pieces
¾ cup (6 oz/170 g) unsalted butter, cut in 2-tablespoon (1-oz/28-g) pieces

2 tablespoons (30 ml) light corn syrup
1 tablespoon (15 ml) water

1. Place the chocolate and butter in a food processor with the steel blade. Pulse chocolate and butter together with quick on/offs until finely chopped. Place the chocolate-butter mixture with the corn syrup and water in a microwave-safe bowl and microwave on 50% power for about 2 minutes, stirring every 30 seconds. Alternatively, prepare a hot water bath. Fill a large skillet with ½ inch (1.3 cm) of water and heat to a simmer. Place all ingredients in a heatproof bowl and place the bowl in the simmering water. Stir constantly with a spatula or wooden spoon. After 30 seconds, turn off the heat. Continue to stir until all the chocolate is melted and the mixture is smooth.

2. Divide the glaze in half. When the temperature of one half drops to 90°F/32°C, ice the cake. The cake should be cold. After you have spread the first half of the glaze on the cake and chilled it for 30 minutes as directed in the Double-Icing Technique (page 141), heat the last half of the glaze, strain it, and, when it cools down to 90°F/32°C, pour over the cake. Refrigerate immediately after icing.

Corn Syrup in Ganache

Using a small amount of corn syrup in recipes from salad dressings to icings produces an attractive glossy sheen. Corn syrup is a miracle ingredient for shine. As my friend Harold McGee puts it, "Corn syrup is a liquid that attracts water and fills in spaces between fine sugar particles to produce a glass-smooth surface." One tablespoon (15 ml) of corn syrup in a ganache will give it a deep, rich shine. The same is true in other icings—1 or 2 tablespoons (15 to 30 ml) of corn syrup gives icings and glazes a beautiful gloss, which you may or may not want. In some icings, you may want a flat matte look with no shine. In such cases, avoid corn syrup.

Corn syrup in a butter ganache produces a deep velvet glow (see Velvety Ganache Glaze, page 98) instead of the glossy sheen that you get with corn syrup in a cream ganache like the my Shiny Ganache Glaze, page 97, or Satin-Smooth Ganache Glaze, see below.

Satin-Smooth Ganache Glaze

MAKES ABOUT 2½ CUPS (591 ML)

Sherry Yard, the executive pastry chef at Spago and a winner of the James Beard Foundation's Pastry Chef of the Year award, is a wonderfully creative pastry chef. I love her work. In her ganache glaze, she adds apricot jelly, which sweetens, adds subtle flavors, and adds a little pectin to slightly firm the glaze. Sherry says, "It has a beautiful velvety shine." As we have seen in other ganache glazes, corn syrup adds a gloss or deep shine. I have patterned this ganache after hers. With my severe sweet tooth, I added a little sugar, too.

What This Recipe Shows

Corn syrup adds a handsome gloss to the surface.

A small amount of jelly adds sweetness, complexity of flavor, and a little pectin to slightly firm the glaze.

---

16 ounces (454 g) semisweet chocolate (I love
   Guittard, but it may be difficult to find in
   your area)
½ cup (118 ml) apple jelly

1 cup (237 ml) heavy cream
½ cup (118 ml) whole milk
½ cup (3.5 oz/99 g) sugar
2 tablespoons (30 ml) light corn syrup

1. Place the chocolate in a food processor with the steel blade and finely chop.

2. In a small saucepan over medium heat, heat the jelly just to melt. Stir in the cream, milk, sugar, and corn syrup and bring carefully to a boil. Pour into a wide metal mixing bowl. All at once, dump and spread the chocolate across the top of the hot cream mixture. Jar to settle the chocolate. Allow to stand about 1 minute, then, starting in the middle, slowly stir to blend the cream and chocolate together well.

3. Divide the ganache in half. Put the cake to be frosted on a cake cardboard exactly the size of the cake. When one half of the glaze cools to 90°F/32°C follow the Double-Icing Technique, page 141.

Why I Worry about Ganache Techniques

Ganache is a smooth, creamy mixture of heavy cream and chocolate. When it is thin, it can be chilled and whipped into a mousse; when it is medium, it is used as a glaze for a cake or for making chocolate truffles; when thick, it is used for truffles or candy or, mixed with eggs, it can be baked as a torte. So what's to worry about here?

If the cream and chocolate are not successfully combined, the ganache can contain little hard, undissolved chocolate specks, or it can separate to create an oily, shiny glaze on top.

Classic ganache is a fat-in-water emulsion. Fats from the cocoa butter and cream are dispersed in tiny droplets in the water-type liquid from the cream, just as oil is dispersed as droplets in liquid in mayonnaise.

The classic ratio for a medium ganache is equal weights of heavy cream and bittersweet or semisweet chocolate. The classic method of preparation is to place the coarsely chopped chocolate in a heatproof bowl, bring the heavy cream to a boil, pour the hot cream over the chocolate, and stir together rapidly until it is smooth.

Young pastry chefs are taught to approach ganache in exactly this manner—always worrying about the emulsion.

Now, ganache can fail. In a tiny kitchen in Erice, Sicily, I watched as a French restaurant owner/chef poured the boiling cream over finely chopped chocolate while a famous French pastry chef stirred vigorously. The famous chef got a product that he was unhappy with two out of five times. He pointed out the tiniest chocolate specks in the otherwise smooth mixture. There were only the three of us there; the two chefs spoke little or no English, and I spoke no French. So I could not ask my burning questions or suggest something to try to remedy the problem. And, after all, this was one of the most famous pastry chefs in France. I remained respectfully silent.

I wanted to ask: "Why not add the chocolate to the cream instead of the cream to the chocolate? That has always worked for me."

If one insists on the classic procedure of adding the cream to the chocolate, one of the most successful and fail-safe ways to do this is in a food processor. Pour boiling cream down the feed tube onto the chopped chocolate. Alice Medrich does caution you that this should take no longer than 15 seconds.

My approach has always been from a completely different direction. I am worried about the amount of water-type liquid, the amount of cocoa particles, and seizing.

Beautiful, satiny, flowing melted chocolate can suddenly become a rock-hard, grainy mass when mixed with a small amount of water-type liquid. Because chocolate is composed of fine dry particles (cocoa and sugar) in rich fat (cocoa butter), all you have to do is mix melted chocolate with a few drops of water, or even steam, and suddenly these dry particles glue together (see Moisture—Seizing, page 93).

If you have enough liquid to wet all the fine cocoa particles, they will not seize or stick together. With both regular American and European chocolates, which previously contained 50 to 55% chocolate liquor (crushed cocoa beans containing cocoa butter and 20 to 22% cocoa particles), 1 tablespoon (15 ml) of water-type liquid for every 2 ounces (57 g) of chocolate was enough to prevent seizing.

We now have high-percentage chocolates that contain 60 or 70% or more chocolate liquor and 28 to 30% cocoa particles. Alice Medrich, as mentioned before, recommends using 1½ tablespoons (22 ml) water-type liquid for every 2 ounces (57 g) of these chocolates.

Watching the voluptuous, flowing, melted chocolate turn instantly into a grainy rock is a startling, terrifying experience. Never even think of combining melted chocolate with ingredients unless there is enough water-type liquid in the ingredients to wet all the chocolate particles and always add melted chocolate to other ingredients. If you add a liquid to melted chocolate, you risk having the terrible situation of some of the chocolate getting too little liquid. Even if this lasts for just a second, small seized groups of particles of chocolate can appear.

So, with my panic over seizing, I designed my Smoothest-Ever Truffles and Secret Marquise in *Cook Wise* with enough water-type liquid to prevent seizing, and I made sure that I added the chocolate to the hot liquid. In all of my ganache glazes, I add the grated chocolate to the hot cream—never the hot cream to the chocolate. I cannot bring myself to risk having a large amount of chocolate and a small amount of liquid, even for seconds.

In addition to the correct amounts of each ingredient and the proper sequence, there is the temperature of the cream. Everything has to be hot enough to melt the chocolate and hot enough to dissolve the sugar (semisweet and bittersweet chocolates contain sugar). If you heat the cream in a large skillet, place the skillet on a hot pad, and then add the grated chocolate and stir, you have the advantage of a heated pan and heated cream. If you pour the cream into a cold bowl of cold chocolate, you have to warm the bowl and the chocolate. It is no wonder that the cream must be near boiling to melt the chocolate.

I did notice that for her truffles Alice Medrich partially melts the chocolate

I add the grated chocolate to the hot cream—never the hot cream to the chocolate. I do not want to risk having a large amount of chocolate and a small amount of liquid, even for seconds.

before she adds the hot cream. This would definitely give her truffles an advantage over the ordinary procedure.

Now, there is one more thing when I make truffles. I want egg yolks in my ganache. I want an incredibly creamy, satiny, shiny, smooth texture when you bite into them. There are truffles containing egg yolks, so this is nothing unusual. I also have butter in my recipe but, here again, some truffle recipes contain butter.

In order to kill salmonella, I just barely melt the butter in a large, deep, heavy skillet. I remove it from the heat, stir in the heavy cream, and then the egg yolks. I return the pan to low heat and carefully continue to heat, constantly scraping the bottom of the pan with a flat-edged spatula. I carefully heat until I see steam rising, or bubbles around the edges, or feel the mixture thickening. I want to get the mixture above 150°F/65°C, but avoid scrambling the yolks. Then, I remove the pan from the heat, stir in the grated chocolate, and continue stirring until it's all melted. If it does not completely melt, I return the pan to the heat for about 15 seconds and then remove from the heat and stir for a full minute. I reheat again if I see even a tiny trace of unmelted chocolate.

I did question why I have never worried about maintaining an emulsion in ganache. I thought that, since I had egg yolks in my truffles, I knew that my ganache emulsion could not break. But I have never had any trouble with ganache glazes, see pages 96–100, which do not contain egg yolks. So maybe we should worry more about the problem of seizing than maintaining an emulsion.

The truffle recipe on page 103 is essentially a slightly different version of one that I have in *Cook-Wise*. It has been a very popular recipe and illustrates ganache in action.

Famous Smoothest-Ever Truffles with Chambord and Macadamia Dust

MAKES ABOUT THIRTY 1 TO 1½-INCH (2.5 TO 3.8-CM) TRUFFLES

When you bite into one of these, it is so smooth that your tooth marks on the truffle are shiny, satiny smooth like dark glass. This is a slight variation of my truffle recipe in *Cook Wise*.

What This Recipe Shows

Egg yolks, nature's great emulsifiers, create sensual smoothness.

Egg yolks are diluted with cream and carefully heated to kill salmonella.

The 17 ounces (482 g) of chocolate in this recipe will require 8½ tablespoons (128 ml) of water-type liquid to prevent seizing. This comes from the 5 yolks (between 2 and 3 tablespoons/30 and 45 ml), the butter (between 1 and 2 tablespoons/15 and 30 ml), the cream (about 3 tablespoons/45 ml), and the Chambord (less than 3 tablespoons/45 ml).

The chocolate is finely chopped for smooth, even melting.

Using nuts that are already roasted gives great flavor.

---

11 ounces (312 g) good-quality semisweet chocolate, such as Lindt, Tobler, or Guittard, or 4 king-size bars (2.6 oz/74 g each) Hershey's Special Dark, broken into 1-inch (2.5-cm) pieces

6 ounces (170 g) milk chocolate, broken into 1-inch (2.5-cm) pieces

5 tablespoons (2.5 oz/71 g) unsalted butter

⅓ cup (79 ml) heavy cream

5 large egg yolks (3.25 oz/92 g) (see Note, page 104)

3 tablespoons (45 ml) Chambord liqueur

2 cups (9.3 oz/264 g) macadamia nuts, roasted and salted (those in jars are just fine)

1. Combine the semisweet and milk chocolates in a food processor with the steel blade and process until finely chopped. Set aside.

2. In an 8 or 9-inch (20 or 23-cm) skillet, heat the butter over low heat until just melted. Mix in the cream, and then the egg yolks, stirring constantly with a fork or spatula flat against the bottom of the pan. The split second that you start to feel thickening, remove the skillet from the heat and keep stirring. Stir in the Chambord. All at once, add the finely chopped chocolate. Stir constantly until the chocolate melts. Continue to stir for 1 minute.

3. When the chocolate is completely melted, place the pan in the refrigerator to cool.

4. While the chocolate is cooling, very finely chop the nuts, in 2 batches, in a food processor with the steel blade using quick on/offs. Set aside.

5. When the chocolate is partly firm, with a tiny ice cream scoop or a teaspoon, spoon up 1 to 1½-inch (2.5 to 3.8-cm) balls and roll each in the chopped macadamia nuts. Keep the truffles covered and refrigerated. Serve in gold-fluted candy cups.

> NOTE: Because of the threat of salmonella, the egg yolks and cream are heated together nearly to a boil to kill possible bacteria. If you use pasteurized yolks, or are confident about the safety of your eggs, you can simply mix together the yolks and cream and heat until just hot enough to melt the chocolate.

Another Problem When Blending Chocolate with Other Ingredients

As discussed on page 93, seizing can be avoided by melting chocolate with an adequate amount of liquid or by adding the melted chocolate to other recipe ingredients slowly with stirring to ensure that there is always an adequate amount of water-type liquid.

A different problem arises when blending cool chocolate with ice-cold ingredients. When you add cool melted chocolate to ice-cold ingredients, the cold makes the cocoa butter in the chocolate harden instantly. For example, if cool melted chocolate is drizzled into ice-cold whipped cream, tiny flecks of solid chocolate may form instantly (a chocolate-chip mousse!) rather than giving you an even blend of chocolate and cream.

To avoid a chocolate-chip mousse, chocolate that you are adding should be a little warm, right at body temperature. This will not be hot enough to deflate the whipped cream, but warm enough to blend smoothly.

Another solution to the problem is to blend the chocolate and cream together before the cream is whipped. Melt the chocolate and cream together and then cool well, about 5 hours or overnight. This chocolate cream whips beautifully just like you would whip cream for a perfect chocolate mousse—see Simple Chocolate Mousse, page 96.

Tempering Chocolate

When you simply melt chocolate and allow it to cool, it may not cool into the shiny, firm chocolate that we know. Melting and cooling chocolate so that it will be beautiful, firm chocolate is called "tempering." Most chocolate that is sold has been tempered but, when you melt it, the fat crystals melt and the right crystals are lost. To get the good crystals to form, the chocolate has to be retempered.

Cocoa butter, the fat in chocolate, crystallizes in any one of six different forms or polymorphs, as they are called; see table on page 107. Unfortunately, only one of these, the Form V crystals, hardens into the firm, shiny chocolate that we want. Form VI is also a stable, hard crystal, but only small amounts of it form from the good beta (Form V) crystals upon lengthy standing. Most commercial chocolate is in the form of Form V crystals.

When you melt chocolate and get the temperature above 94°F/34°C, you melt the much-desired Form V crystals, and other types of crystals can set up upon cooling. If you simply let melted chocolate cool, it will set up in a dull, soft, splotchy, disgusting-looking form of chocolate. Even the taste is different. What you want is fine chocolate (Form V) that has a snap when you break it and a smooth, totally different mouthfeel from the other forms of cocoa butter.

How can we get chocolate to set up in these hard, shiny beta crystals? By tempering. Tempering is necessary only for real chocolate, which contains cocoa butter, not for compound chocolate or summer coating, see page 117, which contain fats other than cocoa butter.

You need a truly accurate thermometer for tempering. Most kitchen thermometers (even the digital instant-read type) can be off by 10°F/5.5°C. If you do much chocolate work you'll need a laboratory-quality thermometer.

Easy Tempering

When I asked chocolate expert Dr. Paul Dimick about tempering, he said that the easy way to temper is to never heat the chocolate to over 91 to 92°F (32.8 to 33.3°C). Form V crystals do not melt until 94°F/34.4°C. So, your melted chocolate is already tempered because you never lose all of those prized Form V crystals. What a wonderful idea!

Your goal is to barely melt the chocolate. All of these crystals have a range over which they melt, and chocolate melts at 89 to 90°F (31.7 to 32.2°C) even though all the good crystals do not melt until above 94°F/34.4°C. You can place the chocolate over a very low heat source and, with *constant stirring*, melt two-thirds of it. Then remove the chocolate from the heat and patiently continue stirring until all the chocolate is melted. For dark chocolate, ideally you want to end up with a final temperature of 89 to 91°F (31.7 to 32.8°C); the final temperature for milk or white chocolate should be 87 to 89°F (30.6 to 31.7°C). If you have kept the chocolate below 92°F/33.3°C during all of this, it is still tempered and ready for use.

To melt the chocolate evenly, chop the chocolate or process it in a food processor until it is finely chopped. (See page 92 for tips on melting chocolate.) You can use any method that allows you to keep the heat at 90 to 92°F (32.2° to 33.3°C). You can use a warm water bath, but you must take great care not to get even one drop of water in the chocolate, since this tiny amount of water will cause it to seize (for more about seizing, see page 93).

If you get the chocolate over 94°F/34.4°C, you melt your prized Form V crystals and you must go through the full tempering process.

More Low-Temperature Tempering

Bruce Healy has a procedure for making chocolate fans that essentially uses low-temperature melting. He heats an upside-down baking sheet in a preheated 300°F/149°C oven, removes it, and then rubs a piece of chocolate back and forth across the hot surface to form a thin layer. He lets this layer cool and then shaves off, or makes curls, pencils, or fans. This method produces shiny, tempered chocolate products.

Tempering the Old-Fashioned Way

As emphasized before, if you get chocolate over 92°F/33.3°C, the Form V crystals melt and you must completely melt the chocolate to temper it. The risk at higher temperatures is melting and irreversible separation of the chocolate into golden cocoa butter and burned, grainy, black cocoa particles. You can use the cocoa butter as a great hand cream, but your chocolate is gone—essentially ruined. Most cooking literature advises you not to heat chocolate over 120°F/48.9°C. Melting curves of chocolate in the technical literature indicate that most of the fats in cocoa butter are melted by 122°F/50°C. Some processors, such as Valrhona, recommend heating their chocolate slightly higher—up to 131°F/55°C (see page 92).

As is true with most natural fats, cocoa butter is a complex mixture. One of the major factors causing separation is inadequate stirring of this mixture of fats.

Ideally, consult the chocolate manufacturer for the best temperature for melting your chocolate to temper it. As an overall guideline, I suggest melting dark chocolate no higher than 122°F/50°C, or for milk or white chocolate 110 to 118°F (43.3 to 47.8°C), with constant stirring.

To temper, after melting, the chocolate must be rapidly cooled to about 82°F/27.8°C for dark chocolate (79°F/26.1°C for milk or white). *Always stir constantly.* Cooling to this low temperature allows some undesirable crystals to form, but it gets good crystallization of the Form V crystals started. Next, the chocolate is warmed gently to raise the temperature to 86°F/30°C for dark chocolate, or 84°F/29°C for milk or white. It should be held at this temperature for a few minutes, then warmed up to 91 to 92°F (33.3 to 38.8°C) for dark, 87 to 89°F (30.1 to 31.7°C) for milk or white. Bringing the chocolate up to this higher temperature melts and gets rid of the undesirable crystals that may have formed.

There are a number of methods to achieve this rapid cooling. Regardless of the method, the one thing that you must do is to *stir constantly.* Some chefs like to spoon two-thirds of the heated chocolate out onto a cold surface such as a marble slab, and then scrape the chocolate back and forth with a spatula until it is about 82°F/27.8°C. One must work fast doing this and it is difficult to get a quick temperature reading on the slab. Then, the cooled chocolate is blended with the warm reserved chocolate to bring it back to the desired temperature.

Dr. Dimick uses a cold water bath. He places a stainless steel bowl of melted chocolate into a bowl of ice water and stirs constantly until the chocolate cools to 82°F/27.8°C for dark, 79°F/26.1°C for milk or white. Then he warms it to 86°F/30°C for dark, 84°F/29°C for milk or white. He lets it remain at this temperature for a couple of minutes then heats it back up to 91 to 92°F (32.8 to 33.3°C) for dark, 89°F/31.7°C for milk or white.

A fairly simple way to lower the temperature fast is to use a big lump (3 inches/7.6 cm, or so) of tempered chocolate to stir the chocolate, or to stir in some grated chocolate. While it melts, the chocolate lump both cools and seeds the chocolate with the right kind of crystals. Lift out and reuse the lump of chocolate when you reach the correct temperature. If using grated chocolate to cool, add only one tablespoon at a time to ensure that you do not end up with unmelted chocolate particles. Chocolate expert Alice Medrich uses an immersion blender to constantly stir while cooling, taking care to keep the blade submerged. This is certainly an excellent way to stir large batches of chocolate.

Some chefs like to temper melted chocolate by simply stirring constantly in a cool room or walk-in refrigerator.

Commercially available tempering machines have the advantages of constant stirring and accurate temperature control. I notice that some of the machines recommend placing a lump of tempered chocolate in front of the machine's stirrer blade to seed the chocolate and encourage the growth of Form V crystals. These machines are available for under $400 and are worth it if you do a lot of quality chocolate work.

Checking the Temper

There are a number of ways to check to see if your chocolate is tempered. Spread a smear out on a piece of waxed paper—if it dries shiny and hard within 5 minutes, you are fine.

Dr. Dimick uses the "string" test. After he has cooled and, then, brought the chocolate back to the correct final temperature, he spoons up a little and drizzles a string of chocolate on the surface of the melted chocolate. If it disappears instantly, he knows that he does not have enough crystals formed to hold it up for a few seconds, and it is not tempered. Stirring constantly after adding a lump of tempered chocolate may fix it. But if it is simply not tempered and you have the wrong kind of crystals, you must begin again and go through the entire melting and cooling process as described.

Different Forms (Polymorphs) of Cocoa Butter

Form	Melting Range
Form I (beta-prime 2)	61 to 67°F (16.1 to 19.4°C)
Form II (alpha)	70 to 72°F (21.1 to 22.2°C)
Form III (mixed)	78°F (25.6°C)
Form IV (beta-prime 1)	81 to 84°F (27.2 to 28.9°C)
Form V (beta 2)	93 to 95°F (33.9 to 35°C)
Form VI (beta 1)	97°F (36.1°C)

Chocolate At a Glance

What to Do	Why
Chop chocolate into small pieces before melting it.	For quicker and more even melting, as chocolate may burn before large lumps melt.
Melt chocolate over very low heat, warm not boiling water, or heat in the microwave.	If chocolate is heated beyond 120°F/49°C, it separates and burns.
Stir chocolate as it melts.	To keep the temperature even.
Use at least 1 tablespoon (15 ml) of liquid for every 2 ounces (57 g) of 55% chocolate. Use 1½ tablespoons (22 ml) for each 2 ounces of 60 to 70% chocolates and 2 tablespoons (30 ml) of liquid for unsweetened chocolate.	These minimum amounts of liquids are necessary to prevent the dry cocoa particles from sticking together (seizing).
Avoid getting even a drop of water or steam into melted chocolate.	A small amount of water causes dry cocoa particles in chocolate to stick together and seize.
When possible, melt chocolate with other liquid ingredients in a recipe.	Adding adequate liquid at the beginning of melting prevents seizing.
Add water to seized chocolate to bring it back to a liquid state.	Sufficient liquid wets all the cocoa particles so that they no longer stick together, but the chocolate is not suitable for all uses (such as coating).
Do not mix cool melted chocolate into ice-cold ingredients.	Cold ingredients cause the cocoa butter to harden immediately.

COCOA POWDER

Contrary to what some think, cocoa powder is not fat-free—it can contain between 10 and 35% fat. In 1828, the Dutch chocolate maker Van Houten developed hydraulic pressing of the nibs to remove 65 to 90% of the cocoa butter from the chocolate liquor. The resulting pressed cake of cocoa particles, containing 10 to 35% of cocoa butter, is finely ground and sieved to produce cocoa powder.

Cocoa powder is a favorite of many pastry chefs because of its intense chocolate flavor, and it is ideal for the Improved Tunnel of Fudge Cake (page 74). This famous, intensely chocolate, chocolate cake has a wet fudgy center—literally a tunnel of fudge.

Acidity

Cacao beans are naturally tart and acidic. So this powder, which is a very concentrated part of the bean, is acidic with a pH of about 5.5. Natural cocoa powder's acidity is an advantage since it causes the proteins in baked goods to set rapidly. You do not have to worry about your cake or cookies becoming firm.

Natural cocoa powder's acidity is an advantage since it causes the proteins in baked goods to set rapidly.

Natural Cocoa

You may not always find the words "natural cocoa" on the label. Some natural cocoa is just labeled "cocoa" or "nonalkalized cocoa." (See Dutch Process Cocoa, below.)

Cocoa can be somewhat harsh. Alice Medrich points out that, unfortunately, with a few exceptions the best cacao beans are normally reserved for producing chocolate, not cocoa.

There are differences in cocoa powders. The cocoa butter content runs from 10 to 35% and there can be different flavors resulting from the variety of the tree, the fermentation, and the roasting of the beans, as well as the fineness of the grind of the powder. I am partial to Scharffen Berger's Natural Cocoa Powder, but you should taste several different brands and decide for yourself which brand is your favorite. (I recently found out that Scharffen Berger's Natural Cocoa contains a little over 30% cocoa butter. No wonder I like it.)

Dutch Process Cocoa

About the same time that Van Houten developed his process for making cocoa powder, he also began treating the beans, nibs, liquor, or powder with an alkaline solution. This changes the color dramatically, as well as the flavor, produces a slight physical swelling of the cocoa particles, and neutralizes free acids. You can see a dramatic difference between the color of a cake with natural cocoa and the same cake made with Dutch process cocoa. In Dutch process, the color change is variable; it can go from a reddish-brown to a deep brown to almost black. If a baked product is very alkaline, it becomes very dark like Oreo cookies or the Deep, Dark Chocolate Cake (page 112).

Dutch process cocoa is neutral or slightly alkaline, with a pH of about 7 or 8. The darker color, milder flavor, and lower acidity make Dutch process cocoa a favorite with many pastry makers. However, I also have seen many disasters caused by Dutch process cocoa. When a baked product is no longer acidic, it may not set. Cookies that resemble a big flat amoeba, and cakes that will not get done, are no fun. Unless I know that a recipe was designed to use Dutch process cocoa, I usually avoid it. It is not interchangeable with natural cocoa powder because of the problems that its alkalinity can cause. (For more information, see below.)

I had a call from a chef in Los Angeles. She made biscotti every week for her restaurant. Someone had given her some very good Dutch process cocoa and she used it to make chocolate biscotti. She did not even look in the oven until it was time to remove the biscotti. To her shock, there were not her usual loaves that she

The color change with alkalinization can go from reddish brown to almost black. The more alkaline, the darker the color.

could cut into slices and dry, but a big chocolate puddle! She had made this recipe for years—what on earth happened?!

I explained that it was the Dutch process cocoa. Her batter was no longer acidic enough for the eggs (biscotti recipes have several eggs) to set, so she had a huge chocolate puddle.

Soon after that, the famous cookbook writer Susan Purdy called. She was working on her high-altitude baking book *Pie in the Sky,* and at 9,000 feet (2,700 m) all of her cakes worked except the chocolate. I asked if she was using Dutch process cocoa. She was stunned. "How did you know?" I knew because at high altitudes, acidity is vital to set cakes quickly before they lose their leavening and fall. No Dutch process cocoa for cakes at high altitudes!

Working with Cocoa Powder

Many recipes using cocoa powder contain hot water or a hot liquid. More intense chocolate flavor can be obtained from cocoa by pouring a small amount of boiling water over the cocoa powder. Natural cocoa does not dissolve as readily as Dutch process and a hot liquid will certainly aid in dissolving cocoa.

While alkalinity (see above) is a problem specific to Dutch process cocoa, both natural and Dutch process cocoas present several other problems—a baked product with cocoa can be dry. The fine particles found in both cocoa and chocolate can act like flour in a recipe.

When you convert a plain cake recipe to a chocolate cake, if you use cocoa, you need to consider it as flour. Subtract the amount of cocoa that you use from the quantity of flour; otherwise the cake will have too much flour and may be dry. Many recipes with cocoa make dry cakes just because the cook writing the recipe did not reduce the amount of flour to compensate for the cocoa. You can reduce the amount of flour in the recipe or add liquid by increasing the amount of buttermilk or milk to compensate for the additional starch.

Another starch-related problem is thinning. A recipe containing cocoa powder and uncooked egg yolks (for example, chocolate mousse) can thin in the refrigerator overnight. An enzyme in the egg yolks, alpha-amylase, destroys the starch gel formed by starch in the cocoa (which contributes to the thickening of the mousse) just as uncooked egg yolks are known to thin starch custards. Heating after adding the egg yolks to the ingredients inactivates the alpha-amylase, and will prevent this thinning. You need to bring the mixture to a full boil. This is difficult because the mixture sticks to the bottom of the pan and is thick, going blop, blop, blop. Stir, constantly scraping the bottom. You have to get the entire mixture above 170°F/77°C to kill all of the enzymes.

Getting Dark Chocolate Color in Recipes

Experienced bakers and test kitchen staff know this—that they can get a very dark, rich color in a recipe with cocoa by alkalizing it with baking soda. There is the very dark Hershey's Black Magic cake. But there can be problems.

I got a call from a staff member at a major dairy product test kitchen. They were developing a recipe for one of these dark chocolate cakes. They had tried it with 2 teaspoons (9 g) baking soda, as used in the Black Magic cake. It was wonderfully dark, but it sank in the center. Being very knowledgeable, they realized that it was because the cake was overleavened. So they cut the baking soda to 1½ teaspoons (7 g). Alas, they lost the really dark color that they wanted. Was there a way to have the dark color and yet avoid the sunken center caused by the overleavening?

I suggested that they use the procedure that I have in the Deep, Dark Chocolate Cake (page 112). Combine the cocoa and the baking soda, and maybe the sugar, with boiling water, bring back to a boil, and then allow to stand in the hot saucepan for 10 minutes. This allows the baking soda to react with the cocoa and darken it. And the heat also makes some of the baking soda react to release carbon dioxide, reducing the amount of leavening. This works beautifully in the Deep, Dark Chocolate Cake, and it worked nicely for them too. They called back very happy with their perfectly level, dark cake recipe.

There is an extremely alkaline cocoa called "black cocoa." It is primarily for color, not flavor, and is normally used with another cocoa.

Hershey's has a fairly new very dark Dutch process cocoa (possibly strongly alkalized) available in my grocery stores called Hershey's Special Dark. We used this in the Improved Tunnel of Fudge Cake with Dutch process cocoa. You will see how dark it is.

I called Hershey's for more information on their Special Dark Cocoa. I also noticed that their Dutch process cocoa called European Style was no longer available. Their customer service person explained that they found that consumers were not really aware of the characteristics of European Style cocoa, that it produced smoother-tasting baked goods that were also darker.

They knew that consumers were very fond of their Special Dark candy. So they felt that this would be a good name for their dark Dutch process cocoa. And certainly consumers would know that they would get a rich, dark color from this cocoa. The Hershey's Special Dark Cocoa came on the market at least three years ago.

At some time after that Hershey's research found that Dutch process cocoas do not have as high an antioxidant level as natural cocoa. Wanting the best for their consumers, they mixed their Dutch process with 50% natural cocoa. So, for the last two baking seasons, the Hershey's Special Dark that is on the market is the mixture, which the Hershey's representative assured me was still very dark. Since the Special Dark that we used in the Improved Tunnel of Fudge Cake was purchased recently, we assume that it is the 50% mixture and, indeed, it is still very dark. Just bake it and see.

With the Deep, Dark Chocolate Cake (page 112), you can see how alkalinity turns chocolate dark. You can make this cake with Dutch process cocoa or simply add more baking soda to natural cocoa. This recipe makes an almost black cake even with natural cocoa.

For chocolate-on-chocolate cakes, see Chocolate-on-Chocolate: Dark Moist Cake with Chocolate-

Walnut Frosting (page 113), Satin-Glazed Midnight Black Chocolate Cake (page 115), and Deep, Dark Chocolate Cake with Ganache and Chocolate Ruffles (page 116).

Deep, Dark Chocolate Cake

MAKES ONE 13 X 9 X 2-INCH (33 X 23 X 5-CM) SHEET CAKE OR TWO 9 X 2-INCH (23 X 5-CM) ROUND LAYERS

This is an incredibly dark, very moist cake—a serious chocolate lovers' cake. It is so chocolaty that I like it with a fluffy white icing like the Italian Meringue (page 187).

This cake has a tendency to really stick to the pan. Be sure to spray the pan well with nonstick cooking spray and line the bottom of the round pans, or use parchment or Release foil in the rectangular pan.

What This Recipe Shows

Dutch process cocoa and baking soda make the chocolate so alkaline that the cake is almost black.

Adding boiling water to cocoa enhances its flavors.

This cake is extremely overleavened and would be sunken in the center, but adding boiling water to the soda and cocoa causes the soda to react and give off a lot of carbon dioxide, which reduces the leavening and prevents sinking.

Nonstick cooking spray
2¾ cups (19.3 oz/546 g) sugar
¾ teaspoon (4.5 g) salt
¾ cup (2.4 oz/69 g) Dutch process cocoa
   powder
1 teaspoon (5 g) baking soda
1 cup (237 ml) water

1 cup (237 ml) canola oil
2 teaspoons (10 ml) pure vanilla extract
1¾ cups (7.7oz/218 g) spooned and leveled
   bleached all-purpose flour
4 large egg yolks (2.6 oz/74 g)
2 large eggs (3.5 oz/99 g)
¼ cup (59 ml) buttermilk

1. Arrange a shelf in the lower third of the oven, place a baking stone on it, and preheat the oven to 350°F/177°C.

2. Spray VERY GENEROUSLY a 13 x 9 x 2-inch (33 x 23 x 5-cm) rectangular pan or two 9 x 2-inch (23 x 5-cm) round cake pans with nonstick cooking spray. Line the bottom of the round pans with parchment and spray on top of the parchment. With the rectangular pan, line and extend up the long sides with a piece of Release foil or parchment sprayed lightly with nonstick cooking spray.

3. In a heavy saucepan, stir together the sugar, salt, cocoa, and baking soda. In another saucepan, bring 1 cup (237 ml) water to a boil. Stirring constantly, pour boiling water a little at a time into the cocoa mixture. It will bubble up at first and then get dark and thicken. Stir the cocoa mixture briskly. Place on the heat and bring back to a boil. Turn off the heat and *allow to stand in the hot saucepan for at least 10 minutes.*

4. Pour the hot cocoa mixture into a mixing bowl. Add the oil and vanilla and beat on low speed for about 10 seconds. On low speed, beat the flour into the batter and then, with a minimum of beating, beat in the egg yolks, whole eggs, and buttermilk. This is a thin batter. Pour the batter into the prepared pan or pans. Place in the oven on the stone and bake until the center feels springy to the touch, about 25 minutes for round layers or 35 minutes for the sheet cake. Allow to cool in the pan for about 10 minutes on a rack. Run a thin knife around the edge and jar the edge of the pan to loosen. Invert onto the serving platter. Cool completely before icing.

Chocolate-on-Chocolate: Dark Moist Cake with Chocolate-Walnut Frosting

MAKES ONE 9-INCH (23-CM) 2-LAYER ROUND CAKE

Chocolate lovers' heaven! Midnight-black, moist, sweet layers with chocolate icing and walnuts. This cake is sweet but the icing is not, so I wanted to add a little more sweetness to the cake.

What This Recipe Shows

Roasting enhances the flavor of nuts.

On chocolate cakes a soaking solution is not able to soak in unless the solution is hot enough to melt the chocolate.

2½ cups (8.7 oz/50 g) walnut pieces
1 tablespoon (0.5 oz/14 g) butter
¼ teaspoon (1.5 g) salt
1 recipe Deep, Dark Chocolate Cake (page 112), prepared as two 9-inch (23-cm) round layers, baked and cooled

1 recipe Luscious, Creamy Chocolate Icing (page 143)
Chocolate-on-Chocolate Cake Soaking Solution (recipe follows)

1. Arrange a shelf in the lower third of the oven, place a baking stone on it, and preheat the oven to 350°F/177°C.

2. Spread nuts out on a baking sheet, place in the oven on the stone, and roast 10 minutes. While nuts are hot, stir in the butter and salt. When cool, coarsely chop and set aside.

3. To keep the serving platter clean, cut a 10-inch (25-cm) long piece of waxed paper, cut it in half lengthwise, then cut each half lengthwise in half again. Now you have four 3 x 10-inch (7.6 x 25-cm) strips. Lay the strips in a square on the serving platter with their outside edge touching the outer edge of the platter. Place one cooled cake layer on the platter, partially on the strips. (These strips, which can be pulled away later, will keep the platter clean while you ice the cake.)

4. Heat the soaking solution almost to a boil so that it will soak into the chocolate layer and drizzle about 3 tablespoons (45 ml) on the layer. Ice this prepared bottom layer with about ½-inch (1.2-cm) thickness of the icing, making the icing just a little thicker around the outer edge. Sprinkle with about ½ cup (1.7 oz/50 g) of the roasted walnuts.

5. Place the second layer on top of the iced layer. Drizzle evenly with 3 tablespoons (45 ml) of the soaking solution. Using a long metal spatula, ice the top and sides with the remaining icing. With the back of a greased tablespoon, make decorative swirls in the top, if desired. Press the remaining 2 cups (7 oz/200 g) roasted walnuts into the icing around the sides of the cake. Remove the waxed paper by pulling each strip out.

Chocolate-on-Chocolate Cake Soaking Solution

½ cup (3.5 oz/99 g) sugar
½ cup (118 ml) hot water

2 tablespoons (30 ml) Frangelico or walnut liqueur, optional
1 teaspoon (5 ml) pure vanilla extract

Stir the sugar into the water to dissolve. Stir in the liqueur and vanilla.

Satin-Glazed Midnight Black Chocolate Cake

MAKES ONE 9-INCH (23-CM) 2-LAYER ROUND CAKE

Satin-smooth, shiny ganache glaze over pitch-black chocolate layers. This cake is beautiful and heavenly delicious! The double-icing technique is used so that even a beginner can get a spotlessly smooth iced cake.

What This Recipe Shows

The double-icing technique produces a perfect, smooth, professional-looking chocolate coating.

---

1 recipe Deep, Dark Chocolate Cake (page 112), prepared as two 9-inch (23-cm) round layers

1 recipe Satin-Smooth Ganache Glaze (page 99)

1. Place one layer of the cooled cake on a cardboard circle that is slightly smaller than the cake. You want to be able to hold the cake and tilt it as necessary. Place the cake on a cooling rack over a large piece of parchment paper or a nonstick baking sheet. You want something that you can drip icing on and scrape it up if you need it.

2. Pour slightly less than half of the Satin-Smooth Ganache Glaze into a 2-cup (473-ml) measuring cup. You want the icing almost cool enough to set, about 90°F/32°C. Pour the icing to cover the cake layer, top with the second layer, and pour icing on until the icing starts to overflow and run down the edges. Lift the cake and tilt to encourage icing to run where there isn't any. With a metal spatula, smooth the icing around the edge. Do what you can to get icing over the top and around the edges. Allow the cake to cool for about 30 minutes.

3. No spatula from here on! Heat the remaining half of the icing just until it flows easily. Strain it into a warm 2-cup (473-ml) measuring cup. Hold the cake up with your left hand (if you are right-handed), keeping it over the parchment. With your right hand, pour icing into the center of the cake. Allow the icing to run down the edges and tilt to get it to run where it is needed. Pour more icing on as needed, but do NOT touch it with a spatula. You want this coating untouched, as smooth as a lake at dawn—a perfect, shiny, dark surface. Replace the cake on the cooling rack and allow to cool. Serve at room temperature.

Deep, Dark Chocolate Cake with Ganache and Chocolate Ruffles

MAKES ONE 9 X 2-INCH (23 X 5-CM) 2-LAYER ROUND CAKE

This is the wonderfully moist, midnight-black Deep, Dark Chocolate Cake turned into a breathtaking show stopper with ruffled chocolate ribbons.

What This Recipe Shows

Combining three great individual units, the Deep, Dark Chocolate Cake, Shiny Ganache Glaze, and Chocolate Ribbons, produces a delicious, breathtaking cake.

---

1 recipe Deep, Dark Chocolate Cake (page 112), prepared as two 9-inch (23-cm) round layers, baked and cooled

1 recipe Shiny Ganache Glaze (page 97)
1 recipe Chocolate Ribbons (page 118)
Confectioners' sugar, for dusting

1. When cake layers are completely cooled, place one layer on a cake cardboard.

2. Divide the ganache in half. Reserve one half. Cool the other half to about 90°F/32°C and use to ice the cake. Spread a thin layer of ganache over the first layer, place the second layer on top, and ice the top and sides, smoothing with a long spatula. Chill the cake in the refrigerator for about 30 minutes to set the icing well.

3. Heat the reserved icing to thin it, and strain it into a 2-cup (473-ml) measuring cup with a pouring spout. When it has cooled a little, pour the ganache on top of cake and tilt to spread. DO NOT touch with a spatula. This will create a glossy, smooth, professional-looking chocolate cake.

4. When the icing has set, flute a length of chocolate ribbon into a ruffled circle and arrange on top of the cake with the outer edge slightly larger than the cake. You can do this with several pieces of ribbon slightly overlapping at the edge or one long piece. Arrange two or three progressively smaller ruffle circles on the cake. Garnish with a light sprinkle of confectioners' sugar. Serve at room temperature. See picture on the cover.

Cocoa At a Glance

What to Do	Why
Reduce the amount of flour by the amount of cocoa added.	Cocoa acts like flour in baking.
Recipes like chocolate mousse that contain raw egg yolks and cocoa need to be brought to a boil.	Alpha-amylase in raw egg yolks will destroy the starch gel and cause the mousse to thin upon standing.
Use natural cocoa in recipes unless Dutch process is listed.	The alkalinity of Dutch process cocoa can reduce the acidity of a batter to a point that the proteins will not set.
Pour boiling water over cocoa.	Boiling water aids in dissolving cocoa and releases more flavors from cocoa.
To make cocoa darker use baking soda, or Dutch process cocoa, or Dutch process cocoa and baking soda.	The more alkaline it is, the darker the cocoa becomes.

Compound Chocolate (Summer Coatings, Compound Coatings)

When chocolates contain fats other than cocoa butter they may look a lot like chocolate, and their taste may be similar to chocolate, but they don't necessarily feel or act like chocolate. They may not melt in your mouth, or have the shine of real chocolate.

Major chocolate companies produce complete lines of these compound chocolates, which are sometimes called "compound coatings," or "summer coatings." Many are of excellent quality and often contain some quantity of cocoa butter. They are like real chocolate in that you must melt them with tender, loving care and not get them over 120°F/49°C, and you must store them in a cool, dry place. They are simpler to use than real chocolate. You do not have to temper them; you can use them as a coating just by melting.

There are two types of compound coatings: those made from palm kernel oil (lauric acid), and those made from soybean and cottonseed oil. Both can be used without tempering, although a simple tempering procedure is recommended for palm kernel–based coatings. Soybean and cottonseed oil–based coatings may be used with "real chocolate," but palm kernel oil–based coatings cannot be mixed with chocolate, and will even develop a bloom when in contact with chocolate.

Elaine Gonzalez is a master of working with compound chocolate. I highly recommend her books, *Chocolate Artistry* and *The Art of Chocolate*. If you do anything with this chocolate, you need her books. And by all means, if you get an opportunity to see her do a demonstration, don't miss it. Even if you don't work with chocolate, you will love watching her. You will learn so much.

Modeling Chocolate for Chocolate Ribbons

Chocolate ribbons are one of my favorite things to make. You can get such high drama on finished cakes and desserts with little effort. They look gorgeous and they are not that hard to make.

Cooks sometimes try modeling chocolate once but it is hard to work, so they get discouraged. The one place that you can go wrong is not having enough corn syrup. Be sure to oil or spray the measuring cup with nonstick cooking spray so that you do not lose some that is stuck to the cup. Also, work the chocolate well before you wrap it to stand in the refrigerator.

This is just melted chocolate and corn syrup, but it can be rock hard and totally unworkable if you do not have the full measure of corn syrup. The standard recipe has $1/3$ cup (79 ml) corn syrup, but I have added $1/2$ teaspoon (2.5 ml) more just to make sure that you have enough.

10 ounces (283 g) semisweet chocolate	$1/3$ cup (79 ml) plus $1/2$ teaspoon (2.5 ml) light
Nonstick cooking spray	corn syrup

1. Chop the chocolate and melt it as described on pages 92 to 93. When the chocolate is melted, spray a measuring cup and a $1/2$-teaspoon (2.5-ml) measuring spoon with nonstick cooking spray so that all of the syrup will drain out. Measure $1/3$ cup (79 ml) and $1/2$ teaspoon (2.5 ml) corn syrup and pour into the melted chocolate and stir. The chocolate will tighten but still be a soft dough.

2. Most recipes call for simply wrapping the dough and refrigerating, but I think it is important to work the dough right now. Flatten it out and fold it up, tripling it over. Smush it flat again, squeezing it between your fingers or rolling it out between plastic wrap. Do this flattening and folding several times. Finally, flatten the chocolate out to about 6 inches (15 cm) and wrap it tightly in plastic wrap. Permit to stand for several hours or overnight in the refrigerator. The modeling chocolate is now ready to shape into forms or ribbons.

Chocolate Ribbons

MAKES ENOUGH CHOCOLATE RIBBONS TO RUFFLE AND COVER ONE 9-INCH (22.8-CM) CAKE

1. Prepare one recipe of Modeling Chocolate for Chocolate Ribbons (page 118). The chocolate will be hard straight from the refrigerator but will become more pliable as it warms up. Warm under a gooseneck lamp or by working with your fingers. If it is very hard, soften it with a 10-second burst in the microwave on 30% power. If the dough gets too soft, let it stand to harden.

2. When the dough is pliable, roll it into a 3-inch (8-cm) long cylinder between your hand and the counter. Flatten it into a thick ribbon. Roll this thick ribbon between sheets of waxed paper with a rolling pin. Fold it over several times, then roll out again. Roll the dough through a pasta machine on the widest setting. Treat it like pasta. Fold it back together and flatten again. Do this four or five times, until it is extremely pliable.

3. Still with the widest setting on the pasta machine, run it through. You may want to divide it into two or three pieces and work each one. When the chocolate is very flexible, run the strip through progressively narrower settings until you get the thickness you want. Use the ribbon to create bows, ruffles, and other elaborate decorations. When left uncovered, the ruffles or bows harden into firm shapes that hold well.

Cake Techniques

With chemically leavened cakes, the techniques are: measuring, mixing, baking, icing, and storing. Mixing methods are the most involved and deserve considerable explanation (pages 119 to 135). Measuring flour is discussed on page 6. Baking tips begin on page 135, and the icings and storing section begins on page 141.

MIXING METHODS

In cake baking, much depends on mixing. Most think of mixing only as the uniform blending of ingredients. Mixing does do this, but the role of mixing in successful leavening is vital. Leaveners do not create a single new air bubble. They only enlarge bubbles that already exist in the dough or batter. So we depend on mixing to incorporate large quantities of fine bubbles into the batter.

Some of the subtle goals of mixing are: good emulsification for a creamy batter, reduction of air-bubble size for a fine-textured cake, and minimum gluten development for a tender cake.

Unfortunately, this whole area is a mess. The same mixing method is frequently known by a number of different names, and there are all kinds of variations on a specific method. The two methods that most home cooks commonly use are the creaming method and the muffin method. I will go into each of the major methods and give their advantages and disadvantages, but to give you an idea of how many there are, here is a list of some of the "named" mixing methods:

> Creaming Method (also called the Sugar/Batter, Sugar-Shortening, or Conventional Method)
> Two-Stage Method (also called Blending or Pastry Blend Method)

> Leaveners do not create bubbles; they only enlarge existing bubbles. We depend on mixing to incorporate large quantities of fine bubbles into the batter.

> The goals of mixing are: to achieve a uniform blending of all ingredients; to incorporate a maximum number of fine air cells for volume and texture; and to develop a minimum amount of gluten for tenderness, texture, and volume.

Flour/Batter Method
Single-Stage Method (also called "Dump," One-Bowl, or Quick-Mix Method)
Muffin Method
Dissolved-Sugar Method
Sugar/Flour Batter Method
Emulsion Method

Overview

Bakers are passionate about their preferred mixing method. One baker will explain to you why his or her method is the best, and you will be completely convinced that this is the method to use. Then another baker will convince you that his or her method is the best.

Different mixing methods do produce different kinds of cakes. I give you my Magnificent Moist Golden Cake prepared by three different methods—Creaming Method, page 124; Two-Stage Method, page 126; and Dissolved-Sugar Method, page 37—so that you can experience the difference in mixing methods for yourself.

The cake's texture and lightness are where you will see differences in mixing methods. Are your priorities light and airy, or velvety smooth, melt-in-your-mouth tender?

If a light texture is your primary goal, you should choose the creaming method, which gives prime importance to volume and aeration. Since the creaming method is the primary home-use method, I will go into detail on creaming. Unfortunately, it does have a number of possible pitfalls.

If velvety smooth texture and tenderness are your first concerns, you may want to use the two-stage method, which prevents gluten development, and a higher oven temperature, so that the bubbles won't expand too much and ruin the smooth, fine texture.

I like to think that my personal favorite method lets me have it all—lightness and velvety texture—and it allows me to make a very moist, sweet cake without too many places to go wrong. I love a little-known method called the dissolved-sugar method. An example of this method is given in the Magnificent Moist Golden Cake (Dissolved-Sugar Method) recipe, page 37.

Creaming Method (Sugar/Batter, Sugar-Shortening, or Conventional Method)

This is the method most familiar to everyone. Many cooking teachers prefer this method. Flo Braker, in *The Simple Art of Perfect Baking*, says, "I prefer the creaming method over all the others because, if you do it properly, you will produce a perfect butter cake with a fine-grained texture and a velvety crumb *every single time*."

If you keep the fat cool, and beat the fat alone and the fat-sugar mixture sufficiently long to incorporate massive amounts of fine air bubbles, this method will produce a light, well-aerated cake.

If you are careful to minimize stirring once the flour and liquid are together in the batter, you can limit the amount of gluten formed, and you will get a very tender cake, too.

To begin, you beat solid fat (butter or shortening), and then fat and sugar, on medium speed to incorporate as many fine bubbles in the fat as possible. At all times, the fat must be kept cool enough to hold the air well. In my recipes, I advise: "While creaming, feel the bowl; if it does not feel cool, place in the freezer for 5 minutes, then continue creaming."

In bakeries, in large commercial batches, creaming should be continued for about 10 minutes. This aeration of the fat and the fat and sugar are the crucial steps for a light cake. Once you add the eggs, you are no longer increasing final cake volume.

When I started baking I had always made poor cakes (very heavy) and didn't really know why. I would just barely beat the butter and the butter and sugar. Because they didn't fluff right up, I would add the eggs (which did fluff up) and beat longer at that point. I had no idea that I was breezing over the major steps that were vital for final cake volume.

> In the creaming method, once you add the eggs, beating no longer increases final cake volume. The aeration of the fat and the fat and sugar are the crucial steps for a light cake.

Bruce Healy, the famous pastry chef and author of *Mastering the Art of French Pastry, The Art of the Cake,* and *The French Cookie Book,* asked me exactly which parts of the creaming procedure contributed to final cake volume. I had always considered beating the butter, butter and sugar, and the butter, sugar, and eggs as "creaming." It never occurred to me to evaluate each of the three separate steps. Bruce and I were amazed when neither of us could find any research in this area.

We are all indebted to Bruce's diligent work, making closely controlled cake after cake to determine that beating the fat and beating the fat and sugar contributed to final volume, but that once you added the eggs, beating no longer increased final volume. Cake expert Susan Purdy, author of *Have Your Cake and Eat It, Too,* agrees completely with Bruce that the creaming of the butter and sugar is the vital step for volume. Learning this dramatically improved my cakes.

> Since fat is a major flavor carrier, adding the flavorings directly to the fat ensures their thorough dispersion of flavoring throughout the batter.

After getting the butter and the butter and sugar very light and fluffy, I like to add the flavoring or flavorings (vanilla, lemon zest, brandy, etc.). Most recipes instruct adding the flavorings last. I noticed that Maida Heatter, the grande dame of baking and my hero, added flavorings directly to the fat. I thought, "What a great idea!" Since fat is a major flavor carrier, adding the flavorings directly to the fat ensures that they are carried throughout the cake. If I am using oil as part of the fat, I add it with the butter, sugar, and flavoring.

> Excessive beating of the batter once the eggs are added can create a separate, meringue-like crust on the top of baked goods.

After adding the flavoring and oil, I mix in the egg yolks first, then the whole eggs, one at a time, on low speed. Beating too much after you add the eggs can create a separate, meringue-like crust on a baked good. You may have seen brownies with this crust, which is lighter in color and may be totally separated from the brownie (see page 409). To prevent this, keep the beating to a minimum, on the lowest speed, or stir by hand once you add the eggs.

I do not think that sifting is effective at blending dry ingredients and dispersing the leaveners (see page 58). I like to mix the flour and baking powder in a separate bowl by beating with a hand mixer for a full 30 seconds, or even beating with a fork to thoroughly blend.

Most recipes tell you to alternate adding the flour mixture and the liquid to the batter, beginning with the flour. I like to blend in at least half of the flour mixture first. At this point, the only water-type liquids present are the egg whites. So here you have the perfect opportunity to grease a lot of the flour proteins without forming much tough gluten before you add any other liquid.

Next, I stir the salt into the liquid (buttermilk, cream, etc.) and add only a small portion of it, to keep the batter from getting too thick. Then I go back and add the rest of the flour. Now that you have liquid and flour together, any further mixing produces tough gluten. To make the cake very tender (and keep gluten formation to a minimum), mix just enough to blend the ingredients. Finally, I stir in the last of the liquid or, in some cases, fold in the whipped cream.

Possible Creaming Pitfalls

There are several steps where you can go wrong in this method. Possible pitfalls are: temperature of the butter, eggs, sugar, and mixing bowl; insufficient creaming; insufficient blending of baking powder and flour; and development of too much gluten.

Butter and bowl temperature—Most recipes call for softened or room-temperature butter. Room temperature may be fine for European home kitchens, which are usually considerably colder than U.S. home kitchens. For typical U.S. home kitchens "room temperature" is not a good idea. The butter needs to be colder. To incorporate and hold fine air bubbles, the butter cannot be melted. Butter has a sharp melting point; it can go from hard to melted within a narrow temperature range. Most experts recommend between 65 and 70°F (18 and 21°C). Bruce Healy, a classic French pastry expert, says that butter actually melts between 67 and 68°F (about 20°C), so his preferred starting temperature for the butter is 65°F/18°C.

Since the butter temperature is so important, Bruce recommends rinsing the mixing bowl and beater with ice water and drying them thoroughly. A hot bowl can lead to melted butter and a disastrously heavy cake. Bruce says to prevent the butter from starting to melt he recommends frequently stopping creaming briefly and dipping the bottom of the bowl in an ice-water bath to cool it down. I usually suggest that if the bowl does not feel cool to the touch, put it in the freezer for 5 minutes and then continue. He is now considering placing the sugar in the freezer for 20 minutes before mixing to see if cold sugar will better maintain the temperature below 68°F (about 20°C).

Bowl, kitchen, and ingredient temperatures present no problem at all in aerating shortening since it remains the same consistency over a wide temperature range and already contains 12% fine nitrogen bubbles.

Temperature of the eggs—Most books recommend room-temperature eggs. Bruce Healy says that his experimentation shows slightly, but definitely, reduced volume with cold eggs. Eggs from the refrigerator can be warmed fairly rapidly by placing them still in their shells in a bowl of hot tap water.

Insufficient creaming—With butter, most of the air bubbles in a cake are created in the creaming step. Baking powder only enlarges bubbles already in the dough. Shortening, which is already "aerated" by the nitrogen bubbles, will produce a light cake even with a poor job of creaming, but butter will not. In addition to using 65°F/18°C butter, the length of beating time, the speed and type of the mixer, and the bowl and room temperature are all important to get the fat and sugar very light and airy.

Flo Braker, author of *The Simple Art of Perfect Baking*, recommends creaming 4 to 5 minutes, and Carole Walter recommends 6 to 10 minutes. Susan Purdy points out that the type of mixer influences the time for good creaming. Hand mixers frequently take several minutes longer to cream than a stand mixer does. She also points out that, when using a hand mixer, it is important to move it around the bowl and scrape down the sides several times for complete creaming.

For very large commercial batches, bakers usually recommend a minimum of 10 minutes at no higher than medium speed, because at higher speeds the mixing can heat the batter and cause the butter to melt.

Insufficient blending of leaveners and flour—This is my personal Waterloo. I am always in a hurry, and this seems like such a minor step—but for cakes, it is actually very important to blend the flour and leavening thoroughly. If the leavening is not uniformly distributed in the flour, the cake can have a velvety texture but numerous unsightly large holes. Unfortunately, even sifting the ingredients together several times does not ensure that they are well blended and you won't have some big holes in the cake (see page 58 for more details). To get the best blending I prefer beating flour and leaveners together with a beater for a full 30 seconds.

Development of gluten—When adding flour and liquid alternately to the cake batter, gluten can be developed that makes the cake tough or leads to tunnels in the cake. Typically, the only liquids

Creaming Method At a Glance

What to Do	Why
Beat the fat, and the fat and sugar well to create fine bubbles in the fat.	Since leaveners enlarge, but do not create bubbles, leavening depends on the creaming step to create fine bubbles in the batter.
Keep the fat cool during this creaming step.	If the fat starts to melt, it will lose the bubbles.
Add the flavorings (extracts, zest, brandies) directly to the fat-sugar mixture.	Fat is a major flavor carrier.
Beat the flour and leavening together with a hand-held mixer, or beat well with a fork.	For a uniform-textured cake
When alternating the addition of flour and liquid to the batter, add more than half of the flour initially.	For a tenderer cake

present when you make the first addition of flour are egg whites. So this first addition of flour is well coated with fat and does not form much gluten, but once the liquid such as milk or buttermilk is added, the uncoated flour proteins can combine with liquid to form tough gluten. Because of this I like to add a lot of the flour in the first addition (over half of the flour mixture). Once the liquid and the last part of the flour are added, limit the mixing to prevent the development of gluten. Simply stated, overbeating the batter at this point can develop gluten.

High-ratio cakes can curdle when using the creaming method. If too much liquid is added at one time, the batter can curdle (switch from the water-in-oil emulsion that you want to an oil-in-water emulsion). This is immediately remedied with the addition of more flour. There is no real problem other than frightening you when you see the curdled mess.

In spite of all the possible pitfalls, the creaming method probably produces the lightest cakes. It gives maximum aeration of the fat, which results in maximum volume of the batter and the cake.

Magnificent Moist Golden Cake (Creaming Method)

MAKES ONE 9 X 2-INCH (23 X 5-CM) ROUND LAYER

This is a wonderfully moist, sweet cake that I developed because I can't stand dry cakes. This makes a single thick layer that can be sliced horizontally into three layers and used for many different cakes. Having moist, sweet layers can dramatically improve any cake creation. This is a level, perfectly shaped cake. The top does brown but, since you invert the cake, this is not a problem.

The creaming method does have many challenges. Read the section on Possible Creaming Pitfalls, page 122, before making this cake.

What This Recipe Shows

A balanced recipe (balanced weights of tenderizing and toughening ingredients) creates a successful cake.

The creaming method incorporates a maximum amount of fine air bubbles into the batter for a light cake.

The correct butter, sugar, egg, bowl, and room temperatures, as well as creaming time, contribute to lightness in the texture of the cake.

Adding the flavorings to the fat, which is an excellent flavor carrier, distributes the flavors well.

Whipped cream adds moisture and great flavor, and gives the cake a soft, velvety texture.

Nonstick cooking spray with flour

4 tablespoons (2 oz/57 g) unsalted butter, cut in 1-tablespoon (0.5-oz/14-g) pieces

1½ cups (10.5 oz/298 g) sugar

2 teaspoons (10 ml) pure vanilla extract

⅓ cup (79 ml) canola oil

3 large egg yolks (1.95 oz/55 g)

2 large eggs (3.5 oz/99 g)

1¾ cups (7.1 oz/201 g) spooned and leveled cake flour (NO SUBSTITUTE—the cake will be sunken in the center and simply will not work correctly if other flour is used; see page 60.)

1¾ teaspoons (8 g) baking powder

½ teaspoon (3 g) salt

⅓ cup (79 ml) buttermilk

½ cup (118 ml) heavy cream

1. Arrange a shelf in the lower third of the oven, place a baking stone on it, and preheat the oven to 350°F/177°C.

2. Spray a 9 x 2-inch (23 x 5-cm) round cake pan with nonstick cooking spray with flour and line with a parchment circle. (I very lightly spray the top of the parchment, too.)

3. In a mixer on medium speed, beat the butter to soften. Beat until it is light in color, about 3 minutes. Add the sugar and continue to beat (cream) until very light, scraping down the sides and across the bottom of the bowl at least once. While creaming, feel the bowl; if it does not feel cool, place in the freezer for 5 minutes, then continue creaming.

4. Beat in the vanilla. On medium speed, blend in the oil.

5. On the lowest speed, blend in the yolks, one at a time, mixing just to blend. Blend in the whole eggs, one at a time, mixing just to blend.

6. In a medium mixing bowl, beat the flour, baking powder, and salt for a full 30 seconds at medium speed with a hand mixer or with a fork or whisk by hand.

7. On the lowest speed, blend over half of the flour mixture into the batter. Continue on lowest speed and blend in half of the buttermilk. Continue adding the remainder of the flour until all is incorporated. Blend in the remaining buttermilk.

8. In a cold bowl with cold beaters, whip the cream until soft peaks form when the beater is lifted. Beat just a little beyond this soft-peak stage. Stir about one-quarter of the whipped cream into the batter to lighten. Then fold the rest of the whipped cream into the batter.

9. Pour the batter into the prepared pan. Drop the pan onto the counter from a height of about 4 inches (10 cm) to knock out bubbles. Place the cake in the oven on the stone and bake until the center springs back when touched, or a toothpick inserted in the center comes out clean but moist, about 40 minutes. Ideally, the cake should not pull away from the sides until it has just come out of the oven. The center temperature should be about 209°F/98°C if you check by inserting an instant-read thermometer.

10. Place the cake in the pan on a rack to cool for about 10 minutes, then shake the pan to loosen the cake all around. Spray a cooling rack with nonstick cooking spray and invert the cake onto the rack to finish cooling. Peel off the parchment. Cool completely before slicing into layers (see page 39), storing, or icing.

Two-Stage, Blending, or Pastry Blend Method

Different experts have slightly different procedures, but the basic method is the same. First, blend all the dry ingredients and all the fat with a tiny bit of liquid, and then add the remaining liquid. Since you blend the flour with the fat before any liquid gets to it, the flour proteins are well greased and as a result a minimum of gluten is formed. This is a way to get melt-in-your-mouth tenderness, but the cake may be heavy because that wonderful aeration that you get when you cream the fat and the fat and the sugar together is missing.

Rose Levy Beranbaum, author of *The Cake Bible*, swears by this two-stage method. She says that, from her observations, bakers have better and more consistent results with the two-stage method when exactly followed according to the recipe. While the two-stage method does not produce quite as good aeration as the creaming method, this method produces cakes so tender that the mouthfeel is a sensation of lightness as the cake dissolves in your mouth. There are fewer pitfalls with the two-stage method, but you definitely get a heavier cake than with the creaming method.

Magnificent Moist Golden Cake (Two-Stage Method)

MAKES ONE 9 X 2-INCH (23 X 5-CM) ROUND LAYER

This is a wonderfully moist, sweet cake that I developed because I can't stand dry cakes. This makes a single thick layer that can be sliced horizontally into three layers and used as the base for many different cakes. Having moist, sweet layers can dramatically improve any cake creation.

What This Recipe Shows

A balanced recipe (balanced weights of tenderizing and toughening ingredients) creates a successful cake.

This two-stage method of blending the fat with the flour produces incredible tenderness.

Whipped cream adds moisture and great flavor, and gives the cake a soft, velvety texture.

Nonstick cooking spray with flour

2 large eggs (3.5 oz/99 g) at room temperature

3 large egg yolks (1.95 oz/55 g) at room temperature

1/3 cup (79 ml) buttermilk, divided

2 teaspoons (10 ml) pure vanilla extract

1 3/4 cups (7.1 oz/201 g) spooned and leveled cake flour (NO SUBSTITUTE—the cake will be sunken in the center and simply will not work correctly with other flour; see page 60.

1 1/2 cups (10.5 oz/298 g) sugar

1 3/4 teaspoons (8 g) baking powder

1/2 teaspoon (3 g) salt

4 tablespoons (2 oz/57 g) unsalted butter, cut in 1-tablespoon (0.5-oz/14-g) pieces, and slightly softened

1/3 cup (79 ml) canola oil

1/2 cup (118 ml) heavy cream

1. Arrange a shelf in the lower third of the oven, place a baking stone on it, and preheat the oven to 350°F/177°C.

2. Spray a 9 x 2-inch (23 x 5-cm) round cake pan with nonstick cooking spray with flour and line with a parchment circle. (I very lightly spray the top of the parchment, too.)

3. Stir the eggs, yolks, 3 tablespoons (45 ml) of the buttermilk, and the vanilla together in a medium bowl.

4. Mix together the flour, sugar, baking powder, and salt in a mixer with the whisk attachment on low speed for a full 30 seconds. Add the butter and oil and the remaining 2 tablespoons (30 ml) buttermilk. Mix on low speed to moisten the dry ingredients, then increase to medium speed and beat 1 1/2 minutes. Scrape down the sides and across the bottom of the bowl. Add one-third of the egg mixture and beat for 20 seconds. Repeat, adding thirds until all of the egg mixture is incorporated. Scrape down the sides with each addition.

5. In a cold bowl with cold beaters, whip the cream until soft peaks form when the beater is lifted. Beat just a little beyond this soft peak stage. Stir about one-quarter of the whipped cream into the batter to lighten it. Then fold the rest of the whipped cream into the batter.

6. Pour the batter into the prepared pan. Drop the pan onto the counter from a height of 4 inches (10 cm) to knock out bubbles. Place the cake in the oven on the stone and bake until the center springs back when touched, or a toothpick inserted in the center comes out clean but moist, about 40 minutes. Ideally, the cake should not pull away from the sides until it has just come out of the oven. The center temperature should be about 209°F/98°C if you check by inserting an instant-read thermometer.

7. Place the cake in the pan on a rack to cool, about 10 minutes, then shake the pan to loosen the cake all around. Spray cooling rack with nonstick cooking spray and invert the cake onto the rack to finish cooling. Peel off the parchment. Cool completely before slicing into layers (see page 39), storing, or icing.

Flour/Batter Method

In this method, you blend the flour with an equal weight of fat, and blend the eggs with an equal weight of sugar. Whip the eggs and sugar at medium speed to form a medium-firm foam. Blend the flour mixture and the egg mixture together in three portions: cream one-third of the egg mixture into the flour mixture, beat the second third of the egg mixture in on low speed, and stir the last third in by hand. Stir the milk in, adding it a little at a time. Stir in any remaining ingredients.

Advantages of the flour/batter method are that you have a thorough dispersion of fat, which produces an extremely fine grain and uniform texture. This allows the use of higher amounts of sugar and liquids than is possible with the creaming method. However, less air incorporation and more gluten development can produce heavier and tougher cakes!

Single-Stage Method ("Dump," One-Bowl, or Quick-Mix Method)

In this method, all the dry ingredients except the baking powder are sifted together, and then combined with all the wet ingredients. The batter is blended with a paddle attachment on low speed for 1 to 2 minutes, on a higher speed for several minutes, and finally on low speed for an additional 2 minutes. The baking powder is added near the end of the beating time. Another version of the single-stage method is to combine all the ingredients except the eggs and then whisk with the whisk attachment on high speed for 1 minute. Finally, the eggs are stirred in on low speed for 30 seconds.

This method really works only if a shortening with emulsifiers such as Crisco, or some egg yolks, is used. Since there is no creaming step to provide aeration, the shortening, which is already aerated, is needed. You also need emulsifiers to help disperse the fat. Advantages of this method are its simplicity and speed, not quality. Without emulsified shortening such as Crisco, it generally produces poor results.

Muffin Pan Sizes

There are a number of different sizes of muffin pans. The 6-cup muffin tins sold frequently in grocery stores are 2¾ x 1⅛ inches (7 x 2.8 cm). Standard bakery muffin size is 2¾ x 1⅜ inches (7 x 3.5 cm) and holds almost twice as much batter as the shallower grocery store pans. Giant muffin pans are 3 x 1¼ inches (7.3 x 3.2 cm), and mini muffin pans are 1¾ x ¾ inches (4.4 x 2 cm). If you make muffins in a pan that is a different size than the recipe indicates, you will need to adjust baking time, and the yield will be different.

Muffin Method

In this method, dry ingredients are combined in one bowl and the eggs, milk, and melted fat are combined in another. Then the wet ingredients are stirred together with the dry ingredients by hand using a large spatula. This is a poor method of cake mixing, since it gives uneven dispersion of ingredients, large cells, and a coarse crumb. In hearty muffins or cornbread, when a coarse crumb is not objectionable, this method works perfectly fine. Three recipes for muffins follow.

If you make muffins in a pan that is a different size than the recipe indicates, you will need to adjust baking time and the yield will be different.

Dena's Great Apple-Walnut Muffins

MAKES 12 MEDIUM (2$\frac{3}{4}$ X 1$\frac{1}{8}$-INCH/7 X 2.8-CM) MUFFINS

Dena Dougherty loves horses and now runs a riding school in Alabama for underprivileged children. Several years ago, I worked in her bakery in Atlanta that sold sensational brownies and desserts. No matter what someone would request, Dena would say, "Oh yes, we make those." Then Dena would call and ask me to "come over quick" and figure out how to make it. We had some wild times in the bakery. (Our cookie-machine episode looked like Lucy in the chocolate factory.) This is a recipe that I developed to fill orders in the bakery.

Please note the size of the muffin tins. If you use a different size, you will need to adjust cooking time and the yield will be different.

What This Recipe Shows

Roasting nuts enhances flavors.

Using baking powder instead of baking soda when using buttermilk makes the batter more acidic so the muffins will have a better peak.

Crisp, sweet Fuji apples hold up well in baking.

Oil helps make the muffins moist.

Baking at a high oven temperature produces a better peak on the muffins.

Whipped cream adds moisture and great flavor, and gives the muffins a softer texture.

1½ cups (5.2 oz/150 g) walnut pieces
¾ teaspoon (4.5 g) salt, divided
1 tablespoon (0.5 oz/14 g) butter
2 cups (8.8 oz/249 g) spooned and leveled
    bleached all-purpose flour
2 teaspoons (9 g) baking powder
1 teaspoon (2 g) ground cinnamon
½ teaspoon (1 g) freshly grated nutmeg
1 cup (7 oz/198 g) sugar, divided
⅔ cup (4 oz/113 g) English toffee bits,
    available in bags near the chocolate chips

2 large eggs (3.5 oz/99 g)
½ cup (118 ml) canola oil
½ cup (118 ml) buttermilk
2 teaspoons (10 ml) pure vanilla extract
Zest (grated peel) of 1 orange
½ cup (118 ml) heavy cream
1½ cups (5.8 oz/165 g) peeled, cored, and
    coarsely chopped apples (Fuji apples are
    my favorite)
Nonstick cooking spray

1. Arrange a shelf in the lower third of the oven, place a baking stone on it, and preheat the oven to 350°F/177°C.

2. Spread the nuts out on a baking sheet, place in the oven on the stone, and roast 10 minutes. While nuts are hot, stir in the butter and ¼ teaspoon (1.5 g) of the salt. When cool, coarsely chop and set aside.

3. Turn oven up to 425°F/218°C.

4. In a large mixing bowl, beat together the flour, baking powder, the remaining ½ teaspoon (3 g) salt, the cinnamon, nutmeg, and ⅔ cup (4.7 oz/132 g) of the sugar for 30 seconds to blend well. Stir in the toffee bits by hand.

5. In a medium mixing bowl, stir the eggs with a fork, then stir in the oil, buttermilk, vanilla, and orange zest.

6. Make a well in the dry ingredients and pour in the wet ingredients. Stir together by hand.

7. In a cold bowl with cold beaters, whip the cream until soft peaks form when the beater is lifted. Beat just a little beyond this soft peak stage. Stir about one-quarter of the whipped cream into the batter to lighten. Then fold the rest of the whipped cream into the batter.

8. Fold the apples and roasted, chopped walnuts into the batter.

9. Spray two 6-cup medium (2¾ x 1⅛-inch/7 x 2.8-cm) muffin pans with nonstick cooking spray. (See Muffin Pan Sizes, page 128. If you make muffins in a pan that is a different size, you will need to adjust baking time, and the yield will be different.)

10. Fill the muffin cups almost full. Sprinkle the remaining ⅓ cup (2.3 oz/66 g) sugar on top of the muffins. Turn the oven down to 400°F/204°C and leave the oven door open for about 10 seconds. Place the muffin tins in the oven on the hot stone and close the door. Bake until muffins are well risen and lightly browned, about 15 to 20 minutes.

11. Cool the muffins in the pans for about 5 minutes. Jar the edge of the pans on the counter to loosen the muffins, and carefully remove them to a cooling rack.

Blueberries and Cream Muffins

MAKES 12 MEDIUM (2¾ x 1⅛-INCH/7 x 2.8-CM) MUFFINS

Creamy, moist, wonderful muffins! The texture is actually soft. They just barely have enough gluten developed to hold them together. Don't hesitate to stir this batter vigorously before you add the cream and blueberries. Select large blueberries; they are sweeter. These muffins really depend on good ripe blueberries.

If these muffins are too tender and crumbly, you can solve the problem by first stirring the buttermilk alone into the flour mixture, then mixing in the oil and eggs. This will develop more gluten to hold the muffins together well.

What This Recipe Shows

Using baking powder instead of baking soda when using buttermilk makes the batter more acidic, so the muffins will have better peaks.

Using the muffin mixing method does not produce as light a result as creaming.

Oil and cream help make the muffins moist.

Whipped cream adds moisture, a wonderful flavor, and an incredibly soft texture.

Baking at a high oven temperature produces better peaks on the muffins.

---

2 cups (8.8 oz/249 g) spooned and leveled
    bleached all-purpose flour
2 teaspoons (9 g) baking powder
½ teaspoon (3 g) salt
1¼ cups (12.3 oz/349 g) sugar
1 large egg (1.75 oz/50 g)
½ cup (118 ml) canola oil
⅓ cup (79 ml) buttermilk
1 teaspoon (5 ml) pure vanilla extract

1 teaspoon (5 ml) lemon zest (grated peel)
1 tablespoon (15 ml) orange zest (grated peel)
½ cup (118 ml) heavy cream
1½ cups (7.4 oz/208 g) fresh blueberries
    (select large berries, which are sweeter)
Nonstick cooking spray
¼ cup (1.8 oz/52 g) coarse sugar or
    granulated sugar, for topping

1. Arrange a shelf in the lower third of the oven, place a baking stone on it, and preheat the oven to 425°F/218°C.

2. In a large mixing bowl, beat together the flour, baking powder, salt, and sugar for a full 30 seconds.

3. In a medium mixing bowl, beat the egg with a few strokes, then beat in the oil, buttermilk, vanilla, and lemon and orange zests.

4. Make a well in the dry ingredients and pour in the wet ingredients. Beat together with a hand mixer or by hand. Stir or beat well. This batter is almost too tender, so do not hesitate to stir vigorously.

5. In a cold bowl with cold beaters, whip the cream until soft peaks form when the beater is lifted. Beat just a little beyond this soft peak stage. Stir about one-quarter of the whipped cream in to lighten the batter. Then, fold the rest of the whipped cream into the batter. Fold the blueberries into the batter.

6. Spray two 6-cup medium (2¾ x 1⅛-inch/7 x 2.8-cm) muffin pans with nonstick cooking spray. (See Muffin Pan Sizes, page 128. If you make muffins in a pan that is a different size than the recipe indicates, you will need to adjust baking time, and the yield will be different.)

7. Fill muffin pans almost to the top. Sprinkle the muffins with coarse sugar. Turn the oven down to 400°F/204°C and leave the oven door open for about 10 seconds. Place pans in the oven on the stone and close the oven door. Bake until well-risen and lightly browned, about 20 minutes.

8. Cool the muffins in the pans for about 5 minutes. Jar the edges of the pans on the counter to loosen the muffins, and carefully remove them to a cooling rack.

Sweet Pears and Crunchy, Roasted Walnut Muffins

MAKES 12 MEDIUM (2¾ X 1⅛-INCH/7 X 2.8-CM) MUFFINS

Incredibly flavorful, moist wonderful muffins! Like the Blueberries and Cream Muffins, these have just barely enough gluten developed to hold them together. Don't hesitate to stir this batter vigorously before you add the cream, pears, and nuts.

If these muffins are too tender and crumbly, you can solve the problem by adding the buttermilk alone to the flour mixture first before you mix in the oil and eggs. This will develop more gluten to hold the muffins together well.

What This Recipe Shows

Roasting nuts enhances flavor.

Using the muffin method does not produce as light a result as creaming.

Using baking powder instead of baking soda when using buttermilk makes the batter more acidic so the muffins will have better peaks.

Oil and cream help make the muffins moist.

Whipped cream adds moisture, a wonderful flavor, and an incredibly soft texture.

Baking at a high oven temperature produces better peaks on the muffins.

---

1 cup (3.5 oz/100 g) walnut pieces
1 tablespoon (0.5 oz/14 g) butter
¾ teaspoon (4.5 g) salt, divided
2 cups (8.8 oz/249 g) spooned and leveled
    bleached all-purpose flour
2 teaspoons (9 g) baking powder
1¼ cups (12.3 oz/349 g) sugar
2 large egg yolks (1.3 oz/37 g)
1 large egg (1.75 oz/50 g)
½ cup (118 ml) canola oil
½ cup (118 ml) buttermilk

1 teaspoon (5 ml) pure vanilla extract
1 tablespoon (15 ml) orange zest (grated peel)
3 tablespoons (45 ml) finely chopped candied
    ginger
½ cup (118 ml) heavy cream
1½ cups (7.4 oz/208 g) canned pears, drained
    well on a paper towel and chopped into
    ½-inch (1.3-cm) chunks or slightly larger
Nonstick cooking spray
¼ cup (1.8 oz/52 g) coarse sugar for topping

1. Arrange a shelf in the lower third of the oven, place a baking stone on it, and preheat the oven to 350°F/177°C.

2. Spread the nuts out on a baking sheet, place in the oven on the stone, and roast 10 minutes. While nuts are hot, stir in the butter and ¼ teaspoon (1.5 g) salt. When cool, coarsely chop and set aside.

3. Turn the oven up to 425°F/218°C.

4. In a large mixing bowl, beat together the flour, baking powder, the remaining ½ teaspoon (3 g) salt, and the sugar for a full 30 seconds.

5. In a medium mixing bowl, beat the egg yolks and egg a few strokes, then beat in the oil, buttermilk, vanilla, and orange zest.

6. Make a well in the dry ingredients and pour in the wet ingredients. Beat with a hand mixer or by hand with a fork. Stir or beat well. Stir in the candied ginger. This batter is almost too tender, so do not hesitate to stir vigorously.

7. In a cold bowl with cold beaters, whip the cream until soft peaks form when the beater is lifted. Beat just a little beyond this soft peak stage. By hand, stir about one-quarter of the whipped cream in to lighten the batter. Then fold the rest of the whipped cream into the batter. Fold the pears and walnuts into the batter.

8. Spray two 6-cup medium (2¾ x 1⅛-inch/7 x 2.8-cm) muffin pans with nonstick cooking spray. (See Muffin Pan Sizes, page 128. If you make muffins in a pan that is a different size than the recipe indicates, you will need to adjust baking time, and the yield will be different.)

9. Fill the muffin pans almost to the top. Sprinkle some coarse sugar on top of each muffin. Turn the oven down to 400°F/204°C and leave the oven door open for about 10 seconds. Place the pans into the oven on the stone and close the oven door. Bake until well-risen and lightly browned, about 20 minutes.

10. Cool the muffins in the pans for about 5 minutes. Jar the edges of the pans on the counter to loosen the muffins, and carefully remove them to a cooling rack.

Dissolved-Sugar Method

In this method of mixing, the sugar is dissolved in liquid equaling about half of its weight. Next the dry ingredients (flour, salt, and baking powder) and fat (emulsified shortening or butter if extra yolks are used) are blended together and then added to the sugar and mixed for 5 minutes. Then the remaining liquid, flavoring, and eggs are blended in on low speed for 1 minute. This is the method that I use for one version my Magnificent Moist Golden Cake (page 37).

This method provides excellent aeration by blending the dry ingredients with fat, and fine texture and tenderness by preventing gluten formation by coating the flour proteins with fat. This has all the advantages of using liquid sugar, an ingredient used commercially, to achieve better volume of cakes. The crust color is a little deeper brown than usual, but not enough to matter when covered with most icings.

Sugar/Flour Batter Method

In this method, the sugar is dissolved into the eggs instead of beaten in. The fat, flavoring, flour, and leavening are mixed together, and then the salt is added to the sugar-egg mixture, which is poured into the fat-and-flour mixture in a stream with the mixer on the lowest speed.

Emulsion Method

In this method, first cream the fat and sugar. Add the milk in several portions while beating continuously at medium speed for 5 minutes to get a light, fluffy mass. Add the flour over a 2-minute period, and then the eggs, and mix for 4 to 5 minutes—total mixing time is a continuous 12 to 15 minutes.

BAKING

A Good Rise

When baking, you are dealing with a constant fight in the oven. You need to get the dough or batter hot so that the baking powder and/or baking soda produces gases vigorously to enlarge bubbles and create a good rise in the batter or dough before the heat from the top of the oven starts setting (crusting) the top of the baked good and holding it down.

The best way to solve this is to create heat from the bottom of the oven to warm the dough or batter quickly. Also, you need the baked good to be as far away from the hot top of the oven as possible. However, if you bake too close to the oven bottom you run the risk of burning the bottom of what you're baking.

So how can you get heat from the bottom and a good distance from the top of the oven, without burning the bottom of the baked good?

A heavy baking stone can be your salvation. I use a heavy rectangular (14 x 16-inch/36 x 41-cm) baking stone (pizza stone) (about ¾ inch/2 cm thick) and place it on a shelf in the lower third of the oven. The thick stone keeps the heat even on the bottom of the pan—a great first step to avoid burning. For cakes, the preheated hot stone gives instant even heat to the batter. This works beautifully since the stone is below the center of the oven, so I have a little more distance from the hot top of the oven to prevent my cake's top from setting prematurely.

Steam is an ideal solution for yeast doughs. With yeast doughs baked in commercial steam ovens, the baker simply keeps the oven filled with steam to prevent the top from drying and crusting. This allows the bread to rise to its maximum height before the baker cuts off the steam and lets the oven dry out and crust the loaf. However, steam is not the best idea for cakes, because they don't form a solid top crust like a loaf of bread. Cakes have a porous structure, and you run the risk of creating a soggy cake top with steam.

Texture

For a level cake layer, you have to decide whether to bake the cake at 325°F/163°C or at 350°F/177°C. At the slightly higher temperature of 350°F/177°C, the cake rises for a shorter time and will set a little sooner, and the texture is finer. At 325°F/163°C, the cake rises slightly longer, producing a lighter cake but with a slightly coarser texture. (Read more about mixing methods starting on page 119.)

Is It Done?

Normally, cake baking directions will read something like, "cook until it springs back to the touch or until a toothpick inserted in the center comes out moist but without crumbs." Ideally, a cake should not pull away from the sides until it has just come out of the oven. The center temperature should be about 209°F/98°C if you check by inserting an instant-read thermometer.

Sometimes "not done" (not completely cooked dry) is "done." The famous Improved Tunnel of Fudge Cake (page 74) and the Intense Chocolate Lava Cakes (page 229) are examples. With the Improved Tunnel of Fudge Cake, the chocolate center is runny when the cake is slightly warm, but becomes firm fudge when cooled overnight in the refrigerator.

The wonderful Queen of California Cake by Alice Medrich, author of *Cocolat* and *Chocolate and the Art of Low-Fat Desserts,* is a good example of an intentionally undercooked cake. Alice wanted it very moist. She directs that a toothpick inserted 1 inch (2.5 cm) from the outer edge should come out moist. A rim of about 1 inch (2.5 cm) is completely risen and completely cooked, but the rest of the cake is sunken. Alice says, "Don't worry about a thing." She then tells you to press down the cooked outer edge so that it is level with the sunken undercooked center.

Shape

Muffins

For layer cakes you want a level top, but for muffins, you want a peak. Possibly for a loaf cake you may want the cake to have a nice ridge. How do you get a peak? If the outside edge sets while the center is juicy and still rising, you get a peak. The smaller diameter of the muffin cup helps the outside to set. Combine that with a higher oven temperature for muffins to deliberately set the outside fast, and you can get nice peaks on muffins.

Unfortunately, many muffin recipes give a baking temperature of 350°F/177°C. You will not get a peak at 350°F/177°C unless you have too many eggs in the recipe. If you have too many eggs in the recipe, the excessive protein will set the outside very fast. So you can get a peak, but with an incredibly dry muffin from the excess egg whites!

I think an oven temperature of at least 400°F/204°C works beautifully to produce a peak on muffins. What I have done successfully in some muffin recipes is to preheat the oven to 425°F /218°C for at least 30 minutes to get the baking stone really hot. I open the oven door for about 10 seconds to cool slightly, and lower the oven temperature to 400°F/204°C. Then I place the muffins on the hot stone and close the oven door. Bake the muffins until they slightly spring back to the touch, about 20 minutes. Dena's Great Apple-Walnut Muffins (page 129) is an example of muffins cooked in this manner.

Loaf Cakes

With loaf cakes, you may want an attractive peaked loaf, or you may prefer an extremely moist loaf that has no peak. You can invert the moist loaf so that the level or sunken top is hidden and you can ice or decorate the bottom (now the top) for a handsome presentation.

The proper oven temperature depends on the pan size and the texture desired. In a pound cake, for a finer texture, you may go with 350°F/177°C, but for a basic fruit quick-bread loaf, 375°F/191°C is a good temperature.

I like to use smaller loaf pan (8 x 4½ x 2½ inches/20 x 11 x 6 cm) simply because it is easier to get the cake done without the risk of drying it.

Moist Banana Nut Bread

Makes one 8 x 4½ x 2½-inch (20 x 11 x 6-cm) loaf

A delicious, moist loaf.

What This Recipe Shows

Oil helps make a very moist loaf.

Using the muffin method (see page 129) works fine for products with nuts and fruits that do not suffer from a coarse texture.

Whipped cream adds moisture, a wonderful flavor, and an incredibly soft texture.

1½ cups (5.2 oz/149 g) pecans
1 tablespoon (0.5 oz/14 g) butter
¾ teaspoon (4.5 g) salt, divided
Nonstick cooking spray with flour
1¾ cups (7.7 oz/218 g) spooned and leveled
    bleached all-purpose flour
1 teaspoon (5 g) baking powder
¼ teaspoon (1 g) baking soda

1½ cups (10.5 oz/298 g) sugar
½ cup (118 ml) canola oil
1 teaspoon (5 ml) pure vanilla extract
2 large eggs (3.5 oz/99 g)
½ cup (118 ml) buttermilk
2 cups (15.8 oz/448 g) mashed very ripe
    bananas (about 5 medium)
½ cup (118 ml) heavy cream

1. Arrange a shelf in the lower third of the oven, place a baking stone on it, and preheat the oven to 350°F/177°C.

2. Spread the nuts out on a baking sheet, place in the oven on the stone, and roast 10 minutes. While nuts are hot, stir in the butter and ¼ teaspoon (1.5 g) salt. When cool, coarsely chop and set aside.

3. Turn oven up to 375°F/191°C.

4. Spray an 8 x 4½ x 2½-inch (20 x 11 x 6-cm) loaf pan with nonstick cooking spray with flour and line it with an 8-inch (20-cm) piece of parchment paper that hangs over each long side by about 1 inch (2.5 cm). (I very lightly spray the top of the parchment, too.)

5. In a large bowl, with a mixer on medium speed, beat together the flour, baking powder, baking soda, the remaining ½ teaspoon (3 g) salt, and the sugar for at least 30 seconds.

6. In a medium bowl, with a fork, stir together the oil, vanilla, eggs, and buttermilk just to blend. Stir in the bananas to blend.

7. Make a well in the dry ingredients and pour the banana mixture into the well. Stir to blend well.

8. In a cold bowl with cold beaters, whip the cream until soft peaks form when the beater is lifted. Beat just a little beyond this soft peak stage. Stir about one-quarter of the whipped cream into the batter to lighten. Then fold the rest of the whipped cream into the batter.

9. Fold in the roasted nuts.

10. Spoon the batter into the prepared pan and place in the oven on the hot stone. Bake until the center springs back when touched, or a toothpick inserted in the center comes out clean but moist, about 35 minutes. Ideally, the bread should not pull away from the sides until it has just come out of the oven. The center temperature should be about 209°F/98°C when checked with an instant-read thermometer.

11. Place the bread in the pan on a rack to cool, about 10 minutes, and then shake the pan to loosen the loaf all around. Use the parchment to lift the loaf out of the pan. Peel off the paper and finish cooling on the rack.

French Cake aux Fruits

MAKES ONE 8 X 4½ X 2½-INCH (20 X 11 X 6-CM) LOAF

A deeply browned, jeweled loaf—a perfect gift. This is the French version of a fruit cake—a cake with a little fruit and nuts. It's very different from the U.S. version—fruit and nuts with a little cake. This is patterned after a cake from the famous Paris pastry shop Ladurée, as featured in Linda Dannenberg's book *Paris Boulangerie-Pâtisserie*. In the recipe below, I used Grand Marnier, but you can use a quality rum like Myers's or the liqueur of your choice.

What This Recipe Shows

Soaking raisins for 1 hour limits the amount of moisture that they will remove from the dough.

Roasting nuts improves the flavors immensely.

Fruit

1 cup (3.5 oz/99 g) pecan halves
1 tablespoon (0.5 oz/14 g) butter, for pecans
¼ teaspoon (1.5 g) salt, for pecans
1 cup (237 ml) water
1 cup (7 oz/198 g) sugar

¼ cup (59 ml) Grand Marnier liqueur
⅓ cup (1.7 oz/48 g) golden raisins
2 tablespoons (1 oz/28 g) butter, for greasing
   the pan

Batter

2 cups (8.8 oz/249 g) spooned and leveled
   bleached all-purpose flour
2 teaspoons (9 g) baking powder
¼ teaspoon (1.5 g) salt
½ cup (4 oz/113 g) unsalted butter, cut in
   2-tablespoon (1-oz/28-g) pieces
1⅓ cups (9.3 oz/264 g) sugar

⅓ cup (79 ml) canola oil
2 tablespoons (30 ml) Grand Marnier liqueur
2 large egg yolks (1.3 oz/37 g)
3 large eggs (5.25 oz/149 g)
¼ cup (59 ml) buttermilk
½ cup (118 ml) heavy cream

1 cup (5.5 oz/156 g) mixed fruit such as candied
   cherries, pineapple, and orange peel

¼ cup (59 ml) apricot preserves, heated and
   strained

1. Arrange a shelf in the lower third of the oven, place a baking stone on it, and preheat the oven to 350°F/177°C.

2. For the fruit, spread the nuts out on a baking sheet, place in the oven on the stone, and roast 10 minutes. While nuts are hot, stir in the butter and salt. Pick out about 15 nice-looking pecan halves to decorate the top of the cake. Coarsely chop the remaining pecans and set all aside.

3. In a small saucepan, bring the water to a boil. Turn off the heat and stir in the sugar to dissolve. Stir in the Grand Marnier and golden raisins. Set aside.

4. Butter an 8 x 4½ x 2½-inch (20 x 11 x 6-cm) loaf pan and line with parchment paper, running down one long side, across the bottom, and up the other long side. Butter the parchment well too.

5. For the batter, in a medium bowl beat together the flour, baking powder, and salt for at least 30 seconds. Set aside.

6. In a mixing bowl, beat the butter and sugar on medium speed until light and fluffy. On low speed, beat in the oil and Grand Marnier. Then beat in the yolks, one at a time, then the eggs, one at a time with a minimum of beating. On the lowest speed, beat in over half of the flour mixture. By hand, stir in the buttermilk. Gently stir in the rest of the flour mixture, just to blend in.

7. In a cold bowl with cold beaters, whip the cream until soft peaks form when the beaters are lifted. Beat just a little beyond this soft peak stage. Stir in about one-quarter of the whipped cream. Then gently fold the rest of the whipped cream into the batter.

8. Drain the raisins, reserving the Grand Marnier–sugar water mixture. (You need this to brush on the cake after it is baked.) Dump the raisins onto a piece of paper towel. Cover with another paper towel, roll up, and press gently to dry.

9. Reserve 3 or 4 candied cherries to decorate the top of the cake. Coarsely chop the rest of the candied fruit. Fold the nuts, candied fruit, and drained raisins into the batter and stir to distribute them throughout the batter. Pour the batter into the prepared pan. Smooth the top, and press the reserved pecan halves into a casual pattern on the top of the cake. As the cake rises, these will move some. Don't worry about it. You can use candied cherry halves to make a pleasant design after it is baked.

10. Place the loaf in the oven on the stone. Bake until well browned, about 55 to 60 minutes or until well-risen and browned. Cool in the pan on a cooling rack for 10 minutes. Loosen by jarring the edges. Dump the loaf out. Remove the parchment paper and turn cake upright. While it is still hot, brush the top of the cake with the reserved Grand Marnier–sugar water. Turn the cake on one side and brush the up side. Rotate and brush the syrup over the top, the sides, and the ends of the cake. Garnish the top by placing candied cherry halves or slices around among the pecans to form an attractive pattern. Brush over and over several times with the apricot preserves and allow to dry.

ICINGS—FROSTINGS

In addition to being decorative, the goal of cake icings (frostings) is to retain moisture and extend the time that you have a really good cake. Prolonging freshness depends on the type of icing. Icings that do not have any fat can rob the cake of moisture and actually reduce the keeping time.

Some icings use sugar particles that are fine enough not to be grainy (4X to 10X confectioners' sugar) and just enough liquid to make very fine sugar spreadable. While icings like this are useful as a decorative drizzle, such sugar-liquid icings do not provide a good moisture barrier. A combination of fat and sugar makes an icing that is much better at preserving the cake's moisture.

Many of the wonderful desserts in this book use icings. There are some icings that are for a specific cake; those are a part of the cake recipe and located with that cake. Some icings belong in the place that explains the technique or the science behind the icing. For example, ganaches are in the chocolate section, page 95, where I explain the possible problems with the chocolate in a ganache; classic buttercreams, which require a meringue or egg foam, are in the section on meringues in Chapter 2, Puff, The Magic Leavener—Steam, page 167.

Then there are icings that can be used on many different cakes, such as many confectioners' sugar icings and the Luscious, Creamy Chocolate Icing. These are the icings in this section.

Double Icing

Spreading icing on a cake takes practice. I was thrilled when I learned what I call a double-icing technique for ganache in Alice Medrich's book *Cocolat*. This technique allows inexperienced cooks to produce a magnificent cake with a perfect, satin-smooth icing that looks as if it came from an expensive bakery.

Since this has now become my favorite icing technique, there are a number of recipes that make use of it: Velvety Ganache Glaze (page 98), Shiny Ganache Glaze (page 97), and Satin-Smooth Ganache Glaze (page 99).

Double-Icing Technique

1. Place the cooled cake on a cardboard circle that is slightly smaller than the cake. This allows you to hold the cake with the sturdy cardboard bottom and tilt it as necessary. Next, place the cake on a cooling rack that is sitting on a large piece of parchment paper or a nonstick baking sheet. You want something that catches icing drips and allows you to scrape them up if you need to.

2. Pour slightly less than half of the ganache or glaze into a 2-cup (473-ml) glass measuring cup with a spout. You want the glaze almost cool enough to set, about 90°F/32°C. Pour a puddle of icing in the center of the cake and continue pouring until the icing starts to overflow and run down the edges. Lift the cake and tilt to encourage the glaze to run where there isn't any. With a metal spatula, smooth the icing around the edge. Do what you can to cover the top and all around the edges. Allow the cake to cool for about 30 minutes.

3. No spatula from here on! Heat the remaining half of the ganache or glaze just until it flows easily. So that it will be perfectly smooth, strain it into a warm 2-cup (473-ml) glass measuring cup with a spout. If you are right-handed, hold the cake up with your left hand, keeping it over the parchment. With your right hand, pour the glaze into the center of the cake. Allow the glaze to run down the edges and tilt to get it to run where it is needed. Pour more glaze on as needed, but do NOT touch it with a spatula. You want this coating untouched, as smooth as a lake at dawn—a perfect, shiny, dark surface. Place the cake on the cooling rack and allow to cool.

Whipped Cream Icings

A whipped cream icing can be very easy to use and fluffy and luscious looking. If you are dealing with warm weather conditions, or a cake that must remain at room temperature for a while, you will want to add a small amount of gelatin to the whipped cream to make it more stable. For more information about whipping cream and the directions for adding gelatin to a whipped cream icing to make it more stable, see page 318.

Soft Chocolate Icings

I love icings that behave beautifully, like the Luscious, Creamy Chocolate Icing. It doesn't harden and it doesn't run. You can smooth it out, or make decorative swirls, or use it in a pastry bag. It can stand overnight in the refrigerator. It will firm up, but you can whip it a minute and it is ready to go again.

Luscious, Creamy Chocolate Icing

MAKES ENOUGH ICING FOR ONE 9-INCH (23-CM) 3-LAYER ROUND CAKE

This icing is a miracle to work with. It doesn't harden and it doesn't run. You can smooth it out or make swirls with a spoon, spatula, or a pastry bag. This is my version of Maida Heatter's recipe Chocolate Sour Cream Icing. Her recipe is large enough for a four-layer cake. I have reduced the volume and added a little brown sugar for my severe sweet tooth, and a little corn syrup to ensure that the chocolate does not seize (for more information on seizing, see page 93).

What This Recipe Shows

Finely chopping the chocolates helps it melt evenly.

Brown sugar adds a fudgy taste to chocolate.

The corn syrup will give a bit of a sheen, and it adds a little liquid to ensure that the chocolate will not seize (for more information on seizing, see page 93).

---

12 ounces (340 g) milk chocolate (I love Hershey's), cut into medium pieces
9 ounces (255 g) semisweet chocolate, cut into medium pieces
2 tablespoons (1 oz/28 g) light brown sugar
$\frac{1}{8}$ teaspoon (pinch) salt
1 teaspoon (5 ml) pure vanilla extract
3 tablespoons (45 ml) light corn syrup
$1\frac{1}{2}$ cups (12.9 oz/366 g) sour cream

1. Place both chocolates in a food processor with the steel blade. Use quick on/offs to finely chop, or alternatively finely chop the chocolate with a sharp knife. Place the chocolate in a microwave-safe bowl. Heat in the microwave on 50% power, stirring every 30 seconds. Stop and remove it from the microwave when most of the chocolate is melted. Continue to stir until all of the chocolate is melted and smooth.

2. In a mixing bowl, stir together the brown sugar, salt, vanilla, and corn syrup. Stir in the sour cream with 1 or 2 strokes only. Add the melted chocolate. Beat on low until very smooth. It will be beautiful. If it is too thin, allow it to stand for an hour or so at room temperature until slightly thickened. Use about a $\frac{1}{4}$-inch (0.6-cm) layer of icing between the cake layers.

Cream Cheese Icings

Cream cheese makes very spreadable, manageable icings that hold up better than butter in warm rooms. Here are two of my favorites. I use the White Chocolate Cream Cheese Icing for a cheesecake wedding cake, but it can be used on any cake. The Cherry-Chambord Butter Icing is a variation of my favorite biscuit spread.

White Chocolate Cream Cheese Icing

MAKES A LITTLE OVER 1 CUP (237 ML)

This is a beautiful, very manageable pale ivory icing. This recipe can be multiplied for larger cakes.

What This Recipe Shows

The addition of cream cheese makes the temperamental white chocolate into an easily spreadable icing that is smooth yet firm.

---

8 ounces (227 g) white chocolate, chopped or grated

One 8-ounce package (227 g) cream cheese

1. Bring 1 inch of water to a boil in a large skillet, remove from the heat, and let stand for 3 minutes. Place the chocolate in a well-dried stainless steel bowl and cover tightly with plastic wrap that does not come down the sides of the bowl far enough to touch the water. Place the bowl of chocolate in the hot water and let stand 5 minutes. Remove the bowl from the water bath, dry the bottom well, and stir the melted chocolate with a dry spatula. If not completely melted, re-cover the chocolate and return it to the skillet of hot water for a few minutes longer.

2. Beat the cream cheese until smooth in a food processor with the steel blade or in a mixer. Beat in the melted white chocolate. Spread evenly on a cold cake. If desired, fill a pastry bag fitted with your chosen tip and pipe a border or decoration of your choice.

Cherry-Chambord Butter Icing

MAKES ABOUT 2 CUPS (473 ML)

This is wonderful on anything!

What This Recipe Shows

Cold butter can be hard, so it is blended first to make blending in the cream cheese easy.

Stir the preserves in by hand to retain the fruit shape.

¾ cup (6 oz/170 g) butter
Two 8-ounce packages (454 g) cream cheese
1 cup (4 oz/120 g) confectioners' sugar

2 tablespoons (30 ml) Chambord liqueur
½ cup (118 ml) good cherry preserves

In a food processor with the steel blade, process the butter until it is soft. Add the cream cheese and sugar and process to blend well. Process in the Chambord. By hand, stir in the preserves. Refrigerate until ready to use.

Meringue Icings

Italian meringue makes a beautiful fluffy white icing. You can make an Italian meringue dramatic by cooking briefly under the broiler or touching with a tiny blowtorch to brown the tips of swirls. For detailed information, see page 186.

There Are Buttercreams and There Are Buttercreams: Confectioners' Sugar Buttercream

What many American cooks know as buttercream icing is not related to the classic buttercreams (see pages 208 to 215), which are made with butter and an egg yolk, egg white, or whole egg foam that is partially cooked with a hot syrup. Confectioners' sugar buttercream is made with either butter or shortening (or a combination of the two) plus confectioners' sugar. A third type of buttercream, which I don't recommend, is made with granulated sugar instead of confectioners' by making a flour-sugar-milk paste, cooling, and stirring in butter and flavorings. Confectioners' sugar icings are easier and offer more advantages.

American cooks who are professional cake makers admit loving classic buttercreams—those rich, creamy, wonderful, butter-sugar-egg emulsions. But they explain that elaborate cakes that have to hold up in a hot room for several hours force them to use confectioners' sugar buttercreams.

They also explain that for elegant cakes, like wedding cakes, these confectioners' sugar buttercreams icings can be made as smooth as a draped fondant by using a Viva paper towel technique as described on page 149. And, although they do not taste as wonderful as classic buttercream icing, they do taste much better than fondant, in my opinion.

Ingredients

CONFECTIONERS' SUGAR

The sugar particles need to be fine enough that the icing is not perceived as grainy. This means 4X to 10X confectioners' sugar is the best choice for buttercreams.

Sugar comes from two sources—sugarcane and sugar beets. Professional cake bakers express a strong preference for cane sugar, saying that with beet sugar they have had inconsistent results. I don't have a scientific reason for this, but I do know in some cases (such as crème brûlée) that beet sugar can burn rather than melt smoothly. So I am willing to accept that there may be a difference.

CORNSTARCH

Confectioners' sugar already contains some cornstarch to aid in keeping it dry. But some bakers who work in humid areas recommend adding $\frac{1}{4}$ cup (32 g) cornstarch per pound (454 g) of confectioners' sugar. This helps the icing hold up under humid conditions and it cuts the sweetness a little.

MERINGUE POWDER

Meringue powder, made of dried egg whites, sugar, starch, gum, stabilizers, and possibly flavoring, is available at Wilton and other cake supply stores (see Sources, page 510). Michaels crafts stores and some J. C. Penney stores also sell Wilton supplies. Meringue powder can help stabilize under humid conditions. If you are making flowers with the icing, meringue powder is very helpful in maintaining their shape.

SALT

I try to dissolve salt in any liquid in the recipe for better dispersion, but some bakers recommend using very finely ground popcorn salt instead of table salt.

CORN SYRUP

As my friend Harold McGee says, "Corn syrup is a liquid that attracts water and fills in spaces between fine sugar particles to produce a glass-smooth surface." A tablespoon of light corn syrup in a ganache will give it a deep, rich shine. The same is true in other icings. You will get a sheen, which you may or may not want. In some icings, you may want a flat matte look with no shine or gloss. In such cases, avoid corn syrup.

EXTRACTS OR FLAVORINGS

For a whiter icing, bakers frequently use clear vanilla (which, to my surprise, I saw recently in my local supermarket), available at cake supply companies like Wilton (see Sources, page 510). Specific flavorings are optional. In icings with shortening as the primary fat, bakers may add butter flavoring. I personally like a tiny bit of pure almond extract, too.

FAT

Shortening or butter? Even if you love the taste of real butter, using some shortening with emulsifiers (mono- and diglycerides) such as Crisco is a good idea. You can check a shortening label for mono- and diglycerides to make sure you have these emulsifiers. That will help the icing retain water without curdling.

For a whiter icing that still uses butter, you may be able to get a paler butter from natural food stores.

Basic Confectioners' Sugar Buttercream

MAKES 3 CUPS (710 ML)

This is a beautiful, easy-to-use wedding cake–type icing that actually tastes good.

What This Recipe Shows

Butter enhances the flavor of the buttercream.

A shortening with emulsifiers, such as Crisco, helps the icing retain water without curdling and also helps the icing to retain its shape in a warm room.

Very finely ground (10X) confectioners' sugar makes a smooth icing.

Use corn syrup if a sheen or gloss is desired.

$\frac{1}{2}$ cup (4 oz/113 g) unsalted butter

$\frac{1}{2}$ cup (3.4 oz/95 g) Crisco or other shortening with emulsifiers

$\frac{1}{8}$ teaspoon (4 drops) pure almond extract

1 teaspoon (5 ml) clear vanilla flavoring

$\frac{1}{2}$ teaspoon (2.5 ml) butter flavoring, optional

4 cups (16 oz/454 g) 10X confectioners' sugar

$\frac{1}{4}$ teaspoon (1.5 g) salt

2 tablespoons (30 ml) whole milk

1 tablespoon (15 ml) light corn syrup (if a sheen is desired), optional

1. With the paddle attachment of a mixer, whip the butter until soft, and then whip in the shortening. On low speed, beat in the extract and flavorings.

2. Sift the sugar through a large strainer with medium mesh just to remove any lumps. Add and beat into the fat mixture on the lowest speed. Scrape down the sides of the bowl as needed.

3. Stir the salt into the milk to dissolve, and mix into the icing on low speed just until smooth and creamy.

4. Beat in the corn syrup, if using.

5. Adjust consistency as desired with a little more milk or confectioners' sugar.

6. This icing can be stored in an airtight container in the refrigerator for up to 2 weeks. Whip with a mixer or a hand beater before using.

Ratio of Fat to Sugar

Confectioners' sugar buttercreams vary in their ratio of fat to sugar. Those with a higher ratio of fat to sugar remain soft and do not form a crust. Those with a higher ratio of confectioners' sugar to fat form a very thin crust after drying for about 10 minutes. These crusting buttercreams can be smoothed with a very smooth paper towel like Viva immediately after they crust.

Crusting Confectioners' Sugar Buttercream

MAKES ABOUT 4 CUPS (946 ML)

This icing looks like a smooth draped fondant, but tastes much better. When the icing forms a thin crust, it is amazing how you can get a perfectly smooth surface by using a Viva paper towel.

What This Recipe Shows

Butter enhances the flavor.

A shortening with emulsifiers, such as Crisco, helps the icing retain water without curdling and helps the icing to retain its shape in a warm room.

Very finely ground (10X) confectioners' sugar makes a smooth icing.

To get an absolutely smooth draped fondant look, Viva paper towels are used because they are the smoothest of the supermarket paper towels.

½ cup (4 oz/113 g) unsalted butter
1½ cups (10 oz/285 g) Crisco or other
    shortening with emulsifiers
¼ teaspoon (1.25 ml) pure almond extract
2 tablespoons (30 ml) clear vanilla flavoring
8 cups (2 lb/907 g) 10X confectioners' sugar

2 tablespoons meringue powder (see Sources,
    page 510)
¼ teaspoon (1.5 g) salt
4 to 5 tablespoons (60 to 75 ml) water
Plain white Viva paper towels

1. With the paddle attachment of a mixer, whip the butter until soft, and then whip in the shortening. Beat in the extract and flavoring on low speed.

2. Sift the sugar through a large strainer with medium mesh just to remove any lumps. Beat the sugar and the meringue powder into the fat mixture on the lowest speed. Scrape down the sides as needed.

3. Stir the salt into the water to dissolve and mix it into the icing thoroughly on low speed only.

4. Adjust consistency to a spreadable icing with a little more water or confectioners' sugar. Do not overmix or mix on high speed.

5. This icing can be stored in an airtight container in the refrigerator for up to 2 weeks. Rewhip before using.

6. For a very smooth cake, similar to a cake draped with rolled fondant, let the icing dry just until a dry Viva paper towel touched to the side does not stick, 10 to 15 minutes, depending on the humidity. To create an absolutely smooth surface, use a plain white Viva paper towel, remove any rings from your fingers, and start with the sides. Place the towel against the side and smooth up and down gently with your fingers or palm. Do not allow the towel to pleat or fold. If desired, smooth a contour edge and smooth the top. (The first time you try this technique, it may take some playing with, but stick with it a few minutes and you will love it.)

Chocolate or Mocha Confectioners' Sugar Buttercreams

You can convert either of the confectioners' sugar icings just given (pages 148 and 149) to chocolate icings by adding ½ cup (1.5 oz/43 g) natural cocoa powder for each pound (16 oz/454 g) of confectioners' sugar.

For mocha icing, substitute an equal amount of very strong freshly brewed coffee for the liquid in the recipe.

WRAPPING AND STORING CAKES

Plain cakes, such as unglazed pound cake or plain cake layers, keep well-wrapped for one day at room temperature, 6 or 7 days in the refrigerator, or up to 3 months in the freezer. Cool the cake thoroughly, all the way through, before wrapping. And remember, some plastic wraps are very porous. I like to wrap in regular Saran wrap first, then in plastic cling wrap to hold the Saran on tightly, and finally place the cake or layer in a freezer-type zip-top bag. The large 2-gallon (7.6-L) freezer bag will hold large cakes, even those made in a tube or Bundt pan.

Doughs—Biscuits and Scones

Biscuits and scones are in a league of their own. They are chemically leavened doughs, while muffins, cakes, and quick breads are batters. We are still faced with some of the problems of batters, such as even distribution of the leaveners (page 58), correct amount of leaveners (page 49), as well as sufficient liquid for good leavening.

A GREAT BISCUIT

There are many kinds of biscuits. To name a few, there are light, moist biscuits; flakey biscuits; and John Egerton's beaten biscuits (which are like hardtack but, with a sliver of country ham on one, they are heavenly). Some people like one type of biscuit more than others.

I do know biscuits. I have made biscuits all over the United States and Canada, and as far away as Europe. I even got a standing ovation for my biscuits at a meeting of food science writers in Erice, Sicily.

When I say I made biscuits, I *mean* I made biscuits. Many times, Belinda Ellis from White Lily flour and I made up to 800 biscuits a day for shows like the Fancy Food Show. You could look up all the aisles and see smooth maroon carpet, but our aisle had a huge soft, white cloudy area—biscuit crumbs!

I will, and have, put my biscuits up against anyone's. At a food meeting, Chuck Williams, founder of the Williams-Sonoma stores, and I got into an argument over biscuits. Chuck said that the Zuni Café in San Francisco made the best biscuits. I was outraged. I said, "How can you say that when you haven't had my biscuits?"

The minute I got home I mailed Chuck my recipe and a 2-pound (907-g) bag of White Lily self-rising flour. I said, "All right, Chuck, you make my biscuits exactly as I direct. Get the dough to the consistency of cottage cheese, coat the biscuits with flour exactly as I describe, and then tell me that Zuni Café makes the best biscuits."

I did not hear from Chuck, but about a week later, someone from White Lily called. "What on earth did you do to Chuck Williams?"

I didn't know what they were talking about. "What do you mean?"

They replied, "He is putting White Lily flour in every Williams-Sonoma store because he says it makes the best biscuits."

I did not hear from Chuck, but I think I can assume that he said "Uncle." However, his stores no longer sell White Lily flour. But you can get it from Smuckers, the new owner of White Lily (see Sources, page 510).

What makes my biscuits so outstanding? The wet dough. The dough looks like cottage cheese. In the hot oven, all the liquid turns to steam and it makes the most incredibly light, moist biscuits!

And, right here and now, let me say that these are my grandmother's biscuits. Arrie Piper Ogletree ("Nanny" to me) was a remarkable woman. She had done everything from farming to running a boarding house to making chevrons on a big commercial sewing machine for the Civilian Conservation Corps during the Depression. When I was growing up, she and my grandfather had a house on Milstead Avenue, the road from Main Street in downtown Conyers, Georgia, out to the mill. We were only a block from downtown, but Nanny had an acre garden, a huge chicken yard, two cows, and a batch of pigs.

My father was a business executive who was in charge of the all of his company's branches in the Eastern states. Travel was primarily by railroad and not the quick option that it is today. To keep his branches running at top performance, my father would move us to the city of any branch that needed help and we would live there for six months to a year or so while he hired good people and got the office running well. Then we would move on to the next new or troubled branch.

During all of these moves, while my parents were looking for a house, I got to stay with Nanny. I adored it. I was her first grandchild and she spoiled me. She would let me use her big sterling silver spoon to make frog houses in the front sand walk. I had a little bucket of water and would pack wet sand over my foot, then, carefully pull it out leaving a perfect frog house. I would make dozens of them. At dusk every night I had to take the stick broom and sweep them all down. But that was all right. I could build them back tomorrow. For years I followed Nanny around the kitchen. You can read the story of her biscuits in the recipe that follows.

Shirley Corriher's "Touch-of-Grace" Southern Biscuits

MAKES 12 TO 14 MEDIUM BISCUITS

As a little girl, I followed my grandmother around the kitchen. For breakfast, lunch, and dinner she made the lightest, most wonderful biscuits in the world. I used her bread bowl, her flour, her buttermilk—I did everything the same, and I shaped the biscuits just like she did. But mine always turned out a dry, mealy mess. I would cry and say, "Nanny, what did I do wrong?" She was a very busy woman with all my uncles and grandfather to feed three meals a day, but she would lean down, give me a big hug, and say, "Honey, I guess you forgot to add a Touch of Grace."

It took me over twenty years to figure out what my grandmother was doing that I was missing. I thought that the dough had to be dry enough to shape by hand, but she actually had a very wet dough. She sprinkled flour from the front of the bowl onto the dough, pinched off a biscuit-size piece, and dipped it in the flour. She floured the outside of the wet dough so that she could handle it. This wet dough in a hot oven creates steam to puff and make feather-light biscuits. A wet dough was the big secret. Now I make biscuits almost as good as my grandmother's, and so can you, with a good wet dough and a Touch of Grace.

What This Recipe Shows

Low-protein flour like White Lily helps make tender, moist biscuits.

A very wet dough makes more steam in a hot oven and creates lighter biscuits.

Nonstick cooking spray
2 cups (9 oz/255 g) spooned and leveled
    self-rising flour (low-protein Southern
    U.S. flour like White Lily or any
    self-rising flour)
¼ cup (1.8 oz/51 g) sugar
½ teaspoon (3 g) salt
¼ cup (1.6 oz/45 g) shortening
⅔ cup (158 ml) heavy cream

1 cup (237 ml) buttermilk, or enough for
    dough to resemble cottage cheese (if you
    are not using low-protein flour it will
    take more than 1 cup)
1 cup (4.5 oz/127 g) plain all-purpose flour,
    for shaping
3 tablespoons (1.5 oz/43 g) unsalted butter,
    melted, for brushing
Cherry-Chambord Butter (recipe follows),
    optional

1. Preheat the oven to 425°F/218°C and arrange a shelf slightly below the center of the oven. Spray an 8 or 9-inch (20 or 23-cm) round cake pan with nonstick cooking spray.

2. In a large mixing bowl, stir together the self-rising flour, sugar, and salt. Work the shortening in with your fingers until there are no large lumps. Gently stir in the cream, then some of the buttermilk. Continue stirring in buttermilk until THE DOUGH RESEMBLES COTTAGE CHEESE. It should be a wet mess—not soup, but cottage-cheese texture. If you are not using a low-protein flour, this may require considerably more than 1 cup (237 ml) of buttermilk.

3. Spread the plain (not self-rising) flour out on a plate or pie pan. With a medium (about 2-in/5-cm, #30) ice cream scoop or spoon, place 3 or 4 scoops of dough well apart in the flour. Sprinkle flour over each. Flour your hands. Turn a dough ball in the flour to coat, pick it up, and gently shape it into a round, shaking off the excess flour as you work. Place this biscuit in the prepared pan. Coat each dough ball in the same way and place each shaped biscuit SCRUNCHED UP AGAINST ITS NEIGHBOR so that the biscuits rise up and don't spread out. Continue scooping and shaping until all of the dough is used.

4. Place the pan on the arranged shelf in the oven. Bake until lightly browned, about 20 to 25 minutes. Brush with the melted butter. Invert onto one plate, and then back onto another. With a knife or spatula, cut quickly between biscuits to make them easy to remove. Serve immediately. "Butter 'em while they're hot," or spread with Cherry-Chambord Butter.

Cherry-Chambord Butter

This is also excellent substituting orange marmalade for the cherry preserves and Grand Marnier for the Chambord.

½ cup (4 oz/113 g) unsalted butter
One 8-ounce package (227-g) cream cheese
2 tablespoons (30 ml) Chambord or other raspberry liqueur

⅓ cup (1.3 oz/38 g) confectioners' sugar
4 tablespoons (about 2 oz/59 ml) good cherry preserves

Place the butter, cream cheese, liqueur, and confectioners' sugar in a food processor with the steel blade. Process to blend well. Stir in the preserves by hand. Chill well before serving. Keeps well in the refrigerator for several weeks in a closed jar.

SCONES

English "biscuits" are cookies. Scones, the classic sweet nibble for the British to eat with tea, are made from a dough similar in consistency to an American biscuit. However, that is about where the similarities stop.

Scones used to contain an egg or eggs, which made them quite dry. Nowadays, the egg has been dropped but scones are frequently made with cream, which makes them crumbly, unless the dough has been overworked.

At any rate, I have tried to eat scones. Some are flavorful and some contain a tasty combination of ingredients like raspberries and white chocolate, but I always feel like I'm eating a dry crumbly mess.

Admittedly, I have not had the pleasure of eating scones around the English countryside, where they may be quite wonderful. I have tried many an English or Canadian scone recipe, but after becoming accustomed to my moist biscuits, I haven't been happy with them. So I came up with my moist biscuit with a scone-type raspberry and white chocolate filling, Shirley's Not-So-Sconey Scones.

Shirley's Not-So-Sconey Scones

MAKES ABOUT 12 SCONES

This is definitely not a true scone recipe, but these are absolutely delicious—light, moist, and sweet, with great flavors—a perfect accompaniment to a good cup of coffee or tea. This is actually my "Touch-of-Grace" southern biscuit recipe with more sugar plus vanilla and white chocolate chips. You can add fruit like blueberries, or apples with roasted walnuts and toffee chips. Whatever you like.

What This Recipe Shows

Low-protein flour like White Lily helps make tender, moist scones.

A very wet dough makes more steam in a hot oven and creates a lighter scone.

Nonstick cooking spray

2 cups (9 oz/255 g) spooned and leveled self-rising flour (low-protein Southern U.S. flour like White Lily or any self-rising flour)

1/3 cup (2.3 oz/65 g) sugar

1/2 teaspoon (3 g) salt

1/4 cup (1.6 oz/45 g) shortening

2/3 cup (158 ml) heavy cream

1 cup (237 ml) buttermilk, or enough for dough to resemble cottage cheese (if you are not using low-protein flour it will take more than a cup)

1 teaspoon (5 ml) pure vanilla extract

1 tablespoon orange zest (grated peel)

1 1/2 cups (9 oz/255 g) white chocolate chips

2 small flats of fresh raspberries, as firm as you can find (about 1 cup)

1 cup (4.4 oz/124 g) plain all-purpose flour, for shaping

3 tablespoons (1.5 oz/43 g) unsalted butter, melted

Scone Icing (recipe follows), optional

1. Preheat the oven to 425°F/218°C and arrange a shelf slightly below the center of the oven. Spray an 8 inch or 9-inch (20 or 23-cm) round cake pan with nonstick cooking spray.

2. In a large mixing bowl, stir together the self-rising flour, sugar, and salt. Work the shortening in with your fingers until there are no large lumps. Gently stir in the cream, then some of the buttermilk and the vanilla. Continue stirring in buttermilk until THE DOUGH RESEMBLES SLIGHTLY THICK COTTAGE CHEESE. This dough should be just slightly drier than when you make it for "Touch-of-Grace" Southern Biscuits (page 152). It should have a wet texture like thick cottage cheese but not the least bit soupy. If you are not using a low-protein flour, this may require considerably more than 1 cup (237 ml) of buttermilk.

3. Stir in the orange zest and the white chocolate chips. Very carefully fold in the raspberries.

4. Spread the plain (not self-rising) flour out on a plate or pie pan. With a medium (about 2-in/5-cm, #30) ice cream scoop or spoon, place 3 scoops of dough well apart in the flour. Sprinkle flour over each. Flour your hands. Turn a dough ball in the flour to coat, pick it up, and gently shape it into a round, shaking off the excess flour as you work. Place the scones in the prepared pan. Coat each dough ball and place each shaped scone SCRUNCHED UP AGAINST ITS NEIGHBOR so that the scones rise up and don't spread out. Continue scooping and shaping until all the dough is used.

5. Place the pan in the oven on the arranged shelf. Bake until lightly browned, about 20 to 25 minutes. Brush with the melted butter. Invert onto one plate, and then back onto another. With a knife or spatula, cut quickly between scones to make them easy to remove. Drizzle each scone with icing, if desired, and serve.

Scone Icing

1 cup (4 oz/120 g) confectioners' sugar
1 to 2 tablespoons (15 to 30 ml) heavy cream

1 teaspoon (5 ml) pure vanilla extract

In a 2-cup (473-ml) glass measuring cup with a spout (so that you can pour a drizzle easily), stir together the sugar, cream, and vanilla. You want the consistency thick because it will melt slightly when it hits the hot scone. Add more sugar or cream as needed to reach the proper thick consistency. Drizzle icing on solid to cover the top with drools that run down the side.

Cornbread and Spoon Bread

Cornbreads and spoon breads are the other end of the spectrum that runs from doughs to thin batters. These are made with thin batters. Some cornbread batters are almost as thick as a cake batter, but most are thinner, and spoon breads can be very thin. My favorite cornbread, All-Time Favorite E-Z, Dee-licious Sour Cream Cornbread, is what I call a "going-around" recipe. Everybody claims that it's their recipe. Here's mine!

All-Time Favorite E-Z, Dee-licious
Sour Cream Cornbread

MAKES ONE 9-INCH (23-CM) ROUND CORNBREAD

Preparation is in one bowl—quick and easy. This recipe is in *CookWise,* but I wanted it here, too, because I consider it a classic and I have made a slight improvement in the recipe. This is a favorite Southern recipe and you will see many variations. One is published as Mrs. Dean Rusk's cornbread. Nathalie Dupree has a version in her book *New Southern Cooking* called Snackin' Cornbread.

What This Recipe Shows

The oil, sour cream, and creamed corn make this cornbread very moist.

---

3 large eggs (5.25 oz/149 g)
1½ cups (11 oz/315 g) canned creamed corn
1½ cups (12.9 oz/366 g) sour cream
¾ cup (177 ml) canola oil
1½ cups (6.5 oz/184 g) cornbread MIX, or
 self-rising cornmeal

2 tablespoons (0.5 oz/15 g) all-purpose flour
¾ teaspoon (4.5 g) salt
½ teaspoon (2.5 g) baking powder
Nonstick cooking spray
3 tablespoons (1.5 oz/43 g) lightly salted
 butter, melted

1. Arrange a shelf in the upper third of the oven and preheat the oven to 425°F/218°C.

2. In a medium mixing bowl, beat the eggs slightly. Stir in the creamed corn, sour cream, and oil. Add the cornbread mix, flour, salt, and baking powder. Stir to blend well. Spray a 9-inch (23-cm) ovenproof skillet with an ovenproof handle, or a 9-inch (23-cm) round cake pan, with nonstick cooking spray. Pour in the batter.

3. If using a skillet, place it on a burner over medium-high heat for 1 minute. Then place in the oven. Turn oven down to 375°F/191°C and bake for 35 to 40 minutes. Slide under broiler about 4 inches (10 cm) from the heat for 45 to 60 seconds to brown the top. Watch carefully. Brush top with the melted butter for a shiny finish.

4. If using a cake pan, pour batter into the pan. Place in the oven and bake 40 minutes. Brown under broiler and brush with butter as directed above.

SPOON BREADS

Spoon breads typically have thinner batters than cornbread. Many spoon breads are made with cornmeal, but I have run across some made with leftover mashed potatoes and even with rice. Some spoon breads contain chemical leaveners, while others simply depend on the steam and eggs. I have included recipes for a very pure Old-Fashioned Spoon Bread, which contains baking powder, and a rice spoon bread that I love that does not contain any chemical leaveners.

Old-Fashioned Spoon Bread

MAKES ONE 8-INCH (20-CM) SQUARE PUDDING

I couldn't resist adding Parmesan, but you can also add bacon or cracklings or shredded Cheddar.

What This Recipe Shows

The cornmeal will swell amazingly when mixed with the boiling liquid.

---

5 tablespoons (2.5 oz/71 g) unsalted butter, divided
1 cup (4.3 oz/122 g) cornmeal, stone-ground if available
1 teaspoon (6 g) salt
¼ teaspoon (0.5 g) white pepper
½ teaspoon (1 g) freshly grated nutmeg

¼ teaspoon (0.5 g) ground cayenne
2 cups (473 ml) whole milk
3 large eggs (5.25 oz/149 g)
1 cup (237 ml) heavy cream
2 teaspoons (9 g) baking powder
1 cup (3.5 oz/99 g) grated Parmesan

1. Arrange a shelf in the lower third of the oven, place a baking stone on it, and preheat the oven to 350°F/177°C. With 1 tablespoon (0.5 oz/14 g) of the butter, grease an 8-inch (20-cm) square glass baking dish.

2. In a medium mixing bowl, stir together the cornmeal, salt, pepper, nutmeg, and cayenne. In a small saucepan over medium heat, bring the milk to a boil. To avoid lumps, stir the cornmeal constantly, gradually adding boiling milk. Stir in the remaining 4 tablespoons (2 oz/56 g) butter.

3. In a small bowl, beat the eggs until the yolks and whites are well combined. Beat in the cream a little at a time. Add this mixture to the cornmeal mixture. Stir in the baking powder and the Parmesan. Beat with a hand mixer to blend well. Pour the batter into the prepared baking dish. Place the dish in the oven on the stone and bake until firm, about 30 minutes. Serve with plenty of butter.

Golden Brown Puffed Cheesy Rice Spoon Bread

MAKES ONE 2-QUART (1.9-L) CASSEROLE

This is a slightly sophisticated, true comfort food. An unbelievably easy do-ahead casserole that is a gorgeous puffed, golden brown, rice version of macaroni and cheese. This great recipe is a corruption of Damon Lee Fowler's Savannah Rice Puff in his book *Damon Lee Fowler's New Southern Baking*.

What This Recipe Shows

The cayenne and nutmeg are added to the butter mixture because fats are great flavor carriers.

The rice is soft, well puffed, and not rinsed after cooking so that there is enough starch in the mixture to prevent the eggs from curdling.

I elected to use Gruyère or Swiss instead of the traditional Cheddar because I wanted a milder flavor from the cheese.

Nonstick cooking spray
2 tablespoons (1 oz/28 g) unsalted butter
4 medium shallots, finely chopped
6 scallions, all of the green included, sliced
    into thin rings
1/2 teaspoon (1 g) ground cayenne
1/2 teaspoon (1 g) freshly grated nutmeg
2 large eggs (3.5 oz/99 g)
1 1/2 cups (355 ml) whole milk

1/2 cup (118 ml) heavy cream
2 cups (11 oz/316 g) cooked rice (see Note)
1 tablespoon (0.25 oz/7 g) cornstarch (necessary
    only if rice has been chilled, which causes it
    to lose its thickening ability)
1 1/2 cups (6 oz/170 g) grated Gruyère or
    Swiss, divided
1/2 teaspoon (3 g) salt, and more as needed
1/4 teaspoon (0.5 g) white pepper

1. Arrange a shelf just below the center of the oven and preheat the oven to 375°F/191°C.

2. Spray a 2-quart (1.9-L) heatproof casserole with nonstick cooking spray.

3. In a large skillet, melt the butter and sauté the shallots over medium-low heat until soft, 5 to 10 minutes. Stir in the scallions and cook another 3 or 4 minutes. Remove from the heat and stir in the cayenne and nutmeg.

4. In a large mixing bowl, stir the eggs briefly to combine the whites and yolks, and then stir in the milk, cream, rice, cornstarch (if needed), 1 cup (113 g) of cheese, salt, pepper, and the shallot mixture. Pour into prepared casserole and sprinkle the remaining ½ cup (57 g) cheese on top. Place on the arranged shelf and bake until a rich golden brown, 30 to 40 minutes.

> NOTE: To cook the rice "Carolina style," rinse 1 cup (6.5 oz/185 g) long-grain white rice in cool water. Place the rice and 2 cups (473 ml) water in a large saucepan. Stir and bring to a boil over medium heat, reduce the heat to a simmer, stir again, and cover, leaving the lid slightly ajar. In a large skillet, heat to a simmer enough water to come 1 inch (2.5 cm) up the side of the rice pan. After cooking the rice for 12 minutes, use a fork to fluff the rice. Completely cover the pan and place the pan of rice in the skillet of hot water over very low heat for about 15 minutes more. Remove from the heat.

Puff, The Magic Leavener—Steam

Priceless Knowledge in This Chapter

The techniques to make great billowing meringues that do not shrink, that cut smoothly—no tearing—and that have a bone-dry seal between the meringue and the pie—no puddle

The science behind the temperature, beating speed, and time for incredibly stable egg foams to make the perfect "trapped air" cakes, génoise

Egg whites and reduced fat to make the cream puffs of your dreams, huge and crisp

The recipe for truly over 6-inch-tall, great, crisp explosions—popovers!

Recipes Include

Perfect meringues—even an easy meringue with marshmallow creme!

Silky classic buttercream icings

Magnificent soufflés

Génoise so light and moist that they are exquisite "sips" of liqueur-flavored sweet liquid

Crisp, huge popovers

The Recipes

The magic of steam—with only eggs, water, and flour, we will see the most incredible puff. A tiny ball of dough (pâte à choux) in a hot oven becomes a great crisp, airy fluff; a steam-leavened cake (génoise) so light that you hardly know you have anything in your hand.

Most baked goods, whether they are chemically leavened (baking powder/baking soda) or yeast leavened, also depend on steam as part of their leavening. We saw that steam from the wet dough made incredibly light biscuits in Shirley Corriher's "Touch-of-Grace" Southern Biscuits (page 152)—much lighter than firmer doughs. In the yeast section, we will see that one of the great secrets of moist, light bread is a soft dough. Very firm doughs make heavy, tight-structured breads. Now, we are going to see steam all by itself as the star.

Hand-in-hand with steam, we will see the wonder of egg-white foams—thin films of protein and water entrapping air to form billowing clouds of meringue. Cooks can take a thick liquid containing protein and water (egg whites) and turn it into great, airy, snow-white puffs. We see egg-white foams and egg foams create magnificently delicate, light, incredibly strong structures that we can further inflate with heat and steam. Foams can be the structural wonders that lighten cakes.

We will see lavish, rich buttercream icings that innocently begin with a meringue. At first thought, you may wonder, "What are icings doing here with meringues and soufflés? Shouldn't they be back in the chapter with cake recipes?" However, since meringues are the building blocks of classic buttercreams, buttercreams would be difficult to make until you have mastered meringues.

Cream puffs, éclairs, Paris-Brest, St. Honoré, croquembouche, Yorkshire pudding, popovers, and all types of pâte à choux puff magnificently without baking powder or yeast. Delicate, airy cakes—génoise, sponge cakes (French *biscuits*), chiffon cakes, and cloud-like meringues—all get their ethereal lightness from trapped air and steam. For steam, we will need heat, but let's begin at the beginning with trapped air—foams.

Egg-White Foams

HOW PROTEINS WORK

Egg whites are essentially proteins and water. Raw, natural proteins are individual units. These are like little pieces of ribbon with bonds holding the ribbon folded or twisted around into wads. These proteins are totally separate, so there is plenty of room for light to go between them. You can see right through a raw egg white in a skillet.

As you heat, or beat air into the proteins, or expose them to acid, their bonds come apart, and the ribbon partially unwinds. This is now a denatured protein; it has been changed from its natural form. Almost immediately, this partially unwound (denatured) protein, with its bonds sticking out, runs into another denatured protein with its bonds sticking out and they bind together. Now there is no longer room for light to go between. The egg white turns solid white.

The same thing happens when you cook raw fish, chicken, or shrimp. They appear glassy, partially translucent, when raw, and turn opaque white when cooked. When the proteins first bind, they trap water between them; some proteins have water bound to them so the cooked proteins are moist and juicy. However, if you continue to heat, beat, or expose proteins to acids, their bonds will tighten up and squeeze out the moisture and they will become tough and dry. Even an overcooked egg can become tough, and shrimp marinated in too acidic a marinade can be so tough that you need a steak knife to cut them.

The secret of protein cookery is to be gentle. Don't overheat or heat too long, don't overbeat or leave in acid too long. We will see that all of this applies when beating egg whites into a foam.

How Egg-White Foams Work

How do egg-white foams work? When you beat egg whites, air makes some of the proteins in the egg whites unwind. The bonds holding together the natural protein coils pop apart. The unwound (denatured) proteins bump into neighboring unwound proteins and they join together, forming a lining or reinforcement around each air bubble.

WORKING WITH EGGS

Simply getting the egg whites in the bowl involves an amazing amount of know-how—just in cracking eggs, separating yolks and whites, and keeping everything scrupulously clean.

Cracking Eggs

I had always cracked eggs on the edge of the bowl or on the edge of the counter. However, the literature points out that cracking an egg on a flat surface gives you less shell shatter and less likelihood of having a piece of shell in your egg.

They do crack nicely on a flat surface and I try to crack them this way, but old habits die hard, and frequently I have to stop myself when I am aiming for the edge of the bowl!

No Yolk in the Whites

The absolute must in beating egg whites, whether from a fresh or an older egg, is that the whites have no yolk contamination. The tiniest trace of fat from an egg yolk can wreck an egg-white foam. Fat slows down foaming and dramatically reduces volume. Fats in egg yolk and olive oil are worse than other fats for that. The smallest trace of egg yolk will deflate egg-white foam.

Three-Bowl Method for Separating Whites and Yolks

Since even a trace of egg yolk will deflate an egg-white foam, I use the three-bowl technique for separating whites and yolks. Eggs are easier to separate when warm, but the yolks break more easily.

Crack the egg, open it carefully, let the white drop into a small scrupulously clean bowl, and place the yolk in another bowl. If the yolk did not break, and the white is absolutely pure, pour the white from the small bowl into the larger bowl in which it will be beaten. Continue this until all the eggs are separated. If you break a yolk, even if you do not see any yolk in the white, throw out that white and wash the small bowl, rather than contaminate the big bowl of whites with a minute trace of yolk.

I used to separate an egg by breaking it in my hand and letting the white run through my fingers into one little bowl and then drop the yolk into the other bowl. When I did this at La Varenne Cooking School in Paris, Chef Albert Jorand slapped my fingers and shook his head, "No." He explained that the oil from my hands could make my soufflé not rise as well.

Old White or Fresh White? Thin Whites or Thick Whites?

Fresh eggs are definitely better for separating into whites and yolks. Membranes in the egg become weaker with age, and the yolk sac becomes weaker and eventually breaks. Old eggs can be almost impossible to separate without breaking the yolk. You may crack an egg very carefully, but it's quite possible that the yolk will break anyhow. In some cases, it is even possible that the yolk sac can be broken inside an uncracked egg. When you crack an egg onto a plate, you will see that there is a thick part of the white that clings around the yolk and a thin runny part that spreads out. A fresh egg's white is nearly all thick. As the egg ages, this thick part deteriorates into runny white. Notice the two chalazae (the cords at each end of the yolk). Prominent chalazae are another sign of a fresh egg.

Older egg whites whip faster and to slightly more volume; however, fresh whites produce a more stable foam that will hold up better in a soufflé or cake.

Some chefs save egg whites and say that older, thin whites are better for egg-white foams. Actually, older whites do whip faster and to slightly more volume; however, fresh whites produce a more stable foam, one that will hold up better in a soufflé or cake.

Frozen whites, if they have not been pasteurized (heat treatment of eggs prolongs beating time), whip more easily than fresh and make good foams and cakes of high quality. Dried egg whites or meringue powders that have been pasteurized require a longer beating time.

Beating

Beating involves both equipment and techniques. Everything matters.

Everything Squeaky Clean

Beat egg whites in a scrupulously clean copper, glass, ceramic, or metal bowl with a clean whisk. The tiniest trace of fat can wreck an egg-white foam. A slightly dirty whisk or a seemingly clean plastic bowl (plastic can hold hidden traces of fat) can be devastating to an egg-white foam.

Beaters

Beaters with many tines incorporate air into egg whites much faster than those with a few tines. Select a large flexible, balloon whisk with lots of tines for easier hand beating. The type of electric mixer also makes a difference. A mixer with beaters that rotate around the bowl incorporates air into a foam faster and better than one with stationary beaters. If you are using a handheld mixer, move it around the bowl for better results.

Overbeating

The secret of a good egg foam is to beat the egg whites long enough for them to unwind and join together around the bubbles, but to still be loosely bound so that the bubbles can expand in the oven when the soufflé or cake is baked.

If you overbeat egg foams you tighten the bonds between the proteins so that the lining of each bubble is firmly bonded (essentially, it's already "cooked"). The bubbles cannot expand when you bake the product and your soufflé or cake will have a poor rise. There are cases when you do not want a product to rise, and overbeating is the proper technique, but not for soufflés, cakes, and pie meringues.

Overbeaten egg whites lose their smooth, shiny, moist surface and become dry and lumpy. In cooking school, we were taught to beat the whites until they lost enough moisture to no longer slip around in the bowl. We were taught to beat them until they were dry enough to hold to the bowl so that we could hold the bowl upside down over our heads without getting blobs of white on our hair.

I disagree with this, and like to keep the foam moister. I want my egg whites to slip a little in the bowl. I feel that they are more elastic this way and I will get a better rise in my soufflé or cake.

EGG-WHITE FOAMS BECOME MERINGUES

Egg-white foams, which start out as air bubbles with a thin film of water stabilized by proteins in the liquid, can easily drain and collapse. They simply drain into a puddle. A meringue is an egg foam that is preserved with heat, and sugar, and sometimes with the aid of an acid and/or starch. Meringues are a cook's way to preserve a foam—basically a way to hold air.

If you overbeat an egg foam you tighten the bonds between the proteins, and the lining of each bubble is firmly bonded (essentially, it's already "cooked"). The bubbles cannot expand when heated and your soufflé or cake will have little rise.

Stop beating soon enough that the egg whites still slip a little in the bowl. They are more elastic this way and the soufflé or cake rises better.

Techniques for Meringues

Heat

Not only do you need heat to cook (coagulate) the proteins around bubbles in a foam, you need heat to inflate the bubbles. Keep the big picture in mind: meringues are steam leavened. For steam, you need liquid and heat. Both Swiss and Italian meringues (coming up on pages 184 and 186) require heat before or during the actual beating of the egg whites. One of the reasons an Italian meringue is so stable is that the foam is both inflated and "cooked" by the hot syrup.

Heat is a major part of steam-leavened products. Heat both inflates bubbles in the dough and cooks (coagulates) the proteins around bubbles to set the baked good.

And, one of the major problems of most traditional pie meringues is weeping—liquid draining from undercooked, unstable meringue. The meringue recipes that follow—Italian Meringue (Magnificent Pie Meringue), Greenwood's Great High Meringue, Carole Moore's Easy Magnificent Meringue, and Alice Medrich's Procedure for Safe Meringues—all pay great attention to heat. You simply can't have steam without it.

Ingredients for Meringues

We have covered egg whites, the main ingredient in a meringue, so now we will turn to sugar.

Sugar

The best sugar to use in a meringue is finely ground sugar, sometimes called superfine, baker's, bar, or berry sugar. It dissolves much faster in the foam than granulated sugar and creates a superior textured foam. If superfine sugar is not available in your grocery store, you can make your own by processing regular granulated sugar in a food processor for a minute or two. Most pastry chefs do not like confectioners' sugar except for hard meringues (it makes very light hard meringues and the cornstarch that it contains aids in drying).

In a stable meringue, whether it is a soft meringue pie topping or a hard meringue crust, omitting sugar is not an option—sugar is a vital part of the structure. Dissolved sugar both pulls some water from the delicate protein network to strengthen it and forms a syrup coating to prevent the foam from drying and draining. When a soft meringue is cooked, the proteins set to form a firm network and some of the water evaporates to leave a still-slightly-moist but stronger sugar-coated foam. In French or hard meringues (page 174), with beating and cooking you completely dry out the moisture from the sugar syrup coating on the egg-white foam to produce a delicate spiderweb network of sugar-crusted proteins.

Some pastry chefs feel that superfine sugar, which dissolves much faster than regular granulated sugar, gives a superior textured foam.

Sometimes food writers or recipe developers have written recipes for "healthy" meringues that contain less sugar. They obviously never tested such a recipe because it simply won't work. The meringue will drain into a big puddle. Equal weights of egg whites and sugar, which is about 2 tablespoons (25 g) sugar per egg white, will produce a meringue that will hold but it is not as stable as the higher-sugar meringues. Greenwood's Great High Meringue (page 191), which is about equal weights of sugar and egg whites, holds with the aid of heat, cream of tartar, and cornstarch. The Italian meringue is the most stable, with the sugar at double the weight of the egg whites, and made with a high-temperature sugar syrup.

When to Add Sugar

When you beat sugar into an egg-white foam, it is like coating the unwound proteins in syrup so they won't dry out. If you add the sugar early in beating it takes longer to get good volume. You can get a good volume of foam faster by waiting until soft peaks begin to form before adding the sugar. However, be careful not to wait too long or you will allow the foam to start drying out. Without sugar, the foam can dry and lose its elasticity. It is better to add sugar too soon and have to beat longer than to add it too late, after the foam has started to dry.

In a meringue, sugar is not an optional ingredient; it is a vital part of the meringue's structure. Dissolved sugar both pulls some water from the delicate protein network to strengthen it and also forms a syrup coating to prevent the foam from drying and draining.

Floating Islands

MAKES 6 SERVINGS

The dessert Floating Islands is made of a basic simple meringue with a near minimum amount of sugar. I use 2 tablespoons (25 g) of sugar per egg white—the ratio that is used in soft pie meringue (see page 188). However, some recipes for floating islands use even less sugar. The meringues do not have to hold up long since they are cooked immediately in small portions. Large-serving-spoon-size scoops are poached in either milk or water. They are flipped over during cooking so that both sides are poached in the hot liquid, which immediately cooks the whites all the way through.

What This Recipe Shows

Warming the eggs by letting them sit in very hot water speeds up the beating.

Superfine sugar dissolves fast and makes excellent meringues.

Meringues are delicately flavored with vanilla and salt.

It is not necessary to add starch to these meringues because they are poached and will never reach a temperature hotter than boiling liquid. Thus, there is no danger of their shrinking or becoming tough.

---

4 large eggs, in the shells
½ teaspoon (1.5 g) cream of tartar
½ cup (3.5 oz/99 g) superfine sugar (see Note)
1 teaspoon (5 ml) pure vanilla extract

Pinch of salt
2 to 3 cups (473 to 710 ml) whole milk for poaching
2 recipes Crème Anglaise (page 331)
Caramel (recipe follows)

1. Place the eggs in a bowl and cover with several inches of very hot tap water. While you are gathering ingredients, pour the water off one time (it will have cooled after a few minutes) and cover the eggs again with very hot tap water.

2. Read Egg-White Foams and Meringues At a Glance (page 194). Follow the precautions—scrupulously clean bowl and beaters. Separate the eggs using the Three-Bowl Method (page 165).

3. In a mixer with the whisk attachment, beat the egg whites and cream of tartar, slowly at first, then building up speed. Beat on medium-high until soft peaks form when the beater is lifted. Beat in the sugar a little at a time until peaks form but droop when the beater is lifted. The whites should still slip a little in the bowl when it is tilted. Beat in the vanilla and salt.

4. In a medium skillet, bring at least 1 inch (2.5 cm) of milk to a gentle boil. Reduce heat to a simmer.

5. Use 2 large serving spoons to shape 6 to 8 oval meringues of beaten egg whites and drop them into the simmering milk. Poach until firm, turning each after 2 to 3 minutes. Remove from the liquid with a slotted spoon and drain on paper towels for up to 30 minutes.

6. Pour the Crème Anglaise into a shallow serving bowl. Float the meringue ovals on the custard and drizzle with hot Caramel. Serve at room temperature or chilled.

NOTE: If you do not have superfine sugar, process granulated sugar in a food processor with the steel blade for about 1 minute.

Caramel

MAKES ABOUT 1 CUP (237 ML)

With care you can get light, medium, or dark caramel using this method.

What This Recipe Shows

At high heat, table sugar (sucrose) breaks down. From one single sugar many different sugars with different tastes are formed as sugars form, break, and join with the heat. As many as 128 different sugars have been identified when sugars go from a pale caramel to a dark caramel. We know a light caramel tastes very different from a dark caramel. It is a different collection of sugars.

---

1 cup (7 oz/198 g) sugar
2 tablespoons (30 ml) light corn syrup

4 or 5 drops (about 1 ml) lemon juice
3 to 4 tablespoons (45 to 60 ml) water

1. Place the sugar in a 2-cup (473-ml) glass measuring cup and add corn syrup and lemon juice. Stir in the water until no white patches of dry sugar are left. Add a little more water if needed to dampen all of the sugar.

2. Place the dampened sugar in the microwave and heat on 100% power until bubbles start piling up on top of each other. The time depends on the amount of sugar and water, and the power of the microwave. Watch carefully.

3. As soon as you see a color change—the melted sugar going to pale tan—be on the alert. Permit the color to darken only slightly, then remove the caramel and let it stand. It will continue to darken and may get as dark as you want. If not, microwave for about 10 seconds longer and, if needed, in additional 10-second increments until you get a color slightly lighter than the color you want. It will continue to darken after you remove the caramel from the microwave.

Cream of Tartar

Cream of tartar, a mildly acidic salt produced from grapes, gives stability to egg-white foams. Adding acid (cream of tartar or vinegar) makes egg whites denature faster and speeds up the unwinding of proteins around the air bubbles in the foam. This reinforces the air bubbles faster and creates a good foam that will hold up until heat can coagulate the proteins and set the soufflé, cake, or meringue.

> I cannot stress too much how important cream of tartar or an acidic ingredient (vinegar or lemon juice) is to the stability of an egg-white foam. Without it, our Italian meringue was floating in an inch of liquid.

Many recipes add either cream of tartar or white vinegar to the egg whites at the beginning of beating. The usual amount is $1/8$ teaspoon (0.5 g) cream of tartar or $1/8$ teaspoon (about 4 drops) of distilled white vinegar per egg white.

Marty Thompson, an excellent young chef, was testing recipes for me. I had been so intent on writing an Italian meringue recipe to include starch for a better texture that I had forgotten to add the cream of tartar. Marty knew that the cream of tartar should be in the recipe, but he followed the recipe exactly as I wrote it to see if it would make a difference. The texture was magnificent. Thanks to the starch, the meringue cut smoothly and did not tear. It was beautiful—however, after 10 minutes the Italian meringue was sitting in an inch of water. Without the cream of tartar, it had leaked that much!

Copper Bowl

You ordinarily would think of the bowl as a piece of equipment, but in the case of the copper bowl, it is actually an ingredient. The whites remain in the bowl long enough for some of the egg-white proteins—conalbumin—to react with the copper, forming copper conalbumin, which has a slightly higher temperature of coagulation than conalbumin. The bubbles coated with copper conalbumin get slightly larger in the hot oven before they set, producing a cooked foam of higher volume. This could be why soufflés made with egg whites beaten in a copper bowl are higher than those that are not beaten in a copper bowl.

I am into wretched excess, so I thought why not use cream of tartar *and* a copper bowl? But my friend Harold McGee said, "Not a good idea." The increased acidity could cause the egg whites to leach considerably more copper from the bowl. Copper in a small amount is a good thing in the diet, but not in excess.

Water

Water increases the volume of an egg-white foam almost as much as if you added an equivalent amount of egg white, but it changes the texture of the cooked product. For example, water in an egg-white foam makes a cake softer. You can replace up to almost a quarter of the total volume of egg whites with water, but it makes a less-stable, softer foam.

This can be useful information. When Rose Levy Beranbaum wanted to soften snow-white layers for a wedding cake (they were essentially hard meringues), I suggested that she add water. It worked like a charm.

Starch—Cornstarch or Tapioca Starch

Why starch in a soft meringue? In custards and puddings, starch prevents eggs from coagulating (cooking) at their normal temperature and allows you to heat them without fear of curds (for more details, see page 328). Starch can do somewhat the same with egg whites. When the egg-white proteins are cooked and tightened, the meringue shrinks dramatically. Food stylists always "anchor" the meringue to the sides of the pie to keep it from pulling away. These tightened cooked egg-white proteins can make a meringue very difficult to cut. The meringue tears and is impossible to cut smoothly.

Adding tapioca starch or a little cornstarch to the egg whites solves all of these problems. Just as starch prevents tightening of egg bonds to make unwanted curds in custards, starch also prevents tightening of egg-white protein bonds and prevents meringues from shrinking. This tender meringue with starch cuts like a dream.

I have previously used a cornstarch paste to do all these wonderful things. Cornstarch is a grain starch and does not start to swell until over 190 to 200°F (88 to 93°C); the egg white will start to tighten before this swelling temperature. So the starch needs to be swollen before you add it to prevent tight coagulation of the proteins. Dissolve 1 tablespoon (7 g) of cornstarch in 1/3 cup (79 ml) of water and heat it until a thick paste forms. After all the sugar is added and the meringue is firm, with the mixer running, add about 3 tablespoons (45 ml) of the starch paste, 1 tablespoon (15 ml) at a time, until all is beaten in.

> Just as starch prevents tightening of egg protein bonds to make curds in custards, starch prevents tightening of egg-white protein bonds and prevents meringues from shrinking or from tearing when cut.

An Easier-to-Use Starch

Making the cornstarch paste is an extra step, but back in the 1940s the good old pie king, Monroe Boston Strause, had an easier solution to a cornstarch paste: use tapioca starch (or tapioca flour, *not* tapioca pearls or Minute tapioca), which is a root starch and swells at a much lower temperature than cornstarch (it starts swelling even below 160°F/71°C). You can mix the tapioca starch right in with the sugar—no extra step of making a paste needed. I love that man!

Simply stir a little tapioca starch into the sugar. Tapioca starch is available at Asian markets and health food stores. It is generally less expensive in Asian markets, where 1 pound (454 g) sells for under $2.00. It is beaten in along with the sugar and makes a wonderful tender meringue that does not shrink, and cuts like a dream. A good amount to use is 2 tablespoons (0.7 oz/19 g) of tapioca starch per 1 cup (7 oz/198 g) of sugar, which is enough for 8 egg whites (8 oz/227 g). So, ½ cup (3.5 oz/99 g) sugar and 1 tablespoon (9 g) of tapioca starch stirred together is ideal to use in making a meringue that uses 4 egg whites (4 oz/113 g). Actually, the more that I have used the tapioca starch, the more I realize that you can use less. Two teaspoons (6 g) of tapioca starch is enough for a meringue made with 4 egg whites (4 oz/113 g).

I talked Bill Greenwood, of Greenwood's on Green Street Restaurant in Roswell, Georgia, into trying the tapioca starch in his Greenwood's Great High Meringue, page 191. He said it was wonderfully easy, but he did not think it gave him quite the shine on the surface that the cornstarch did. You may want to experiment to see which you prefer. It really does made a difference in the appearance. Like Bill, I have decided that the cornstarch is worth the trouble if you want a shiny meringue.

THE RECIPES

As I explained on page 168, sugar is not an optional ingredient in meringues; it is a vital structural component. The sugar pulls water out and ties up water, allowing the delicate spiderweb-like protein network to strengthen and eventually become firm enough to hold. For a meringue to be stable you need close to equal weights of egg whites and sugar.

There are three classic meringues: French meringue (sometimes called *meringue ordinaire*), Swiss meringue, and Italian meringue. All three meringues use approximately 1 weight of egg whites (about 1 oz/28 g each) to 2 weights of sugar.

Historically, meringues have used a ratio of 10 egg whites (about 10 oz/283 g) to 1 pound and 2 oz sugar (18 oz/510 g total). *Larousse Gastronomique* (1984 edition) uses 10 egg whites (10 oz/283 g) to 17 oz (482 g) sugar.

All of the three classic meringues (French, Swiss, and Italian) have about twice as much sugar as the typical soft pie meringue (see page 188). Interestingly, many of the classic meringue recipes do not use an acid (cream of tartar, lemon juice, or vinegar), probably because they are stable enough without it. I am chicken and do include an acid in my recipes. We are going to see that with our lower-sugar, less-stable American meringue, we can have many problems.

French Meringues

French meringue (*meringue ordinaire*) is a hard meringue, usually baked into a meringue cake layer, meringue puffs, or meringue shells, or piped into the form of meringue mushrooms or other hard meringues. It is normally made with part granulated sugar and part confectioners' sugar, so that it is very light in texture.

French meringue and nut meringue batter are also used to make larger shells called *vacherins*. A rim consisting of two or more layers is piped on top of each other on a meringue base and baked to form a container, a *vacherin* (named after the cheese wheels).

I have included recipes for Delicate French Meringue (page 175) and a recipe using meringue puffs, Featherlight Meringue Spheres with Silky Crème Anglaise Coffee Buttercream and Chocolate (page 176).

Delicate French Meringue

MAKES ABOUT THIRTY TO THIRTY-FIVE 1½ TO 2-INCH (3.8 TO 5-CM) SHELLS

This is the basic hard meringue for meringue cake layers, puffs, or shells. I have given directions here for puffs. They are light, fragile, and melt-in-the-mouth to eat—perfect for puffs to sandwich together with pastry cream or whipped cream. They are also ideal for meringue shells that can be filled with fruit, mousse, or ice cream.

What This Recipe Shows

Confectioners' sugar makes this meringue extremely lightweight—a sweet bit of trapped air.

Reserving a little superfine sugar (about 2 tablespoons, 0.9 oz/26 g) and blending it with the confectioners' sugar and flour gives a slightly different texture to the mix and aids in its blending in with the meringue.

---

4 large egg whites (4 oz/113 g)
¼ teaspoon (0.8 g) cream of tartar
¾ cup (5.3 oz/150 g) superfine sugar, divided
  (see Note)

1 cup (4 oz/120 g) confectioners' sugar
1 tablespoon (8 g) all-purpose flour

1. Arrange a shelf in the lower third of the oven with a baking stone on it and preheat the oven to 250°F/121°C.

2. Read Egg-White Foams and Meringues At a Glance (page 194). Follow the precautions—scrupulously clean bowl and beater.

3. In a mixer with the whisk attachment, beat the egg whites and cream of tartar, slowly at first, then building up speed. Beat on medium-high until soft peaks form when the beater is lifted. Beat in the superfine sugar a little at a time until all but about 2 tablespoons (0.9 oz/26 g) is incorporated, the whites are smooth and shiny, and very stiff peaks form when the beater is lifted.

4. Stir together the remaining 2 tablespoons (0.9 oz/26 g) superfine sugar, the confectioners' sugar, and the flour. Sprinkle part of the sugar mixture on top of the meringue and fold in with a few strokes of a large spatula. Continue sprinkling and folding until all of the sugar mixture is folded in.

5. Place a sheet of parchment on a large baking sheet. Immediately pipe or spoon the batter into 1½ to 2-inch (3.8 to 5-cm) round or oblong puffs on the parchment.

6. Turn the oven down to 200°F/93°C. Place the sheet on the hot baking stone and bake 1 hour and 45 minutes, until thoroughly dry. Remove from the oven and allow to cool completely. When completely cooled, these will keep several weeks in a sealed container.

> NOTE: If you do not have superfine sugar, process granulated sugar in a food processor with the steel blade for about 1 minute.

Featherlight Meringue Spheres with Silky Crème Anglaise Coffee Buttercream and Chocolate

MAKES ABOUT 12 TO 15 PASTRIES

These airy, crunchy meringue balls are glued together and coated with a thin coating of coffee buttercream and then rolled in fine chocolate shavings. Total yum! These can be made up to three days ahead and held in the refrigerator in a closed container.

What This Recipe Shows

Crisp, airy meringue is a perfect contrast to rich buttercream icing.

Coffee buttercream and chocolate shavings make a classic flavor combination.

---

1 recipe Delicate French Meringue (page 175), shaped and baked into 1 to 1½-inch (2.5 to 3.8-cm) puffs

1 recipe Silky Crème Anglaise Coffee Buttercream (page 216)
1 cup (6 oz/170 g) semisweet chocolate shavings or chocolate sprinkles

1.Generously spread buttercream on the flat bottom of one puff, then press the flat side of another puff against the icing to make a ball glued together in the middle with buttercream. Repeat with all of the remaining meringues. Refrigerate for 30 minutes.

2. Ice each meringue ball with a thin coating of buttercream, then sprinkle each all over with chocolate shavings or chocolate sprinkles. Place in a closed container and refrigerate for at least 30 minutes before serving. These keep refrigerated for 3 days.

Nut Meringue Cakes—Dacquoise and More and More!

This is the stuff of dreams—incredible creations! A crisp, crunchy, nutty layer is a perfect contrast to silky buttercream, a soft mousse, pastry cream, or simply whipped cream. Hundreds of magnificent cakes are made with nut meringue layers—Progrès, Café Noix, Stanislas, Chanteclair, and Paris, just to name a few classic cakes from Bruce Healy's *The Art of the Cake*.

The definition of "dacquoise" is something like "traditional French cake consisting of two to three layers of nut-flavored (almond or hazelnut) discs of crisp meringue sandwiched together with whipped cream or buttercream and sometimes fruit." So, I thought a dacquoise was simply a cake made with French meringue layers with finely ground almonds or hazelnuts added. Not necessarily so!

There is actually an incredible variety of nut meringues, including different nuts—Pierre Hermé uses walnuts in one of his—and different amounts of nuts (the ratio of the weight of nuts to the weight of egg whites runs from 40 to 110%).

Although nut meringues contain primarily just three ingredients (egg whites, sugar, and nuts), their recipes vary considerably.

Some recipes use superfine sugar only, while others use part confectioners' sugar and part superfine. And, the ratios of the weight of sugar to weight of egg whites are all over the place. Roland Mesnier, author of *Dessert University*, former White House pastry chef, and teacher, has a recipe for Meringue Dacquoise (a soft, moist meringue that he uses in many cakes) with a ratio of 131% for the weight of sugar to the weight of egg white. His very fragile Almond Meringue has a ratio of 295%, and his Japonaise has a ratio of 131%. Both his Meringue Dacquoise and his Japonaise have ratios of 50% for the weight of nuts to the weight of egg whites. His Almond Meringue has a ratio of 150% of weight of nuts to egg whites. It is no wonder that he describes this Almond Meringue as "quite fragile." With 295% sugar and 150% nuts to egg whites, there is not as much egg white to hold things together as in other nut meringues.

Bruce Healy's Dijonnaise, which he describes as "lighter, less sweet, and more flavorful" than a French meringue, contains both confectioners' sugar and superfine sugar for a total sugar-to-egg-white ratio of 172%. Bruce's Succès, again with both confectioners' sugar and superfine sugar, has a weight ratio of sugar to egg white of 79%.

> Crisp, crunchy, nutty meringue layers are the building blocks of dream creations—many of the cakes of the great pastry shops of France and Austria.

> Although nut meringues contain primarily just three ingredients (egg whites, sugar, and nuts), their recipes vary considerably.

A few generalizations:
the more nut flour,
the heavier; the more
sugar, the crisper; and
confectioners' sugar
makes the meringue
lighter.

Wayne Gisslen's Almond Meringue uses equal weights of egg whites, sugar, and almonds. His Japonaise contains twice as much sugar as egg whites.

Some generalizations: the more nut flour, the heavier; the more sugar, the crisper; and confectioners' sugar makes the meringue lighter.

I have included two recipes here. One is typical of European coffeehouse or pastry shop pastries—a very crisp, hazelnut and almond thin nut meringue that is a perfect contrast to the Silky Crème Anglaise Coffee Buttercream (page 216) icing that I like with it. The other is patterned after Roland's thicker, soft, moist meringue that is ideal for many cakes, even those with whipped cream and fruit.

Hazelnut-Almond Meringue Layers with Silky Crème Anglaise Coffee Buttercream

MAKES ONE 4 X 10-INCH (10 X 25-CM) 4-LAYER LOAF, ABOUT 8 SERVINGS

Elegant, rich, totally decadent—the crunchy nut layers are a perfect contrast to the silky, voluptuous buttercream. To get very finely ground nuts, I used Bruce Healy's technique of processing nuts with part of the confectioners' sugar, straining through a coarse strainer, and then processing the nut pieces that were left in the strainer with the remaining confectioners' sugar.

What This Recipe Shows

Roasting enhances the flavor of the nuts.

Processing the nuts with confectioners' sugar absorbs some of the oil and allows you to get a finer grind without clumping.

Cream of tartar stabilizes the meringue.

Since the cold, firm fat icing does not soak in as would an icing with liquid, the nut layers of this dessert remain crisp for several days in the refrigerator.

½ cup (2.5 oz/71 g) blanched hazelnuts

¼ cup (1 oz/28 g) blanched almond slivers

2 cups (9.7 oz/227 g) mixed whole blanched hazelnuts and almonds, for garnish

½ cup (2 oz/60 g) confectioners' sugar, divided

1 tablespoon (7 g) cornstarch

5 large egg whites (5 oz/142 g)

½ teaspoon (1.5 g) cream of tartar

1 cup (7 oz/198 g) superfine sugar (see Note)

1 recipe Silky Crème Anglaise Coffee Buttercream (page 216)

1. Arrange a shelf in the lower third of the oven with a baking stone on it and preheat the oven to 350°F/177°C.

2. Spread nuts for the meringue and the nuts for the garnish separately on a baking sheet. Place the sheet on the hot baking stone with the almond slivers near the oven door. Roast until lightly browned, about 10 minutes. Set aside to cool.

3. When nuts are completely cool, coarsely chop the mixed whole nuts for the garnish and set aside. For the meringue, process ½ cup (2.5 oz/71 g) hazelnuts and ¼ cup (1 oz/28 g) almonds with ⅓ cup (1.3 oz/38 g) confectioners' sugar to finely grind the nuts. Stop before the nuts get oily and the mixture starts to clump. Sift through a coarse strainer. Process any nuts left in the strainer with the remaining 3 tablespoons (22 g) confectioners' sugar. Stir together both batches of processed nuts and sugar. Stir in the cornstarch.

4. In a mixer with the whisk attachment, beat the egg whites and cream of tartar, slowly at first, then building up speed. Beat on medium-high speed until soft peaks form when the beater is lifted. Beat in the superfine sugar a little at a time until all is incorporated, the whites are smooth and shiny, and stiff peaks form when the beater is lifted.

5. Sprinkle part of the nut-sugar mixture on top of the meringue and with a large spatula fold it in with a few strokes. Continue sprinkling and folding until all of the nut mixture is folded in.

6. Line a 17 x 11 x 1-inch (44 x 29 x 2.5-cm) baking pan with parchment. Cut slashes in the corners so that the parchment fits into the pan smoothly. With an offset spatula, spread the batter evenly in the pan so that it is equal depth throughout.

7. Place the baking pan on the hot baking stone and bake until lightly browned around the edges and firm to the touch, about 15 to 20 minutes.

8. Cool in the pan a few minutes only, then invert onto a cooling rack and carefully peel off the parchment while the meringue is hot. When the meringue has cooled, place it on a clean countertop and trim the edges using a large pizza cutter to make an even rectangle. Mark off 4 equal sections lengthwise and cut with a pizza cutter so that you have 6 rectangles about 4 x 10 inches (10 x 25 cm) in size.

9. Place one layer on the serving platter and spread with a thin layer of buttercream icing, then arrange another layer on top and spread with buttercream. Continue until the fourth layer is in place. Ice the top and sides with the buttercream. Garnish by pressing the coarsely chopped mixed nuts into the sides. Place in the refrigerator, covered, for an hour or more to set. Can be kept refrigerated for several days. Slice with a serrated knife and serve cold.

NOTE: If you do not have superfine sugar, process granulated sugar in the food processor with the steel blade for about 1 minute.

Hazelnut-Almond Soft Dacquoise

MAKES FOUR 10-INCH (25-CM) ROUND LAYERS

Moist meringue rounds with ground nuts—the perfect layers for breathtakingly delicious cakes.

What This Recipe Shows

Processing the nuts with confectioners' sugar absorbs some of the oil and allows you to get a finer grind without clumping.

Cream of tartar stabilizes the meringue.

Adding a small amount of milk makes a slightly soft, moist meringue.

½ cup (2 oz/57 g) blanched almond slivers
½ cup (2.5 oz/71 g) blanched hazelnuts
½ cup (2 oz/60 g) confectioners' sugar, divided, plus extra for sprinkling
2 tablespoons (0.5 oz/14 g) all-purpose flour
8 large egg whites (8 oz/227 g)

½ teaspoon (1.5 g) cream of tartar
1¼ cups (8.75 oz/248 g) superfine sugar (see Note)
⅓ cup (79 ml) whole milk

1. Arrange a shelf in the lower third of the oven with a baking stone on it and preheat the oven to 350°F/177°C. Place a second shelf in a slot slightly above the center of the oven.

2. On each of two large pieces of parchment, trace two 10-inch (25-cm) circles with a pen dark enough to see through the parchment. Turn the sheets over and place each on a large baking sheet.

3. Process the almonds and hazelnuts with ⅓ cup (1.3 oz/38 g) of the confectioners' sugar to finely grind the nuts. Stop before the nuts get oily and the mixture starts to clump. Sift through a coarse strainer. Process any nuts left in the strainer with the remaining 3 tablespoons (0.8 oz/21 g) confectioners' sugar. Stir together both batches of nuts and sugar. Stir in the flour.

4. In a mixer with the whisk attachment, beat the egg whites and cream of tartar, slowly at first, then building up speed. Beat on medium-high until soft peaks form when the beater is lifted. Beat in the superfine sugar a little at a time until all is incorporated, the whites are smooth and shiny, and stiff peaks form when the beater is lifted.

5. Stir the milk into the nut mixture. Stir about one-third of the egg whites into the nut-milk mixture to lighten it, and then carefully fold in the rest of the egg whites.

6. Fit a large pastry bag with a #8 (¾-inch/2-cm) pastry tip. Fill the bag only half full with batter each time and, starting in the center, pipe to fill in the 4 circles marked on the parchment. Just before placing in the oven, sprinkle each circle very lightly with confectioners' sugar.

7. Arrange one baking sheet on the hot baking stone and the other on the shelf in the upper portion of the oven. Bake for 20 minutes, leaving the oven door open less than 1 inch (2 cm). Swap baking sheet positions. Turn the oven down to 300°F/149°C, leaving the oven door still slightly open, and bake 30 to 40 minutes more, until firm.

8. Slide the cakes out of the pans and cool on cooling racks. Leave on the parchment until you are ready to use.

NOTE: If you do not have superfine sugar, process granulated sugar in the food processor with the steel blade for about 1 minute.

Softer Hard Meringue?

Isn't this a contradiction? How can you have a soft, moist hard meringue? Years ago Rose Levy Beranbaum was trying to make a white cake layer using egg whites. I mentioned this back in the "Water" section of Ingredients (page 172). The problem was that it was very firm—hard almost like a hard meringue. I suggested adding a cup of liquid. And sure enough, the liquid converted her recipe into the soft, white cake layer that she wanted.

So, I was very interested when I saw that Roland's Meringue Dacquoise contained 5 tablespoons (75 ml) of milk and he described it as a "soft, moist meringue"—a perfect layer for many cakes.

Now, my Hazelnut-Almond Soft Dacquoise (page 180) is not as soft as a shortened cake layer, but it is soft compared to a very crisp meringue such as the Hazelnut-Almond Meringue Layers with Silky Crème Anglaise Coffee Buttercream (page 216).

Heavenly Mocha Hazelnut-Almond Meringue Cake

MAKES ONE 10-INCH (25-CM) ROUND 3-LAYER CAKE

Sensuously silky coffee buttercream blended with mildly chocolaty pastry cream between layers of hazelnut-almond meringue. You are truly in heaven when you experience this cake. Roland Mesnier describes meringue cakes like this by saying that "if you eat it the day it is made, you have a wonderful contrast between the crisp meringue and the silky filling. If you eat it after a day or two in the refrigerator, the filling and the meringue layers and flavors have blended into total lusciousness." They are totally different experiences, but both wonderful.

What This Recipe Shows

Finely chopped chocolate or chocolate chips melt more evenly than big chunks.

Roasting enhances the flavor of the nuts.

---

1 cup (3.2 oz/92 g) sliced almonds
3 ounces (85 g) semisweet chocolate, finely chopped
1¾ cups Pastry Cream (page 330)

1¾ cups Silky Crème Anglaise Coffee Buttercream (page 216)
3 layers of Hazelnut-Almond Soft Dacquoise (page 180), baked and cooled

1. Arrange a shelf in the lower third of the oven with a baking stone on it and preheat the oven to 325°F/163°C.

2. Place the almonds on a baking sheet. Place on the hot baking stone and roast for 8 minutes. Set aside.

3. Place the chocolate in a microwave-safe glass cup or bowl and melt in the microwave on 50% power for 1 minute. Stir well. If not completely melted, heat for 15 seconds more and stir. Repeat if necessary.

4. Stir the melted chocolate into the pastry cream. Cover with plastic wrap, pressing against the surface of the pastry cream surface. Refrigerate. When completely chilled, stir the chocolate pastry cream into the coffee buttercream.

5. Place one hazelnut-almond meringue layer on a serving plate and ice generously with the pastry cream–coffee buttercream blend. Top with another layer and ice. Top with the final layer and coat the top and sides of the cake. Gently press roasted almond slices into the sides. Cover loosely and refrigerate immediately for several hours before serving. Keeps for 3 to 4 days refrigerated.

Nut Meringues as "Pie Crusts"

Meringues with nuts make excellent "pie crusts," as in the Blueberries with Honey Mascarpone Cream in Walnut-Oat Meringue (below).

Blueberries with Honey Mascarpone Cream in Walnut-Oat Meringue

MAKES ONE 10-INCH (25-CM) PIE

My friend Judy Falk, who died much too young, was an outstanding Atlanta cook. She was even featured in *Bon Appétit*. She made a raspberry pie in a walnut-oat meringue crust topped with whipped cream. Her delicate crunchy walnut-oat meringue is an excellent complement to any fruit filling. In my recipe, I have used a super-easy blueberry pie filling (page 269) and my favorite Honey Mascarpone Cream (page 270)—a heavenly combination.

What This Recipe Shows

Warming the eggs by letting them sit in hot water speeds up the beating.

Roasting enhances the flavor of the walnuts.

Cream of tartar helps produce a more stable meringue.

Confectioners' sugar makes the meringue crust lighter.

---

3 large eggs, in the shells
$1/2$ cup (1.7 oz/50 g) walnut pieces
$1/4$ teaspoon (0.8 g) cream of tartar
1 cup (4 oz/120 g) confectioners' sugar
$1/4$ teaspoon (1 g) baking powder
$3/4$ cup (2.3 oz/65 g) quick oats
$1/2$ teaspoon (2.5 ml) pure vanilla extract
$1/4$ teaspoon (1.5 g) salt

1 tablespoon (0.5 oz/14 g) butter for greasing the pan
2 tablespoons (0.5 oz/14 g) flour for preparing the pan
1 recipe fresh blueberry filling from Judy Brady's Blueberries and Bordeaux (page 269)
1 recipe Honey Mascarpone Cream (page 270)

1. Place the eggs in a bowl and cover with several inches of very hot tap water. While you are gathering ingredients, pour the water off one time (it will have cooled after a few minutes) and cover the eggs again with very hot tap water.

2. Arrange a shelf in the lower third of the oven with a baking stone on it and preheat the oven to 325°F/163°C.

3. Place the walnuts on a baking sheet. Place on the hot baking stone and roast for 10 minutes. When cool, coarsely chop and set aside.

4. Separate the eggs using the Three-Bowl Method (see page 165).

5. In the mixer with the whisk attachment, beat the egg whites and cream of tartar, slowly at first, then building up speed. Beat on medium-high until soft peaks form when the beater is lifted. Beat in the confectioners' sugar a little at a time until all is incorporated, the whites are smooth and shiny, and stiff peaks form when the beater is lifted. Beat in the baking powder. Fold in the walnuts, oats, vanilla, and salt.

6. Butter and heavily flour a 10-inch (25-cm) pie plate. Spoon the meringue onto the plate. Spread thinly over the bottom and pile higher around the edges to form a shell for filling. Bake until set and lightly browned, about 30 to 40 minutes. Cool completely on a cooling rack.

7. Pile the blueberry filling into the meringue crust (instead of Judy's Bordeaux crumb crust). Refrigerate to chill thoroughly. Just before serving, spoon on Honey Mascarpone Cream.

Swiss Meringues

In a Swiss meringue, the egg whites and sugar are heated to slightly over 120°F/49°C in the mixer bowl before beating. Roland Mesnier describes Swiss meringues as having the bright white that most people associate with meringues, and says that this heating before beating makes the finished hard meringues strong enough to use as containers for ice cream.

Salmonella-Safe Meringue

Fortunately, in the United States, we have not had as big a salmonella issue with eggs as in the UK and other countries. Salmonella is usually in the yolks. The contamination is passed on by the hen as the yolk is formed in her oviduct. So a perfectly good-looking egg with no cracks can be contaminated.

The contaminated yolk can pass salmonella to the egg white, but this is rare. In the few cases of egg-white contamination, the eggs have been incredibly abused. In one case the eggs sat in a very hot storage area for weeks before use.

Alice Medrich's Safe Meringue

MAKES ENOUGH MERINGUE FOR TWO 9-INCH (23-CM) PIES OR ONE "MILE-HIGH" MERINGUE PIE

If you are concerned with egg-white contamination, in her book *Chocolate and the Art of Low-Fat Desserts,* Alice Medrich gives a procedure for killing salmonella. Essentially a Swiss meringue technique, this safe meringue is just heated to a higher temperature. I have also added tapioca starch for a meringue that will cut smoothly and will not shrink. This is a very stable meringue. If you spread it on a pie shortly after preparation, it should still be warm. Even piled very high, it cooks through fast and does not weep. For baking, follow the directions for Greenwood's Great High Meringue on page 191. (For a meringue with a shiny finish, use cornstarch and water instead of tapioca starch, following the procedure on page 187.)

What This Recipe Shows

With constant stirring, you can carefully heat egg whites to the instant-kill temperature for salmonella (160°F/71°C) by diluting the whites with water and adding sugar.

I added starch to the beaten whites to produce a tender, smooth-cutting meringue that does not shrink or bead easily.

Meringue made with egg whites heated in this manner is an excellent, stable meringue.

---

6 large egg whites (6 oz/170 g)
2 tablespoons (30 ml) water
¾ teaspoon (2 g) cream of tartar
¾ cup (5.3 oz/150 g) sugar
2 tablespoons (0.7 oz/19 g) tapioca starch

¼ cup (59 ml) cool water
1 teaspoon (5 ml) pure vanilla extract
⅛ teaspoon (pinch) salt
Flavoring, optional

1. In a medium stainless-steel bowl, stir the whites, water, cream of tartar, and sugar just to blend. In a medium skillet, heat 1 inch (2.5 cm) of water to a simmer and turn the heat off. Place a cup of hot tap water near the skillet and place an instant-read thermometer in it. Place the metal bowl of egg-white mixture in the skillet of hot water and constantly scrape the bottom and the sides of the bowl with a rubber spatula to prevent the whites from overheating. After 1 minute of constant scraping and stirring, remove the bowl of egg whites from the hot water and check the temperature by tilting the bowl so that you have about 2 inches (5 cm) of white covering the thermometer stem. If the temperature is up to 160°F/71°C, the whites are ready to beat. If not, place the bowl of whites back in the hot water and scrape constantly in 15-second increments until the temperature reaches

160°F/71°C. Rinse the thermometer in the hot water in the skillet (to kill salmonella) and replace in the cup of hot water after each use.

2. Beat the egg white–sugar mixture until soft peaks form when the beater is lifted. Stir the tapioca starch into the cool water and beat into the meringue. Continue beating until stiff peaks form when the beater is lifted. Beat in the vanilla, salt, and any other desired flavoring (such as lemon zest for a lemon pie). Set aside while preparing the pie filling.

Italian Meringues

Italian meringues and meringues made with a hot sugar syrup have a great advantage: they are cooked all the way through—no weeping—and are wonderfully stable (see Weeping and Beading, page 189).

> Italian meringues made with a hot sugar syrup have a great advantage: they are cooked all the way through—no weeping.

Italian meringues, the traditional sugar-syrup meringues, can be soft or hard, depending upon the amount of cooking. They are already "cooked" by the very hot sugar syrup and are stable immediately. You can recook them and completely dry them out into a hard meringue, or you can simply brown the peaks in a hot 450°F/232°C oven or with a blowtorch and use them as a very stable soft meringue. This is a way to have a stable white meringue highlighted with dark tips and dark top ridges of the swirls. Normally, when you cook a meringue long enough to make it stable, it will be tan all over. Since this meringue is already cooked all the way through, you do not have to worry about cooking it.

> An Italian meringue is a food stylist's dream. You have snow-white meringue that doesn't need to be cooked to be stable. You can add color as you desire with a blowtorch—magnificent swirls with browned ridge tops and dark tips.

Italian meringues and sugar-syrup meringues are excellent multipurpose meringues, ideal for pie toppings or for frosting a cake. These meringues can be folded in to lighten pastry creams, buttercreams, pie fillings, and puddings. Classic Italian meringue (*Meringue Italienne*) is made of double the weight of sugar to egg whites. It is quite stable and does not weep. Heat the sugar syrup to 248°F/120°C (hard-ball stage) then drizzle very hot syrup into well-beaten egg whites until the meringue is cool and ready to spread.

A Very Stable Pie Meringue

To make the ideal meringue that does not shrink and cuts smoothly (for more details see page 173), I added cornstarch paste to a standard Italian meringue. This makes an incredibly stable pie meringue that does not shrink, cuts beautifully without tearing, and is snow white so that you can brown it as you like.

Pouring Hot Syrup

When you are making an Italian meringue you need to pour a very hot syrup slowly and steadily into an egg foam with the mixer running on high speed, without hitting the beaters or the side of the bowl. To make this tough job a little easier, first pour the hot syrup into a 2-cup (473-ml) heatproof (glass) measuring cup and then pour the syrup from this cup. Certainly, pouring from a measuring cup is much easier than pouring from a heavy saucepan.

Rinse the cup in the hottest tap water and dry it just before using it for the hot syrup. It seems to be asking a lot of even Pyrex to pour 248°F/120°C hot syrup into a cold glass cup.

Italian Meringue (Magnificent Pie Meringue)

MAKES ENOUGH MERINGUE FOR TWO 9-INCH (23-CM) PIES OR ONE "MILE-HIGH" MERINGUE

This very stable meringue is incredibly versatile—it makes magnificent billowy white peaks to brown as you wish. It is a large recipe—6 egg whites—so that you have an abundance of this great meringue. Of course, you can easily halve this recipe.

What This Recipe Shows

Adding the sugar as a hot syrup cooks and swells the meringue immediately—no problems with weeping.

Pouring the hot syrup into a 2-cup (473-ml) heatproof glass measuring cup with a spout makes pouring the hot syrup into the meringue easier.

---

1 tablespoon (7 g) cornstarch
⅓ cup (79 ml) cool water
6 large egg whites (6 oz/170 g)
1 teaspoon (3 g) cream of tartar
2 cups (14 oz/397 g) sugar, divided

1 tablespoon (15 ml) light corn syrup
½ cup (118 ml) water
1 teaspoon (5 ml) pure vanilla extract
¼ teaspoon (1.5 g) salt

1. Place a shelf in the middle of the oven. Place a baking stone on it and preheat oven to 375°F/191°C.

2. In a small saucepan, heat the cornstarch and ⅓ cup (79 ml) cool water over medium heat, stirring steadily with a whisk until thick and cloudy. Reserve until needed.

3. Read Egg-White Foams and Meringues At a Glance (page 194). Follow precautions—scrupulously clean bowl and beater.

4. In a mixer with the whisk attachment, beat the egg whites and cream of tartar until soft peaks form when the beater is lifted. Add in ¼ cup (1.8oz/50g) sugar and continue to beat.

5. In a heavy unlined saucepan, stir together remaining 1¾ cups (12.3 oz/347 g) of the sugar, the corn syrup, and ½ cup (118 ml) water. Bring to a boil, and rinse down the sides of the pan with water on a pastry brush. Attach a candy thermometer to the saucepan, and continue to boil the syrup until it reaches 248°F/120°C (hard-ball stage).

6. Continue beating whites until stiff peaks form. Ideally, have the whites stiff when the syrup reaches 248°F/120°C. Rinse a 2-cup (473-ml) heatproof glass measuring cup with a spout with the hottest tap water and dry well. When the syrup reaches 248°F/120°C, carefully pour the syrup into the cup. Drizzle the hot sugar syrup into the meringue while beating on medium speed. Try to avoid drizzling the syrup on the beaters or the sides of the bowl. The meringue will swell dramatically and fill the whole bowl. Beat until the meringue has cooled, about 10 to 13 minutes. Beat in the vanilla and salt, then beat in about 3 tablespoons (45 ml) of the reserved cornstarch paste, 1 tablespoon (15 ml) at a time. The meringue is essentially cooked but it is still snow white. It is the perfect palette for a masterpiece.

7. Spread the meringue on the pie. Place the pie in the middle of the oven and bake for about 10 minutes—just until the ridges are brown—then remove from the oven and touch up with a blowtorch as desired. (I think that you have to be very experienced to brown a meringue with a blowtorch alone. It is easier to bake just until you start getting color on the ridges, then pull out of the oven and touch up with the blowtorch.)

SOFT PIE MERINGUE

Traditional recipes for soft pie meringue contain equal weights of sugar and egg whites. This is half the amount of sugar used in stable classic pie meringue. French and Swiss meringues are typically baked as hard meringues, but Italian meringue is most frequently used as a soft meringue and does, indeed, give us as close to a perfect pie meringue as imaginable.

Traditional American pie meringue contains a lower amount of sugar and has been with us for a long time. The *Boston Cooking School Cookbook* has a recipe with 2 egg whites (2 oz/57 g), 2 tablespoons (26 g) sugar, and ½ tablespoon (8 ml) lemon juice or ¼ teaspoon (1.25 ml) vanilla extract. The recipe does add 3 tablespoons more sugar for a "sweet meringue" to be baked on top of the pie for 15 minutes at 300°F/149°C. An older *Joy of Cooking* recipe has 2 egg whites (2 oz/57 g), ¼ teaspoon (0.8 g) cream of tartar, 3 tablespoons (1.3 oz/38 g) sugar, and ½ teaspoon (2.5 ml) vanilla extract to be baked on top of the pie at 325 to 350°F/163 to 177°C for 10 to 15 minutes. Both of these use only 2 egg whites (2 oz/57 g) for a thin topping—probably for the very good reason that if we try to make a thicker low-sugar meringue we are going to have major problems.

Soft Meringue Problems

Problems, problems, problems—weeping and beading, meringues that shrink and pull away from the crust, meringues that are tough and tear when you try to cut them. We see that using starch in a meringue (page 190) or switching to an Italian meringue can solve many problems.

Weeping and Beading

The two classic problems with our lower-sugar American soft meringues on pies are "weeping," a puddle of liquid between the meringue and the filling, and "beading," little brownish syrup droplets on the surface of the meringue.

Weeping is caused by undercooking—the meringue does not get hot enough to cook all the way through. Both Swiss and Italian meringues solve this problem by heating the egg whites before or during heating. Bill Greenwood adapted the Swiss meringue technique of heating the whites before beating in his lower-sugar meringue (see Heating Before Beating, page 190). A warm meringue cooks through much faster.

One solution is to prepare the meringue before the filling. Since the meringue is safe to stand once the sugar is beaten in, prepare the meringue before you prepare the filling and then allow the filling to cool just enough to firm up. If you pile the meringue on a totally runny pie filling, the meringue sinks and the filling spills over the crust. The filling needs to be firm enough to hold up the meringue. Finally, pile the meringue on a slightly warm filling. Now the meringue gets a little heat from both underneath and above so you have a better chance of getting it done through. At least, it is not cold underneath.

> Weeping is caused by undercooking—the meringue does not get hot enough to cook all the way through.

Another way of getting a warm filling is to place the pie in the preheated oven for a short time while you are preparing the meringue.

Roland Mesnier has an excellent trick for making a bone-dry seal between the meringue and filling. He sprinkles fine cake crumbs on the hot filling before he piles on the meringue. This combination of hot filling and crumbs can give you an incredibly dry seal between the meringue and the filling.

> Roland Mesnier gets a bone-dry seal between the meringue and filling by sprinkling fine cake crumbs on the hot filling before he piles on the meringue.

The beads on the top of the meringue are caused by overcooking. Actually, you can have two faults at the same time: weeping from undercooking and beading from overcooking. If you pile a cold high meringue on a cool filling and cook at a high temperature of 450°F/232°C for only a few minutes, you will have beads from overcooking the surface and also great puddles of liquid that drained from the uncooked bottom and center of the meringue. Starting with a warm meringue (Swiss meringue or Greenwood's Great High Meringue), a lower temperature, or a shorter baking time can solve the beading problem.

> The beads on the top of the meringue are caused by overcooking.

Shrinking and Tearing

When egg-white proteins join (cook or coagulate), they shrink. This means that a meringue on top of a pie can shrink considerably. Food stylists always anchor a meringue to the crust all the way around so that they will not have an unsightly space between the meringue and the crust.

Starch to the Rescue

As described on page 173, starch in a meringue prevents egg-white proteins from shrinking together tightly when cooked. To prevent this tightening, the starch must be swollen before the tightening occurs in the egg whites. Cornstarch, unfortunately, does not swell until 190°F/88°C or higher. So for it to be effective, you need to swell the starch before adding it to the egg whites. To do so, mix 1 tablespoon (7 g) of cornstarch and ⅓ cup (79 ml) water in a small saucepan. Stir over low heat to form a paste. After all the sugar is added to the egg whites and the meringue is firm, add 3 tablespoons (45 ml) of the starch paste, 1 tablespoon (15 ml) at a time with the mixer running, and beat in well. Please note that it is difficult to make a smaller portion of cornstarch paste. You really only need about three-fourths of this, maybe a little less.

Compared to cornstarch, tapioca starch has a much lower swelling temperature of 160°F/71°C or slightly below. This lower swelling temperature allows you to simply stir the tapioca starch into a little sugar that is added early in the beating, using about 2 teaspoons (19 g) tapioca starch for 4 egg whites (4 oz/113 g).

As I mentioned on page 174, Bill Greenwood tried the tapioca starch, felt it was wonderfully easy, but also thought that he got more of a shine on the surface of his meringues using the cornstarch paste. This is quite true; you get a flat, matte finish with the tapioca starch. You may want to experiment to see which you prefer.

Heating Before Beating

Bill Greenwood's lemon meringue pie easily won "Best Lemon Meringue Pie" in the Best of Atlanta. His "mile-high" meringue looks as if it were a painting. Instead of the evenly brown-colored top that most high meringues get when baked, his ranges from snow-white in the valleys to dark brown tips at the peaks. The ridges are medium dark, and every different level in the meringue is a different shade of brown.

When I asked, "How on earth did you get such a beautiful meringue?" Bill explained that he felt that the warm starting temperature of his egg whites was vital. He places the mixing bowl with the whites, the sugar, and the cream of tartar in a hot water bath and stirs gently. He gets the egg white–sugar mixture to a temperature of between 120 and 140°F/49 and 60°C and then immediately beats at a high speed until the peaks remain when the beater is lifted. This will be a much shorter beating time because of the warm eggs, since the time required to beat a meringue is inversely related to the starting temperature.

Some Swiss meringue recipes beat the egg whites while in the water bath on the heat. Bill does not beat the egg whites until he has removed them from the heat. He does have a hot mixing bowl. But he says that his meringue does have a different texture.

To decorate the pie with meringue, Bill starts by piling all the meringue on top of the pie. To produce the wonderful peaks, starting in the center of the pie, he inserts his spatula down into the meringue and fluffs up and out toward the edge of the pie. As he pulls the spatula from the meringue he makes peaks. He adds more meringue, fluffs it magnificently high, and bakes at 375°F/191°C until the tips of the peaks are dark brown. This produces his picture-perfect meringue that goes from snow-white valleys to dark brown ridges.

If you start baking with a warm meringue, and if you pile it on a warm filling, you will get the meringue cooked through and not have any trouble with weeping. Starting with this warm meringue, you will have a shorter baking time. Also, the warm meringue that will cook through fast allows you to use a higher baking temperature. All of these things give you the beautiful color differentiations.

Using one technique after another, Bill manages to get a lower-sugar soft pie meringue. With the warm whites, the cream of tartar, and the starch, Bill's meringue works and produces a masterpiece—it stands high, doesn't weep or bead, and is bright white with beautiful color variations.

Starting with a warm meringue, you will have a shorter beating time, a shorter baking time, and the meringue cooks through well so that you do not have trouble with weeping. You can cook the meringue at a higher temperature, which produces beautiful color differentiations.

Greenwood's Great High Meringue

MAKES ENOUGH FOR ONE "MILE-HIGH" MERINGUE TOPPING FOR ONE 9 TO 10-INCH (23 TO 25-CM) PIE

This is a picture-perfect, magnificent meringue with dark brown tips on the peaks, snow-white valleys, and golden brown ridges.

What This Recipe Shows

The cornstarch prevents both shrinking and weeping, and Bill Greenwood thinks he gets more "shine" (gloss) on his meringues with cornstarch than with tapioca starch. In my Italian Meringue, which is not dried out by baking, I use only 3 tablespoons (45 ml) of the cornstarch paste. But this baked meringue can handle more liquid.

Heating the whites before beating greatly reduces beating time, and the meringue cooks all the way through, preventing weeping.

Sprinkling dry cake or bread crumbs on the filling before piling on the meringue absorbs excess moisture.

1½ tablespoons (0.4 oz/11 g) cornstarch
  stirred into ½ cup (118 ml) room-
  temperature water
6 large egg whites (6 oz/170 g)
¾ teaspoon (2 g) cream of tartar

¾ cup (5.3 oz/150 g) sugar
1 teaspoon (5 ml) pure vanilla extract
Pinch of salt
Dry fine bread or cake crumbs, for sprinkling

1. Arrange a shelf in the middle of the oven and preheat to 375°F/191°C.

2. In a small saucepan, heat the cornstarch and water over medium heat, stirring steadily with a whisk until thick and cloudy. Reserve until needed.

3. Make a hot water bath by boiling 1 inch (2.5 cm) of water in a large skillet. Turn off the heat.

4. Place the egg whites in a heatproof mixing bowl. Stir together the cream of tartar and the sugar, then stir both into the egg whites. Place the mixing bowl in the hot water bath, stirring constantly until the egg-white mixture reaches between 120 and 130°F/49 and 54°C. Do not overheat. Stirring gently, keep at this temperature for 2 minutes. Move the warm whites immediately to the mixer and beat on the highest speed until you have stiff peaks. Beat in the cornstarch mixture, 1 tablespoon (15 ml) at a time. Whisk in the vanilla and a pinch of salt.

5. When the pie filling has cooled enough to set, sprinkle fine bread or cake crumbs on the filling, then pile the meringue on. To produce wonderful peaks, start in the center of the pie, insert the spatula down into the meringue, and fluff the meringue up and out toward the edge of the pie. Add more meringue and continue to fluff it magnificently high. Bake at 375°F/191°C until the tips of the peaks are dark brown but the valleys are still white.

Carol Moore's Easy Magnificent Meringue

Makes enough meringue for one 9-inch (23-cm) pie

Carol Moore, an outstanding cooking teacher and food writer from Galesburg, Illinois, generously shares her recipe for this excellent meringue with us. I did add cornstarch to it so that is doesn't shrink, and cuts smoothly.

What This Recipe Shows

Using marshmallow creme instead of sugar makes a beautiful meringue with an added touch of gelatin in the marshmallow creme.

Cornstarch prevents the meringue from shrinking and makes it cut smoothly.

---

1 tablespoon (7 g) cornstarch
1/3 cup (79 ml) cool water
4 large egg whites (4 oz/113 g)

1/2 teaspoon (1.5 g) cream of tartar
One 7-ounce (198-g) jar marshmallow creme

1. Preheat the oven to 375°F/191°C and arrange a shelf in the center of the oven.

2. In a small saucepan or a microwave-safe glass cup, stir the cornstarch into the water. Heat, stirring frequently, until a thick paste forms. Set aside until needed.

3. In a mixer with the whisk attachment, beat the egg whites and cream of tartar, slowly at first, then building up speed. Beat on medium-high until soft peaks form when the beater is lifted. Beat in the marshmallow creme a little at a time until all is incorporated, and the whites become smooth and shiny and form stiff peaks when the beater is lifted.

4. Beat in 3 tablespoons (45 ml) cornstarch paste, 1 tablespoon (15 ml) at a time, until at least three-fourths of it is incorporated.

5. Pile the meringue on warm pie filling, make decorative swirls, and place on the middle shelf in the oven. Bake until the tips and ridges are lightly browned, 15 to 20 minutes.

Egg-White Foams and Meringues At a Glance

What to Do	Why
Use scrupulously clean bowl and beaters for egg whites.	Any oil or grease will wreck an egg-white foam.
Use fresh egg whites.	Fresh egg whites take slightly longer to beat and yield slightly less volume than older whites, but are more stable and make better meringues and soufflés.
Use room-temperature eggs.	Warmer eggs are easier to separate. The length of time it takes to beat egg whites is inversely related to how cold the whites are. The colder the whites, the longer the beating time.
Separate the eggs using the three-bowl method.	Even a trace of egg yolk will deflate an egg-white foam.
Use a copper bowl or add $\frac{1}{8}$ teaspoon cream of tartar per egg white.	To get a more stable foam that will hold up better in cooking.
For meringues, add the sugar when soft peaks form when the beaters are lifted. Be sure to add sugar then—do not wait until too late.	Adding sugar too early reduces the volume and increases beating time. If you wait too late to add sugar, meringue can dry out and will not expand.
Do not overbeat egg whites. Beat them only until they are still moist and slip a little in the bowl.	Overbeaten egg-white foams become dry and rigid and will not expand in a hot oven.
Stir tapioca starch into the sugar or make a cornstarch paste and beat in the paste after adding the sugar.	Starch prevents the meringue's shrinking when baked and prevents tearing when the meringue is cut.

Magnificent Soufflés

Soufflés, the cook's majestic way to trap air, can be as simple as puréed fruit stirred into an Italian meringue (Fresh Peach Soufflé à la Roland Mesnier, page 202), as ethereal as the free-form soufflés resembling the mountains around Salzburg (Salzburger Nockerl, page 204), as amazing as soufflés that are dumped out (Incredibly Creamy Soufflés, page 206), or as basically wonderful as a classic French cheese soufflé (page 196).

THINK "HEAT"

Many soufflés contain a thick creamy base (which should be hot) and an egg-white foam.

A good soufflé is dependent on a good egg-white foam (see page 164). And then you need to think "heat." Soufflés are steam-leavened, and steam requires heat. I knew this, but I had not really realized how important it is to have the soufflé base—a béchamel (thick cream sauce) with flavoring—hot when you fold in the yolks and the beaten whites. If this base is hot, and you work reasonably fast when folding in the final ingredients, you will have a warm soufflé going into the oven. This means a faster, better rise and a well-risen soufflé.

In San Francisco, on Grant Avenue between Union Street and Green Street, is Café Jacqueline, a very small restaurant. Both walls are lined with tables for two, each with a white tablecloth and a clear vase with two pink roses. Chef Jacqueline, the proprietor and sole chef of Café Jacqueline, reminded me that it is important to have the base hot.

Chef Jacqueline serves, essentially, soufflés: main-course soufflés and dessert soufflés. Her soufflés are magnificent, puffed, browned creations that are luxuriously creamy in the center. She makes one size, a 6-inch (15-cm) soufflé, which is a generous serving for two as a main course and easily enough for four as a dessert.

She also serves classic French onion soup made from mountains of thinly sliced onions, cooked and cooked and cooked, and an excellent endive salad—fresh endive leaves with a few flecks of Roquefort and a drizzle of wonderful olive oil. The endive that I have always had was bitter—how is it that hers was not bitter? She explained that you must look for endive with absolutely no green, and tips as pale yellow as possible. I later mentioned this to Kristine Kidd, food editor at *Bon Appétit*. She, too, thought that this was a great tip.

The restroom is located in an open courtyard garden out the back door, a well-lit door to the right. Even if you don't need to visit the restroom, you may want to stroll back just to see the courtyard or to visit with Chef Jacqueline. She is usually standing near the open courtyard door, at a high counter beating egg whites in a very old, small KitchenAid mixer. Next to her is the biggest crudely chiseled wooden bowl that I've ever seen, containing dozens and dozens of eggs.

> Steam requires heat. In steam-leavened soufflés, it is vital to have the soufflé base with the yolks hot when you fold in the beaten whites. A warm soufflé going into the oven means a faster, better rise and a well-risen soufflé.

> For endive that is not bitter, select endive with absolutely no green and the palest possible yellow tips.

There also are two white plastic 5-gallon (19-L) containers, one with freshly grated Gruyère and the other with a hot, thick, cream-sauce soufflé base.

Chef Jacqueline will happily chat with you as she beats egg whites, one hand resting on top of the mixer. She graciously answers questions about soufflés, withholding nothing. She gives you the oven temperature, 400°F/204°C, and time, 10 minutes for convection ovens and 25 for regular home ovens, for her perfectly cooked soufflés.

Chef Jacqueline stressed how important it is for the béchamel (the soufflé base) to be hot when you fold in the egg yolks and the beaten whites. Here we are again. The secret of dramatic steam-leavened dishes—heat.

She stressed how important it is for the béchamel (the soufflé base) to be hot when you fold in the egg yolks and the beaten whites. Wow! Here we are again—the secret of dramatic steam-leavened dishes—*heat*. If the batter is warm, it takes a shorter time for steam to form and create a great rise, making a magnificent, tall soufflé. In my soufflé recipes that follow, I made sure to incorporate this tip, and my instructions tell you to beat the whites first, then make the base, and immediately fold in the yolks and the whites and cheese, if used.

Soufflé Magnifique!

MAKES ONE 6-INCH (15-CM) SOUFFLÉ

A soufflé with a gloriously browned crust and a velvety, creamy center is truly a work of art. No matter what is happening when I go to San Francisco, I make sure that I get to Café Jacqueline's for one of her perfect soufflés. I always order the simple cheese soufflé, but her crab soufflés with big chunks of crabmeat are sensational. I just love the brown crust, yet with an amazingly creamy center. The high oven temperature and the exact cooking time contribute to this perfection.

What This Recipe Shows

Warming the eggs helps to get a warm soufflé that will rise faster.

Keeping everything scrupulously clean and using the three-bowl method to separate eggs will help produce a good egg-white foam.

Cream of tartar aids in producing a more stable foam.

Beating whites first enables you to use the soufflé base while it is very hot. This will give you a warm soufflé going into the oven, which will rise faster.

---

6 large eggs, in the shells
½ teaspoon (3 g) salt
⅛ teaspoon (pinch) white pepper
¼ teaspoon (1.5 g) sugar
⅛ teaspoon (pinch) freshly grated nutmeg
5 tablespoons (2.5 oz/71 g) butter, divided

1¼ cups (5 oz/142 g) finely grated Gruyère, divided
½ teaspoon (1.5 g) cream of tartar
¼ cup (1.1 oz/31 g) bleached all-purpose flour
1 cup (237 ml) hot whole milk

1. Read Egg-White Foams and Meringues At a Glance (page 194). Follow precautions—scrupulously clean bowl and beater.

2. Arrange a shelf in the lower third of the oven with a baking stone on it and preheat the oven to 400°F/204°C.

3. Place the eggs in a bowl and cover with several inches of very hot tap water. While you are gathering ingredients, pour the water off one time (it will have cooled after a few minutes) and cover again with very hot tap water.

4. Measure out and stir together the salt, white pepper, sugar, and nutmeg. Set aside.

5. Grease one 6 x 4-inch (15 x 10-cm) round soufflé dish with 1 tablespoon (0.5 oz/14 g) of the butter. Add ¼ cup (1 oz/28 g) grated Gruyère and rotate the dish to coat the sides well. Set dish aside in a warm place, perhaps on the back of the stovetop or near the oven.

6. Separate the eggs using the Three-Bowl Method (see page 165) until you have 6 yolk-free whites and 6 yolks. Stir the cream of tartar into the 6 egg whites and with a mixer using the whisk attachment, beat on high speed until the whites form soft peaks when the beater is lifted. Set aside.

7. To make the soufflé base, melt the remaining ¼ cup (2 oz/56 g) butter in a heavy saucepan over medium-low heat. Stir in the flour and continue stirring and heating for 2 to 3 minutes, until the flour is well absorbed into the butter. Remove from the heat and whisk in the hot milk a little at a time. Place back on medium heat and, stirring constantly, bring the mixture to a boil. It should thicken well.

8. Remove the hot soufflé base from the heat and stir in the salt, pepper, sugar, and nutmeg. Stir a little of this hot soufflé base into the egg yolks, and then stir the yolks back into the hot soufflé base. Stir about an eighth of the beaten whites into the hot soufflé base mixture to lighten it.

9. Gently push the whites to one side of the bowl, carefully pour the hot soufflé base down the side of the bowl, and slide the hot mixture under the whipped egg whites. Gently fold the whites and the soufflé base together, reaching a large spatula to the bottom, pulling some of the thick base up and smearing it across the whites. Continue in this manner until the whites and the base are fairly well blended. Carefully fold in the remaining 1 cup (4 oz/113 g) Gruyère.

10. Pour the soufflé batter into the warm prepared dish. Run a clean thumb around the inside edge of the soufflé dish to aid in the soufflé's rising straight up. Place it in the oven on the hot baking stone. Bake until soufflé is well risen and well browned, about 25 minutes.

11. Serve immediately, serving each guest some of the firm outside and some of the creamy center. Bon appétit!

SOUFFLÉS WITH AND WITHOUT FOAM?

In recent years, I have been impressed by realizing what thin lines lie between a soufflé and a custard, and between a soufflé and a cake. The way that an ingredient is added or the amount of a single ingredient can mean the difference.

Years ago, Susan Purdy, baker and author of many fine baking books, called me with a question about a loaf cake. It rose beautifully, but when she took it out of the oven it fell.

It behaved like a soufflé. When she described how she made it, I realized that it *was* a soufflé! She had only one egg yolk in the batter and all of the egg whites were beaten until stiff, and then folded into the other ingredients.

Firmly beaten egg whites are partially "cooked" and cannot contribute as much structure as an unbeaten egg can to set and hold up a cake.

I explained that stiffly beaten whites were essentially partially cooked (see page 164). She needed some unbeaten whole eggs or whites that could cook and hold the cake up when it rose. She could still fold in some beaten egg whites, but in the batter she needed either a whole egg or a couple of unbeaten whites to have some completely raw egg to set and hold the cake.

All of this started my thinking in the direction of making soufflés that would hold better—not fall instantly when they came out of the oven. How about making the soufflé base thick enough to include a whole egg, or maybe 2 whole eggs, in addition to the yolks? This should make a more stable soufflé. I encourage you to try this. I have a great soufflé like this in *Cook Wise,* Chocolate Soufflé with White Chocolate Chunks, page 237.

Quick Soufflés—Soufflés with No Egg-White Foam

Since two eggs in the base can help to hold up a soufflé, I decided to go a step further and try a "soufflé" with none of the eggs beaten—no beaten whites. If it would rise decently, it should be more stable.

I raised this question in a conversation with Chef Heather Hurlbert, our very talented and artistic pastry chef at the Cherokee Town Club. In a rare quiet moment, she and some of her staff tried the regular Soufflé Magnifique! and also a version made without beating the egg whites.

The soufflé without beating the egg whites did rise, not as high as the classic soufflé, but her comment gives true insight into the major difference. You would expect a texture difference, and Chef Heather hit it right on when she described the "without-foam" soufflé as having a more custard-like texture.

Of course, depending on how much you beat or do not beat the whole batter, this *is* a custard. I had just never thought of a soufflé as a custard with beaten egg whites, but that is exactly what it is! You can try this quicker soufflé, recipe follows, to experience first-hand the relationship between a custard and a soufflé.

Easy—Without Foam—Soufflé

MAKES ONE 6-INCH (15-CM) SOUFFLÉ

This is a simplified version of Soufflé Magnifique! The eggs are not separated and no egg foam is used. The batter is beaten with the addition of each whole egg. It rises similarly to a soufflé and it is more stable, but it does have a noticeably different texture—not that of an ethereal soufflé that is destined to fall. The high oven temperature and the exact cooking time contribute to this perfection.

What This Recipe Shows

A dish containing eggs whose batter is beaten after the eggs are added will rise almost like a soufflé.

---

6 large eggs, in the shells
1/2 teaspoon (3 g) salt
1/4 teaspoon (1 g) sugar
1/8 teaspoon (pinch) white pepper
1/8 teaspoon (pinch) freshly grated nutmeg
1/4 cup (2 oz/56 g) butter, divided

1 cup (4 oz/113 g) finely grated Gruyère, divided
3 tablespoons (0.8 oz/23 g) all-purpose flour
1 cup (237 ml) hot whole milk
1/2 teaspoon (1.5 g) cream of tartar

1. Arrange a shelf in the lower third of the oven with a baking stone on it and preheat the oven to 400°F/204°C.

2. Place the eggs in a bowl and cover with several inches of very hot tap water. While you are gathering ingredients, pour the water off one time (it will have cooled after a few minutes) and cover again with very hot tap water.

3. In a cup or small bowl, stir together the salt, sugar, white pepper, and nutmeg. Set aside to add later.

4. Grease a 6 x 4-inch (15 x 10-cm) round soufflé dish with 1 tablespoon (0.5oz/14 g) of the butter. Add ¼ cup (1 oz/28 g) grated Gruyère and rotate the dish to coat the sides well. Set dish aside in a warm place, perhaps on the back of the stovetop, or near the oven.

5. To make the soufflé base, melt the remaining 3 tablespoons (1.5 oz/43 g) butter in a heavy saucepan over medium-low heat and stir in the flour. Continue stirring for 2 to 3 minutes until the flour is well absorbed into the butter. Remove from the heat and stir in the hot milk a little at a time. Place back on medium heat and stirring constantly, bring the mixture to a boil. It should thicken well. Remove from the heat and stir in the seasonings and cream of tartar.

6. Scrape the hot mixture into a mixing bowl. With the mixer running on medium speed and using the whisk attachment, add 1 egg and beat it in well. Then add another egg and beat it in well. Continue beating in one egg at a time until all 6 eggs are beaten in. Beat on high for about 1 minute. Add the remaining ¾ cup (3 oz/84 g) Gruyère and mix it in on low speed just to blend in.

7. Pour the soufflé mixture into the warm prepared dish. Run your clean thumb around the inside edge of the dish to aid the soufflé in rising straight up, and place on the hot baking stone. Bake until soufflé is well risen and well browned, about 25 to 30 minutes.

8. Serve immediately, spooning up some of the firm outside and some of the creamy center for each guest.

Stratas—Soufflés or Custards?

Stratas, wonderful breakfast casseroles, are in a broad sense a type of soufflé, too. Cheese and bread (sometimes with sausage, bacon, or ham) are soaked overnight in an egg-milk mixture. When baked, they puff and brown magnificently.

Simply Wonderful Strata—
Browned Billows of Cheesy Puff

This magnificent puffed casserole is an ideal company or family meal. A complete do-ahead—prepare the night before and it is ready to bake the next day. The subtle flavor of nutmeg adds to good ham and cheese. Use an open, porous bread (like French bread) to form a base for eggs and milk and create a soufflé-like puff.

What This Recipe Shows

Eggs, with their abundance of liquid, soak into the bread and create a soufflé-like puff.

Shallots contribute subtle sweet onion flavors.

½ cup (4 oz/113 g) butter
5 shallots, peeled and finely chopped
½ green bell pepper, finely chopped
¾ teaspoon (4.5 g) salt
¼ teaspoon (1 g) white or black pepper
1 teaspoon (4 g) sugar
¾ teaspoon (2 g) dry mustard
⅛ teaspoon (pinch) ground cayenne

⅛ teaspoon (pinch) freshly grated nutmeg
1 loaf (8 oz/226 g) French bread, trimmed and
    torn into 1-inch (2.5-cm) pieces (8 cups)
3 cups (12 oz/340 g) grated Gruyère
1 pound (454 g) coarsely chopped ham
8 large eggs (14 oz/397 g)
2¾ cups (651 ml) whole milk
Nonstick cooking spray

1. Heat the butter in a skillet over medium heat. Add shallots and green pepper and cook, stirring, for about 10 minutes just to soften. Stir in the salt, pepper, sugar, mustard, cayenne, and nutmeg. Pour into a 9 x 13-inch (23 x 33-cm) glass baking dish.

2. Place the bread chunks in the dish on top of the shallots and peppers. Sprinkle the Gruyère over the top, and then spread the ham around evenly on top of the cheese. Beat together the eggs, then slowly beat in the milk. Pour the egg mixture over all in the dish. Cover tightly with plastic wrap and refrigerate overnight.

3. About 20 minutes before baking, arrange a shelf in the lower third of the oven with a baking stone on it and preheat the oven to 350°F/177°C. Place the strata on the hot baking stone and bake until puffed and browned, about 1 hour. Serve hot.

FLOURLESS "SOUFFLÉS"

A "soufflé" can be as simple as a flavored meringue. One of Roland Mesnier's White House desserts is his Fresh Fruit Soufflé, essentially a fruit-flavored Italian meringue. Italian meringue, which is already cooked by the hot sugar syrup, is wonderfully stable. (Read more about Italian Meringue on page 186.) However, it is important not to overcook these soufflés.

Fresh Peach Soufflé à la Roland Mesnier

MAKES SIX 6-OUNCE (177-ML) INDIVIDUAL SOUFFLÉS

A delicate fresh fruit dessert. Once you have prepared the Italian meringue, the soufflé is practically done. I love the technique of using a potato masher to mash fresh peaches to make a sauce, and just a touch of Grand Marnier elevates this dish to simple elegance. These soufflés are absolutely delicious all by themselves and the sauce is wonderful over vanilla ice cream.

What This Recipe Shows

The stable Italian meringue (with puréed fruit stirred in) can become a soufflé.

Peach Sauce (recipe follows), divided
½ recipe Italian Meringue (Magnificent Pie Meringue), page 187
2 tablespoons (1 oz/28 g) butter, to prepare ramekins

3 tablespoons (1.3 oz/38 g) sugar, for ramekins
1 pound (454 g) fresh peaches (about 3 medium), peeled, pitted, and sliced or 2 cups (473 ml) frozen peaches, thawed

1. Prepare the Peach Sauce and Italian Meringue first. Set the sauce aside.

2. Arrange a shelf in the lower third of the oven with a baking stone on it and preheat the oven to 400°F/204°C.

3. Butter six 6-ounce (177-ml) ramekins, sprinkle with the sugar, and rotate the sugar around in each dish to coat generously.

4. In a food processor with the steel blade or in a blender, process 1 cup of the Peach Sauce to a purée. Measure out 1 cup (237 ml) of the purée into a large mixing bowl.

5. Stir one-third of the Italian meringue into the peach purée to lighten it. Then gently push the Italian meringue to one side of its bowl and pour the lightened peach purée mixture down the side of the bowl to slide under the Italian meringue. Carefully fold together the peach purée mixture and meringue. Fill the prepared ramekins to the top and smooth with a spatula. Run your clean thumb around the inside edge of each ramekin.

6. Place the ramekins on the hot baking stone and bake just until the soufflés are well risen and firm to the touch, no longer than 10 minutes. They can become watery if overcooked. Serve immediately with the remaining Peach Sauce.

Peach Sauce

Makes about 2 cups (473 ml)

A quick fresh-fruit sauce with big chunks of peaches.

What This Recipe Shows

Just a pinch of salt suppresses some of the bitterness (sharpness) of acidic fresh fruit.

---

4 fresh peaches, peeled, pitted, and sliced or about 2 cups (473 ml) frozen peaches, thawed
½ cup (2 oz/60 g) confectioners' sugar

1 tablespoon (15 ml) Grand Marnier or amaretto liqueur
1 teaspoon (5 ml) lemon juice
Pinch salt

In a large bowl, toss together all the ingredients. With a potato masher, break the peaches into large chunks. Use immediately, or cover and refrigerate for up to 2 days.

FREE-FORM SOUFFLÉS

After all those years of greasing and coating soufflé dishes with grated cheese or sugar, and being told that the soufflé needed the coarse surface to climb (a batch of baloney!), I was totally amazed by the free-form soufflé Salzburger Nockerl. This soufflé is piled in the shape of three ridges (to resemble mountains) into an oblong au gratin baking dish with some delicious hot, steaming cream.

I have made no attempt to make this an authentic recipe. There seems to be great license as to what a Salzburger Nockerl contains, so I took the liberty of including whatever I wanted.

Salzburger Nockerl

MAKES ABOUT 6 SERVINGS

This impressive free-form soufflé is formed in ridges to resemble the mountains of Salzburg. It is said that every housewife in Salzburg has a different version, and that originally Salzburg dumplings were pâte á choux puffs poached in milk, rather than a soufflé. I make no attempt at authenticity, but have made a simple and impressive soufflé. Serve immediately after baking. It is wonderful served with Crème Anglaise (page 331).

What This Recipe Shows

In a more authentic recipe, a few drops of lemon juice would be used to stabilize the whites, but I am very partial to using cream of tartar instead.

Both the whites and the yolks are beaten for light soufflés.

Starting with a very thin layer of hot, steaming cream in the pan is a great boost to inflating and setting the soufflés fast.

---

7 large eggs, in the shells
1 teaspoon (3 g) cream of tartar
1 cup (7 oz/198 g) superfine sugar (see Note)
⅓ cup (1.4 oz/38 g) cake flour
⅓ cup (79 ml) heavy cream

¼ cup (59 ml) cherry preserves
½ teaspoon (2.5 ml) lemon zest (grated peel)
1 teaspoon (5 ml) pure vanilla extract
⅛ teaspoon (pinch) salt
Confectioners' sugar, for dusting

1. Arrange a shelf in the lower third of the oven with a baking stone on it and preheat the oven to 400°F/204°C.

2. Place the eggs in a bowl and cover by several inches with very hot tap water. While you are gathering ingredients, pour the water off one time (it will have cooled after a few minutes) and cover again with very hot tap water.

3. Separate the eggs using the Three-Bowl Method (see page 165). Set aside all 7 egg whites and 3 of the egg yolks.

4. Beat the egg whites and cream of tartar until soft peaks form. Beat in the superfine sugar a little at a time. Beat just until stiff peaks form and the egg whites are very shiny. Sift the flour a little at a time over the whites and fold into the whites in several batches.

5. Stir together the cream and preserves and pour into an 8 x 10 x 2-inch (20 x 25 x 5-cm) oval baking dish. Place in the oven on the hot baking stone to get hot while finishing the soufflés.

6. Stir together the 3 egg yolks, lemon zest, vanilla, and salt. Stir about one-quarter of the beaten egg whites into the yolk mixture to lighten and then fold the rest of the whites into the yolks.

7. Remove the hot dish from the oven. Pour most of the hot cream mixture into a 2-cup (473-ml) glass measuring cup with a spout and reserve. With a large spatula, pile the egg whites into the hot dish in 3 or 4 mounds, at an angle (slant) across the dish, narrower at the top edge (they are supposed to resemble a mountain range). Place back in the oven on the stone and bake until lightly browned on the outside, about 10 to 12 minutes. Pour the rest of the cream mixture back into the dish to flow at the base of the mountains.

8. Dust with confectioners' sugar and serve immediately.

NOTE: If you do not have superfine sugar, process granulated sugar in a food processor with the steel blade for about 1 minute.

SOUFFLÉS THAT ARE DUMPED OUT?

Not only do you not have to have rough-textured walls of grated cheese or sugar for these soufflés to rise, you can dump them out! I love these soufflés, not only because they are inconceivably delicious but also because they break all of the rules.

I first had these soufflés at Michael's Waterside Inn in Santa Barbara, California. At first, I could not figure out how they were made—sensationally delicious, simply standing straight up in a bowl of cream like a perfectly shaped 3-inch cake!

Incredibly Creamy Soufflés

MAKES 6 SERVINGS

The first freestanding soufflés in cream that I had were at Michael's Waterside Inn in Santa Barbara, California. I was impressed with how delicate they were, but I couldn't figure out how they were prepared. Were they baked in a metal ring in the dish, then the ring removed? I was surprised to find out that the soufflés were baked in a metal tart pan and dumped out into the dish of hot cream.

I couldn't wait to try my own soufflés in cream. First, they are baked in very well-greased muffin pans, not ceramic dishes, and in an outrageously hot oven for a soufflé—425°F/218°C. And, as if that's not enough, they are then dumped out of the pan into a shallow dish of hot cream, sprinkled lightly with cheese, and slipped back into the oven until the cheese melts and the cream is bubbly. I think that once you have dumped out a soufflé you will be over any fear of soufflés forever.

What This Recipe Shows

Soufflés do not have to have containers with textured sides—grated Parmesan or sugar—to rise. These are baked in well-greased muffin tins.

Soufflés can be baked in muffin tins as well as ceramic ramekins.

These soufflés can be baked and dumped into the cream a day ahead, then reheated when ready to serve.

Nonstick cooking spray

3 tablespoons (1.5 oz/43 g) softened butter, to grease pans

3½ cups (828 ml) heavy cream, divided

3 tablespoons (1.5 oz/43 g) butter

¼ cup (1.1 oz/31 g) bleached all-purpose flour

1 cup (237 ml) milk

1 teaspoon (6 g) salt, divided

¼ teaspoon (1 g) white pepper, divided

4 large eggs (7 oz/198 g)

½ teaspoon (1.5 g) cream of tartar

½ cup (2 oz/56 g) grated Gruyère

1. Spray one 12-cup (2¾ x 1⅜-inch/7 x 3.5-cm) nonstick muffin pan or two 6-cup muffin pans with nonstick spray, place in the freezer for at least 10 minutes, and then grease with the softened butter. Place the pan back in the freezer until ready to fill. This double greasing is important for the success of these soufflés.

2. Place 3 cups (710 ml) of the cream in a large saucepan. Bring to a boil over low heat and allow to boil gently until reduced by half. Transfer the cream from the saucepan to a shallow gratin or oval baking dish. Set aside.

3. Arrange a shelf in the lower third of the oven with a baking stone on it and preheat the oven to 425°F/218°C.

4. To prepare the soufflé base, melt 3 tablespoons (1.5 oz/43 g) butter in a heavy saucepan. Whisk in the flour, and cook over low heat for several minutes, stirring constantly. Remove from heat. In another saucepan, heat the milk and the remaining ½ cup (118 ml) cream until hot. Slowly whisk into the flour mixture. Return the pan to the heat and cook, stirring slowly, until quite thick. Remove from the heat. Season with ½ teaspoon (3 g) salt and ⅛ teaspoon (pinch) white pepper.

5. Carefully separate the eggs using the Three-Bowl Method (see page 165). Be certain that the whites are absolutely free of even a trace of yolk. Place the yolks in a medium mixing bowl. Place the whites in a mixing bowl and add the cream of tartar.

6. Stir a few tablespoons of the warm soufflé base into the egg yolks, then stir the yolks into the rest of the base.

7. In a mixer with the whisk attachment, beat the egg whites until soft peaks form that do not fall over when you lift the whisk. The egg whites should still slip just a little in the bowl. Stir one-quarter of the beaten whites into the soufflé base. Then carefully fold the rest of the whites into the base. Fill the prepared muffin cups with the soufflé mix. Place the soufflés in the oven on the baking stone and turn the oven up to 450°F/232°C. Bake until the soufflés are well puffed but not brown, about 5 to 10 minutes.

8. Season the reduced cream with the remaining ½ teaspoon (3 g) salt and ⅛ teaspoon (pinch) white pepper. Move the gratin dish of hot cream to a trivet on a clean counter top. When the soufflés are risen and set, turn the muffin pan upside down and dump the soufflés into the hot cream. If a soufflé falls onto the counter, scoop up with a spatula and place it in the cream.

9. The soufflés will fall at first, but they will puff up again during the second baking. Sprinkle Gruyère over the top of the soufflés and return them to the oven. Bake until the cream is bubbly and the cheese melts and begins to brown, about 4 minutes. Serve with a large serving spoon. Be sure to serve a generous portion of cream with each soufflé.

VARIATION: Stir in any desired cooked ingredients right after you have dumped the soufflés into the hot cream. Fresh crabmeat or pieces of cooked chicken are wonderful.

NOTE: These soufflés can be dumped into reduced cream, then refrigerated and held—even overnight—and reheated when ready to serve. The puff may fall, but the hot cream repuffs them. They may not be quite as high as they were when served directly, but there is a hardly discernible difference.

Soufflés At a Glance

What to Do	Why
Use a scrupulously clean bowl and beaters for beating egg whites.	Any oil or grease will wreck an egg-white foam.
Use fresh egg whites.	Fresh egg whites take slightly longer to beat and yield slightly less volume than older whites, but they are more stable and make better soufflés.
Use room-temperature eggs.	The length of time it takes to beat egg whites is inversely related to how cold the whites are. The colder the whites, the longer the beating time. Warmer eggs are also easier to separate.
Separate the eggs using the Three-Bowl Method described on page 165.	Even a trace of egg yolk will wreck an egg-white foam.
Use a copper bowl or add $1/8$ teaspoon cream of tartar per egg white for beating.	To get a more stable foam that will hold up better in cooking.
If the recipe calls for sugar, add when soft peaks form when the beaters are lifted.	Adding sugar too early reduces the volume and requires longer beating time.
Have the base warm when you fold in the beaten whites.	A warm base will give you a warm batter that will rise better.
Run a clean thumb around the edges of the soufflé before baking.	Helps the soufflé rise straight up.

Classic Buttercreams

Just as there are a number of buttercreams made with confectioners' sugar (page 141), there are also a number of classic buttercreams. Swiss and Italian buttercreams are made with egg whites, French buttercreams are made with egg yolks or whole eggs, and crème anglaise buttercreams are made with custard. Let's take a quick look at ingredients and techniques.

INGREDIENTS

With the eggs, butter, and sugar in buttercream, the primary concern is that they are fresh and of high quality. When a shortening with emulsifiers, such as Crisco, is substituted for part of the butter in Swiss or Italian buttercreams, it provides a little more stability and enables the buttercream to hold up better in a warm room.

TECHNIQUES

Pouring Hot Syrup

When you are making an Italian meringue, and some buttercreams, you need to pour a very hot sugar syrup slowly and steadily into an egg foam with the mixer running on high speed, taking care not to hit the beaters or the side of the bowl. To make this tough job a little easier, some bakers, Rose Levy Beranbaum included, recommend pouring the hot syrup into a 2-cup (473-ml) heatproof measuring cup with a spout first and then pouring from this. Certainly, pouring from a measuring cup is much easier than pouring from a heavy saucepan.

Just before adding the hot syrup, rinse the cup in the hottest tap water and dry it well. It seems to be asking a lot of even Pyrex to pour 248°F/120°C syrup into a cold glass cup.

Combining Egg Foam and Butter

A buttercream is essentially whipped butter lightened with an egg foam. We have been careful to keep fat away from our meringues (egg-white foams). How are we going to pull this off?

SWISS AND ITALIAN BUTTERCREAMS

There are two types of lighter egg-white buttercreams. Swiss buttercream is made with Swiss meringue combined with beaten butter, and Italian buttercream uses an Italian meringue combined with beaten butter.

Swiss and Italian buttercreams are made with only egg whites—no whole eggs or yolks—and do not have the emulsifiers that yolks provide. Consequently, they are less stable. To make these magnificent egg-white buttercreams a little more stable and enable them to hold up under warmer conditions, many pastry chefs substitute a little shortening with emulsifiers, such as Crisco, for part of the butter.

I asked Chef Heather Hurlbert of the Cherokee Town Club in Atlanta, Georgia, which buttercream was better for a large, busy pastry kitchen. She felt that the Swiss buttercream has many advantages. Large kitchens frequently have many apprentices and an inexperienced chef may not realize how crucial the syrup temperature is in making Italian buttercream. If a busy chef takes the syrup off the heat a few degrees below the set temperature, it means there will be more water in the buttercream, which can cause the emulsion to break.

Swiss buttercream is easier to make than Italian buttercream, because you do

Egg white–based Swiss and Italian buttercreams are missing the emulsifiers found in egg yolks. To make the buttercream more stable, substitute a little shortening with emulsifiers, such as Crisco, for part of the butter.

The temperature of a syrup indicates its water concentration. In making an Italian meringue, if the syrup is not allowed to reach the correct temperature it can contain too much water and possibly cause the buttercream to separate.

Emulsions

Emulsions are a combination of two liquids that usually do not mix, such as oil and water. To make an emulsion, you need to break one liquid into tiny droplets while at the same time making the other liquid "juicy" (break its surface tension) so that it can run between the droplets.

What emulsifiers do that is vital to holding the two liquids together is to break the surface tension, or the "pull into itself," of one of the liquids. This allows the liquid to flow freely between the droplets of the other liquid, preventing these droplets from coming together (coalescing) and the mixture from separating.

Any of the classic buttercreams can look curdled if the ingredients are too cool, because the butter is not soft enough to act as a liquid. French buttercream is the most stable because of all the emulsifiers in the egg yolks.

Water-Type Liquid in Buttercreams

There are two kinds of emulsions—oil-in-water emulsions like mayonnaise, and water-in-oil (fat) emulsions like butter.

In mayonnaise, the emulsifiers in the egg yolks reduce the surface pull of the water-type liquid (lemon juice). When you very slowly drizzle the oil into the egg and lemon juice in the blender, you break the oil into tiny droplets. As you add more oil, the tiny droplets become tightly packed in the water-type liquid and the mayonnaise thickens.

Emulsifiers in dairy products reduce the surface tension of the fats and allow tiny droplets of water to be held in the fat. Buttercreams are just such a water-in-fat emulsion. Most directions in buttercream recipes tell you to beat the butter into the egg foam that has been partially cooked with hot syrup. When you have an egg-white foam without emulsifiers from the yolks, and also have a small amount of butter, there may not be enough emulsifiers to hold the emulsion, so the buttercream looks curdled. As you add more butter, as long as it is not too cool, the emulsion forms nicely.

To successfully combine the butter with these egg-white foams, beat the butter until very soft and fluffy, and also substitute a little shortening with emulsifiers for some of the butter. Then, carefully fold about one-quarter of the foam into the butter to further lighten it. Finally, fold the rest of the foam and the butter mixture together.

With the French buttercream you use an egg-yolk or whole-egg foam, and therefore have plenty of emulsifiers—you can simply beat the butter into the foam a little at a time. The only reason for this buttercream to appear curdled is that it is too cold for the butter to act as a liquid.

not have to pour a hot sugar syrup into a batter in a fast-running mixer. Also, Swiss buttercream can be made more stable and suitable for use on cakes that must stand in a hot room by substituting a shortening with emulsifiers for about one-quarter of the butter.

Swiss Buttercream

MAKES ENOUGH TO ICE ONE 9-INCH (23-CM) LAYER CAKE

With this buttercream, you do not have to deal with pouring hot sugar syrup. Also, a small amount of shortening with emulsifiers makes the buttercream more stable and enables it to hold up at warm room temperature. Step 1 in this recipe is essentially a Swiss meringue.

What This Recipe Shows

Cream of tartar speeds up the unwinding of the egg-white proteins and aids in forming and stabilizing the meringue.

A small amount of shortening with emulsifiers helps to hold the buttercream together and enables it to hold up better in a warmer room.

---

1 cup (7 oz/198 g) sugar
½ teaspoon (1.5 g) cream of tartar
4 large egg whites (4 oz/113 g)
1 cup plus 2 tablespoons (9 oz/255 g)
    unsalted butter

7 tablespoons (3 oz/85 g) shortening with
    emulsifiers (such as Crisco)
1 teaspoon (5 ml) pure vanilla extract

1. Stir the sugar and cream of tartar together, then stir both into the egg whites in a mixing bowl. Heat the bowl over a hot water bath (about 140°F/60°C), stirring constantly until the egg-white mixture reaches 120 to 130°F (49 to 54°C). Do not overheat. (You may be able to use only the pilot light of a gas stove to keep the water bath warm.) Stirring gently, keep the whites at this temperature for about 2 minutes. Then move the warm whites immediately to a mixer and beat on high speed for 5 minutes. Lower the speed and beat for 5 more minutes until cool and stiff.

2. Transfer the meringue from the mixer to another bowl. In the mixing bowl, with the whisk attachment, whip the butter, shortening, and vanilla until very light and fluffy. With a large spatula, fold about one-quarter of the meringue into the butter to lighten it—then fold the rest of the meringue into the butter mixture.

Italian Buttercream

MAKES ENOUGH TO ICE ONE 9-INCH (23-CM) LAYER CAKE

Italian meringue makes a wonderfully light, but fragile, buttercream. It is missing the emulsifiers found in egg yolks that you have in French buttercreams made with whole eggs or yolks. For this reason, I like to substitute a little shortening with emulsifiers for part of the butter to help hold the emulsion together. Also, the icing with a little shortening holds up better in a warm room than an all-butter icing.

What This Recipe Shows

Cream of tartar speeds up the unwinding of the egg-white proteins and aids in forming and stabilizing the meringue.

Adding a little sugar to the beaten egg whites when they reach the soft peak stage helps to prevent overbeating before the syrup is added.

Adding corn syrup to the sugar syrup avoids crystallization.

Pouring the hot syrup into a heatproof glass measuring cup with a spout makes it easier to avoid the beaters when drizzling it into the meringue.

Adding a little shortening with emulsifiers makes a more stable emulsion and also helps the buttercream to hold up better in a warm room than a buttercream made with butter alone.

1½ cups (12 oz/340 g) unsalted butter, cut in
    2-tablespoon (1-oz/28-g) pieces
6 large egg whites (6 oz/170 g)
1 teaspoon (3 g) cream of tartar
2 cups (14 oz/397 g) sugar, divided
1 tablespoon (15 ml) light corn syrup
½ cup (118 ml) water

⅔ cup (4 oz/113 g) shortening with
    emulsifiers (such as Crisco)
1 tablespoon (15 ml) pure vanilla extract, or
    2 tablespoons (30 ml) Grand Marnier,
    Frangelico, or other liqueur of choice
¼ teaspoon (1.5 g) salt

1. Read Egg-White Foams and Meringues At a Glance (page 194) and follow precautions—scrupulously clean bowl and beater. Place the butter on the counter to soften slightly while you are preparing the meringue.

2. In a mixer with the whisk attachment, beat the egg whites and cream of tartar, slowly at first, then building up speed. Beat on medium-high until soft peaks form when the beater is lifted. Beat in ¼ cup (1.8 oz/50 g) of the sugar a little at a time. Let the whites stand while you make the syrup, and until the syrup is near 248°F/120°C.

3. In a heavy unlined saucepan, bring the remaining 1¾ cups (12.3 oz/347 g) sugar, the corn syrup, and the water to a boil. Rinse down the sides of the pan with water on a pastry brush, attach a candy thermometer, and boil the syrup until it reaches 248°F/120°C (hard-ball stage).

4. Turn the mixer back on and continue beating whites until stiff peaks form. Ideally, have the whites stiff when the syrup reaches 248°F/120°C. Rinse a 2-cup (473-ml) heatproof glass measuring cup with a spout with the hottest tap water available and dry well. When the syrup reaches 248°F/120°C, pour it into the measuring cup and immediately drizzle the hot sugar syrup into the meringue while beating on medium speed. Try to avoid drizzling the syrup on the beaters or the sides of the bowl. The meringue will swell dramatically and fill the whole bowl. Beat until the meringue has cooled, over 5 minutes. The meringue is essentially cooked but it is still snow-white. Carefully remove the meringue from the mixing bowl to another bowl.

5. In the mixing bowl, with the whisk attachment, whip the softened butter, shortening, flavoring, and salt until very light and fluffy. With a large spatula, stir about one-quarter of the meringue into the butter, then very carefully fold the rest of the meringue into the butter mixture.

6. You can use the buttercream immediately or store it tightly sealed in the refrigerator for up to 4 days, or in the freezer for up to 1 month. Thaw in the refrigerator and rewhip with the paddle attachment.

FRENCH BUTTERCREAMS

If you are making a French buttercream, the egg yolk contributes plenty of emulsifiers to hold the emulsion together. You simply beat the butter into the egg foam. Your only problems can come from either the egg mixture being too cold, so that the butter isn't soft enough to act as a liquid, or trying to incorporate too much liquid.

Roland Mesnier says that he loves the lightness and mousse-like texture of Italian buttercream and will use it on cakes that are made and served the same day. But, for cakes that are made more than a day in advance, he uses French buttercream, which is made with yolks, whole eggs, or a mixture, and is more stable because of all the emulsifiers in egg yolks.

Roland gives a recipe for whole-egg buttercream in *Dessert University*. Although most French buttercreams are made with yolks, I think that the whole-egg buttercream is a breath lighter, while still luxuriously rich. And this is a really good idea for those of us less experienced than professional pastry chefs. Drizzling hot syrup into yolks alone can result in lumps of cooked yolk (yolks cook between 150 and 158°F/66 and 70°C), but drizzling hot syrup into beaten whole eggs is a little safer (whole beaten eggs cook at about 165°F/74°C).

Silky French Buttercream à la Roland Mesnier

MAKES ABOUT 7 CUPS (1.7 L)

This is a magnificent pure silky, rich adornment for a most elegant cake. If you are a purist and long for more yolks, by all means substitute 2 yolks for 1 egg and go with 2 yolks and 4 whole eggs.

What This Recipe Shows

Adding corn syrup to the sugar syrup avoids crystallization.

Pouring the hot syrup into a heatproof glass measuring cup with a spout makes it easier to avoid the beaters when drizzling the syrup into the meringue.

---

5 large eggs, in the shells
2 cups (14 oz/397 g) sugar
1 tablespoon (15 ml) light corn syrup
1/2 cup (118 ml) water
2 1/2 cups (20 oz/567 g) unsalted butter, softened

1 tablespoon (15 ml) pure vanilla extract, or up to 1 1/2 tablespoons (22 ml) Grand Marnier, Frangelico, Chambord, or pear brandy
1/8 teaspoon (pinch) salt

1. Place the eggs (in their shells) in a bowl and cover with several inches of very hot tap water. While you are gathering ingredients, pour the water off one time (it will have cooled after a few minutes) and cover again with very hot tap water.

2. In a mixer with the whisk attachment, beat the eggs until very light and silky, like thick mayonnaise.

3. In a heavy unlined saucepan, bring the sugar, corn syrup, and water to a boil. Rinse down the sides of the pan with water on a pastry brush, attach a candy thermometer, and boil the syrup until it reaches 248°F/120°C (hard-ball stage).

4. Rinse a 2-cup (473-ml) heatproof glass measuring cup with the hottest tap water available and dry well. When the syrup reaches 248°F/120°C, carefully pour the hot syrup into glass measuring cup with a spout and then, with the mixer running on high speed, drizzle the hot syrup into the eggs. Try to avoid the beater or the sides of the bowl. Beat until the mixture reaches warm room temperature, not cool.

5. In another bowl with a hand mixer, beat the butter, flavoring, and salt until soft and light. Turn the mixer containing the egg foam to medium speed. Spoon the butter into the egg foam, a little at

a time, until all is added. If the mixture is not warm enough, it may look curdled, but just keep adding the butter; it will all come together.

6. You can use the buttercream immediately or store it tightly sealed for up to 4 days in the refrigerator or up to 1 month in the freezer. Thaw in the refrigerator and rewhip with the paddle attachment before using.

Bruce Healy's Italian Meringue—Lightened French Buttercream

Many pastry chefs add a little Italian Meringue, page 186, to French buttercream to lighten the buttercream. Since home cooks may not have Italian meringue on hand, in *The Art of the Cake* Bruce Healy has a recipe that combines the making of a small amount of Italian meringue in the beginning steps of making French buttercream. He starts the recipe as if making an Italian meringue, beating on high 2 or 3 egg whites with cream of tartar, and then drizzles in sugar syrup made with 1¾ cups (12.5 oz/354 g) sugar. When three-quarters of the syrup has been added, he whips in 5 egg yolks, added all at once, and then drizzles in the remaining syrup. Finally, he beats in 2¼ cups (18 oz/510 g) butter a little at a time.

CRÈME ANGLAISE (CUSTARD-BASED) BUTTERCREAMS

Crème anglaise (custard-based) buttercreams are wonderfully smooth and rich in taste. They taste lighter and creamier than a French buttercream. The egg yolks are totally cooked like a crème brûlée, adding a creamy custardy taste to the buttery flavor.

This is an ideal buttercream to flavor with coffee. You are limited in the amount of liquid that you can add to a buttercream and still maintain the emulsion, so you cannot add much liquid coffee. The crème anglaise preparation allows you to steep real coffee beans in the milk, eliminating the need to use instant coffee powder as is frequently done in many other coffee buttercream recipes.

I patterned this recipe after Roland Mesnier's in *Dessert University*. Roland said that he included it in his book because he had so many requests for it through the years.

The amount of liquid used in a buttercream is a tricky thing. You can only incorporate a few tablespoons of liquid into the butter without getting into trouble with the emulsion. I think the reason that Roland's recipe successfully incorporated almost 2 cups (473 ml) of thin custard is that the custard contains 8 egg yolks (an incredible amount of emulsifiers) so the custard is a sturdy emulsion itself. Also, Roland's technique for incorporating the custard and the butter may allow more milk in the buttercream. Other recipes whip the custard, whip in the butter, and then whisk to lighten. Roland whips the butter in mixer with the whisk attachment until it is very light, and then whips in the custard. It is quite possible that aerating the butter first helps make the large addition of custard possible.

Silky Crème Anglaise Coffee Buttercream

MAKES ENOUGH TO ICE ONE 9-INCH (23-CM) LAYER CAKE

A wonderfully smooth and rich buttercream—lighter and creamier than most French buttercreams. You steep crushed coffee beans in the milk, eliminating the instant coffee powder that you may find in other coffee buttercream recipes. (You may omit the coffee for a plain version.)

What This Recipe Shows

Adding some sugar to the coffee-flavored milk allows you to bring it almost to a boil without curdling.

Heating the stirred custard on direct, but low, heat (not in a double boiler), stirring constantly, and bringing it almost to a simmer ensures that you have gotten it as thick as possible. By heating it on direct heat and bringing it almost to a simmer you may have a small amount of coagulated egg, which can be removed by straining.

Whisking the butter to aerate it well and slowly whisking in the cooled custard allows you to incorporate an unusually large amount of liquid (milk in the custard) into the buttercream.

½ cup (1.2 oz/34 g) whole coffee beans
1¾ cups (414 ml) whole milk
2 cups (14 oz/397 g) sugar, divided

8 large egg yolks (5.2 oz/147 g)
3 cups (24 oz/680 g) unsalted butter, out of
   the refrigerator for about 25 minutes

1. Coarsely crush the coffee beans a little at a time with a mortar and pestle or coarsely grind in a coffee grinder. In a medium saucepan, stir together the milk and coffee and bring to a boil. Remove from the heat, cover, and allow to steep for 10 minutes. Strain through a fine-mesh strainer into a heavy saucepan.

2. Stir ¼ cup (1.8 oz/51 g) of the sugar into the coffee-flavored milk. Place over medium heat and bring almost to a simmer to dissolve the sugar.

3. In a medium bowl, whisk the eggs yolks and the remaining 1¾ cups (12.3 oz/349 g) of sugar together. Whisk in ¼ cup (59 ml) of the hot milk. Then pour the yolk mixture into the saucepan with the remaining hot milk. Heat over low heat, stirring constantly and scraping the bottom of the pot with a flat-end spatula until the custard begins to thicken. Continue heating until almost to a simmer and the custard coats a spoon. Strain into a cool, stainless-steel bowl. To cool, place the bowl of custard in a bowl of ice water and constantly scrape the custard from the sides of the cold bowl with a spatula. The custard will thicken a little more as it cools.

4. In a mixer with a whisk attachment, beat the butter until it is very light and fluffy. Slowly whisk in the cooled custard until light and creamy. Use immediately or keep tightly covered up to 3 days in the refrigerator. Rewhip before using.

Foam Cakes

In chemically leavened cakes, we saw that baking powder and baking soda produce carbon dioxide to inflate air bubbles in the batter. Now we are going to see heat produce steam to inflate the fine bubbles in foams. Here are unbelievably light cakes. They are trapped air held by a strong egg foam. They may be dry, but they are strong enough to hold a generous amount of liqueur-flavored sugar syrup, and can be heavenly.

Foam cakes are frequently referred to as sponge cakes. Technically, foam cakes fall into several categories: egg white–only foam cakes (angel food); whole-egg cakes (with or without extra yolks) with additional fat (génoise and chiffon cakes); and whole-egg cakes (with or without extra yolks) without additional fat (sponge cakes, known to the French as *biscuit,* pronounced Bees-Kwee). We will go into detail on these cakes, one at a time, starting with the one that is probably most familiar to everyone, angel food cakes (below), then génoise (page 219), chiffon cakes (page 231), and sponge cakes (233).

EGG WHITE–ONLY FOAM CAKES (ANGEL FOOD CAKES)

An angel food cake is essentially a meringue with flour added.

The Recipe

According to E. J. Pyler in *Baking Science and Technology,* the proportions for angel food cake are: the weight of the sugar equals the weight of the egg whites, and the weight of the flour is one-third the weight of the sugar. Interestingly enough, Mimi's Magnificent Angel Food Cake recipe (page 218) falls perfectly within these guidelines even though I'm sure that Mimi (Sibyl Moore), a great Southern cook, never heard of "proper proportions" for angel food cakes. My friend Mary Moore, Mimi's granddaughter, has generously shared her grandmother's recipe with us.

Mary is a very talented, successful, hard-working culinary professional here in Atlanta. She started her culinary career at three years old following her mother and Mimi around the kitchen. She has been a chef, kitchen manager, and an actress on national commercials, and is the founder and owner of a thriving business. In 1995, she began Cook's Warehouse, a marvelous cookware shop and cooking school. She now operates three large stores in different areas of Atlanta and is a talented chef.

Ingredients

You want to use very fresh egg whites for stability, and definitely use cream of tartar. Cream of tartar is the acid of choice with a number of advantages over lemon juice or vinegar (acetic acid). Research indicates that the cream of tartar increases volume, whitens the crumb, makes a finer grain, and makes an angel food cake that shrinks less.

Mimi's Magnificent Angel Food Cake does not have any additional water, but some cakes have a little water for a slightly softer, but less stable, foam.

Techniques

Pour the batter into an ungreased pan that has been rinsed with hot water. The warm pan gets the cake off to a good start and any drops of water left just add a little steam.

Cooling upside down allows the cake to stretch, not sink and compress as it cools.

Mimi's Magnificent Angel Food Cake

MAKES ONE 9 OR 10-INCH (23 OR 25-CM) CAKE

A magnificent big cloud of a cake—heavenly delicious! This is from a great Southern cook, Sibyl Moore (Mimi). My friend Mary Moore, the founder of Cook's Warehouse cookware shops and cooking schools, had the great good fortune of getting to spend much of her childhood following her loving Grandmother Mimi around the kitchen in Cullman, Alabama. Mary has generously shared Mimi's recipe with us.

For chocolate lovers, Mary pours a ganache icing over the cake. Any of the ganache recipes, pages 97 to 99, will work just fine.

What This Recipe Shows

Cream of tartar increases the volume, whitens the crumb, produces a finer texture, and makes an angel food cake that shrinks less.

Completely cooling the cake upside down stretches the cake as it cools, producing the lightest texture.

The pan is not greased because the fat can deflate the batter. The pan is rinsed in hot water and not dried. This gives the batter a little warmth.

1$\frac{1}{2}$ cups (10.5 oz/298 g) sugar, divided
1$\frac{1}{8}$ cups (3.5 oz/99 g) sifted cake flour
$\frac{1}{4}$ teaspoon (1.5 g) salt

10 to 12 large egg whites (10 to 12 oz/283 to 340 g), about 1$\frac{1}{2}$ cups (355 ml) of liquid
1$\frac{1}{4}$ teaspoons (4 g) cream of tartar
1 teaspoon (5 ml) pure vanilla extract

1. Arrange a shelf in the lower third of the oven with a baking stone on it and preheat the oven to 375°F/191°C.

2. Read Egg-White Foams and Meringues At a Glance (page 194). Follow precautions—scrupulously clean bowl and beater.

3. In a medium bowl, combine $\frac{3}{4}$ cup (5.3 oz/149 g) of the sugar, the flour, and the salt, and whisk to blend.

4. In a mixer with the whisk attachment, beat the egg whites until frothy, add the cream of tartar, and beat until soft peaks form when the beater is raised. Gradually beat in the remaining $\frac{3}{4}$ cup (5.3 oz/149 g) sugar, beating until very stiff peaks form when the beater is raised slowly.

5. Add the vanilla to the egg-white mixture. Gently sprinkle the flour mixture over the whites in four additions, and fold in quickly but gently. After the last addition, fold a few extra times to make sure that it is well blended, but it doesn't have to be perfect.

6. Rinse a 9 or 10-inch (23 or 25-cm) ungreased tube pan with hot water. Pour in the batter and drop the pan once on the counter to release any air bubbles. Bake 30 to 35 minutes for a 9-inch (23-cm) cake, and 35 to 40 minutes for a 10-inch (25-cm) cake, or until a cake tester comes out clean and the cake springs back when lightly pressed.

7. Remove from oven and invert the pan suspended by the tube on an upside-down metal funnel. Cool completely, upside down, in the pan (1 to 1$\frac{1}{2}$ hours).

8. Loosen around the sides and the tube with a thin metal spatula. Remove the center core of the pan if a removable bottom pan was used, or remove cake from solid pan. Invert onto a serving plate. Serve or wrap airtight.

GÉNOISE

I had considered génoise a strange French cake and, with my technical knowledge, I knew that they had to be bone dry with all those eggs. How totally wrong I was! A liqueur-flavored, sugar-syrup-soaked génoise is like biting into a sip of the best thing that you ever tasted. What joys I have missed not discovering génoise sooner!

Since a génoise is simply trapped air, it is so light that a génoise with fruit, a fruit syrup, and whipped cream is still a "light" cake. Eggs create a strong but light, airy cake. Here is the perfect base for unlimited creations—it can be layers of a magnificent cake, or a single layer cut and elegantly decorated to make delicate petit fours.

Chef Roland Mesnier points out génoise's wonderful chameleon ability to take on the flavors of the soaking solution and the icing to create cakes that are a perfect harmony of ingredients. And a génoise can contribute great flavors itself. For example, when flavored with cocoa powder or espresso powder, a génoise can be magnificent with Silky Crème Anglaise Coffee Buttercream and a Kahlúa soaking solution.

Buttercream icings get firm when refrigerated and can fall off of a baking powder and baking soda–leavened cake in chunks, but buttercreams adhere to génoise, cold or warm.

The Recipe

Adding some extra egg yolks and using the techniques for a stable foam (below) are vital for producing a great génoise. There are some ballpark guidelines for génoise recipes: the weight of flour and sugar are close to equal, and the amount of sugar should not exceed a ratio of 1 to 1.25 to the eggs. In my génoise (page 224), the weight of the flour and the cornstarch is about 3.8 oz (108 g), and the weight of the sugar is about 3.9 oz (110 g). So it does fall within the first guideline.

The weight of the eggs in the recipe is 8.3 oz (235 g), making the ratio of sugar to eggs about 1 to 2—well below the 1 to 1.25 limit.

Ingredients

Eggs + Extra Yolks

According to E. J. Pyler in *Baking Science and Technology,* modern eggs may be deficient in yolk solids, so it is a common practice to add 20 to 50 percent more yolks to whole eggs to improve both their aerating ability and the stability of the foam. E. B. Bennion in *The Technology of Cake Making* says the best amount of yolks to add is 20 percent the weight of the eggs.

Adding more egg yolks to the whole eggs improves their aerating ability and the stability of the foam.

Bruce Healy adds two yolks to his génoise because he needs to reduce the effect of the higher-protein all-purpose flour that he uses. He also adds potato starch to reduce the overall protein content.

Even though I am using cake flour and don't have to fight for a fine texture in my génoise recipe (page 224), I went with the 20 percent addition of yolks for stability and better aeration.

Flour

Flour in génoise is sifted in small amounts over the egg foam and folded or beaten in on the lowest speed. If this is not done carefully, tiny clumps of white flour will be very visible in the final cake.

Some bakers use a mixture of all-purpose flour and cornstarch. I really like cake flour, not just for its silky, fine texture, but also for its acidity, which helps the foam set beautifully. Cake flour's fine texture makes a beautiful génoise.

In the Techniques section, below, I explain how to add a little sugar to the flour to aid in its blending into the egg foam.

Butter

You will have a lighter génoise without butter, and one that absorbs syrup better; however, if you add enough butter (Roland Mesnier's recipe is 4 tablespoons for 4 eggs) you can have a wonderfully buttery taste. Sherry Yard uses even more. If you want to go for sensational flavor you can use browned butter or, as Kate Zuckerman, the talented pastry chef at Chanterelle, does, you can add a split vanilla bean to your butter as you are browning it. Wow! Colossal flavor! But, remember, you get an incredibly light génoise that is quite marvelous with liqueur-flavored syrup and no fat at all.

Whipped Cream

By all means, try a génoise once with lightly whipped heavy cream instead of butter. I noticed that Flo Braker uses whipped cream in one of her génoise recipes. With my love of the taste of cream, this was a natural for me.

Techniques

Temperature

Temperature is important. I use an instant-read thermometer, but you can use body temperature—you are 98.6°F/37°C—so as you will see, you want the foam just barely cool at 86 to 90°F/30 to 32°C. You heat the eggs, sugar, and salt so that the foam comes up faster; however, too much heat produces a foam with poor stability. You will have large bubbles that combine, float to the top, and pop! According to Bennion, the best beating temperature is 70°F/21°C. Below 70°F/21°C, the foam comes up much slower and never reaches full volume.

Pyler says that the rate of foam formation and foam stability depend on the temperature, which should be between 75 and 80°F/24 and 27°C.

This would seem to be a contradiction to the traditional heating of the mixture to 90 to 110°F/32 to 43°C. But, remember that European room temperature is much cooler than U.S. room temperature; it could well be that some initial heating was necessary to have the mixture at the desired 70°F/21°C for a major part of the beating.

In Gaston Lenôtre's génoise directions, he heats the egg mixture over—not touching—boiling water with constant whisking for 1 minute only, and he further cautions, "Do not overheat the egg mixture . . . or the génoise will dry out too fast when baking."

Roland Mesnier is very specific: heat the mixture to between 86 and 90°F/30 and 32°C. I have a feeling that Roland is right on. If you start between 86 and 90°F/30 and 32°C, your initial beating will probably not be below 80°F/27°C and a fair amount of the beating will take place in Pyler's proclaimed 75 to 80°F/24 to 27°C—the best temperature for foam formation and foam stability.

Bruce Healy directs you to whisk the egg foam over—not touching—simmering water until warm (about 100°F/40°C), frothy, and pale yellow.

Basically, you do not want the mixture ice cold but, rather, practically neutral to the touch—no more than 90°F/32°C.

Beating the Egg Foam

For génoise your goal is to get a thick egg foam of very fine bubbles. The warmed eggs and sugar will foam up to triple their volume, but patience is required. Lenôtre recommends beating on high speed for 2 minutes, then 5 minutes more on low speed. Roland Mesnier cautions that reducing the speed when you are whipping the eggs is vital because lengthy whipping at high speed produces large air bubbles, which will rise to the surface and pop during baking and produce a heavy cake. It is the same principle as overleavening a shortened cake (see page 48). Roland's beating times are 5 minutes on high and 12 minutes on medium, until the foam is completely cool, thick, and shiny.

In *Baking Boot Camp,* Darra Goldstein describes Chef Paul Prosperi showing the students how to observe the foam during beating. When beaten on high, eventually the foam falls, and the same happens when beating on low. But when beaten on medium, the foam remains high regardless of the beating time.

As beating time on medium speed is extended, the stability of the foam increases. Some chefs recommend beating on medium speed the entire time. Pyler says that, as beating time is extended, the stability of the foam increases. The one thing all agree on is that a stable, fine foam takes time—from Lenôtre's 7 minutes to Wayne Gisslen's "it may take as long as 15 minutes" to Roland's 17 minutes. Most of my recipes use a time of 12 to 17 minutes.

Adding Sugar to Flour

The step of folding the flour into the very light egg foam is an extremely delicate one. There is the problem of having little white clumps of flour in the baked cake.

Adding a little sugar to the flour aids in blending the flour into the batter. Flo Braker first brought to my attention the technique of adding a little sugar to the flour for easier blending of the flour into the batter. I believe she said that she got this technique from Lenôtre. He adds vanilla sugar to his flour. The slight difference in texture with the added sugar makes spreading the flour across the top of the batter easier.

Folding In the Flour

As mentioned, the folding in of the flour is a delicate step. You can clearly see lumps of flour in the finished cake if this is not done carefully.

Pastry chefs have mentioned the problem of flour sticking to the edge of the bowl. If you scrape it down into the batter, you will have permanent white flour lumps. Some chefs recommend spreading a little of the foam batter up the side of the bowl to pick up flour. I have a feeling that a little sugar in the flour will also help with this problem.

My daughter, Terry Infantino, who tests recipes for me, has not had formal pastry chef's training, and she feels insecure folding. She prefers sifting a light coating of flour on the batter and then beating on low speed until the flour is incorporated, stopping the mixer, sifting another layer of flour, and again beating in on low speed. She continues in this manner until all the flour is incorporated. She found that working in this careful way that she would never have any flour lumps. You may find this a comfortable way to incorporate the flour, too.

Flour First or Fat First?

Most chefs recommend folding the flour in before the fat. Bruce Healy says that the flour aids in reducing the fat's deflating the foam. Pyler says, "the fat must be added at the final mixing stage to minimize the loss in volume."

> Add the flour before you add the fat. The fat must be added at the final mixing stage to minimize the loss in volume.

A Small Amount of Batter Added to Butter First

Folding anything into the foam can be tricky, so I love the technique of blending a cup of the batter with the butter or cream first, and then folding this mixture into the rest of the batter.

Baking

You should grease and flour the pan, and definitely line the bottom with parchment. Since the cake sets around the edge first, starting in the center, you should smooth the batter level in the pan.

Baking time for a 9-inch (23-cm) round pan at 375°F/191°C is 20 to 30 minutes, depending on your oven. The cake surface should be dry, but not have a hard crust. The center should slightly spring back to the touch. A toothpick or the tip of a thin knife inserted into the center of the cake should come out dry. Ideally, the cake should just be pulling away from the sides right after you take it out of the oven.

Immediately after removing the cake from the oven, run a thin knife or thin spatula around the edge between the cake and the pan so that the cake can settle as it cools. Allow it to cool 3 to 5 minutes in the pan on a cooling rack, then invert the cake onto the cooling rack, remove the pan, peel off the parchment, and reinvert the cake onto another rack. If you allow the cake to cool upside down on the rack, you will have ridges from the rack on top of the cake.

Improved Génoise

This is truly captured air. The cake is so light that when the whole cake is in your hand, you hardly feel anything. When you fold in the butter, the cake definitely becomes heavier and, as Roland Mesnier says, if he is using a flavored syrup he prefers not to add the butter—the cake absorbs the syrup better if you do not add the butter. I always want to add the syrup because I think that the génoise is dry without it. I love Flo Braker's technique of adding a little whipped cream instead of butter. Feel free to leave the butter out, or to go with a little whipped cream. I like the French Buttercream icing (page 214) flavored with the same liqueur used in the soaking solution.

What This Recipe Shows

Beating on high speed creates larger bubbles, which can run together, float to the top, and pop! creating a heavier cake. So it is important to beat right at or just below medium speed for smaller bubbles for the last part of the beating.

Longer beating on medium speed makes the foam more stable.

Extra egg yolks improve aeration and stability of the foam.

Adding a littler sugar to the flour makes it a little easier to blend into the batter.

Blending the butter with a cup of the batter first makes it easier to thoroughly incorporate into the batter.

Egg-foam cakes like génoise are strong enough to hold a soaking liqueur-flavored syrup.

Nonstick cooking spray with flour

6 large eggs, in the shells

1/2 cup plus 1 tablespoon (4 oz/110 g) sugar, divided

3/4 cup (3 oz/85 g) spooned and leveled cake flour

3 tablespoons (0.8 oz/22 g) cornstarch

1/8 teaspoon (pinch) salt

1 teaspoon (5 ml) pure vanilla extract

2 to 4 tablespoons (1 to 2 oz/28 to 56 g) butter, browned butter, or vanilla browned butter, or 1/4 cup (59 ml) heavy cream whipped until soft peaks form when beater is lifted, optional. If you are going to use a syrup, I recommend not using this optional butter or whipped cream (see Butter, page 221).

Génoise Syrup (recipe follows)

1. Arrange a shelf in the lower third of the oven with a baking stone on it and preheat the oven to 375°F/191°C.

2. Spray a 9 x 2-inch (23 x 5-cm) round cake pan with nonstick cooking spray with flour, and line with a parchment circle.

3. Place the eggs in a bowl and cover by several inches with very hot tap water. While you are gathering the rest of the ingredients, hold the eggs, drain the water, and cover again with hot tap water.

4. In a medium bowl, beat together well 1 tablespoon (0.4 oz/11 g) of the sugar, the flour, cornstarch, and salt. Set aside until needed.

5. Separate 2 eggs, reserving the yolks, using the Three-Bowl Method (page 165).

6. In a large skillet, heat about 2 inches (5 cm) of water to 110°F/43°C. Rinse a mixer bowl with tap water as hot as possible to warm, then dry well. Whisk 4 whole eggs, 2 egg yolks, and the remaining ½ cup sugar together in the warm bowl. Check the temperature of the mixture. You want to get the mixture between 86 and 90°F/30 and 32°C. This is not warm, but feels almost neutral—just barely cool to touch. You may not need any further heating. If the temperature of the mixture is lower than 86°F/30°C, place the bowl with the eggs into the warm water in the skillet. Whisk constantly. Keep whisking and checking the temperature until you get the mixture to between 86 and 90°F/30 and 32°C.

7. Place the bowl of warm egg mixture on the mixer with the whisk attachment. Beat on high speed for 2 minutes only. Turn the speed down to medium or just below medium and beat for 10 minutes, until the foam is completely cool, thick, and shiny.

8. Sift part of the flour mixture on top, avoiding the edges of the bowl. Very carefully fold once only by dipping a large spatula into the foam at the 12 o'clock position, dragging it across the bottom. At the 6 o'clock position, lift up some foam and spread it across the top. Sift more of the flour mixture and fold again. Try to incorporate all the flour in about three to five batches and fold carefully to blend.

9. If you are adding the optional melted butter, browned butter, or whipped cream, place it in a medium mixing bowl with the vanilla. Spoon in 1 cup (237 ml) of the batter and fold together. When this is well blended, fold this mixture into the main batter.

10. Pour the batter into the prepared pan.

11. Place in the oven on the hot baking stone and bake for about 20 minutes. The surface should be dry but not a hard crust. The center should slightly spring back to the touch. A toothpick or thin knife inserted in the center should come out almost dry. Immediately after removing the cake, run a thin knife or a thin spatula around the edge between the cake and the pan so that the cake can settle as it cools.

12. Allow the cake to cool 3 to 5 minutes in the pan on a cooling rack, then invert the cake onto the rack, remove the pan, peel off the parchment, and reinvert the cake onto another rack. (If you allow the cake to cool upside down on the rack, you will have ridges on the top from the rack.)

13. When the cake is completely cooled, place in the freezer for about 20 minutes. Slice the cake horizontally into 2 layers (see page 39 for basic slicing techniques). Slip a large spatula or a flat removable pan bottom under the top layer and invert it on a cardboard cake circle or serving plate so that the cut side is up. If using a syrup (recipe below), sprinkle 3 to 4 tablespoons (44 to 59 ml) evenly over both layers.

14. Spread a generous portion of icing over the bottom layer. Invert the remaining layer onto the icing so that the cut side is down and the top of the layer is up. Spread the icing over the top and then down the sides.

15. Cover with a cake dome and refrigerate several hours before serving.

Génoise Syrup

A thinner syrup is more easily absorbed. Diluting the Basic Heavy Syrup with water and the liqueur of your choice makes a perfect syrup to sprinkle on génoise layers.

½ cup (118 ml) Basic Heavy Syrup (recipe
    follows)
¼ cup (59 ml) water

¼ cup (59 ml) liqueur of choice (Kahlúa,
    Frangelico, Grand Marnier, framboise,
    Chambord, rum, pear brandy, etc.)

In a bowl, mix together the heavy syrup, water, and flavoring of choice. Reserve until ready to use.

Basic Heavy Syrup

2 cups (14 oz/397 g) sugar
1 tablespoon (15 ml) light corn syrup

1 cup (237 ml) water

In a heavy saucepan, bring the sugar, corn syrup, and water to a boil. Set aside to cool. This can be kept in a sealed container in the refrigerator for up to 3 weeks.

Delicate Hazelnut Génoise

Subtle flavors create a most magnificent cake. It is heavenly good. Combined with a buttercream—an ethereal experience.

What This Recipe Shows

Roasting nuts enhances flavor.

Egg-foam cakes like génoise are strong enough to hold a soaking liqueur-flavored syrup.

---

3 cups (14.6 oz/414 g) blanched hazelnuts
1 recipe Improved Génoise (page 224), made without butter or whipped cream

1 recipe Génoise Syrup flavored with Frangelico (page 226)
1 recipe Silky Crème Anglaise Coffee Buttercream (page 216)

1. Arrange a shelf in the lower third of the oven with a baking stone on it and preheat the oven to 350°F/177°C.

2. Roast the hazelnuts on a baking sheet in the center of the oven until lightly browned, about 10 minutes. When cooled, chop the nuts in the food processor in two batches with quick on/offs until they are ground between a fine and a coarse chop.

3. When Improved Génoise is completely cool, wrap it well and place in the freezer for about 20 minutes to making cutting easier. Slice the génoise horizontally into 2 equal layers (see page 39 for basic slicing techniques).

4. Slip a large spatula or a flat removable pan bottom under the top layer and invert it on a cake cardboard or serving plate, cut side up. Sprinkle each layer with about 4 tablespoons (59 ml) of the Génoise Syrup. Spread the bottom layer generously with buttercream. Place the second layer on top, cut side down. Ice the cake with buttercream and chill in the refrigerator for about 30 minutes.

5. Working over a jelly-roll pan to catch spills, press the hazelnuts into the sides of the cake all around. Cover the cake in a cake container and refrigerate overnight. Use a serrated bread knife to cut the cake, and wipe the knife with a paper towel between each cut.

Génoise At a Glance

What to Do	Why
Heat the egg and sugar mixture to 86 to 90°F/30 to 32°C.	If this mixture is too warm, the bubbles will be large, run into each other, float to the top, and POP and your cake will be heavy.
Starting at 86 to 90°F/30 to 32°C produces a very stable foam.	Beating at room temperature, this starting temperature ends up keeping the foam at between 75 and 80°F/24 and 27°C, which is the ideal temperature for a stable foam for a good portion of the time during foam formation.
When the temperature is right, beat the egg-sugar mixture on high speed for 3 to 5 minutes, then beat on medium for over 12 minutes.	Lengthy beating on medium speed produces a very stable thick foam of fine bubbles.
Add 2 extra egg yolks.	Extra yolks improve the foaming ability and the stability of the foam.
Add a small amount (2 tablespoons) of sugar to the flour.	Makes blending of the flour into the foam easier.
Sift a small portion of flour on the foam, then fold or beat on the lowest speed to incorporate.	Great care must be taken in incorporating the flour to avoid tiny clumps of white flour in the final baked cake.
If you are adding butter, blend it first with a cup of the batter, then fold this mixture into the batter.	This procedure produces a more even blending of the foam and the fat.

Intense Chocolate Lava Cakes

MAKES SIX 4-OUNCE (118-ML) INDIVIDUAL CAKES

These cakes are actually a variation of génoise! Chocolate lovers delight in this dessert. These sensuous individual chocolate cakes ooze dark, rich chocolate lava when you cut into them. The origin of this recipe is reported to be from the Valrhona Chocolates Company. These are superb made with Valrhona chocolate.

What This Recipe Shows

The eggs, yolks, and sugar are beaten on medium speed for a long time (15 minutes) to produce a very stable foam.

Extra yolks are added for both a stable foam and a velvety texture.

To ensure a runny center some chocolate is cut into pieces and pressed in the batter just before they are intentionally underbaked.

Nonstick cooking spray
8 ounces (227 g) semisweet or bittersweet
    chocolate, cut into pieces, divided
1 cup (8 oz/227 g) unsalted butter

3 large eggs (5.25 oz/149 g)
3 large egg yolks (1.95 oz/55 g)
6 tablespoons (2.6 oz/74 g) sugar
5 tablespoons (1.4 oz/40 g) all-purpose flour

1. Arrange a shelf in the lower third of the oven with a baking stone on it and preheat the oven to 325°F/163°C.

2. Spray six 4-ounce (118-ml) custard cups or ramekins with nonstick cooking spray and line the bottom of each with a parchment circle. (I very lightly spray the top of the parchment, too.)

3. Coarsely chop 6 tablespoons (2.3 oz/65 g) of the chocolate and set aside. In a food processor with quick on/offs, chop the remaining chocolate (5.7 oz/162 g) and butter together. Place in a stainless-steel bowl. In a medium skillet, bring 1 inch (2.5 cm) of water to a simmer. Turn off the heat and allow the water to stand for 1 to 2 minutes. Place the bowl of chocolate and butter in the hot water. Stir the chocolate-butter mixture constantly until melted and smooth. Set aside to cool.

4. In a mixer with the whisk attachment, beat the whole eggs, yolks, and sugar on medium speed until pale and thick, a full 15 minutes. Turn the speed to low and blend in the flour. Mix in the melted chocolate and continue to beat until thick and glossy, about 5 minutes.

5. Evenly divide the batter among the custard cups. To each, add 1 tablespoon (0.4 oz/11 g) of the reserved chocolate. Place on the hot baking stone and bake until the outer edge of each cake is done, but the center is jiggly, about 10 minutes. Cool slightly.

6. Run a thin knife around the edge of each cake and invert onto a serving plate. Serve immediately with a scoop of vanilla ice cream, or sweetened freshly whipped cream.

Financiers

Makes about 12 small cakes

This very rich cake was created by a baker in the financial district of Paris and named for his wealthy customers. Pastry Chef Sherry Yard loves this cake. It's a dream cake—just imagine almonds, browned butter, and sugar. It's so good!

And, wonder of wonder, it's easy, and the batter keeps in the refrigerator for up to 2 weeks, ready for you to whip together a great dessert! Chef Sherry uses it to create individual desserts in a hurry. A round of the rich cake is the perfect base for all kinds of creative desserts.

I couldn't resist using a tip from Chef Kate Zuckerman of Chanterelle in New York City for making vanilla browned butter. You add a split vanilla bean to the butter when you are browning it. Flavor, flavor, flavor! I love the traditional financiers—little cakes topped with browned sliced almonds (see photograph insert).

What This Recipe Shows

A vanilla bean and some scrapings from it are added for superflavorful browned butter.

Part of the almond flour is lightly browned for additional flavor.

---

1 cup (8 oz/227 g) unsalted butter
1 plump vanilla bean, split in half lengthwise
Nonstick cooking spray with flour
1¼ cups (3.8 oz/108 g) almond flour (available at Whole Foods, Middle Eastern markets, or from King Arthur Flour (see Sources, page 509)
¾ cup (3 oz/85 g) spooned and leveled cake flour

2½ cups (10 oz/283 g) confectioners' sugar
⅛ teaspoon (pinch) salt
8 large egg whites (8 oz/227 g), room temperature
1 cup (3.2 oz/92 g) sliced unblanched almonds
3 tablespoons (1.5 oz/43 g) butter, melted
3 tablespoons (45 ml) melted and strained orange marmalade, for glaze

1. Place 1 cup (8 oz/227 g) butter in a heavy saucepan. With the tip of a small knife, scrape some of the inside of the vanilla bean into the butter and add the bean to the butter. Heat over medium-low heat until the dairy solids settle to the bottom and begin to brown to a deep gold, about 8 minutes. Remove from the heat, take out the vanilla bean, and allow to cool to room temperature. The butter needs to be melted, but not hot.

2. Arrange a shelf in the lower third of the oven with a baking stone on it and preheat the oven to 350°F/177°C. Spray small round or rectangular pans, miniature savarin rings, or small barquette pans with nonstick cooking spray with flour.

3. Spread half of the almond flour in a baking dish and roast until golden brown, 5 to 10 minutes.

4. With a mixer, beat together on low speed for at least 30 seconds the almond flour, cake flour, confectioners' sugar, and salt. Add the egg whites all at once and beat on medium speed for 3 minutes. Dump in all of the melted vanilla butter, scraping the bottom of the pan to get all of the browned bits. Beat on medium speed for about 3 minutes. Scrape down the sides and across the bottom of the mixing bowl at least once.

5. Pour into the prepared pans. In the photograph insert we used fluted individual tins. Place on the hot baking stone and bake until the small cakes are lightly browned, 15 to 20 minutes.

6. In a small skillet, toss the almond slices with the melted butter and heat with constant stirring until lightly browned.

7. Allow the cakes to cool in the pans on a rack for about 5 minutes, and then carefully remove from the pans and place on the rack to cool completely. Invert the little cakes one at a time out of the pan and place the cakes on a baking sheet. Brush the cake bottoms (now tops) with strained marmalade for a shiny glaze. Sprinkle with the toasted almonds and glaze the top of the almonds too.

8. This batter keeps in the refrigerator for up to 2 weeks. It is actually better made a day ahead. Before using, stir the batter well, scraping the bottom, and beat for 1 minute by hand or with a mixer to warm up and blend together well.

CHIFFON CAKES

General Mills touted their Chiffon Cake, which used vegetable oil in place of shortening, as the first truly original cake in 100 years. Harry Baker, a Los Angeles insurance agent who baked cakes for the movie stars, invented the Chiffon Cake in 1927. For twenty years, he carefully guarded his recipe and baked the cake only for the famous in Hollywood at The Brown Derby Restaurant. Finally, in 1947 he sold his recipe secret to General Mills for the women of America.

In the May 1948 *Better Homes and Gardens* magazine, General Mills presented the recipe with its secret ingredient—vegetable oil—to the world.

Lemon-Orange Cream Chiffon Cake

MAKES ONE 10-INCH (25-CM) TUBE CAKE

A light white cloud of a cake, tender and moist.

What This Recipe Shows

Oil coats flour proteins to prevent gluten formation for an extremely tender cake.

The acidity of cake flour helps the egg proteins to set well.

---

2 cups (8.2 oz/232 g) spooned and leveled
    cake flour
2 teaspoons (0.3 oz/9 g) baking powder
1 teaspoon (3 g) salt
1 cup (7 oz/198 g) granulated sugar, divided
6 large egg whites (6 oz/170 g)
3/4 teaspoon (2 g) cream of tartar
1/2 cup (3.5 oz/99 g) superfine sugar (see
    Note)
5 large egg yolks (3.25 oz/92 g)

1 large egg (1.75 oz/50 g)
1/2 cup (118 ml) canola oil
Zest (grated peel) of 1 large lemon
Zest (grated peel) of 1 medium orange
1 teaspoon (5 ml) pure vanilla extract
1/4 teaspoon (1.2 ml) pure lemon extract
1/4 teaspoon (1.2 ml) pure almond extract
1/2 cup (118 ml) whole milk
1/4 cup (59 ml) heavy cream
Confectioners' sugar, for dusting, optional

1. Arrange a shelf in the lower third of the oven with a baking stone on it and preheat the oven to 325°F/163°C. Have an ungreased 10-inch (25-cm) two-piece tube pan (angel food cake pan) ready.

2. In a medium bowl, with a hand mixer, whisk, or fork, beat together to blend well the flour, baking powder, salt, and 1/2 cup (3.5 oz/99 g) of the granulated sugar. Set aside until needed.

3. Place the egg whites in a mixing bowl and sprinkle the cream of tartar over them. With a mixer, beat the whites slowly for a few seconds, then gradually increase speed to high. If you overbeat the whites, they will not expand in the oven. You want to get some volume before you add the superfine sugar, but if you wait too long to add any sugar, you run the risk of overbeating. Beat just until the foam is white, billowy, and looks like it has very fine bubbles. It should slip a little in the bowl. Start adding the superfine sugar. Add about one-third of the superfine sugar and beat in well and then add one-third more and beat. Continue until all the superfine sugar is beaten in. Set aside until ready to fold into the batter.

4. In another large mixing bowl, beat the egg yolks and whole egg just to blend. Beat in the oil just to blend. Add the lemon and orange zests, and then the vanilla, lemon, and almond extracts. Beat just to blend in. Beat in the remaining ½ cup (3.5 oz/99 g) of granulated sugar. Add about one-quarter of the flour mixture and blend in. Continue adding flour until all is well blended in. On the lowest speed, blend in the milk and then the cream.

5. Add about one-quarter of the beaten egg whites and fold in well. Pile the remaining whites on top and very carefully fold in. Dip a large flat spatula into the back side of the bowl and scrape it across the bottom, picking up batter from the bottom and spreading it across the top of the batter. Rotate the bowl a quarter turn and repeat until you no longer see white streaks in the batter. Pour the batter into the ungreased pan.

6. Place on the hot baking stone and bake until springy to the touch, about 60 to 65 minutes. Invert the pan on a metal funnel to cool upside down.

7. When the cake is completely cool, run a thin knife around the tube and around the edge of the pan. Remove the cake and the tube from the outside rim. Invert the cake onto a flat dish, then reinvert onto a platter. If using, sprinkle with confectioners' sugar or drizzle with a confectioners' sugar icing, page 18.

NOTE: Superfine sugar is perfect because it dissolves fast in meringues, but I have had trouble finding it in my stores. Some large grocery stores carry it with the bar supplies. When I can't find it, I put the required amount of granulated sugar in the food processor with the steel blade and run it for 30 seconds to a minute.

SPONGE CAKES

Recipes for sponge cakes, or *biscuits* (pronounced Bees-Kwee) as the French call them, are all over the place—some made with a whole-egg foam, but many with the eggs separated and the yolks and whites beaten separately. Some are flat roulades, while others are prepared in a tube pan.

Much of the ingredients and techniques information for génoise (pages 219 to 223) apply to sponge cakes. A great technique tip from Bruce Healy: if you sift the flour over the yolk foam and then cover with part of the egg-white foam, you can minimize the folding necessary for an extremely light batter.

La Joconde

This is my favorite sponge cake—an opinion shared by many. The French pastry chefs thought that this sponge cake was so magnificent that they called it "La Joconde" (The Mona Lisa).

In his book *The Art of the Cake,* Bruce Healy fills us in on the history of this splendid sponge cake. Leonardo da Vinci's famous masterpiece, the *Mona Lisa,* was called *La Gioconda* by the Italians. Leonardo and his painting spent the later years of his life in France as the guest of the French king, François I. So it was that the *Mona Lisa* came to reside in France, where it was called *La Joconde.*

The French pastry chefs had incredibly high regard for this sponge cake to name it after the famous work of art. It contains powdered almonds, whole eggs rather than just yolks, and meringue.

Simplified La Joconde

MAKES FOUR 7 X 10-INCH (18 X 25-CM) LAYERS.

I love this magnificent, delicate almond cake. There are many Joconde recipes published in baking books. Bruce Healy's Joconde recipe in *The Art of the Cake* is very close to the original Clichy cake. Dorie Greenspan has Dalloyau's Joconde in the Opera Cake recipe in her book, *Paris Sweets*.

What This Recipe Shows

Folding in the flour and the meringue at the same time minimizes the folding for maximum batter volume.

Cream of tartar adds stability to egg-white foam.

Mixing a little sugar with the flour make blending with the batter a little easier.

Using Release foil avoids sticking.

---

6 large egg whites (6 oz/170 g)
½ teaspoon (1.5 g) cream of tartar
7 tablespoons (3.1 oz/88 g) sugar, divided
2 cups (6.2 oz/176 g) almond flour
2 cups (8 oz/227 g) confectioners' sugar

6 large eggs (10.5 oz/298 g)
½ cup (2.1 oz/58 g) spooned and leveled cake flour
3 tablespoons (1.5 oz/43 g) unsalted butter, melted and cooled

1. Arrange a shelf in the lower third of the oven with a baking stone on it. Place another shelf slightly above the center of the oven and preheat the oven to 425°F/218°C.

2. Line two 15½ x 10½ x 1-inch (39 x 27 x 2.5-cm) jelly-roll pans with Release foil (nonstick side up) or parchment brushed with melted butter and lightly floured.

3. In a mixer with the whisk attachment, beat the egg whites and cream of tartar slowly at first, increasing the speed until on medium-high, and beat until soft peaks form when the whisk is lifted. Add 6 tablespoons (2.6 oz/75 g) of the sugar a little at time until stiff peaks form. If you have only 1 mixing bowl, scoop the meringue into another bowl.

4. In a mixer with the paddle attachment, beat the almond flour, confectioners' sugar, and eggs on medium speed until very light, about 6 minutes.

5. With a fork or whisk, stir together the cake flour and the remaining 1 tablespoon (0.5 oz/13 g) sugar.

6. Sift the cake flour mixture on top of the almond-egg mixture and allow to stand a few seconds. Spread about one-third of the beaten whites on top and fold in. Add the remaining whites and fold in. Stir about 1 cup (237 ml) of batter into the melted butter, then fold the mixture back into the batter. Divide the batter between the two pans. With a long spatula, smooth out and spread evenly over each entire pan.

7. Arrange the two large baking sheets in the oven, one on the hot baking stone and the other on the shelf in the upper portion of the oven. Bake for 5 minutes. Swap baking sheet positions and bake about 5 more minutes, or until lightly browned and the surface springs back when lightly pressed. Remove from the oven.

8. Grab the foil by the ends and pull each cake onto a cooling rack. Cool about 1 minute and then invert onto another rack. Carefully peel the foil off the cakes and reinvert onto a cooling rack so that they are right side up to cool.

9. When the cakes are completely cool, move to a cutting board and, using a ruler and a sharp knife or a large pizza cutter, trim any rough edges and cut each Joconde sheet in half lengthwise to make a total of four 7 x 10-inch (18 x 25-cm) rectangular layers.

Shirley's Simplified Clichy Cake (Opera Cake)

MAKES ONE 7 X 10-INCH (18 X 25-CM) 4-LAYER CAKE

Louis Clichy presented his magnificent cake at the Exposition Culinaire of 1903 in Paris. It has been the signature cake of Clichy's shop on Boulevard Beaumarchais. Paul Bugat, Bruce Healy's collaborator in his fine French pastry books, continues to make the Clichy by the original recipe at this shop.

Dalloyau, a famous pastry shop is Paris, makes a cake called The Opera Cake patterned after the Clichy. It is a delicate almond cake lightly soaked with coffee syrup, layered with coffee buttercream, and topped with chocolate ganache. The original Clichy has a slab of tempered chocolate on top instead of the simple ganache and it also has a layer of ganache in the middle. This requires considerable time for cooling the cake. The ganache is warm and will melt the buttercream. Even if you put the ganache on the almond cake layer, you must get it cold before you can cover it with buttercream. I adore the Joconde almond cake, and I go nuts over the Silky Crème Anglaise Coffee Buttercream. When you are eating this cake, you have only to close your eyes and you are transported to one of the elegant Paris pastry shops.

1 recipe Simplified La Joconde (page 234)
Espresso Syrup (recipe below)

1 recipe Silky Crème Anglaise Coffee
    Buttercream (page 216)
1 recipe Shiny Ganache Glaze (page 97)

1. Prepare all of the component parts above.

2. To assemble, place one layer of the cake on a piece of cake cardboard cut the same size as the layers. Sprinkle with 3 to 4 tablespoons (44 to 59 ml) of the Espresso Syrup. Spread with a layer of the Silky Crème Anglaise Coffee Buttercream.

3. Arrange a second layer of cake on top of the buttercream and sprinkle with 3 to 4 tablespoons (45 to 60 ml) of the espresso syrup. Spread with a layer of buttercream.

4. Place the third layer of cake on top, sprinkle with syrup as before, and spread with buttercream. Arrange the final cake layer on top, and spread with buttercream. Refrigerate for two to three hours to chill through.

5. Make sure that the ganache is about 90°F/32°C. Pour ganache over the top, and tilt to cover and run down the sides. Chill overnight in the refrigerator in a covered cake dish.

Espresso Syrup

A thinner syrup is absorbed easier, so diluting a heavy syrup with water or the liqueur of your choice makes a perfect syrup to sprinkle on génoise layers.

½ cup (118 ml) Basic Heavy Syrup (page 226)

½ cup extra-strong espresso or 1 tablespoon
    instant espresso powder dissolved in ½
    cup (118 ml) water

In a small bowl, mix together the Basic Heavy Syrup and strong espresso or espresso powder dissolved in water. Use as directed in recipe.

Chocolate Pecan Torte with a Hint of Bourbon

MAKES ONE 9-INCH (23-CM) TORTE

Talk about heavenly—roasted pecans and chocolate! If desired, serve in a puddle of sweetened heavy cream, whipped to cream-sauce consistency only.

What This Recipe Shows

Both finely ground nuts and cocoa particles in chocolate can act as flour in flourless cakes.

Melting the chocolate with butter avoids the danger of having the chocolate seize.

A small amount of cream of tartar ensures that the batter will be acidic.

---

1 cup (3.5 oz/99 g) pecans
Nonstick cooking spray
6 ounces (170 g) semisweet chocolate
¾ cup (170 g) unsalted butter
4 large egg yolks (2.6 oz/74 g)
1¼ cups (8.8 oz/248 g) sugar, divided

2 tablespoons (0.8 oz/22 g) potato starch
1 tablespoon (15 ml) bourbon
4 large egg whites (4 oz/113 g)
¼ teaspoon (0.5 g) cream of tartar
1 recipe Shiny Ganache Glaze (page 97)

1. Arrange a shelf in the lower third of the oven with a baking stone on it and preheat the oven to 350°F/177°C.

2. Spread the pecans on a baking sheet. Place the sheet on the hot baking stone. Bake until lightly browned, about 10 minutes.

3. When nuts are completely cool, place them in a food processor with a steel blade and process with quick on/offs until finely chopped. Stop before the nuts get oily and the mixture starts to clump.

4. Increase oven temperature to 375°F/191°C.

5. Spray a 9 x 2-inch (23 x 5-cm) round cake pan with nonstick cooking spray and line with a parchment circle. (I very lightly spray the top of the parchment, too.)

6. Place the chocolate and butter in a microwave-safe bowl. Melt chocolate and butter for 2 minutes in the microwave on 50% power. Allow to cool.

7. In a large bowl, beat the egg yolks and ¾ cup (5.3 oz/150 g) of the sugar until pale. Stir in the chocolate, roasted pecans, potato starch, and bourbon.

8. Place the egg whites and cream of tartar in a mixing bowl. Beat slowly at first, increasing speed until almost on high. Beat until soft peaks form when the beater is lifted. Beat in the remaining ½ cup (3.5 oz/99 g) sugar. Fold one-quarter of the whites into the chocolate mixture. Now fold the lightened chocolate mixture into the remaining whites.

9. Pour the batter into the pan; smooth the top if necessary. Bake until a toothpick in the center comes out with moist crumbs, about 40 to 45 minutes.

10. Cool the cake completely in the pan on a rack. The center will sink a little. Gently press down the outside edge to level. Jar the edge of the pan on the counter to loosen or run a thin knife around the edge, and invert onto an 8-inch (20-cm) cardboard cake circle. Cool completely before icing with Shiny Ganache Glaze.

Roulades or Rolled Sponge Cakes

Basic Formula

The basic formula for a roulade is 100% flour, 200% eggs, and 140% sugar (see page 32 for more about Baker's Percentages). In the Great Flower Cake (recipe follows) the percentages are close to this. The weight of finely ground pecans, which act as flour, is about 3 oz (85 g) per cup or about 6 oz (173 g) for the 1¾ cups in the recipe, and the total weight of the 6 egg yolks (3.9 oz/111 g) plus 6 egg whites (6 oz/170 g) equals 9.9 oz (281 g), which is about 188%, not far from 200%. The sugar comes in at 7 oz (198 g), close enough to the 7.3 oz (207 g) indicated by the formula.

The Great Flower Cake in *CookWise* is a different—but also delicious and spectacular—sponge cake. Here is an updated version. There is a little baking powder in the recipe, but this is essentially a sponge cake. You will find many sponge cake recipes using a little baking powder.

Great Flower Cake

MAKES ONE 12-INCH (30-CM) ROUND CAKE

This is a spectacular cake—a spiral of a dark nut roll and snow-white whipped cream topped with thin slices of strawberries arranged like the petals of a big flower.

What This Recipe Shows

Roasting enhances the flavor of the pecans.

Both finely ground nuts and cocoa particles in chocolate can act as flour in flourless cakes.

When beating the yolks and sugar, 1 tablespoon (15 ml) water is added to ensure dissolving the sugar.

Cream of tartar added to the egg whites helps make a stable foam.

A little shaved or finely crushed ice added to the cream aids in fast whipping.

Roulade

1¾ cups (6 oz/173 g) pecans
½ teaspoon (3 g) salt, divided
6 large egg yolks (3.9 oz/111 g)
1 teaspoon (5 ml) water
1 cup (7 oz/198 g) superfine sugar, divided (see Note 1)

1 teaspoon (5 g) baking powder
1 teaspoon (5 ml) pure vanilla extract
6 large egg whites (6 oz/170 g)
¾ teaspoon (2 g) cream of tartar
Confectioners' sugar, for dusting
Nonstick cooking spray with flour

Whipped Cream and Fruit

2 cups (473 ml) heavy cream
2 tablespoons (30 ml) shaved or finely crushed ice
5 tablespoons (1.3 oz/37 g) confectioners' sugar

2 tablespoons (30 ml) Grand Marnier liqueur, divided
1 quart (946 ml) strawberries, hulled and each cut lengthwise into several slices
½ cup (118 ml) red currant jelly

1. Arrange a shelf in the lower third of the oven. Preheat the oven to 350°F/177°C. Spread the pecans in a single layer on a baking sheet and roast for 10 minutes. Sprinkle with ¼ teaspoon (1.5 g) of the salt. Let cool. Finely chop the pecans in a food processor with the steel blade, using quick on/offs.

2. Turn up the oven to 400°F/204°C. Prepare a 17 x 11 x 1-inch (43 x 30 x 2.5-cm) jelly-roll pan by lining with Release foil, nonstick side up. Alternatively, you can use a nonstick or silicone baking sheet liner (see Note 2) or parchment sprayed with a nonstick cooking spray with flour, or greased with shortening and coated with a light dusting of flour.

3. Place the egg yolks in the bowl of a mixer with the whisk attachment. Add 1 teaspoon (5 ml) water and all but 2 tablespoons (0.9 oz/26 g) of the superfine sugar. Whip on medium speed until well aerated and light in color, about 4 minutes. By hand, stir in the chopped pecans, baking powder, the remaining ¼ teaspoon (1.5 g) salt, and the vanilla.

4. Beat the egg whites and cream of tartar in a clean, dry mixing bowl until soft peaks form when the beater is lifted. Add the remaining 2 tablespoons (0.9 oz/26 g) of sugar and beat in well. Spoon about one-quarter of the beaten egg whites into the yolk mixture with a large spatula. Stir in well to lighten the yolk mixture. Add the rest of the whites to the yolk mixture and gently fold in.

5. Spread the batter evenly in the jelly-roll pan and bake until springy to the touch, 10 to 12 minutes. Dust a clean dish towel heavily with confectioners' sugar. Invert the cake onto the towel and carefully peel off the foil or liner. Let stand to cool thoroughly.

6. For the whipped cream, place a bowl and beaters in the freezer for 10 minutes to chill well. Place the cream in the freezer for 5 minutes to chill. Pour the cream into the chilled bowl. Add the ice and whip to firm peaks. Stir in the confectioners' sugar and 1 tablespoon (15 ml) of the Grand Marnier.

7. Spread the whipped cream evenly in a thick layer on top of the cooled nut cake. With a serrated knife, slice the cake lengthwise into 8 equal strips, about 1⅜ x 17 inches (3.5 x 43 cm). The easiest way to do this is to slice the cake in half lengthwise, slice each half in half lengthwise, and then each piece in half again.

8. To assemble, take one strip and roll it up like a jelly roll. Now turn the spiral over on one side like a cinnamon roll and place it flat in the center of a large serving platter. Take another strip and carefully curl it around the first one to make a larger spiral. Continue adding 1 strip at a time until all 8 strips are used. The cake is now a spiral of dark cake and white whipped cream, about 1⅜ inches (3.5 cm) high and a little more than 10 inches (25 cm) in diameter.

9. Starting at the outside edge, arrange strawberry slices with the tips of the berries pointing outward, overlapping all the way around the outside edge. Arrange another circle just inside the first so that the inner circle overlaps the first circle about halfway. Continue with another overlapping circle inside the first two, and so on, until the entire cake is covered and looks like a great red flower blossom.

10. In a small saucepan, warm the jelly just enough to melt. Stir in the remaining 1 tablespoon (15 ml) Grand Marnier to thin. Brush the entire top heavily with jelly glaze. Refrigerate and serve cold.

VARIATION: Peaches, ripe mangos, or plums may be substituted for the strawberries. Use an appropriate liqueur such as amaretto with peaches or mangos, or Chambord with plums.

NOTES: 1. If you do not have superfine sugar, process granulated sugar in a food processor with the steel blade for about 1 minute.

2. Nonstick silicone baking sheets are available through mail order sources and at kitchen supply stores (see Sources—baking sheet liners, page 507).

Magic Puffs, Pâte à Choux

That such a tiny ball of dough can puff to a great fluffy-looking, crisp pastry is breathtaking—truly magic! And the real magic is that these crisp puffs open up an amazing world of delicate French pastries. The hollow shell begs for a filling of satiny pastry cream. Flavored with hazelnuts, almonds, and caramel, it becomes a Paris Brest, a wheel of pâte à choux celebrating the brave cyclists who endure the grueling Paris-to-Brest-and-back bicycle race.

A little cream puff filled with coffee-flavored or chocolate pastry cream is perched atop a larger filled puff and is covered with a chocolate or mocha glaze to resemble a little nun (Religieuses, page 251). The new bridge in Paris at the end of the sixteenth century (which is now the oldest bridge in Paris) was celebrated with a puff pastry tartelette filled with a mixture of pâte à choux and pastry cream (Pont Neuf, page 254). Pâte à choux is also the basis for simple wonders like Cream Puffs (page 250) and Éclairs (page 251) and elegant pastries like a towering croquembouche.

Bruce Healy in his true masterpiece, *Mastering the Art of French Pastry,* guides you through this amazing world of delicacies. This book is a must for pastry chefs. Unbelievably, it is out of print, so the price is dear!

Pâte à choux can also be savory like the you-can't-eat-just-one nibble, cheesy Gougères (page 255), impressive appetizers like Cocktail Puffs with Escargots (page 259), or a ring of cheesy pastry encasing a savory dish (Turkey Gougère, page 257).

The wonderful thing about pâte à choux is that it is not terribly difficult! This is true bang for the buck. With some attention to detail, you can get breathtaking results.

INGREDIENTS

The basic ingredients are simple enough: water, butter, flour, and eggs. However, the type of liquid (water or milk), the amount of butter, the type of flour, and whether you use all whole eggs or part whole eggs and part whites matter greatly. Let's take a look at the individual ingredients.

Eggs

Both the type of eggs (whole eggs or whites) and the amount of eggs are important. Eggs are not just eggs, but yolks *and* whites. Yolks are nature's great emulsifiers, while whites are incredible drying agents. One of the problems with cream puffs, especially larger puffs, is how to get the puffs dry enough so that they will not collapse. And, even if they do not collapse, medium to large puffs are usually gooey inside in spite of techniques such as puncturing the puff to dry out the inside. Many recipes may even tell you to scoop out the gooey inside.

Until I started teaching it, I had never seen a pâte à choux recipe with anything but whole eggs. But I knew that using part egg whites would give a bigger, crisper puff that would hold up and be easier to dry, and would not be as gooey inside. My puffs made with 1 to 2 whole eggs and 3 whites were great. Since then, I have even talked many people, including my friend Rose Levy Beranbaum, into using whites in puffs.

Now, about the amount of eggs—the more eggs, the more puff. However, we don't want to add too many eggs because the dough must be firm enough to pipe or spoon into balls, or the puffs will not rise.

Flour

High-protein flour, such as bread flour, forms good elastic sheets of gluten and produces higher and lighter puffs. High-protein flour also absorbs more liquid so that the initial liquid-butter-flour dough is firm enough to add at least 3 large eggs or 1 large egg plus 3 whites. Lower-protein flour such as all-purpose does not absorb as much water; a pâte à choux dough made with it will be thinner and fewer eggs can be added. As a result, the puffs will be heavier when made with a lower-protein flour from both using fewer eggs and less gluten formation. Dough puffs much better when there are strong elastic sheets of gluten to hold in the steam.

Liquid

Pâte à choux ordinaire made with water and less butter produces a very light, crisp puff, while pâte à choux spéciale made with milk and a greater amount of butter makes a richer, softer, but not as large puff.

I was taught to make pâte à choux with water, but I noticed in *Dessert University* that Roland Mesnier used whole milk, which I thought was a great idea. The milk gives a richer flavor to the puffs, plus the sugar in the milk makes them brown much better.

Bruce Healy, in *Mastering the Art of French Pastry,* defines the whole situation. Bruce explains that the texture of pâte à choux depends on the choice of milk or water and the amount of butter used. Pâte à choux ordinaire uses water and less butter and is light and crisp, while pâte à choux spéciale with milk is richer and softer and better suited for small pastries. You can also use slightly less water initially (¾ cup instead of 1 cup), but you need the liquid for steam. Rose Levy Beranbaum, in *The Pie and Pastry Bible,* comments that the milk makes the eggs coagulate faster, making smaller puffs. In *The Secrets of Baking,* Sherry Yard uses half water and half milk. I also noticed in *Lenôtre's Desserts and Pastries* that Gaston Lenôtre, the famous French pastry chef, used half water and half milk. Perhaps this is the way to go for the richer version. In my recipes, I have combined all of these techniques.

Fat

The type of fat does not matter much except for flavor. You can make pâte à choux with butter, lard, shortening, margarine, or even olive oil, white truffle oil, or chicken fat. The amount of fat *does* matter. With less fat, you can add more egg and get a bigger puff; with more fat, you get a tenderer puff, and using less butter coats fewer flour proteins, allowing the flour to absorb more liquid. With less butter, you will get more gluten formed and a lighter puff.

Remember, some fats like butter and margarine are only 80 percent fat. If you substitute another fat such as lard, chicken fat, shortening, or oil for the 4 tablespoons (57 g) of butter in my recipe, use only 3¼ tablespoons (49 ml) of the alternative fat.

Ammonium Bicarbonate

This is a chemical leavener like baking soda. It totally evaporates when it reacts—all of its by-products go off as a gas. It can be difficult to find, but may be available from King Arthur Flour or a baking supply shop. It is desirable in products that are baked at a high temperature or baked long enough to dry, such as biscotti. Lisa Yockelson, an outstanding baker, likes to use ammonium bicarbonate in her biscotti.

TECHNIQUES

Mixing

Traditionally, all of the flour is added at once to the hot water and butter mixture and stirred vigorously so that the starch in the flour swells uniformly and does not form any lumps. I have seen Nathalie Dupree very successfully make pâte à choux by making a roux with the butter and flour and then incorporating the water as you would make a sauce or gravy.

Beating in the eggs by hand is tough, but it is easier with either a food processor or a heavy-duty stand mixer with the paddle attachment. Lenôtre cautions not to "work this dough too long or else the puffs will not rise correctly." However, with our higher-protein flour that may not be a problem. I prefer a food processor because it is a fast way to add the eggs, and the dough stays a little warmer, meaning that I can get the puffs in the oven a little warmer. We have real advantages with a higher-protein flour: the puffs rise higher and brown better.

Sticking

Liquid proteins from the eggs in the dough can seep into imperfections in the surface of a pan and then, when heated, literally cook into the pan. Always use a nonstick surface such as the wonderful Release foil (foil with a nonstick surface on one side) or those super-Teflon or silicone nonstick sheets (see Sources—baking sheet liners, page 507) or nonstick cooking spray. If you are caught in a sticky situation without your trusty nonstick cooking spray, use the old double-grease technique used in Step 1 of the Incredibly Creamy Soufflés, page 206. You can also use well-greased foil (or well-greased parchment paper, except in a convection oven). If you brush an egg wash on baked puffs or pastries, be careful not to get any between the puffs and the pan.

Piping and Shaping

You can pipe pâte à choux directly onto your nonstick surface to make round puffs or cylinders for éclairs using a pastry bag fitted with a #6 ($\frac{1}{2}$-inch/1.3-cm) fluted or plain round pastry tip. Bruce Healy says that fluted tips are most frequently used because the grooves make the batter rise more evenly. You can also spoon portions of the dough for puffs, using a teaspoon or tablespoon, depending on the size you want.

Professional pastry chefs have their own techniques for piping and shaping pâte à choux. It was a joy to watch Chef Albert Jorand, who taught baking at La Varenne in Paris, pipe perfectly spaced puffs or éclairs. He insisted they be spaced evenly for even cooking. When he finished piping puffs, he would oil the back of a fork and gently press each puff on the top from one angle and then again at an angle perpendicular to his first press. They would be slightly flattened and have a light crisscross pattern from the fork. This, he said, makes them rise more evenly.

Baking: Heat from the Bottom

Heat from the bottom is vital. You want to get the puffs to rise as much as possible before the heat from the top of the oven makes the puffs crust on top, holding them down. In days gone by, heat in ovens came from a unit in the bottom of the oven. So you could preheat the oven to a lower temperature, put the puffs in, turn the oven up, and be confident that the bottom unit would come on and heat the puffs from the bottom. However, with ovens today you may have no clue where the heat is coming from. They are made to heat up very fast. So, if the oven is preheating or if the oven temperature is much too low, every heating element in the oven comes on, burning any food in the oven.

That is why I use a baking stone to save me. I preheat the oven to a high temperature to get the stone hot. Then I can turn the oven down, leave the oven open for one minute, or even spray a mist of water on the top of the oven (ONLY if the oven has sealed heating elements—with no heating coils exposed) to cool it down. My heavy stone remains hot, so I place the puffs on the hot baking stone and set the oven at the desired baking temperature. I like to mist the tops of the puffs lightly with water just before putting them in. This keeps them moist and rising as long as possible. Creating another source of steam, like pouring boiling water over a pan of hot rocks, as I describe on page 246, is also a great idea.

Shirley's Boston Cream Pie (Page 43)

Sweet Pears and Crunchy,
Roasted Walnut Muffins (Page 133)

Cream Puff (Page 250)

Chocolate-Walnut Frosted
Golden Layer Cake (Page 41)

Shirley Corriher's "Touch-of-Grace"
Southern Biscuits (Page 152)

Rustic Pear Tart (Page 289)

Financiers
(Page 230)

Memorable Silky Chocolate Meringue Pie (Page 336)

Great Shell with Fresh Crabmeat
and Sweet Creamed Corn (Page 364)

Chocolate Crinkle Cookies
(Page 395)

Shirley's Fudgy Brownies (Page 411)
and Shirley's Cakey Brownies (Page 413)

Snowflake Cookie (Page 419)

Roasted Pecan Chocolate Chip Cookie (Page 375)

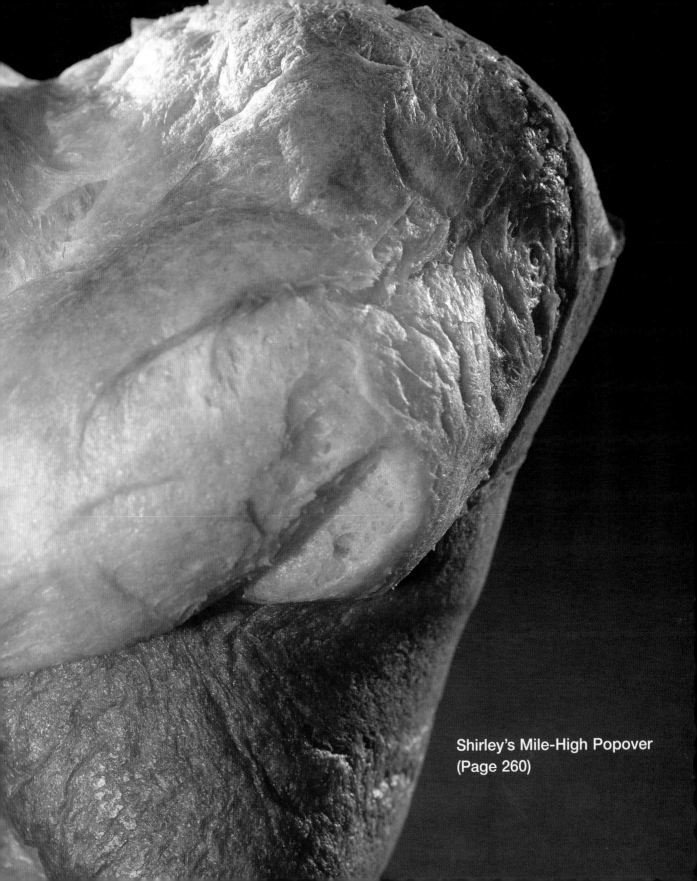

Shirley's Mile-High Popover
(Page 260)

Fougasse (Page 439)

Judy Brady's Blueberries and Bordeaux (Page 269)

Pâte à Choux Ordinaire

MAKES ABOUT 30 HORS D'OEUVRE PUFFS OR ABOUT 15 LARGE PUFFS

This pâte à choux dough rises to a magnificent height and is crisp on the outside and moist but not gooey inside. For a better puff, your goal is to add as many eggs as you can and still have a thick enough dough that will hold its shape when piped or spooned onto the pan. If the dough is too soft and spreads out, it will not rise well. In this recipe you need one slightly packed cup of flour, so I have given measuring directions.

Your overall goal is to have everything warm (the eggs, the pan) so that you will get steam in the dough in the oven faster. You are trying to get the puffs to rise as much as possible before the hot oven crusts the tops and holds them down.

What This Recipe Shows

Using a smaller amount of butter than traditionally used in many recipes allows the flour to absorb more liquid, allowing the addition of more eggs.

High-protein flour like bread flour absorbs more liquid, allowing the use of more eggs, plus a higher-protein flour will form more gluten for a great rise and the puffs will brown better.

Egg whites are incredible drying agents, so using some extra egg whites instead of the usual all whole eggs produces crisp puffs that are still moist but less gooey on the inside.

Starting with a hot baking stone gives you great heat from the bottom to get these puffs to rise fast.

About 2½ cups (593 ml) water, for steam
6 large eggs, in the shells
1 cup (237 ml) water
4 tablespoons (2 oz/57 g) unsalted butter
½ teaspoon (3 g) salt
½ teaspoon (2 g) sugar
⅛ teaspoon (4 drops) pure vanilla extract

1 cup (5.7 oz/162 g) bread flour (measured by scooping and gently packing against the inside of the bag)
1 teaspoon ammonium bicarbonate, available from King Arthur Flour or a bakery supply store, optional
Nonstick cooking spray
1 large egg (1.75 oz/50 g), beaten, for glaze, optional

1. Arrange a shelf in the lower third of the oven with a baking stone on it and preheat the oven to 450°F/232°C.

2. Place a few clean small rocks (about 2 inches/5 cm in diameter each) in a metal pan with 2-inch (5-cm) sides and place the pan on the floor of the oven near the door. You are going to pour about 2 cups (473 ml) of boiling water over the rocks just before you place the puffs in the oven. This will create a steam bath to keep the oven moist for a little while to allow the puffs to rise well before they crust. For the boiling water, place a saucepan with about 2½ cups (593 ml) of water on a back burner and bring to a very low boil.

3. Place the 6 eggs in a bowl and cover them with hot tap water to warm them. As you get other things ready, pour off the water, which will have cooled, and cover the eggs again with hot water.

4. Place a heavy baking sheet on the top of the stove near the back vents so that it will get hot. If you do not have a warm spot such as this, warm the sheet in the oven while you are beating the eggs into the dough.

5. Separate 2 of the eggs, saving the whites to add later. Store or discard the yolks.

6. Bring 1 cup (237 ml) water, butter, and salt to a full boil in a medium, heavy saucepan. Remove from the burner. Stir in the sugar and vanilla. Add the bread flour *all at once* and stir vigorously. This will make a dough ball that pulls away from the pan. Place the pan back on medium heat and, using a heavy wooden spoon, heat and stir for at least 3 minutes, spreading the dough out and gathering it back up. Your goal is to dry the dough out as much as possible but not let it brown. Remove from the heat and place the dough in the bowl of a food processor with the steel blade.

7. In a small bowl, lightly beat 3 of the eggs. Stir the ammonium bicarbonate (if using) into the eggs. Process this egg mixture into the dough a little at a time. As soon as the eggs are well incorporated, beat the 2 egg whites in until well blended. This may be all the egg that you can add. You want to add as much egg as you can, but the dough must remain thick enough to spoon or pipe it into balls that will hold their shape. Place a spoon of dough on a plate to see if it will stand without spreading out. If it is firm enough, and not spreading too much, beat 1 more egg, and add about half of it, and process to beat in well. If you think it will hold the last half of the beaten egg, process it in too.

8. Spoon or pipe the dough onto the heavy baking sheet covered with Release foil (nonstick side up) or sprayed well with nonstick cooking spray. The puffs will triple in size when baked. For small individual puffs, spoon or pipe evenly spaced balls about 1 to 1½ inches (2.5 to 3.8 cm) in diameter and about 1 inch (2.5 cm) high. You can use a #5 (³⁄₈-inch/about 1-cm) or a #6 (½-inch/about 1.3-cm) fluted or plain pastry tip. For medium to large puffs, spoon or pipe evenly spaced balls about 1½ to 2 inches (3.8 to 5 cm) in diameter, about 1 inch (2.5 cm) high. Alternatively, you can use a #6 (½-inch/about 1.3-cm) or a #7 (⁵⁄₈-inch/about 1.6-cm) fluted or plain tip.

9. With the back of a greased fork, press the top of each puff gently at an angle to level it slightly. Then, go back and press each puff at an angle 90° to the first light press. Brush the puffs with beaten egg if a glossy surface is desired, taking care not to get any egg between the puff and the baking sheet. With a spritz bottle filled with water, spray the puffs fairly heavily to keep them moist and rising a little longer.

10. Wearing oven mitts, and being *careful* to keep your arm and face out of the way of the blast of steam that shoots up, pour the boiling water from the back of the stove into the pan with the hot rocks and *immediately* close the oven door.

11. Turn the oven down to 425°F/218°C. Place the baking pan in the oven on the hot baking stone. Do not open the oven door during baking. Bake until the puffs are risen and well browned, about 25 minutes. Turn the oven down to 350°F/177°C and bake for another 20 minutes to dry the puffs out well. Remove from the oven and cut a small slit in the side of each puff to let steam escape and dry the inside.

12. Puffs can be used right away, or cooled completely and stored in heavy-duty zip-top plastic bags, and frozen for up to 2 months. (The puffs are moist and contain eggs; if they are kept in a warm, moist spot, they will mold in a single day!) To reheat and crisp, bake for about 5 minutes in a 325°F/163°C oven.

Pâte à Choux "Somewhat Spéciale"

MAKES ABOUT 30 HORS D'OEUVRE PUFFS OR ABOUT 15 LARGE PUFFS

Because of the milk in this recipe, the puffs brown faster and are a breath more tender than the Pâte à Choux Ordinaire. This pâte à choux dough rises to a magnificent height and is crisp on the outside and moist, but not gooey, inside.

Your overall goal is to have everything warm (the eggs, the pan) so that you will get steam in the dough in the oven faster. You are trying to get the puffs to rise as much as possible before the hot oven crusts the tops and holds them down.

What This Recipe Shows

Using a little less than the usual 1 cup (237 ml) of liquid allows the addition of more egg for more puff without getting the dough too thin to rise.

High-protein bread flour absorbs more liquid, allowing more egg to be added, plus it forms more gluten for a great rise and the puffs will brown better.

Egg whites are incredible drying agents, so using some whites instead of the usual all whole eggs will produce crisp puffs that are still moist but not gooey on the inside.

About 2½ cups (593 ml) water, for steam
6 large eggs, in the shells
⅓ cup (79 ml) water
½ cup (118 ml) whole milk
4 tablespoons (2 oz/57 g) unsalted butter
½ teaspoon (3 g) salt
½ teaspoon (2 g) sugar
⅛ teaspoon (4 drops) pure vanilla extract

1 cup (5.7 oz/162 g) high-protein bread flour
  (measured by scooping and gently
  packing against the inside of the bag)
1 teaspoon ammonium bicarbonate, available
  from King Arthur Flour or a bakery
  supply store, optional
Nonstick cooking spray
1 large egg (1.75 oz/50 g), beaten, for glaze,
  optional

1. Arrange a shelf in the lower third of the oven with a baking stone on it and preheat the oven to 450°F/232°C.

2. Place a few clean small rocks (about 2 inches/5 cm each) in a metal pan with 2-inch (5-cm) sides and place the pan on the floor of the oven near the door. You are going to pour about 2 cups (473 ml) of boiling water over the rocks just before you place the puffs in the oven. This will create a steam bath to keep the oven moist for a little while to allow the puffs to rise well before they crust. For the boiling water, place a saucepan with about 2½ cups (593 ml) of water on a back burner and bring to a very low boil.

3. Place the 6 eggs in a bowl and cover them with hot tap water to warm them. As you get other things ready, pour off the water, which will have cooled, and cover the eggs again with hot water.

4. Place a heavy baking sheet on the top of the stove near the back vents so that it will get hot. If you do not have a warm spot such as this you will need to warm the sheet in the oven while you are beating the eggs into the dough.

5. Separate 2 of the eggs, reserving the whites to add to the dough, and store or discard the 2 yolks.

6. In a medium, heavy saucepan, bring ⅓ cup (79 ml) water, the milk, butter, and salt to a full boil. Remove from the heat, then stir in the sugar and vanilla. Add the bread flour *all at once* and stir vigorously. This will make a dough ball that pulls away from the pan. Place the saucepan back on medium heat, and using a heavy wooden spoon, stir and heat for at least 3 minutes, spreading the dough out and gathering it back up. Your goal is to dry the dough out as much as possible but not let it brown. Remove from the heat and place the dough in a food processor with the steel blade.

7. In a small bowl, lightly beat 3 of the eggs. Stir the ammonium bicarbonate, if using, into the eggs. Process this egg mixture into the dough a little at a time. As soon as the eggs are well incorporated, beat in the 2 egg whites until well blended. This may be all the egg that you can add. You want to add as much egg as you can, but the dough must remain thick enough to spoon or pipe it into balls that will hold their shape. Place a spoon of dough on a plate to see if it will stand and not spread out. If it is firm enough, beat 1 more egg, add about half of it, and process to beat in well. If you think it will hold the last half of the beaten egg, process it in.

8. Spoon or pipe the dough onto the heavy baking sheet covered with Release foil (nonstick side up) or sprayed well with nonstick cooking spray. The puffs will triple in size. For small individual puffs, spoon or pipe evenly spaced balls about 1 inch to $1\frac{1}{2}$ inches (2.5 to 3.8 cm) in diameter and about 1 inch (2.5 cm) high. You can use a #5 ($\frac{3}{8}$-inch/about 1-cm) or a #6 ($\frac{1}{2}$-inch/about 1.3-cm) fluted or plain pastry tip. For medium to large puffs, spoon or pipe evenly spaced balls about $1\frac{1}{2}$ to 2 inches (3.8 to 5 cm) in diameter, about 1 inch (2.5 cm) high. Alternatively, you can use a #6 ($\frac{1}{2}$-inch/about 1.3-cm) or a #7 ($\frac{5}{8}$-inch/about 1.6-cm) fluted or plain tip.

9. With the back of a greased fork, press the top of each puff gently at an angle to level it slightly. Then press each puff at a 90° angle to the first press. Brush the puffs with beaten egg if a glossy surface is desired, taking care not to get any glaze between the puff and the baking sheet. With a spritz bottle filled with water, lightly spray the puffs to keep them moist and rising a little longer.

10. Wearing oven mitts, and being *careful* to keep your arm and face out of the way of the blast of steam that shoots up, pour the boiling water from the back of the stove into the pan with the hot rocks and *immediately* close the oven door.

11. Turn the oven down to 425°F/218°C. Open the door and quickly place the baking sheet in the oven on the hot baking stone. Bake until the puffs are risen and well browned, about 25 minutes. Do not open the oven door. Turn the oven down to 350°F/177°C and bake for another 20 minutes to dry the puffs out well. Remove from the oven and cut a small slit in the side of each puff shortly after you remove them from the oven to let steam to escape and dry the inside.

12. Puffs can be used right away, or cooled completely and stored in a heavy-duty zip-top plastic bag, and frozen for up to 2 months. To reheat and crisp, bake for about 5 minutes in a 325°F/163°C oven. The puffs are moist and contain eggs; if they are kept in a warm, moist spot, they will mold in a single day!

Cream Puffs

I love the contrast of the crisp puff and a satiny smooth vanilla pastry cream. My favorites are cream puffs filled with pastry cream, but you can fill them with flavored sweetened whipped cream if that is your preference.

1 recipe Pastry Cream (page 330)

1 recipe Pâte à Choux Ordinaire (page 245) or Pâte à Choux "Somewhat Spéciale" (page 247), baked and completely cooled

1. Fill a pastry bag fitted with a #5 ($^3/_8$-inch/about 1-cm) tip with pastry cream. Punch a hole in the bottom of each puff and fill with pastry cream.

2. Another way to fill the puffs is to cut off the top third of the puffs with a serrated bread knife. Spoon the pastry cream into the puffs or use a pastry bag fitted with a #6 ($^1/_2$-inch/about 1.3-cm) tip. Fill above the puff with a swirl of pastry cream and then lightly place the lid on top.

Orange Cream Puffs

Flavor the pastry cream with 2 tablespoons (30 ml) Grand Marnier and 1 tablespoon (15 ml) grated orange peel (zest).

Chocolate Cream Puffs

Stir 4 oz (113 g) chopped semisweet chocolate into the hot pastry cream.

Coffee Puffs

Stir 1$^1/_2$ teaspoons (1.5 g) instant espresso powder into the hot pastry cream.

Éclairs

Boy, oh boy! Chocolate icing on a crisp puff filled with velvety pastry cream.

1 recipe Pâte à Choux Ordinaire (page 245) or Pâte à Choux "Somewhat Spéciale" (page 247) piped as directed below	1 recipe Pastry Cream (page 330) ½ recipe Velvety Ganache Glaze (page 98) Confectioners' sugar, as needed

1. For miniature éclairs, use a pastry bag fitted with a #5 (³⁄8-inch/about 1-cm) fluted or smooth tip and pipe thirty 2 to 2½-inch (5 to 6.4-cm) fingers of dough. For regular éclairs, use a #6 (½-inch/about 1.3-cm) fluted or smooth tip and pipe fourteen 4½-inch (11.4-cm) fingers of dough. Bake according to directions for Pâte à Choux Ordinaire.

2. Fill a pastry bag fitted with a #5 (³⁄8-inch/about 1-cm) tip with pastry cream. Punch a hole in the end of each puff and half fill with pastry cream.

3. If necessary, thicken the ganache with a little confectioners' sugar, and then spoon a coating across the top of each éclair.

Religieuses (Little Nuns)

These adorable "little nuns" are made with a medium puff filled with a satiny chocolate pastry cream and a head made of a small filled puff. A mocha icing drizzled overall forms the nun's habit.

Nonstick cooking spray, optional 1 recipe Pâte à Choux "Somewhat Spéciale" (page 247) 1 recipe Pastry Cream (page 330)	3 ounces (85 g) semisweet chocolate, melted 1 recipe Caramel (page 171) 1 recipe Mocha Glaze (recipe follows)

1. Prepare 3 baking sheets with Release foil (nonstick side up) or spray well with nonstick cooking spray. Pipe and bake the Pâte à Choux "Somewhat Spéciale" according to directions: 14 large puffs and 14 small puffs on separate baking sheets (2 sheets with 7 large puffs on each sheet, and 1 sheet with 14 small puffs).

2. For large puffs, use a #6 (½-inch/about 1.3-cm) plain or fluted tip. Pipe mounds 2 inches (5 cm) in diameter and 1 inch (2.5 cm) high. For small puffs, use a #5 (⅜-inch/about 1-cm) plain or fluted tip and pipe mounds about ¾ inch (2 cm) in diameter and ¾ inch (2 cm) high.

3. Stir the pastry cream and chocolate together. Let the pastry cream cool. Fill a pastry bag fitted with a #5 (⅜-inch/about 1-cm) tip with pastry cream. Punch a hole in the bottom of each puff and fill all the puffs with pastry cream.

4. Prepare the caramel. Dip a small filled puff in caramel and then place it on top of a large puff to make a "head." Repeat with all of the small puffs. Prepare the Mocha Glaze and pour a coating to look like a cloak over the back of the head and backside of each little "nun." Serve immediately.

Mocha Glaze

MAKES ABOUT 1 CUP (237 ML)

1 cup (4 oz/120 g) confectioners' sugar
½ teaspoon (0.5 g) instant espresso powder
1 teaspoon (3 g) natural cocoa powder

1 teaspoon (5 ml) pure vanilla extract
2 to 4 tablespoons (30 to 60 ml) heavy cream
   or whole milk

Stir together the confectioners' sugar, espresso powder, and cocoa powder. Stir the vanilla into the cream or milk. Stir the milk into the confectioners' sugar mixture until smooth.

Puits d'Amour (Wells of Love)

MAKES 6 PASTRIES

A truly amorous pastry—puff pastry, pâte à choux, pastry cream, and caramel—much of a pastry chef's arsenal. Lenôtre's Puits d'Amour is made of pâte à choux dough pressed into a tartlet shell and baked, the rim is dipped in caramel, and then the shell is filled with pastry cream. Bruce Healy's version is a little easier. He cuts a puff pastry circle, pipes pâte à choux on top around the edge, bakes, fills with pastry cream, and sprinkles the rim with confectioners' sugar that he melts under the broiler for a few seconds.

One 17.3-ounce (490-g) package of frozen puff pastry sheets, thawed
Nonstick cooking spray, optional
½ recipe Pâte à Choux Ordinaire (page 245), not baked

1 recipe Pastry Cream (page 330)
Confectioners' sugar
¼ cup (59 ml) Shiny Apricot-Orange Glaze (recipe follows)

1. Arrange a shelf in the lower third of the oven with a baking stone on it and preheat the oven to 425°F/218°C.

2. Cut six 4-inch (10-cm) circles from the pastry. Place pastries on a heavy baking sheet covered with Release foil (nonstick side up) or spray the baking sheet well with nonstick cooking spray. Fill a pastry bag fitted with a #5 (⅜-inch/about 1-cm) tip with pâte à choux dough and pipe the dough on top around the edges of the pastry circles.

3. IF the inside top of your oven is a sealed metal surface (NO heating coils exposed), spray with a mist of water to cool. You need heat from the bottom before the tops of the puffs cook and hold them down. Place the baking sheet on the hot baking stone. Spray a light mist over the puffs to keep them moist and rising a little longer. Bake until well puffed and browned, about 15 to 20 minutes. Turn the oven down to 325°F/163°C and continue to bake 15 to 20 minutes longer to dry well. The pastries should be well browned.

4. When the pastries are completely cooled, fill each with pastry cream or crème chiboust (¾ cup pastry cream lightened with ¼ cup Italian meringue). Sprinkle the pastry cream heavily with confectioners' sugar. Melt and caramelize the sugar under the broiler, or carefully with a miniature blowtorch.

5. Brush the pâte à choux rim with the glaze.

Shiny Apricot-Orange Glaze

2 tablespoons (30 ml) apricot preserves
2 tablespoons (30 ml) orange marmalade

1 tablespoon (15 ml) light corn syrup
1 teaspoon (5 ml) Grand Marnier liqueur

In a small saucepan, heat the apricot preserves and orange marmalade. Strain, reserving the melted preserves that come through the strainer. Stir together the melted preserves, corn syrup, and Grand Marnier. Brush and rebrush onto the pastry several times.

Pont Neuf

MAKES 8 MAGNIFICENT PASTRIES

French pastry chefs love to create pastries in honor of events. Back in the late sixteenth century, when Paris had a new bridge, it was truly an event to be celebrated with a pastry creation. The new bridge creation was a puff pastry shell that contains a filling of pastry cream mixed with pâte à choux dough topped with a very narrow puff pastry cross. Diagonally opposite sections created by the cross are brushed with apricot or red currant jelly, and the remaining two sections are sprinkled with confectioners' sugar.

Nonstick cooking spray
One 17.3-ounce (490-g) package of frozen puff pastry sheets, thawed (it is important to have the pastry sheets as cold as possible going into the oven to prevent overbrowning on the bottom)
1 recipe Pastry Cream (page 330)

$1\frac{1}{2}$ tablespoons (22 ml) rum or Grand Marnier
1 recipe Pâte à Choux "Somewhat Spéciale" (page 247) or Pâte à Choux Ordinaire dough (page 245) (not baked)
Confectioners' sugar
$\frac{1}{4}$ cup (59 ml) Shiny Apricot-Orange Glaze (page 253)

1. Arrange a shelf in the lower third of the oven with a baking stone on it and preheat the oven to 425°F/218°C.

2. Spray eight 4-inch (10-cm) tartlet pans with nonstick cooking spray.

3. Roll out enough puff pastry to get eight 4-inch (10-cm) circles plus some narrow strips. With a very sharp knife, cut out the circles and eight 4-inch-long narrow strips to go across the top. Press the dough circles down into the tartlet pans.

4. While the pastry cream is still warm, stir in the rum or Grand Marnier, then stir in the pâte à choux dough. Fill each tart with this mixture (use all of the filling), and arrange a cross of the narrow strips of puff pastry on top of each tart. Place the tarts on a heavy baking sheet.

5. Place the baking sheet on the hot baking stone, and bake until well puffed and browned, about 15 to 20 minutes. Turn the oven down to 325°F/163°C and continue to bake for about 20 minutes more. Cool in the pans for 10 minutes, then remove to a rack to completely cool. When cooled, sprinkle diagonally opposite quarters with confectioners' sugar. In a small saucepan, heat the glaze just enough to melt, and brush it on the remaining diagonally opposite quarters and on the pastry strips. Chill until served.

Gougères—Magnificent Little Bits of Cheese Clouds

MAKES ABOUT 30 HORS D'OEUVRE PUFFS OR 15 LARGE PUFFS

These are perfect cheesy nibbles for an elegant party or simply for hungry children. The great news is that they can be completely prepared, baked, and frozen ahead. Then you can pull out as many or as few as you like, crisp them a few minutes in the oven or toaster oven, and you have wonderful fresh, crisp puffs. For a restaurant, they could be the reason your guests come back.

Although long, this recipe is straightforward and actually easy. It just has many little things that you need to be nitpicky about that make it seem long. Please read through it before starting.

What This Recipe Shows

High-protein flour like bread flour absorbs more liquid to allow the use of more eggs, plus the flour forms more gluten for a great rise and the puffs will brown better.

Using part water and part whole milk or half-and-half gives you a more flavorful and browner puff.

Egg whites are an incredible drying agent, so substituting 2 whites for 1 whole egg instead of the usual all whole eggs will produce crisp puffs that are still moist but not as gooey on the inside.

Starting with a hot baking stone gives you a head start on heat from the bottom.

About 2½ cups (20 oz/591 ml) water, for steam

5 large eggs, in the shells

1 cup (5.7 oz/161 g) bread flour, measured by dipping the cup into the flour bag, slightly packing and leveling the cup against the bag. If you measure by spooning the flour into the cup and leveling, you will need 1¼ cups bread flour.

½ teaspoon (1.5 g) dry mustard

¼ teaspoon (1 g) sugar

¼ teaspoon (1 g) ground cayenne

⅛ teaspoon (pinch) freshly grated nutmeg

¾ cup (177 ml) water

¼ cup (59 ml) whole milk or half-and-half

4 tablespoons (2 oz/57 g) unsalted butter

½ teaspoon (3 g) salt (sea salt is my first choice)

¼ cup (1 oz/28 g) grated Gruyère

½ cup (1.5 oz/42 g) grated Parmesan

Nonstick cooking spray

1 large egg (1.75 oz/50 g), beaten, for glaze, optional

---

1. Arrange a shelf in the lower third of the oven with a baking stone on it and preheat the oven to 450°F/232°C.

2. Place a few clean small rocks (about 2 inches/5 cm in diameter each) in a metal pan with 2-inch (5-cm) sides and place the pan on the floor of the oven near the door. You are going to pour about 2 cups (473 ml) of boiling water over the rocks just before you place the puffs in the oven. This will create a steam bath to keep the oven moist for a little while to allow the puffs to rise well before they crust. For the boiling water, place a saucepan with about 2½ cups (591 ml) of water on a back burner and bring to a low simmer. (Your overall goal is to have everything warm—the eggs, the pan—so that you will get steam in the dough in the oven faster. You are trying to get the puffs to rise as much as possible before the hot oven crusts and holds them down.)

3. Place the eggs in a bowl and cover them with hot tap water to warm them. While you get other things ready, pour off the water, which will have cooled, and cover the eggs again with hot water.

4. Place a heavy baking sheet on the top of the stove near the back vents so that it will get hot. If you do not have a warm spot such as this, you will need to warm the sheet in the oven while you are beating the eggs into the dough.

5. Have a food processor with the steel blade ready along with the bowl of eggs in hot water beside it. Separate 2 eggs, and reserve the whites. Save the yolks for another use. Have a spritz bottle filled with water to spray water on the puffs just before you put them in the oven, or have a bowl of water that you can dip your fingers into and flick water on the puffs.

6. In a medium bowl, stir together the flour, mustard, sugar, cayenne, and nutmeg. Bring ¾ cup (177 ml) water, the milk, butter, and salt to a full boil in a medium heavy saucepan. Dump in the flour mixture *all at once,* and immediately stir vigorously. This will make a dough ball that pulls away from the pan. Keep the dough on the heat and turn the heat down to medium. You want to dry out the dough ball as much as possible without burning the dough. Lift the ball, then "smush" it onto the bottom of the pan. Do this pulling the dough together, then smearing the dough on the bottom, gathering together, and smearing on the bottom for about 2 minutes.

7. Dump the dough into a food processor with the steel blade. Run the processor 3 or 4 seconds. With the processor running, add whole 1 egg. Wait until it has been absorbed, 1 or 2 seconds, then add the next egg. Add a total of 3 whole eggs, one at a time, processing 1 to 2 seconds for each egg. Finally, add half of the 2 egg whites. Stop the processor and spoon up a scoop of dough. The dough should be just firm enough to hold its shape when spooned up. If it looks like it will hold its shape, process in the rest of the egg white. Add both cheeses and process just to blend

8. Spray the hot baking sheet with nonstick cooking spray. Spray your clean fingers and a spoon, then spoon rounds of dough about 1½ inches (3.8 cm) wide and about 1 inch (2.5 cm) high on the sheet, using your fingers as necessary. (Or you can put the dough into a large pastry bag fitted with a #6 [½-inch/about 1.3-cm] round or fluted pastry tip. Fill the bag only half full and twist the top to squeeze and pipe the puffs the size above.) If desired, touch a brush just to the top of each puff with a beaten egg glaze. With a spritz bottle filled with water, spray the puffs lightly.

9. Wearing oven mitts, and being *careful* to keep your arm and face out of the way of the blast of steam that shoots up, pour the boiling water from the back of the stove into the pan with the hot rocks and *immediately* close the oven door. Turn the oven down to 425°F/218°C. Open the door and quickly place the baking sheet in the oven on the hot baking stone. Bake until the puffs are risen and well browned, about 25 minutes. Do not open the oven door during baking. Turn the oven down to 325°F/163°C and bake for another 20 minutes to dry out well.

10. Puffs can be used right away or cooled completely. Store cooled puffs sealed in a heavy-duty zip-top plastic bag and freeze for up to 2 months. To reheat and crisp, bake for about 5 minutes in a 325°F/163°C oven. The puffs are moist and contain eggs; if they are kept in a warm, moist spot, they will mold in a single day.

Turkey Gougère

MAKES 4 TO 6 SERVINGS

A magnificent crisp, puffed cheesy ring surrounds a creamy turkey filling. The slight sweetness of the fruit in the filling and the crisp cheese of the puff make a perfect bite.

Prepare the gougère ring first, and then prepare the filling. Serve hot.

Gougère Ring

About 2½ cups (593 ml) water, for steam
Nonstick cooking spray

½ recipe Gougère dough (page 255)
1 large egg (1.75 oz/50 g), beaten

Turkey Filling (recipe follows)

1. Arrange a shelf in the lower third of the oven with a baking stone on it. Place 2 to 4 small clean rocks in a metal pan with 2-inch (5-cm) sides on the oven floor near the door. This is for a home-made steamer. Preheat the oven to 450°F/232°C. For the boiling water for the steam bath, place a saucepan with about 2½ cups (593 ml) of water on a back burner and bring to a very low boil. Place an oblong metal or heatproof au gratin casserole (about 10-inch/25-cm size) on the top of the stove near the back vents so that it will get hot. If you don't have a warm spot such as this, place it in the oven for 3 minutes to warm. Spray the hot casserole with nonstick cooking spray.

2. Spray a spoon and clean fingers with nonstick cooking spray and spoon balls of dough about 1½ to 2 inches (3.8 to 5 cm) in diameter and about 1 to 1½ inches (2.5 to 3.8 cm) high around the edge of the casserole about ¾ inch (1.9 cm) apart (or you can pipe using a large pastry bag with a #6 [½-inch/1.3-cm] fluted or plain pastry tip). Very lightly glaze just the tops of the puffs with a beaten egg. With a spritz bottle filled with water, spray the puffs lightly.

3. Wearing oven mitts, and being *careful* to keep your arm and face out of the way of the blast of steam that shoots up, pour the boiling water from the back of the stove into the pan with the hot rocks and *immediately* close the oven door. Turn the oven down to 425°F/218°C. Open the door and quickly place the baking sheet in the oven on the hot baking stone. Bake until the puffs in the casserole are risen and well browned, about 25 minutes. Turn the oven down to 325°F/163°C and bake for another 20 minutes to dry out well. The puffs should be well browned and form a magnificent crown.

4. Fill the ring with the filling, garnish, and serve hot.

Turkey Filling

1 tablespoon (1 oz/28 g) butter
2 tablespoons (30 ml) canola oil
½ teaspoon (0.5 g) dried thyme or 1½
  teaspoons (1.5 g) fresh thyme leaves
1 bay leaf
1 medium onion, chopped (about 1 cup/237 ml)
1 tablespoon (15 ml) Worcestershire sauce
1 kiwi, peeled and chopped
1 ripe Golden Delicious apple, peeled, cored,
  and chopped into about ¼-inch (0.6-cm)
  dice

1 teaspoon (2 g) dried chicken bouillon
  granules
2 tablespoons (0.5 oz/15 g) all-purpose flour
1 cup (237 ml) chicken stock or broth
1 teaspoon (5 ml) "B-V The Beefer-Upper,"
  (see Sources, page 509) or Maggi
  Seasoning
1 pound (454 g) coarsely chopped cooked
  turkey, chicken, beef, or pork
4 sprigs parsley, chopped
4 green onions, chopped

1. In a large skillet, melt the butter. Stir in the oil, thyme, and bay leaf. Add the onions and sauté briefly. Turn the heat down to low and simmer for about 8 minutes, until the onions are very soft. Turn the heat up to lightly brown the onions, then stir in the Worcestershire, kiwi, and apple. Turn the heat to medium and allow to simmer several minutes, stirring regularly, until the apples soften. Stir in the dried bouillon, then sprinkle the flour over and stir in well. Add about one-third of the chicken stock, stir in well, add the B-V, then add the rest of the stock. Keep at a low simmer, stirring constantly until the sauce thickens to a gravy consistency. REMOVE and discard the bay leaf. Set aside.

2. When the gougère ring is baked and you are ready to assemble, reheat the sauce, stir in the turkey, and bring back to a simmer. Pour into the ring, garnish the filling with parsley and green onions, and serve hot. Serve everyone some of the pastry ring with some filling.

Cocktail Puffs with Escargots

MAKES 24 COCKTAIL PUFFS

Once when I was teaching in Santa Barbara, California, Julia and Paul Child came over to join us in eating the goodies that we had prepared in class. After Julia had three of these little puffs, she asked, "Shirley, what are these? They are delicious." "Escargots, Julia." She replied, "No wonder they're so good." I was thrilled to have prepared a dish that Julia enjoyed so much.

What This Recipe Shows

The secret of fine snail butter is high-quality salted butter (such as Plugra or Kerrygold), and a little freshly grated nutmeg.

---

2 cans (7 oz/198 g each) medium snails (see Note)

2 shallots, peeled

4 cloves garlic, peeled

About 10 fresh curly parsley florets

1/2 pound (8 oz/227 g) lightly salted butter, softened

Dash of hot pepper sauce or ground cayenne

Pinch of freshly grated nutmeg

1/4 teaspoon (1.5 g) salt

Freshly ground white pepper to taste

1 recipe Pâte à Choux Ordinaire (page 245), formed into 1-inch (2.5-cm) balls, baked, and cooled

1. Preheat the oven to 450°F/232°C.

2. Drain the snails and place on a paper towel. Chop the shallots, garlic, and parsley in a food processor with the steel blade. Add the softened butter, hot sauce, nutmeg, and salt, and blend in. Taste and add salt and pepper as needed. (Snail butter can be prepared 1 or 2 days ahead and kept tightly sealed in the refrigerator.)

3. Cut tops from the puffs, place a snail or snails in each, add a generous teaspoon (6.5 ml) of snail butter, and replace the top. Warm puffs in the oven just long enough to melt butter, about 4 minutes. Serve immediately.

NOTE: Canned jumbo snails, 12 to a can, are the most commonly available. If you have jumbo snails, you may have to cut them in half. With small snails, add 2 or 3 to a puff.

Shirley's Mile-High Popovers

MAKES 6 LARGE POPOVERS

These are magnificent and delicious! They are deep brown and crusty and oh so good! These deserve the best butter that you can buy.

The big secret of popovers is that everything is as warm as you can get it—the pan, heat from the bottom, the batter—everything.

What This Recipe Shows

The milk and flour need to stand about an hour so that the flour is fully hydrated.

Adding hot cream to warm the batter just before it goes in the oven helps the batter to heat fast, producing steam for a great rise.

The hot stone is vital in providing instant heat from the bottom to make the batter explode into a great puff.

Egg whites will make drier, crisper puffs.

---

5 large eggs, in the shells
1½ cups (355 ml) whole milk
1¾ cups (8.4 oz/238 g) spooned and leveled
    Pillsbury bread flour

⅓ cup (79 ml) heavy cream
¾ teaspoon (4.5 g) salt
Nonstick cooking spray

1. Place the eggs in a bowl of very hot tap water to warm. After a while, drain and cover again with very hot tap water.

2. In a heavy saucepan, heat the milk until it feels warm to the touch. Place the flour in a large mixing bowl (if you have a large measuring cup with a spout, that is great) and, with a fork or whisk, beat in the milk a little at a time to prevent forming lumps. Allow the flour/milk mixture to stand at room temperature for at least an hour.

3. After the flour/milk mixture has been standing for about 15 minutes, place a shelf in the lower third of the oven with a baking stone on it and preheat the oven to 475°F/246°C. If you think that your oven is low, turn it to 500°F/260°C. It is important that the oven be very hot.

4. After the flour/milk mixture has stood for over an hour, place the popover pan in the oven on the stone to heat.

5. Separate 3 of the eggs, saving the whites and storing the yolks. Beat the 2 whole eggs and 3 egg whites together, beat in about ½ cup of the flour/milk mixture and then beat the egg mixture into the flour mixture.

6. Heat the cream almost to a boil. Sprinkle the salt over the batter and whisk in the hot cream.

7. Pull the hot popover pan out of the oven. I like to place the pan over the sink. Spray one cup of the popover pan well with nonstick cooking spray and immediately pour batter into that cup, filling over three-quarters full. This 6-cup batch of filling is exactly enough for 6 cups. Repeat spraying and filling each cup. Place the popover pan on the hot stone and bake for 9 minutes. Do NOT open the oven. Turn down the heat to 425°F/218°C, and bake for 7 minutes more. Do NOT open the oven. Turn down the oven to 325°F/162°C, and leave the popovers in 20 to 25 minutes more for the popovers to dry out.

8. Dump the popovers onto a rack to cool a minute. Serve immediately with really good butter and preserves. You can make these several hours ahead and rewarm them at 300°F/149°C for 5 minutes. Or, when they are completely cool, you can seal them in heavy freezer zip-top bags and freeze. Reheat in a 300°F/149°C oven for about 5 minutes.

Pâte à Choux At a Glance

What to Do	**Why**
Use bread flour for a higher, lighter puff.	A high-protein flour like bread flour has more gluten-forming proteins for higher, lighter puffs, and it absorbs more water, allowing the use of more eggs.
Use 4 tablespoons of butter instead of the usual 8.	With less butter, you will get more gluten formed for a lighter puff.
Add flour all at once to boiling liquid-fat mixture.	Flour stirred in all at once will quickly swell the starch and dry the dough.
Replace at least one whole egg with 2 whites for crisp, dry puffs.	Egg whites are excellent drying agents.
When adding eggs, stop while the consistency is firm enough to hold its shape.	Puffs will not rise if the dough is too thin.
Bake puffs on nonstick foil (Release) or parchment sprayed with nonstick cooking spray.	Doughs with eggs stick badly.
Bruce Healy suggests a fluted pastry tip for piping.	The slight ridges help the dough expand easily.
With round puffs, gently press the top of each puff with the back of a greased fork.	Pressing very lightly levels the top for an even rise.
Preheat the oven with a baking stone on a low shelf to get the stone very hot. Place the puffs on the hot stone and turn down the oven to the cooking temperature.	Heat from the bottom makes the puffs rise before the top crust sets and holds them down.
Cut a small slit in the side of each puff shortly after you remove it from the oven.	This allows steam to escape and the inside to dry.
Make a steamer by placing rocks in a pan in the bottom of the oven and pouring boiling water in just before baking.	Steam keeps the tops of the puffs moist so they can rise to a maximum.
Spray the puffs lightly with a mist of water just before baking.	To keep the puffs moist and rising and prevent their crusting on top as long as possible.

CHAPTER THREE

Pie Marches On and On
The Thrill of the Pie!

Priceless Knowledge in This Chapter

Interesting pie and pastry techniques—brushing off pastry with ice water before folding to make it easy to roll

What pie and pastry ingredients work, and why—how sugar preserves the shape of fruit

A sure-fire way to keep cream pies from becoming soupy upon standing

Explanations of many basic pastries and pastry problems

The thrill of making one great pie after another

Recipes Include

Puff pastry that is easy to roll even when made with high-protein flour

A custard pie that is firm and cuts smoothly, but in your mouth it is ethereal, melting deliciousness and the crust is dry and firm even after days in the refrigerator

An easy-to-make crust that is magnificently flakey

A pumpkin pie crust that does not get soggy even after days

Fruit pies that are just shiny, luscious pieces of fruit in fabulous pastry

The Recipes

Two Great Pie Masters

MY HERO—THE PIE KING

Pie Marches On by Monroe Boston Strause (his father was Boston Monroe Strause) came from the 1930s, the days when pie was America's dessert and Monroe was the undisputed King of Pies. In many printings, there is a picture of the big, handsome Monroe holding a pie while tiny Mary Pickford (who in spike heels comes just to Monroe's chest) looks adoringly up at Monroe and daintily secures a bite of pie on a fork.

Discovering *Pie Marches On* was like discovering a lost art. Here are amazing cures for pie problems written in the deep, dark jungles of the past. I will pass his cures along to you with my own know-how and explanations of the science behind the techniques. Monroe may not have known why an ingredient or technique was scientifically correct but, as a great baker, he knew what worked and what didn't.

Monroe was more passionate about a soggy bottom (pie crust, that is) than most people are about their stock portfolios. He has invaluable solutions for one problem after another from rock-hard crumb crusts to watery fruit pies.

I cannot understand how we lost this knowledge. Here was a man who was an icon in his own time—a man who trained the best of the best bakers. Even though he wrote articles and books, until I started raving about him back in the 1980s, chefs didn't know who he was. We have had to blunder along trying to improve pies, pastries, and meringues without even considering his valuable direction.

ATLANTA'S PIE KING

Bill Greenwood of Greenwood's on Green Street in Roswell, Georgia, makes over a hundred spectacular pies every day. His double-crusted pies are great domed masterpieces with an amazing pastry braid around the base of the domes. His mile-high meringue pies are billowing puffs with colors from snow-white in the valleys to splashes of golden brown and finally dark brown tips on the peaks. I was amazed! How could he cook a deep meringue like that without its being solid brown all over? Bill has generously shared some of his secrets (see pages 191 and 327).

Throughout this chapter I quote these experts and share their techniques.

Pie Crusts: Crusts Without Rolling Pins

Crumb crusts, press-in crusts, and meringue crusts are all easy, nonrolled crusts.

Some cooks are terrified of rolling out a pie crust. Some cooks, like those in tiny New York apartments, don't have counter space to roll a pie crust on. Fear not, there are many delicious crusts that rolling pin– and space-challenged cooks can make. Three types of nonrolled crusts are: crumb crusts, press-in crusts, and meringue crusts.

TO THE LAST CRUMB—CRUMB CRUSTS

A basic crumb crust is easy enough. You stir together the crumbs, a little sugar, and a little melted butter. Press it into a greased pan, bake a few minutes, and you have a crust. So what could possibly go wrong? A look at the basic ingredients reveals all.

Ingredients

"Crumbs"—Crackers to Nuts

Crumbs for crusts can be made of everything from crackers to nuts, with dozens of cookies or cereals in between. The cookie list goes on and on—Bordeaux cookies as in the Bordeaux Macadamia Crust (page 268), chocolate cookies as in the Chocolate Cookie Crumb Crust (page 275), lemon cookies, gingersnaps as in the Gingersnap-Pecan Crust (page 277), to crackers like zwieback and even saltines, with or without nuts. Cereals like Honey Bunches of Oats make great crust. In *The Artful Pie* by Lisa Cherkasky and Renée Comet, there are many unusual pies including an excellent coconut cream pie made with a saltine and salted-nut crust. I have my version of a saltine and nut crust in the Cracker-Nut Crust (page 273).

Sugar

The large amount of sugar in cookies crystallizes as the cookies cool to make them firm. The same thing can happen in a crumb crust. If you are using sweet cookies like lemon cookies or Pepperidge Farm Bordeaux cookies, even without additional sugar the crust can be cement-hard—virtually uncuttable.

Fortunately, we have solutions to a cement-hard crust made with cookies. You can add some bread crumbs or zwieback crumbs that are more or less flavorless, to "dilute" the sugar. Or another way to get the sugar concentration down to a cuttable amount is to add finely chopped nuts as I do in my Bordeaux cookie crust (page 268).

Now let's turn to the old master, Monroe Boston Strause, the originator of the crumb crust. (He invented the crumb crust to go with the Black Bottom Pie, which he also created.) He had the perfect solution all along for a tender

Crumbs for crusts can be made of everything from cereal, cookies, and crackers, to nuts.

If you make a crumb crust with sweet cookie crumbs, even without additional sugar, the crust can be cement-hard.

You can add bread crumbs or finely chopped nuts to a cookie crumb crust to "dilute" the sugar and make a cuttable sweet-cookie crumb crust.

In his original crumb crust, Monroe Boston Strause solved the problems of cement-hard crusts by substituting corn syrup mixed into water for the sugar. Cold butter can be very hard, too. Monroe, our pie master, solved this by mixing shortening with the butter for a perfectly cuttable crust at any temperature.

crumb crust: instead of sugar, he used corn syrup, which interferes with sugar crystallization. (See Monroe's crust on page 272.)

If you have too much butter in a crumb crust, it will melt in the hot oven and the sides of the crust will slide down the side of the pan.

Butter

If you have too much butter in the crumb crust, it will melt in the hot oven and the sides of the crumb crust will slide down to the bottom of the pan.

Bordeaux Macadamia Crust

MAKES ONE 9-INCH (23-CM) CRUST

Delicious, sweeter-than-shortbread Pepperidge Farm Bordeaux cookies combined with macadamia nuts make an incredible crust—perfect for cold fruit pies like Judy Brady's Blueberries and Bordeaux (page 283), mousse or chiffon pies, or even cheesecakes!

What This Recipe Shows

Even without additional sugar, the large amount of sugar in these cookies makes the crust uncuttable. To cut the sugar concentration in the crumbs, I could add bread crumbs, zwieback crumbs, or nuts. I selected macadamia nuts.

Because of the richness of the macadamia nuts, I used less butter than in a plain graham cracker crumb crust.

Nonstick cooking spray
27 Pepperidge Farm Bordeaux cookies (about 1½ cups/355 ml crumbs)

¾ cup (3.5 oz/99 g) roasted, salted macadamia nuts
3 tablespoons (1.5 oz/43 g) butter, melted

1. Place a shelf in the center of the oven and preheat the oven to 350°F/177°C.

2. Spray a 9-inch (23-cm) pie pan with nonstick cooking spray.

3. In a food processor with the steel blade, process the cookies and nuts to fine crumbs. Then drizzle in the melted butter while processing with quick on/offs.

4. Spread the crumbs around in the prepared pan. Press up the sides about 1½ inches (4 cm) high and across the bottom. Bake for 8 minutes until set. Cool completely before filling.

Judy Brady's Blueberries and Bordeaux

MAKES ONE 9-INCH (23-CM) PIE

From my friend Judy Brady, a long-time great cook in Ft. Walton Beach, Florida—fresh cold blueberries in a cookie crust. This is hard to beat—the perfect summertime dessert. And it is incredibly easy! You can use this same technique—heating the preserves, stirring in the gelatin and fresh fruit—with other fruits. And, of course, you can always add a tablespoon or two of good fruit-flavored liqueur. For example, use cherry preserves, a tablespoon of Chambord, and fresh dark pitted cherries.

What This Recipe Shows

Sugar in the jam prevents the pectic substances "glue" between the fruit cells from changing to water-soluble pectins and dissolving. (See page 310 for details.) This preserves the shape and texture of the fruit. You will not get this if you use sugar-free jams, and can end up with mushy fruit.

Salt suppress bitterness to allow other flavors to come out. Pastry chefs always say "a pinch of salt brings out the sweetness."

This amount of gelatin just sets the pie. A little juice will trickle from the slice. If you want a completely firm pie use 1⅓ to 1½ teaspoons (4 to 5 g) of gelatin.

¼ cup (59 ml) cool water
1 teaspoon (3 g) unflavored gelatin
1 cup (237 ml) red or black seedless raspberry
    jam (I usually use Smucker's)
⅛ teaspoon (pinch) salt

5 to 6 cups (a little less than 1½ quarts/1.4 L)
    fresh blueberries (I like a full pie), quickly
    rinsed in a colander and drained
1 Bordeaux Macadamia Crust (page 268),
    baked and cooled
Honey Mascarpone Cream (recipe follows)

1. To prepare the filling, pour the water into a small saucepan. Sprinkle the gelatin on top of the water and let stand 2 minutes. Over very low heat, warm just to dissolve the gelatin. (Never boil gelatin, since this will reduce its ability to gel.) Alternatively, in a microwave-safe glass measuring cup or small bowl, sprinkle the gelatin over the water and allow to stand to soften. Microwave gelatin on 100% power for about 20 seconds, just long enough to dissolve.

2. Place the jam in a medium saucepan. Over medium heat, stir to melt the jam. Stir in the softened gelatin. Remove from the heat. Stir in the salt and the blueberries. Stir gently with a wooden spatula so that all the blueberries are coated, then pour into the prepared crust.

3. Refrigerate for an hour or more to chill well. Spread with the Honey Mascarpone Cream. Serve cold.

> NOTE: I adore the Honey Mascarpone Cream more than anything, but instead you could spread on the blueberry filling 2 cups (17 oz/482 g) sour cream sprinkled with ¼ cup (1.9 oz/54 g) dark brown sugar or 1 cup (237 ml) heavy cream, whipped and sweetened with 2 tablespoons (0.9 oz/25 g) granulated sugar.

Honey Mascarpone Cream

MAKES ABOUT 2½ CUPS (591 ML)

This is my absolute favorite topping in the whole world for fruit. Food writer and teacher Michele Scicolone introduced me to the joy of mascarpone and honey. I just adore this—a hint of honey, the richness of the cheese, and the billowing lightness of the cream. A dignified judge friend was helping us with a class in North Carolina and there was a full cup of this left when we were cleaning up. He ate the whole thing, smiled, and sighed with total contentment.

What This Recipe Shows

Stirring honey into the mascarpone lightens it to make blending with the whipped cream easier.

Having the cream, bowl, and beaters cold helps fat stick together around air bubbles to hold the whipped cream firm.

---

1 cup (237 ml) heavy cream	3 tablespoons (45 ml) honey
½ cup (4 oz/113 g) mascarpone cheese	

1. Place a medium bowl and beaters in the freezer for 5 minutes. Pour the cream into the chilled bowl.

2. Whip the cream with cold beaters to medium-firm peaks. In a small bowl, whisk together the mascarpone and honey. Fold the mascarpone mixture into the whipped cream. Chill until ready to serve. Serve cold.

Modern Basic Honey Graham Crumb Crusts

Here are some ratios for basic honey graham cracker crumb crusts. Four square crackers (2½ inches/6 cm) produce about ¼ cup (1 oz/28 g) crumbs. This chart gives a good ballpark figure, but you still need to use some personal judgment. After mixing the crumbs, sugar, and butter, pinch a little of the blended mixture between your thumb and forefinger to see if it holds together. You need to be able to press the mixture against the side of the pan and have it hold.

Crust Size	Crumbs	Sugar	Butter
8-inch (20-cm)	1¼ cups (5 oz/142 g) about 20 squares (2½ inches/6 cm)	2 tablespoons (0.9 oz/25 g)	¼ cup (2 oz/57 g)
9-inch (23-cm)	1½ cups (6 oz/170 g) about 24 squares (2½ inches/6 cm)	3 tablespoons (1.3 oz/38 g)	5 tablespoons (2.5 oz/71 g)
10-inch (25-cm)	1¾ cups (7 oz/198 g) about 28 squares (2½ inches/6 cm)	¼ cup (1.8 oz/51 g)	6 tablespoons (3 oz/85 g)

1. Arrange a shelf in the center of the oven and preheat to 350°F/177°C.

2. In a food processor with the steel blade, process the crackers and sugar to fine crumbs. With the processor running, drizzle in the melted butter until the crumbs begin to clump.

3. Spray the appropriate size pie pan or springform pan (see Note) with nonstick cooking spray. Sprinkle crumbs around the bottom of the prepared pan, then press up the sides about 1½ inches (4 cm) and across the bottom of the pan. Bake about 8 minutes until set. Cool completely before filling.

NOTE: Springform pans labeled 8 inch (20 cm) may actually be 8½ inches (22 cm), and springform pans labeled 9 inch (23 cm) may actually be 9½ inches (24 cm). Either is fine.

Monroe Boston Strause's Crumb Crust

MAKES ONE 9-INCH (23-CM) CRUST

Monroe, the perfectionist, created the first crumb crust for his famous Black Bottom Pie, and his crust remains outstanding to this day. Monroe used shortening, but since the cooked flavor of butter-flavored shortening (which was not available in his time) is so good, I have substituted it.

What This Recipe Shows

Monroe's use of corn syrup prevents the sugar from crystallizing when the crust cools, so it will always give you an easy-to-cut crust.

Adding some shortening to the melted butter also avoids rock-hard cold butter and makes an easy-to-cut crust even when ice cold.

---

24 squares (2½ inch/6 cm) graham crackers (6 oz/170 g)
2 tablespoons (1 oz/28 g) butter
1 tablespoon (0.4 oz/11 g) butter-flavored shortening

⅛ teaspoon (pinch) salt
1 tablespoon (15 ml) water
1 tablespoon (15 ml) light corn syrup
Nonstick cooking spray

1. Place a shelf in the center of the oven and preheat the oven to 350°F/177°C.

2. In a food processor with the steel blade, process the crackers to fine crumbs.

3. In a small saucepan, melt the butter and shortening. Stir in the salt. With the processor running, drizzle in the melted butter, shortening, and salt. Stir together the water and corn syrup and drizzle in with processor running.

4. Spray a 9-inch (23-cm) pie pan or springform pan (see Note) with nonstick cooking spray. Sprinkle crumbs around the bottom of the prepared pan, then press up the sides about 1½ inches (4 cm) and across the bottom of the pan. Bake in the preheated oven for 8 minutes. Cool completely before filling.

NOTE: Springform pans labeled 9 inch (23 cm) may actually be 9½ inches (24 cm). Either is fine.

Cracker-Nut Crust

MAKES ONE 9-INCH (23-CM) CRUST

Buttery, salty, crunchy, nutty—what more could you ask?

What This Recipe Shows

The blend of flavors of salty nuts, crackers, and butter is excellent for a savory crust.

About 24 square (2-inch/5-cm) saltine
crackers
1½ cups (6 oz/170 g) store-bought roasted
salted mixed nuts without peanuts

1 tablespoon (0.4 oz/11 g) sugar
½ teaspoon (3 g) salt
5 tablespoons (2.5 oz/71 g) butter, melted
Nonstick cooking spray

1. Arrange a shelf in the center of the oven and preheat the oven to 350°F/177°C.

2. In a food processor with the steel blade, process the saltines, nuts, sugar, and salt to fairly fine crumbs. With the processor running, drizzle in the melted butter.

3. Spray a 9-inch (23-cm) pie or tart pan or a springform pan (see Note) with nonstick cooking spray. Sprinkle the crumbs around the bottom of the prepared pan, then press up the sides and across the bottom of the pan. Bake 8 minutes until set. Cool completely before filling.

NOTE: Springform pans labeled 9 inch (23 cm) may actually be 9½ inches (24 cm). Either is fine.

Herb-Crusted Goat Cheese Tart

MAKES ONE 8-INCH (20-CM) TART

Wonderful served with cold mixed greens tossed with olive oil, salt, and pepper, and no more than 1 tablespoon (15 ml) balsamic vinegar. Sometimes I prepare this in a 9 x 9 x 1½-inch (23 x 23 x 4-cm) pan lined with Release foil and press the crust in the bottom only, bake, and cool. Then I prepare and bake the filling as directed. When it has cooled, I lift out the pie in the foil. I can then cut it into 16 slightly-larger-than-2-inch (5-cm) squares to serve on the side of the salad plate with the simple salad described above.

What This Recipe Shows

Cream cheese and mayonnaise dilute the sharpness of the fresh goat cheese.

A little salt suppresses bitterness.

---

1 recipe Cracker-Nut Crust (page 273), baked and cooled in a springform pan
¼ cup (59 ml) room-temperature water
1 teaspoon (3.0 g) unflavored gelatin
6 ounces (170 g) Montrachet (plain fresh goat cheese)
Two 8-ounce (454-g) packages cream cheese
½ cup (118 ml) mayonnaise

Zest (grated peel) of 1 lemon
2 teaspoons (0.3 oz/8.5 g) sugar
¼ teaspoon (1.5 g) salt
¼ teaspoon (0.5 g) ground cayenne
¼ cup (2 oz/57 g) unsalted butter
½ cup (1.9 oz/54 g) Italian-seasoned fine bread crumbs

1. Pour the water into a small saucepan, sprinkle the gelatin on top, and let stand 2 minutes. Over very low heat, warm just to dissolve the gelatin. (Never boil gelatin, since this will reduce its ability to gel.) Alternatively, in a microwave-safe glass measuring cup or small bowl, sprinkle the gelatin over the water and allow to stand to soften. Microwave gelatin on 100% power for about 20 seconds, just long enough to dissolve.

2. In a food processor with the steel blade, process to blend the goat cheese, cream cheese, mayonnaise, lemon zest, sugar, salt, and cayenne. With the food processor running, drizzle the gelatin into the cheese mixture. Immediately spoon the mixture onto the cooled crust. Refrigerate while preparing the bread-crumb topping.

3. Meanwhile, in a medium skillet, melt the butter over medium-high heat. Add the crumbs and cook, stirring, until the crumbs are lightly browned. Cool the crumbs about 10 minutes. Turn on the

broiler. Spread the crumbs on top of the cheese mixture. Slip the cheesecake under the broiler just to brown—about 3 to 4 minutes only—watch carefully.

4. Chill well before serving. Just before serving, expand the springform pan and remove the sides.

5. This can be impressive served on a pedestal cake dish. I usually cut it "wedding cake" style: cut an inner circle about 2 inches (5 cm) from the outer edge, then cut thick slices 1 to 1½ inches (2.5 to 4 cm) wide by 2 inches (5 cm) deep (into the inner circle cut). This makes serving small portions easier.

CHOCOLATE COOKIE CRUMB CRUSTS

Chocolate cookie crumb crusts are probably next in popularity to graham cracker crusts. Cooks use a great variety of chocolate cookies from Oreo crumbs (even whole Oreos, filling and all) to chocolate graham crackers to Nabisco Famous Chocolate Wafers. Here is an example of a typical chocolate cookie crumb crust.

Chocolate Cookie Crumb Crust

MAKES ONE 9-INCH (23-CM) CRUST

A truly versatile crust—you can use it for everything from a chocolate mousse to a cherry pie. I use it for one of my favorite pies in the world—the Rum Cream Pie on page 276.

What This Recipe Shows

No sugar is added, to prevent an uncuttable crust.

Salt reduces bitterness and brings out the sweetness of the cookies.

1½ cups (about 6 oz/170 g) chocolate cookie crumbs (Nabisco Famous Chocolate Wafers are my favorite; in the grocery store, they are usually found near the ice cream)

¼ cup (2 oz/57 g) butter, melted
½ teaspoon (2.5 ml) pure vanilla extract
⅛ teaspoon (pinch) salt
Nonstick cooking spray

1. Arrange a shelf in the center of the oven and preheat the oven to 350°F/177°C.

2. In a food processor with the steel blade, process the cookies to fine crumbs. Drizzle in the melted butter. Add the vanilla and salt and process in.

3. Spray a 9-inch (23-cm) pie or tart pan or a springform pan (see Note) with nonstick cooking spray. Spread the crumbs around in the prepared pan and press up the sides and across the bottom. Bake about 10 minutes until firm. Cool completely before filling.

NOTE: Springform pans labeled 9 inch (23 cm) may actually be 9½ inches (24 cm). Either is fine.

Rum Cream Pie

MAKES ONE 8-INCH (20-CM) PIE

This is one of the most delicious pies imaginable! Technically, it is a rum chiffon pie, but when you say chiffon, people think of a beaten-egg-white, light, low-fat dessert. I did not want to go under any false pretenses here. This is rich and wonderful from the days of old. It is an adaptation of a recipe in an older version of *The Joy of Cooking*. Note: This recipe contains raw egg yolks. Also, do not substitute rum flavoring for the dark rum.

What This Recipe Shows

Emulsifiers in egg yolks create a velvety texture.

If you have the ingredients to be added at room temperature, they incorporate beautifully into whipped cream.

Having the bowl, beaters, and cream cold enhances whipping.

---

1 recipe Chocolate Cookie Crumb Crust (page 275) prepared in an 8-inch (20-cm) springform pan lined with parchment or foil circle, baked and cooled in the pan

2 cups (473 ml) heavy cream

6 large egg yolks (3.9 oz/111 g)

1 cup (7 oz/198 g) sugar

½ cup plus 1 tablespoon (133 ml) water, divided

¼ cup (59 ml) dark rum (Myers's is the best; you can drink the leftovers!)

1½ envelopes (10.5 g) unflavored gelatin

1 ounce (28 g) bittersweet or semisweet chocolate, for garnish

⅓ cup (about 1.5 oz/37 g) shelled pistachio nuts, for garnish

1. In a cold bowl with cold beaters, whip the cream until peaks form and the cream is slightly firm. Set aside.

2. In a medium mixing bowl, beat the egg yolks, sugar, and 1 tablespoon water until pale yellow. Beat the rum into the yolks and sugar.

3. Pour the remaining ½ cup (118 ml) water into a small saucepan. Sprinkle the gelatin on top of the water and let stand 2 minutes. Over very low heat, warm just to dissolve the gelatin. (Never boil gelatin, since this will reduce its ability to gel.) Alternatively, in a microwave-safe glass measuring cup or small bowl, sprinkle the gelatin over the water and allow to stand to soften. Microwave gelatin on 100% power for about 20 seconds, just long enough to dissolve.

4. Beat in the dissolved gelatin. Fold this gelatin-rum mixture into the whipped cream, and pour into the cool crust. Refrigerate until firm.

5. In a food processor with the medium shredding disc, or with a Mouli hand grater, grate the chocolate and pistachio nuts, or finely chop by hand on a cutting board. Sprinkle on top to garnish. Just before serving, expand the springform pan and remove the sides.

Gingersnap-Pecan Crust

MAKES ONE 8-INCH (20-CM) CRUST

Gingersnaps with their crisp texture and distinctive flavor make a great crumb crust. When mixed with roasted pecans, gingersnaps make the perfect crust to enhance a delicately flavored cheesecake. When I saw Carole Walter's Gingersnap with Pecan Crust in her book *Great Pies & Tarts,* I thought, "What a great flavor combination."

What This Recipe Shows

Finely chopped pecans cut the sugar concentration so that the crust cuts easily.

The gingersnaps complement the pecan flavors.

1½ cups (5.2 oz/149 g) pecans
8 ounces (227 g) gingersnaps
Nonstick cooking spray

2 tablespoons (0.9 oz/25 g) sugar
¼ teaspoon (1.5 g) salt
¼ cup (2 oz/56 g) butter, melted

1. Arrange a shelf in the center of the oven and preheat the oven to 350°F/177°C.

2. Spread the pecans on a baking sheet. Place in the oven and roast for about 10 minutes, until lightly browned and fragrant. Remove from oven to cool.

3. Spray an 8-inch (20-cm) springform pan (see Note) with nonstick cooking spray.

4. In a food processor with the steel blade, process the cookies, nuts, sugar, and salt to fine crumbs. Then drizzle in melted butter with the processor running until clumps begin to form.

5. Spread the crumbs around in the prepared pan and press up the sides and across the bottom. Bake for about 10 minutes. Cool completely before filling.

NOTE: Springform pans labeled 8 inch (20 cm) may actually be 8½ inches (22 cm). Either is fine.

PRESS-IN-THE-PAN CRUST

If a crust is so tender that it is impossible to roll, it can be pressed into the pan.

A crust may be so tender that it is nearly impossible to roll. If the ratio of sugar to flour is high, or if the ratio of fat to flour is high (see the savory crust on page 340), it is easier to simply press the crumbly dough into the pan. This is a cross between a traditional flakey pastry crust and a crumb crust.

E-Z Delicious Chocolate-Nut Crust

MAKES ONE 9-INCH (23-CM) CRUST

This press-in-the-pan crust was adapted from a recipe by the great master dessert maker Maida Heatter. I adore this gracious lady's recipes. This crust would be delicious filled with the Rum Cream Pie filling on page 276.

What This Recipe Shows

The high ratio of butter to flour, plus the sugar, nuts, and chocolate, make this crust so tender that rolling it out would be just short of impossible.

Brown sugar gives the chocolate a fudgy taste.

¾ cup (2.6 oz/75 g) walnut pieces

½ cup (4 oz/113 g) butter, cut in 1-tablespoon (0.5-oz/14-g) pieces, divided

¼ cup (1.9 oz/54 g) light brown sugar, packed

1 cup (4.4 oz/124 g) spooned and leveled all-purpose flour

½ teaspoon (3 g) salt

1 ounce (28 g) unsweetened baking chocolate

1 teaspoon (5 ml) pure vanilla extract

1 tablespoon (15 ml) water

Nonstick cooking spray

1. Place a rack in the center of the oven and preheat the oven to 375°F/191°C.

2. Spread the walnuts out on a baking sheet, place in the oven, and roast for 10 minutes. While nuts are hot, stir in 2 tablespoons (1 oz/28 g) of the butter. Allow to cool.

3. In a food processor with the steel blade, process the brown sugar, flour, salt, and roasted walnuts until the nuts are very finely chopped. Add the remaining 6 tablespoons (3 oz/85 g) butter and process with quick on/offs until the butter is incorporated into the flour mixture.

4. Dump the sugar-flour-butter mixture into a medium mixing bowl. Using a hand grater such as a Mouli with a fine grating wheel, or a Microplane, grate the chocolate into the flour mixture and stir well.

5. Mix together the vanilla and water. Sprinkle half of it over the flour mixture and toss well with a fork. Sprinkle the remaining half and continue tossing with a fork. The mixture should be crumbly.

6. Spray a 9-inch (23-cm) pie pan with nonstick cooking spray. Dump the crust mixture into the pan and spread it around, pressing the sides in place first, then up the sides and across the bottom. Bake for about 15 to 20 minutes, until set. Cool completely before filling.

ANGEL PIES—MERINGUE CRUSTS

Hard meringues make ideal, very light pie crusts, thus the name "Angel Pies." Hard meringues are classically used as meringue cake layers with nuts like dacquoises and meringue shells like vacherins. (For more on hard meringues, and the Walnut-Oat Meringue crust, see page 183.)

PHYLLO CRUSTS

You can make dramatic but easy desserts with phyllo dough—store-bought or homemade. The Croustade on page 281 looks like a breathtaking giant tea rose.

I have been at events with "Anna" in Blacksburg, Virginia, a number of times, but I have no idea what her last name is. She is known to all as Anna. I've had the great opportunity to watch Anna make phyllo, and it is a truly humbling experience. Many years ago, Anna and her husband opened a restaurant on the square in Blacksburg, a small college town. With Anna's good cooking and her husband's warm hospitality, the restaurant was a big success. However, instead of calling the restaurant by its original name, everyone referred to it as "The Greeks." Finally, Anna's husband took down the restaurant sign and put up "The Greeks."

When I heard that Anna made her own phyllo, I begged my friends in Blacksburg to ask if I might come and watch her. Of course, Anna generously took me home with her and I watched the true art of phyllo making. Anna would lean against the dough, pressing it between her stomach and the table edge. Then she would wrap the dough around a dowel that was 3 feet (91 cm) long and pull the dowel up and out to stretch the dough. She would let the dough fall down in front of her, anchor a new spot farther up on the dough with her stomach against the table, and again stretch the dough with the dowel.

For successful phyllo dishes, buy phyllo at a store that has good turnover, thaw overnight in the refrigerator, work fast, keep everything but the sheet that you are working on well covered with a damp cloth and plastic wrap, and brush the edges of the phyllo first to prevent their cracking.

I was in awe. This was true art. I decided right then and there that I would always have to settle for store-bought phyllo.

It is best to buy phyllo in a store that has a rapid turnover. If you get phyllo that has been in the freezer for a long time and has frozen and thawed and frozen and thawed, it can be dreadful to handle; the sheets may be stuck together and dried out and impossible to work with.

On the other hand, relatively fresh frozen phyllo thawed in the refrigerator overnight can be a joy to use—but use caution because phyllo sheets dry out quickly when exposed to air. Work fast and keep all sheets, except the sheet that you are working with, well covered with a damp cloth and plastic wrap. When spreading melted butter on the phyllo, use a large pastry brush and brush the edges first to prevent them from cracking, then work your way into the center.

Croustade

MAKES 8 SERVINGS

This dramatic dessert resembles a large tea rose. The texture combination is nice with crispness from the flakey phyllo and toasted almonds in contrast to the soft, sweet apples and pears.

Phyllo sheets are available in frozen packages. For best results, place frozen phyllo in the refrigerator to thaw overnight.

This croustade takes a large amount of counter space to assemble. Allow room around the pizza pan for the phyllo rectangles to extend 4 to 6 inches (10 to 15 cm) beyond the pan edge.

What This Recipe Shows

The big secret in working with phyllo is to work as fast as you can. These sheets dry out rapidly in air. Keep all but the sheet that you are using covered with a damp towel and plastic wrap.

Brushing the edges with melted butter first and working in toward the center prevents the edges from cracking.

---

1 cup (3.5 oz/99 g) pecans or almonds

1/2 cup plus 2 tablespoons (5 oz/141 g) unsalted butter, divided

3/4 teaspoon (4.5 g) salt, divided

3 apples, cored and sliced into 1/2-inch (1-cm) slices (I like Fuji or ripe yellow Golden Delicious)

3 ripe pears, cored, peeled, and sliced into 1/2-inch (1-cm) slices

2/3 cup (6 oz/161 g) light brown sugar, packed

1/2 cup (118 ml) amaretto liqueur

1/2 teaspoon (1 g) freshly grated nutmeg

Eight to ten 14 x 18-inch (36 x 46-cm) phyllo sheets

1/2 cup (4 oz/113 g) salted butter, melted

1/4 cup (1 oz/28 g) confectioners' sugar

1. Preheat oven to 350°F/177°C.

2. On a baking sheet, roast the nuts for 10 minutes. While nuts are hot, stir in 2 tablespoons (1 oz/28 g) of the butter and 1/4 teaspoon (1.5 g) of the salt.

3. Turn up the oven to 375°F/191°C.

4. In a medium mixing bowl, toss the apple and pear slices with the brown sugar, amaretto, nutmeg, and remaining 1/2 teaspoon (3 g) salt. Cover and let sit for at least 30 minutes at room temperature.

5. Melt the remaining ½ cup (4 oz/113 g) butter in a small saucepan or in the microwave.

6. Carefully unroll the phyllo dough. Remove one sheet and lay it on the countertop. Cover the remaining phyllo with a damp towel and plastic wrap. Brush the sheet with melted butter and fold in half lengthwise to form a long rectangle. Place one end of rectangle in the center of a 16-inch (41-cm) pizza pan like the spoke of a wheel with part of the sheet outside the pan. Continue brushing one sheet at a time of the remaining phyllo with butter and arranging partially overlapping, so that the center of the pan is completely covered and sheets stand out in all directions.

7. Drain the apples and pears and place them in the center of phyllo circle. Sprinkle the roasted nuts evenly over them. Pick up the outside end of the last phyllo leaf that was placed down, bring toward the center over the apples, and twist the leaf over so that the bottom side is now on top. This forms a slightly cupped petal. Continue to bring leaves to the center one at a time, forming "petals" with each so that a large "tea rose" is formed. Drizzle any remaining melted butter over the top. Bake in the preheated oven for 35 to 40 minutes, until golden brown. Sprinkle with the confectioners' sugar. Serve hot or at room temperature.

Shaped and Prebaked Phyllo Shells

Already prepared and baked miniature phyllo shells are available in most grocery stores in the freezer section. They can be used to make instant savory hors d'oeuvres. Fill with chicken salad or salmon mousse made by blending equal parts cream cheese and lox or nova.

Although the shells are already baked, they taste and look much better if you dip or brush them in melted butter—holding them upside down—for a quick in-and-out dip. Then arrange them right side up on a baking sheet and bake for 10 minutes at 375°F/191°C.

The shells make perfect hand-held desserts. One batch of cheesecake batter will fill about 60 miniature phyllo shells. You can make a spectacular dessert platter by garnishing these mini cheesecakes with a variety of fruit such as a single strawberry, a few blueberries, and overlapping kiwi slices. To glaze, brush the top of the fruit with melted apple jelly and refrigerate until ready to serve. The Lemon Tartlets, recipe follows, are a marvelous light dessert after a seafood dinner. They can also be filled with the filling for chocolate pie (page 336), butterscotch pie (page 338), or with Pastry Cream (page 330).

Lemon Tartlets

MAKES ABOUT 60 SMALL TARTLETS

For a quick, elegant dessert, these little lemon tartlets are made using packaged mini phyllo shells available in the freezer section of most grocery stores. They are unbelievably crisp and make a perfect light hand-held dessert for buffets or large parties.

For real elegance, each can be garnished with a single candied violet.

What This Recipe Shows

Cold drops of fat glue to each other around air bubbles in whipped cream to create its texture. It is vital to keep the cream and utensils cold so that the fat drops do not melt. It is helpful to whip cream in a cool room so that you are not beating hot air into it.

You need to whip the cream until stiff, but keeping it very cold will allow you to carefully fold in the lemon curd without having the cream go to butter.

---

4 boxes mini phyllo shells (each box contains 15 shells; available in the freezer section)

½ cup (4 oz/113 g) butter, melted

1½ cups (355 ml) Lemon Curd (recipe follows)

2 cups (473 ml) heavy cream

1 tablespoon (15 ml) lemon zest (grated peel), for garnish

1. Arrange a shelf in the center of the oven and preheat the oven to 375°F/191°C.

2. Holding each shell upside down, dip each quickly (an in-and-out dip) in the melted butter. Arrange the shells right side up on a baking sheet. Bake for 10 minutes to lightly brown.

3. Remove from the oven to a rack to cool.

4. Chill the Lemon Curd well. Place the mixer bowl, beaters, and cream in the freezer for 5 minutes. Whip the cream until firm, but be careful not to whip it too long or it will turn to butter. Gently fold in lemon curd and taste. If you would like it more lemony, stir in more lemon curd until you achieve the intensity that you desire. Keep refrigerated.

5. Shortly before serving, and when the shells are completely cool, pipe or spoon the lemon curd–cream mixture into each shell. Garnish each with a sprinkle of lemon zest and serve immediately.

Lemon Curd

Makes about 2½ cups (593 ml)

Lemon curd is a wonderful thing. It is marvelous spooned on a soft warm biscuit. You can use it to fill tart shells or folded into whipped cream as a tart filling.

I remember this recipe as 5, 4, no 3, 2, 1—5 yolks, 4 lemons, no 3, 2 cups (14 oz/397 g) of sugar, and 1 stick (4 oz/113 g) of butter. Roland Mesnier scared the daylights out of me by getting me to make this over direct heat: bring it to a boil and strain it. I just knew that I was going to have a mass of curds. But Roland knew his recipe. When I strained it, I had maybe a teaspoon of curds, but I also had a well-thickened lemon curd in just minutes instead of the thirty minutes or so that it would take to make lemon curd in a double boiler. I still stick to the double boiler, partially because I am chicken, and partially because I love the texture when the custard is slow-cooked.

What This Recipe Shows

Sugar slows the setting of the egg yolks.

A double boiler is used to control the heat and prevent the eggs from scrambling. Heating slightly slower in a double boiler also produces a better texture.

The lemon curd is removed from the heat when it is only the thickness of a light to medium cream sauce—"coats a spoon." It becomes thicker as it cools.

---

5 large egg yolks (3.25 oz/92 g)
Zest (grated peel) and juice of 4 lemons

2 cups (14 oz/397 g) sugar
½ cup (4 oz /113 g) butter

1. Combine all ingredients in the top of a heavy double boiler, or in a heavy metal mixing bowl placed over a pot of boiling water. Make sure that the top bowl does not touch the water. Whisk ingredients constantly or scrape the bottom with a large flexible spatula until thickening begins to occur. With the water at a low boil, this will take about 5 minutes. Remove the top of the double boiler and continue to whisk. The heat of the pan should be enough to thicken the custard until it "coats the spoon" (when you run your finger across a spoon dipped in the lemon curd, the streak where your finger went across should last for a little).

2. Strain the curd into a cool bowl. Cover with plastic wrap touching the surface or dot with butter and then chill. Keeps well refrigerated for 2 weeks.

The Best-Ever Chess Tarts

MAKES ABOUT 45 SMALL TARTS

This sweet, incredibly delicious Southern chess pie filling is fabulous baked in the mini phyllo shells available in most grocery stores in the freezer case. They are unbelievably crisp and make a perfect hand-held dessert for buffets or large parties.

You can also bake this filling in an 8-inch (20-cm) prebaked pie crust, but the filling will be a little shallow.

What This Recipe Shows

The large amount of sugar plus the acidity from the vinegar keep the eggs from curdling, but I did add 1 tablespoon (12 g) of cornmeal just to be sure.

Vinegar cuts the sweetness for a perfect rich-tasting dessert.

---

3 boxes mini phyllo shells (each box contains 15 shells; available in freezer section)
1 cup (8 oz/227 g) butter, melted, divided
3 large eggs (5.25 oz/149 g)
2 large egg yolks (1.3 oz/37 g)

1½ cups (10.5 oz/297 g) sugar
¼ teaspoon (1.5 g) salt
1 tablespoon (12 g) cornmeal
1 tablespoon (15 ml) apple cider vinegar
1 tablespoon (15 ml) pure vanilla extract

1. Arrange a shelf in the lower third of the oven and preheat the oven to 375°F/191°C. Holding each shell upside down, dip quickly in ½ cup (118 ml) of the melted butter. Arrange the mini shells right side up on a baking sheet. Bake 10 minutes to lightly brown.

2. In a medium mixing bowl, stir together the eggs, yolks, remaining ½ cup (118 ml) melted butter, the sugar, salt, cornmeal, vinegar, and vanilla until well blended. Pour the filling into the mini shells, filling each shell completely. Place in the oven and bake until set, 15 to 20 minutes.

Pastry Crusts

I do not want to mislead. I love things that are quick and easy, and try to make recipes as quick and easy as possible. Pastry crusts are not difficult, but they are not quick. To make a good pie crust requires time and patience. After putting the dough together, you need to leave it in the refrigerator at least two hours for the moisture to distribute more evenly. If you roll a crust immediately after putting it together, the wet spots stick to the counter and the dry places tear. There are a few recipes that are exceptions, but they clearly state "roll out immediately." Before baking, you need to leave the crust in the freezer long enough to thoroughly freeze. Do not enter into the endeavor of making pie crust expecting "quick," but with time and patience, you can make a magnificent, memorable crust.

IMPORTANCE OF TECHNIQUES

In making a pastry crust, everything matters: the techniques, the recipe, and the ingredients.

The techniques, the recipe, and the ingredients all influence the kind of pie crust that you make. I normally discuss a subject in this order: recipe, ingredients, and finally techniques. However, before you can even make a simple crust, you have to know the techniques to experience how the recipe and different ingredients affect the crust. Also, pastry techniques are different. You don't just stir things together.

Easy Does It

When making pastry crust, there are many things that matter, and it is impossible to start with everything first. To ease into the topic we will start with rolling techniques, then with a delicious recipe for a cream cheese crust that is easy to put together and roll. You can make a simple rustic fruit tart with this crust.

Techniques for Rolling

Wrapping the dough in plastic wrap and refrigerating for at least 2 hours or overnight allows the moisture to distribute more evenly.

The Dough

The dough should hold together well but not be wet. Press the dough together into a 6-inch (15-cm) disc. Wrap in plastic wrap and refrigerate for at least 2 hours or overnight. This will allow the moisture to distribute more evenly. If you roll a crust immediately after making it, the wet spots will stick to the surface and the dry spots will tear.

The Surface for Rolling

Roll on a lightly floured counter, a pastry cloth or plastic sheet, or between two pieces of lightly floured wax paper. Carole Walter, in *Great Pies & Tarts,* recommends a canvas pastry cloth and rolling pin cover made by Ateco (available in some cookware shops). Rose Levy Beranbaum in *The Pie and Pastry Bible* says that the ideal surface for rolling pastry is marble covered with a pastry cloth. She recommends a 16 x 20 x ¾-inch (41 x 51 x 2-cm) piece of marble available in gourmet shops or from marble supply companies. A marble slab stays cold and helps to keep the pastry cool.

Gourmet shops sell a plastic sheet that is marked with circles for the different size pie pans. It is very helpful to have a guide when trying to roll an even circle. My early pie crusts looked like strange-shaped amoebas!

Some cooks like to roll the dough between two sheets of wax paper or plastic wrap, or a layer of foil on the bottom and plastic wrap or wax paper on top. You may need to peel the paper or plastic off once or twice during rolling and reposition and smooth it out. Regardless of the surface—pastry cloth or countertop—you want to flour lightly to prevent the dough from sticking.

Rolling Pins

There are many different sizes and shapes of rolling pins available. Those that are straight cylinders are called straight French rolling pins and are usually 17 to 19 inches (43 to 48 cm) in length. There is one that is fat in the center and tapers narrower toward the ends—tapered French—and is about 19 inches (48 cm) long. This tapered French pin is designed to prevent the edges of the dough from getting too thin. Carole Walter feels that it is a little easier to roll evenly with the traditional ball-bearing rolling pin with handles. These come in lengths of 12 to 15 inches (30 to 38 cm).

Your choice of the rolling pin and the rolling surface are personal preferences. Feel free to go with whatever works best for you.

Rolling in Detail

On limited counter space, rotating the dough works very well. This technique also ensures that the dough does not stick to the counter or pastry cloth. Flour the rolling pin and place it in the center of the dough disc and roll forward. Place the pin back in the center of the dough disc and roll back, taking care not to roll over the dough edges, making them too thin. Gently lift and rotate the dough 45 degrees, roll forward and back again, rotate, and so on. Keep a little bleached all-purpose flour on the counter to one side. If the dough tends to stick when rotating, drag the dough through the flour when rotating and repositioning the dough. If you enlarge the dough a little at a time, in different positions, it helps to keep the circle even.

> Rotating the dough prevents sticking and aids in rolling an even circle.

Try to avoid rolling the dough thinner in one area. These thin spots will brown or burn before the rest of the crust is done. To get a very even thickness, stop when the dough is nearing the desired thickness. Place a ruler or a strip of wood (which is the thickness that you want) on one side of the dough, and another the same thickness on the other side. Rest the rolling pin on the two rulers or wood strips, and roll across the dough.

Keeping the dough an even thickness prevents excessive browning or burning in the thin spots. Another way to get a very even dough thickness is with rolling pin rings that are available in some gourmet cookware shops (see also Sources, rolling pin rings, page 509). Pairs of these elastic rings are of various thickness and fit on both ends of the pin. They keep the pin an exact distance from the counter so the dough is rolled to an even thickness.

Cream Cheese Crust

MAKES TWO 9-INCH (23-CM) CRUSTS

This is an easy-to-use-and-work-with dough resulting in a marvelously flakey crust. The technique for blending in the butter makes the crust extra flakey.

What This Recipe Shows

Cream cheese makes the dough very easy to handle.

The cream cheese is blended with the flour to add tenderness so that all the butter can be left in larger pieces (flattened) for flakiness.

½ teaspoon (3 g) salt
1 teaspoon (5 ml) apple cider vinegar
1 tablespoon (15 ml) water
One 8-ounce package (227 g) cream cheese, cut in 8 pieces

2 cups (9.2 oz/261 g) spooned and leveled all-purpose flour
1 cup (8 oz/227 g) butter, cut in ½-tablespoon (0.25-oz/7-g) pieces and frozen

1. In a small measuring cup, stir the salt and vinegar into the water. Refrigerate while you are putting the other ingredients together.

2. In a food processor with the steel blade, process the cream cheese and the flour until the cream cheese is blended in. Place the bowl and the cheese-flour mixture in the freezer for 15 to 20 minutes.

3. Place the bowl back on the processor, add the frozen butter, and process with a few quick on/offs to blend. With the processor running, drizzle in the salt-vinegar-water mixture. The dough should come together nicely.

4. Shape the dough into two 6-inch (15-cm) discs. Wrap tightly with plastic wrap, and refrigerate for at least 2 hours or overnight.

5. Shape and bake according to the specific pie recipe directions.

Rustic Pear Tart

MAKES ONE 9-INCH (23-CM) TART

Pears in a nut paste with sensationally flakey, crisp crust! Wow! How good can it get? Can be made with mixed fruits, as in the photograph insert, such as nectarines and pears.

What This Recipe Shows

Fine bread crumbs pressed into the bottom of the crust dry the crust, making it crisp and flakey.

½ recipe Cream Cheese Crust (page 288), refrigerated
Frangipane—Almond-Hazelnut Paste (page 291)
1½ pounds (24 oz/680 g) pears, peeled, cored, and sliced (about 4 or 5 pears)
1 cup (7.7 oz/220 g) light brown sugar
1 tablespoon (9 g) tapioca starch stirred into 3 tablespoons (45 ml) cool water

½ cup (3.5 oz/99 g) granulated sugar
½ teaspoon (3 g) salt
2 tablespoons (30 ml) Grand Marnier
Nonstick cooking spray
2 tablespoons (0.5 oz/14 g) very fine dry unseasoned bread crumbs
¼ cup (2 oz/57 g) butter, melted
¼ cup (59 ml) red currant jelly, melted

1. Toss the pear slices with the brown sugar and place them in a colander over a bowl to drain for 3 hours.

2. Pour all of the liquid from the pears into a skillet and bring to a boil over medium heat. Simmer until the juice is reduced to a syrup.

3. Stir in the tapioca-water mixture with a flat-end spatula and scrape the bottom to prevent scorching. Bring to a boil. (The boiling causes changes in the starch so that it can no longer continue to thicken when the pie is baked, which would make the filling a thick, starchy mess—see page 310 for more details.)

4. After the thickened juice comes to a boil, stir in the granulated sugar and the salt. The filling will thin. Again, it is necessary to bring this mixture back to a boil while stirring to prevent scorching. Remove from the heat and stir in the Grand Marnier. Pour the pears into a bowl, pour the cooked mixture over the drained fruit, and carefully stir with a wooden spatula. Do not refrigerate, but allow this to cool before pouring it into the crust to bake.

5. While the fruit is cooling, you can roll out the crust. Unwrap the dough disc. Roll the dough between two pieces of lightly floured wax paper. Start by placing the rolling pin in the middle of the dough, and roll forward but do not roll over the edge of the crust. Lift the pin, move it back to the middle, and start rolling again in the middle of the dough. This time roll back toward you, but not off the edge of the dough. Rotate both pieces of paper and the dough circle a quarter of a turn and repeat the forward and backward rolling. Keep rotating the circle, paper and all, and roll until the dough is a 12-inch (30-cm) circle. You will need to peel the paper off once or twice and relocate it during rolling. (For detailed rolling directions, see page 287).

6. Arrange a shelf in the lower third of the oven, place a baking stone on it, and preheat the oven to 450°F/232°C.

7. Spray a round pizza pan with nonstick cooking spray. Sprinkle the crumbs over an area 4 inches (10 cm) smaller than the pastry circle—for a 12-inch (30-cm) circle, make an 8-inch (20-cm) circle of crumbs in the center of the pan.

8. Cut a 12-inch (30-cm) circle from pastry and place on the pizza pan so that the crumb circle is under the center of the dough. Roll a rolling pin across the center of the dough so that the crumbs are pressed into the bottom of the dough. Spread about 2½ cups (591 ml) of the frangipane on the pastry, leaving a 3-inch (8-cm) border around the edges. Spoon the fruit on top of the nut paste. Fold the edges of the dough up and over the fruit. Place the pizza pan on the hot baking stone.

9. Bake for about 25 minutes, until the crust is golden brown, the nut paste is set, and the fruit has softened. Brush the folded-over crust edge with the melted butter. Brush the cooked fruit with the melted red currant jelly. Serve warm, at room temperature.

Frangipane—Almond-Hazelnut Paste

MAKES ABOUT 3 CUPS (710 ML)

Ground nuts, butter, and sugar—all the good stuff! Frangipane is a wonderful addition to many desserts.

1 cup (4.8 oz/138 g) store-bought roasted salted almonds
1 cup (4.8 oz/138 g) hazelnuts or deluxe mixed nuts without peanuts
1/2 cup (4 oz/113 g) butter
1 1/2 cups (10.5 oz/298 g) granulated sugar
1 cup (8.4 oz/238 g) dark brown sugar, packed
1/2 teaspoon (3 g) salt
2 large eggs (3.5 oz/99 g)
1/2 cup (2.2 oz/62 g) spooned and leveled bleached all-purpose flour

In a food processor with the steel blade, process the nuts until finely chopped, using caution not to turn the nuts to nut butter. Add the butter, granulated sugar, brown sugar, and salt, and process to blend well. Add one egg at a time, blending after each addition. Sprinkle in the flour, and then do quick on/offs just to blend in the flour. Can be refrigerated in a sealed container, for up to a week.

Rustic Cherry Tart

MAKES ONE 9-INCH (23-CM) TART

Cherries in a nut paste with sensationally flakey, crisp crust! Wow! And, I love Marcona almonds, the round Spanish almonds. I think they have a more almondy flavor. Thank goodness, they are becoming more available. I sprinkled them on the top of this tart. Do try them if you can. Trader Joe's, Whole Foods Market, and some of our gourmet grocers carry them. If you can get fresh cherries, by all means, use them. With a good cherry pitter they are not too much trouble. Also, some brands of frozen cherries are excellent.

What This Recipe Shows

Fine bread crumbs pressed into the bottom of the crust dry the crust, making it crisp and flakey.

½ recipe Cream Cheese Crust (page 288), refrigerated

1 recipe Frangipane—Almond-Hazelnut Paste (page 291)

One 15-ounce can (425 g) pitted dark sweet cherries, drained and liquid reserved

One 15-ounce can (425 g) pitted sour red cherries, drained and liquid reserved

1 cup plus 2 tablespoons (7.9 oz/223 g) sugar, divided

⅓ cup (1.8 oz/50 g) tapioca starch plus 1 tablespoon cornstarch (7 g) stirred into ¼ cup (59 ml) cool water

½ teaspoon (3 g) salt

3 tablespoons (1.5 oz/42 g) unsalted butter

2 tablespoons (30 ml) Chambord

1 tablespoon (15 ml) light corn syrup

Nonstick cooking spray

2 tablespoons (0.5 oz/14 g) very fine dry unseasoned bread crumbs

¼ cup (2 oz/57 g) butter, melted

½ cup (2.4oz/69 g) Marcona almonds, roasted and salted, or canned roasted and salted almonds

1. Pour the drained juice from both cans of cherries into a large, heavy saucepan. Add 1 cup (7oz/198 g) of the sugar and bring to a boil over medium heat. Reduce until about ½ cup (118 ml) remains. With constant stirring using a flat-end wooden spatula, drizzle in the starch-and-water mixture and bring back to a simmer. This liquid should be almost a stiff paste. *Bring to a boil.*

2. Keep stirring this thick mixture on the heat. Add the remaining 2 tablespoons (0.9 oz/25 g) of the sugar and the salt. Cook, stirring steadily, for several minutes. The mixture will thin a little when you add the sugar. *It is important to bring this mixture back to a good boil. Keep scraping the bottom to prevent burning.*

3. Stir in the butter, Chambord, and corn syrup. Pour this mixture into a bowl and carefully fold in the drained cherries with a spatula until all the fruit is coated. Allow to cool for about 30 minutes. *Do not refrigerate.*

4. Arrange a shelf in the lower third of the oven, place a baking stone on it, and preheat the oven to 450°F/232°C.

5. While the fruit is cooling, you can roll out the crust. Unwrap one of the dough discs. Roll the dough between two pieces of lightly floured wax paper. Start by placing the rolling pin in the middle of the dough, and roll forward but do not roll over the edge of the crust. Lift the pin, move it back to the middle, and start rolling again in the middle of the dough. Roll this time back toward you, but not off the edge of the dough. Rotate both pieces of paper and the dough circle a quarter of a turn and repeat the forward and backward rolling. Keep rotating the circle, paper and all, and roll until the dough is a 12-inch (30-cm) circle. You will need to peel the paper off once or twice and relocate it during rolling. (For detailed rolling directions, see page 287.)

6. Spray a round pizza pan with nonstick cooking spray. Sprinkle bread crumbs over an area 4 inches (10 cm) smaller than the pastry circle—say for a 12-inch (30-cm) circle, make an 8-inch (20-cm) circle of bread crumbs in the center of the pan.

7. Cut a 12-inch (30-cm) circle from the pastry and place it on the pizza pan so that the bread crumb circle is under the center of the dough. Roll a rolling pin across the center of the dough so that the bread crumbs are pressed into the bottom of the dough. Spread about 2½ cups (591 ml) of the frangipane on the pastry, leaving a 3-inch (8-cm) border around the edges. Spoon the fruit on top of the frangipane. Fold about 2 inches (5 cm) of the edges of the dough up and over the fruit. Place on the hot baking stone.

8. Bake for about 25 minutes, until the crust is golden brown, the frangipane is set, and the fruit is soft. Brush the folded-over crust edge with the melted butter. Sprinkle the almonds over the top to garnish. Serve hot, cold, or at room temperature.

Shaping the Pastry Crust

Now that you have mastered a beautiful crisp rustic tart, let's delve into details of placing a crust in the pan and shaping.

Cut the Dough to Shape

Many cooks like to trim the dough after it is in the pan. I like to start with the dough close to the right size. Rose Levy Beranbaum, in *The Pie and Pastry Bible*, has an excellent section on sizes of dough circles. Here are a few of the more common size pies:

- Cut or roll a 12 to 13-inch (30 to 33-cm) circle for a single-crust 9-inch (23-cm) pie pan. For pies with a fluted edge use a 13-inch (33-cm) circle.
- Cut or roll a 12-inch (30-cm) circle for a 9½ x 1-inch (24 x 2.5-cm) tart pan.
- Cut or roll the bottom crust 12 inches (30 cm) and the top crust about 14 inches (36 cm) to allow for a generous filling for a double-crust 9-inch (23-cm) fruit pie.
- Cut or roll a 13 to 14-inch (33 to 36-cm) circle for a 10-inch (25-cm) pie pan.
- For tartlets, cut the dough circle ¾ inch (2 cm) larger than the tartlet pan.

Selecting a Baking Pan

Black pan, dull pan, shiny pan, clear heatproof glass dish, removable-bottom quiche pan, springform pan, or flan ring—which is best? The primary consideration is that the crust needs to cook fast. The shape and the flakiness of the crust will both be lost if the fat melts before the protein structure starts to set. Also, if the filling is being baked in, such as in an apple or pumpkin pie, fast heat is vital to prevent the bottom crust from becoming soggy.

Clear heatproof glass pie dishes allow cooking by both conduction and radiant heat energy, which goes through the glass directly to the crust. Other pans cook by heat conduction only. Many bakers swear by Pyrex, but since I am so dedicated to freezing the crust and using a high baking tempera-

The crust needs to set fast. If the fat melts before the flour proteins start to set, the sides cave in, any decorative edges melt, and the flakiness is lost. Also, high heat fast helps to prevent a soggy bottom crust in pies that are baked with the filling in.

Air trapped between the crust and the pan makes the crust bubble up when it is heated. Cooks punch holes in the crust or "dock" the crust with a fork before baking to allow the trapped air to escape; however, this allows the filling to leak out and bake between the crust and the pan. A mess! *Punching holes in the pan, not in the crust, is a great idea!*

ture (450°F/232°C), I stay away from it. I think that you are asking a lot even of Pyrex to go directly from the freezer into a hot oven and not shatter or break.

In baking pans, the color and type of metal also affect the cooking speed. Dark or dull metal pans absorb heat faster and therefore cook faster than shiny pans.

A heavy pan made of a good heat conductor like aluminum is certainly going to give you a more evenly baked crust than a thinner, less conductive metal surface such as tin-plated steel. For a traditional pie pan, my favorite is heavy, dull aluminum, ideally with holes.

Advantages of Pans with Holes

Air trapped between the crust and the pan expands when the crust is heated, and makes the crust bubble up. When pre- or blind-baking a crust, it is recommended to "dock" the crust (punch holes in the crust), by rolling over it with a spiked roller or by punching holes with a fork to allow this trapped air to escape. However, more than once I have had the filling leak through these holes. The filling then bakes on between the crust and the pan and it is impossible to get the pie out of the pan.

When I read Strause's recommendation to punch holes in the pan, not the crust, I thought it was brilliant. The holes in the pan prevent air from getting trapped under the crust and bubbling up as a result, and without holes in my crust the filling stays in the crust, not baked under the crust.

Pie pans with holes were popular in the thirties and you may find one in an antique shop; unfortunately, it may be rusty. There are some thin, cheap pans with holes that are undesirable and would contribute to burning. However, Chicago Metallic makes an outstanding heavy aluminum 9-inch (23-cm) pan with holes that makes fabulous crusts. It is available by mail order from Amazon, and others (see Sources, pie pans with perforated bottoms, page 509).

Advantages of Baking Rings (Flan Rings)

Actually, my preference is no pan at all. A baking ring (flan ring) on a heavy baking sheet provides great heat fast. Maury Rubin of City Bakery, who has been producing classic tarts in New York since the late eighties, loves flan rings. With his dough, he bakes perfect 4¾-inch (12-cm) tarts (even baking blind without pastry weights) in flan rings.

You get fast high heat to set the crust quickly by using a baking ring (flan ring) on a heavy baking sheet. This very fast heat allows you to blind bake a pie or tart crust without using pie weights, which can have their disadvantages. (See page 326 for discussion about baking blind and pie weights.)

Placing the Dough in the Pan

To get the dough circle into the pan, fold the dough circle in half, then fold in half again to form a quarter of a circle. Spray the baking ring, pan with holes, or tart pan with nonstick cooking spray. If you are using a ring on a baking sheet, you may want to anchor the ring to the baking sheet by pressing small pieces of scrap dough in four places around the outside of the ring.

Carefully lift the folded dough, place the point in the center of the pan, and unfold halfway. Check to see if the overhanging dough is about the same width on both sides and the back. If not, gently move the crust so that it is centered in the pan, and then unfold all the way.

The crust is going to shrink, so you want to press a little extra dough down the sides—ease as much dough as you can down into the pan. If you are right-handed, hold a section of the overhang up with your left hand and with your right hand gently push the crust down into the pan with a stroking motion.

The crust shrinks during baking, so you want to press extra dough down inside the pan—gently ease as much dough as you can down into the pan.

Some cooks like to roll the dough around the rolling pin, carry it to the pan, and unroll across the top of the pan. If you use this technique, be sure to roll most of the dough around the pin—do not leave half of it dangling down. If the dough stretches and thins out it will shrink more during baking.

Shaping and Decorating

In a baking ring or tart pan, you want to make sure that the upper edge of the dough is slightly thicker than the sides. You can do this by running your index finger along the inside and gently pressing with your thumb on the top of the dough.

For a fluted or rope-edged 9-inch (23-cm) pie, a 13-inch (33-cm) circle of dough is the perfect size. After the dough circle is centered in the pan, turn the edge under about ½ inch (1.3 cm) all around and let it rest on the rim of the pie pan. You now have a double thickness of dough around the edge to flute. To flute the edge, place the thumb of one hand on the inside edge, then place the other thumb and index finger on the outside. Pinch the pastry around the inside thumb. Repeat this pinching all the way around the dough edge. For a rope edge, place a thumb on the inside and the knuckle of the index finger on the outside. With the knuckle, press the pastry toward the thumb and slightly toward the inside of the pan. Move your thumb along the inside and repeat.

For a crust that is to be baked upside down (see page 326 for more details) or for a simple decorative edge, use a fork and simply press the edge of the dough gently against the top edge of the pan. You can trim if needed, but remember, the crust is going to shrink a little when baked, so I always like to trim a little outside the pan. Spray the back of the fork with nonstick cooking spray and press fork into the edge, leaving its imprint. Repeat all around the edge.

GETTING THE PIE CRUST THAT YOU WANT

For some, perfection in a pie crust is layers of delicate flakes. For others, it is an almost disintegrating tenderness. What is important is that you know how to get the crust that you want.

Tenderness

For tenderness, you need to coat or grease the flour proteins well so that they cannot join together with water and each other to form tough gluten. The softer the fat and the more it is worked into the flour, the better the flour proteins are greased. The cook can rub the fat and flour together, or run the flour-fat mixture in a mixer or food processor until the fat is well incorporated into the flour.

Flakiness

The goal for flakiness is to achieve large, flat, cold pieces of fat coated with flour. The fat needs to be large enough to remain unmelted long enough for the dough above and below the fat to partially set. The fat acts as a spacer. Then the fat melts and steam from the dough puffs the dough apart where the fat once was. The pieces of fat also need to be flattened. If you have a big lump of fat, it will go all the way through the crust and leave a hole when it melts.

You can already see that the techniques for a tender crust are going to be very different from the techniques for a flakey crust. For a tender crust, you want to work warm, soft fat into the flour very thoroughly. For a flakey crust you want to create large, flat, cold pieces of fat.

Techniques, Step One—Combining Flour and Fat

The very nature of the crust depends on the way that you incorporate the fat with the flour. Right here, at the beginning, you are determining the total character of the crust. Will it be flakey, will it be tender, will it be tough? All of this will depend on how you combine the flour and fat.

If you work the fat into the flour until the mixture resembles fine meal (as many recipes direct), that fat is going to melt instantly in the hot oven. This will coat the flour proteins well and produce a very tender crust, but not a single flake.

If you work the fat into the flour so that you get large, flat, cold pieces of fat coated with flour, you will have a flakey crust. If you work about a fourth of the fat in well, but three-fourths of the fat into large, flat, cold pieces, you will have a crust that is both tender and flakey.

Tender Crust Only—No Flakes

I love flakey pastry and normally have had little use for crusts made by working the fat in well. To my astonishment, a tender crust like this can be waterproof (the flour is so well greased that it does not get wet) if cooked properly. My version of Monroe Boston Strause's Special Crust for Pumpkin Pie on page 298 is a crust that does not get soggy.

I have given food processor directions, but you can easily make this amazing waterproof crust by hand or in a mixer.

There are times when you do not want a crust to be tender. Hand-held pies need to be sturdy. For such a pastry, it's important to develop some gluten to hold the crust together. I like to add an egg to the crust, which makes it stronger. Later, I will go into how to make pies tough when needed (see page 306).

Crusts made by working the fat in thoroughly can be waterproof if cooked properly.

Tender Crusts by Hand

You goal is to coat the flour proteins really well with fat. Start with room-temperature or warm fat. Work the fat in well, but not quite to the point that it is pasty. You want to develop a tiny bit of gluten to keep the crust from falling apart. After you have worked the fat into the flour very well, sprinkle the flour with 1 to 2 tablespoons (15 to 30 ml) of the liquid. Toss the dough with your hands and press a little of the dough between your fingers. The dough should be wet enough to hold together but not feel sticky or gooey. Sprinkle and toss 2 more tablespoons (30 ml) of the liquid in at a time until you get a dough that holds together. Since the gluten-forming proteins are greased and cannot combine with water, this dough should not absorb much water. Shape the dough into a 6-inch (15-cm) disc, wrap well with plastic wrap or place in a zip-top plastic bag, and refrigerate for at least 2 hours or overnight.

Tender Crusts in a Mixer

Your goal is the same as by hand: to coat the flour proteins really well with fat. Place the room-temperature or warm fat and the flour in the mixer bowl. Mix on low to medium speed until the fat and flour are well blended, just short of being pasty. I like to finish off by hand since I have more control. Sprinkle with 1 to 2 tablespoons (15 to 30 ml) of the liquid. Toss the dough and press a little between your fingers. The dough should be wet enough to hold together but not sticky or gooey. Sprinkle and toss in 2 tablespoons (30 ml) of the liquid at a time until you get a dough that holds together. This dough should not absorb much water. Shape the dough into a 6-inch (15-cm) disc, wrap well with plastic wrap or place in a zip-top plastic bag, and refrigerate for at least 2 hours or overnight.

Tender Crusts in a Food Processor

Again, your goal is to coat the flour proteins very well with fat. Place room-temperature fat and flour in a food processor with the steel blade and process until they are well blended, almost pasty. Again, just like with the mixer, I like to add the liquid by hand so that I have more control. Transfer the flour-fat mixture to a bowl and sprinkle with 1 to 2 tablespoons (15 to 30 ml) of the liquid. Toss the dough and press a little between your fingers. You want the dough wet enough to hold together but not

This crust is astonishing. Even after several days in the refrigerator with the nice moist pumpkin pie filling in it, this crust does not get soggy!

sticky or gooey. Sprinkle and toss in 2 tablespoons (30 ml) of the liquid at a time until you get a dough that holds together. This dough should not absorb much water. Shape the dough into a 6-inch (15-cm) disc, wrap well with plastic wrap or place in a zip-top plastic bag, and refrigerate at least 2 hours or overnight.

I never liked crust with the fat worked in this well until Monroe Boston Strause explained that such a crust, cooked properly, can be waterproof—a crust that doesn't get soggy. What a find! You have got to try Monroe Boston Strause's Special Crust for Pumpkin Pie, below.

Shirley's Adaptation of Strause's Special Crust for Pumpkin Pie

MAKES ONE 9-INCH (23-CM) CRUST

This crust is astonishing. After several days in the refrigerator with the nice moist pumpkin pie filling in it, this crust is not soggy! It is still as if it had just been brought out of the oven.

The very nature of the crust depends on the method in which you combine the fat and flour. Monroe baked at 450°F/232°C and added that, since your oven temperature drops significantly when the door is opened, you need to account for this. Since all ovens drop when the door is opened even briefly, I recommend preheating to 475°F/246°C and then, immediately after placing the pie in the oven, turning the oven down to 450°F/232°C.

What This Recipe Shows

Working the shortening into the flour extremely well makes this crust waterproof so it does not get soggy even when cooked with the filling.

The corn syrup acts as a binder to make the dough easier to handle. You don't really have enough gluten to hold the crust together well.

The corn syrup is also a major color enhancer. Since you do not have the amount of gluten (which is a protein and a color enhancer) that you do in a regular crust, this is a big help.

Nonfat dry milk provides proteins and sugars that are also color enhancers.

Instant flours like Wondra and Shake & Blend are low in gluten-forming proteins and have an excellent taste from the barley malt in them.

1²⁄₃ cups (7.7 oz/217 g) instant flour (such as Wondra or Shake & Blend), poured into a measuring cup and leveled

7 tablespoons plus 1¹⁄₂ teaspoons (3.2 oz/90 g) butter-flavored shortening

1 teaspoon (6 g) salt

2 scant teaspoons (5 g) nonfat dry milk powder

1¹⁄₂ teaspoons (8 ml) light corn syrup

1 teaspoon (5 ml) apple cider vinegar

¹⁄₄ cup (59 ml) plus 2 teaspoons (10 ml) water

Nonstick cooking spray

2 tablespoons (13 g) very fine dry unseasoned bread crumbs

1. Place the flour and shortening in a food processor with the steel blade and process with quick on/offs until clumpy—almost pasty. Be aware that this is more than you would normally work the shortening into the flour for a pie crust.

2. In a small bowl or measuring cup, stir together the salt, nonfat dry milk, corn syrup, vinegar, and water. Drizzle this liquid into the flour-shortening mixture a little at a time, processing with quick on/offs after each addition. Process until dough comes together.

3. Do NOT refrigerate as you normally do with pie crust. This is a dry dough, but if you roll it out immediately it works well. Roll between two pieces of wax paper or plastic wrap lightly sprinkled with flour into a 12-inch (30-cm) circle. (See page 286 for detailed rolling directions.)

4. Spray a 9-inch (23-cm) springform pan (see Note) with nonstick cooking spray and sprinkle the bread crumbs very evenly over the bottom only. To get the dough centered in the pan, fold the dough in half, and then fold in half again to make a quarter section. Place the point of the folded section in the center of the pan, and then unfold the dough circle. With your fingertips, press well across the whole bottom of the pan to press the crumbs into the dough. Run your fingers around the sides to press against the pan and use your thumb to even and press down the top edge very slightly—just so it is not thin on the upper edge. Set aside unbaked until the filling is finished.

NOTE: Springform pans labeled 9 inch (23 cm) may actually be 9¹⁄₂ inches (24 cm). Either is fine.

Memorable Creamy Pumpkin Pie

MAKES ONE 9-INCH (23-CM) PIE

Creamy, smooth, and flavorful—this is no wimpy pumpkin pie.

What This Recipe Shows

Allowing the pumpkin to stand a few minutes with the spices and liquid incorporated permits it to soak in both well.

Cracking in the pie filling is caused by overcooking, but the corn syrup keeps the pie very moist and helps some to prevent cracking.

---

1 recipe Shirley's Adaptation of Strause's Special Crust for Pumpkin Pie (page 298), prepared in a 9-inch (23-cm) springform pan

2 tablespoons (0.5 oz/15 g) bleached all-purpose flour

1¼ cups (10.5 oz/298 g) dark brown sugar, packed

1 teaspoon (6 g) salt

2 teaspoons (4 g) ground cinnamon

½ teaspoon (1 g) ground ginger

½ teaspoon (1 g) freshly grated nutmeg

½ teaspoon (1 g) ground allspice

1 tablespoon (15 ml) pure vanilla extract

⅓ cup (79 ml) light corn syrup

One 14-ounce can (414 ml) sweetened condensed milk

½ cup (118 ml) heavy cream

1¾ cups (15-ounce/443-ml can) pumpkin puree

1 large egg (1.75 oz/50 g)

3 large egg yolks (1.95 oz/55g)

Sour Cream Topping (recipe follows), optional

1. Arrange a shelf in the lower third of the oven, place a baking stone on it, and preheat the oven to 475°F/246°C.

2. In a large heavy saucepan, stir together the flour, sugar, salt, cinnamon, ginger, nutmeg, and allspice. Stir in the vanilla, corn syrup, sweetened condensed milk, cream, and pumpkin. Allow to stand on the counter for at least an hour for full absorption to take place.

3. After 1 hour, place the pan over medium-low heat for 3 to 4 minutes, stirring constantly, to take the chill off of the ingredients and slightly shorten baking time. Remove from the heat.

4. In a small bowl, mix together the egg and egg yolks. Beat 1 heaping tablespoon (about 30 ml) of the warm filling into the eggs, then pour the tempered eggs into the filling and mix well. Pour into the prepared crust.

5. Place on the baking stone. Close the door and immediately turn the oven down to 450°F/232°C. Bake for about 40 minutes. The center will still be very jiggly when the pie is done, so do not overcook. The center will firm up when the pie is cool.

6. If desired, top with Sour Cream Topping.

Sour Cream Topping

MAKES ENOUGH FOR ONE 9-INCH (23-CM) PIE

This is from Maida Heatter. She covers fresh strawberries with this topping and says that after 3 hours, the brown sugar becomes a dark brown layer of "deliciousness."

One 8-ounce carton (227 g) sour cream $^2/_3$ cup (5.5 oz/157 g) dark brown sugar, packed

When the pie is completely cool, and 3 to 6 hours before you are ready to serve, carefully and without stirring (which thins the sour cream) spread the sour cream over the top of the pie. With your fingers and a coarse strainer, sprinkle the sugar evenly over the sour cream, covering the pie heavily. Allow to stand 3 to 6 hours in the refrigerator before serving.

For Flakey Crusts—Preparing the Fat and Flour

If you want a fall-apart tender crust with no sign of a flake, you can work with warm fat or even oil. But if you want a crust that is tender but has at least a hint of flakiness, before combining the fat and flour you need to cut the fat into workable-size pieces, and you need to chill the fat and the flour so that the fat will not melt the minute you start working with it.

For a crust that is tender but has some flakiness, before combining the fat and flour, cut the fat into workable-size pieces, toss with the flour, and chill.

Cutting the Butter

My favorite way to cut butter is with a butter slicer. It is easy and fast. You can get butter slicers at most gourmet cookware shops. Mine is called Endurance Butter Slicer, and it's made by R.S.V.P. International, Inc. in Seattle, Washington. It cuts thin slices, about ½ tablespoon (0.25 oz/7 g). I simply take a stick of cold butter directly from the refrigerator and place it in the bottom of a pan or dish containing the flour called for in the recipe. I turn the butter over and over, pressing it into the flour on each side so that I'm starting with the edges coated with flour. Then I press the butter cutter down almost all the way through the stick of butter. I pick up the cutter with the butter still stuck in it, turn the cutter over, and run a finger across a wire of the cutter to finish cutting the slices all the way through. This allows a single slice or two at a time to fall into the flour and saves me the job of separating the slices. I toss the butter around to coat all the slices, then place the bowl or pan in the freezer for about 10 minutes.

Shortening and lard, even cold, are too soft to cut with the butter slicer. Instead, I place them in the freezer for 10 to 20 minutes and then slice by hand into pieces of 1 tablespoon (0.5 oz/14 g) or less. I then toss well with flour, and place the flour and fat in the freezer for 10 minutes. I love to use the shortening sticks, too, because they make measuring so much easier.

"Super Flakey" Crust

Whether you are mixing the crust by hand, with a mixer, or with a food processor, cut the fat into workable-size pieces (as described above), toss in the flour, and place in the freezer for 10 minutes.

Flakey Crust By Hand

By preparing the fat and flour as directed above, you are well on your way to a flakey crust. Your goal is to flatten the pieces of fat without making them too small. You can do this by squishing the pieces of fat between your fingertips and thumb. Work fast and take not care to let the fat melt.

My favorite way to flatten the butter is Chef Jim Dodge's flatten-on-the-counter technique. After cutting the fat into slices, tossing with flour, and placing the fat and flour in the freezer for 10 minutes, dump the cold fat-butter mixture out onto a clean counter. Flour a rolling pin and roll it over the fat and flour mixture to flatten the butter or shortening. Some butter may stick to the pin. Scrape it off and scrape the mixture together. Roll over the mixture again. If the butter becomes soft at any time during the rolling, return the mixture immediately to the bowl and freeze for 5 minutes. Rapidly continue rolling and scraping together at least three times. The mixture should look like paint flakes that have fallen off a wall. Scrape the mixture back into the bowl and return it to the freezer for 10 minutes.

For a flakey crust, keep the fat cold. If the fat gets warm and melts into the flour, flakiness is lost.

Simple Very Flakey Crust

MAKES 1 INCREDIBLY FLAKEY 9-INCH (23-CM) CRUST

I love this crust! When I made it for the first time, I was thrilled. I couldn't believe that, right at home, without much trouble, I made this magnificent flakey masterpiece. Some think it is too flakey, but I think it's wonderful.

This crust is perfect for making rustic tarts, like the Rustic Pear Tart on page 289. The dough is rolled out in a circle, placed on a heavy baking sheet, filled (usually with fruit) piled high, and the dough turned up around the edges. The crust is so flakey and puffed in the bottom of a pie pan that it takes up some of the filling space, but that doesn't matter in a rustic tart that can be as high as it comes out.

Because this crust is extremely flakey, when making it a regular crust, I like to bake it upside down or in a deep-dish pie pan. The bottom and the sides are puffed with flakes and you do not have a lot of space for filling unless you have the sides stretched full length, as baking upside down does, or have deep sides, like a deep-dish pie pan. (For detailed upside-down baking directions, see page 326.)

What This Recipe Shows

Keeping the butter cold and flattening it into the flour by rolling over the flour and butter, scraping it together and rerolling several times, produces hundreds of flour-coated flakes of butter that bake into an incredibly flakey crust.

Sour cream acts as a tenderizer because the fat in the sour cream coats the proteins in the flour.

Since none of the fat is worked into the flour, this crust could be tough if it were not for the sour cream and the low-protein instant flour.

---

1 cup (4.6 oz/130 g) instant flour (such as Wondra or Shake & Blend), poured into a measuring cup and leveled

½ cup (2.2oz/62 g)spooned and leveled bleached all-purpose flour

½ cup (4 oz/113 g) very cold unsalted butter, cut in ½-tablespoon (0.25-oz/7-g) pieces

1 teaspoon (6 g) salt

One 8-ounce carton (227 g) sour cream

Cold whole milk, as needed

1. In a medium bowl, stir together both flours. Add the butter to the flour and stir to coat the butter slices well. Place in the freezer for 10 minutes.

2. Dump the cold flour-butter mixture out onto a clean countertop. Flour a rolling pin and roll it over the mixture to flatten the butter. Some butter may stick to the pin. With a pastry or bench scraper, scrape it off and scrape the mixture together. Roll over the mixture again. If the butter becomes soft at any time during the rolling, immediately return the mixture to the bowl and freeze for 5 minutes. Working quickly, continue rolling and scraping the butter and flour mixture together at least three times in all. The mixture should look like paint flakes that have fallen off a wall. Scrape the mixture back into the bowl and return it to the freezer for 10 minutes.

3. Stir together the salt and sour cream. Gently stir the sour cream mixture into the flour-fat mixture. Add milk 1 tablespoon (15 ml) at a time only if needed to get the mixture wet enough to hold together. Press the dough together to make a 6-inch (15-cm) disc. Wrap well in plastic wrap and refrigerate for at least 2 hours or overnight.

4. Roll the disc into a 12 to 13-inch (30 to 33-cm) circle.

5. See pages 290 and 295 for detailed directions for rolling and placing in the pan.

Flakey Butter Crust in a Mixer

MAKES TWO 9-INCH (23-CM) CRUSTS

You can make a wonderfully flakey crust in the mixer. Jim Stacy, the founder of Tarts Bakery in San Francisco, developed a fast mixer method for making high-quality crusts. This recipe is prized by caterers and those who have to produce numerous crusts. I have altered his recipe to accommodate my personal hang-ups like vinegar and fine crumbs.

You can use a 9 x 1-inch (23 x 2.5-cm) tart or pie ring or adjustable baking ring on a heavy baking sheet.

What This Recipe Shows

The vinegar slightly tenderizes, and makes the crust easier to roll and set faster.

Using a baking ring on a heavy baking sheet allows you to bake the unfilled crust without any pie weights.

An alternative to baking rings is to use a tart pan (see page 294).

Pressing the crust into a light coating of bread or cracker crumbs sprinkled in the bottom of the pan or on the baking sheet produces a very dry, crisp crust. (See Rolled-In Crumbs Crust, page 324.)

½ teaspoon (3 g) salt
2 teaspoons (10 ml) apple cider vinegar
⅓ cup (79 ml) cold water
1 cup (8 oz/226 g) cold unsalted butter, cut in
    ¼-inch (0.6-cm) cubes

2½ cups (11 oz/312 g) spooned and leveled
    bleached all-purpose flour
Nonstick cooking spray
3 tablespoons (20 g) very fine dry unseasoned
    bread crumbs

1. In a small bowl, stir together the salt, vinegar, and water. Place the butter and flour in mixer work bowl. Refrigerate both the water mixture and the flour and butter for at least 30 minutes.

2. Place the flour and butter in a mixer with the paddle attachment, and cut the butter into the flour using the lowest speed, mixing until the butter resembles flakes of oatmeal, about 2 minutes. With the mixer running, pour in the cold salted water and mix until the dough forms a ball, about 30 seconds.

3. Divide the dough into 2 equal pieces Shape each into a 6-inch (15-cm) disc. Wrap each disc separately in plastic wrap and refrigerate for at least 2 hours or overnight. (Refrigerate or freeze the remaining crust for later use. Thaw overnight in the refrigerator.)

4. Arrange a shelf in the lower third of the oven and place a baking stone on it. Preheat the oven for at least 30 minutes to 450°F/232°C.

5. Spray a 9 x 1-inch (23 x 2.5-cm) ring or tart pan with nonstick cooking spray and sprinkle 1 tablespoon (7 g) of the fine crumbs over the bottom only. Roll out one dough disc into a 12-inch (30-cm) circle. To get the dough centered in the pan, fold the dough in quarters. Place the point of the folded section in the center of the pan, and then unfold the dough circle. With your fingertips, press the whole bottom well, starting at the center and pressing outward to press into the crumbs and to squeeze out any air between the crust and the pan. Press the edges well all the way around. Lift the top edges, fold under slightly and press down so that edges are slightly thicker. Freeze the crust in the tart pan or on the baking sheet for at least 45 minutes.

6. Remove from the freezer and bake immediately on the hot baking stone for 20 minutes. Use as directed in the recipe.

Flakey Crust in a Food Processor

It is so easy to overprocess a pie crust that I like to do a combination of starting in the processor and finishing by hand. This assures a flakey crust. To use this method, prepare the fat and flour as described in Step 1 of the Simple Very Flakey Crust, page 302. Place the work bowl of a food processor and the steel blade in the freezer, too. Stir the salt and vinegar into the water in a small glass measuring cup and refrigerate.

1. Place the cold food processor bowl back on the processor. Dump in the cold butter-flour mixture and process with 5 or 6 quick on/offs. It is so easy to overprocess that I like to finish by hand. Dump the butter-flour mixture onto a clean countertop. Flour the rolling pin and roll over the mixture to flatten the butter. Some butter may stick to the pin. Scrape it off and scrape the mixture together. Roll over the mixture again. If the butter becomes soft at any time during the rolling, return the mixture immediately to the freezer for 5 minutes. The flattened, flour-coated pieces of butter should look like pieces of paint flaking off a wall. Scrape together and roll one more time if necessary. Place in a mixing bowl and put back in the freezer for 5 minutes.

2. Sprinkle with 2 tablespoons (30 ml) of the cold salt-vinegar-water mixture. Toss the mixture lightly with a large spoon, sprinkle with 2 more tablespoons (30 ml) of the liquid, toss again, then sprinkle the rest of the liquid over the pastry. Squeeze the pastry together 2 or 3 times with your hands. If the dough is not moist enough to hold together, sprinkle with a little more ice water, toss, and press the dough together.

3. Press the dough together into a 6-inch (15-cm) disc. Wrap in plastic wrap and refrigerate for at least 2 hours or overnight. This will allow the moisture to distribute more evenly.

4. Roll into a 12 to 13-inch (30 to 33-cm) circle. See pages 290 and 295 for detailed directions for rolling and placing in the pan. See page 323 for baking directions.

Flakey Strong Crust—For Hand-Held Pies

Sometimes—for hand-held pies, for example—you need a crust that is strong and will hold together. You can deliberately develop gluten in the dough, which makes the crust strong but a little tough, and/or you can add an egg or egg white for strength.

Crust for Hand-Held Pies

MAKES ENOUGH DOUGH FOR TWELVE 5-INCH (13-CM) PIES

This is a wonderfully flakey crust yet it is strong. The lard, vinegar, and buttermilk keep it from being tough.

What This Recipe Shows

Using all-purpose flour instead of lower-protein flour allows more gluten development. (See page 343 for more on flours.)

Egg white will make the fried crust stronger without absorbing as much fat as would a crust made with a whole egg.

Vinegar and buttermilk will make the dough slightly more tender, which may be needed since the crust has been made tough by ingredients and techniques.

Buttermilk enhances color.

¼ cup (1.8 oz/51 g) lard, cut in ½-inch (1.3-cm) pieces

1 teaspoon (6 g) salt

½ teaspoon (2 ml) apple cider vinegar

3 tablespoons (45 ml) cold buttermilk, plus extra as needed

¼ cup (2 oz/57 g) very cold unsalted butter, cut in small pieces

1½ cups (6.6 oz/187 g) spooned and leveled bleached all-purpose flour

1 large egg white (1 oz/28 g), stirred with 1 tablespoon (15 ml) water

1. Place the lard in the freezer for at least 5 minutes. Stir the salt and vinegar into the buttermilk and place in the refrigerator.

2. Toss the butter and chilled lard with the flour in a medium mixing bowl, coating the pieces of fat with flour, and place in the freezer for 10 minutes.

3. Dump the cold flour-butter-lard mixture out onto a clean countertop. Flour the rolling pin and roll over the mixture to flatten the butter and lard pieces and coat them with flour. Some butter or lard may stick to the pin. Scrape it off, flour the rolling pin, and scrape the mixture together. Roll over the mixture again. If the butter or lard becomes soft at any time during the rolling, immediately return the mixture to a bowl and freeze for 5 minutes. Working quickly, continue rolling and scraping together the butter-lard-flour mixture at least three times in all. The mixture should look like paint flakes that have fallen off a wall. Scrape the mixture back into the bowl and return it to the freezer for 10 minutes.

4. Sprinkle half of the egg white–water mixture over the flour and toss, then sprinkle the rest over and toss. Sprinkle the salt-vinegar-buttermilk mixture over the flour, a little at a time, tossing between additions. Press the dough together to see if it will hold; if it is too dry, continue adding cold buttermilk a little at a time. When the dough holds together, place it on the counter and knead it with two quick push-and-pull-back-together motions.

5. Press the dough together into a 6-inch (15-cm) disc. Wrap in plastic wrap and refrigerate for at least 2 hours or overnight. This will allow the moisture to more evenly distribute.

6. After the filling is prepared and just before frying, roll out dough (see page 287) and cut into 5-inch (13-cm) circles. You want the pies small enough to fry easily but big enough to hold enough filling.

Fried Apple Pies Extraordinaire

MAKES TEN TO TWELVE 5-INCH (13-CM) FRIED PIES

To a child a fried pie is an incredible joy. What the heck, to an adult a fried pie is an incredible joy, too. These are wonderfully flakey and delicious. Chef Marty Thompson's Aunt Jane is famous for her fried pies. Cooking the dried apples in orange juice is one of the techniques she uses that make her pies outstanding.

What This Recipe Shows

Cooking the dried apples in orange juice is a major flavor enhancer.

---

1 recipe Crust for Hand-Held Pies (page 306), cut into 5-inch (13-cm) circles

$\frac{1}{2}$ cup (3 oz/85 g) dried apple slices

$1\frac{1}{2}$ cups (355 ml) orange juice

1 large (about $\frac{1}{2}$ pound/227 g) ripe Fuji or Golden Delicious apple, peeled, cored, and chopped (about $1\frac{1}{2}$ cups/360 ml; if you peel and chop the apple early, dip the pieces in orange juice to prevent discoloration)

$\frac{1}{2}$ cup (2 oz/57 g) grated sharp cheddar

$\frac{1}{2}$ cup (3.8 oz/108 g) light brown sugar, packed

3 tablespoons (1.5 oz/43 g) butter

1 teaspoon (2 g) ground cinnamon

$\frac{1}{2}$ teaspoon (3 g) salt

Fresh canola oil, for frying

$\frac{1}{2}$ cup (2 oz/60 g) confectioners' sugar

1. In a large heavy saucepan over low heat, simmer the dried apples in the orange juice until puffed and soft, about 10 minutes. Add the chopped fresh apple and cook for about 10 minutes more. This filling should be fairly thick. Simmer a little longer if necessary to reduce and thicken the juice; this can take as long as 5 minutes more.

2. Stir in the grated cheddar, sugar, butter, cinnamon, and salt. Allow the filling to cool.

3. Spoon 2 tablespoons (30 ml) of filling in the center of each dough circle. With a pastry brush, paint water very lightly around the edge of half of the circle. Fold the pastry over the filling to create a half-moon shape. Press the edges together with a fork to seal.

4. In a 9 to 10-inch (23 to 25-cm) heavy skillet, heat $\frac{1}{2}$ inch (1.3 cm) of oil to 375°F/191°C. Gently lay 2 or 3 pies in the oil without crowding the skillet. Fry in batches until golden brown, about 2 minutes on each side. Drain on paper towels. Sprinkle with confectioners' sugar and serve warm or at room temperature.

Pastry At a Glance

What to Do for More	Why
TENDERNESS	
Use a low-protein flour.	Less gluten will be formed.
Use a soft or liquid fat.	Soft or liquid fat greases flour proteins well.
Work the fat into the flour well.	To coat flour proteins and prevent their joining to form tough gluten.
Add sugar to the pastry dough.	Sugar can reduce the amount of gluten formed.
Add acid like a little vinegar to the dough.	Acid can cut long gluten strands to tenderize.
FLAKINESS	
Use cold large pieces of fat.	The fat needs to be big enough and cold enough to hold the dough apart in the hot oven long enough for the dough on top of the fat and the dough under the fat to partially set.
CRISPNESS	
Bake crust well.	The dough has to be thoroughly dried to crisp.
COLOR	
Use dairy products such as milk, cream, sour cream, cream cheese, or cheese.	Dairy products contain both sugar and protein to aid in browning.
Use a tiny amount of light corn syrup.	Corn syrup is a major browning aid.

Fruit Pies

GLAZED FRESH FRUIT

Fruit in pies can be essentially uncooked, with a glaze coating like the blueberries in Judy Brady's Blueberries and Bordeaux on page 269. A sweet fruit-flavored glaze is made with a little gelatin added and then gently stirred with the uncooked fruit and immediately placed in the pie shell and chilled to set. This is a great way to preserve the flavors and texture of delicate fresh fruit like berries. Sugar

Tossing delicate berries in a hot sugar syrup not only gives the fruit a shine, but also helps preserve the shape of the fruit.

works magic in preserving the texture and shape of fresh fruit. Tossing delicate berries in a hot sugar syrup not only gives the fruit a shine, but also helps preserve the shape of the fruit (see the following for more information).

COOKED FRUIT

When you heat fruits or vegetables, their cell walls shrink and they begin to leak. The pectic substances "glue" between the cells changes to water-soluble pectin and dissolves. The cells start leaking and falling apart. The fruit or vegetable softens and can become mushy.

Sugar to the Rescue

Sugar and/or calcium prevent this "glue" from changing. In the presence of sugar, the cells stay together and the fruit or vegetable holds its shape and preserves texture. You can see this clearly with navy or pinto beans. If you cook them without sugar, in about four hours they are mush—refried beans. But if you cook them with molasses (which contains both calcium and sugar) and brown sugar, they are Boston baked beans and will hold their shape for days.

Sugar is a vital tool for the cook in preserving the shape of fruits in desserts. A cook can sauté apple wedges until they are as tender as desired, and then add sugar to preserve their shape and texture from that point on.

In addition to losing their shape when heated, fruits lose water. Fruits are full of water. As my friend Harold McGee, author of *On Food and Cooking,* says, "fruits are pretty wrappers for water." Even apples, which are firm, contain 86% water. When fruit is heated, it loses a lot of this water, which dilutes the filling and causes a "boil-over" (a large amount of liquid that boils out of the pan and creates a sticky mess in the oven).

In a pie, when the fruit cooks it also shrinks, leaving a large gap between the fruit filling and the top crust of a double-crusted pie. Monroe Boston Strause has a great solution. He carefully stirs the peeled and sliced fruit with a portion of the sugar in the recipe and allows this to stand for 3 hours in a colander over a bowl. This partially sweetens the fruit, preserves the shape of the fruit, and draws out a considerable amount of water, which is caught in the bowl.

He then cooks the drained liquid to concentrate the flavors and thickens the concentrate with cornstarch or tapioca starch (flour). If you bring the thickened juice to a boil, it will form a stiff paste. (Stir to prevent scorching—I love to use a flat-end wooden spatula so that I can scrape the bottom.) Bringing this thickened juice to a boil causes changes in the starch so that it can no longer continue to thicken, which would make the filling a thick, starchy mess when the pie is baked.

After the thickened juice comes to a boil, stir in the remaining sugar and the salt. The filling will thin. Again, it is necessary to bring this mixture back to a boil, stirring to prevent scorching. Pour this cooked mixture over the drained fruit and carefully stir with a wooden spatula. Do not refrigerate, but allow this to cool before pouring it into the crust to bake.

The sugar used in preparing the fruit helps it retain its shape. The fruit's juices have been converted to a syrup glaze that will not become cloudy. The fruit and its glaze have shine and luster. The fruit is not mashed up or broken, and the filling is not a thick starchy mess—just luscious, beautiful, and delicious fruit.

Monroe's incredibly valuable technique of letting the fruit and sugar stand and drain solves the problems of "boil-over," watery fillings, starchy, cloudy fillings, and the gap between the fruit and top crust in a double-crusted pie. Best of all, the fruit retains its shape and creates a gorgeous sweet fruit pie filling.

When I heard that Rose Levy Beranbaum was going to write a pastry book, I told her she had to find a copy of Strause's *Pie Marches On,* that it was invaluable for pastry. She did, and I noticed that she too uses his technique for tossing the fruit with sugar. This technique is applied here in *BakeWise* to fresh or frozen fruit in Golden-Leafed Peach Pie (page 312) and Dark, Sweet Bing Cherry Pie with Pastry Lattice (page 314), and in a number of the other fruit pies. They are all luscious and delicious. In Cherries and More Cherries, Cherry Pie with Streusel Topping (page 316) I use a technique for a high-quality canned-fruit pie.

There are fruits like blueberries that have a leathery skin and can sit for days tossed with sugar and not lose any liquid. Roland Mesnier, the White House pastry chef for many administrations, has a solution for this type of fruit that can apply to many other fruits. He keeps the fruit beautiful in cold desserts with a strong sugar syrup made by boiling 3 cups (21 oz/595 g) sugar in 1 cup (237 ml) water. He keeps this syrup barely at a simmer, adds the fruit, and simmers for less than 15 minutes (smaller fruits less time—blueberries less than a minute). He lifts the fruit out to drain, and boils down the fruit-sugar-water until it is an intensely fruit-flavored syrup. He now has beautiful fruit. The sugar preserves the fruit's shape and produces an incredible syrup to flavor parts of his dessert. Some of this syrup can be thickened by Monroe's procedure (see page 310) and added back to the fruit for a great pie filling or it can be used as a syrup to soak into a cake layer or as a sauce.

Dishes thickened with cornstarch can become cloudy if refrigerated. If you know that pies are going to be refrigerated, use tapioca starch (flour) for thickening instead of cornstarch. Tapioca starch is available in Asian markets and some health food stores.

When fruit is heated, it loses a lot of its water, which dilutes the filling and causes "boil-over" in the oven—a real mess. The fruit shrinks with this water loss, leaving a large gap between the fruit and the top crust.

Tossing the fruit for a pie with sugar and allowing it to stand for 3 hours removes a considerable amount of water, which solves the problems of "boil-over" and watery fillings, and the sugar helps to preserve the shape of the fruit. It also reduces the gap between the fruit and the crust in a pie.

Solve the problem of keeping cooked fruit beautiful by dipping it in a very strong sugar syrup. You can then reduce the flavored syrup to use, too.

TOPPINGS

Pastry Cutouts

Many different shaped cutouts (hearts, leaves, diamonds) can serve as pastry decorations. I love decorative leaves for a crust edge (small to medium leaves) or for a topping (large leaves). Different leaf cutters are available in gourmet cookware shops, or you can cut your own shapes. For dramatic leaves, cut veins as deeply as you can without going all the way through the dough.

Sometimes, too, on a double-crust pie, the pastry cutout is a clue about the flavor of the pie and the delicious filling under the crust.

Pastry cutouts can be used to cover the whole top or just around the edges. You can bake the cutouts on a baking sheet (with some lying across small wads of foil to give them a curled shape) and simply arrange them on the finished pie, or you can arrange leaves around the edge, placed on just before baking the dough.

Golden-Leafed Peach Pie

MAKES ONE 9-INCH (23-CM) PIE

This pie is incredibly beautiful, with shiny pastry leaves around the edge and extending slightly over the filling. The filling is golden brown. Unfortunately, ripe peaches are usually unavailable in most of our markets, and I find that I get a much better dish using frozen peaches instead of the rock-hard fresh ones. If you can get fresh, ripe peaches, by all means use them instead of frozen peaches.

What This Recipe Shows

Tossing the peaches with sugar and allowing them to stand for 3 hours removes a considerable amount of liquid so that the peaches will not shrink so much when baked.

Bringing the filling to a boil after the starch is added causes irreversible changes in the starch so that it will not continue to thicken, preventing the fruit filling from becoming pasty during the baking.

Pastry leaves line the edge of the crust to cover a little of the filling while leaving most of the filling open. This gives you the beauty of a small "top crust" without the problems of a double-crusted pie.

---

1 recipe Cream Cheese Crust (page 288)

1 pound (454 g) frozen sliced peaches, thawed

1¼ cups (8.75 oz/248 g) sugar, divided

Nonstick cooking spray

¼ cup (1 oz/28 g) very fine vanilla wafer crumbs

⅓ cup (1.8 oz/50 g) tapioca starch plus 1 tablespoon cornstarch (7 g) stirred into ¼ cup (59 ml) cool water

½ teaspoon (3 g) salt

3 tablespoons (1.5 oz/42 g) butter

2 tablespoons (30 ml) orange marmalade

1 tablespoon (15 ml) light corn syrup

2 teaspoons (10 ml) pure vanilla extract

¼ cup (1 oz/28 g) crushed amaretti cookies or crumbled date-nut bread

¼ cup (about 1.5 oz/43 g) English toffee bits (available in bags near the chocolate chips), optional

1 large egg yolk (0.65 oz/18 g)

2 tablespoons (30 ml) heavy cream or whole milk

1. In a large bowl, toss together the peaches and 1 cup (7 oz/198 g) of the sugar. Pour the fruit into a colander to drain and place a bowl under the colander to catch all the liquid. Drain for 3 hours.

2. Arrange a shelf in the lower third of the oven, place a baking stone on it, and preheat the oven to 450°F/232°C.

3. You will have two 6-inch (15-cm) dough discs of pastry. Keep one refrigerated for the leaves and roll the other disc into a 13-inch (33-cm) circle (see page 286). Fold the dough circle in half, then fold in half again to form a quarter of a circle. Spray a 9-inch (23-cm) heavy aluminum pie pan (preferably with holes) with nonstick cooking spray. Sprinkle the vanilla wafer crumbs evenly over the bottom only of the pan. Place the point of the folded dough in the center of the pan and unfold halfway. Check to see if the overhang is about the same on both sides and the back. If not, gently move the crust so that it is centered, then unfold all the way. Place the dough in the pan and shape (see page 293). Starting in the center, gently press the dough with your fingers into the crumbs all across the bottom. Allow to stand at room temperature for 30 minutes, and then freeze for 5 minutes.

4. While the pastry is resting and freezing, pour off and measure the liquid from the peaches. If you do not have 1 cup (237 ml) of liquid, add water to make 1 cup (237 ml). Take three of the worst-looking peach slices, chop and smush them, and add them to the liquid. Place the liquid in a heavy saucepan and bring to a boil over medium-high heat. With constant stirring using a flat-end wooden spatula, drizzle in the starch-and-water mixture and bring back to a simmer. This liquid should be almost a stiff paste. *Bring back to a boil.*

5. Keep stirring the thick mixture on the heat and add the remaining ¼ cup (1.8 oz/51 g) sugar and the salt. Cook for 2 minutes, stirring steadily. The mixture will thin when you add the sugar. *It is important to bring this mixture back to a good boil. Keep scraping the bottom to prevent burning.*

6. Stir in the butter, orange marmalade, corn syrup, and vanilla. Pour this hot mixture into a medium bowl and carefully stir in the drained peaches. Stir gently with a spatula until all of the fruit is coated. Stir in the amaretti crumbs and the toffee bits, if using. Allow to cool for about 30 minutes.

7. Roll out the second pastry disc and cut about thirty 2½-inch (6-cm) leaves. For attractive leaves, press deep veins in them with a small sharp knife, being careful not to go all the way through the pastry. Remove the pastry shell from the freezer and pour the filling into the uncooked pastry shell. Arrange the leaves around the edge of the pie, extending partially over the filling. Make sure that no leaves extend over the outer edge of the crust. Stir together the egg yolk and cream and brush the pastry leaves with this mixture.

8. Bake on the baking stone for about 25 minutes, until the crust is well browned and the peaches are bubbly. Serve at room temperature. It's excellent with a scoop of vanilla ice cream.

Dark, Sweet Bing Cherry Pie with Pastry Lattice

MAKES ONE 9-INCH (23-CM) PIE

Deep red cherries peek through a shiny golden-brown pastry lattice. This is real cherry pie. The taste of the cherries dominates. The cherries are perfectly cooked, holding their shape and just slightly softened.

What This Recipe Shows

Bringing the filling to a boil after the starch is added causes irreversible changes in the starch so that it will not continue to thicken during baking, making the pie too pasty.

A pastry lattice gives you the beauty of a crust without the disadvantages of a double crust.

---

1 recipe Cream Cheese Crust (page 288)
1 recipe Frangipane—Almond-Hazelnut Paste
    (page 291), made with almonds only
2 pounds (907 g) frozen Bing cherries, thawed
1¼ cups (8.5 oz/248 g) sugar, divided
Nonstick cooking spray
¼ cup (1 oz/28 g) very fine vanilla wafer
    crumbs
⅓ cup (1.8 oz/50 g) tapioca starch plus 1
    tablespoon cornstarch (7 g) stirred into
    ¼ cup (59 ml) cool water

½ teaspoon (3 g) salt
2 tablespoons (30 ml) Chambord or
    raspberry liqueur
1 tablespoon (15 ml) light corn syrup
½ teaspoon (2.5 ml) pure almond extract
3 tablespoons (1.5 oz/43 g) butter
1 large egg yolk (0.65 oz/18 g)
2 tablespoons (30 ml) heavy cream or whole
    milk

1. In a large bowl, toss together the thawed cherries and 1 cup (7 oz/198 g) of the sugar. Pour into a colander to drain, and place a bowl under the colander to catch all the liquid. Drain for 3 hours.

2. You will have two 6-inch (15-cm) dough discs of pastry. Keep one refrigerated for the lattice and roll the other disc into a 13-inch (33-cm) circle (see page 286). Fold the dough circle in half, then fold in half again to form a quarter of a circle. Spray a 9-inch (23-cm) heavy aluminum pie pan (preferably with holes) with nonstick cooking spray. Sprinkle the vanilla wafer crumbs evenly over the bottom only of the pan. Place the point of the folded dough in the center of the pan and unfold halfway. Check to see if the overhang is about the same on both sides and the back. If not, gently move the crust so that it is centered, then unfold all the way. Starting in the center, gently press the dough with your fingers into the crumbs all across the bottom. Allow to stand at room temperature for 30 minutes, and then freeze.

3. Roll out the reserved portion of dough. With a sharp knife or pastry cutter, cut 12 strips of pastry (about ½ inch/1.5 cm wide) equal in length to the diameter of the pie dish. Place in the freezer until needed.

4. Arrange a shelf in the lower third of the oven, place a baking stone on it, and preheat the oven to 450°F/232°C.

5. While the pastry is resting and freezing, measure the liquid from the cherries. If you do not have 1 cup (237 ml) of liquid, add water to make 1 cup (237 ml). Take 3 or 4 of the worst-looking cherries, chop and smush them, and add them to the liquid. Place this juice in a heavy saucepan and bring to a boil over medium-high heat. With constant stirring using a flat-end wooden spatula, drizzle in the starch-and-water mixture and bring back to a simmer. This liquid should be almost a stiff paste. *Bring back to a boil.*

6. Keep stirring the thick mixture on the heat and add the remaining ¼ cup (1.8 oz/51 g) sugar and the salt. Cook, stirring steadily, for several minutes. The mixture will thin when you add the sugar. *It is important to bring this mixture back to a good boil. Keep scraping the bottom to prevent burning.*

7. Stir in liqueur, corn syrup, almond extract, and butter. Pour this mixture into a bowl and stir in the drained cherries. Fold carefully with a spatula until all fruit is coated. Allow to cool for about 30 minutes. *Do not refrigerate.*

8. Remove pastry shell from the freezer. Spread a thick layer of frangipane over the bottom of the pastry shell.

9. Pour the filling into the pastry shell. With the pastry strips, weave a lattice on the top. Trim any overhang so that nothing extends over the outer edge of the crust. Stir together the egg yolk and cream and brush pastry with this glaze.

10. Bake on the stone for about 25 minutes, until the pastry is well browned. Serve at room temperature. This pie is excellent with a scoop of vanilla ice cream.

STREUSEL TOPPING

Many pies, cobblers, and muffins have wonderful streusel toppings made with butter, brown sugar, and flour. I love adding nuts and some of the fruit from the product.

Cherries and More Cherries, Cherry Pie with Streusel Topping

MAKES ONE 9-INCH (23-CM) PIE

Dried cherries add intense flavor to sour cherries and dark sweet cherries. What a cherry pie!

What This Recipe Shows

Bringing the filling to a boil after the starch is added causes irreversible changes in the starch so that it will not continue to thicken during baking, making the fruit filling pasty.

A little of the fruit added to the Streusel Topping adds a surprising great taste.

---

1 recipe Cream Cheese Crust (page 288)
Streusel Topping (recipe follows)
¼ cup (59 ml) boiling water
⅓ cup (1.7 oz/48 g) dried cherries
¾ cup (5.3 oz/150 g) sugar, divided
¼ cup (1 oz/28 g) very fine vanilla wafer
    crumbs
⅓ cup (1.8 oz/50 g) tapioca starch plus 1
    tablespoon cornstarch (7 g) stirred into
    ¼ cup (59 ml) cool water
½ teaspoon (3 g) salt

3 tablespoons (1.5 oz/42 g) butter
1 tablespoon (15 ml) light corn syrup
½ teaspoon (2.5 ml) pure almond extract
One 15-ounce can (425 g) pitted dark sweet
    cherries, drained and liquid reserved
One 15-ounce can (425 g) pitted sour red
    cherries, drained and liquid reserved

1. Pour the boiling water over the dried cherries and add ¼ cup (1.8 oz /51 g) of the sugar. Stir, and allow to stand at least 30 minutes.

2. You will have two 6-inch (15-cm) dough discs of pastry. Freeze one for later use and roll the other disc into a 13-inch (33-cm) circle (see page 286). Fold the dough circle in half, then fold in half again to form a quarter of a circle. Spray a 9-inch (23-cm) heavy aluminum pie pan (preferably with holes) with nonstick cooking spray. Sprinkle the vanilla wafer crumbs evenly over the bottom only of the pan. Place the point of the folded dough in the center of the pan and unfold halfway. Check to see if the overhang is about the same on both sides and the back. If not, gently move the crust so that it is centered, then unfold all the way. Starting in the center, gently press the dough with your fingers into the crumbs all across the bottom. Allow to stand at room temperature for 30 minutes, and then freeze until needed.

3. Arrange a shelf in the lower third of the oven, place a baking stone on it, and preheat the oven for at least 30 minutes to 450°F/232°C.

4. Place 1 cup (237 ml) of the reserved cherry juices and the dried cherry mixture in a heavy saucepan over low heat. Add ¼ cup (1.8 oz /52 g) of the sugar. Bring to a boil and reduce to about 1 cup (237 ml).

5. With constant stirring using a flat-end wooden spatula, drizzle in the starch-and-water mixture and bring back to a simmer. This liquid should be almost a stiff paste. *Bring back to a boil.*

6. Keep stirring the thick mixture on the heat and add the remaining ¼ cup (1.8 oz /51 g) sugar and the salt. Cook, stirring steadily, for 1 minute. The mixture will thin a little when you add the sugar. *It is important to bring this mixture back to a good boil. Keep scraping the bottom to prevent burning.*

7. Stir in the butter, corn syrup, and almond extract. Pour this hot mixture into a bowl. Carefully stir in the drained canned cherries. Fold carefully with a spatula until all of the fruit is coated. Allow to cool for about 30 minutes. *Do not refrigerate.* Spoon filling into the prepared crust.

8. Sprinkle heavily with all of the Streusel Topping.

9. Bake on the stone for about 25 minutes, until the topping is browned and the filling is hot. Allow to cool 2 hours before serving.

Streusel Topping

MAKES ENOUGH TOPPING TO GENEROUSLY COVER ONE 9-INCH (23-CM) PIE

This is one of my favorite things. My grandson liked to eat just icing off a cake when he was little. I love to eat just the streusel off of desserts! This is an excellent topping for cobbler, and it is wonderful as a topping on muffins. Use the same fruit in the streusel that you have in the pie, cobbler, or muffin.

What This Recipe Shows

Chopped fruit and nuts make this streusel extra special.

½ cup (2.4 oz/ 69 g) roasted, salted almonds (canned roasted almonds are fine)

½ cup (118 ml) canned cherries, well drained and chopped

1¼ cups (5.5 oz/156 g) spooned and leveled bleached all-purpose flour

½ cup (3.8 oz/110 g) light brown sugar, packed

⅛ teaspoon (pinch) salt

½ cup (4 oz/113 g) butter, cut in ½-inch (1-cm) slices

In a food processor with the steel blade, process the almonds with a few quick on/offs just to coarsely chop. Add the cherries to the processor. In a bowl, stir together the flour, sugar, and salt, then dump in the processor on top of the cherries. Add the butter and process with quick on/offs just to blend all ingredients. Sprinkle on desserts before baking.

Meringue Toppings

For all about meringues, see pages 167–194.

Whipped Cream Toppings

Cold, cold, cold—the big factor in successfully whipping cream is to keep the cream cold. Cold fat droplets that are stuck to each other hold whipped cream firm. If these fat droplets get warm, they melt and the cream is no longer firm. This is exactly what happens to whipped cream if it gets warm.

> Temperature is the major factor in getting cream to whip. Everything must be cold—cold cream, cold bowl, cold beaters, and a cool room.

When air is beaten into cold heavy cream, the air bubbles are coated with a water film filled with fat droplets. As more and more air bubbles are whipped into the cream, the film around the bubbles becomes thinner and the fat droplets, robbed of their water film and coating, touch each other and stick together. The whipped cream gets firmer. Eventually, enough air is beaten into the cream that all the air bubbles are lined with fat droplets stuck to each other, and the cream becomes firm and ready to use.

Cooks usually take the precaution of placing the beaters and the bowl in the freezer for 5 minutes before whipping cream. However, even if you have a cold bowl, beaters, and cream, if you beat 90°F/32°C air from your hot kitchen into your cream, it may fail to whip. A cool room is a big help. To ensure having the cream cold, some chefs add 2 or 3 tablespoons (30 to 45 ml) of shaved or finely crushed ice to the cream just before whipping.

Another major factor in producing firmly whipped cream is the amount of fat in the cream. The fat droplets lining the air bubbles are what hold whipped cream up, so you need to buy a cream with a good supply of fat, cream with at least 30% fat. Half-and-half has 10 to 18% fat; light cream, sometimes called coffee cream, has 18 to 30%; whipping cream 30 to 36%; and heavy cream a minimum of 36%. Because of its high fat content, heavy cream will whip much faster and to a firmer consistency than whipping cream.

Three other factors affect whipped cream. First, there is an enzyme in milk that encourages fat globules to clump together. Unfortunately, since heat destroys this enzyme, pasteurized and ultra-pasteurized creams do not whip as easily as raw cream, which used to be more readily available. Most cream sold in the United States today is ultra-pasteurized and this high-heat treatment increases whipping time. Second, large fat globules clump together more easily than small fat globules; therefore, homogenized milk or cream whose fat has been broken into tiny globules does not whip as well as unhomogenized. For this reason, whipping cream is not homogenized. Finally, the breed of cow matters. Jerseys and Guernseys produce milk with large fat globules, and Holsteins produce milk with smaller fat globules—not that we can exercise much choice over that.

Fats absorb odors easily, so don't store whipped cream in a refrigerator with foods with strong odors. Cover whipped cream tightly to protect it from odors when storing it in the refrigerator.

Liquid drains out of whipped cream as it stands. You can whisk the cream back together with a few strokes. If you want to keep the cream very firm, line a large strainer with a piece of cheesecloth or a paper towel and pile in the whipped cream. Place the strainer over a clean bowl, cover the strainer with heavy plastic wrap, and refrigerate the cream until ready to use; simply discard the small amount of liquid that has dripped out.

Whipped Cream Stabilizers

Packaged stabilizers for whipped cream are available in some grocery stores. One called "Whip it," from Dr. Oetker, is the most widely available. It contains sugar (dextrose), modified cornstarch, and tricalcium phosphate as its active ingredients. Some modified starches can thicken when cold. "Whip it" can keep cream stiff for hours.

I have never tried it, but Rose Levy Beranbaum, in *The Pie and Pastry Bible,* says that she likes Cobasan. This flavorless and colorless stabilizer is a commercial product from Albert Uster Imports, and has to be ordered in a large batch—maybe not practical for home use.

You can also dissolve a tiny amount of gelatin in water and add it to the cream near the end of whipping. Such a whipped cream is firmer and holds up well in hot weather. There is a problem, however, in adding the gelatin. Whether mixed with water or cream, you must heat the gelatin to dissolve it, and adding something hot to whipped cream can be a disaster.

Sprinkle the gelatin on cold liquid and let it stand until the gelatin has softened, then heat the gelatin just enough to dissolve it. (Never boil gelatin, since this will reduce its ability to gel.) Let the gelatin cool to about body temperature before whisking it into the cream.

The gelatin needs to be neither too hot nor too cold when it is incorporated into the cream. Body temperature or slightly above is ideal (it should feel just tepid to the touch). If you let the gelatin cool too much, it will set up the second it hits the cold cream, before you have a chance to whisk it in. This will give you a splatter-shaped piece of gelatin that you can peel from the top of the cream.

A sneaky way to add a tiny amount of gelatin to whipped cream is to incorporate a near-melted marshmallow into the cream at the end of whipping. One large marshmallow per cup of heavy cream will hold whipped cream well. Cut large marshmallows into quarters (easiest with greased scissors), place them in a warm spot (such as a warm toaster oven) or microwave for a few seconds until they are quite soft and almost melted, then whisk them a little at a time into the cold whipped cream. If you try to whisk a whole, cold marshmallow into whipped cream, the beater may sling the cream-covered marshmallow right into your face!

One final precaution about incorporating whipped cream into other ingredients: If the whipped cream is too warm or is overwhipped, it will turn into butter and a thin liquid. I remember well my first lobster mousse. I was trying to do everything just right, so I whipped my cream nice and firm, then began to whisk in my puréed lobster. I noticed what looked like a tiny yellow streak. Before my eyes, my lovely firm white whipped cream melted into a thin liquid with small yellow blobs of butter. Why? I had whipped the cream too long. It was too firm. Whipped cream that is to be blended with other ingredients should be whipped to form medium to medium-firm peaks—not firm. You must be able to continue to whisk it a little more to thoroughly incorporate the other ingredients without turning the cream into butter.

Whipped Cream Topping

MAKES ABOUT 2 CUPS

1 cup (237 ml) heavy cream
2 tablespoons (30 ml) shaved or finely
    crushed ice

1 large plain marshmallow, optional
2 tablespoons (0.9 oz/25 g) sugar

1. Place a bowl and beaters in the freezer for 5 to 10 minutes to chill well. Place the cream in the freezer for 5 minutes to chill. Pour the cream into the chilled bowl. Add the ice to the cream and whip to soft peaks.

2. If using, cut the large marshmallow into quarters (easiest with greased scissors), and place in a warm spot (such as a warm toaster oven) or microwave for a few seconds until quite soft and almost melted.

3. Whip the partially melted marshmallow into the cream, and then gently stir in the sugar. If you try to whisk a whole, cold marshmallow into whipped cream, the beater may sling the cream-covered marshmallow right into your face! Whip the cream until it forms firm peaks.

Whipped Cream At a Glance

What to Do	Why
Have the cream, bowl, and beaters cold, and whip the cream in a cool room. Keep whipped cream cold at all times.	Fat droplets need to stay cold and firm so that they will stick to each other around the air bubbles.
Whisk only a small amount of a warm ingredient into whipped cream.	Cream has to stay cold so that the fat around the air bubbles will not melt.
Whip cream that is to be combined with other ingredients to medium-firm peaks only.	The cream needs to be whisked more to combine it with other ingredients. If it is already firm, additional beating will turn it to butter.
Keep whipped cream covered in the refrigerator.	Fats are great holders and carriers of flavor. Uncovered whipped cream will pick up tastes and odors from other items in the refrigerator.

Clide Ogletree's Famous Strawberry Pie

MAKES ONE 9-INCH (23-CM) PIE

My friend Leah Marie's mother, Margaret Rawls, felt that girls needed to know how to sew and she very generously took on the task. On Tuesday afternoons, she guided eight teenage girls through making blue dotted-Swiss dresses. My mother, Clide Ogletree, supplied one of her luscious strawberry pies every Tuesday. Today, we all burst into laughter when we remember those blue dotted-Swiss dresses. We had such good times and we are very grateful for our skills. We have been able to make clothes for our children. When remembering those days, we also sigh with longing for the pie.

What This Recipe Shows

The strawberries are not cooked, so that their fresh goodness is preserved.

The starch glaze is brought to a boil so that it will not thicken further to make a pasty coating.

Having the cream, bowl, and beaters cold allows a good, thick whipped cream.

---

1 prebaked 9-inch (23-cm) crust: Cream Cheese Crust (page 288), or your favorite prebaked crust (see page 325 for baking instructions)
1 recipe Whipped Cream Topping (page 321)

1 quart (25 oz/720 g) fresh strawberries (4 to 5 cups)
1 cup (237 ml) water
1 cup (7 oz/198 g) sugar, divided
$\frac{1}{3}$ cup (1.5 oz/43 g) cornstarch stirred into $\frac{1}{4}$ cup (59 ml) cool water

1. Using a sharp knife, slice the stem end off each strawberry, creating a small flat surface. Place the strawberries in a colander and just barely rinse. Lay the berries on a double layer of paper towels to drain, and gently mop with another paper towel to wick away excess water.

2. Pick out the crushed or not-so-good-looking berries and place them in a heavy saucepan with 1 cup (237 ml) water and $\frac{3}{4}$ cup (5.3 oz/149 g) of the sugar. Bring to a boil over medium-high heat. Stir in the cornstarch mixture and continue stirring gently as the mixture thickens. Boil until no longer cloudy, and then stir in the remaining $\frac{1}{4}$ cup (1.8 oz/51 g) sugar. Bring the mixture back to a boil. It will thin a little. This is normal.

3. Brush the inside bottom of the crust with this thickened strawberry mixture. With the flat side down, stand up the prettiest berries in the bottom of the crust.

322 BAKEWISE

4. Place the rest of the berries in a medium mixing bowl. Pour the starch-sugar mixture over them. Very gently fold together with a spatula. Carefully spoon into the crust and allow to cool. Refrigerate until ready to serve.

5. Just before serving, pipe or spoon the Whipped Cream Topping in billows onto the pie.

Baking Techniques

The type of pie can dictate both the type of crust needed and the baking method. Pumpkin pies and pecan pies need to be baked in the crust, while cream pies, lemon meringue pies, chiffon pies, and some fresh fruit pies (Clide Ogletree's Famous Strawberry Pie on page 322, for example) can be made in a prebaked shell.

A custard pie, though, is a challenge. It needs a crust that will not become a soggy mess, but the custard needs to be baked in the crust. There are techniques for baking the custard in a dish and slipping it into a prebaked crust, but these are not really satisfactory.

The Custard Pie Supreme (page 332) is quite remarkable. It is baked at 450°F/232°C in the Rolled-In Crumbs Crust (page 324) and both the crust and filling are fantastic. The crust is dry and firm even after overnight in the refrigerator. This is unbelievable because custards are notorious for soaking into the crust and producing a soggy mess. And the custard itself is surreal. It cuts and looks like a very firm slice, but when you bite into it, it is as soft and dissolving as air.

BAKING WITH THE FILLING IN

A big problem with custard pies and pumpkin pies, which are baked in the crust, is a soggy crust. On page 298, the special crust for pumpkin pies has the fat worked into the flour well for a tender, nearly moisture-proof but not flakey crust. The crust is baked near the oven floor at a high temperature (450°F/232°C) to thoroughly dry it and set the filling next to the crust.

The pumpkin pie on page 300 and the custard pie on page 332 are quite remarkable; they can sit in the refrigerator for several days and yet the crust does not get soggy. The first time that I baked the Custard Pie Supreme, I could not believe it. Every other custard pie that I had made was a mess—a totally soaked crust holding a miserable tough, eggy filling. The combination of the cracker crumbs to dry the crust and a high oven temperature to set the crust fast can produce miracles.

Monroe Strause's Rolled-In Graham-Cracker Crust baked with a filling in it can give you a marvelously dry crust. The bottom of the crust (the part touching the pan) has fine graham cracker or vanilla wafer crumbs pressed into the crust. This dries out the dough so that it bakes through bone dry. The slightly darker color also absorbs heat faster to ensure thorough baking. The vanilla

The Memorable Creamy Pumpkin Pie and the Custard Pie Supreme are quite remarkable; they can sit in the refrigerator for several days and yet the crust will not get soggy.

wafers are not as dark as the graham cracker crumbs, but they work just as well and I love their flavor.

Rolled-In Crumbs Crust

MAKES ONE 9-INCH (23-CM) CRUST

This crust is unbelievable. The combination of the cracker crumbs to dry the dough and baking the pie on a low shelf in a hot 450°F/232°C oven produces a crust that you can fill and then bake with the filling in it. The crust remains dry and firm even after several days in the refrigerator with a custard filling. (See page 332 for the Custard Pie Supreme, a remarkable experience.)

What This Recipe Shows

Working the shortening into the flour extremely well helps to make this crust waterproof.

Cracker crumbs absorb moisture from the dough and give you a dry, firm crust even when the filling is baked in it.

3¾ tablespoons (56 ml) ice water
1½ teaspoons (7.5 ml) apple cider vinegar
1 teaspoon (6 g) salt
1½ cups (6.2 oz/174 g) pastry flour

9 tablespoons (3.6 oz/102 g) shortening
⅓ cup (1.5 oz/42 g) very, very fine honey graham or vanilla wafer crumbs
Nonstick cooking spray

1. In a small glass measuring cup, stir together the water, vinegar, and salt. Refrigerate until needed.

2. Place the flour and shortening in a food processor with the steel blade and process with quick on/offs until the dough clumps together and the shortening is blended in well.

3. Drizzle the cold water-salt-vinegar mixture into the flour-shortening mixture a little at a time, processing with quick on/offs after each addition. Process until the dough comes together.

4. Pull the dough together and press into one 6-inch (15-cm) disc. Wrap well in plastic wrap, and refrigerate overnight. It is important for this dough to stand overnight.

5. Sift the crumbs through a wire mesh strainer. You can process any larger crumbs left in the strainer and strain again.

6. Spray a 9-inch (23-cm) baking ring placed on a baking sheet or a 9-inch (23-cm) pan with non-stick cooking spray.

7. Roll out the dough into a 9-inch (23-cm) circle. Spread the fine crumbs evenly on the counter in an 8-inch (20-cm) circle. Roll the rolling pin over the crumbs to spread them evenly. Fold the dough into a quarter circle and position the point in the center of the crumbs. Unfold the dough and roll over it several times to enlarge the dough to a 12-inch (30-cm) circle and press crumbs into the crust well. Fold the dough in quarters and position the point in the center of the prepared baking ring or pan crumb side down. Unfold. Allow to stand at room temperature at least 30 minutes for the crumbs to absorb liquid from the crust.

8. Prepare the filling and bake as directed.

Top and Bottom Rolled-In Crumb Crust

In making the Rolled-In Crumbs Crust, cracker or vanilla wafer crumbs are rolled into the bottom side of the crust only. The Rolled-In Crumbs Crusts are ideal for baking pies with the filling in, such as custard or pumpkin pie.

You can use this crust for pies that are not baked, too, such as a fresh strawberry pie, lemon meringue, or cream pie. To do so, roll ⅓ cup (1.5 oz/42 g) crumbs into each side of the crust. Bake blind the crust and you get a dry crisp crust.

Follow the directions for the Rolled-In Crumbs Crust, but roll crumbs into both the top and bottom of the crust.

BAKING BLIND

Using a specialty crust that is designed to bake dry and firm with the filling in, like the Rolled-In Crumbs Crust, page 324, or Shirley's Adaptation of Strause's Special Crust for Pumpkin Pie on page 298, produces incredible crusts that remain dry and firm even after several days in the refrigerator.

However, with a flakey crust, baking blind (prebaking the crust) produces a superior crust. For a demonstration, I baked two pies made with the same dough and same filling. One was baked with the filling in, the other baked blind, then glazed, filled, and baked. The crust baked blind is always definitely crisper. A crisp, thoroughly cooked and glazed crust has a good chance of staying crisp when the filling is added.

You can bake blind (prebake) a pie crust right-side up or upside down. Baking upside down does give the advantage of not having to use weights. These techniques are described below.

Baking Blind Right-Side Up

To bake a crust right-side up in a traditional pie pan, cover the frozen crust with parchment or foil and fill the covered crust with weights to hold it down. (For weights, you can use uncooked rice, dried beans, pie weights, or—my favorite—pennies that have been sterilized by boiling.) Using weights, you do have the problem of uneven baking. The uncovered rim can overcook while the covered bottom is undercooked.

Problem with Pie Weights

Pie weights (special weights, dried beans, or uncooked rice) prevent the sides from caving in, and they prevent bubbling up of the bottom crust due to trapped air between the crust and the pan. But as the weights weigh down the bottom crust, they cause it to bake unevenly. The rim is exposed and gets overbaked while the sides and bottom are covered with the weights and often go undercooked. But if the crust is frozen, you bake in a hot (450°F/232°C) oven on a baking stone, and use a baking ring, you may be able to avoid using weights. It is imperative that the crust be well frozen before baking if you choose to use this technique.

Pie weights cause a crust to bake unevenly— the exposed rim gets overbaked while the covered bottom is underbaked. Using the weights is not as damaging for tarts with straight sides as it is for a regular crust. For small tarts (up to 5 inches/13 cm) baked in a baking (flan) ring on a heavy baking sheet, it may be possible to blind bake the crusts without using any pie weights. If the crust is well frozen and is baked with fast, high heat on a baking stone that was preheated in a 450°F/232°C oven, you may be able to bake small tart shells without weights. (See the tartlets on page 283.) For other crusts, you may have to experiment to determine which you can or cannot bake blind in a ring without weights.

Baking Blind Upside Down

For a plain-edged (not fluted) crust, baking blind upside down is a little easier and may give you a better crust. This procedure stretches the sides and gives you a slightly higher crust. Baking upside down also gives you the advantage of not having to use weights.

To bake blind upside down, arrange a shelf in the lower third of the oven, place a baking stone on it, and preheat the oven to 450°F/232°C. Place the crust in the pan and then freeze. Remove the crust from the freezer and cover it with a sheet of parchment (first crumple the parchment up, then straighten it out so that it is more flexible and will fit better) and place a pie pan of the same size as the one the crust is in on top of the parchment. Turn both pans upside down, with the crust in the middle. Remove the pan that is now on top to expose the bottom of the crust. Bake like this—upside down—on the baking stone for about 12 minutes. Replace the empty pie pan on top of the crust, turn the crust right-side up, and remove the inside pan and parchment. Bake on the hot stone about 10 minutes more to dry the inside well. Glaze the inside of the crust with your choice of glazes, such as egg white or Dijon mustard, and bake for 3 or 4 minutes to cook the glaze.

BAKING DOUBLE-CRUSTED PIES

Double-crust pies (top and bottom crusts) are not prebaked (baked blind; see page 326), so it is easy to get an improperly baked, soggy bottom crust, with a gap between the fruit and the top crust.

In the *CookWise* recipe for Big Chunk Fresh Apple Pie, I solved these problems by baking everything separately. The bottom crust was baked blind with rolled-in crumbs on the bottom for crispness (see page 324). The top crust was baked over an upside-down metal bowl and the filling prepared in a large pot on the stove. When ready to serve, the three completely cooked components were assembled for a beautiful apple pie.

Bill Greenwood's Great Dome with a Braided Base

We have our own present-day Pie King here in the Atlanta area. Chef Bill Greenwood of Greenwood's on Green Street restaurant in Roswell makes fruit pies—apple and cherry—that are works of art. They are smooth, high-domed creations with a magnificent wide braid at the base of the dome joining top and bottom crusts. Bill said he designed the crust after seeing a program on how Wedgwood sculpted his porcelain.

1. Arrange a shelf in the lower third of the oven and place a baking stone on it. Preheat the oven for at least 30 minutes to 450°F/232°C.

2. See Greenwood's Great Buttermilk Crust (page 347), and follow the directions for placing the bottom crust in the pan. There are about 1½ inches (4 cm) of dough beyond the outer edge of the pan. Brush this 1½-inch (4-cm) rim of dough lightly with water.

3. Toss thin-sliced apples with brown sugar, cinnamon, etc. (pie ingredients). You could use Monroe's technique of allowing the apple slices and sugar to drain over a colander (see page 310). After draining and concentrating the liquid, toss the slices with all ingredients and pile these sliced apples in a mountain that is about 5 inches (13 cm) above the crust. Push the apples in around the edges so that you have somewhat of a trough between the apples and the sides of the crust. Now, for one pie, grate 2 ounces (57 g) of butter, shape the grated butter into a 4-inch (10-cm) disc, and place on the peak of the apple mountain. Press down gently. This will help form the top of the dome.

4. Bill's bottom crust dough is quite thin, 1/16 inch (0.2 cm). He rolls the top crust slightly thicker. Drape the top crust over the butter-topped apple mountain, and trim it so that when it is pressed together with the bottom crust overhang, the top crust is ½ inch (1.3 cm) smaller than the bottom crust. Fold a small section of the dough over so that the outer edge of the arch touches the dough right at the inside edge of the pan rim.

5. Now, place your left index finger on the outer edge of the arch to hold the dough down. With your right hand, fold another small section of the dough over, partially overlapping the earlier fold, and tuck it under with your thumb. Then, move your left index finger over to hold the new fold. Continue holding and folding all around. Now, go around the whole crust to gently press the outer edge of this "braid" up straight and slightly toward the center.

6. Brush the crust very lightly with beaten egg, then sprinkle heavily with sugar. Bake on the hot stone until the crust is well browned, 25 to 35 minutes.

7. There will be a gap between the top crust and the apples. However, when the pie is sliced, the top crust slides forward (the melted butter undoubtedly helps this) so that the slice ends up with the crust right on top of the apples.

Two Types of Custards

Cream and custard pies have been a problem even for experienced chefs. The two basic types of custards are *crème anglaise* (also called stirred custard or boiled custard) and pastry cream (sometimes called *crème pâtissière*). The ingredients are almost the same. Crème anglaise contains flavored milk and/or cream, sugar, and eggs. Pastry cream contains flavored milk and/or cream, sugar, eggs, and a little starch to thicken it, usually cornstarch or flour.

This small amount of starch makes an enormous difference in the two custards in both preparation techniques and texture. You heat crème anglaise in a double boiler, stirring steadily to keep the temperature even throughout. Different chefs have different techniques for stirring—Paula Wolfert may say to stir with a wooden spoon in one direction only, Giuliano Bugialli may say to pray over your left shoulder to your grandmother. I say do whatever works for you, but it's most important to keep the temperature under 180°F/82°C. The custard thickens at about 160°F/71°C and curdles (turns into scrambled eggs in a watery juice) at 180°F/82°C—not much room for error.

> The small amount of starch in pastry cream makes an enormous difference between it and crème anglaise in both preparation techniques and texture.

> Custards without starch, such as crème anglaise, thicken around 160°F/71°C and turn into scrambled eggs at 180°F/82°C.

With pastry cream, you simply heat and stir over direct heat until it thickens, somewhere near boiling temperature (212°F/100°C). Boy! What a difference a little starch makes! All natural starches that I have tried, such as cornstarch, tapioca starch, and arrowroot, work well to prevent curds, but some modified starches do not. In a commercial honey mustard recipe that I had developed, we had been using plain cornstarch. Even though the cornstarch worked beautifully in their manufacturing plant for several years, the processing people thought they would modernize us and use a more expensive modified starch. They ended up with a 300-gallon batch of curds.

Scientists don't know exactly how starch prevents proteins from coagulating at their normal temperature. Normally, raw proteins are long molecules curled around or wadded up like a piece of ribbon. Bonds across the coils keep each individual protein bound in a separate unit with space between. There is plenty of room for light to travel between the proteins. You can see this with a raw egg white in a frying pan. You can see right through the white, and you could see through the yolk, too, if it did not contain all the yellow stuff.

When you heat proteins or expose them to acid or even to air, the protein bonds break and proteins partially unwind into longer pieces with their bonds sticking out (now called a "denatured protein" because it has changed from its natural form). Almost immediately this unwound protein runs into another unwound protein and they join (coagulate or cook). Now there is no longer room for light to go between them. The egg white goes from clear to solid white, and fish or chicken turns from glassy to solid white.

How starch prevents this joining of proteins may simply be that the starch swells enough below the temperature at which egg proteins join, to literally be in the way of this process. Swollen starch granules act like boulders keeping unwound (denatured) egg proteins apart.

Whatever the mechanism, many cooks know that plain cornstarch prevents curdling in many situations. When you are trying to make a low-fat version of a cream sauce, the minute you heat the sauce with low-fat milk or yogurt, it turns to a mass of curds. There is no problem heating heavy cream, because there are only a few proteins and a lot of fat to grease these proteins and keep them apart. But with low-fat dairy products, you have tons of proteins and little fat to keep them apart. Starch to the rescue!

A friend who teaches low-fat classes stirs a tablespoon of cornstarch into a quart of yogurt then she can use it for low-fat sauces or quiches without fear of curdling.

Custards with starch such as pastry cream can be stirred over direct heat and thicken near boiling temperature (212°F/100°C).

Cornstarch can prevent curdling in custards and low-fat sauces.

Pastry Cream (Crème Pâtissière)

MAKES ABOUT 2 CUPS (473 ML)

What This Recipe Shows

Starch prevents the egg proteins from curdling, so this can be prepared over direct heat, without a double boiler.

Stir in any additions or flavorings while the finished pastry cream is still warm. Once it cools and the starch begins to bond, any stirring will thin the custard.

---

1 large, plump vanilla bean
1 cup (237 ml) whole milk
$\frac{1}{2}$ cup (118 ml) heavy or whipping cream
$\frac{1}{3}$ cup (2.3 oz/65 g) sugar

$\frac{1}{4}$ teaspoon (1.5 g) salt
3 tablespoons (0.8 oz/22 g) cornstarch
5 large egg yolks (3.25 oz/92 g)

1. Pry a vanilla bean open with the tip of a knife and scrape some of its grainy black interior into a medium saucepan. Add the vanilla bean, milk, and cream. Heat over medium heat until the mixture just begins to steam. In another medium saucepan, stir together the sugar, salt, and cornstarch. Remove the vanilla bean (see Note). Drizzle the hot milk into the sugar mixture, whisking constantly. Return the saucepan to the heat and cook over medium heat, stirring constantly, until the mixture thickens.

2. In a medium bowl, stir together the egg yolks. Stir about $\frac{1}{4}$ cup (59 ml) of the hot mixture into the yolks, then scrape the yolk mixture into the saucepan. Return it to the heat and bring to a boil, stirring constantly, scraping the bottom until the custard becomes thick and smooth. This will be very thick and go *blop, blop,* but you must be sure to get this entire mixture to a good boil to kill enzymes in the yolks or these enzymes will destroy the starch and the custard will thin and turn to soup while standing.

3. Transfer the custard to a bowl. Add any additional flavorings. If this is a part of another recipe, stir the pastry cream and other components together while the pastry cream is warm. Dot the surface with butter or cover with a piece of plastic wrap touching the entire surface of the custard. If this custard is stirred after it is cooled, starch bonds will be broken and it will thin. Keep refrigerated.

NOTE: Vanilla beans can be rinsed, dried, and reused. They will have less flavor after you have scraped out the insides but can still contribute a rich vanilla taste to a dish.

Crème Anglaise

MAKES ABOUT 2 CUPS (473 ML)

This delicious dessert sauce is a thin custard sometimes called stirred custard or boiled custard.

What This Recipe Shows

Stirring constantly as the custard sets prevents firm setting to produce the texture of a thick sauce.

---

1 large, plump vanilla bean
1 cup (237 ml) whole milk
$\frac{1}{2}$ cup (118 ml) heavy cream

5 large egg yolks (3.25 oz/92 g)
$\frac{1}{2}$ cup (3.5 oz/99 g) sugar
$\frac{1}{4}$ teaspoon (1.5 g) salt

1. Pry a vanilla bean open with the tip of a knife and scrape some of its grainy black interior into a medium saucepan. Add the vanilla bean, milk, and cream. Heat over medium heat until the mixture just begins to steam. Set aside and allow to steep for 5 minutes. Remove the vanilla bean (see Note).

2. Stir the egg yolks, sugar, and salt together in another bowl. Drizzle the hot milk mixture into the yolk mixture, whisking constantly. Strain the yolk mixture into the top of a double boiler.

3. Bring about $1\frac{1}{2}$ inches (4 cm) of water to a boil in the bottom of the double boiler. Make sure the water does not touch the top pan. Stir the custard mixture constantly, scraping the bottom and sides until it just begins to thicken. Remove from the double boiler and continue stirring. Dip a large spoon into the custard, then remove it. The custard should be "thick enough to coat a spoon"; it will leave a line when you drag your finger across the back of the spoon.

4. Transfer the custard to a bowl. Dot the surface with butter or cover with a piece of plastic wrap touching the entire surface of the custard. Refrigerate immediately until needed.

NOTE: Vanilla beans can be rinsed, dried, and reused. They will have less flavor after you have scraped out the insides but can still contribute a rich vanilla taste to a dish.

Texture Differences

Just as starch makes a tremendous difference in the techniques used to prepare a custard, it also makes a major difference in the texture of the custard. Custards held with an egg-only network, or a bare minimum of starch (like the Custard Pie Supreme), are firm enough to cut, but are fragile and dissolve in your mouth—an incredible silky sensation.

Custard Pie Supreme

MAKES ONE 9-INCH (23-CM) PIE

This is an amazing pie! The filling cuts with a clean, smooth cut and looks very firm, but in your mouth, it is dissolving, silky deliciousness—like nothing you've ever tasted before. And, wonder of all wonders, the crust is dry and firm—not the soft, soggy mess of every custard pie crust that I have ever had.

This recipe makes 1 cup (237 ml) too much filling. I tried cutting down the proportions to perfect pie size. But the custard exactly as it is has this remarkable, ethereal texture that I have never experienced before. Reduced proportions lose this indescribable texture. To keep this texture, I am happy to have extra filling, which I can bake later as a small custard.

What This Recipe Shows

The small amount of tapioca starch gives a little insurance against curdling, and allows the high baking temperature, but there is not enough to wreck the custard texture.

Emulsifiers in the egg yolks produce the incredible smoothness.

---

1 recipe Rolled-In Crumbs Crust (page 324)
1⅓ cups (9.3 oz/263 g) sugar
1 teaspoon (3 g) tapioca starch
⅛ teaspoon (pinch) salt
3 large eggs (5.25 oz/149 g)
4 large egg yolks (2.6 oz/74 g)

2 cups (473 ml) heavy cream
1 cup (237 ml) whole milk
1 tablespoon (0.5 oz/14 g) butter, melted
1 teaspoon (5 ml) pure vanilla extract
Freshly grated nutmeg

1. Arrange a shelf in the lower third of the oven, place a baking stone on it, and preheat the oven to 450°F/232°C.

2. In a medium mixing bowl, stir together the sugar, tapioca starch, and salt. Stir in the eggs and yolks one at a time, stirring well after each addition. A little at a time, stir in the cream and milk. Stir in the melted butter and vanilla. Place the filling and the nutmeg right by the stove.

3. Working quickly, open the oven door and pull out the shelf with the stone slightly. Place the prepared crust on the hot baking stone. Quickly pour in the filling until the crust is almost full and sprinkle the top with nutmeg. Gently ease the shelf back into the oven. Try to keep the oven open as short a time as possible during the whole procedure.

4. Bake 30 minutes. The custard should puff only an inch around the edges. The pie will be very shaky and not look done. Have faith; it will finish cooking as it cools. Refrigerate and allow the pie to cool thoroughly before serving.

Custards, Custards, and More Custards—Cheesecakes

Cheesecakes, custards by another name, reflect this difference in starch, too. There is an enormous difference in the texture of the Herbed Parmesan Cheesecake, page 341, which contains starch, and one without starch. Its texture is sturdy, yet smooth from emulsifiers in the egg yolks. The absolute creaminess of The Creamiest Ever Amaretto Cheesecake is the velvety texture of a custard without starch.

The Creamiest Ever Amaretto Cheesecake

MAKES ONE 8-INCH (20-CM) ROUND CHEESECAKE

I tried my beloved whipped cream in a cheesecake. It is even creamier than I imagined! I'll never be able to go back to ordinary cheesecakes.

Cooks frequently ask, "Why do cheesecakes crack?" It is because they are overcooked. Cheesecakes are the most deceptive dish in cooking. They look completely undercooked when they are done. When a cheesecake is done, not just the center but a whole 3-inch (8-cm) circle in the center jiggles like Jell-O. You know that it can't possibly be done. You have to have faith and place it in the refrigerator. A few hours later, you will be stunned to see that it is perfectly cooked.

What This Recipe Shows

This is a custard that contains no starch and needs to be baked in a water bath or a very low-temperature oven (just below 200°F/93°C).

Since the cheesecake contains no starch, its texture is satiny smooth and creamy.

Beating the cream cheese until it is completely smooth prevents lumps. If you add all the egg and get it too juicy before it is smooth, the lumps scoot away from the beater and you can't get it smooth.

Crust

12 amaretti cookies

3 tablespoons (1.5 oz/43 g) butter, melted

Nonstick cooking spray

Filling

¾ cup (177 ml) heavy cream

Two 8-ounce packages (454 g) cream cheese

1 cup (7 oz/198 g) sugar

3 large eggs (5.25 oz/149 g)

¼ cup (59 ml) amaretto liqueur

2 teaspoons (10 ml) pure vanilla extract

¼ teaspoon (1.5 g) salt

2 cups (17 oz/482 g) sour cream

Boiling water for a water bath, about 4 cups (946 ml)

1. Arrange a shelf in the lower third of the oven, place a baking stone on it, and preheat the oven to 350°F/177°C.

2. In a food processor with the steel blade, process the amaretti cookies until fine crumbs. With the processor running, drizzle in the melted butter.

3. Line the bottom of an 8 x 3-inch (20 x 8-cm) round cake pan with a parchment circle. Spray the lined pan with nonstick cooking spray. Pour the crumbs into the prepared pan and press in the crumbs to form a crust.

4. Place a bowl, beaters, and heavy cream in the freezer for 5 minutes. In a mixer with the whisk attachment, whip the cream to the soft-peak stage and then beat just a little longer. Refrigerate until needed.

5. In a food processor with the steel blade, or in a large mixing bowl with a beater, blend the cream cheese and sugar well to remove all the lumps. Beat in the eggs, one at a time, and blend well after each addition. Blend in well the amaretto, vanilla, and salt. If using the processor, pour the batter into a mixing bowl. With a large spatula, blend in the sour cream. Gently fold in the whipped cream. Pour into the prepared crust.

6. To prepare a water bath, fold a small terrycloth towel and place it in the bottom of a roasting pan or large pan that is at least 1 inch (2.5 cm) larger on all sides than the cake pan. Place the cake pan on the towel in the larger pan.

7. Pull the oven shelf with the baking stone out slightly. Place the larger pan on the stone. Carefully pour into the larger pan enough boiling water to come at least 1 inch (2.5 cm) up the side of the cake pan. Ease the shelf back in and close the oven door. Bake the cheesecake for 45 minutes. Do *not* open the oven during the baking time. Turn off the oven and leave the cheesecake in for 1 more hour. The cheesecake will not look done, and a 3-inch (8-cm) circle in the center will still wiggle. Have faith. Remove it from the oven and refrigerate overnight.

8. Turn a burner on low and place the cheesecake pan on the burner to heat the bottom of the pan for just seconds for easy removal. Run a thin knife around the edges and jar the pan on one side. Since the cheesecake is in a cake pan, you have to invert it twice. Cover a baking sheet with plastic wrap. Turn the cheesecake upside down onto the baking sheet. Peel off the parchment. Place a pedestal cake dish on the bottom and invert again. Refrigerate. Serve cold.

CREAM PIES

Modern techniques for making cream pie fillings usually first thicken the milk or cream, sugar, and flavoring ingredients with cornstarch or flour, and then add the egg yolks or eggs. After the eggs are added, a good recipe directs the cook to return the custard to the heat and bring it back to a boil. Because of the starch, you don't have to worry about the eggs curdling. This very important step inactivates the enzyme alpha-amylase in egg yolks and prevents its breaking apart the starch network that makes the filling thick. If you do not first heat the custard to inactivate these enzymes, as the custard cools, the enzymes gobble up the starch just like Pac-Man. Several hours later you have soup instead of a nice, thick, creamy pie filling.

> Many thick cream pie fillings turn to soup upon standing because the filling was not brought back to a boil after the eggs were added and an enzyme, alpha-amylase, destroyed the starch network.

Another problem is that after you add the eggs, probably right out of the refrigerator, and start heating again, the custard gets very thick and begins to stick to the bottom of the pan. You have to keep scraping the bottom and the custard is so thick that it is going *blop! blop!* The cook's instinct is to say, "Oh, it's at a boil," and take the custard off the heat before the custard gets even close to 180°F/82°C (the temperature at which enzymes are inactivated) all the way through. Even if you have inactivated a high percentage of the alpha-amylase, one enzyme can catalyze thousands of reactions in a second and, since alpha-amylase enzymes can react over and over again, it doesn't take many to turn a beautiful, thick cream pie filling to soup upon standing.

Monroe Boston Strause uses a different and, I think, better technique. He mixes the starch and eggs with part of the milk, then whisks this mixture into the other ingredients at a boil. The filling does not get terribly thick until most of the starch-egg mixture has been added. So there is only a brief time that the mixing is difficult. Since the filling was already close to boiling until then, you need only a brief time at this difficult-to-stir stage to be sure that the whole mixture has gotten well above 180°F/82°C and all of the enzymes are inactivated.

> Even if you get the custard hot enough to inactivate a high percentage of the alpha-amylase, one enzyme can catalyze thousands of reactions in a second, and enzymes react over and over again, so it doesn't take many to thin the filling.

Unfortunately, the fact that you need to get all the filling above 180°F/82°C after the eggs or yolks are added does not seem to be thoroughly understood, and many pie books give poor directions for this step. With Monroe's method, you are almost assured of getting the temperature high enough.

Memorable Silky Chocolate Meringue Pie

MAKES 1 CREAMY, SILKY 9-INCH (23-CM) PIE

This is a pie to dream about—once you taste it, you will not forget this sensationally smooth, creamy chocolate.

What This Recipe Shows

Starch in the custard prevents the egg yolks from curdling at their usual temperature, enabling you to bring the custard to a boil.

Adding the starch and the egg yolks at the same time, drizzling in slowly, allows the eggs to get hot enough to kill the enzyme that attacks the starch.

Boiling the custard after the egg yolks are added ensures that the whole mixture gets over 180°F/82°C to kill enzymes in the egg yolks that will thin the pie overnight.

Egg yolks, nature's great emulsifiers, make a sensationally smooth custard.

Corn syrup gives a magnificent shine because it is a liquid that attracts water and fills between crystals on the surface to produce a perfectly glass-smooth finish.

Sprinkling fine crumbs on the filling will give you a dry seal between the meringue and the filling.

---

1 recipe Rolled-In Crumbs Crust (page 324)
1 recipe Italian Meringue (Magnificent Pie Meringue) (page 187)
⅓ cup (1.5 oz/43 g) cornstarch
2 tablespoons (0.5 oz/14 g) bleached all-purpose flour
1 cup (237 ml) whole milk, divided
6 large egg yolks (3.9 oz/110 g)
1 cup (7 oz/198 g) sugar
¼ teaspoon (1.5 g) salt

¾ cup (177 ml) heavy cream
3 tablespoons (45 ml) light corn syrup
3 ounces (85 g) unsweetened baking chocolate, finely chopped
10 ounces (283 g) milk chocolate, broken into pieces
2 tablespoons (1 oz/28 g) butter
1 teaspoon (5 ml) pure vanilla extract
3 tablespoons (0.8 oz/21 g) fine dry cake or unseasoned bread crumbs

1. Arrange a shelf in the lower third of the oven, place a baking stone on it, and preheat the oven to 450°F/232°C.

2. Prepare the Rolled-In Crumbs Crust, place it in a 9-inch (23-cm) pie pan, and bake it on the baking stone, using your favorite blind-baking method (see page 325). Remove the pie shell from the oven and allow it to cool completely. Turn off the oven, and when it is cool, remove the baking stone.

3. Meanwhile, prepare the Italian Meringue, reserving the egg yolks for the pie filling.

4. Arrange a shelf in the upper third of the oven and preheat the oven to 400°F/204°C.

5. In a small mixing bowl or a 2-cup (473-ml) measuring cup, stir together the cornstarch and flour. A little at a time, stir in ½ cup (118 ml) of the milk. Stir the egg yolks into the mixture until you cannot see any egg streaks.

6. In a large, heavy saucepan, stir together the sugar and salt. Place over low to medium heat and stir in the cream a little at a time. Then add the remaining ½ cup (118 ml) milk and the corn syrup.

7. Bring this mixture to a boil. *With a whisk,* whisk in the cornstarch–egg yolk mixture a little at a time and bring back to a boil. When at a boil, use a spatula with a straight end to scrape the bottom to prevent burning. Keep at a low boil for at least 1 minute. It is a very thick mixture and difficult to boil throughout, but *it is imperative that you get the whole mixture over 180°F/82°C to kill the enzymes in the egg yolks that will thin the pie filling overnight.*

8. Stir in both chocolates, the butter, and the vanilla. Pour the hot filling into the crust.

9. Allow the filling to stand uncovered to firm. You need it to cool and become firm enough to hold up the meringue. When the filling is set but barely warm, sprinkle the top with the bread crumbs. Pile on the prepared meringue, spread the meringue into decorative whirls, and make peaks—some that stand up and others that flop over.

10. Bake until the swirls start to brown, about 10 to 15 minutes. Serve cold.

Butterscotch Meringue Pie

Makes 1 memorable 9-inch (23-cm) pie

This is truly memorial butterscotch—indescribably delicious!

What This Recipe Shows

Starch in the custard prevents the egg yolks from curdling at their usual temperature, enabling you to bring the custard to a boil.

Adding the starch and the egg yolks at the same time, drizzling in slowly, allows the eggs to get hot enough to kill the enzyme that attacks the starch.

Boiling the custard after the egg yolks are added ensures that the whole mixture gets over 180°F/82°C to kill enzymes in the egg yolks that will thin the pie overnight.

Egg yolks, nature's great emulsifiers, make a sensationally smooth custard.

Corn syrup gives a magnificent shine because it is a liquid that attracts water and fills between crystals on the surface to produce a perfectly glass-smooth finish.

Sprinkling fine crumbs on the filling will give you a dry seal between the meringue and the filling.

---

1 recipe Rolled-In Crumbs Crust (page 324)
1 recipe Italian Meringue (Magnificent Pie Meringue) (page 187)
6 tablespoons (3 oz/85 g) butter
¾ cup (6.3 oz/178 g) dark brown sugar, packed
2 tablespoons (30 ml) light corn syrup
¾ cup (177 ml) heavy cream
1½ cups (355 ml) whole milk, divided

⅓ cup (1.5 oz/43 g) cornstarch
2 tablespoons (0.5 oz/14 g) bleached all-purpose flour
6 large egg yolks (3.9 oz/111 g)
½ teaspoon (3 g) salt
1 tablespoon (15 ml) pure vanilla extract
3 tablespoons (0.8 oz/ 21 g) fine dry cake or unseasoned bread crumbs

1. Arrange a shelf in the lower third of the oven, place a baking stone on it, and preheat the oven to 450°F/232°C.

2. Prepare the Rolled-In Crumbs Crust, place it in a 9-inch (23-cm) pie pan, and bake it on the baking stone, using your favorite blind-baking method (see page 325). Remove the pie shell from the

oven and allow it to cool completely. Turn off the oven, and when it is cool, remove the baking stone.

3. Meanwhile, prepare the Italian Meringue, reserving the egg yolks for the pie filling.

4. Arrange a shelf in the upper third of the oven and preheat the oven to 400°F/204°C.

5. In a large, heavy saucepan, on low heat, stir together the butter, brown sugar, and corn syrup until the butter melts and the sugar is dissolved. Leave on very low heat and simmer gently until it reaches 220°F/104°C on a candy thermometer, about 5 minutes.

6. With the heat on low, add the cream, stirring steadily with a wooden spatula or spoon until the sugar mixture (butterscotch) dissolves. When the butterscotch is dissolved, stir in 1 cup (237 ml) of the milk.

7. In a small mixing bowl or a 2-cup (473-ml) measuring cup, stir together the cornstarch and flour and stir in the remaining ½ cup (118 ml) milk a little at a time. Beat in the egg yolks until you can't see any egg streaks. Bring the butterscotch mixture up to a boil. *With a whisk,* whisk in the cornstarch–egg yolk mixture a little at a time and bring back to a boil. When at a boil, use a spatula with a straight end to scrape the bottom to prevent burning. Keep at a low boil for at least 1 minute. It is a very thick mixture and difficult to boil throughout, but *it is imperative that you get the whole mixture over 180°F/82°C to kill the enzymes in the egg yolks that will thin the pie filling overnight.*

8. Stir in the salt and vanilla. Pour the hot filling into the crust.

9. Allow the filling to stand uncovered to firm a little. You need to let it cool and become firm enough to hold up the meringue. When the filling is set but barely warm, sprinkle the top with the crumbs. Pile on the prepared meringue, spread the meringue into decorative whirls, and make peaks—some that stand up and others that flop over.

10. Bake until swirls start to brown, 10 to 15 minutes. Serve cold.

Pastry Crust—The Recipe

The recipe is just a ballpark starting point. Crusts with the same basic formula will turn out very different according to the individual ingredients and techniques that are used. A basic formula for a manageable crust is one volume fat (a little more for a rich crust) to three volumes flour, plus salt and liquid.

Here is an example of a basic crust formula:

Crusts with the same recipe can be very different, depending on the techniques.

1½ cups (approximately 6.9 oz/196 g) pastry, instant, or low-protein soft winter wheat flour

½ cup fat (butter, 4 oz/113 g; shortening or lard, 3.4 oz/95 g)

½ to 1 teaspoon (3 to 6 g) salt

A cold acidic liquid like buttermilk, or a cold plain liquid like water plus a small amount of an acidic ingredient like vinegar or lemon juice

The type of flour, the type of fat, the technique used, and the type of liquid will all influence the amount of liquid needed in a crust.

The amount of liquid depends on how many gluten-forming proteins in the flour are left uncoated with fat and are available to absorb water. The type of flour, the type of fat, the technique used to work the fat into the flour, and the type of liquid will all influence this. So many variables! Alas, the complexity of a simple pie crust.

RATIO OF FAT TO FLOUR

If amounts of ingredients vary too far from these basic ratios, there can be problems. For example, if the recipe has a high ratio of fat to flour, it will be extremely tender, but can be impossible to roll out. The tender, flavorful E-Z Crust with the Fresh, Sparkling Taste of Lemon Zest (below) has a high ratio of fat to flour and is difficult—nearly impossible—to handle and to roll. In this case, the dough should be put into the pan using the press-in technique on page 278.

E-Z Crust with the Fresh, Sparkling Taste of Lemon Zest

MAKES ONE 8 TO 9-INCH (20 TO 23-CM) CRUST

This wonderfully flavorful crumbly dough is sprinkled into the pan and simply pressed in. It bakes into an extremely tender, rich crust and is an ideal accompaniment for the Herbed Parmesan Cheesecake, page 341.

What This Recipe Shows

The large ratio of butter to flour makes this crust so tender that it is almost crumbly.

Lemon zest (grated peel) is an intense flavoring agent, ideal for a pie crust since a little bit can have a major influence.

---

1 cup (4.4 oz/124 g) spooned and leveled
   bleached all-purpose flour
½ teaspoon (3 g) salt
Zest (grated peel) of 1 lemon

½ cup (4 oz/113 g) unsalted butter, cut in 8
   pieces
3 tablespoons (45 ml) lemon juice
1 large egg yolk (0.65 oz/18 g)
Nonstick cooking spray

1. Process the flour, salt, lemon zest, and butter in a food processor with the steel blade for several seconds. Some butter should remain in lumps. Add the lemon juice and egg yolk. Process with a few on/offs just to mix.

2. Spray an 8 or 9-inch (20 or 23-cm) springform pan (see Note) with nonstick cooking spray. Crumble a third of the dough into the bottom of pan and using your fingertips press it out evenly across the bottom of the pan. Press the remaining dough around the sides of the pan. Place the pan in the freezer while mixing the filling.

NOTE: Springform pans labeled 8 inch (20 cm) may actually be 8½ inches (22 cm) and springform pans labeled 9 inch (23 cm) may actually be 9½ inches (24 cm). Either is fine.

Herbed Parmesan Cheesecake

MAKES 25 TO 30 HORS D'OEUVRE SERVINGS

This unusual hors d'oeuvre cheesecake with fresh herbs in the filling and lemon zest in the crust is deep brown on top, with golden sides. On a pedestal cake dish encircled with a garland of fresh herbs, or garnished with a cluster of tomato roses and fresh basil leaves, it attracts attention instantly. It is excellent for large parties and a favorite of caterers because it is dramatic and unusual and neither expensive nor difficult to prepare. It can be made several days ahead.

What This Recipe Shows

The starch (flour) in this custard produces a firm texture and protects the eggs from curdling, which enables the cheesecake to be baked at 325°F/163°C without a water bath.

Blending the eggs in well one at a time prevents the batter from becoming too wet with floating lumps of cream cheese.

---

1 recipe E-Z Crust with the Fresh, Sparkling
    Taste of Lemon Zest (page 340),
    prepared and frozen
Three 8-ounce packages (680 g) cream cheese
3 tablespoons (0.8 oz/23 g) bleached
    all-purpose flour
2 large egg yolks (1.3 oz/37 g)
3 large eggs (5.25 oz/149 g)
1 teaspoon (6 g) salt
$^{1}/_{2}$ teaspoon (2.5 ml) hot pepper sauce
2 tablespoons (30 ml) lemon juice
1$^{1}/_{2}$ teaspoons (1.5 g) minced fresh oregano
    or $^{1}/_{2}$ teaspoon (0.5 g) dried

1$^{1}/_{2}$ teaspoons (1.5 g) minced fresh tarragon
    or $^{1}/_{2}$ teaspoon (0.5 g) dried
1 tablespoon (3 g) chopped fresh basil
    or 1 teaspoon (1 g) dried
1 teaspoon (1 g) minced fresh rosemary or
    $^{1}/_{3}$ teaspoon (0.5 g) dried
$^{1}/_{2}$ cup (30 g) chopped fresh parsley
1 cup (3 oz/85 g) freshly grated Parmesan
4 large shallots, finely chopped
3 large tomatoes, for garnish
3 sprigs fresh basil, for garnish

1. Place an oven shelf slightly above center. Preheat the oven to 400°F/204°C.

2. In a food processor with the steel blade, process the cream cheese until smooth. Add the flour and the egg yolks. Process in well, and scrape down sides of bowl. Add the whole eggs, one at a time, processing after each egg addition. Add the salt, hot sauce, lemon juice, herbs, Parmesan, and shallots. Process just to blend well.

3. Pour the filling into the prepared crust. Bake for 15 minutes. Turn the oven down to 325°F/163°C and bake until the top is medium brown, about 50 more minutes. Cool 10 minutes on a cooling rack. Loosen the crust from the springform by running a thin knife between the crust and pan. Open the springform ring and remove. Let come to room temperature, at least 1 hour. Refrigerate if not serving immediately (see Note).

4. Carefully peel the tomatoes deeply with a sharp paring knife, in one long piece of peel if possible. Wind each peel into a tomato rose. Arrange three roses on top of the cheesecake with basil leaves to garnish them.

5. To make it easy for the guests to serve themselves, precut a number of portions by cutting an inner circle about 1$^{1}/_{2}$ inches (4 cm) from the edge, then cut, but do not remove, $^{3}/_{4}$-inch (2-cm) slices around the edge to this circle. Serve at room temperature.

VARIATION: Decorate with fresh herbs and edible flowers instead of tomato roses. Wrap the cheesecake in garlands of fresh thyme sprigs, for example, interspersed with flowers from flowering herbs or other edible flowers.

NOTE: This cheesecake can be prepared 1 or 2 days ahead and refrigerated, or it can be prepared several weeks ahead and frozen. Thaw overnight in the refrigerator.

INGREDIENTS

Flour

When the cook adds water to flour and stirs, two flour proteins (glutenin and gliadin) grab water and each other to form strong, elastic, bubblegum-like sheets called gluten. Pie crusts need just enough gluten to hold them together. More gluten will not only make the crust tough, it will also make the crust shrink badly when baked. The simplest way to limit the amount of gluten formed is to start with a flour that contains a lower amount of the gluten-forming proteins (8 to 9 grams of protein per cup, about 8%) in the first place; examples are pastry flour, instant flour, cake flour, or a low-protein Southern all-purpose flour like White Lily.

> The simplest way to limit the amount of gluten formed is to start with a low-protein flour.

Commercial buyers have access to pastry flour. Home cooks outside of the Southern states where White Lily is available usually need to go to a health food store for pastry flour.

Other lower-protein flours available in the grocery store are cake flour and instant flours such as Wondra or Shake & Blend. Cake flour produces good textured crusts. It is low protein (8 grams per cup, about 8%) and acidic. A slightly acidic dough is easier to roll and sets a little faster to help the crust hold its shape. (See Acidic Ingredients, page 355.) However, cake flour does have a definite taste.

> Low-protein flours available to the home cook are pastry flour (health food stores), Southern low-protein all-purpose flours like White Lily (see Sources, flour, page 510), cake flour, and instant flours like Wondra and Shake & Blend.

I love the taste of the instant flours like Wondra or Shake & Blend. These flours are steam processed to make lump-free sauces and gravies. Some malted barley flour is added for flavor and to lower their gluten-forming protein content. Because of the barley, the label indicates a higher protein content, but the proteins are not gluten-forming proteins. In supermarkets these are available in cylinders, and occasionally in boxes or bags. Commercially, they are available in large bags, and some pastry chefs use 100% instant flour for pie crusts. Actually, I know a number of good home cooks—Carol Evans in Jackson, Mississippi, for example—who love to make their crusts with these flours.

For a lower-protein flour outside of the Southern states, you can use Wondra or Shake & Blend flour or you can mix one part of this lower-gluten-forming protein flour with one part of a national brand bleached all-purpose.

Crust with Instant Flour

MAKES ONE 9-INCH (23-CM) CRUST

Carol Evans, a great home cook in Jackson, Mississippi, is very specific about using instant flour such as Wondra in her pie crust. Carol likes to use margarine, but I prefer butter or a mix of butter and shortening or lard.

What This Recipe Shows

Lower-protein instant flour produces a tender crust.

The malted barley flour in these instant flours enhances browning.

Buttermilk is mildly acidic to make the crust easier to roll and to make it set faster.

Protein and sugars in buttermilk are also color enhancers.

1½ cups (6.9 oz/196 g) instant flour (such as Wondra or Shake & Blend Flour) poured into a measuring cup and leveled

6 tablespoons (3 oz/85 g) butter, cut in ½-tablespoon (0.25-oz/7-g) pieces and frozen

3 tablespoons (1.3 oz/36 g) butter-flavored shortening, cut in ½-tablespoon (0.25-oz/6-g) pieces and frozen

1 teaspoon (6 g) salt

⅓ cup (79 ml) cold buttermilk

Nonstick cooking spray

1 large egg (1.75 oz/50 g), separated, for glazing

2 tablespoons (1 oz/28 g) butter, melted

1. In a medium mixing bowl, stir together the flour and frozen butter and shortening.

2. Cut the fat in with a pastry cutter or by hand. For flakiness, it is important to keep the pieces of fat fairly large (large lima bean–size, or like large paint flakes falling off a wall).

3. Stir the salt into the buttermilk. Sprinkle a little of this over the flour-butter mixture and toss. Continue sprinkling and tossing until all the buttermilk is incorporated. The dough should hold together and even be a little sticky, but not wet. Press the dough together. If it is dry and crumbly, add a little more buttermilk. Shape the dough into a 6-inch (15-cm) disc, wrap tightly with plastic wrap, and refrigerate for at least 2 hours or overnight. This will allow the moisture to distribute more evenly.

4. For a 9-inch (23-cm) pan, roll out to a 13-inch (33-cm) circle on a lightly floured pastry cloth or counter or between two pieces of lightly floured wax paper. For detailed instructions on rolling pastry see page 286. If you are going to bake the crust and filling together, use the roll-in-crumbs technique to avoid a soggy crust on page 324. Otherwise, use regular directions—placing in the pan (page 295), and baking (page 323).

Salt

Salt is vital both technically and flavorwise. Technically, it enhances gluten strength to hold the crust together but, perhaps even more important, it is a major flavor enhancer. Salt suppresses bitterness to allow other flavors to come out. To quote the pie master Monroe Boston Strause, "I have often tasted an otherwise excellent pie crust, the flavor of which was ruined by the lack of salt." (For more about salt and flavor see page 481.)

> Salt is vital for flavor and enhances gluten strength.

Adding Salt to Pastry Dough

Different cooks have different preferences for adding salt to pastry dough. Some like the ease of adding it to the flour in the beginning and feel that it gets distributed well enough. Others like to add it to the liquid for more even distribution. Professional bakers insist on adding the salt to the liquid.

Salt enhances gluten formation. I thought that if it was mixed with the flour, some salt would be greased and probably would not increase gluten formation. However, bakers say otherwise—that adding the salt to the flour gives you a tougher crust. My beloved Monroe Boston Strause says to never add salt to the flour—always dissolve it in the liquid. So that is gospel for me and I will henceforth always add my salt to the liquid.

> Bakers say that adding the salt to the flour gives you a tougher crust. Also, adding it to the liquid allows more even distribution.

You may not be sure exactly how much liquid that you will use. To make sure that you get all the salt in, add it to part of the liquid, add that first, then add the rest of the liquid as needed.

Fat

Fats tenderize by coating flour proteins, which prevents their joining to form gluten, and fats create flakiness by serving as a spacer between layers of dough. Another role of fat (which I had never realized before) is to waterproof, preventing a crust from becoming soggy. My adaptation of Monroe Boston Strause's pumpkin pie crust on page 298 directs you to rub the shortening into the flour extremely well until it is on the verge of becoming pasty. This crust is amazing. Even though the filling and crust are baked together, this crust never gets soggy or soft.

> Fats can tenderize, create flakes, or even waterproof to prevent a soggy crust.

Some fats grease or coat the flour proteins more easily than others. Shortening, for example, is softer and easier to work into flour than cold butter. The temperature matters, too. Warm fat will be softer or runnier and coat better than cold, firm fat. The ultimate tender crusts are the hot-oil crusts popular in the thirties. These crusts are fall-apart tender but have not a single flake.

For flakiness, you need large, cold, firm pieces of fat that remain unmelted and keep layers of dough apart in the hot oven just long enough for the dough above and below the fat to begin to set. The fat melts, then steam from the dough forms and puffs the layers apart. Different types of fat—butter, margarine, shortening, lard, or oil—have different protein-coating abilities, and different abilities to serve as a spacer.

For flakiness you need large, cold, firm pieces of fat that remain unmelted and keep layers of dough apart in the hot oven just long enough for the dough above and below the fat to begin to set. The fat acts as a spacer. When the fat melts, steam comes out of the dough and puffs the dough apart where the fat was.

Fat Content of Different Fats

Solid fats like shortening and lard are 100% fat, and make flakier pastry than butter or margarine, which are only about 80% fat. Since there is a lower percentage of fat when you use butter or margarine, the same amount of butter or margarine will produce a less tender and/or less flakey crust than other fats such as shortening or lard under the same conditions. Spreads contain gums and vary all over the place in the amount of fat and water that they contain. Some of the low-fat spreads are 50% or even more water.

Texture, Temperature, and Melting Characteristics

At the same temperature, butter, shortening, margarine, lard, and oil can have very different textures. So they have very different protein-coating abilities and are different in ease of use. Using the same techniques, oil and softer fats such as Crisco or lard will coat many more proteins and make a more tender crust.

Because of the difference in melting temperature, it is much easier to work with a shortening crust than a butter crust. When the butter is cold, it is hard and the crust is difficult to roll. If you let the crust get too warm, the butter softens and may soak into the dough, destroying flakiness. Shortening, on the other hand, is designed to remain about the same consistency over a wide range of temperatures and it is considerably easier to handle.

For a flakey crust, the fat must remain solid in the hot oven long enough for the dough on either side of it to begin to set. Most of the fats that are solid at room temperature can do this, but butter must be very cold going into the oven to hold up long enough. Fats that hold their shape over a wide range of temperatures, like shortening, lard, and some margarines, hold up well and create flakiness more easily.

It is much easier to work with a shortening or lard crust than a butter crust, which can be rock hard when cold.

Shortening Crust

Because shortening greases the flour so well, it can produce a tender crust and, because it holds its shape to act as a spacer between layers of dough, it can make a very flakey crust.

The shortening crust of good old pie bakers like those in *American Pie: Slices of Life (and Pie) from America's Back Roads* by Pascale Le Draoulec, and *Blue Ribbon Pies* (from state, local, and county fairs), contain 6 to 6.6 tablespoons (66 to 73 g) of shortening per cup of flour. Monroe Boston Strause uses about 6.7 to 7 tablespoons (67 to 77 g) per cup of pastry flour, while gourmet pastry bakers like Rose Beranbaum use 6 tablespoons (66 g) of shortening per cup of pastry flour. Bill Greenwood, our pie master of Atlanta, uses 6 to 6.6 tablespoons (66 to 73 g) per cup.

Chef Greenwood makes 100 pies a day (400 pies a day during holidays) and prepares this recipe in batches using 10 pounds (4.5 kg) of flour. Amazingly enough, he prepares the dough by hand.

Greenwood's Great Buttermilk Crust

MAKES 1 GORGEOUS, FLAKEY 9-INCH (23-CM) CRUST

Not too many chefs who own large, busy restaurants are generous enough to share their prize-winning recipes with the world. I really appreciate the gift that Bill has made allowing me to print some of his recipes. In this great crust, his secret ingredient is buttermilk. His dough is easy to work, and roll, and bakes into a magnificent, golden brown, flakey crust. I have described his procedures for you to use in your kitchen.

What This Recipe Shows

Buttermilk provides wonderful taste, enhances the color of the crust, and is acidic, which will make it a little more tender and easier to roll and help the crust set faster.

½ teaspoon (3 g) salt
¼ cup (59 ml) buttermilk
9 to 10 tablespoons (3.6 to 4.2 oz/102 to 119 g) butter-flavored shortening (I like to use the sticks of shortening because they are so easy to measure)

1½ cups (6.6 oz/187 g) spooned and leveled bleached all-purpose flour
3 tablespoons (45 ml) ice water, or as needed

1. In a small measuring cup, stir the salt into the buttermilk and refrigerate.

2. Cut the shortening in ½-tablespoon (0.2-oz/6-g) slices, toss the shortening and flour together in a medium mixing bowl, and place in the freezer for 30 minutes.

3. Work the shortening into the flour by rolling them together. Dump the cold shortening and flour mixture onto a clean countertop, flour a rolling pin, and roll over the mixture to flatten the shortening pieces and coat them with flour. Wipe any shortening off the rolling pin, push the mixture back together with a pastry scraper, and roll over it again. Working fast to keep the mixture cold, push it back together and roll over it again, making a total of 3 times that you flatten and coat the shortening with flour. The mixture will look like paint peeling off of a wall. Scrape it together, place it back in the bowl, and freeze for 5 minutes.

4. Add all the buttermilk at once and knead the dough to work in the buttermilk. Add ice water as needed to get the dough to hold together. Place the dough back on the counter, flatten it out, and fold it together to layer it similarly to making puff pastry (fold the top down, the bottom up, both sides to the middle). Flatten again and refold. Shape the dough into a 6-inch (15-cm) disc. Wrap tightly with plastic wrap and refrigerate for 1 hour or overnight.

5. Arrange a shelf in the lower third of the oven, place a baking stone on it, and preheat the oven to 450°F/232°C.

6. Bill has a machine that is like a very wide pasta roller. He rolls the dough through on a thick setting just to flatten a little, then reduces the thickness to roll thinner and thinner until he has a dough about ⅛ inch (0.3 cm) thick. Then he folds the circle to layer (top down, bottom up, sides to the middle). He shapes it again into a 6-inch (15-cm) disc, and now he runs it through the rollers for the final times, getting the thickness thinner and thinner until the dough is about 1/16 inch (0.15 cm).

7. For a single crust, he drapes the dough across the pie pan loosely so that it falls down into the center, then he drops the pan to get the dough to drop farther down into the pan. Holding the excess dough up with his left hand, he strokes the dough down well into the pan. He trims the dough so that he has about 1½ inches (4 cm) extending beyond the outer edge of the rim of the pan.

8. He folds a small section of the dough over so that the outer edge of the arch touches the dough right at the inside edge of the pan rim. Now he places his left index finger on the outer edge of the arch to hold the dough down. With his right hand, partially overlapping the first fold he folds another small section of the dough over, tucking it under with his thumb. Next, he moves his left index finger over to hold the new fold, and continues making folds all around. He goes around the whole crust, gently pressing the outer edge of this "braid" up straight and slightly toward the center.

9. He uses square delicatessen paper (one of the kinds that comes in a box like Kleenex) to place in each crust and then fills the paper with beans. He presses the beans out against the edges and fills in a few more in the center. He bakes the crust in a commercial pizza oven at a little over 400°F/204°C. At this temperature, on the floor of the very even-temperature oven he can get the bottom browned inside and out without overbrowning the edges. (See Problem with Pie Weights, page 326.)

Structure of the Fat

The size and type of fat crystals can influence the kind of job that a fat does in cooking.

Lard Crust

The structure—the type of crystals—of some types of lard, such as leaf lard, which comes from the fat around the hog's kidneys, produces the flakiest pastry of all. The dough is soft and easy to roll, and it will hold its shape during baking.

The problem I have found with lard is that, with the exception of a few brands that are consistently good, the products in the grocery stores may be off-tasting. Lard is 56% mono- and polyunsaturated fat, which reacts more readily than saturated fat and can change taste more easily. Since there is such limited use of lard in the United States, the shelf turnover is probably slow in many grocery stores.

Lard Crust

MAKES TWO 9-INCH (23-CM) CRUSTS

This crust is wonderfully flakey yet tender. Perfect for savory pies. Be sure to purchase a reliable brand of lard.

What This Recipe Shows

Vinegar and buttermilk will make the crust slightly more tender.

Buttermilk enhances color and flavor.

Lard produces an incredibly flakey crust.

½ cup (3.6 oz/102 g) lard, cut in
   ½-tablespoon (0.2-oz/16-g) pieces
1 teaspoon (6 g) salt
1 teaspoon (5 ml) apple cider vinegar
3 tablespoons (45 ml) buttermilk, plus
   additional as needed

1 cup (4.6 oz/130 g) instant flour (such as
   Wondra or Shake & Blend) poured into
   a measuring cup and leveled
½ cup (2.2 oz/62 g) spooned and leveled
   bleached all-purpose flour

1. Place the lard in the freezer for at least 5 minutes.

2. Stir the salt and vinegar into the buttermilk and place in the refrigerator. In a medium mixing bowl toss the lard with both flours, coating the pieces of lard well with flour, and place in the freezer for 10 minutes.

3. Dump the cold flour-lard mixture out onto a clean countertop. Flour a rolling pin and roll over the mixture to flatten the lard pieces and coat them with flour. Some lard may stick to the pin. Scrape it off, flour the rolling pin, and scrape the mixture together. Roll over the mixture again. Working quickly, continue rolling and scraping together at least three times in all. The mixture looks like paint flakes that have fallen off a wall. Scrape the mixture back into the bowl and return it to the freezer for 10 minutes.

4. Sprinkle the salt-vinegar-buttermilk mixture over the flour, a little at a time, tossing between additions. Press the dough together to see if it will hold; if it is too dry, continue adding additional cold buttermilk, a little at a time. When the dough holds together, place it on the counter and knead it with one quick push-and-pull-back-together motion.

5. Press the dough together into a 6-inch (15-cm) disc. Wrap in plastic wrap and refrigerate for at least 2 hours or overnight. This will allow the moisture to more evenly distribute.

6. Roll out dough (see page 286), cut, and place in the pan (see page 295).

7. For shaping and baking directions, see pages 295 and 323.

Taste of Fat

Nothing tastes like real butter and because of its rich, creamy flavor, butter is frequently the fat of choice for pie crust. It is, however, difficult to handle, and does not make as flakey or as tender a crust with the same amounts and conditions as 100% fats such as shortening. Lard, which produces marvelously flakey pastry and is very easy to work with, unfortunately may have off-flavors.

To have the best of both worlds, I like to use some butter for flavor and some lard or shortening for ease of handling and flakiness.

The Crust for Hand-Held Pies (page 306) is an excellent example of a butter-lard crust. It is wonderfully flakey with good flavor. You have butter for great flavor plus the flakiness that you get from lard.

Sugar

Sugar wrecks gluten formation (page 485). When plenty of sugar is around, the gluten-forming proteins do not join together. Glutenin (one gluten-forming protein) combines with sugar, gliadin (the other gluten-forming protein) combines with sugar, and very little gluten is formed. Too much sugar can wreck a yeast dough, but it is ideal to tenderize a pie crust.

Three basic types of basic French pastry doughs are: *pâte brisée, pâte sucrée* (sugar pastry), and *pâte sablée* (crumbly crust). This classification used to make no sense to me. Pâte brisée is what we would call a regular crust with little or no sugar. Pâte sucrée has some sugar—up to about 5 tablespoons (2 oz/55 g)—but pâte sablée has more sugar than that.

Why didn't they call pâte sablée "sugar pastry," since it is the one with the most sugar? Sablée means "sandy," and, indeed, it is crumbly. Sometimes pâte sablée crusts do not even have enough gluten to roll them out. The crust has to be sprinkled in the pan and then pressed in with the fingers. This is exactly what a high amount of sugar will do: prevent gluten formation to the point that the crust is crumbly, like sand.

In *Mastering the Art of French Cooking, Volume Two* by Julia Child and Simone Beck, pâte sucrée is listed as the same as pâte brisée but with the salt reduced and with 5 tablespoons of sugar added. (This is for a 3½ cups, 16 oz/456 g of flour recipe.) Pâte sablée on the other hand (for a 4⅓ cups, 20 oz/561 g of flour recipe) calls for 8 to 18 tablespoons (3.5 to 7.8 oz/99 to 221 g) of sugar. In this case, there is significantly more sugar in the pâte sablée. However, when I started looking at pâte sucrée and pâte sablée recipes I found that many of them have about the same amount of sugar.

What *was* significant was that the fat was worked into the flour better in the pâte sablée recipes. This would reduce the amount of gluten formed, just like containing more sugar. So these crusts would be crumbly, too.

Then I noticed something else interesting. Some pastry chefs say that pâte sucrée is perishable and should be used for tarts that do not contain a juicy filling and will be consumed quickly. Other pastry chefs say that the sugar crust keeps its crispness even after prolonged refrigeration. Who is right?

Actually, I think that they both are. If you have a crust prepared like a flakey crust, or a brisée with sugar, the sugar is certainly water soluble and the fat has not been worked in well enough to protect the crust from moisture. So it would tend to get soggy with any liquid in the filling. On the other hand, a dough that has been prepared by working the fat into the flour well will tend to resist moisture and is somewhat "waterproof."

Modern pastry chefs call their sweet crust "cookie crust," but one defines it as pâte sucrée and another as pâte sablée. So when you see a crust called a "cookie crust," you don't know whether it will absorb liquid quickly or not. You can best judge by looking at the directions for combining the fat with the other ingredients. If there is a reasonable amount of fat and it is worked into the flour well, it will not absorb liquid fast. But, if the fat is worked into the flour as for a flakey crust, it will absorb liquid fast.

Maury Rubin of City Bakery has been producing classic tarts in New York since the late eighties. His *Book of Tarts* is a true tart bible. Not only are his tarts delicious, they are beautiful (read about his tart shell on page 394). In his basic recipe, he works the butter into the flour very well and even uses an egg yolk and cream (more fat) for the liquid in the crust. So his tarts probably do not absorb liquid easily. His 4-inch (10-cm) tarts bake beautifully in tart rings without pie weights.

Some pastry chefs use confectioners' sugar in their sweet crusts, while others use granulated sugar. Maury Rubin and Bruce Healy stick pretty closely to classic French recipes and use confectioners' sugar.

Pâte Sablée

Makes enough dough for eight 4-inch (10-cm) tarts

This easy-to-prepare, reliable, and delicious recipe is for eight 4-inch (10-cm) tart shells, but you can use this dough for larger crusts as well. This is my adaptation of Maury Rubin's Basic Tart Pastry.

What This Recipe Shows

Working the fat into the flour well makes the crust not absorb liquid as easily as flakey crust.

Freezing the dough and baking it in tart rings allow cooking without pie weights.

---

1 large egg yolk (0.65 oz/18 g)
2 tablespoons (30 ml) heavy cream
½ cup plus 5 tablespoons (6.5 oz/184 g)
   unsalted butter cut in ½-tablespoon
   (0.25-oz/7-g) pieces
⅓ cup (1.3 oz/38 g) confectioners' sugar

1½ cups (6.6 oz/187 g) spooned and leveled
   bleached all-purpose flour
½ teaspoon (3 g) salt
1 teaspoon (5 ml) apple cider vinegar
Nonstick cooking spray

1. Stir together the yolk and cream and refrigerate.

2. In a mixer with the paddle attachment, cream the butter and sugar well. Add half of the flour and beat in. Add half of the yolk mixture and beat in briefly. Add the remaining flour and beat in. Stir the salt and vinegar into the rest of the yolk mixture. Drizzle in the remaining yolk mixture with the mixer running. Beat until the dough forms a sticky mass. The dough should hold together and even be a little sticky, but not wet.

3. Press the dough together. If it is dry and crumbly, add a little more cream. Shape the dough into a 6-inch (15-cm) disc, wrap tightly with plastic wrap, and refrigerate for at least 2 hours or overnight.

4. Arrange a shelf in the lower third of the oven, place a baking stone on it, and preheat the oven to 400°F/204°C.

5. See page 287 for rolling directions.

6. Cut the dough into eight 5½-inch (14-cm) circles. Spray a baking sheet and the eight tart rings with nonstick cooking spray. Place the rings on the baking sheet. Place the dough into the tart rings and press into the rings well. (I like to leave the pastry standing about ½ inch [1.3 cm] above the pan when I trim it because it will shrink.) Freeze for at least 30 minutes.

7. Place on the baking stone and bake until well browned, about 10 minutes.

Liquids

An almost endless variety of liquids from water to sour cream can be used in a pie crust. In the *Cook's Illustrated* November/December, 2007 issue, J. Kenji Alt makes a pie crust using ¼ cup (59 ml) vodka and ¼ cup (59 ml) water for a very moist, easy-to-roll crust (it does have ½ cup, 3.4 oz/95 g, shortening with the 12 tablespoons, 6 oz/170 g, of butter also making it easy to handle).

As discussed on page 343, the two gluten-forming proteins in wheat flour must have water to join together and form gluten. An easy way to prevent their joining is to cut their water supply. You may have read an Italian pastry recipe that called for 1 to 2 tablespoons (15 to 30 ml) of oil (100% fat), or a pastry recipe that called for 1 egg yolk (34% fat) as part of the liquid. Many pastry recipes use cream, sour cream, or cream cheese. In all of these cases, some of the water in the recipe is replaced with liquid fat—a good idea for cutting down the water supply and minimizing gluten formation.

Dairy Products

In addition to replacing some of the water with liquid fat, dairy products add flavor and enhance color. The protein and sugar in dairy products produce a browner crust. Cream and sour cream are excellent examples of liquids that are part fat for making pastry tender. Just think about all the nice things that sour cream does. It is cold, so it maintains flakiness by keeping the dough cold. It is acidic, so it tenderizes. It contains sugar (lactose), so it tenderizes. It is part fat, so it tenderizes by replacing some of the water.

Cheese

Cream cheese is another favorite pie crust ingredient. Regular (not low-fat) cream cheese has a high fat content so you are adding a soft, cold, malleable, part-fat ingredient instead of water. Like cream and sour cream, cream cheese makes tender, easy-to-work crusts that have good color—perfect crusts for pastry beginners. See Cream Cheese Crust (page 288).

Cheeses like cheddar and Parmesan are good additives for flavor and color. A crust with cheddar or Parmesan is ideal for a pear or apple pie.

Adding Cheese to a Pie Crust Dough

There are several ways to incorporate cheese or cream cheese into a crust. You can blend the cheese with the butter (this is essentially the way that you make cheese straws), you can blend the cheese into the flour, or you can add grated cheese to the dough after it is put together.

Blending the cheese with the butter or with the flour produces a crust with even color, but adding grated cheese to the finished dough makes the crust spotty—an orange spot everywhere there is a piece of cheddar cheese. With Parmesan, you can grate it fine enough so that the color is even but, by adding grated cheddar, you will get an uneven-colored crust.

I thought that processing the cheese into the flour well would be the best way to go because that would coat flour proteins to produce a tender crust, then I could add the butter in larger pieces for flakiness. This is the procedure I selected for Cream Cheese Crust (page 288), and it is a lovely, tender flakey crust.

Flakey Cheddar Crust

MAKES TWO 9-INCH (23-CM) CRUSTS

This crust is so good, people break it off and eat it all by itself.

What This Recipe Shows

Cheddar cheese adds tenderness, color, and flavor, makes the dough easy to handle, and pairs well with fruit.

The cheese is blended with the flour to add tenderness so that all the butter can be left in larger pieces (flattened) for flakiness.

Using a combination of butter and lard creates extra flakiness.

½ teaspoon (3 g) salt

1 teaspoon (5 ml) apple cider vinegar

3 tablespoons (45 ml) water

2½ cups (11 oz/312 g) spooned and leveled all-purpose flour

½ teaspoon (1 g) ground cayenne

8 ounces (227 g) extra-sharp cheddar, coarsely grated

¾ cup (6 oz/170 g) butter, cut in ½-tablespoon (0.25-oz/7-g) pieces and frozen

3 ounces (85 g) lard, cut in 1-tablespoon (0.4-oz/12-g) pieces and frozen

Ice water

1. In a small measuring cup, stir the salt and vinegar into the water and refrigerate.

2. In a food processor with the steel blade, process the flour and the cayenne to mix. Add the grated cheese and process until well blended. Place the bowl with the cheese-flour mixture in the freezer for 10 minutes.

3. Place the bowl back on the processor, add the frozen butter and lard, and process with a number of quick on/offs to cut the fats into large lima bean–sized pieces. With the processor running, drizzle in the salt-vinegar-water mixture. The dough should come together. If not, add ice water a little at a time until it does come together.

4. Shape the dough into two 6-inch (15-cm) discs. Wrap tightly with plastic wrap, and refrigerate for at least 2 hours or overnight.

5. Shape and bake according to the specific pie recipe directions.

Acidic Ingredients

Many pastry recipes contain lemon juice, vinegar, buttermilk, sour cream, or some other acidic ingredient. Cooks think that it is primarily to tenderize, which is true, but it is also very valuable in making the crust set faster so the sides don't droop or slide down in the pie pan.

Acidic ingredients do three different things. In addition to tenderizing, they make the crust set faster, and they make it easier to roll and handle. Unfortunately, they can make a dough slightly paler in color—not necessarily what you want.

An acidic batter speeds up the cooking of proteins and the setting of dough. In the cookie chapter (see page 404), we learn that this faster setting of the dough helps limit how much the cookies spread. In a pie crust, faster setting will help preserve the shape and designs on any decorative touches, as well as preserve the shape of the crust itself. If you are trying to preserve every detail of a pastry decoration, use butter-flavored shortening for fat and add an acidic ingredient to the dough.

You may have seen mild acids used to tenderize in marinating meat. Acids tenderize by breaking down long, stringy protein molecules into smaller pieces. Acidic ingredients can cut long gluten strands to make the dough easier to roll and the crust more tender.

The problem of acidic ingredients making a crust paler can be offset. Acidic dairy products like sour cream or buttermilk are a great idea for a pie crust. They not only tenderize, they also enhance color.

A tiny amount (as little as a teaspoon) of a reducing sugar like corn syrup can make a major color change in a baked product (see page 424). Also, a colored ingredient can be used. We have a good old Southern chef in Atlanta who makes great pie crust using a tablespoon of frozen orange juice concentrate. It is partially frozen, so it helps chill the crust for flakiness. It is acidic, so it tenderizes. It is sweet, so it tenderizes. It also adds a nice hint of flavor and color. What a good idea!

Egg or No Egg?

As in other baking, eggs do many things. They bind ingredients together, they add strength, they can leaven, and they add taste and color. Whole eggs and/or egg whites add a little puff and considerable strength to a crust. For a hand-held crust that is baked, a whole egg may be a good idea. For a fried pie, an egg white is a better idea because yolks in a batter or dough absorb fat.

Eggs are not just whole eggs. They can be whole eggs, or whites, or yolks. The whites are a great drying agent, and a good binding agent, but they definitely add puff. In a bakery where I was working, we rolled a crust very thin, but the baked crust was considerably thicker—thicker than we wanted. When I looked at the recipe, sure enough, there was an egg white. We dropped the white and the crust came out much thinner—just like we wanted.

I personally like all the puff in my crust to come from flakey puffing, so I rarely use whole eggs or whites (except in baked or fried hand-held pie dough). Yolks, on the other hand, do add color and taste and contribute some binding and some emulsification (holding liquid and fat together), all without making the crust puff.

The yolks are great emulsifiers, holding fat and liquid together. They also bind and contribute taste and color. Yolks are a great idea for sweet crust (see page 352).

Techniques for Puff Pastry—The Ultimate Flakey Crust

Puff pastry is super flakey and is basically made the same way that you make flakey pastry pie dough—by creating layers of cold, firm fat that serve as spacers to keep the thin layers of dough apart in the hot oven just long enough for the dough to begin to set. When the fat melts, steam comes from the liquid in the dough and puffs the layers apart. The pastry puffs beautifully.

Now for puff pastry, how do we get so many thin layers of dough between thin layers of fat? Classically, you wrap a block of butter with dough, roll it out, then fold it like an envelope (bottom up, top over to create three layers), roll it out flat again, and repeat. Folding in this manner to make three layers at a time is called a "single fold." Another way of folding (called a "double turn") is to fold the bottom to the middle, the top to the middle, and then fold one double layer on top of the other, creating four layers.

For puff pastry, the fat must remain cold and unmelted during the whole folding operation. If the butter melts and soaks into the dough, there goes the flakiness!

You can see that by doing multiple folds and turns, you get many layers, which can puff magnificently. But there can be challenges. The fat must remain cold and unmelted during the whole folding operation. If the butter gets warm and starts to melt and soak into the dough, there goes the flakiness!

The other challenge is that as you roll the dough out, which is similar to kneading it, it becomes more elastic and firm. The additional gluten forms as you roll, absorbs water from the dough, and makes it firmer and firmer.

Classic directions tell you to brush off the flour before each turn, but I do not think that this is enough. You need to add liquid to keep the dough soft. Not only does this make the dough much easier to roll, but the additional liquid provides more steam and puffs the pastry higher. After rolling out the dough and brushing off the flour, I like to brush the dough with ice water, then do the folds and turns. I keep the dough soft throughout the rolling process by brushing on ice water as needed.

Some chefs solve the problem of having difficulty rolling by using a lower-protein flour, but this is a bad idea. Lower-protein flours do not form enough gluten to hold the steam as well and give you less puff.

Puff pastry contains no eggs for structure and is solely dependent on paper-thin layers of dough to hold the steam and puff. The higher-protein flours, which make stronger layers of dough, create much lighter puff pastry. The big secret is to keep the dough moist and soft; then puff pastry can be made with high-protein flour in spite of the elasticity. If the dough becomes tight, brush it with ice water just before folding. My brushing-with-ice-water technique produces puff pastry of wonderful height.

> The big secret is to keep the dough moist and soft—then puff pastry can be made with high-protein flour in spite of the elasticity. My "Brush-It-with-Ice-Water" technique produces puff pastry of wonderful height.

EXPERIENCE

Years ago, I went on a puff pastry binge. I made puff pastry every day for two or three weeks. I made it with different types of flour, with different kinds of cheese, with different liquids. I made it with a little wine, and I made it with a lot of wine. I should have drunk the wine—the puff pastry with all wine (no water) was a total disaster. The wine evaporated before the pastry set so there was no steam to puff the layers apart. It was completely flat!

Some Things That I Learned

Immediately, from my research using different flours, I learned that the higher the protein content of the flour, the higher the puff. But, with the higher protein flour and the great amount of gluten, the stronger the dough became and the more difficult to roll.

Shirley's "Brush-It-with-Ice-Water" Technique

I knew that the solution to the difficulty in rolling was a softer (wetter) dough. So, when I brushed off the excess flour before I folded the dough, I brushed the dough lightly with ice water and then made the folds—the beginning of my "brush-it-with-ice-water" technique. By adding more water to the dough turn by turn, I could keep the dough very soft and easy to roll even with high-protein flour, which gave a great puff.

In addition to making the rolling easier, brushing the dough lightly with water added water to the pastry. This water became steam—more water—more steam—more puff!

When you have rolled out the dough and are making the turns, brush off any excess flour, then brush the dough lightly with ice water. This keeps the dough softer, making it easier to roll, and also adds liquid for more steam and a greater puff.

So keeping the dough soft did two things. It enabled me to use a higher-protein flour that gave me a greater puff, and the additional liquid in the soft dough made more steam for a higher puff. From my all-wine puff pastry, I truly learned how important water is: no water, no steam!

Years ago, when I first started teaching this technique of brushing on ice water, it was radical and people acted as if I were crazy. Now this technique has been picked up, is more accepted, and is taught enough that it is no longer as startling.

To create steam for the puff, puff pastry needs to be baked at an initial high temperature (about 450°F/232°C).

CLASSIC PUFF PASTRY

There are actually a number of ways to make puff pastry. "Classic" puff pastry, as I was taught, is made by wrapping a flat slab of butter in dough, rolling it out, folding, rolling, and refolding several times to produce a dough with over a thousand layers of unmelted fat between layers of dough.

Greg Patent, in his outstanding book *A Baker's Odyssey,* describes a puff pastry made in Terceira in the Azores that uses a totally different technique. He makes it by spreading 4 ounces (113 g) of fat into a thin layer over a 16-inch (41-cm) square of dough, folding it a single turn (like folding a letter to fit in an envelope) right to left to create three layers, and then doing another single turn from top to bottom to create nine layers. The dough is wrapped and chilled, then rolled out again into a 16-inch (41-cm) square, spread again with a layer of fat and again folded, envelope style, right to left and top to bottom, wrapped, and chilled. This same procedure of rolling out to a 16-inch (41-cm) square, spreading with fat, and folding is repeated two more times for a total of four times. This technique makes sense and makes beautiful puff pastry.

Greg uses 4 cups (17 oz/482 g) flour, 1 teaspoon (6 g) salt, and 1 pound (454 g) butter. In the Azores they use margarine (a fat that is softer and easier to roll than butter and probably does not melt as easily as butter). Greg used unsalted butter with ½ cup (2.2 oz/62 g) of the flour worked into it to make it easier to roll. He also used one-quarter cake flour and three-quarters unbleached all-purpose flour, because he was trying to duplicate the flour in the Azores. When I make it, I use bread flour or unbleached all-purpose flour and use my brush-it-with-ice-water technique to keep the dough soft and give me a little more puff.

Pierre Hermé, in his book *Chocolate Desserts by Pierre Hermé,* has what he calls Inside-Out Puff Pastry. The layer that contains the butter and some flour is the larger outside layer. A soft dough is placed inside the butter layer. He does two double turns and one single turn. I have a feeling that with the dough wrapped inside the butter, his dough stays soft and easy to roll.

Quick Puff Pastry or "Rough Puff"

MAKES ENOUGH TO COVER THREE 9-INCH (23-CM) PIES OR MAKES MANY SMALL PIECES

Rough puff or quick puff pastry, less formal and faster, is made by rolling, folding, and rerolling large frozen pieces of butter into the dough. The result is a magnificent, flakey treasure—buttery flakes that add wonder to any dish. At any time if the butter gets soft, chill the dough immediately. If the butter melts and works into the dough, you lose flakiness. If dough gets too firm and elastic (difficult to roll), brush with ice water just before folding.

What This Recipe Shows

Folding and rerolling produces many layers of butter between the dough, creating much flakiness.

Keeping the dough cold at all times prevents the butter from melting and soaking into the flour and preserves flakiness.

Brushing the dough with ice water before rolling will soften a firm, hard-to-roll dough and add liquid for more steam.

---

4 sticks (16 oz/454 g) cold unsalted butter
3 cups (14.5 oz/411 g) spooned and leveled
    bread flour
1/2 teaspoon (3 g) salt

1 cup (8.5 oz/241 g) sour cream
Ice water as needed
1 cup (4.8 oz/136 g) spooned and leveled
    bread flour, for rolling

1. Cut each stick of butter in half lengthwise, then each in half lengthwise again, making four long logs from each stick. Cut each log into three pieces. Place 3 cups bread flour, the butter, and the salt in a large heavy-duty zip-top plastic bag. Squeeze out the air and seal the bag. Toss the butter and flour together in the bag to break butter up and coat well. Place the bag in the freezer for 10 minutes to firm the butter.

2. Dump the cold flour-butter mixture onto a clean counter and roll over it with a large rolling pin to flatten the butter lumps. Scrape the butter off the pin and scrape the mixture back into a pile. Roll over it again, and scrape back together and roll over a third time. Scrape the mixture back into the bag, reseal, and return to the freezer for 10 minutes.

3. Dump the cold butter-flour mixture into a large mixing bowl. Stir in the sour cream, then work in enough ice water to get the dough to come together. It should be slightly sticky rather than too dry. Shape it into a ball, then place back in the plastic bag and refrigerate for at least 2 hours or overnight.

At any time that the butter gets soft, chill the dough immediately. If the butter melts and works into the dough, you lose flakiness. During the rolling and folding that follows, try to keep the dough soft. Lightly dust with flour as needed to roll dough out, but brush off excess flour after rolling. If the dough is too firm and difficult to roll, brush with ice water before folding.

4. Flour the counter, remove the dough from the bag, and flour the dough. Flour the rolling pin and use flour on the countertop to prevent sticking as needed. Roll the dough into a large square (20 x 20 inches/51 x 51 cm). Brush off excess flour. Using a pastry scraper to help if necessary, fold the top one-quarter of the dough over and down to the center. Fold the bottom one-quarter over and up to the center. Then fold the upper two layers down over the lower two layers. You now have a narrow rectangle about 5 x 20 inches (13 x 51 cm). Roll a little to press the four layers together and to flatten it out a little. Now fold one-quarter of the right side over to the center and then fold one-quarter of the left side over to the center. Fold the left double side on top of the right double side. You now have four layers again, but this time in a 5-inch (13-cm) square. Refrigerate for 30 minutes to chill.

5. Roll the dough into a medium-sized rectangle (about 15 inches/38 cm top to bottom and 10 inches/25 cm across). Brush off the excess flour. Brush the dough lightly with ice water to keep the dough soft. Fold the top one-third down to the center and the bottom one-third up and over the double layer. Roll to flatten a little. Fold the right half on top of the left half. Wrap the dough in plastic wrap and refrigerate for 1 hour to chill well.

6. The dough is ready to roll out and cut into shapes. After rolling out and cutting, bake according to recipe directions.

Pear Tart with Frangipane in Puff Pastry

MAKES 2 IMPRESSIVE SERVINGS

This is a pear half sitting on a puff pastry "pear." A layer of frangipane between the pear and the puff pastry gives sweet richness to this beautiful pastry.

1 ripe or near-ripe pear
Frozen puff pastry large enough for two
    5-inch (13-cm) squares, thawed
½ cup Frangipane—Almond-Hazelnut Paste
    (page 291)

4 tablespoons (2 oz/57g) butter, melted
¼ cup (1.7 oz/49 g) sugar
Nonstick cooking spray
1 large egg (1.75 oz/50 g), beaten

1. Arrange a shelf in the lower third of the oven, place a baking stone on it, and preheat the oven to 425°F /218°C.

2. Peel, halve vertically, and core the pear.

3. With a very sharp knife, cut a 5-inch (13-cm) square from the puff pastry. Using a pear half as a pattern, cut the puff pastry to look like a pear, making it 1 inch (2.5 cm) wider than the pear. Then cut right around the pear but not all the way through the pastry. Repeat with the other pastry square. From the scraps, cut a puff pastry stem and two leaves for each pastry.

4. On the puff pastry that will be under the pear, generously spread frangipane on each pastry. Place the pear half, cut side down, into the frangipane. Cut deep lengthwise slits in each pear but not all the way through. Brush the pear halves heavily with the melted butter and sprinkle heavily with the sugar. Spray a heavy baking sheet with nonstick cooking spray. Place both pieces of puff pastry containing pear halves on the baking sheet. Arrange a stem and two leaves on each using the beaten egg for "glue."

5. Place the baking sheet on the hot stone. Bake until well puffed and browned, 20 to 25 minutes. Serve warm.

Mustard-Dill Salmon en Croûte

Makes 2 servings

Magnificent rich brown puff pastry with deep-cut, dramatic decorations impresses even your most discerning guests. The hint of sweet apple gives an interesting complexity to the mustard and sets off the salmon perfectly.

2 tablespoons (30 ml) apple jelly
½ cup (118 ml) whole-grain prepared
    mustard (with seeds)
1 teaspoon (5 ml) chopped fresh dill
One 17.3-ounce (490-g) package (2 sheets)
    frozen puff pastry, thawed

Nonstick cooking spray
¼ teaspoon (1.5 g) salt
Two 3 to 4-ounce (85 to 113-g) salmon fillets,
    skinned, pin bones removed, and
    trimmed to about the same size
1 large egg (1.75 oz/50 g), beaten

1. Arrange a shelf in the lower third of the oven, place a baking stone on it, and preheat the oven to 450°F/232°C.

2. In a medium saucepan, melt the apple jelly over low heat. Stir in the mustard and continue cooking to reduce to a thick sauce. Remove from the heat and stir in the dill.

3. Unfold the puff pastry and cut a total of four rectangles: two rectangles 1 inch (2.5 cm) wider and longer than one of the salmon fillets, and two rectangles about 2 inches (5 cm) wider and longer than one of the salmon fillets. Save the scraps to decorate. Spray a baking sheet with nonstick cooking spray and place the two smaller rectangles on the baking sheet.

4. Lightly salt the salmon fillets. Place a salmon fillet on top of each of the smaller rectangles of puff pastry and spread each piece of salmon with the mustard-dill mixture. Brush the beaten egg around the edge of each fillet. Cover each piece of salmon with one of the larger puff pastry rectangles. Press around the edges with a fork to seal the edges of the pastry together, and then with a sharp knife trim to a ½-inch (1.3-cm) border around each fillet. Decorate with leaves cut from scraps. Brush with beaten egg.

5. Place the baking sheet on the hot baking stone and turn down the oven to 425°F/218°C. Bake 20 to 25 minutes, until the pastry is well puffed and lightly browned. Reduce heat to 325°F/163°C and bake 10 minutes more. Serve immediately.

Piroshkis

MAKES 15 HORS D'OEUVRE OR 8 FIRST-COURSE SERVINGS

These are incredibly good hors d'oeuvres made with Crust for Hand-Held Pies (page 306). My mother-in-law-to-be and I made these for my wedding. For an elegant first course, make a larger triangular portion with puff pastry, store-bought or homemade such as Quick Puff Pastry (page 359). I love to serve these with béarnaise sauce.

1 pound (454 g) ground chuck
1 large onion, chopped fine
½ teaspoon (0.5 g) dried dill or
    1½ teaspoons (1.5 g) chopped fresh dill
1 teaspoon (6 g) salt
¼ teaspoon (0.5 g) ground white or
    black pepper
3 large eggs (5.25 oz/150 g), hard cooked,
    peeled, and chopped

⅓ cup (79 ml) Cream Sauce (recipe follows)
One 17.3-ounce (490-g) package (2 sheets)
    frozen puff pastry, thawed, or Crust for
    Hand-Held Pies (page 306), Simple Very
    Flakey Crust (page 302), or Quick Puff
    Pastry (page 359)
Nonstick cooking spray
1 large egg (1.75 oz/50 g), beaten, for glaze

1. In a large skillet over medium heat, sauté the beef, onion, dill, salt, and pepper until the beef is no longer pink and the onion is translucent. Drain off excess fat. Stir in the chopped hard-cooked eggs and the Cream Sauce. Season to taste.

2. Roll the pastry fairly thin (about ⅛ inch/0.3 cm). For hand-held hors d'oeuvres, cut the pastry into 3½-inch (9-cm) squares or rounds. For first-course servings, cut the pastry into 4½-inch (11-cm) squares.

3. Place a small spoonful of beef filling in one corner of a pastry square or in the center of pastry round. Leave a ½-inch (1-cm) border of bare pastry. Moisten the edges of pastry with water and fold over the filling to form a filled triangle or half-moon. Press around edges with a fork to seal.

4. Place on a baking sheet sprayed with nonstick cooking spray and freeze or refrigerate to chill for 1 hour.

5. Arrange a shelf in the lower third of the oven, place a baking stone on it, and preheat the oven to 450°F/232°C for at least 20 minutes.

6. Brush the filled pastries with the beaten egg to glaze. For small hors d'oeuvres, bake in the preheated oven about 20 minutes, until browned. For large triangles, bake for 20 minutes, then turn the oven down to 350°F/177°C and bake 15 to 20 minutes more, until browned.

Cream Sauce

MAKES ABOUT 1 CUP (237 ML)

2 tablespoons (1 oz/28 g) salted butter	⅛ teaspoon (pinch) dry mustard powder
2 tablespoons (0.5 oz/15 g) all-purpose flour	½ cup (118 ml) whole milk
¼ teaspoon (1.5 g) salt	½ cup (118 ml) heavy cream

1. In a medium saucepan, melt the butter over low heat. Stir in the flour, salt, and dry mustard. Cook with constant stirring for 2 minutes. Remove from heat and whisk in the milk a little at a time. Whisk in the cream. Return to medium heat and cook with constant stirring until the sauce is thick.

2. Use immediately or dot surface with butter to prevent a film from forming.

Great Shell with Fresh Crabmeat and Sweet Creamed Corn

Makes 8 servings

Fresh crabmeat is sweet and delicate. Creamed white shoe-peg corn adds an extra touch of sweetness but is mild enough to let the delicate crab flavor come through. A great puff pastry shell serves as an eye-catching container for this elegant dish (see photograph insert).

Great Puff Pastry Shell

One 17.3-ounce (490-g) package (2 sheets) frozen puff pastry, thawed, or 1 recipe Quick Puff Pastry (page 359)

Nonstick cooking spray
1 large egg (1.75 oz/50 g), beaten

Fresh CrabMeat and Sweet Corn Filling

5 tablespoons (2.5 oz/71 g) salted butter, divided
1 pound (454 g) fresh crabmeat, picked over for shells
$\frac{1}{4}$ cup (59 ml) dry white wine
1 tablespoon (0.4 oz/11 g) sugar
$\frac{1}{8}$ teaspoon (pinch) ground white pepper
$1\frac{1}{2}$ cups (355 ml) heavy cream
3 tablespoons (0.8 oz/23 g) all-purpose flour

About $3\frac{1}{2}$ cups (828 ml) fresh white shoe-peg corn kernels, or two 10-ounce (283-g) packages frozen shoe-peg corn in butter sauce, thawed and drained
$\frac{1}{2}$ teaspoon (3 g) salt
3 green onions, white and green parts, thinly sliced
3 sprigs parsley, leaves only, finely chopped

1. Arrange a shelf in the lower third of the oven, place a baking stone on it, and preheat the oven to 450°F/232°C.

2. Separate the frozen pastry dough into 2 sheets. Keep one sheet refrigerated while you roll out the other. If using Quick Puff Pastry, divide the dough in half. Roll out half the dough or one sheet into a large rectangle, 14 x 11 inches (36 x 28 cm) and fairly thin, $\frac{1}{3}$ to $\frac{1}{2}$ inch (0.8 to 1.3 cm) thick.

3. On a piece of wax paper or parchment, draw and cut out a pattern for a scallop shell (like the Shell gas station sign) as large as your rolled-out puff pastry will permit, with seven scallops on the rounded section. With a very sharp knife (or an X-Acto knife), follow the pattern and cut the shell shape from the pastry. Spray a baking sheet with nonstick cooking spray and place the pastry shell

on it. This will be the top part of the shell. Place in the freezer. Roll out, cut, place on a baking sheet, and freeze the other piece of pastry the same way. This will be the bottom part of the shell.

4. Take the top part of the shell out of the freezer. Score it with deep lines indicating ridges. Be bold: cut at least halfway (but not all the way) through the pastry. Put the top shell back in the freezer.

5. Take the bottom part of the shell out of the freezer. This will be the container for the crab mixture. With a sharp knife, cut all the way around, about ¾ inch (2 cm) from the outside edge, half to three-quarters of the way through the pastry (not all the way to the baking sheet). Place this back in the freezer and freeze the top and bottom parts of the shell for 15 minutes before baking.

6. Glaze the top shell with the beaten egg. Place both shells in the oven on the hot baking stone and bake 20 minutes. Turn the oven down to 375°F/191°F and bake 20 to 25 minutes more, until the tops are well browned. Remove the shells from the oven.

7. Being careful, hollow out the center of the bottom shell to create a bowl. Place it back in the oven for a few minutes to dry out the now-exposed shell inside. Remove from the oven and place the hollowed-out shell on a large serving platter.

8. To make the filling: In a large skillet over medium heat, melt 2 tablespoons (1 oz/28 g) of the butter. Stir in the crab and cook, stirring for a few seconds. Add the wine, sugar, and pepper. Simmer for several minutes. Stir in the cream and bring just to a simmer.

9. In a small bowl, knead together the flour and the remaining 3 tablespoons (1.5 oz/43 g) butter. Add a little of this kneaded butter to the crab mixture, stirring constantly. Continue adding kneaded butter and stirring until the mixture reaches the consistency of a thick cream sauce. Stir in the corn. Adjust the thickness by adding more cream if too thick, or stirring in more kneaded butter if the sauce is too thin. Taste and add salt if needed. As soon as you get a good consistency, the filling is ready to pour into the shell.

10. To serve, spoon the hot crab filling into the container shell. Prop up the dramatic top shell so that it is resting on one edge of container. Sprinkle green onions and parsley on the crab filling. Serve immediately.

Real Homemade Chicken Pot Pie

A golden brown, crisp, flakey puff pastry lattice tops old-fashioned real chicken pot pie with chunks of chicken and vegetables. The seasonings are just thyme, salt, and pepper with a little sugar and dry sherry as flavor carriers, allowing the good chicken flavor to dominate. Once you have eaten this pie it's hard to be happy with an ordinary chicken pot pie.

As Annie Johnson says in *Cookin' Up a Storm,* "Most people never had homemade chicken pot pie. It's the best." This book contains the marvelous wit and wisdom of a generous, loving Southern cook and her very real Old South recipes—Buttermilk Pound Cake, Fried Chicken and Gravy, Chicken and Dumplin's, Sweet Potato Pie.

This is an adaptation of Annie's Chicken Pot Pie. I have used my chicken cooking techniques and altered ingredient amounts to my personal whims.

Annie covers her pot pie with a good crust, makes decorative edges, and cuts steam vents. I know that it is a lot to ask a home cook to make this pie, and asking a cook to also make a pie crust might be too much. So I covered mine with a puff pastry lattice made with store-bought puff pastry. A little puff pastry elevates a humble pie to an elegant dish, worthy of any company dinner.

As Annie says, "This recipe takes some time to make, but it's worth every minute of it." You can spread out the preparation to two days to make it easier. Cut the puff pastry, weave the lattice on a cardboard covered with foil, cover with plastic wrap, and place in the freezer.

Cook the chicken, strain the stock, and chill the stock fast by placing the bowl of stock in a bowl of ice water. Cover and refrigerate the cooled stock. Pull the chicken from the bones (discard the bones) and place in a tightly sealed heavy-duty zip-top plastic bag in the refrigerator for the night.

1 recipe baked and lightly browned Puff Pastry Lattice (recipe follows)	1/2 cup (2.2 oz/62 g) spooned and leveled all-purpose flour
One 3 1/2 to 4-pound (1.6 to 1.8-kg) chicken	1 teaspoon (0.15 oz/4 g) sugar
3 tablespoons (45 ml) canola or mild olive oil	1/2 teaspoon (3 g) salt
1 large onion, peeled and chopped fairly small	1/4 teaspoon (1 g) ground black pepper
3 stalks of celery, chopped fairly small	1 1/2 cups (10 oz/283 g) frozen peas, still frozen
Leaves from 6 sprigs of fresh thyme	2 tablespoons (30 ml) dry sherry
2 large carrots, peeled and sliced into 1/4-inch (0.6 cm) slices	

1. Prepare puff pastry lattice small enough to fit inside a 2-quart (1.9-L) baking casserole. These vary in size—7 x 11 inches (18 x 28 cm), 8 x 11 inches (20 x 28 cm), 7 x 13 inches (18 x 33 cm). Set aside.

2. Rinse the chicken and cut into 4 to 6 pieces. Cut off both leg and thigh sections, then split the breast down the center and break the back away from the ribs. Place the chicken pieces in a large pot with enough water to cover by about ½ inch (1.3 cm). Bring to a boil, and then turn down immediately to a low simmer, skim off any foam, and cover. Keep the temperature just below a simmer for 10 minutes, then turn off the heat. Do not remove the cover. Allow the chicken to stand for 1 hour.

3. While chicken is cooking, in a large saucepan, heat the canola oil over medium-low heat. Add the onion, celery, and thyme and cook, stirring regularly, until very soft, about 20 minutes.

4. Arrange a shelf in the lower third of the oven and preheat to 325°F/163°C.

5. Remove the chicken from the pot and allow to cool, then remove the meat from the bones, place in a medium bowl, and discard the bones. Remove and strain 3 to 4 cups (710 to 946 ml) of the cooking liquid into another large saucepan. This is the chicken stock. Hopefully this is nearly all the liquid; if there are only 3 cups (710 ml), it is fine. Place over medium-high heat and bring this stock to a boil for about 5 minutes to reduce. Then, add the carrots and cook until tender, about 10 minutes. Turn off the heat, lift the carrots out with a slotted spoon, and add them to the chicken.

6. Stir the flour, sugar, salt, and pepper into the onions and celery. Cook over low heat for 1 to 2 minutes, until the flour is well absorbed. Stir in the reserved stock, a little at a time, until all the liquid is added. Turn up the heat and simmer gently, scraping the bottom constantly to prevent sticking. Simmer about 10 minutes—the sauce should reach at least a thick soup consistency.

7. Remove from the heat and stir in the peas, the dry sherry, and the reserved chicken and carrots. Taste and add salt if needed. Pour into the casserole dish and top with the cooked puff pastry lattice. Bake below the center of the oven 10 to 15 minutes, until casserole is bubbly.

Puff Pastry Lattice

MAKES 1 LATTICE TOPPING FOR A LARGE RECTANGULAR CASSEROLE

One 17.3-ounce (490-g) package (2 sheets) frozen puff pastry, thawed
Nonstick cooking spray

1 large egg yolk (0.65 oz/18 g)
3 tablespoons (45 ml) heavy cream or whole milk

1. Place a baking stone on a shelf in the lower third of the oven and preheat to 475°F/246°C.

2. With a sharp knife or pastry cutter, cut 5 strips of puff pastry about ¾ inch (2 cm) wide, just shorter than the length of the rectangular casserole. Cut 6 or 7 strips a little over ½ inch (1.3 cm) wide, just shorter than the width of the casserole.

3. Spray a light-colored metal, heavy (not dark) baking sheet with nonstick cooking spray. Place the 5 lengthwise strips on the sheet, spaced equal distances apart and close enough together that they will fit inside the casserole. Weave the widthwise strips across, over and under the lengthwise strips.

4. In a small bowl, beat together the egg yolk and cream. Very, very lightly brush the top of the lattice.

5. Turn the oven down to 450°F/232°C. Quickly place the baking sheet on the baking stone and close the oven door. It is vital that the oven not be open any longer than absolutely necessary. Bake about 15 minutes, until the pastry is well puffed. Turn the oven down to 325°F/163°C and bake 10 minutes more to dry and crisp the lattice. Remove from oven and allow to cool before using.

CHAPTER FOUR

As the Cookie Crumbles

Priceless Knowledge in This Chapter

How to keep cookies from being crumbly

How to make cookies spread less

How to make cookies browner

How to make cookies that stay crisp or stay soft

How to make soft, puffy cookies or flat, crisp cookies

The secrets of fudgy brownies and cakey brownies

How to get a crust on a brownie or avoid a crust

Recipes Include

Corrupted Black Gold cookies with a firm, slightly shiny surface, but gooey chocolate and roasted nuts inside

Butter cookies (Buttery Jelly-Jeweled Cookies) that are "to die for." Year after year, I have made these cookies and I think that they can't be as good as I remember, then when I make them they are even better than I remembered.

Chocolate Crinkle Cookies that are rolled lightly in regular granulated sugar before they are rolled in confectioners' sugar to keep the confectioners' sugar from soaking in. They are dramatic snow-white against dark, dark chocolate (see page 395) and they have a slightly crunchy surface against a gooey inside.

The Recipes

There are a million cookies out there—one book alone is titled *1001 Cookie Recipes*. Many books have chapters like drop cookies, rolled cookies, piped cookies, and refrigerator cookies. This is certainly a way of categorizing cookies, but actually these are shaping techniques and can all be used with the same dough with minor adjustments.

So the good news is you don't have to be overwhelmed—even a million cookies can be reduced to some basics. The expert pastry chef Bruce Healy, in his book *The French Cookie Book,* simplified the world of cookies by dividing them into cookies made from batters and cookies made from pastry doughs.

I cover a special meringue-type cookie in the meringue section (see page 176) of the Steam chapter. Other than that, I am not dividing cookies into this type or that type. My goal is to give you the know-how to make your own "perfect" cookie and to solve your cookie problems regardless of the type.

In the low-moisture world of cookies, everything matters—every ingredient, ingredient brands, measuring, weighing—not just the flour and the liquid (many cookie recipes have no liquid as such). But any change in ingredients that changes the available liquid in the dough changes the cookie.

Here, more than anywhere else in baking, all problems are magnified—the tiniest variation can totally change the cookie. Getting the exact cookie that you want can be a thrilling challenge.

> Any change in ingredients that changes the available liquid in the dough changes the cookie.

Ingredients

Since every ingredient matters, here is an overview of basic cookie ingredients and how each can affect the cookie. Later, we can use this ingredient know-how for specific problem solving.

FLOUR

Commercial cookies and crackers are made with soft winter wheat because it is low protein (8 to 10%) and makes tender cookies. As you can see from the following chart of the flours available to home cooks, cake flour, pastry flour, instant flour (sold under the brand names Wondra and Shake & Blend), and many all-purpose flours fall in the "low-protein" range.

Occasionally, there is a need to use a high-protein flour in cookies, too.

Low Protein or High Protein?

The protein content of flour matters in two ways. It can determine whether a baked good is tender or tough. This is normally not a big worry in cookies. And the protein content determines how much liquid the flour absorbs. This is a major concern in cookies.

General Overview of Flours Available to Home Cooks

Flour is a natural product and experiences seasonal and regional changes, so these are always approximate numbers.

Flour	Approximate protein
Cake flour	7.5 to 8.5%
Pastry flour	8 to 9%
Instant flour* (Wondra and Shake & Blend brands)	9.5 to 11%
Southern all-purpose (White Lily)	8%
Southwestern all-purpose (Pioneer)	10 to 11%
National brand bleached all-purpose	9.5 to 12%
National brand unbleached all-purpose	10 to 12%
Northern specialty blended all-purpose (King Arthur Unbleached)	11.7%
Bread flour	11 to 14%

*These instant flours contain proteins other than those that form gluten.

Nearly all of the proteins in plain white flour (not whole wheat) are the two gluten-forming proteins, glutenin and gliadin. High-protein flour can potentially form more tough elastic gluten, which makes a baked product strong, but tough.

Amount of protein in the flour can determine tenderness or toughness.

When the cook adds water to flour and stirs, two proteins in the flour—glutenin and gliadin—grab water and each other to form elastic sheets of gluten. How many of these two proteins a flour contains determines how much water the flour absorbs. Humidity has very little to do with water absorption compared to protein content.

This difference in water absorption can be major. For example, 2 cups (9.6 oz/272 g) of high-protein bread flour absorb 1 cup (237 ml) of water to form a soft, sticky dough. However, 2 cups (8.8 oz/248 g) of low-protein Southern flour or cake flour and 1 cup (237 ml) water make a thick soup. It takes ½ cup (2.2 oz/62 g) more low-protein flour to get the same consistency dough as with the high-protein flour. This means that even a small recipe with 2 cups of flour can be off by ½ cup! This is a difference of 25%; commercial recipes with 20 pounds (9.1 kg) of flour could be off by 5 pounds (2.3 kg).

The amount of protein determines water absorption.

The large amount of fat and sugar in cookies normally prevents much gluten formation. In fact, a big cookie problem is too little gluten—crumbly cookies—that we will address in problem solving (see page 420). The fat coats the flour proteins so that they cannot bind to water and each other to make gluten. Sugar also interferes with gluten formation. Glutenin combines with sugar, gliadin combines with sugar, and you have very little gluten formed. For more details, see page 421.

The fact that the type of flour (high-protein or low-protein) determines how much water is absorbed can be a major problem in the low-moisture world of cookie making. The first thing that you need to realize is that flours labeled "all-purpose" can have varying amounts of protein.

National brand all-purpose flours can run from approximately 9.5 to 12% protein.

If the person writing the recipe was using an all-purpose flour that was on the high end of protein content (about 12% protein) and the person following the recipe is using a lower-protein-content all-purpose flour (8 to 10% protein), the person following the recipe will have a wetter dough and the cookies will spread much more than those of the writer.

> Fat and sugar interfere with gluten formation, so cookies are normally quite tender.

> All-purpose flours can run from 8 to 12% protein.

Cooks Using a Different Flour than the Recipe Writer Used

Actually, our beloved chocolate chip cookies are frequently an example of the cook using a different flour than the recipe writer used. The Original Toll House Chocolate Chip Cookies were created in the 1930s in New England. Ruth Wakefield, their creator, was probably using a local all-purpose flour, which would have been from high-protein spring wheat and would have absorbed liquid well.

So it is not surprising that today a frequent complaint about these famous cookies is that the cookies are very flat. This is because the cook is using a lower-protein flour, which absorbs less liquid and leaves the dough wetter. I have been asked if there is a way to keep the cookies from spreading so much. Actually, if you use high-protein bread flour you will have cookies more like the original. This flour would absorb more liquid than many all-purpose flours and your cookies would spread a little less and they would be a little browner. Or you can simply add a little more flour to the recipe. Some people like to add about ¼ cup (1.1 oz/31 g) more flour.

Ruth Wakefield, the creator of the chocolate chip cookie, not only created the cookies—she was actually responsible indirectly for the creation of chocolate chips! The Original Toll House Chocolate Chip Cookies have been a favorite since Ruth first made them. Ruth and her husband Kenneth purchased a Cape Cod–style toll house on the outskirts of Whitman, Massachusetts. The original toll house (constructed in 1709) had been a rest stop for travelers.

So when the Wakefields opened their lodge, calling it The Toll House Inn, in keeping with the tradition of hospitality, Ruth served wonderful home-cooked meals. She was especially noted for her desserts.

The story goes that one day when she was making cookies, she chopped up a Nestlé semisweet chocolate bar and stirred the chocolate pieces into her cookies. She expected the chocolate to melt and was surprised when the chocolate held its shape and had a creamy texture. Her cookies became very popular fast and the recipe was printed in newspapers all around New England. Sales of Nestlé semisweet chocolate bars went up. Ruth and Nestlé reached an agreement giving Nestlé permission to print her recipe on the candy bar wrapper. Among other things, Ruth was assured a lifetime supply of chocolate.

First, Nestlé scored the bar to make it easier to chop up for the cookies, and in 1939 they began to offer packages of small pieces of chocolate—chocolate chips were born!

Another factor contributing to a difference in Ruth Wakefield's dough and present-day cookie dough is hydration. In her cookbook, she wrote, "at Toll House, we chill this dough overnight." This contributed to a drier dough than one that is just mixed and baked.

Maury Rubin at City Bakery in New York City, who sells 1,000 cookies a day, carries hydration even further. He mixes his dough and refrigerates it for 36 hours, resulting in a drier, firmer dough. Flavorwise, standing time is a gold mine, allowing the doughs' flavors to meld. In a taste test of 12,

Cookie Baking Tips

Before we get into the recipes, here are a few tips that you need. See more about baking on page 420.

Cookie Sheets

Get the heaviest baking sheets that you can, but avoid thin or dark metal cookie sheets that will burn your cookies. I use some heavy pieces of aluminum that I got at a sheet metal company out of their scrap bin. They polished the edges of them for me.

Procedure

I like to bake cookies one sheet at a time. I love using Release foil because it allows me to bake one sheet of cookies after another with only one or two cookie sheets. You can't put cookie dough on a hot baking sheet (the fat will melt), but you can have cookies arranged on sheets of foil on your counter. When you take out a hot baking sheet, you pull the foil with the baked cookies onto a cooling rack, rinse your baking sheet with cold water to cool it fast, dry it, then slide it under a sheet of foil covered with cookies and back into the oven. Working in this way, you can get one pan of cookies back into the oven right after the other comes out.

Unless instructed otherwise, take care to remove cookies to the cooling rack after they have cooled for 2 minutes. Keep all of the cookie dough refrigerated except the portion that you are getting on the pan.

24, and 36-hour batches, the 36-hour cookies won hands down. The cookies had stronger hints of toffee and were more handsome with a very even and deeper shade of brown.

Roasted Pecan Chocolate Chip Cookies

MAKES ABOUT 6 DOZEN COOKIES

The picture of the chocolate chip cookie is not this exact recipe. I was concentrating on showing the chocolate so, for the picture in the photograph insert, I baked the Toll House chocolate chip cookie recipe with chocolate chips only—no pecans.

I love roasted pecans. Growing up in Georgia, a pecan-growing state, cracking pecans was an early job for me. So instead of just adding flour to the Toll House recipe to make cookies that are not so flat, I wanted to add some roasted pecan meal as a thickener, too.

By all means try refrigerating the dough for 36 hours as described on page 374. After the dough is prepared, place the whole batch of dough in a heavy-duty zip-top bag, squeeze out the air and refrigerate for 36 hours before proceeding with the rest of Step 6.

What This Recipe Shows

Roasted pecans ground to a coarse meal help thicken this dough and add great flavor.

The baking soda is excessive and overleavens, but it does aid in making a slightly darker cookie.

In order to make the dough thick enough to shape into rolls that can be chilled and then sliced, I reduced the eggs from 2 to 1.

---

3 cups (10.5 oz/297 g) pecans
1 cup plus 2 tablespoons (9 oz/255 g), unsalted butter, divided
1 teaspoon (6 g) salt, divided
2$\frac{1}{4}$ cups (10 oz/287 g) spooned and leveled unbleached all-purpose flour
1 teaspoon (5 g) baking soda

1$\frac{1}{2}$ cups (10.5 oz/298 g) sugar
1 teaspoon (5 ml) unsulfured molasses
1 tablespoon (15 ml) pure vanilla extract
2 large eggs (3.5 oz/99 g)
2 cups (12 oz/340 g) semisweet chocolate chips
Nonstick cooking spray, optional

1. Arrange a shelf in the center of the oven and preheat the oven to 350°F/177°C.

2. Spread out the pecans on a baking sheet and roast until lightly browned, about 10 minutes. While they are hot, toss the nuts with 2 tablespoons of the butter (1 oz/28 g) and ¼ teaspoon (1.5 g) salt.

3. When the nuts have cooled, place 1½ cups (5.25 oz/149 g) of the pecans in a food processor with the steel blade and process with quick on/offs until very finely chopped to a coarse meal. The nuts will chop unevenly, so do not try to get every nut finely chopped, but watch the overall batch carefully—do not go to pecan butter.

4. In a bowl, beat together the pecan meal, flour, baking soda, and the remaining ¾ teaspoon (4.5 g) salt. Set aside.

5. In a mixer with the paddle attachment, beat the remaining 1 cup butter (8 oz/226 g) with the sugar until light and fluffy. Beat in the molasses and vanilla. On the lowest speed, beat in the eggs. Beat in the flour–pecan meal mixture in several batches.

6. Coarsely chop the remaining 1½ cups (5.25 oz/149 g) pecans. Stir the pecans and chocolate chips into the dough. Work in with your hands, if necessary. Shape into several logs about 1½ inches (4 cm) in diameter, wrap well in plastic wrap, and refrigerate at least 1 hour or up to 36 hours if desired.

7. Turn up the oven to 375°F/191°C. Line a baking sheet with Release foil, nonstick side up, or parchment sprayed with nonstick cooking spray. Slice the dough into ½-inch (1.3-cm) slices. Keep unbaked dough refrigerated. Place on the baking sheet about 1 inch (2.5 cm) apart. Bake until the edges just begin to color, 9 to 11 minutes.

Different Flours Could Make an Even Greater Difference

If it were not for the high fat and sugar content cutting the amount of gluten formed in cookies, different flours would make an even greater difference than they do. It is just that the low-moisture conditions of cookies magnify the effect of even the slightest change in moisture in the dough.

Not only are there differences among brands, but with the large millers, the same brand can have significant seasonal or regional variations. You can use a certain cookie recipe for years and the cookies are perfect, but then one time when you make them even with the same brand of flour, they are different. You can see there are possibilities for all kinds of problems. What can we do about all of this?

Even if you measure exactly and follow a recipe exactly, cookies can come out different depending on the flour.

First and foremost, you need to realize that even if you measure exactly and follow a recipe exactly, the cookies can come out totally different depending on the flour. You can either change flour or address the problem. For example, if the cookie dough is too thin, add more flour.

Commercial bakeries can buy flour that is kept in a very narrow protein range, but home cooks are more limited in their flour availability. The trouble with using all-purpose is its wide range of protein content. Soft winter wheat all-purpose flours like White Lily and Martha White run about 8 to 9% protein. Higher-protein all-purpose King Arthur flours run about 12% protein (their "catalogue" and website list protein contents). National brands like Pillsbury and Gold Medal can run from 9.5 to 12%.

Small specialty mills like White Lily and King Arthur produce a very high-quality product that is always within a very narrow range of protein content—within one-half of 1%. This means great consistency. Home bakers who have access to either or both of these flours may use them exclusively, because they know exactly what they are getting every time.

The problem is availability. White Lily is available in stores only in the southeastern states. King Arthur is not everywhere either. Both of these flours are available by mail order (see Sources, flour, page 510, for more information).

Low-Flour Cookies

Some cookie recipes may contain little or no flour—the beautiful lace cookies, for example. In the Lace Cookie recipe (below), the batter contains only 1 tablespoon (9 g) of flour and is very thin. The cookies spread into a delicate "lace."

In her lace cookie recipe, Maida Heatter, the famous pastry chef and writer, mixes the ingredients in a skillet and heats to melt the butter and warm all of the ingredients. This possibly produces cookies with an even more open lace.

Lace Cookies

MAKES 12 TO 16 COOKIES

Delicate, beautiful, and delicious—Lace Cookies are a work of art. While they are still hot from the oven, they can be curled or formed into a basket for ice cream or fruit. I adore them just as cookies. If you want the cookies to have a slightly more open "lace," add $\frac{1}{2}$ to 1 tablespoon (0.25 to 0.5 oz/7 to 14 g) more butter or use Maida Heatter's technique of heating the ingredients described above.

What This Recipe Shows

The butter is melted and the batter is thin so that it really spreads.

These cookies have very little protein (in the flour and milk), so they rely on the sugar hardening to set them.

Nonstick cooking spray, optional

$^2/_3$ cup (2.5 oz/72 g) slivered blanched almonds

$^1/_2$ cup (3.5 oz/99 g) sugar

6 tablespoons (3 oz/85 g) unsalted butter, melted

1 tablespoon (0.3 oz/9 g) bleached all-purpose flour

2 tablespoons (30 ml) whole milk

1. Position a rack one-third from the top of the oven and preheat the oven to 350°F/177°C.

2. Cover a baking sheet with Release foil (nonstick side up) or parchment lightly sprayed with nonstick cooking spray.

3. In a food processor with the steel blade, process the almonds and sugar until the almonds are finely ground. Don't worry about a few larger pieces of almonds. (If you don't have a food processor, you can grind the almonds with a cheese grater or grind them in batches in a coffee grinder.)

4. With quick on/offs or in a mixing bowl by hand, blend in the melted butter, then the flour and milk.

5. The cookies will spread, so drop heaping teaspoons full of batter about 4 inches (10 cm) apart, only 4 per baking sheet.

6. Bake one sheet at a time, 6 to 7 minutes. Remove from the baking sheet after 1 minute out of the oven.

7. If you want to shape the cookies, it must be done right after they are removed from the oven. Give the cookies less than a minute to cool, lift them off the baking sheet with a wide spatula, and gently curl over a large rolling pin.

Cookies with Flour and Other Grains

There are cookies made with cornmeal, but oatmeal cookies with textured oats are by far America's favorite mixed-grain cookie. The classic recipe on the Quaker Oats box is excellent. This first recipe (below) has cinnamon and nuts, and I love to soak the raisins a few minutes so that they do not rob moisture from the cookie. The other two oatmeal cookie recipes are also unusual.

Cinnamon Walnut Oatmeal Cookies

MAKES ABOUT $2\frac{1}{2}$ DOZEN COOKIES

When I am reaching for another one of these, I tell myself, "Oats and raisins, they have to be good for me."

What This Recipe Shows

Soaking raisins briefly in boiling water prevents their robbing the cookies of moisture.

Roasting enhances the flavor of the nuts.

A small amount of molasses adds a little color and acidity to the dough.

Bread or unbleached flour enhances the color.

These are pretty crumbly, so I sprinkle 1 tablespoon of water over the flour and stir in to make a little gluten.

Nonstick cooking spray, optional
1 cup (237 ml) boiling water
$\frac{1}{2}$ cup (2.6 oz/74 g) raisins
$1\frac{1}{2}$ cups (7 oz/150 g) walnuts
$\frac{3}{4}$ cup plus 2 tablespoons (7 oz/198 g) unsalted butter, cut in 2-tablespoon (1-oz/28-g) pieces, divided
$1\frac{1}{4}$ cups (8.75 oz/248 g) sugar
1 tablespoon (15 ml) unsulfured molasses, such as Grandma's
1 tablespoon (15 ml) pure vanilla extract

2 large eggs (3.5 oz/99 g)
$1\frac{1}{2}$ cups (6.6 oz/187 g) spooned and leveled unbleached all-purpose flour
1 tablespoon (15 ml) water
$1\frac{1}{2}$ teaspoons (7 g) baking powder
$\frac{1}{2}$ teaspoon (3 g) salt
1 tablespoon (6 g) ground cinnamon
$\frac{1}{4}$ teaspoon (0.5 g) freshly grated nutmeg
$2\frac{2}{3}$ cups (8 oz/227 g) old-fashioned oats (not quick-cooking)

1. Position a shelf in the center of the oven and preheat to 350°F/177°C. Cover a baking sheet with Release foil (nonstick side up) or parchment sprayed with nonstick cooking spray.

2. Pour the boiling water over the raisins and allow to soak for about 10 minutes. Drain well and spread out on a paper towel for a while.

3. Spread out the walnuts on a baking sheet and roast for 10 minutes. Toss with 2 tablespoons (1 oz/28 g) of the butter while they are hot. When cool, coarsely chop and set aside.

4. In a heavy-duty mixer with the paddle attachment, beat the remaining ¾ cup (6 oz/170 g) butter with the sugar until light and fluffy.

5. Beat in the molasses and vanilla. Add one egg at a time and beat just to blend.

6. Place the flour in a large mixing bowl. Sprinkle the water over the flour and stir in. Stir in the baking powder, salt, cinnamon, and nutmeg. Then stir in the oats.

7. Add about one-third of the dry mixture at a time to the butter mixture and blend in on the lowest speed. Remove the bowl from the mixer and stir in the nuts by hand. Then stir in the raisins.

8. I like to oil my hands and shape about 1½-inch (4-cm) dough balls. Place them on the prepared baking sheet about 1 inch (2.5 cm) apart and flatten them out slightly.

9. Bake one sheet at a time for about 10 minutes. They don't brown much and they do not look totally done, but they firm as they cool. Place on a cooling rack to cool.

Bourbon Pecan Oatmeal Cookies

MAKES ABOUT 2½ DOZEN COOKIES

This is a family favorite, a slightly more elegant oatmeal cookie. I love the flavor combination of bourbon, pecans, and brown sugar. My daughter-in-law, the opera singer Beth McCool, says that when there are friends around and she makes these, the cookies are gone before they can even cool.

What This Recipe Shows

Roasting enhances the flavor of nuts.

Processing the oats in a food processor makes a slightly smoother texture.

Using shortening limits the cookie's spread.

---

2 cups (7 oz/198 g) pecans

½ cup plus 2 tablespoons (5 oz/142 g)
unsalted butter, divided

1 teaspoon (6 g) salt, divided

1 cup (3 oz/85 g) old-fashioned or
quick-cooking oats

¼ cup (1.6 oz/45 g) butter-flavored
shortening

1 cup (7.7 oz/218 g) light brown sugar,
packed

1 tablespoon (15 ml) pure vanilla extract

2 tablespoons (30 ml) bourbon

2 tablespoons (30 ml) heavy cream

1 large egg (1.75 oz/50 g)

1¼ cups (5.5 oz/156 g) spooned and leveled
bleached all-purpose flour

1 teaspoon (5 g) baking soda

1 teaspoon (2 g) ground cinnamon

½ teaspoon (1 g) freshly grated nutmeg

Nonstick cooking spray, optional

1. Arrange a shelf in the center of the oven and preheat to 350°F/177°C.

2. Spread the pecans on a baking sheet and roast for 10 minutes. While they are hot, stir in 2 tablespoons (1 oz/28 g) of the butter and sprinkle with ¼ teaspoon (1.5 g) of the salt. When cool, coarsely chop and set aside.

3. Process the oats in a food processor with the steel blade for about 10 seconds.

4. With a mixer, in a bowl, beat the remaining ½ cup (4 oz/113 g) butter, the shortening, and sugar until light and fluffy. Beat in the vanilla, bourbon, and cream. Add the egg and beat just to blend.

5. In a mixing bowl, stir together the flour, baking soda, the remaining ¾ teaspoon (4.5 g) salt, the cinnamon, and nutmeg. On the lowest speed, add flour mixture into butter mixture in several portions. Stir in the oats and pecans by hand.

6. Cover a baking sheet with Release foil (nonstick side up) or parchment sprayed with nonstick cooking spray. Drop by heaping tablespoons or with a 1½-inch (#40) ice cream scoop onto the baking sheet. Bake one sheet at a time for about 10 minutes, until puffy and lightly browned on the edges. Allow to cool on the sheet for 2 minutes, and then remove to a cooling rack.

Laura Berry's Extra-Crunchy Oatmeal Cookies

MAKES ABOUT 4 DOZEN COOKIES

These amazingly crunchy morsels are delicious and completely addictive. Laura Berry is a wonderful cook and baker from St. Simons Island, Georgia. She said that this recipe came from a friend (which one, she can't remember) many years ago.

What This Recipe Shows

Roasting enhances the flavor of the nuts.

Using shortening, which retains its shape over a wide range of temperatures, limits the spread of the cookies.

The excessive amount of baking soda is in the recipe for browning, not leavening.

1½ cups (5.2 oz/149 g) pecans
2 tablespoons (1 oz/28 g) unsalted butter
¾ teaspoon (4.5 g) salt, divided
Nonstick cooking spray, optional
1½ cups (6.6 oz/187 g) spooned and leveled
    bleached all-purpose flour
1 teaspoon (5 g) baking soda
½ teaspoon (1 g) ground cinnamon
¼ teaspoon (0.5 g) freshly grated nutmeg

1 cup (6.7 oz/190 g) vegetable shortening
1 cup (7 oz/198 g) granulated sugar
½ cup (3.8 oz/108 g) light brown sugar,
    packed
1 large egg (1.75 oz/50 g)
1 tablespoon (15 ml) water
1 teaspoon (5 ml) pure vanilla extract
1½ cups (4.5 oz/130 g) quick-cooking oats
Additional coarse or granulated sugar for tops

1. Arrange a shelf in the middle of the oven and preheat the oven to 350°F/177°C.

2. Spread the pecans on a baking sheet and roast for 10 minutes. While nuts are hot, stir in the butter and ¼ teaspoon (1.5 g) of the salt. When cool, coarsely chop and set aside.

3. Turn oven up to 375°F/191°C. Line a heavy baking sheet with Release foil (nonstick side up) or parchment sprayed with nonstick cooking spray.

4. In a medium mixing bowl, beat the flour, the remaining ½ teaspoon (3 g) salt, the baking soda, cinnamon, and nutmeg together for a full minute. Set aside.

5. Beat the shortening and both sugars together until fluffy. Break the egg into a measuring cup and beat in the water and vanilla. Blend the egg mixture into shortening and sugar.

6. Stir in the flour mixture until well blended. Work in the oats and pecans. The dough will be very stiff. Work it with your hands if necessary. Chill the dough for about 30 minutes.

7. Take a tablespoon of dough at a time, shape into a ball and flatten, and place on the prepared baking sheet. Space them apart, since they spread a little. Gently press down with a buttered glass bottom that has been dipped in sugar.

8. Place in the oven and bake one sheet at a time for 10 to 12 minutes, until lightly browned around the edge. Allow to cool on the sheet for 2 minutes, and then remove to a cooling rack.

Flourless Cookies

A nut meal can provide all the "flour" needed for a cookie. The outstanding pastry chef and writer Susan G. Purdy has a recipe in *The Family Baker,* Impossible Peanut Butter Cookies, which has just three ingredients: 1 cup (9.1 oz/258 g) peanut butter, 1 cup (7 oz/198 g) granulated sugar, and 1 large egg (1.75 oz/50 g). The ground nut meal in the peanut butter provides the "flour" and flavor, and the egg has the protein to set the cookie. These work beautifully as long as you do not have so much sugar that it interferes with the eggs setting. I chickened out a little when I developed my recipe, below, and went with ¾ cup (5.3 oz/150 g) instead of a full cup of sugar.

E-Z Delicious Peanut Butter Cookies

MAKES ABOUT 2 DOZEN COOKIES

These unbelievably easy cookies are also unbelievably delicious! I saw a flourless recipe years ago and was reminded of it by Susan Purdy's Impossible Peanut Butter Cookies in *The Family Baker.*

What This Recipe Shows

Nut meal—ground peanuts in the peanut butter—acts as flour.

The egg sets these cookies beautifully.

Sugar is limited to ¾ cup, which provides plenty of sweetness but not so much as to interfere with the egg's setting.

Nonstick cooking spray, optional

1 cup (9.1 oz/258 g) extra-crunchy peanut
    butter

¾ cup (5.7 oz/162 g) light brown sugar,
    packed

1 large egg (1.75 oz/50 g)

½ cup (about 3 oz/85 g) English toffee bits
    (available in bags near the chocolate
    chips)

1. Place a rack in the center of the oven and preheat the oven to 350°F/177°C.

2. Cover a baking sheet with Release foil (nonstick side up), or parchment sprayed with nonstick cooking spray.

3. In a medium mixing bowl, stir together the peanut butter, brown sugar, and egg. When well mixed, stir in toffee chips.

4. Spoon a heaping tablespoon or use a 1½-inch (#40) ice cream scoop to place scoops of dough at least 1 inch (2.5 cm) apart on the baking sheet. Grease the bottom of a fork with butter or nonstick cooking spray and gently press cookies down a little. They do not spread a lot and if you have them flattened a little and not just blobs on the sheet, they make a prettier cookie.

5. Bake one sheet at a time, until the edges just begin to color, 9 to 10 minutes. Do not overcook. These can be deceptive. Cool 2 minutes on the pan, then remove to a cooling rack.

FAT

Fats frequently used in home cookie baking are butter, shortening, and butter-flavored shortening. The fat in cookies has a major influence on spread, texture, and taste, and a minor influence on color. Of these, spread and taste are probably the factors that concern cooks the most.

Spread

Butter has a sharp melting point. It is firm at one temperature, slightly warmer it is soft, and still slightly warmer it melts. Butter melts immediately in a hot oven. So cookies made with butter spread fast. Also, butter is only 80% fat, with about 16% water, which contributes to spread.

Cookies made with butter can spread more than those made with shortening.

Shortening, on the other hand, remains the same texture over a wide range of temperatures. Since it does melt immediately in the hot oven, cookies made with shortening do not spread nearly as much as those made with butter.

Flour in Cookies At a Glance

Type of Flour	What It Can Do
Cake flour	Has a consistent low-protein content and is chlorinated so it is slightly acidic, causing cookies to set faster.
Pastry flour	Frequently available only in health-food stores. May have differences in protein content.
Instant flour (Wondra and Shake & Blend, sometimes sold in cylinders)	This flour is wheat blended with barley, which has a consistent low-protein content and excellent flavor. This flour falls grain by grain and will never lump in a sauce. It is presteamed so that the starch is already swollen.
Southern all-purpose (White Lily)	Consistent low-protein content, producing consistent spread.
Southwestern all-purpose (Pioneer)	Very consistent slightly higher protein content than White Lily. It is formulated to make perfect flour tortillas.
National brand all-purpose	Has a range of protein content; water absorption varies, so cookie spread can vary.
Northern specialty blended all-purpose (King Arthur Unbleached)	Very consistent protein content, producing consistent spread.
Bread flour	Has a consistent higher-protein content, which enhances browning. Can absorb slightly more liquid in the dough. Could possibly make cookies tougher.

Taste

Certainly, there are varying opinions on taste. I love the taste of real butter and I am not fond of cookies made with plain shortening. However, the taste of cookies made with butter-flavored shortening can be outstanding. Butter-flavored shortening cookies can beat butter in blind tastings with some recipes, for example chocolate chip cookies.

Magnificent Butter Cookies

When it comes to butter cookies, I love real butter, both for the taste and the delicate golden color. For my husband's fiftieth birthday party, I made Maida Heatter's Swedish Jelly Cookies from her *Book of Great Desserts* and I thought they were the best cookies that I had ever eaten.

When I started gathering material for this chapter, I went right to my battered copy of Maida's book and made the Swedish Jelly Cookies. I prepared myself to be disappointed. You know how your memory can magnify how good something is. But, oh, my goodness, they were better than I remembered! A basic butter cookie is a great thing!

In the world of cookies you will run into butter cookies in all different guises. In fact, in 1998 Leslie Glover Pendleton wrote a little book, *One Dough, Fifty Cookies,* in which she literally made fifty different cookies from one basic butter cookie dough.

Recipes usually start out with ½ pound (227 g) of butter, varying amounts of sugar, salt, flavoring, egg yolks, and about 2½ cups (11 oz/312 g) flour. Here is my butter cookie recipe with a variation. You can prepare most butter cookies by piping, or using a small ice cream scoop, or hand shaping balls, or shaping into rolls to slice before baking (refrigerator cookies), which I find the simplest.

Buttery Jelly-Jeweled Cookies

MAKES ABOUT 3 DOZEN COOKIES

I like to use dark cherry preserves so the jelly center shines like a rich garnet in a pale golden setting. It is very difficult to stop eating these buttery jewels.

What This Recipe Shows

This dough has a relatively small amount of sugar for a cookie, so a tiny bit of jelly is a perfect finishing touch to add both sweetness and flavor.

The relatively small amount of sugar and just a touch of flavoring allow the flavor of the butter to dominate.

By baker's percentages (see page 32) these cookies are 75% butter, but since they have practically no liquid (¼ teaspoon almond extract—alcohol that evaporates fast—and less than a tablespoon of water from the egg yolks), they do not spread much.

Having the dough cold also helps to limit spread.

---

1 cup (8 oz/227 g) unsalted butter, cut in
    2-tablespoon (1-oz/28-g) pieces
½ cup (3.5 oz/99 g) sugar
½ teaspoon (3 g) salt
¼ teaspoon (1.2 ml) pure almond extract
2 large egg yolks (1.3 oz/37 g)

2¼ cups (9.9 oz/281 g) spooned and leveled
    bleached all-purpose flour
¼ cup good preserves (dark cherry is my
    favorite)
Nonstick cooking spray, optional

1. In a heavy-duty mixer with the paddle attachment, beat the butter, sugar, salt, and almond extract until light and creamy. Add the yolks one at a time, and beat with each addition, just to blend in thoroughly.

2. On the lowest speed, beat in the flour, scraping down the bowl and across the bottom twice. Divide the dough into 4 pieces. Roll each into a log about 1½ inches (4 cm) in diameter. Wrap each roll individually in plastic wrap and refrigerate at least 2 hours or overnight.

3. Heat and strain the preserves.

4. About 30 minutes before you are ready to bake, place a shelf in the center of the oven and preheat the oven to 375°F/191°C.

5. Cover a heavy baking sheet with Release foil (nonstick side up), or parchment sprayed with non-stick cooking spray.

6. Slice cookies into ⅜-inch (6-cm) slices and arrange about 1 inch (2.5 cm) apart on the sheet. Immediately after you slice each cookie and place it on the baking sheet, press an indentation in the center with your thumb or a fingertip.

7. After all the cookies are on the sheet, carefully spoon or pipe a small amount of jelly to fill the indentation in each cookie.

8. Place the baking sheet on the arranged shelf. Bake one sheet at a time until the edges just begin to brown, about 14 minutes. Allow to cool on the sheet for 2 minutes, and then remove to a cooling rack.

Stained Glass Cookies

For beautiful cookies that look as if they have patches of stained glass, break up into small pieces about four different colored hard candies like Lifesavers. Instead of making a thumb-print in the cookies as in Step 6, press some red pieces together in one spot on each cookie, and in a separate place, press some yellow pieces, then green or blue pieces in another separate spot. Be sure to keep each color hard candy pressed into a separate area. (When the hard candy melts, it might run together, which can give a muddy color.) Proceed to Step 8.

Diamond-Edged Melt-in-Your-Mouth Butter Cookies

MAKES ABOUT 3 DOZEN COOKIES

Rolling refrigerator cookie rolls in coarse (crystal) sugar, a technique that I got from Bruce Healy, is ideal to dress up and add a little sweetness to a simply wonderful butter cookie. The sugared edges sparkle like diamonds.

What This Recipe Shows

Since these cookies do not have the touch of jelly for sweetness and flavor, they need both more sugar and flavor than the Buttery Jelly-Jeweled Cookies.

By baker's percentages (see page 32) these cookies are 75% butter, but since they have practically no liquid (½ teaspoon almond extract—alcohol that evaporates fast—and less than a tablespoon of water from the egg yolks), they do not spread much.

Having the dough cold also helps limit spread.

---

1 cup (8 oz/227 g) unsalted butter, cut in
    2-tablespoon (1-oz/28-g) pieces
1 cup (7 oz/198 g) granulated sugar
½ teaspoon (3 g) salt
½ teaspoon (2.5 ml) pure almond extract
2 large egg yolks (1.3 oz/37 g)

2¼ cups (9.9 oz/281 g) spooned and leveled
    bleached all-purpose flour
½ cup (3.8 oz/108 g) coarse or crystal sugar
    (see Sources, page 509)
1 large egg (1.75 oz/50 g), beaten
Nonstick cooking spray, optional

1. In a heavy-duty mixer with the paddle attachment, cream the butter, sugar, salt, and almond extract until light and creamy. Add the yolks, one at a time, and beat with each addition, just to blend in thoroughly.

2. On low speed, beat in the flour, scraping down the bowl twice. Divide the dough into 4 pieces. Roll each into a log about 1½ inches (3.8 cm) in diameter.

3. Sprinkle coarse sugar evenly on wax paper, the length of the rolls and about 4 inches (10 cm) wide. Brush a roll lightly with beaten egg, then roll in sugar to coat well. Repeat with each roll. Wrap each roll individually in plastic wrap and refrigerate at least 2 hours or overnight.

4. About 30 minutes before you are ready to bake, place a shelf in the center of the oven and preheat the oven to 375°F/191°C.

5. Cover a heavy baking sheet with Release foil (nonstick side up), or parchment sprayed with nonstick cooking spray. Slice cookies into ⅜-inch (0.9-cm) slices and arrange about 1 inch (2.5 cm) apart on the sheet.

6. Place the baking sheet on the arranged shelf. Bake one sheet at a time until the edges just begin to brown, about 14 minutes. Allow to cool on the sheet for 2 minutes, and then remove to a cooling rack.

Additional Flavors

Without additional flavors, the taste of butter can come through in this butter cookie recipe. But this is also a great recipe with additional flavors, as evidenced by the fantastic Taste Sensation Lemon–White Chocolate Butter Cookies. When I gave lectures at Scripps College in Claremont, California, Suzanne Zetterberg, my hostess, brought us fantastic cookies from A Piece of Crust Bakery. One of my favorites was a lemon–white chocolate chip cookie. The flavor combination of the sharp lemon and the sweet white chocolate was wonderful. I don't have their recipe, but I just had to make a cookie taking advantage of that flavor combination. You will love these!

Taste Sensation Lemon–White Chocolate Butter Cookies

MAKES ABOUT 4 DOZEN COOKIES

Wow! Wait until you taste these!

What This Recipe Shows

A limited amount of liquid and having the dough cold limits the spread of these cookies.

The sharpness of the lemon is balanced by the sweetness of the white chocolate.

---

1 cup (8 oz/227 g) unsalted butter, cut in 2-tablespoon (1-oz/28-g) pieces
¾ cup (5.3 oz/150 g) sugar
1 teaspoon (6 g) salt
1 teaspoon (5 ml) light corn syrup
½ teaspoon (2.5 ml) pure lemon extract

1 tablespoon (30 ml) lemon zest (grated peel)
2 large egg yolks (1.3 oz/37 g)
2 cups (8.8 oz/249 g) spooned and leveled bleached all-purpose flour
1 cup (6 oz/170 g) white chocolate chips
Nonstick cooking spray, optional

1. In a heavy-duty mixer with the paddle attachment, cream the butter, sugar, salt, corn syrup, lemon extract, and lemon zest until light and creamy. Add the yolks, one at a time, and beat with each addition, just to blend in thoroughly.

2. On the lowest speed, beat in the flour, scraping down the sides of the bowl and across the bottom once. Stir in the white chocolate chips. Divide the dough evenly into 4 pieces. Roll each piece into a log about 2 inches (5 cm) in diameter. Wrap each roll individually in plastic wrap and refrigerate at least 2 hours or overnight.

3. About 30 minutes before you are ready to bake, place a shelf in the center of the oven and preheat the oven to 375°F/191°C.

4. Cover a heavy baking sheet with Release foil (nonstick side up), or parchment lightly sprayed with nonstick cooking spray.

5. Slice cookies into ⅜-inch (6-cm) slices and arrange about 1 inch (2.5 cm) apart on the sheet.

6. Place the baking sheet on the arranged shelf. Bake one sheet at a time until the edges just begin to brown, about 15 minutes. Allow to cool on the sheet for 2 minutes, and then remove to a cooling rack.

Texture

Fats grease the flour proteins and prevent their joining to form gluten, so fats are major tenderizers. Of all the fats, oil is the most effective at coating proteins—or, in other words, a great tenderizer.

Since cookies have so much fat and sugar, they are very tender—sometimes to the point of crumbling. There are a few cookie recipes with oil (see Chocolate Crinkle Cookies, page 395) but, in general, oil is rarely needed or used.

Fats in baking are the major aerators. Baking powder and baking soda do not make a single new bubble. They only enlarge bubbles that already exist in the batter or dough. So the bubbles beaten into the fat in the creaming step play a big part in the leavening process. In cookies, this role is not as important as in cakes, muffins, and many other baked goods. As explained under Leaveners (see page 402), many times the baking soda in a cookie recipe is not there for leavening but to enhance color.

Shortening is a better leavener than butter because it has 12% inert gases already beaten into it and it doesn't melt as easily during creaming.

Thin layers of fat between thin layers of dough create puff pastry, as we saw in Chapter 3 (page 359). This next recipe is very interesting. It is a "savory cookie"—a cracker. Store-bought saltine crackers cover a pan. They are topped with a good sprinkling of hot pepper flakes and grated extra-sharp cheddar, then placed in a very hot oven. The oven is so hot that it not only melts the cheese but breaks it down. The fat in the cheese runs down into the crackers and gets between the thin, flakey layers in each cracker and makes them puff like puff pastry. They are delicious!

Roosters' Famous Fire Crackers

MAKES ONE 10 X 15-INCH (25 X 38-CM) SHEET OF CRACKERS

These sensational pepper-hot, crisp, cheesy crackers that you can't stop eating are from Roosters, a gourmet take-out shop and cooking school in Greensboro, North Carolina. They're perfect party food. In a Christmas tin, they make a wonderful home-cooked gift.

What This Recipe Shows

Normally, you keep temperatures low when working with cheese so that it won't separate, but in this case, the separation of the cheese makes the dish outstanding. The oven is so hot that the fat in the cheese separates out and goes into the crackers, making them incredibly flakey and crunchy.

I get the crispest crackers using a heavy commercial pan or a brown or gray (not shiny) nonstick baking sheet (jelly-roll pan)—a pan that holds the heat well.

Nonstick cooking spray
One 15-ounce box (225 g) fat-free saltines
   (such as Keebler's Zesta Fat-Free)

Fresh hot red pepper flakes
One 10-ounce package (283 g) Cracker Barrel
   extra-sharp cheddar, grated

1. Place a shelf in the center of the oven and preheat the oven to 475°F/246°C.

2. Spray a jelly-roll pan (baking sheet with sides) measuring about 10 x 15 inches (25 x 38 cm) with nonstick cooking spray. Arrange the crackers (about 40) in rows so that they are touching each other. One sleeve fits almost perfectly in this size pan and you will have about three sleeves left in the box.

3. Sprinkle with as many pepper flakes as you dare. About 6 to 8 to a cracker is good. Finally, top evenly with the grated cheese.

4. Quickly, place the pan on the arranged shelf and close the oven door. Leave the heat on for no more than 10 seconds, then *turn the oven off.* Leave in the closed oven for at least 2 hours. The hot oven melts and browns the cheese, producing an even crisp brown coating. The fat from the cheese soaks into the crackers and puffs them slightly. Leaving them in the oven also dries them out, so they become super crunchy. Break apart and eat, or store for several weeks sealed in an airtight container.

NOTE: It may take a second time to get this recipe just right. Some ovens are not hot enough or are too hot when set at 475°F/246°C. You want the cheese light to medium brown but not burned. Also, it may take a second time to get the pepper flakes right.

Color

Butter contains small amounts of sugars and proteins in its dairy components. Both of these can enhance color, and butter cookies can have a nice golden color. However, because of the small amount, this is not as big an influence on color as many other ingredients, like the type of sugar (see below) or the type of leavening (see page 402).

Fats in Cookies At a Glance

Type of Fat	What It Does
Butter	Has a sharp melting point and contains about 16% water, which can make cookies spread excessively. Gives cookies an excellent rich taste. Slightly enhances color of cookies.
Shortening	Holds its shape over a wide range of temperatures, which helps limit spread. Can enhance leavening for a slightly puffier cookie.
Butter-flavored shortening	Holds its shape over a wide range of temperatures, which helps limit spread. Produces cookies with a rich buttery taste. Can enhance leavening for a slightly puffier cookie.

SUGAR

The type of sugar used in a cookie can dramatically influence browning and texture, and can influence spread in a minor way.

In large amounts, sugar acts as a hardening agent to make cookies crisp and firm. In lesser amounts, sugar holds moisture and softens a cookie—especially certain forms of sugar like brown sugar or honey.

Browning

Cookies made with even a small amount of corn syrup will be significantly browner.

Corn syrup is primarily glucose, a sugar with a structure that makes it brown at a lower temperature than regular granulated sugar (sucrose). Cookies made with even a small amount (1 tablespoon/15 ml) of corn syrup will be significantly browner.

Texture

Cookies made with granulated sugar tend to stay crisp upon standing, but other sweeteners act differently. Honey contains 42% fructose, a sugar that absorbs water from the atmosphere (it is *hygroscopic*) and makes cookies soften upon standing. Brown sugar is also more hygroscopic than granulated sugar. Maple syrup is high in sucrose, and corn syrup is high in glucose. So cookies made with either do not absorb as much water from the air as those made with honey or brown sugar.

The texture of the sugar itself affects creaming, the spread during baking, and the surface texture of the cookies. The coarser the granule, the less it dissolves, and the less spread. In the hot oven, coarser sugar melts and migrates to the surface where it can contribute to browning and produce a cracked surface. Confectioners' sugar can cause the greatest spread because it dissolves easily.

The coarser the sugar granule, the less it dissolves and the less spread.

Brown sugar is slightly acidic, so brown sugar can help limit spread by making proteins set faster. The amount of sugar also influences spread. Cookies with an excessive amount of sugar will spread more.

Cracked Surface

I love cracked-surface cookies. You can get this on a lot of cookies but gingersnaps, more consistently, have a cracked surface. You have to have coarse sugar—at least, granulated sugar—and a very-low-moisture dough so that the sugar does not dissolve well and migrates to the surface. In my gingersnap recipe, I used regular granulated sugar, which dissolves slower than superfine or confectioners' sugar.

Cracked-Surface Crunchy Gingersnaps

MAKES ABOUT 3½ DOZEN COOKIES

Crispy, crunchy, spicy, and with a lovely brown crinkled surface—these are yummy.

What This Recipe Shows

With the low moisture content and high sugar, the sugar does not dissolve well and in the hot oven migrates to the surface to create a cracked, crisp top.

I used regular granulated sugar, which does not dissolve as well as superfine, to contribute to the cracked surface.

---

2 cups (14 oz/397 g) sugar, divided
¾ cup (6 oz/170 g) unsalted butter
¼ cup (59 ml) unsulfured molasses,
    such as Grandma's
1 large egg (1.75 oz/50 g)
2¼ cups (9.9 oz/281 g) spooned and leveled
    bleached all-purpose flour

2 teaspoons (0.3 oz/9 g) baking soda
½ teaspoon (3 g) salt
1 tablespoon (5 g) ground ginger
1 teaspoon (2 g) ground cinnamon
½ teaspoon (1 g) ground cloves
¼ teaspoon (0.5 g) freshly grated nutmeg
Nonstick cooking spray, optional

1. In a heavy-duty mixer, beat 1¾ cups (12.3 oz/349 g) of the sugar and the butter until fluffy. Add the molasses and beat to blend in well. Add the egg and beat on low just to blend in.

2. In a medium mixing bowl, stir together the flour, baking soda, salt, ginger, cinnamon, cloves, and nutmeg. Add this dry mixture to the mixer and blend on lowest speed. Cover and chill dough for at least 1 hour or overnight.

3. Place a rack in the center of the oven and preheat the oven to 350°F/177°C.

4. Cover a baking sheet with Release foil (nonstick side up), or parchment lightly sprayed with nonstick cooking spray.

5. Roll the dough into 1¼-inch (3.2-cm) balls. Place the remaining ¼ cup (1.8 oz/51 g) sugar in a small bowl and roll each ball in sugar. Place on the baking sheet, 2 inches (5 cm) apart. Bake until edges just begin to color, about 10 minutes, but check on them at 8 minutes.

6. Remove the foil and cookies to a rack to cool completely.

Crunchy Surface but Gooey Center

In addition to giving you crunch all the way through like a gingersnap, sugar can give you a crunchy surface only. In the eye-catching Chocolate Crinkle Cookies, the cookies are rolled in granulated sugar and then in confectioners' sugar just before baking. Rolling in granulated first does several things. It prevents the confectioners' sugar from soaking in, so that you have dramatic snow-white splotches on the dark chocolate surface, and it gives you a great crunchy surface to contrast with the gooey chocolate center.

Chocolate Crinkle Cookies

MAKES 3 TO 5 DOZEN, DEPENDING ON SIZE

Striking snow-white and black, these wonderful cookies are slightly crunchy on the surface but gooey chocolate inside—oh, yum!

What This Recipe Shows

By rolling the dough balls in plain sugar first, the confectioners' sugar does not soak in so much and stays on the surface better.

Corn syrup in the dough helps prevent crystallization to produce the soft chocolate center.

Oil greases flour proteins to produce a tender to the point of gooey chocolate center.

$1^{3}/4$ cups plus 2 tablespoons (8.2 oz/232 g) spooned and leveled bleached all-purpose flour

$1^{1}/2$ teaspoons (7 g) baking powder

$^{1}/2$ teaspoon (3 g) salt

8 ounces (227 g) semisweet chocolate, finely chopped

$2^{3}/4$ cups (19.3 oz/547 g) sugar, divided

$^{1}/3$ cup (79 ml) canola oil

2 tablespoons (30 ml) light corn syrup

2 large eggs (3.5 oz/99 g)

1 large egg yolk (0.65 oz/18 g)

2 teaspoons (10 ml) pure vanilla extract

1 cup (4 oz/120 g) confectioners' sugar

1. In a medium bowl, beat together well the flour, baking powder, and salt, and set aside.

2. Melt the chocolate in the microwave on 50% power for 1 minute, stir, and microwave for 15 seconds more and stir.

3. In a mixer with the paddle attachment, beat together $2\frac{1}{2}$ cups (17.5 oz/496 g) of the sugar, the oil, and corn syrup to blend. Beat in the eggs, egg yolk, and vanilla. Then on low, beat in the melted chocolate. Add the flour mixture and beat in on low speed.

4. Wrap the dough in plastic and refrigerate for several hours or overnight.

5. About 30 minutes before you are ready to bake, arrange a shelf in the middle of the oven and preheat the oven to 325°F/163°C. Line a baking sheet with Release foil (nonstick side up).

6. Take out about one-quarter of the dough at a time to shape. Roll the dough into $1\frac{1}{2}$ to 2-inch (3.8 to 5 cm) balls. Pour the remaining $\frac{1}{4}$ cup (1.8 oz/51 g) granulated sugar into one bowl and the confectioners' sugar in another bowl. Roll each cookie dough ball lightly in granulated sugar first, then very heavily in confectioners' sugar. (By rolling in plain sugar first, the confectioners' sugar does not soak in so much and stays on the surface better.)

7. Arrange cookies 2 inches (5 cm) apart on the foil. For crisp cookies, bake 12 to 14 minutes. You can have several sheets of foil covered with cookies ready.

8. When one sheet is done, you can pull off the foil and cookies to a cooling rack. Rinse the baking sheet with cold water to cool and then slip the sheet under another sheet of foil with cookies on it and get it right back into the oven. Allow the cookies to cool for 2 minutes, then remove to a rack to cool completely.

Sugars in Cookies At a Glance

Type of Sugar	What It Does
Sucrose (table sugar)	In high proportions, makes a very crisp cookie that stays crisp. In lesser amounts, it keeps cookies moist.
Coarse sucrose	In a limited-moisture cookie, it does not dissolve fast and in the hot oven migrates to the surface to create a cracked, crisp surface.
Turbinado sugar	Is more coarse than granulated sugar and acts in the same way that coarse sucrose does.
Confectioners' sugar	Dissolves fast and can make cookies spread faster. Makes an attractive surface.
Brown sugar	Is more hygroscopic than sucrose, so cookies made with it will absorb moisture from the atmosphere and soften on standing.
Honey	Contains 42% fructose and is very hygroscopic. Baked goods containing honey absorb moisture from the atmosphere and stay moist.
Corn syrup	Is glucose, a reducing sugar, and even in small amounts will enhance browning.

EGGS

A Major Structural Ingredient

Eggs and flour are the two proteins that hold cookies together. We saw that if flour is missing, eggs become more important and, if eggs are missing, flour becomes more important. Grandmother's Pecan Macaroons, page 398, have no flour and are just barely held together. You can see how vital the egg white is to bind, and the wonderful tenderness of a cookie with limited structural proteins.

Grandmother's Pecan Macaroons

MAKES ABOUT 40 COOKIES

Carol Hacker of Lakewood, Ohio, is an outstanding food professional, a home economist who works for many food companies. Carol worked for years to get this recipe for her grandmother's pecan macaroons exactly right. Every year her family would inhale the cookies, but then add that they weren't like Grandmother's. After years, Carol finally got cookies that were just like Grandmother's.

What This Recipe Shows

Without flour, egg whites are the sole binder for these cookies.

Pecans and brown sugar produce great flavors subtly touched off by 3 drops of honey.

Nonstick cooking spray, optional
7 cups (24.4 oz/692 g) pecans
1 tablespoon (0.4 oz/11 g) granulated sugar, divided

2 cups (15.4 oz/437 g) light brown sugar, packed
½ teaspoon (3 g) salt
2 large egg whites (2 oz/57 g)
3 drops honey

1. Arrange a shelf in the center of the oven and preheat the oven to 325°F/163°C. Line a baking sheet with Release foil (nonstick side up), or parchment sprayed with nonstick cooking spray.

2. In a food processor with the steel blade, process the pecans in three batches with 1 teaspoon (0.15 oz/4 g) of the granulated sugar in each batch. You want to get the pecans finely ground but not to a powder or a butter. Measure out 6 cups (21 oz/593 g) ground pecans and place in a mixing bowl.

3. Add the brown sugar, salt, egg whites, and honey. With clean hands, work the ingredients into an evenly mixed dough. Shape dough into small (about 1-inch/2.5-cm) balls and place on the baking sheet. Place in the refrigerator for at least 30 minutes.

4. Place in the oven on the arranged shelf and bake for 20 minutes, until set. Allow to cool for 2 minutes, then remove to a cooling rack. When completely cooled, seal in a cookie tin or heavy-duty zip-top plastic bag. These cookies will keep well for months and are better made several weeks ahead.

Meringues

Meringues are a whole world of cookies. In Chapter 2 (Puff, The Magic Leavener—Steam) you have an introduction to this world. The cookies can be small rounds of Delicate French Meringue (page 195) or more complex with buttercream and chocolate like the magnificent Featherlight Meringue Spheres with Silky Crème Anglaise Coffee Buttercream and Chocolate (page 176). Bruce Healy's *The French Cookie Book* is an entire book of marvelous meringue cookies.

Eggs Setting

Eggs are proteins, which must cook (coagulate) to set the cookie. If the dough is acidic, the proteins will set faster. This can be a major aid in limiting the spread.

I am really impressed with the power of eggs and an acidic dough to control the shape of a cookie. Evan Kleiman, a chef and radio talk show hostess in Los Angeles, called me about her biscotti, a recipe that she had done over and over and loved to do with different flavors and different additions. The biscotti had always come out perfectly until she tried a chocolate version.

> If the dough is acidic, eggs will cook faster— this can be a major aid in limiting the spread.

She wanted a nice dark color and rich taste, so she used Dutch process cocoa. Instead of holding its shape nicely, as it always did, the biscotti spread all over the place.

Her high-egg dough, which had been acidic so that the eggs set fast and did not spread much, was now alkaline (not at all acidic) with the Dutch process cocoa, and the eggs did not set fast. The dough became a big puddle of chocolate. (For more about eggs, acidic doughs, and spread, see the Spread section on page 425.)

An Egg Is Three Ingredients

An egg can be three different ingredients: a whole egg, an egg white that dries things out, or an egg yolk that contains natural emulsifiers and can produce a moist interior or silky smooth texture. Butter cookies should not be dry, and it is all right for them to be tender almost to the point of crumbly. So you definitely want nothing but yolks in butter cookie recipes.

> An egg can be three different ingredients: a whole egg, an egg white that dries things out, or an egg yolk with natural emulsifiers that can produce a moist interior or silky smooth texture.

For cookies that you want to have a crisp surface, but a soft—almost gooey—inside, like the Lava Cookies, page 400, you want whole eggs. You need the whites for the dry, crisp surface and the yolks for the moist center.

Lava Cookies

MAKES ABOUT 16 COOKIES

Crisp on the outside and runny chocolate in the middle—magnificent cookies—my version of a great recipe from the fine chocolate maker Guittard. These are outstanding cookies made with any chocolate chips, but they are truly memorable made with Guittard. Cookbook author Sheilah Kaufman brought these cookies to my attention, and I am ever grateful. My daughter took a batch to my granddaughter's school. Everybody who tried one came back for four!

What This Recipe Shows

Roasting nuts enhances flavor.

Melting the chocolate with the butter avoids any risk of seizing (see page 93 for more details about seizing).

1½ cups (5.2 oz/149 g) pecans or walnuts
½ cup (4 oz/113 g) unsalted butter, divided
Nonstick cooking spray, optional
2 cups (12 oz/340 g) semisweet chocolate chips
2 large eggs (3.5 oz/99 g)

⅔ cup (4.6 oz/130 g) sugar
1 teaspoon (6 g) salt
2 teaspoons (10 ml) pure vanilla extract
1 cup (4.4 oz/125 g) spooned and leveled bleached all-purpose flour
½ teaspoon (2.5 g) baking powder

1. Arrange a shelf in the middle of the oven and preheat the oven to 350°F/177°C.

2. On a baking sheet, roast the nuts 10 minutes. While nuts are hot, stir in 2 tablespoons (1 oz/28 g) of the butter. When cool, coarsely chop and set aside.

3. Turn oven up to 375°F/191°C. Line a baking sheet with Release foil (nonstick side up), or parchment sprayed with nonstick cooking spray.

4. In a medium saucepan, melt the remaining 6 tablespoons (3 oz/85 g) butter over medium heat; remove it from the heat, add the chocolate and allow it to stand for 1 minute, then stir. If all the chocolate is not melted, place the pan on very low heat for 1 minute, remove, and stir. Allow to stand a minute and continue stirring. Repeat until all of the chocolate is melted. Set aside.

5. In a mixer, beat the eggs, sugar, salt, and vanilla on high speed until light and pale yellow, 2 to 3 minutes. Turn the mixer down to low and pour in the melted chocolate and butter.

6. In a medium bowl, beat together thoroughly the flour and baking powder. Stir flour into the dough in several batches. Scrape down the bowl and across the bottom. Stir in the roasted nuts.

7. Cover the bowl with plastic wrap and refrigerate for 20 to 30 minutes.

8. Scoop with a 2-inch (#30) ice cream scoop and place dough about 2 inches (5 cm) apart on the prepared baking sheet.

9. Place the sheet in the oven. Bake one sheet at a time exactly 12 minutes. Cool 3 to 5 minutes. Best served warm, but you can reheat each cookie in the microwave on 100% power for 10 seconds for runny centers. You can also freeze them, thaw, and microwave as above to get a runny center.

Shirley's Corrupted Black Gold

MAKES ABOUT 28 COOKIES

Marcel Desaulniers, a famous cookbook author and the executive chef of the Trellis Restaurant in Colonial Williamsburg, is a true chocolate expert and a loyal friend. His Black Gold cookies have a great following. They are crisp and slightly shiny on the surface but pure, soft chocolate underneath. I went crazy over them. Marcel brought me a huge platter of his cookies to serve at a book signing that he arranged for *CookWise*.

Marcel would want nothing to do with my version because he loves intense bittersweet chocolate, but as a spoiled child, I lived off of Hershey's milk chocolate. So I can't resist throwing it into my favorite recipes.

What This Recipe Shows

Eggs produce a slightly paler, slightly shiny crisp surface while the inside of the cookies is soft chocolate heaven.

1¹⁄₂ cups (5.2 oz/149 g) pecans
¹⁄₂ cup (4 oz/113 g) unsalted butter, cut in
    1-tablespoon (0.5-oz/14-g) pieces, divided
1 cup (6 oz/170 g) semisweet chocolate chips
4 ounces (113 g) milk chocolate, chopped
2 ounces (57 g) unsweetened chocolate, chopped
¹⁄₂ cup (3.5 oz/99 g) sugar

2 large eggs (3.5 oz/99 g)
2 teaspoons (10 ml) pure vanilla extract
¹⁄₂ cup (2.2 oz/62 g) spooned and leveled
    bleached all-purpose flour
¹⁄₂ teaspoon (2.5 g) baking powder
¹⁄₂ teaspoon (3 g) salt
Nonstick cooking spray, optional

1. Arrange a shelf in the center of the oven and preheat the oven to 350°F/177°C.

2. Spread the pecans on a baking sheet and roast for 10 minutes. While the nuts are hot, stir in 2 tablespoons (1 oz/28 g) of the butter. When cool, coarsely chop and set aside.

3. In a large heatproof glass bowl, arrange the remaining 6 tablespoons (3 oz/85 g) of butter around the edge of the bowl. Place the semisweet chocolate, milk chocolate, and unsweetened chocolate in the center. Microwave on 50% power for 1 minute and stir. If all the chocolate is not melted after stirring well, heat in 10-second increments, stirring thoroughly, until all chocolate is melted.

4. Beat together the sugar and the eggs until pale and light. Stir in the melted chocolate and then the vanilla.

5. Measure the flour into a medium bowl. Stir in the baking powder and salt. Stir this dry mixture into the chocolate mixture. Stir in the roasted chopped pecans. Mix well.

6. Line a heavy baking sheet with Release foil (nonstick side up) or parchment sprayed with nonstick cooking spray. Spoon a heaping tablespoon of dough for each cookie. I use a 1½-inch (#40) ice cream scoop. Place the baking sheet on the arranged shelf. Bake one sheet at a time, about 10 minutes, until cookies just start to darken around the edges. Cool the cookies on the sheet for 2 minutes, then remove to a cooling rack. Store in an airtight container.

LEAVENERS

The leavening in most cookies is minimal. In many cookies, for example chocolate chip or oatmeal cookies, a slightly puffed cookie is more attractive than an absolutely thin flat cookie. Actually, many things contribute to spread and puff (see Spread on page 425). As previously mentioned, baking soda's role in color or baking powder's role to limit spread may be more important than leavening, per se.

> Leaveners do not make a single new bubble. They only enlarge bubbles that already exist in the batter or dough.

> In most recipes, 1 teaspoon (5 g) baking powder or ¼ teaspoon (1 g) baking soda will perfectly leaven 1 cup (4.4 oz/125 g) of flour.

Leaveners do not make a single new bubble. They only enlarge bubbles that already exist in the batter or dough. So the bubbles beaten into the fat in the creaming step play a big part in the leavening. Shortening is a better leavener than butter because it has 12% inert gases already beaten into it and it doesn't melt easily during the creaming.

In home baking, baking powder or baking soda are the primary leaveners in cookies. Commercially, ammonium bicarbonate, a leavener that breaks down into carbon dioxide gas and ammonia gas, is sometimes used. However, this works only on flat cookies and crackers or cookies that are baked dry like biscotti. The ammonia gas generated must completely escape in the hot oven. Otherwise, the cookie or cracker could have a horrible ammonia taste.

In most recipes, 1 teaspoon (5 g) baking powder or ¼ teaspoon (1 g) baking soda leavens 1 cup (4.4 oz/125 g) of flour. When the leavening is much over this, the bubbles get big, rise to the surface, pop! There goes your leavening. In most cookie recipes the amount of baking soda is excessive for leavening and is there primarily for alkalinity or color.

Self-Rising Flour

Self-rising flour, which contains leaveners and a little salt, is both a short-cut (you don't have to add leaveners) and insurance that you have a low-protein flour. Millers know that chemical leaveners like baking powder and baking soda work best with lower-protein flour, so self-rising flour usually has a slightly lower protein content than plain all-purpose flour. The super crispy cheese coins below take advantage of self-rising flour.

Crispy, Flakey Cheese Coins

MAKES ABOUT 5 DOZEN CHEESE "QUARTERS"

Crisp on the surface, light, flakey airiness, and totally cheesy. These are incredibly addictive.

What This Recipe Shows

Self-rising flour is used for its correct leavening and low-protein content.

---

1 pound (454 g) extra-sharp cheddar, cut in
 $1/2$-inch (1.3-cm) chunks
$1/2$ cup (4 oz/113 g) butter, cut in
 1-tablespoon (0.5-oz/14-g) pieces and
 frozen, divided
1 large egg white (1 oz/28 g)

$1 1/2$ cups (6.75 oz/191 g) spooned and leveled
 self-rising flour, divided
$1/2$ teaspoon (3.5 g) salt
$1/4$ teaspoon (0.5 g) ground cayenne (or adjust
 to personal taste)
Nonstick cooking spray, optional

1. In a food processor with the steel blade, process the cheddar into very small pieces. Add half of the frozen butter (2 oz/57 g) and the egg white and process just until blended, but leave the butter in lumps.

2. Add ¾ cup (3.4 oz/96 g) of the flour, sprinkle the salt and cayenne around on the top, and process until dough begins to come together. Add the remaining ¾ cup (3.4 oz/96 g) flour. Process just until a dough ball forms. Add the remaining (2 oz/57 g) frozen butter and process only until the butter is incorporated in frozen lumps. Divide into 2 pieces, and shape in 2 rolls about 1½ inches (4 cm) in diameter. Wrap tightly in plastic wrap. Refrigerate for about an hour.

3. Place a shelf in the center of the oven and preheat the oven to 400°F/204°C.

4. Cover a heavy baking sheet with parchment sprayed with nonstick cooking spray or Release foil (nonstick side up). Slice the dough into ¼-inch-thick (0.6 cm) discs and place at least 2 inches (5 cm) apart on the prepared baking sheet. Be sure to space the dough apart as they spread a bit. Place one sheet at a time on the arranged shelf and bake 4 minutes. Reduce the heat to 325°F/163°C and bake until the very edges start to color, about 10 to 15 more minutes. Do not let them brown all over; they can have a terrible burned taste.

5. Allow to cool on the baking sheet 1 to 2 minutes only, then remove to a cooling rack. When completely cooled, store in an air-tight container.

Acidity

Leaveners in cookies play a role not just in leavening, but in the acidity of the dough.

If something is too acidic, it will not brown. Since baking soda reduces acidity, it can make a big difference in the color of a cookie, allowing the cookie to brown more. (See Pitifully Pale Cookies on page 423 for more details.)

> Leaveners in cookies play a role not just in leavening, but in the acidity of the dough.

> An acidic dough speeds up the cooking of the proteins and the setting of cookies and helps limit spread.

An acidic dough speeds up the cooking of the proteins and the setting of cookies, and helps limit spread. So when baking soda neutralizes the acids in the dough, the cookies will not set ("cook") as fast.

Baking powder does not influence the dough's acidity. So using it will not slow the setting of the cookies. Baking powder contains baking soda, an acid or acids to react with the soda, and cornstarch to keep everything dry. There is exactly the right amount of acid to neutralize all of the soda so that you will never have a soapy aftertaste or an influence on the acidity of the dough.

Many baking powders are double acting. One of the acids dissolves immediately to produce bubbles the minute that liquid is added, but other acids do not dissolve to enlarge the bubbles until a specific higher temperature is reached in the oven.

Intentional Improper Leavening

With too much leavening, bubbles in the batter are puffed up immediately. They get larger and larger, run into each other, float to the surface, and pop! There goes your leavening, and the product falls and is dense and heavy. In some recipes like Old New England Hermit Bars (below), this is exactly what you want.

The other day someone sent me a recipe for a hermit bar saying that it had a nice taste, but it was cake-like and she wanted an old-fashioned chewy hermit bar. What did she need to do to get that?

Sometimes it is not clear what is meant by "chewy." In a yeast bread, when someone says it is too chewy or not chewy enough, this normally means that it has too much or too little gluten developed.

With cookies, when someone says "chewy," they usually mean moist and dense as opposed to crisp and crunchy. This was clearly her meaning. She did not like the light cake-like bars. Her recipe was perfectly leavened—2 teaspoons (9 g) baking powder for 2 cups (8.8 oz/249 g) flour and 2 large eggs (3.5 oz/99 g)—just right for the amount of fat that she had. So she did, indeed, have a perfect light cake.

Historically, hermit bars were from the time when the great clipper ships docked in New England ports. They were moist, dense bars with dried fruit and nuts, which retained their taste and texture for a long period, perfect for sailors to tuck away in their sea chests. Some recipes that I found are indeed dense. One recipe had 2 teaspoons (9 g) of baking soda (proper leavening for 8 cups, 34 oz/964 g, of flour) but used only 2 cups (8.8 oz/249 g) of flour. These would fall immediately in a hot oven and would have a nice deep color.

Old New England Hermit Bars

MAKES ABOUT 30 COOKIES

These moist, flavorful bars that didn't dry out easily were treasures hidden away in the sea chests of sailors on the great clipper ships. Directions here are for "bars," but these can be baked as drop cookies—drop generous tablespoons of dough 2 inches (5 cm) apart.

What This Recipe Shows

Intentionally, these are greatly overleavened so that they fall immediately in a hot oven to be dense and well browned.

The excess sugar, cinnamon, and mashed raisins (which contain propionic acid, a preservative) slow staling and extend the shelf life of these bars.

Baking soda destroys cell walls to soften dates.

4 cups (946 ml) water

1 cup (5.1 oz/147 g) chopped dates

¼ teaspoon (1 g) baking soda

1 cup (5.1 oz/145 g) raisins

½ cup (1.5 oz/43 g) chopped dried apples or mixed chopped dried fruit

3 tablespoons (45 ml) dark rum (I like Myers's)

6 tablespoons (90 ml) unsulfured molasses, such as Grandma's, divided

1 cup (3.5 oz/106 g) walnuts

½ cup plus 2 tablespoons (5 oz/142 g) unsalted butter, room temperature, divided

Nonstick cooking spray, optional

2½ cups (11 oz/312 g) spooned and leveled all-purpose flour

2 teaspoons (9 g) baking soda

2 teaspoons (4 g) ground ginger

2 teaspoons (4 g) ground cinnamon

1¾ teaspoons (3.5 g) ground cloves

½ teaspoon (1 g) ground allspice

¼ teaspoon (0.5 g) freshly grated nutmeg

½ teaspoon (3 g) salt

1 cup (7.7 oz/218 g) light brown sugar, packed

1 large egg (1.75 oz/50 g), at room temperature

1. Boil about 4 cups (946 ml) of water to have enough for dates, raisins, and dried apples. Place the dates in a container large enough to allow bubbling up (say, a 2-cup/473-ml measuring cup), sprinkle with the baking soda, and pour boiling water over to cover. Ideally, this should stand for about 1 hour—the longer it stands, the softer the dates get.

2. In a small bowl, cover the raisins and dried fruit with boiling water. Stir in the rum and 2 tablespoons (30 ml) of the molasses. Allow to soak at least 10 minutes.

3. Place a shelf in the center of the oven and preheat to 350°F/177°C.

4. Spread out the walnuts on a baking sheet and roast for 10 minutes. Remove from oven and while hot, stir in 1 tablespoon (0.5 oz/14 g) of the butter. When cool, coarsely chop and set aside.

5. Increase oven temperature to 375°F/191°C. Line two baking sheets with Release foil (nonstick side up) or parchment paper sprayed with nonstick cooking spray.

6. In a medium bowl, stir together the flour, baking soda, ginger, cinnamon, cloves, allspice, nutmeg, and salt.

7. In the bowl of a mixer with the paddle attachment, beat the remaining ½ cup plus 1 tablespoon (4.5 oz/127 g) butter and the brown sugar until light and fluffy, about 2 minutes. Add the egg, and beat on low speed until just combined, scraping down the sides of the bowl. Add the remaining 4 tablespoons (60 ml) molasses, and beat until just blended; scrape down sides of bowl. On the lowest speed add the dry ingredients. Mix in the walnuts.

8. Drain the raisins and dried apples and dump out onto a paper towel for a few minutes to further dry. Then place in a mixing bowl. With the back of a spoon, smush the raisins and fruit against the side of the bowl a bit. (Raisin pulp is a good anti-staling agent, so you want to make some of it available.) Drain the dates well and pat off excess moisture with a paper towel. Add the raisins, apples, and dates to the dough, and mix by hand until the dough comes together.

9. Divide the dough into 4 pieces. Shape each piece into a log about 1½ inches (4 cm) in diameter. Arrange 2 logs on each baking sheet, leaving 3 inches (8 cm) between them.

10. Bake until golden (and puffy in the center), but still very soft to the touch, about 15 minutes. The logs will flatten out and lengthen as they bake. Cool logs on the baking sheet. While they are still warm, slice into 1-inch (2.5-cm) pieces. Allow to cool completely, then store in an airtight container for up to several weeks, or longer in a sea chest on a clipper ship!

SALT

Salt has complex indirect influences on flavor. Pastry chefs have always said, "Add a pinch of salt to desserts to bring out the sweetness." Dr. Gary Beauchamp and researchers at Monell Chemical Senses Center in Philadelphia have demonstrated the interplay between salt and sweetness. He has a diagram representing bitterness in a dish. When sugar is added, the bitterness drops significantly so that sweetness and bitterness are now equal in strength. Then he adds a little salt. The bitterness drops almost to nothing and there is only the sweetness left.

To experience this, taste tonic water, which has both bitter quinine and sweetness to moderate it. Pour two samples of the tonic water. Taste one plain; to the second sample, add a pinch of salt. Amazingly, bitterness is dramatically reduced and the sample is almost like sugar water!

Salt suppresses bitterness.

When you think about this, you have experienced it many times. You have seen people put salt on grapefruit or cantaloupe to make it more sweet.

CHOCOLATE

There are many great chocolate cookie recipes, but brownies are perhaps the most widely known.

The Brownie Chronicles

Brownies today contain everything imaginable, from Chambord-soaked dried cherries to chocolate-covered coffee beans and everything in between. Prices of some "gourmet" brownies start at fifty dollars a dozen.

The plain, wonderful chocolate brownie, as we know and love it, probably came from the creativity of Fannie Merritt Farmer when she drastically reduced the flour in one of her chocolate cookie recipes.

History of Brownies

In 1897, the Sears Roebuck catalog had a sweet named for the cartoon characters "Brownies," but it was not similar to brownies. There was also a recipe called "Brownies" in the 1896 *The Boston Cooking-School Cook Book,* but the recipe contained molasses and nuts—no chocolate. It was not until the 1906 revision of this book that Fannie Merritt Farmer had a chocolate brownie. It was very close to her 1896 chocolate cookie recipe with a greatly reduced amount of flour.

Maria Willett Howard, who had been trained by Fannie Farmer, added an egg to the Fannie Farmer recipe to create Lowney's Brownies for the Wilbur M. Lowney Co., a chocolate manufacturer in Boston. According to *The Oxford Encyclopedia of Food and Drink in America,* Mark H. Zanger says that the two-egg Lowney's Brownies was the recipe most often reprinted in New England community cookbooks before 1912.

The other popular early (by 1912) recipe was for Bangor Brownies, with $\frac{1}{4}$ cup butter, 1 cup brown sugar, 1 egg, 3 squares unsweetened chocolate, $\frac{1}{2}$ to $\frac{3}{4}$ cup flour, 1 cup nut meats, and $\frac{1}{4}$ teaspoon salt.

Hang On to a Good Thing

It was startling to me how little this great all-American recipe has changed through the years. Two of our modern recipes (Nick Malgieri's famous Supernatural Brownies, a current recipe, and my flavor chemist friend Dr. Sara Risch's recipe out of the sixties) are similar to that early Lowney's brownie recipe. It may appear that Nick's has twice as much chocolate; however, unsweetened chocolate has about twice as many cocoa particles as semisweet or bittersweet, so the recipes are close. For sugar, Nick uses half dark brown sugar for a wonderful fudgy taste.

Modern Popular Recipe Nick's Supernatural Brownies ($\frac{1}{2}$ recipe)	Early Recipe Lowney's Brownies	Sara Risch's Brownies from *A World of Baking* 1968
4 oz butter	4 oz butter	4 oz butter
4 oz bittersweet or semisweet chocolate	2 oz unsweetened chocolate	2 oz unsweetened chocolate
2 eggs	2 eggs	2 eggs
$\frac{1}{4}$ teaspoon salt	$\frac{1}{4}$ teaspoon salt	$\frac{1}{4}$ teaspoon salt
$\frac{1}{2}$ cup sugar	1 cup sugar	1 cup sugar
$\frac{1}{2}$ cup packed dark brown sugar		
1 teaspoon vanilla	1 to 2 teaspoons vanilla	
$\frac{1}{2}$ cup all-purpose flour	$\frac{1}{2}$ cup flour	$\frac{3}{4}$ cup all-purpose flour
	$\frac{1}{2}$ cup nuts, chopped	1 cup nuts, chopped (optional)

Brownie Techniques

Separate Shiny Crust or No Crust?

Have you ever baked or eaten a brownie with a separate crust that is lighter in color than the brownie? This crust appears on cakes frequently, too. It may look sugary, but it is actually a *meringue*. And I have just learned that it can even crop up on a chocolate chip cookie.

Whether brownies—or even some cakes and pound cakes—have a crust on top depends on how much you beat the batter after the eggs are added. The more you beat, the more crust you get. If you beat vigorously with a mixer, you can get a dramatic crust. Depending on how much you beat, this crust can be barely noticeable or a crisp, shiny crust that is totally puffed and separated above the cake or brownie. It is also usually lighter in color. The color and shine are especially noticeable on brownies.

This is a meringue-like crust and is actually caused by a mixture of egg white and sugar—or a "meringue." Your beating of the batter after the eggs are added creates the meringue-like crust. This seems not to be widely known even among chocolate experts.

My friend Dena Kalin ran a small bakery, DK's Desserts, providing primarily brownies for restaurants and caterers. She made hundreds of pans of brownies every day. This is a product that she knows inside out, but when they moved two stores down to a larger space in the same little strip shopping center, the brownies suddenly had this meringue-like crust.

I had seen this before in both cakes and brownies and knew that it was truly a meringue caused by excessive beating after the eggs were added.

Beating the butter and sugar until they are light and fluffy significantly increases the volume of baked goods, but pastry chef Bruce Healy discovered that once you add the eggs, beating no longer increases final volume. So there is no technical reason to beat beyond blending the eggs in well, and excessive beating does produce this shiny meringue-like crust. Usually you do not want it, but if you do, that is the way to get it.

The sudden crust at DK's was baffling. I knew that it had to be because the batter was being over-beaten after the eggs were added. But this was the same recipe, the same ingredients, the same procedure—same beating speed settings and time with the same equipment.

We solved the problem by reducing the mix time after the eggs were added. We did notice that the big commercial mixer, a large Hobart, seemed to beat slightly faster at the same speed setting. When we spoke with the electrician, he said it was possible because of the wiring in this section of the building—there was slightly more "juice" (voltage) available. I'm no electrician, but I do know that any change in beating speed or beating time can affect a product.

I had never seen this separate crust in chocolate chip cookies until the other day. Pat and Betty at the Reynolds test kitchen e-mailed me a photo of their cookies with a shiny crust. And sure enough, they had been beating them vigorously in a heavy mixer after the eggs were added. They were stunned at the difference when they cut the mixing to just enough to blend the eggs in well. The crust totally disappeared.

More Brownie Techniques

Alice Medrich, our Queen of Chocolate, has explored many techniques in her search for magnificent brownies. Here are a few of them.

Allowing the Batter to Mellow Before Baking

Alice will sometimes prepare the brownies, place them in the pan, cover tightly, and refrigerate overnight or for 2 or 3 days to allow the flavors to meld.

High-Temperature Baking

Most brownies are baked at 325 to 350°F/163 to 177°C. Alice wants a crisp outside and gooey inside, so she bakes for about half the normal baking time at the higher temperature of 400°F/204°C and then instantly cools the brownies by placing the brownie pan on ice in a larger pan.

Cutting Brownies

Many brownie experts prefer to well wrap completely cooled brownies and refrigerate or leave at room temperature overnight, and then place them on a cutting board and cut into individual pieces. Most think that they cut easier this way. Brownies keep best individually wrapped.

Your Perfect Brownie

Some want a cake-like brownie, while others love a fudge-like brownie. Some like a firm brownie; others want a softer brownie. Some like a crust on a brownie; others do not want a crust. Brownies can have a fudgy or a plain chocolate taste. Again, some like them one way and some the other.

Cake-Like or Fudge-Like

Remember that the brownie was literally created by drastically reducing the amount of flour in a chocolate cookie. So the ratio of flour to the other ingredients is a big deal with brownies.

The difference between fudgy and cakey brownies is the difference in the ratio of fat and chocolate to flour. The 75th anniversary edition of the *Joy of Cooking* estimates a range of fat and chocolate from 1½ cups (12 oz/340 g) butter and 5 ounces (142 g) unsweetened chocolate to 2 tablespoons (1 oz/28 g) butter and 2 ounces (57 g) unsweetened chocolate for 1 cup (4.4 oz/125 g) of flour.

For fudgy brownies use less flour; for cakey brownies, more flour. Here are recipes for both fudgy and cakey brownies. The picture in the photograph insert shows clearly the difference in the two types of brownies.

Shirley's Fudgy Brownies

MAKES ONE 13 X 9-INCH (33 X 23-CM) PAN, ABOUT 24 BROWNIES

These are truly fudgy—moist, chocolaty deliciousness!

What This Recipe Shows

Melting the chocolate with the butter prevents chocolate's seizing.

Since these brownies contain more cocoa butter than brownies made with cocoa, they will be firmer than cocoa brownies using butter as their primary fat.

Salt suppresses bitterness to bring out the sweetness of brownies.

Dark brown sugar gives chocolate a fudgy taste.

1$\frac{1}{2}$ cups (5.2 oz/149 g) pecans
1$\frac{1}{2}$ cups plus 2 tablespoons (13 oz/369 g) unsalted butter, cut in 1-tablespoon (0.5-oz/14-g) pieces, divided
Nonstick cooking spray, optional
12 ounces (339 g) semisweet chocolate, finely chopped
1 ounce (28 g) German's Sweet Chocolate
4 large eggs (7 oz/198 g)
3 large egg yolks (1.95 oz/55 g)

1$\frac{1}{2}$ cups (12.6 oz/357 g) dark brown sugar, packed
1 cup (4 oz/120 g) confectioners' sugar
2 tablespoons (0.9 oz/25 g) granulated sugar
3 tablespoons (45 ml) light corn syrup
1 tablespoon (15 ml) pure vanilla extract
$\frac{3}{4}$ teaspoon (4.5 g) salt
1$\frac{1}{2}$ cups (6.6 oz/187 g) spooned and leveled bleached all-purpose flour

1. Arrange a shelf in the middle of the oven and preheat the oven to 300°F/149°C.

2. Spread the pecans on a baking sheet and roast for 10 minutes. While the nuts are hot, stir in 2 tablespoons (1 oz/28 g) of the butter. When cool, coarsely chop and set aside.

3. Line a 13 x 9 x 2-inch (33 x 23 x 5-cm) pan with parchment sprayed with nonstick cooking spray or Release foil (nonstick side up), allowing overhang on both long sides to make removal easier.

4. Place the remaining 1$\frac{1}{2}$ cups (12 oz/340 g) butter around the edge of a microwave-safe glass bowl. Place the semisweet and sweet chocolate in the center. Melt the butter and chocolate in the microwave on 100% power for 1 minute, stirring at least 2 times, and then 15 seconds more, stirring 1 time. Or, place the chocolates and butter together in a stainless-steel bowl. In a large skillet, bring water to a simmer. Set aside until the water is no longer steaming. Place the bowl of chocolate and butter in the hot water, being careful not to get water or steam into the chocolate. Stir the chocolate every few minutes until melted.

5. In a large bowl, beat the eggs with a fork just to blend whites and yolks. With a minimum of hand stirring, stir together the eggs, egg yolks, brown sugar, confectioners' sugar, granulated sugar, corn syrup, vanilla, and salt.

6. By hand, with a minimum of stirring, stir together the egg mixture and the chocolate mixture. Stir in the flour. Pour the batter into the prepared pan and smooth out. Soak cake strips in water and wrap around the outside edge of the pan as directed. (See Sources, cake strips, page 508.)

7. Place the pan on the arranged shelf and bake until brownies just begin to pull away from the edge of the pan, about 1 hour. *Err on the side of undercooking* rather than risk drying out the brownies. A toothpick inserted should come out wet with gooey chocolate.

8. Cool completely in the pan on a rack. Remove the brownies from the pan, using the parchment or foil overhang to help lift out the brownies. When completely cool, wrap the brownies well with plastic wrap and refrigerate overnight.

9. Place the brownies on a cutting board and remove the parchment or foil. Place another cutting board on top and turn over so that the brownies are right side up. Trim the edges and cut into 2-inch (5-cm) squares. Wrap individually in plastic wrap and store refrigerated.

Shirley's Cakey Brownies

MAKES ONE 13 X 9-INCH (33 X 23-CM) PAN, ABOUT 24 BROWNIES

I am a fudgy brownie lover, but for those who like cakey brownies, these are heavenly.

What This Recipe Shows

Melting the chocolate with the butter prevents chocolate's seizing.

Since these brownies contain more cocoa butter than brownies made with cocoa, they will be firmer than cocoa brownies using butter as their primary fat.

Salt suppresses bitterness to bring out the sweetness of brownies.

1½ cups (5.2 oz/149 g) pecans
1½ cups plus 2 tablespoons (13 oz/369 g)
    unsalted butter, cut in 2-tablespoon
    (1-oz/28-g) pieces, divided
Nonstick cooking spray, optional
12 ounces (339 g) semisweet chocolate, finely
    chopped
1 ounce (28 g) German's Sweet Chocolate
4 large eggs (7 oz/198 g)
3 large egg yolks (1.95 oz/55 g)
1 cup (4 oz/120 g) confectioners' sugar

¾ cup (5.3 oz/150 g) granulated sugar
¾ cup (6.3 oz/179 g) dark brown sugar,
    packed
3 tablespoons (45 ml) light corn syrup
1 tablespoon (15 ml) pure vanilla extract
2¼ cups (9.9 oz/281 g) spooned and leveled
    bleached all-purpose flour
1 teaspoon (5 g) baking powder
¾ teaspoon (4.5 g) salt
⅓ cup (79 ml) whole milk

1. Arrange a shelf in the middle of the oven and preheat the oven to 300°F/149°C.

2. Spread the pecans on a baking sheet and roast for 10 minutes. While the nuts are hot, stir in 2 tablespoons (1 oz/28 g) of the butter. When cool, coarsely chop and set aside.

3. Line a 13 x 9 x 2-inch (33 x 23 x 5-cm) pan with parchment sprayed with nonstick cooking spray or Release foil (nonstick side up), allowing overhang on both long sides to make removal easier.

4. Place the remaining 1½ cups (12 oz/340 g) butter and the semisweet and sweet chocolates in a microwave-safe bowl. Microwave on 100% power for 1 minute, stirring at least 2 times, and then 15 seconds more, stirring 1 time. Or, place chocolates and butter together in a stainless-steel bowl. In a large skillet, bring water to a simmer. Set aside until the water is no longer steaming. Place the

bowl of chocolate and butter in the hot water, being careful not to get water or steam into the chocolate. Stir the chocolate every few minutes until melted.

5. In a large bowl, beat the eggs with a fork just to blend whites and yolks. Beat together the eggs, egg yolks, confectioners' sugar, granulated sugar, dark brown sugar, corn syrup, and vanilla.

6. By hand, with a minimum of stirring, stir together the egg mixture and the chocolate mixture. Beat together the flour, baking powder, and salt. Stir the flour mixture into the batter, then stir in the milk. Pour the batter into the prepared pan and smooth out. Soak cake strips in water and wrap around the outside edge of the pan as directed. (See Sources, cake strips, page 508.)

7. Place the pan on the arranged shelf. Bake until the brownies just begin to pull away from the edge of the pan, about 1 hour. *Err on the side of undercooking* rather than risk drying. A toothpick inserted should come out wet with gooey chocolate.

8. Cool completely in the pan on a rack. Remove the brownies from the pan, using the parchment or foil overhang to help. When completely cool, wrap the brownies well with plastic wrap and refrigerate overnight.

9. Place the brownies on a cutting board and remove parchment. Place another cutting board on top and turn over so that the brownies are right side up. Trim the edges and cut into 2-inch (5-cm) squares. Wrap individually in plastic wrap and store refrigerated.

Much Depends on the Chocolate

There are many chocolate choices, more now than ever: unsweetened, semisweet or bittersweet, sweet chocolate (like German's), high-percentage chocolates, and natural and Dutch process cocoa. We will see below that cocoa is a necessity for a softer brownie whose primary fat is butter.

My daughter Terry Infantino, who helps me test recipes, adores Robert Steinberg's Fudgy Brownies in *The Essence of Chocolate* (his book with John Scharffenberger). They are made with a large amount of 70% Scharffen Berger bittersweet chocolate. His recipe contains the usual ½ cup (2.2 oz/62 g) flour, and 2 large eggs (3.5 oz/99 g). His amount of sugar, ¾ cup plus 2 tablespoons (6.2 oz/175 g), is only 2 tablespoons (0.9 oz/56 g) less than the original brownie recipe (page 408). It is the chocolate that makes the difference in his brownies.

My husband's absolute favorite brownies were made by Dena Kalin, a friend who owned an Atlanta bakery that specialized in brownies, and made hundreds of pounds of brownies a week for restaurants and restaurant chains. Dena used quality commercial brands of both semisweet and sweet chocolate in her outstanding brownies.

Firm Brownie or Softer Brownie

If a brownie contains chocolate, it will have cocoa butter, which is firm when cold. If the brownie contains cocoa, it will have much less cocoa butter than chocolate and will contain butter as its primary fat. Since firm butter is softer when cool than firm cocoa butter, cocoa brownies will be softer than chocolate brownies.

Alice Medrich also points out that cocoa brownies have more granulated sugar since they don't have superfinely ground sugar like the sugar in sweetened chocolate. And, she feels that granulated sugar gives them a crunchier crust.

Brown Sugar

In addition to different chocolates for different flavors, many years ago Marcel Desaulniers, another chocolate expert, taught me that brown sugar (with a touch of molasses) gives chocolate dishes a fudgy taste. Even with other flavors, brown sugar enhances taste, as evidenced in the Super Rich Espresso Brownies recipe below. Espresso brownies are a popular brownie variation. I love the crunch of the chocolate-covered espresso beans.

Super Rich Espresso Brownies

MAKES ONE 8 X 8-INCH (20 X 20-CM) PAN, ABOUT 16 BROWNIES

These are very moist, very chocolaty, great brownies.

1½ cups (7 oz/150 g) walnuts
1 cup plus 2 tablespoons (9 oz/254 g) unsalted butter, cut in 1-tablespoon (0.5-oz/14-g) pieces, divided
Nonstick cooking spray, optional
7 ounces (198 g) semisweet chocolate, chopped (my favorite is Hershey's Special Dark, available in most grocery stores with the candy bars, not the chocolate chips)
1 scant cup (5 oz/142 g) milk chocolate chips
1 cup (7.7 oz/218 g) light brown sugar, packed
1 tablespoon (15 ml) pure vanilla extract

2 large eggs (3.5 oz/99 g)
3 large egg yolks (1.95 oz/55 g)
1 cup (4.4 oz/125 g) spooned and leveled bleached all-purpose flour
2 tablespoons (0.2 oz/5 g) instant espresso powder
½ teaspoon (3 g) salt
½ cup (3.5 oz/99 g) chocolate-covered espresso beans (available at coffee shops)
4 ounces (113 g) milk chocolate chunks (chocolate nuggets, cut in half, or from a big candy bar cut in chunks) or mini kisses

1. Arrange a shelf in the center of the oven and preheat the oven to 350°F/177 °C.

2. Spread out the walnuts on a baking sheet and bake for 10 minutes. Remove from the oven and while still hot, stir in 2 tablespoons (1 oz/28 g) of the butter. When cool, coarsely chop and set aside.

3. Line an 8 x 8-inch (20 x 20-cm) pan with parchment sprayed with nonstick cooking spray, or Release foil (nonstick side up).

4. In a large microwave-safe glass bowl, arrange the remaining 1 cup (8 oz/227 g) butter around the edge of the bowl. Place the semisweet chocolate and milk chocolate chips in the center and microwave on 100% power for 1 minute, stir, and then microwave 1 minute more. Allow to stand a few minutes, and then stir again. If all the chocolate is not melted, microwave another minute and stir.

5. Stir in the sugar and vanilla. In a small bowl, stir together the eggs and yolks, then stir this mixture into the chocolate mixture, just enough to blend well.

6. Stir in the flour, espresso powder, and salt. When well blended, stir in the walnuts, espresso beans, and chocolate chunks. Pour into the prepared pan and bake 30 to 35 minutes. The brownies should just start to pull away from the edge of the pan. Allow to cool about 5 minutes. Invert on a cutting board, then reinvert so that the top is up. Cut into 16 brownies. Wrap individually in plastic wrap and store refrigerated.

Cookie Techniques

Cookie-making techniques are fortunately simpler than those of many other baked goods. Cakes, for example, can have a number of mixing and baking techniques, while there are fewer for cookies.

MIXING

Mixing is usually pretty straightforward—butter and sugar are creamed, eggs stirred in, dry ingredients stirred in.

The creaming step (which is a major contributor to leavening) is not nearly as important in cookies as it is in cakes. I like to use cold butter, cut in 1 to 2-tablespoon (14 to 28-g) chunks, and I usually beat until the butter and sugar are light and fluffy. Be sure to scrape down the bowl and beat again. If any lumps of butter are left at this stage, you cannot get them out when the batter becomes more liquid with the eggs.

Beat in each egg just enough to blend. It is vital not to beat much once you have added the eggs. This can produce a separate meringue-like crust on top. This is especially a problem with brownies. (See page 409 for more details.)

With cookies, the dough can be very thick and many times it is best to work the last of the flour in by hand rather than strain a mixer.

In small cookie batches at home, blending of ingredients is usually not a problem, but with big batches this can be a disaster. Rose Concepcion, the former executive pastry chef at EatZi's and now owner of MIX The Bakery in Vancouver, explained to me that scraping down and proper blending with each ingredient is a big factor in making huge batches of cookies with commercial mixers. If the ingredients are not thoroughly blended, there can be more butter in the bottom and more flour in the top. So for the batches scooped off the top, the cookies are dry, while those off the bottom spread too much.

SHAPING

Many doughs can be shaped by a number of different techniques. The dough for Buttery Jelly-Jeweled Cookies (page 386) can be piped, rolled into balls then flattened, scooped with an ice cream scoop (drop cookies), or shaped into logs, chilled, and then sliced (refrigerator cookies). Many times, the shaping technique is a matter of personal preference.

But there are some cookies that must be shaped in a certain way, like the paper-thin Moravian cookies (page 418) or molded springerle cookies that are pressed with a beautiful three-dimensional design.

Drop Cookies

Many cookie recipes give "drop cookie" directions saying something like, "Spoon the dough in tablespoon-size portions onto the baking sheet, 2 inches (5 cm) apart." I love to use ice cream scoops for drop cookies so that they are all the same size. I have several different-sized scoops to cover most of the cookie sizes.

Many cooks like to use a large pastry bag with different tips, and others prefer a cookie shooter (cookie press).

Refrigerator Cookies

The refrigerator cookie technique—rolling cookie dough into logs, chilling, then slicing off and baking—has a number of advantages. It is quick and easy and the dough keeps for several days, so you can slice off just what you need and refrigerate the rest.

Rolled Cookies

The ultimate rolled cookies are the paper-thin Moravian Molasses Cookies, page 418. Properly rolled, this dough is so thin that you can see through it. These are the cookies sold in cardboard tube containers at Christmas.

Great Grandmother Schorr's recipe (below) is from Janice, my daughter-in-law, who is a wonderful cook. Her mother, Bonnie Wagner, has always made these cookies, so I consulted with Bonnie.

Actually, several years back, I had gotten the recipe from Bonnie for my friend Rose Levy Beranbaum for her *Rose's Christmas Cookies* book. Bonnie's recipe makes over 900 cookies and takes all day just to roll out and bake. Rose divided the recipe by eight and I agree that that makes a good-sized batch, over 100 cookies.

I have been accustomed to eating these spicy cookies, both commercial and homemade, for years and love them with Bonnie's exact spice ratios. This amount of spice gives you a slight after-sting like a mild chili pepper.

If this cookie dough is rolled fairly thin, not as paper thin as for the Moravian cookies, but less than $\frac{1}{8}$ inch (0.3 cm), it is an ideal dough to use for intricate cut-out cookies like snowflake patterns. The beautiful snowflake cookies (see photograph insert) were made by my very patient son-in-law, Carmelo Infantino. This dough does not spread much when rolled this thin and preserves the intricate patterns. A cookie cutter set of seven snowflake designs is available from specialty cookie-cutter suppliers (see Sources, cookie cutters, page 508). To get the beautiful cookies that Carmelo made requires not only the snowflake cookie cutter for the outside pattern, but infinite patience with a tiny cutter, cutting out the interior design.

Great Grandmother Schorr's Moravian Molasses Cookies

MAKES ABOUT 100 VERY THIN COOKIES

These are classic Christmas cookies, and make perfect gifts.

What This Recipe Shows

Letting the dough stand overnight allows the moisture to be evenly spread. In other words, there are not wet spots that will stick when rolling and there are not dry spots that will tear. This is vital for a dough that is rolled so thin.

¼ cup (1.6 oz/45 g) shortening

⅓ cup (2.5 oz/72 g) light brown sugar, packed

½ cup (118 ml) unsulfured molasses, such as Grandma's

1¼ cups (5.7 oz/162 g) spooned and leveled all-purpose flour

1½ teaspoons (7 g) baking soda

1½ teaspoons (3 g) ground cloves

1½ teaspoons (3 g) ground cinnamon

1½ teaspoons (3 g) ground ginger

Nonstick cooking spray, optional

1. In a large mixing bowl, beat the shortening and sugar with a mixer until fluffy. Add the molasses and beat until well blended. In a large mixing bowl, stir together the flour, baking soda, cloves, cinnamon, and ginger. Add one-third of the dry mixture to molasses mixture and blend in on the lowest speed. Add another third and blend in, then add the final third and blend in. Cover the dough with plastic wrap and leave on the counter overnight.

2. Bonnie uses a large flour sack that is well floured as a surface to roll out the dough. I think a floured pastry cloth will work perfectly. Take a handful of dough and shape it into an 8-inch (20-cm) disc, about 1 inch (2.5 cm) high, as you might do in making a pie crust. Keep the rest of the dough tightly covered.

3. You want to use only the smallest amount of flour possible to keep the dough from sticking. This takes practice. Roll as thin as you are comfortable. Bonnie said sometimes when Grandmother Schorr was in a hurry she didn't bother to roll them really as thin as they should be. Your first time or two making these, you may want to settle for a little short of see-through thin.

4. Place a rack in the center of the oven and preheat the oven to 325°F/163°C.

5. Cover a baking sheet with Release foil (nonstick side up), or parchment sprayed with nonstick cooking spray.

6. Cut the cookies with a fluted 2½-inch (6-cm) cookie cutter and place on the baking sheet about 1 inch (2.5 cm) apart.

7. Bake for 8 to 10 minutes, until edges just begin to color.

8. Remove the foil or parchment with the cookies to a rack. Allow the cookies to cool 2 minutes, then remove to a rack to cool completely. Store in an airtight container.

Snowflake Cookies

Prepare one recipe of the dough for Great Grandmother Schorr's Moravian Molasses Cookies, above. Roll out the dough according to the directions above. Cut with a snowflake cookie cutter. Bake as directed in Steps 4 to 8 of the recipe. This will make about 30 intricate snowflakes.

BAKING

Baking cookies requires care and attention. The baking sheet, the oven, the position in the oven, and the time all matter.

Baking sheets are a personal preference. A heavy sheet is an advantage. You don't want a sheet so thin that it may warp violently in the middle of baking and plaster your cookies against the oven wall. Primarily, a heavy sheet distributes the heat for more even baking.

The darker the sheet, the more heat it will absorb and the faster the bottoms of the cookies will brown. Some cooks are accustomed to the dark sheets and use oven positions and temperatures to account for their fast cooking.

My personal preference is for heavy, dull aluminum pans because of their wonderfully even heat conductivity. At a good cookware shop, you can buy commercial-quality aluminum half-sheet pans that are excellent.

My favorite pans in the world are flat sheets of very heavy aluminum (more than twice the thickness of any that you can buy) that I got out of the scrap bin at a sheet metal company. They polished the sharp edges so that I would not be cut by them.

Some people like insulated cookie sheets. These are not going to provide much heat from the bottom. Cooks whose ovens or cooking techniques are such that they constantly burn cookies on the bottom like these types of sheets.

New expensive ovens cook very evenly throughout and really do cook evenly with several pans on different racks. But most ovens do not, so I have always advised cooking one pan at a time in the center or slightly above the center of the oven.

Many chefs advise rotating the pan once during cooking for more even baking.

The cooking time for cookies is so short that a minute matters and some cookies will taste burned if they are allowed to brown.

As far as cooking time goes, cookies really need to be watched. I think most cookies should be removed from the oven when they just start to brown around the edges. The cooking time is so short that a minute matters, and some cookies will taste burned (for example, the cheese coins, page 403) if they are allowed to brown.

Cookie Problems

One of the big problems across the board with cookies is spread, puff, and shape. Because of the complexity, I will save that for last and take care of the other problems first.

Some of the other cookie problems are: crumbly cookies, shiny crust, pale cookies, limp cookies, sticking, and overbaking.

CRUMBLY COOKIES

As one grandmother put it, "My cookies are delicious, but when I send them to my grandchildren, they arrive as a tin full of crumbs."

The problem is not enough gluten to hold the cookies together. When a cook adds water to flour and stirs, two proteins (glutenin and gliadin) in the flour grab water and each other to form tough, elastic, bubble-gum-like sheets of gluten. Gluten is tough and strong, and holds baked goods together.

Gluten holds baked goods together.

Sometimes, like in a pie crust, you want only a little gluten, just enough to hold the crust together. Too much will make it tough. To make a tender pie crust, the cook works fat into the dry flour, greasing the two proteins so that there is no way that they can grab water and each other to make gluten. Ideally, the cook coats a lot of the proteins for tenderness, but leaves enough uncoated with fat to make a little gluten to keep the crust from being crumbly.

Adding sugar is another way to prevent gluten from being formed. If a lot of sugar is present, glutenin combines with sugar, gliadin combines with sugar, and very little gluten is formed. The classic French pie crust called pâte sablée contains more sugar than the crust called pâte sucrée (sugar crust). "Sablée" means sandy, and this crust has so much sugar and is so crumbly that it is usually pressed into the pan with your fingers instead of being rolled.

Now you have the picture. Both fat worked into flour and the sugar can prevent gluten from being formed. It is no wonder cookies are crumbly—they are full of fat and sugar. What can you do?

Fat and sugar prevent gluten from being formed.

Make gluten first—before you let the fat or the sugar get near the flour, make a little gluten. Take the flour or part of the flour that you are using in the cookies and, before mixing with other ingredients, stir in about half a tablespoon (8 ml) of water per cup (4.4 oz/124 g) of flour in the recipe. For a recipe using 2 cups (8.8 oz/249 g) of flour, stir in 1 tablespoon (15 ml) of water. It will make some little lumps. Don't worry; they disappear when everything else is mixed together.

This amount of water on the flour will usually give you cookies that hold together but are not tough. You can get any texture you want by the amount of water that you work into the flour. You can even make a cookie so tough that you can throw it across the room and it won't break!

You can get any texture you want by the amount of water that you work into the flour. You can make a cookie so tough that you can throw it across the room and it won't break!

The Wedding Cookies (page 422), which have plenty of butter, and ground pecans to replace some of the flour, are notoriously crumbly. You will see that adding water to the flour, before it is blended with the butter, makes a little gluten and makes these cookies a little less crumbly than most Wedding Cookies.

Wedding Cookies

MAKES ABOUT 4 DOZEN COOKIES

These snow-white, delicate cookies are sweet, nutty morsels of delight. They literally fall apart in your mouth.

What This Recipe Shows

A tablespoon of water is sprinkled over the flour, and stirred in to make a little gluten to limit crumbling of these delicate cookies.

These cookies are notoriously crumbly because of the large amount of finely chopped nuts and the fact that, in a traditional recipe, the only water in the recipe is in the butter.

Nonstick cooking spray, optional
1 cup (8 oz/227 g) unsalted butter
2½ cups (10 oz/286 g) confectioners' sugar, divided
1 tablespoon (15 ml) pure vanilla extract
1 tablespoon (15 ml) water
2 cups (9 oz/255 g) spooned and leveled all-purpose flour
¼ teaspoon (1.5 g) salt
¾ cup (2.9 oz/82 g) finely chopped pecans

1. Place a rack in the center of the oven and preheat the oven to 325°F/163°C.

2. Cover a baking sheet with Release foil (nonstick side up), or parchment sprayed with nonstick cooking spray.

3. In a heavy-duty mixer with the paddle attachment, beat the butter and ½ cup (2 oz/60 g) of the confectioners' sugar until fluffy. Beat in the vanilla.

4. In a medium mixing bowl, sprinkle the water over the flour and stir, then stir in the salt. Add the flour mixture to the mixer in several batches and beat on the lowest speed just to blend in. When all the flour is added, add the pecans and blend in.

5. Roll the dough into balls about the size of a walnut and place on the baking sheet about 1 inch (2.5 cm) apart. Bake until set but not browned, about 20 minutes.

6. While the cookies are warm, lift them with a spatula, one at a time, into a large mixing bowl with the remaining 2 cups (8 oz/227 g) confectioners' sugar. Gently roll them in the confectioners' sugar several times to coat generously, then place on a rack to cool. Reroll once again in confectioners' sugar before storing in an airtight container.

SHINY CRUST

Shiny crust in cookies is usually a desirable, rather than undesirable, trait. In Shirley's Corrupted Black Gold (page 401), we see this slightly shiny, crisp surface as a perfect contrast to the soft chocolate center. It is produced by beating the dough after the eggs are added (see page 409 for more on separate shiny crusts).

PITIFULLY PALE COOKIES—BROWNING

"My cookies taste good, but they are pale and unappetizing looking." Three ingredients determine color: the amount of a specific type sugar (reducing sugar), the amount of protein, and the acidity.

More Reducing Sugar

Using even a small amount of corn syrup (glucose), which is a reducing sugar, is a major browning enhancer. Adding 1 tablespoon (15 ml) of corn syrup to your cookie dough will dramatically increase browning. That is, as long as the cookies are not strongly acidic. Too much acidity prevents browning.

Using even a small amount of corn syrup (glucose), which is a reducing sugar, is a major browning enhancer.

More Protein

To enhance browning, you can increase the protein by switching to a higher-protein flour like bread flour or unbleached all-purpose flour. Cake flour helps limit spread because it is acidic, and it is low in protein, but both acidity and low-protein content reduce browning.

Less Acidity

Baking powder contains baking soda and enough acid or acids to neutralize the baking soda, therefore baking powder does not influence the color of cookies. Baking soda by itself is alkaline and is a major contributor to browning.

Some cookie recipes that contain acidic ingredients like brown sugar may contain baking soda—not for leavening, but to reduce the acidity and improve browning.

LIMP COOKIES

"My cookies are crisp and perfect the day I make them, but the next day they are soft and limp." If your recipe calls for brown sugar, molasses, or honey, they all contain some fructose, a sugar that is hygroscopic (absorbs water out of the air). Honey contains 42% fructose and baked goods made with honey keep well. They stay soft and don't dry out easily. Some cookie recipes with part brown sugar stay firm for a day or so, but if you want really crisp cookies stick with plain granulated sugar.

STICKING

Some recipes say to bake on an ungreased pan to limit spread. This is a bad idea. It doesn't limit spread, and the cookies can stick as if they were cemented to the pan.

I love the new Reynolds Release foil. It is a miracle for cookies. It is aluminum foil with a nonstick coating on one side. (This stuff is great. It may not be in every supermarket yet, but it is pretty widely available.) Just twist a cookie and lift off. I like it even better than parchment, because sometimes cookies can stick to even parchment. You can slide the foil off the cookie sheet and onto the cooling rack. Your pan is free for the next batch.

You can already have the next batch on foil. Cool the hot pan by running cold water over it, dry, and slide the foil with your next batch onto it. No more washing dirty cookie pans.

In the past I used parchment, but if I did not have it I always sprayed the pan with nonstick cooking spray or a nonstick cooking spray with flour such as Baker's Joy.

You can get cookies that are "glued" to the pan off by reheating for a couple of minutes.

Without Release foil or parchment, there is an ideal time to remove cookies from the baking sheet. If you try to remove them immediately after they come out of the oven, they come apart, but if you wait 1 to 2 minutes, they will lift off the pan easily. If you wait longer, they may be "glued" to the pan. You can reheat the cookies for a couple of minutes, then remove them.

OVERBAKING

Overcooked cookies can be rock hard. Since cookies require a short baking time, some as short as 6 minutes, and for most 10 to 12 minutes, 1 minute more or less can make a world of difference. Take cookies out of the oven when they just start to brown around the outer edge. Don't wait for the center to brown.

Other Cookie Problems At a Glance

Problem	What to Do
Crumbling	Stir 1 tablespoon (15 ml) water into the flour before you mix it with other ingredients.
Lighter, shiny separated crust ("meringue")	Stir just enough to incorporate each egg. Keep any beating to a minimum once eggs are added.
Cookies are pale	Add 1 tablespoon (15 ml) light corn syrup. Use baking soda. Use a higher-protein flour like unbleached or all-purpose bread flour.
Cookies are limp	Use granulated sugar only, no honey.
Cookies stick to pan	Use Release foil (foil with a nonstick coating).
Cookies are overbaked	Do not wait for cookies to brown. Remove from the oven when the edges start to brown.

Spread in a Low-Moisture World

Unfortunately, one man's perfect cookie is another man's disaster. Personal preference is a very real consideration in cookie making. Some people love a soft, puffy cookie, others go for flat, crisp cookies. My goal is to give you information so that you can get the kind of cookie that you want.

Spread is a frequent cookie problem. "The cookies were very flat with the chocolate sticking up like little bumps. I wanted a nice puffy cookie."

Controlling spread would seem to be a simple matter. If the dough is wet, the cookies will spread more. If it is firmer, they will spread less. Some doughs are clearly too wet. The minute you scoop a spoon onto the baking sheet you see it spreading out bigger and thinner than you wanted. It is clear that you have to reduce the liquid or increase the flour.

There are also doughs that are thick—the cookie is a solid ball when you put it on the cookie sheet, but after a few minutes in the oven, it spreads out to make a thin cookie. What happened here?

Cookies are a microcosm of cooking. The role of each ingredient is magnified in this low-liquid situation. Not just a change in the amount of liquid (many cookies have no liquid as such), but any change in ingredients that changes the available liquid in the dough can change the spread of the cookies—the type

Any change in ingredients that changes the available liquid or the acidity in the dough can change the spread of the cookies.

and amount of fat, the type and amount of flour, the type and amount of liquid, the acidity of the dough, the type and amount of sugar, and even the type of chocolate.

We will go over each of these ingredients and how they can change spread.

Type of Fat

The type of fat in a cookie has a major influence on the spread. Cookies made with butter, which has a sharp melting point, can spread significantly. Of course, other ingredients influence the spread, too. Butter cookies, although they are made from a high percentage of butter, do not spread much because the only liquid is from the butter (16% water in butter) and the egg yolks.

Cookies made with butter-flavored shortening that stays the same consistency over a range of temperatures hold their shape much better. If you have an all-butter cookie that is spreading too much, one of the easiest ways to limit spread is to substitute butter-flavored shortening for part or all of the butter. As I mentioned earlier, there is no bigger butter lover than me, but, in many recipes, the flavor of cookies made with butter-flavored shortening can beat cookies made with butter in a blind taste test.

Amount of Fat

The amount of fat, or to be more exact the fat-to-flour ratio, can control spread. But as you see in the section in *CookWise* entitled "Three different cookies from the same recipe" (pages 131 to 132), you can totally change the spread using the same amount, but a different type of fat. So in many cases, the type of fat has more control of the spread than the amount.

Type and Amount of Flour

With flour, the reverse is true. Ordinarily, the amount of flour has more influence on spread than the type. Some chefs use the amount of flour or, more correctly, a high flour-to-fat ratio as their main method of limiting spread.

In most baked goods, the type of flour (high-protein or low-protein) has a major influence on the amount of liquid absorbed. It still does in cookies, but to a limited degree. Flour absorbs water when its proteins join to form gluten. But because of the large amount of fat and sugar in cookies, the amount of gluten formed is limited.

Nevertheless, type of flour can still influence the amount of liquid absorbed and thus have a little control over spread. Flour has more influence in some cookies than others. The sequence of combining ingredients—whether the flour can get to the liquid before it is totally coated with fat—can give flour more or less spread control. In the section on Crumbly Cookies (see page 421), I add a tablespoon of water directly to the flour to deliberately make some gluten to hold the cookie together. This water is completely absorbed and does not influence spread at all.

Type and Amount of Liquid

The amount of liquid, just like the amount of flour, determines the wetness of the dough and, thus, the spread. Many cookies have no liquid, per se—only the water in the butter or egg.

If the liquid in the dough is eggs, the softness of the dough may be deceiving. Eggs are proteins that can set pretty fast in a hot oven. A dough with eggs may appear wet but actually will not spread much. And, of course, you can always go with one or two egg yolks instead of a whole egg to limit spread.

Acidity of the Dough: Choice of Leaveners, Choice of Cocoa

Whether you use baking soda or baking powder can have a major influence on spread. An acidic dough speeds up the cooking of the proteins and the setting of cookies, and helps limit spread. Baking soda neutralizes acidity while baking powder does not.

Brown sugar, chocolate, and other cookie ingredients are mildly acidic, so a lot of cookie doughs are nicely acidic to set well. But if you add baking soda, an alkali, the dough is no longer acidic and the cookies may spread significantly more.

The type of cocoa that you choose—plain or Dutch process—makes a major change in the acidity of the dough and can make a drastic change in the cookie. Earlier in this chapter, on page 399, I told the story of the perfectly setting biscotti that was reduced to a puddle by the alkaline Dutch process cocoa.

Type and Amount of Sugar

The coarser the sugar granule, the less it dissolves and the less the cookie spreads. Confectioners' sugar can cause the greatest spread because it dissolves easily.

Brown sugar is slightly acidic, so brown sugar can help limit spread by making proteins set faster. Amount of sugar also influences spread. Cookies with an excessive amount of sugar will spread more.

Type and Amount of Chocolate

I have realized for a long time that cocoa, which is a fine dry powder, acts like flour in a recipe. If you change a recipe to make a chocolate version and add cocoa, you should subtract the amount of cocoa from the amount of flour. For example, if you add 1/2 cup of cocoa, you should reduce the flour by about 1/2 cup.

Recently, I was impressed with how much difference the types of chocolate can make on the dough texture. Chocolate's basic ingredients are cocoa particles, cocoa butter, and sugar. Since unsweetened baking chocolate does not have as much sugar as semisweet, for the same amount it contains more cocoa particles. Just like cocoa, this can act to thicken the dough and limit spread.

If you have a chocolate cookie with melted semisweet chocolate that is spreading more than you want, you can replace a little of the semisweet chocolate with melted unsweetened chocolate or cocoa.

Substituting melted unsweetened baking chocolate or cocoa for melted semisweet will reduce the spread.

Fine-Tuning Cookies At a Glance

What to Do for More Spread

Use all butter.

Increase the amount of fat.

Add 1 to 2 tablespoons liquid (water, milk, or cream—not egg).

Use a low-protein flour like bleached all-purpose (but not one that is chlorinated).

Cut the amount of flour.

Add 1 to 2 tablespoons sugar.

Use semi- or bittersweet chocolate.

Use Dutch process cocoa.

Use room-temperature ingredients or let dough stand at room temperature.

What to Do for More Puff

Everything under Less Spread.

What to Do for More Tenderness

Use cake flour (low-protein flour).

Add a few tablespoons of sugar. Add a few tablespoons of fat.

What to Do for More Color

Use an egg for liquid.

Use unbleached all-purpose or bread flour.

Substitute 1 to 2 tablespoons of light corn syrup for sugar.

What to Do for Less Spread

Use shortening or reduced fat that spreads.

Decrease the amount of fat.

Use an egg for liquid.

Use cake flour.

Increase the amount of flour.

Cut the sugar by a few tablespoons. Switch from baking powder to baking soda (which is alkaline).

Use unsweetened chocolate.

Use regular cocoa.

Use cold ingredients or chill dough before going into the oven.

What to Do for Less Puff

Everything under More Spread.

What to Do for Less Tenderness

Use unbleached or bread flour (high-protein flour).

Cut the sugar by a few tablespoons. Cut the fat by a few tablespoons.

Add a tablespoon or more of water to the flour before combining with other ingredients.

What to Do for Less Color

Use water for liquid.

Use cake flour or bleached all-purpose.

CHAPTER FIVE

Great Breads—Great Flavors

Priceless Knowledge in This Chapter

Techniques and ingredients to get wonderful flavors from the most basic bread ingredients (flour, water, yeast, and salt)

Techniques that apply across the board to all kinds of breads

Simple techniques for wonderful, complex flavors—like making a predough of a small amount of yeast and some flour and water and allowing this to stand (ferment) overnight

How mixing flour and water and allowing it to stand for 20 minutes or more before making the dough enhances the extensibility of the dough for better-volume loaves, and reduces oxidation for better-flavored loaves

Recipes Include

Incredibly flavorful, crusty French breads from baguettes to fougasse

Runny cheese–filled focaccia

Open-textured rustic rounds

Milk-and-honey whole wheat

Golden, buttery brioche

The Recipes

Throughout this chapter, my emphasis is on techniques and ingredients that produce not just handsome, successful breads, but breads that taste wonderful. In many breads, there are only flour, water, yeast, and salt, but the type of flour and the choice of techniques can create thousands of different flavors. This is the difference between good bread and great bread.

There is much interest in breads like those of Old World village bakers. We love the wonderful flavors from slower rising and longer fermentation, and the flavors of the grain. In this fight for great flavors, I quote frequently from the French master Professor Raymond Calvel, author of *The Taste of Bread*. And my whole world of bread making was changed by classes from the U.S. teacher Didier Rosada, one of the coaches who has taken our Team U.S.A. to victory in the World Cup of Baking (Coupe du Monde de la Boulangerie) that is held every three years. Team U.S.A. won in 1999 and again in 2005. Can you believe it—our American bakers made better baguettes than the French and the Italians!

In a bread chapter, everything needs to come first—details about the ingredients, which flour to use and why; the vital techniques, why you should do this or that for great bread. I have decided to start with all-important techniques. If you have burning questions about an ingredient, feel free to skip ahead and read all about the ingredients.

We will see below that bread-making techniques are very much involved in this fight for flavor. Holding on to the flavorful carotenoid compounds requires attention through kneading, rising, and baking. For example, I can easily lose these precious flavors when oxygen combines with them during kneading. So I am going to carefully knead minimally.

QUICK OVERVIEW OF INGREDIENTS

Flour

Didier Rosada turned everything that I thought I knew about flour upside down. I had wanted the highest protein hard spring wheat for the strongest doughs and the fastest rise. I felt confident that I would get the highest loaves with this flour.

But, from Didier, I learned that using unbleached hard red winter wheat flour, a medium-protein flour treasured for its flavorful carotenoid compounds, not only made more flavorful breads, but because it makes doughs with great extensibility, it can make even higher loaves than the higher-protein flours! (See page 468 for more about flour.)

> Unbleached hard red winter wheat flour is prized for its flavorful carotenoid compounds.

"Strange" Ingredients

Yes, I do use tiny amounts of "strange" ingredients. These "strange" ingredients are used by bakers in French bakeries.

Vitamin C

I use a very small amount of vitamin C. It increases loaf volume and speeds up the maturation of the dough, cutting rising time. You can get 500-mg vitamin C (ascorbic acid) tablets in grocery or drug stores. Divide one tablet into quarters. With the back of a spoon, smush one of the pieces to a powder. Use about one-tenth of this powder (about 10 mg) in your doughs.

Lecithin

Lecithin is an emulsifier found in egg yolks. It enhances the keeping quality of bread. It is both a lubricant and an antioxidant, which helps preserve the precious flavorful carotenoid compounds of flour. You can purchase lecithin powder in health food stores or Whole Foods Market. Or, you can simply use ½ teaspoon (2.5 ml) of raw egg yolk.

Malted Barley Flour

Barley malt syrup does not contain a live enzyme, and contributes only a little flavor to breads. But diastatic malt or malted barley flour contains an active enzyme that helps break down starch in the flour to provide a constant supply of sugar to feed yeast during long rises. Both of the hard red winter wheat flours that I recommend—King Arthur Unbleached All-Purpose and Gold Medal Harvest King Unbleached—contain a small amount of malted barley flour. So using these flours totally relieves you of needing to add malted barley flour.

BAKER'S PERCENTAGES

Baker's percentages are explained on pages 000 to 000. Essentially, the weight of the key ingredients of a recipe are expressed as a percentage of the weight of flour. Flour is taken as 100%. For example, if the weight of water in a recipe is half as much as the weight of the flour, the water is said to be 50%.

In several recipes throughout this chapter, baker's percentages are used.

Bread-Making Techniques

I am going to start with the steps that you go through in putting together a loaf of bread and then move into specific procedures for different types of doughs.

KNEADING?

One would think that kneading was a technique that has to be mastered for good bread making. Well, not necessarily.

Something that has come up in the press in the past few years as the new thing in bread—the no-knead bread—is actually old stuff. Years ago, I talked to Dr. Carl Hosney, one of the country's top starch and flour experts, about kneading. He had startled me by saying that you didn't really need to knead bread because, when bread rises, it kneads itself on a molecule-by-molecule basis.

What does kneading actually do? When you add water to flour and stir, two proteins in the flour, glutenin and gliadin, grab water and each other and form an elastic network. As you work the dough, proteins come in contact with other proteins and form more and more networks. In this way, kneading forms large elastic sheets of gluten.

Carl pointed out that rising does this. The yeast exudes a liquid. The second that this liquid touches an air bubble in the dough, it releases carbon dioxide and alcohol—puff! It is like someone blowing up bubblegum with tiny puffs. The dough moves. Proteins touch other proteins and cross-link. With every tiny rise of the dough, molecule by molecule, the dough "kneads" itself.

> Years ago, Dr. Carl Hosney explained that, when bread rises, it kneads itself; as the dough moves in rising, more proteins link together.

Kneading and Flavor

How does no-kneading or minimal kneading fit into the fight for flavor? The flavorful carotenoid compounds in hard red winter wheat are easily oxidized by the oxygen introduced in kneading. Didier got us to stand around a large mixer and watch the dough as it kneaded. He pointed out that the dough was getting whiter and whiter. As you knead, more and more oxygen combines with the dough. These flavorful carotenoid compounds oxidize and lose their color. The dough becomes whiter and less flavorful.

To save these precious flavor components, Didier does not want to knead much—just long enough to combine ingredients well, about 2 to 3 minutes.

Bakers test a dough to see if it is properly kneaded by stretching a small piece of it in all directions. If the dough has been kneaded enough, you can pull the piece so thin that you can almost see through it. Bakers call this a windowpane test.

Didier wants a dough that still tears and has holes when you pull a window-pane. This may be great to save flavor compounds, but will a dough that is not kneaded rise and make a loaf with good volume?

Didier's final loaves (from a dough that had the ingredients just mixed by minimal kneading) are magnificent. When you cut the bread and look at the inside crumb, it is a pale ivory, a slightly deeper color than a kneaded loaf made side by side. And the taste! Wonderful flavors.

> No regular kneading— Didier feels you lose too much flavor. He wants the dough kneaded only 2 to 3 minutes—just long enough to combine ingredients well.

MUCH DEPENDS ON TEMPERATURE—DOUGH TEMPERATURE

Dough temperature has a major role in fermentation activity and bread flavor. Jeffrey Hamelman, author of *Bread,* tells us that fermentation can occur anywhere from 30 to 130°F/-1 to 54°C for wheat doughs, but the optimum range is 75 to 78°F/24 to 26°C, and the optimum range for rye is at least 5°F/3°C higher. For the maximum yeast activity and gas production, the temperatures are 80°F/27°C and above, up to yeast death temperature at about 138°F/59°C.

Professor Calvel stresses that dough temperature during mixing has an effect on flavor loss.

Calvel stresses that dough temperature has an important effect on oxidation during mixing and the accompanying flavor loss.

Average mixing temperatures vary between 75 to 77°F and 24 to 25°C.

Deterioration of flavor is much more pronounced at dough mixing temperatures between 78 to 80°F and 26 to 27°C.

Bread flavor is enhanced by lower mixing temperatures in the range of 71 to 73°F/22 to 23°C.

And Then There Are Bacteria

In a yeast dough, both yeast and bacteria can be active. Temperature controls which of the two is the more active at any given time. Warmer temperatures (above 70°F/21°C) give yeast an advantage, while colder temperatures limit yeast activity and give the advantage to bacteria. Bacterial activity produces many flavorful compounds but also increases acidity, making it more difficult for baker's yeast to thrive.

Both yeast and bacteria are one-celled organisms that need oxygen to reproduce. When you stir or knead dough, you are incorporating oxygen. When dough rises, it exposes a little more of the dough to oxygen; when you knead, fold, or "punch down" the dough, you introduce more oxygen. Yeast and bacteria use oxygen to process their food (sugars in dough). Without oxygen, they are struggling to survive and cannot reproduce. Bacteria, a more primitive organism, reproduce by asexual fission, while different types of yeast reproduce both asexually by budding and sexually.

There is a tightrope to walk here. You want some oxygen so that the yeast cells can thrive and produce carbon dioxide to raise the dough, but you don't want so much oxygen that you oxidize the flavorful carotenoid compounds. So, what is the ideal dough temperature and how can you control dough temperature?

Dough Temperature

When mixing doughs, the warmer the temperature, the more oxidation takes place and the more flavor loss occurs.

So, a baker's technique is to add ice to the water before mixing to reach a cooler mixing temperature. Professor Calvel recommends a mixing temperature of 71 to 73°F/22 to 23°C, while Hamelman suggests 75 to 77°F/24 to 25°C.

Calvel gives Wayne Gisslen's method for dough temperature calculation (from *Professional Baking*):

> (Desired dough temperature x 3) - (flour temperature + room temperature + machine friction) = water temperature

This formula uses 20°F/11°C as the machine friction factor:

(72 x 3) - (70 + 70 + 20) = water temperature in Fahrenheit
216 - 160 = 56°F/13°C is the desired water temperature.

When mixing doughs, the warmer the temperature, the more oxidation takes place and the more flavor loss occurs.

Controlling Dough Temperature

Dough mixing temperature is a troublesome detail that home bakers would love to forget, but this is vital to bread flavor. How can you control dough temperature? Using crushed ice to lower dough temperature has been a time-honored practice.

Since I am making small home batches (without much "machine friction"), I do not bother with figuring how much ice I need, as professional bakers do. I usually use some ice to get the water that I am going to use in the bread down to the temperature that I want, and then throw out the ice. In my kitchen—and since I minimally knead—I can usually get a 72°F/22°C dough if I use 68°F/20°C water.

AUTOLYSIS

Autolysis is an important technique in our fight for flavorful breads. Autolysis is slow-speed premixing of flour and water only. This premix stands for 15 to 30 minutes, which allows the flour to more fully hydrate. This improves the extensibility of the dough, reduces final dough kneading time, and reduces dough oxidation by about 15%. Another way of enhancing flavor is by use of pre-ferments (see page 447).

Recipes Using Autolysis

The recipes that follow, Straight Dough with Autolysis Baguettes, Straight Dough with Autolysis Bâtards, and Straight Dough with Autolysis Fougasse, are step-by-step directions using the technique of autolysis—slow-speed premixing of flour and water only. These three recipes use the straight dough method that is the most common method of bread making (see page 444).

For more details about basic techniques that we have not covered yet, see pages 441 through 465.

Straight Dough with Autolysis Baguettes

MAKES 2 BAGUETTES

This is the straight dough method using autolysis. I used Calvel's basic ratios, but I did add my little bit of semolina, which I love for flavor. This is a good basic French bread dough that you can use as pizza dough or to make small loaves or shape as fougasse (see page 439).

What This Recipe Shows

Allow the flour and water to stand to permit the flour proteins and starch to hydrate well. This cuts the kneading time.

Using a hard red winter wheat flour such as Gold Medal Harvest King Unbleached or King Arthur Unbleached All-Purpose (both of which have a good carotenoid content) and limiting kneading, which would oxidize these flavorful compounds, produces loaves with excellent flavor.

Both Gold Medal Harvest King Unbleached and King Arthur Unbleached All-Purpose have a small amount of malted barley flour, which contains active enzymes to break flour starch into sugars to feed yeast.

The lecithin contained in egg yolks is an antioxidant that helps to preserve flavor compounds, and it is an emulsifier that will give the bread a little better shelf life.

---

4 cups (18 oz/510 g) spooned and leveled King Arthur Unbleached All-Purpose or Gold Medal Harvest King flour
2 tablespoons (0.7 oz/21 g) semolina flour
1½ cups plus 2 tablespoons (370 ml, 12.5 oz/355 g) water (about 68°F/20°C), divided
1 package (2¼ teaspoons) plus ⅛ teaspoon (7.5 g) instant yeast, such as RapidRise or Quick-Rise

Pinch (0.4 g) lecithin powder (available at health food stores or Whole Foods Market *or* ½ teaspoon (2.5 ml) raw egg yolk
1/10 of a crushed quarter of a 500-mg vitamin C (ascorbic acid) tablet (about 10 mg)
1¾ teaspoons (10 g) fine sea salt
2 tablespoons (30 ml) olive oil, divided
Nonstick cooking spray

Baker's Percentages—Flour, total: 18.7 oz/531 g, 100%; water, total: 13 oz/369 g, 69%; yeast: 0.25 oz/7.5 g, 1.4%; salt: 0.4 oz/10 g, 2%.

1. Place both flours in a mixer with the paddle attachment. Add 1½ cups (355 ml) of water and mix on the lowest speed for about 20 seconds just to blend. Cover with plastic wrap and allow to stand for 30 minutes.

2. Sprinkle the yeast over 1 tablespoon (15 ml) of the water. Allow to stand for 1 minute only, then stir and sprinkle over the dough. Mix on low speed for a few seconds. Stir the lecithin, vitamin C, and salt into the remaining 1 tablespoon (15 ml) water and sprinkle over the dough. Mix on the second speed for 2 minutes. Check the dough temperature with an instant-read thermometer; ideally, it should be about 72°F/22°C.

3. Oil your hands with about 1 teaspoon (5 ml) of the oil. Oil a bowl with about 1 tablespoon (15 ml) of the oil. Scrape the dough into the oiled bowl, turn the dough in the bowl by hand to lightly coat, and cover with plastic wrap. Allow to rise about 45 minutes.

4. Wipe a clean counter with a lightly oiled paper towel. Dump out the dough onto the counter so that the smooth top of the dough is now on the bottom. Allow it to spread out as much as it will. Pick up the dough on the left side, lift up about one-third of the dough, and gently fold it across to the right. Allow it to spread a few seconds, then lift up about one-third of the right side of the dough and bring it across to the left. Again, allow the dough a few seconds to spread. Pick up the bottom edge of the dough and bring about one-third of it up and across to the top. After it settles, pick up the top edge, lift about one-third of it up, and bring it across toward you.

5. Place the dough back in the bowl, turning it over so that the smooth top that was against the counter is back on top. Cover with plastic wrap and allow to rise for another 45 minutes. After this bulk fermentation, lift out the dough and place it on the lightly oiled counter, smooth top up.

6. Divide the dough in half. Using both hands with a gentle cupping and tucking action, shape each half into a smooth round. With both hands, grab the sides of the round and stretch it sideways into an oval. Let it spring back slightly, then pull it out again. Cover each with plastic wrap sprayed with nonstick cooking spray and leave on the counter for 20 minutes. The dough is now ready to shape.

7. Arrange a shelf with a baking stone on it in the lower third of the oven and preheat the oven to 460°F/238°C.

8. Shape one baguette at a time. Cup a piece of dough with both hands, fingers spread out behind the loaf on either side and thumbs in front of the loaf. Press your thumbs into the dough and down against the table. This pulls in or tucks part of the bottom half of the dough. At the same time, pull the top of the dough tight and forward with your fingers. Now move your thumbs down slightly and press down and in again, pulling the top forward with your fingers to knead and tuck again. Repeat this motion two or three times until the loaf is stretched taut and tucked in well. The loaf will lengthen as you stretch and tuck and may be long enough if you have pulled your hands outward in the process. If not, lengthen the loaf by placing both hands, spread out, palms down, on top of the center of the loaf. Simultaneously push away against the table with your right hand and pull toward you with your left, pulling the dough out in opposite directions. Repeat this pulling once or twice more, if necessary. Now pinch the bottom seam together.

9. Spray a double-trough French bread pan with nonstick cooking spray and place the loaves in the pan to rise. Cover with a damp cloth or a piece of plastic wrap that is lightly sprayed with nonstick cooking spray. Allow to rise at 76°F/24°C for 1 to 1½ hours.

10. Place a few clean small rocks (about 1 to 2 inches/2.5 to 5 cm each) in a pan with 2-inch (5-cm) sides and place the pan on the floor of the oven near the front. You are going to pour about 1 cup (237 ml) of boiling water over the rocks just before you place the dough in the oven. The moisture will condense on the relatively cool dough and keep it a little moister, allowing the dough to rise well before it crusts. For the boiling water, place a saucepan with about 1¼ cups (296 ml) of water on a burner and bring to a low boil.

11. To slash the baguettes, see the instructions on page 442.

12. With oven mitts on, *very carefully* pour the boiling water into the pan with the stones. Keep your head and arms out of the way of the great billow of steam that comes up. Close the oven door briefly.

13. Place the baguettes, in the pan, on the stone in the oven. Bake for 34 to 38 minutes. The dough needs to be crisp. Do not be tempted to remove it too soon. If it is getting too brown, lower the oven temperature by about 10°F/6°C. Place on a rack to cool.

Straight Dough with Autolysis Bâtards

MAKES 4 BÂTARDS

These are essentially slightly fatter and about half the length of baguettes. They are a little easier to shape than baguettes.

1 recipe Straight Dough with Autolysis Baguettes (page 436) followed through Step 5	Nonstick cooking spray

1. Divide the dough into four pieces. Using both hands with gentle cupping and tucking action, shape each piece into a smooth round. With both hands, grab the sides of each round and stretch it sideways into an oval. Let it spring back slightly, then pull it out again. Cover each with plastic wrap

lightly sprayed with nonstick cooking spray and leave on the counter for 20 minutes. The dough is now ready to shape.

2. Arrange a shelf with a baking stone on it in the lower third of the oven and preheat the oven to 460°F/238°C.

3. To shape bâtards, cup each piece of dough with both hands, fingers spread out behind the loaf on either side and thumbs in front of the loaf. Press your thumbs into the dough and down against the table. This pulls in or tucks part of the bottom half of the dough. At the same time, pull the top of the dough tight and forward with your fingers. Now move your thumbs down slightly and press down and in again, pulling the top forward with your fingers to knead and tuck again. Repeat this motion two or three times until the loaf is stretched taut and tucked in well. Pinch the bottom seam together on each loaf. Spray a double-trough French bread pan with nonstick cooking spray and place two bâtards in each trough to rise. Cover with a damp cloth or a piece of plastic wrap lightly sprayed with nonstick cooking spray and allow to rise at 76°F/24°C for 1 to 1½ hours.

4. Place a few clean small rocks (about 1 to 2 inches/2.5 to 5 cm each) in a pan with 2-inch (5-cm) sides and place the pan on the floor of the oven near the front. You are going to pour about 1 cup (237 ml) of boiling water over the rocks just before you place the dough in the oven. The moisture will condense on the relatively cool dough and keep it a little moister, allowing the dough to rise well before it crusts. For the boiling water, place a saucepan with about 1¼ cups (296 ml) of water on a burner and bring to a low boil.

5. To slash the bâtards, follow the instructions on page 442 for slashing baguettes.

6. With oven mitts on, *very carefully* pour the boiling water into the pan with the stones. Keep your head and arms out of the way of the great billow of steam that comes up. Close the oven door briefly.

7. Place the pan on the stone in the oven. Bake 34 to 38 minutes. The dough needs to be crisp. Do not be tempted to remove it too soon. If it is getting too brown, lower the oven temperature by about 10°F/6°C. Place on a rack to cool.

Straight Dough with Autolysis Fougasse

MAKE 3 FOUGASSES

Fougasse is a French term related to the Latin *focus* or center, which referred to the hearth—the fireplace—the center of the home. The Italian *focaccia* is of similar origin. Fougasse is much thicker than pizza, but relative to a thick loaf it is thin, with deep holes that create an abundance of wonderful crust to contrast with its soft interior.

1 recipe Straight Dough with Autolysis Baguettes (page 436) followed through Step 5

Cornstarch for dusting dough
Nonstick cooking spray

1. Divide the dough into three pieces. With both hands in a cupping motion, tuck the sides slightly under each quarter to create a smooth top. With both hands, grab the sides of the each round and stretch it sideways into an oval. Let it spring back slightly, then pull it out again. Flatten out a little, cover each with plastic wrap lightly sprayed with nonstick cooking spray and leave on the counter for about 20 minutes. The relaxed dough is now much easier to shape.

2. Shape one dough piece at a time, for a total of three. It is a good to look at a picture of a fougasse before you start shaping one (see the photograph insert). Cut a piece of Release foil 12 to 14 inches (30 to 36 cm) long. Place the dough on the nonstick side. You want to shape each piece of the dough into a large, fat "leaf" a little over 1 inch (2.5 cm) thick, with roughly an 8 to 10-inch (20 to 25-cm) base, 10 inches (25 cm) long in the center, coming to a fat point at the top. Roll or press the dough out into a large leaf shape. The cuts in the dough are not slits, but holes running from $\frac{1}{2}$ to 1 inch (1.3 to 2.5 cm) wide.

3. With a sharp dough scraper, cut a slit up the middle to resemble the major center vein of the leaf. Pull the dough apart so that you have a 1-inch (2.5-cm) wide hole. This slit should run from $\frac{3}{4}$ inch (2 cm) from the bottom to $\frac{3}{4}$ inch (2 cm) from the point. Dust your fingers with cornstarch and widen the slit, running about $\frac{1}{2}$ inch (1.3 cm) wide at the top and bottom and 1 inch (2.5 cm) wide in the center, so that a hole will remain when the dough rises. Next make three slits (holes) on each side of this main "vein." Near the base of the "leaf," parallel to the base, cut a slit on one side of the main slit, running from almost the corner of the base to almost the main "vein" hole. Cut another slit like this on the other side of the main "vein" slit. Widen these two base slits to $\frac{1}{2}$ inch (1.3 cm) wide near the ends and almost 1 inch (2.5 cm) in the center. Again, use your fingers to widen these slits so that they will remain open after the dough rises.

4. Cut two more short "veins" on each side running up some from the main "vein" slit at an angle, almost to the outer edge of the "leaf." Widen all of these slits to $\frac{1}{2}$ to 1-inch (1.3 to 2.5-cm) holes. Sprinkle the shaped leaf lightly with cornstarch. Cover loosely with plastic wrap that has been sprayed lightly with nonstick cooking spray and allow to rise 30 minutes to an hour.

5. As soon as you have shaped the dough for its final rise, arrange a shelf in the lower third of the oven, place a baking stone on it, and preheat the oven to 460°F/238°C.

6. Place a few clean small rocks (about 1 to 2 inches/2.5 to 5 cm each) in a pan with 2-inch (5-cm) sides and place the pan on the floor of the oven near the front. You are going to pour about 1 cup

(237 ml) of boiling water over the rocks before you put the bread in the oven. You want a good steam-filled oven for the bread to go in. This steam will condense on the dough to keep it moist and allow a good oven rise. For the boiling water, place a saucepan with about 1¼ cups (296 ml) of water on a back burner and bring to a low simmer. When the bread is risen, turn the heat up on the water and bring to a boil. *Very carefully,* with oven mitts on, making sure your arms and face are out of the way of the steam that will burst up, pour the boiling water into the pan of hot rocks. Close the oven door to allow it to fill with steam.

7. I do not have a baker's peel, so I slip a thin, flat baking sheet with no raised edges on three sides under the fougasses on the foil, and slide the foil and fougasse onto the hot stone. It will take only 13 to 16 minutes to bake. Be sure to brown well. This magnificent, crunchy crust is wonderful. Place the fougasses on a rack to cool.

FOLDING OR PUNCHING DOWN?

When yeast is active, it reproduces by dividing—one cell divides into two, then each of those divides. So, soon you have a clump of yeast. Yeast needs both oxygen and food (sugar) to thrive and divide. The yeast in the center of these clumps can no longer get this necessary oxygen and food.

If you move the dough around, you break up these clumps and spread out the yeast, giving it a fresh supply of food and oxygen.

In folding, you are not trying to remove air bubbles, but just to stretch the dough and trap a little air. Instead of the violent punching down of the dough, simple stretching and folding does several things. It spreads out the yeast beautifully and it also develops gluten.

> Folding the dough instead of "punching down" does an excellent job of spreading the yeast and it also develops gluten.

On a clean counter wiped with a lightly oiled paper towel, dump out the dough so that the smooth top of the dough is now on the bottom. Allow it to spread out as much as it will. Pick up the dough on the left side, lift up about one-third of the dough, and gently fold it across to the right, trapping some air as you make the fold. Allow it to spread a few seconds, then lift up about one-third of the right side of the dough and bring it across to the left. Again, allow the dough a few seconds to spread. Now pick up the bottom edge of the dough and bring about one-third of it up and toward the top. After it settles, pick up the top edge, lift about one-third of it up, and bring it across the dough toward you.

ROUNDING (PRESHAPING)

Rounding or preshaping—tucking the dough pieces into smooth rounds before shaping—does several things. It allows the dough to relax, making final shaping much easier. And this tucking into smooth rounds creates a covering to better hold gases. Rounding also helps to align gluten. In good gluten development, protein strands are aligned and stretched in the same direction.

> Preshaping the dough relaxes it to make final shaping easier, holds the gases in the dough better, and helps to align gluten.

Cover the rounds with plastic wrap that has been sprayed lightly with nonstick cooking spray and let them rest on the counter for 15 minutes. The relaxed dough is now much easier to shape.

SHAPING

Individual recipes give shaping directions.

SLASHING

Yeast is a one-celled organism that exudes a liquid. When this liquid touches an air bubble in the dough, it releases carbon dioxide gas and alcohol. The carbon dioxide slowly inflates the dough.

> When a dough goes into the hot oven, the alcohol that the yeast has exuded during the rises evaporates all at once, producing a sudden great rise of the dough called "oven spring."

When the dough goes into the hot oven, one of the first things that happens as the dough gets warm is that all of the alcohol evaporates at once, giving the dough a great rise. Bakers call this "oven spring."

The surface of the dough can't stretch fast enough and actually holds the dough down. To take advantage of this sudden rise, if you have some cuts on the surface, the dough can burst open there and rise fully. This is why you make slashes on the surface of the dough just before you put it in the oven.

With rounds, or large loaves, you can make deeper cuts and arrange them decoratively to create handsome loaves.

Baguette Slashes

To slash loaves you need a single-edge razor blade or an X-Acto knife. Bakers use a tool that looks like a razor blade at the end of small stick, called a lame (pronounced *lahm*). These are available from the King Arthur Flour company (see Sources on page 508). The slashes should not be straight down or deep. You want to make slashes at an angle of about 30 degrees to the horizon so you are slashing a thin flap of dough.

Although proper baguette slashes end up looking as if they are across the dough, they begin as cuts down the center. Imagine a line right down the center of the baguette. Each slash should begin less than ¼ inch (0.6 cm) to the right of this center line and end up less than ¼ inch (0.6 cm) to the left of this line. Each slash should be 4 to 5 inches (10 to 12 cm) long. Each slash should begin so that it overlaps (but does not cross) the slash before it by about one-quarter of its length.

BAKING

Baking Stone

A baking stone gives you wonderful even heat and is vital for many baked goods. With bread, you have a constant battle between getting the dough hot enough to rise well before the heat from the top of the oven forms a crust on the baked good, holding it down and preventing maximum rise.

Place the heavy stone in the lower third of the oven, as far away from the top as possible. The even heat of the stone will prevent burning on the bottom. Also, the stone stays hot when the oven temperature fluctuates (see page 3) or when you open the oven door. This keeps your baked good at a more uniform temperature.

A baking stone provides even heat and prevents burning on the bottom while allowing you to bake breads in the lower part of the oven away from the hot top of the oven, which can produce an early crust and hold the bread down.

Steaming

Steam actually needs to fill the oven before the bread is put in. You want the steam to condense on the relatively cool surface of the dough. The condensed steam keeps the dough surface moist longer, allowing it to rise longer for better bread volume. This moisture on the surface also dissolves sugar in the dough; when the moisture evaporates, it leaves a little sugar that will produce a browner crust. Ideally, you need the steam-producing water to run out about 15 minutes before the end of the baking time so that the crust can dry out.

A Good Home Steamer

Peter Nyberg, an outstanding sourdough baker, taught me how to make a great steam bath by placing a heavy metal pan in the bottom of the oven with about five stones in it. I got some great 1 to 2-inch (2.5 to 5-cm) smooth black stones from a landscape plants store. The hot stones hold the heat longer and produce steam longer than just the pan alone.

Most of my recipes give directions for placing the pan with the stones on the floor of the oven near the oven door and for placing a saucepan with water on to heat. You need about 1 cup (237 ml) of boiling water to pour into the steam bath. You must be *very careful* to have oven mitts on your hands when you pour the boiling water into this hot pan with hot stones. There is a great rush of steam that can burn your hand and arm badly. Even with oven mitts on, take care to hold your arms and face to the side. BE CAREFUL!

Basic Bread-Making Methods

Many things influence bread taste, and certainly the method of preparation has a major influence on taste.

STRAIGHT DOUGH

The straight dough method used in the recipes above is the way most of us have made bread for years. It is simply mixing the ingredients, allowing the dough to rise, "punching down," shaping the dough, allowing it to rise again, and baking it.

Straight dough breads are not going to have the depth of flavor that you get from pre-ferments. Fougasses, page 439, are great to make with a straight dough because, with their big holes, they have a lot of crunchy, crusty surface and you don't miss the flavor that you get from pre-ferments. And breads with flavorful ingredients such as olives or cheese are good candidates for the straight dough method (see recipe below).

Cheese 'n' Rice Bread

MAKES ONE 9 X 5 X 3-INCH (23 X 13 X 8-CM) LOAF

A salty cheese like Parmesan is a great flavor enhancer. The unusual honeycomb texture and moisture that rice gives a bread make this a striking and delicious savory loaf. It is unbelievably good toasted.

What This Recipe Shows

A good Parmesan cheese is a slightly salty taste enhancer that does not interfere with yeast growth.

Cooked rice adds moisture and good keeping characteristics, and imparts an unusual honeycomb texture.

Olive oil in the loaf imparts flavor and slightly enhances volume.

---

3 cups (13.5 oz/383 g) spooned and leveled King Arthur Unbleached All-Purpose or Gold Medal Harvest King flour

2 tablespoons (0.7 oz/21 g) semolina flour

$1/10$ of a crushed quarter of a 500-mg vitamin C (ascorbic acid) tablet (about 10 mg)

1 tablespoon (0.5 oz/14 g) dark brown sugar

1 teaspoon (6 g) salt

$1/2$ teaspoon (1 g) ground cayenne (bright red and fresh)

$1\frac{1}{3}$ cups (316 ml, 10.6 oz/301 g) water (about 68°F/20°C)

1 package ($2\frac{1}{4}$ teaspoons/7 g) instant yeast, such as RapidRise or Quick-Rise

3 tablespoons (45 ml) warm water (110°F/37°C)

$1/3$ cup (1 oz/28 g) freshly grated Parmesan, preferably Parmigiano-Reggiano

1 cup (5.6 oz/158 g) cooked rice (freshly cooked so that it is still soft and moist)

2 tablespoons (30 ml) olive oil, divided

Nonstick cooking spray

1 large egg (1.75 oz/50 g), beaten

1. Place the flours in a mixer with the paddle attachment. Add the vitamin C, sugar, salt, and cayenne. Mix about 30 seconds to blend well. Switch to the dough hook. Add $1\frac{1}{3}$ cups water and mix on the lowest speed for 2 minutes.

2. Sprinkle the yeast over the barely warm water. Stir and allow to stand for about 10 seconds only, then sprinkle over the dough. Mix on low speed for 30 seconds. Add the Parmesan. Mix on the second speed for 1 minute. Add the rice and 1 tablespoon (15 ml) of the oil. Mix on the second speed for about 1 minute more, to thoroughly mix. The dough should be very soft and almost sticky. Add a little more flour or water as needed. Mix on the second speed a few seconds to incorporate.

3. With the remaining 1 tablespoon (15 ml) of the oil, coat a bowl and your hands. Scrape the dough into the oiled bowl and turn it in the bowl to coat lightly. Cover with plastic wrap. Allow the dough to rise 45 minutes.

4. Wipe a clean counter with a lightly oiled paper towel. Dump out the dough onto the counter so that the smooth top of the dough is now on the bottom. Allow it to spread out as much as it will. Pick up the dough on the left side, lift up about one-third of the dough, and gently fold it across to the right. Allow it to spread a few seconds, then lift up about one-third of the right side of the dough and bring it across to the left. Again, allow the dough a few seconds to spread. Pick up the bottom edge of the dough and bring about one-third of it up and across to the top. After it settles, pick up the top edge, lift about one-third of it up, and bring it across toward you.

5. Place the dough back in the bowl, turning it over so that the smooth top is back on top. Cover with plastic wrap and allow to rise for another 45 minutes.

6. After this bulk fermentation, lift out the dough and place on the lightly oiled counter, keeping the top on top. Using both hands with a gently cupping and tucking action, shape the dough into a smooth round. Grab the sides of the round and stretch it sideways into an oval. Let it spring back slightly, then pull it out again. Cover with a piece of plastic wrap that has been lightly sprayed with nonstick cooking spray and allow to stand for 20 minutes.

7. To shape the loaf, cup the piece of dough with both hands, fingers spread out behind the loaf on either side and thumbs in front of the loaf. Press your thumbs into the dough and down against the table. This pulls in or tucks part of the bottom half of the dough. At the same time, pull the top of the dough tight and forward with your fingers. Now move your thumbs down slightly and press down and in again, pulling the top forward with your fingers to knead and tuck again. Repeat this motion two or three times until the loaf is stretched taut and tucked in well. Pinch the bottom seam together tightly. The ends go down to a slight taper. Tuck them under, then pinch the ends and bottom seam together.

8. Arrange a shelf with a baking stone on it in the lower third of the oven and preheat the oven to 450°F/232°C.

9. Spray a 9 x 5 x 3-inch (23 x 13 x 8-cm) loaf pan with nonstick cooking spray and place the loaf in, seam side down. Brush with the beaten egg. Let the dough rise until more than doubled, about an hour.

10. Place a few clean small rocks (about 1 to 2 inches/2.5 to 5 cm each) in a pan with 2-inch (5-cm) sides and place the pan on the floor of the oven near the front. You are going to pour about 1 cup (237 ml) of boiling water over the rocks just before you place the dough in the oven. The moisture will condense on the relatively cool dough and keep it a little moister, allowing the dough to rise well before it crusts. For the boiling water, place a saucepan with about 1¼ cups (296 ml) of water on a burner and bring to a low boil.

11. About 5 minutes before baking, turn the oven down to 375°F/191°C.

12. With oven mitts on, *very carefully* pour the boiling water into the pan with the stones. Keep your head and arms out of the way of the great billow of steam that comes up. Close the oven door briefly.

13. Place the loaf in the pan on the stone in the oven. Bake until well browned, 45 to 55 minutes total baking time. The loaf should sound hollow when thumped on the bottom. You can also check for doneness by inserting an instant-read thermometer in the bottom center of the loaf and pushing it to the center. The loaf is done when the center is over 200°F/93°C. Remove the loaf from the pan and place it on a rack to cool.

STRAIGHT DOUGH WITH AUTOLYSIS

See pages 436 to 441 for straight dough recipes using the autolysis technique.

PRE-FERMENTS, PREDOUGHS: FLAVOR, FLAVOR, FLAVOR!

Pre-ferments (fermented cultures made before mixing the dough) can be made with baker's yeast or wild yeast (sourdough starter). Pre-ferments develop some acidity, which enhances gluten strength and contributes to better keeping quality of breads.

Pre-ferments with Baker's Yeast

A pre-ferment with baker's yeast gives you some of the wonderful fermentation flavors that you get from wild yeast sourdough starters.

All of the strange terms for pre-ferments—sponge, biga, poolish—used to drive me crazy until I realized that they are nothing but different types of mixtures of a small amount of baker's yeast with flour and water that is allowed to sit around and ferment—typically for 6 to 18 hours—before you make your dough. If this mixture is fairly firm, it is a sponge or, in Italian, a biga. If it is wetter, from equal weights of water and flour, it is a poolish or a biga. Bigas can be firm or wet.

The more yeast, the faster the pre-ferment reaches its prime. Also, the wetter the pre-ferment, the faster it reaches its prime. In the biga recipes on pages 452 and 455 and the poolish recipe on page 448, I describe how to tell when they are ripe.

With a pre-ferment you get an enormous flavor return for minimal effort. You have only to stir together a little yeast, flour, and liquid, cover, and allow to stand overnight. The next day, you simply use this as a beginning mixture to add your yeast, flour, water, and salt.

In addition to marvelous flavors, pre-ferments also become slightly acidic, which aids in gluten development. This acidity also enhances shelf life.

> The more yeast, the faster the pre-ferment reaches its prime. Also, the wetter the pre-ferment, the faster it reaches its prime.

Sponge

Sponge is a reasonably firm pre-ferment mixture of a small amount of baker's yeast, flour, and liquid that is allowed to stand for a number of hours. The firmer Biga (50% water) on page 455 could also be called a sponge.

Poolish

Poolish is a wetter pre-ferment with baker's yeast and equal weights of flour and water.

Poolish

A much more liquid sponge, which allows much faster propagation of yeast.

⅛ teaspoon (0.5 g) instant yeast, such as RapidRise or Quick-Rise

½ cup plus 1 teaspoon (123 ml, 4.2 oz/119 g) water (about 68°F/20°C)

1 cup minus 2 tablespoons (4.2 oz/119 g) spooned and leveled King Arthur Unbleached All-Purpose or Gold Medal Harvest King flour

Baker's Percentages—Flour: 4.2 oz/119 g, 100%; water: 4.2 oz/119 g, 100%; yeast: 0.5 g, 0.4%.

1. In a medium bowl, stir the yeast into the water. Stir in the flour in two batches. Stir or beat with a hand-held mixer about 1 minute, until smooth. (The dough temperature should be 70°F/21°C.) Scrape into a clean, wide-mouth quart (liter) jar. Cover and allow to stand for 6 to 12 hours to ripen. Fine bubbles should cover the surface of a ripe poolish. You can even see a bubble break on the surface. If the poolish is past its prime—has risen and collapsed—there will be a foam line on the glass above the current poolish level.

2. The time is totally dependent on the amount of yeast and the ambient temperature. It may take a try or two playing with amounts of yeast and the temperature to get the time where you would like it for your schedule. My poolish was ripe in a little over 6 hours.

Baguettes Made with Poolish

Makes 2 baguettes

1 recipe Poolish, above

1 cup (237 ml, 8 oz/227 g) water (about 68°F/20°C) plus 2 to 4 tablespoons (30 to 60 ml) as needed

¼ teaspoon plus ⅛ teaspoon (1.5 g) instant yeast, such as RapidRise or Quick-Rise

1¾ teaspoons (0.35 oz/10 g) fine sea salt

1/10 of a crushed quarter of a 500-mg vitamin C (ascorbic acid) tablet (about 10 mg)

3 cups (13.5 oz/383 g) spooned and leveled Gold Medal Harvest King Unbleached or King Arthur Unbleached All-Purpose flour

1 tablespoon (15 ml) olive oil, divided

Nonstick cooking spray

1. Pour the poolish into the mixer bowl. (The ideal mixing temperature is 72°F/22°C.) Add the water, yeast, salt, and vitamin C. With the paddle attachment, mix a few seconds on lowest speed. Add 2 cups (9 oz/255 g) of the flour and mix a few seconds. Add the rest of the flour. Mix on low about 1 minute, then mix on the second speed about 2 minutes. The dough should be soft, on the edge of sticky. Add a tablespoon or so of water if needed.

2. Oil your hands and very lightly oil a large bowl. (The ideal temperature for a place to rise is 72°F/22°C.) Place the dough in the oiled bowl, cover with plastic wrap, and allow to rise, about 1 hour.

3. With an oiled paper towel, very lightly oil an area on a clean countertop. Dump out the dough onto this area so that the smooth top of the dough is now on the bottom. Allow it to spread out as much as it will. Pick up the dough on the left side, lift up about one-third of the dough, and gently fold it across to the right, trapping some air as you make the fold. Allow it to spread a few seconds, then lift up about one-third of the right side of the dough and bring it across to the left. Again, allow the dough a few seconds to spread. Pick up the bottom edge of the dough and bring about one-third of it up and across to the top. After it settles, pick up the top edge, lift about one-third or it up, and bring it across toward you.

4. Place the dough back in the bowl, turning it over so that the smooth top that was against the counter is back on top. Cover with plastic wrap and allow to rise for another hour.

5. After the second hour of bulk fermentation, lift the dough out and place on the lightly oiled counter, smooth top up. Divide the dough in half. For each half, with both hands in a cupping motion, tuck the sides slightly under creating a smooth top. By tucking the dough into a tight smooth round you create a covering to better hold gases. With both hands, grab the sides of each round and stretch it sideways into an oval. Let it spring back slightly, and then pull it out again. Cover each oval with plastic wrap and leave on the counter for about 20 minutes. The relaxed dough is now much easier to shape.

6. To shape baguettes, cup the oval piece of dough with both hands, fingers spread out behind the loaf on either end and thumbs in front of the loaf. Press your thumbs into the dough and down against the table. This pulls in or tucks part of the bottom half of the dough. At the same time, pull the top of the dough tight and forward with your fingers. Now move your thumbs down slightly and press down and in again, pulling the top forward with your fingers to knead and tuck again. Repeat this motion two or three times until the loaf is stretched taut and tucked in well. The loaf will lengthen as you stretch and tuck and may be long enough if you have pulled your hands outward in the process. If not, lengthen the loaf by placing both hands, spread out, palms down, on top of the center of the loaf. Then simultaneously push away against the table with your right hand and pull toward you with your left, pulling the dough out in opposite directions. Repeat this pulling once or twice more, if necessary. Pinch the bottom seam together.

7. Spray a double-trough French bread pan with nonstick cooking spray. Place the loaves seam side down in the pan, cover with a floured smooth-surface towel or plastic wrap, and allow to rise. (The ideal temperature is 76°F/24°C.) This rise will be 1 to 1½ hours.

8. About 20 minutes after you have shaped the dough for its final rise, arrange a shelf in the lower third of the oven, place a baking stone on it, and preheat the oven to 460°F/238°C.

9. Place a few clean small rocks (about 1 to 2 inches/2.5 to 5 cm each) in a pan with 2-inch (5-cm) sides and place the pan on the floor of the oven near the front. You are going to pour about 1 cup (237 ml) of boiling water over the rocks before you put the bread in the oven. You want a good steam-filled oven for the bread to go in. This steam will condense on the dough to keep it moist and allow a good oven rise. For the boiling water, place a saucepan with about 1¼ cups (296 ml) water on a back burner and bring to a low simmer. When the bread has risen, turn the heat up under the water and bring to a boil. *Very carefully,* with oven mitts on and making sure your arms and face are out of the way of the steam that will burst up, pour the boiling water into the pan of hot rocks. Close the oven door to allow it to fill with steam.

10. It is imperative to slash loaves so that they can rise rapidly in the hot oven. See the slashing directions on page 442.

11. Place the baguettes in the pan on the stone in the oven. Bake 34 to 38 minutes. The dough needs to be crisp. Do not be tempted to remove it too soon. If it is getting too brown, lower the oven temperature by about 10°F/6°C. Remove loaves from the pan and place on a rack to cool.

Rustic Boules Made with Poolish

MAKES 2 LARGE OR 3 MEDIUM ROUNDS

This is my adaptation of Jeffrey Hamelman's adaptation of James MacGuire's (bread expert from Montreal) version of a recipe from Professor Calvel, really!

POOLISH

⅛ teaspoon (0.5 g) instant yeast, such as RapidRise or Quick-Rise
2 cups (473 ml) water

3½ cups (15.8 oz /447 g) spooned and leveled Gold Medal Harvest King or King Arthur Unbleached All-Purpose flour

In a mixing bowl, stir the yeast into the water. Add half of the flour and mix with the paddle blade on low for 30 seconds. Add the rest of the flour and mix just to blend, about 2 minutes. Cover and allow to stand at about 70°F/21°C for 12 to 16 hours. Use in the dough, below.

DOUGH

¾ cup (177 ml, 6.1 oz/173 g) water
3½ cups (15.8 oz/447 g) spooned and leveled
    Gold Medal Harvest King or King Arthur
    Unbleached All-Purpose flour
2 tablespoons (21 g) semolina flour

1½ teaspoons (6 g) instant yeast, such as
    RapidRise or Quick-Rise
1 tablespoon (19 g) fine sea salt
Nonstick cooking spray
1 tablespoon (15 ml) canola oil, divided

1. In a mixer with the dough hook, beat together the water, both flours, and the poolish on low speed for about 1 minute. Cover with plastic wrap and allow to stand for about 40 minutes.

2. Sprinkle the yeast over the dough and mix for about 5 seconds. Sprinkle the salt over the dough and mix on the second speed about 2 minutes, until the dough has come together. The dough should not be firm, but not totally soft—a medium consistency. Add water or flour and mix as needed. Cover the dough with plastic wrap lightly sprayed with nonstick cooking spray and allow to ferment, ideally at about 76°F/24°C.

3. After 25 minutes, with an oiled paper towel, lightly oil an area on a clean countertop. Dump out the dough onto the counter. Lift one-third of the dough on the right and pull across to the other side. Lift one-third of the dough on the left and pull across to the other side. Lift bottom one-third of the dough up and across the dough. Lift top one-third of the dough and pull it down across the dough. Lightly oil a bowl and place the dough in the bowl with the side that was on the counter turned up. After 25 minutes, dump the dough on the lightly oiled counter with the top of the dough on the counter. Fold the dough again as before. Place the dough back in the bowl, counter side up. Cover with plastic wrap lightly sprayed with nonstick cooking spray and allow to stand 20 minutes more.

4. Place the dough on the counter and gently divide into two equal pieces. With both hands in a cupping motion, tuck the sides slightly under each piece, creating a smooth top. By tucking the dough into a tight smooth round you create a covering to better hold gases. Cover each oval with plastic wrap sprayed with nonstick cooking spray and leave on the counter for about 20 minutes. The relaxed dough is now much easier to shape.

5. Arrange a shelf in the lower third of the oven, place a baking stone on it, and preheat the oven to 470°F/243°C.

6. Place about 1¼ cups (296 ml) of water in a saucepan and heat to a very low boil for a steam bath.

7. Using your left hand as a backstop, with your right hand, press gently against a dough round and "massage" with a stroke away from you, massaging the side of the round. Rotate the round and again gently "knead" the side of the dough. Repeat with the other round. Place the rounds on a piece of Release foil, nonstick side up, or a piece of parchment sprayed with nonstick cooking spray. Cover with plastic wrap sprayed with nonstick cooking spray. Allow to rise about 25 minutes at about 76°F/24°C.

8. Place a few clean small rocks (about 1 to 2 inches/2.5 to 5 cm each) in a pan with 2-inch (5-cm) sides and place the pan on the floor of the oven. You are going to pour about 1 cup (237 ml) of boiling water over the rocks before you put the bread in the oven. You want a good steam-filled oven for the bread to go in. This steam will condense on the dough to keep it moist and allow a good oven rise. When the bread has risen, turn the heat up under the water and bring to a boil. *Very carefully,* with oven mitts on, making sure your arms and face are out of the way of the steam that will burst up, pour the boiling water into the pan of hot rocks. Close the oven door to allow it to fill with steam.

9. Slash the rounds at an angle using several quick slashes only about ⅛ inch (3 cm) deep. Place the loaves side by side on the foil. I do not have a baker's peel, so I slide a thin, flat baking sheet with no raised edges on three sides under the foil and then slide the foil with the dough on top onto the hot stone. Bake for 35 to 38 minutes until well browned. Remove the loaves to a rack to cool.

Biga

Biga is the Italian term for a baker's yeast pre-ferment that can be fairly stiff (50 to 60% hydration, about half as much water as flour) or wet like a poolish with about 100% hydration (equal weights of flour and water). According to Jeffrey Hamelman in *Bread,* a biga contains a small portion of yeast (0.08 to 1%) and just flour and water, never salt.

Carol Field's Biga from *The Italian Baker* is a little over 75% water. I have included two biga recipes, one an adaptation of Carol Field's (below) and another, firmer biga (50% water) on page 455.

Biga

MAKES ABOUT 2⅓ CUPS (ABOUT 551 ML)

This recipe is based on Carol Field's Biga. I normally use instant yeast, but notice that this recipe calls for active dry yeast.

¼ teaspoon (1 g) active dry yeast
¼ cup (59 ml, 2 oz/57 g) warm water
(about 110°F/43°C)
¾ cup (6 oz/170 g) plus 1 tablespoon (0.5 oz/15 g) plus 1 teaspoon (0.16 oz/5 g) room-temperature water (about 70°F/21°C)

2½ cups (11.3 oz/319 g) spooned and leveled Gold Medal Harvest King or King Arthur Unbleached All-Purpose flour
1 tablespoon (15 ml) olive oil, divided
Nonstick cooking spray

Baker's Percentages—Flour: 11.3 oz/319 g, 100%; water, total: 8.7 oz/247 g, 77%; yeast: 1 g, 0.3%.

1. In a mixing bowl, stir the yeast into the warm water and allow to stand until creamy, about 10 minutes.

2. Stir in the room-temperature water. Stir in the flour, 1 cup (4.5 oz/127 g) at a time. Mix on the lowest speed in a mixer with the paddle attachment, no longer than 2 minutes total.

3. Place the dough in a lightly oiled bowl, turn to coat, and then cover with plastic wrap that was lightly sprayed with nonstick cooking spray. At cool room temperature (about 70°F/21°C), allow the biga to rise for 6 to 24 hours. The biga will triple in volume and be wet and sticky. It should be domed and just beginning to dip in the center. In my kitchen, my biga is ready in about 14 hours. Refrigerate until needed.

Ciabatta with Biga

Makes 2 loaves

This is a bread with a crisp surface but a moist, open interior. The dough is so wet and soft that it spreads out to be slightly thicker than a focaccia.

¾ teaspoon (about 3 g) instant yeast, such as
 RapidRise or Quick-Rise
1½ cups (355 ml, 12 oz/340 g) plus 2
 tablespoons (30 ml, 1 oz/28 g) water
 (about 70°F/21°C)

3¾ cups (16.9 oz/478 g) spooned and leveled
 King Arthur Unbleached All-Purpose or
 Gold Medal Harvest King flour
2 teaspoons (12 g) fine sea salt
About ⅔ recipe (7 oz/198 g) Biga (page 452)
1 tablespoon (15 ml) olive oil, divided

1. In a mixer, stir the yeast into water. Stir in the flour about 1 cup (4.5 oz/127 g) at a time. Stir in salt. With the paddle attachment, beat on the lowest speed for 1 minute. Add the biga in chunks, beating in each chunk on low. When all of the biga is incorporated, beat on the second speed for 2 minutes. (The desired dough temperature is 75°F/24°C.)

2. Oil your hands and very lightly oil a large bowl. Place the dough in the oiled bowl, cover with plastic wrap, and allow to rise about 1 hour.

3. Pour a little oil on a paper towel and rub over an area of clean counter so that you have a very lightly oiled area to prevent the dough's sticking.

4. Dump out the dough onto this area so that the smooth top of the dough is now on the bottom. Allow it to spread out as much as it will. Pick up the dough on the left side, lift up about one-third of the dough, and gently fold it across to the right. Allow it to spread a few seconds, then lift up about one-third of the right side of the dough and bring it across to the left. Again, allow the dough a few seconds to spread or gently pat it out a little. Pick up the bottom edge of the dough and bring about one-third of it up and across to the top. After it settles, pick up the top edge, lift about one-third of it up, and bring it across toward you.

5. Place the dough back in the bowl, turning it over so that the original smooth top that was against the counter is back on top. Cover with plastic wrap and allow to rise for another hour.

6. Once again, place the dough on a clean, very lightly oiled counter and do the folding as described in Step 4. Place it back in the bowl and cover again for a final rise of about one hour.

7. You want to preserve as much air as possible in the dough. Have two pieces about 14 inches (36 cm) long of Release foil, nonstick side up, or two pieces of lightly oiled parchment ready. Very lightly flour the counter. With fingers slightly spread, and with both hands under the dough, lift it out of the bowl and place out on the counter with the original top side up. Divide the dough in half. Again, with both hands gently lift one half to a piece of foil and gently pull a little at a time to a rectangle, about 4 x 10 inches (10 x 25 cm). Repeat with the other half of the dough. Cover with plastic wrap and allow to rise about another hour. The temperature should ideally be about 75°F/24°C. Because of the very moist dough, this is a fairly flat loaf.

8. As soon as you have shaped the dough for its final rise, arrange a shelf in the lower third of the oven, place a baking stone on it, and preheat the oven to 460°F/238°C.

9. Place a few clean small rocks (about 1 to 2 inches/2.5 to 5 cm each) in a pan with 2-inch (5-cm) sides and place the pan on the floor of the oven near the front. You are going to pour about 1 cup (237 ml) of boiling water over the rocks before you put the bread in the oven. You want a good steam-filled oven for the bread to go in. This steam will condense on the dough to keep it moist and allow a good oven rise. For the boiling water, place a saucepan with about 1¼ cups (296 ml) of water on a back burner and bring to a low boil.

10. When the bread has risen, turn up the heat under the water and bring to a rolling boil. *Very carefully,* with oven mitts on and making sure your arms and face are out of the way of the steam that will burst up, pour the boiling water into the pan of hot rocks. Close the oven door to allow it to fill with steam.

11. I do not have a baker's peel, so I slide a thin, flat baking sheet that has no raised edges on three sides under the foil, and slide the foil with the dough on top onto the hot stone. Place the loaves side by side on the stone. Bake 34 to 38 minutes. The dough needs to be crisp. Do not be tempted to remove it too soon. If it is getting too brown, lower the oven temperature by about 10°F/6°C. Remove bread to a rack to cool.

Biga (50% Water)

Makes about 11.8 oz/334 g

This is not dead-on 50% water. I rounded off a little to use easy measures—(½ cup, 4 oz/118 g, water and 1¾ cups, 7.9 oz/223 g, flour).

⅛ teaspoon (0.5 g) instant yeast, such as RapidRise or Quick-Rise
½ cup (118 ml, 4 oz/118 g) water (about 65°F/18°C)

1¾ cups (7.9 oz/223 g) spooned and leveled King Arthur Unbleached All-Purpose or Gold Medal Harvest King flour

Baker's Percentages—Flour: 7.9 oz/223 g, 100%; water: 4 oz/118 g, 53%; yeast: 0.5 g, 0.2%.

1. Stir the yeast into the water and then stir in the flour in two batches. Stir about 2 minutes by hand until smooth. Ideally, you want a dough temperature of 70°F/21°C.

2. Place dough in a lightly oiled bowl, turn to coat, and then cover with plastic wrap. Let stand at cool room temperature, about 70°F/21°C.

3. With this amount of yeast, this should take you 6 to 16 hours until the biga is ripe, but it is important to watch carefully the first time you make it under your conditions. The biga is ripe when it "domes" and is just starting to sink in the middle. The biga will be wet and sticky. Refrigerate until needed.

Basic Dough Made with Biga

MAKES ABOUT 4 CUPS (946 ML)

If your biga has been refrigerated, allow the portion that you need to stand at room temperature for an hour.

5 oz (142 g) Biga (page 452), at room temperature

1 cup plus 2 tablespoons (267 ml, 9 oz/255 g) water (about 70°F/21°C)

½ teaspoon (2 g) instant yeast, such as RapidRise or Quick-Rise

2 tablespoons (0.7 oz/21 g) semolina flour

1¼ teaspoons (7.5 g) fine sea salt

¹⁄₁₀ of a crushed quarter of a 500-mg vitamin C (ascorbic acid) tablet (about 10 mg)

3 cups (13.5 oz/383 g) spooned and leveled King Arthur Unbleached All-Purpose or Gold Medal Harvest King Unbleached flour, divided

1 tablespoon (15 ml) olive oil, divided

1. Stir the biga well, weigh out 5 ounces (142 g), and pour into a mixer. Add the water, yeast, semolina flour, salt, and vitamin C. With the paddle attachment, mix a few seconds on lowest speed. Add 2 cups (9 oz/254 g) of the flour and mix a few seconds. Then add the remaining 1 cup (4.5 oz/127 g) of flour. Switch to the dough hook when the dough becomes very thick. Mix on low for 1 minute, then on the second speed about 2 minutes. The desired dough temperature is about 72°F/22°C. The dough should be soft, on the edge of sticky. Add a tablespoon or so of water if needed.

2. Oil your hands and very lightly oil a large bowl. Place the dough in the oiled bowl, cover with plastic wrap, and allow to rise, about 1 hour. Pour a little oil on a paper towel and rub over an area of clean counter so that you have a very lightly oiled area, to prevent the dough's sticking.

3. Dump out the dough onto this area so that the smooth top of the dough is now on the bottom. Allow it to spread out as much as it will. Pick up the dough on the left side, lift up about one-third of the dough, and gently fold it across to the right, trapping some air as you make the fold. Allow it to spread a few seconds, then lift up about one-third of the right side of the dough and bring it across to the left. Again, allow the dough a few seconds to spread. Pick up the bottom edge of the dough and bring about one-third of it up and across to the top. After it settles, pick up the top edge, lift about one-third of it up, and bring it across toward you.

4. Place the dough back in the bowl, turning it over so that the smooth top that was against the counter is back on top. Cover and allow to rise for another hour. The dough is ready to preshape and, after standing, shape and bake as Fougasse (page 457) or Focaccia Farcita (page 458).

Fougasse with Biga

MAKES 3 FOUGASSES

Because of its shape, this fougasse has a lot of wonderful crust. It is made with a pre-ferment (biga) so it is more flavorful than the fougasse on page 439.

1 recipe Basic Dough Made with Biga (page
   456)

Cornstarch for shaping
Nonstick cooking spray

1. After the dough has completed its second bulk rise, place it on the lightly oiled countertop, smooth top up. Divide the dough into three pieces. With both hands in a cupping motion, tuck the sides slightly under each piece to create a smooth top. With both hands, grab the sides of the each round and stretch it sideways into an oval. Let it spring back slightly, then pull it out again. Flatten out a little, cover each with plastic wrap lightly sprayed with nonstick cooking spray and leave on the counter for about 20 minutes. The relaxed dough is now much easier to shape.

2. Shape one dough piece at a time. Cut a piece of Release foil 12 to 14 inches (30 to 36 cm) long. Place the dough on the nonstick side. You want to shape the dough into a large, fat "leaf" a little over 1 inch (2.5 cm) thick, with roughly an 8 to 10-inch (20 to 25-cm) base, 10 inches (25 cm) long in the center, coming to a fat point at the top. Roll or press the dough out into this large leaf shape. The cuts in the dough are not slits, but holes running from $1/2$ to 1 inch (1.3 to 2.5 cm) wide. (It is helpful if you look at the picture of the Fougasse.)

3. With a sharp dough scraper, cut a slit up the middle to resemble the major center vein of the leaf. Pull the dough apart so that you have a 1-inch (2.5-cm) wide hole. This slit should run from $3/4$ inch (2 cm) from the bottom to $3/4$ inch (2 cm) from the point. Dust your fingers with cornstarch and widen the slit, running about $1/2$ inch (1.3 cm) wide at the top and bottom and 1 inch (2.5 cm) wide in the center, so that a hole will remain when the dough rises. Next make three slits (holes) on each side of this main "vein." Near the base of the "leaf," parallel to the base, cut a slit on one side of the main slit, running from almost the corner of the base to almost the main "vein" hole. Cut another slit like this on the other side of the main "vein" slit. Widen these two base slits to $1/2$ inch (1.3 cm) wide near the ends and almost 1 inch (2.5 cm) in the center. Again, use your fingers to widen these slits so that they will remain open after the dough rises.

4. Cut two more short "veins" on each side running up some from the main "vein" slit at an angle, almost to the outer edge of the "leaf." Widen all of these slits to $1/2$ to 1-inch (1.3 to 2.5-cm) holes. Sprinkle the shaped leaf lightly with cornstarch. Cover loosely with plastic wrap that has been sprayed lightly with nonstick cooking spray and allow to rise 30 minutes to an hour.

5. As soon as you have shaped the dough for its final rise, arrange a shelf in the lower third of the oven, place a baking stone on it, and preheat the oven to 460°F/238°C.

6. Place a few clean small rocks (about 1 to 2 inches/2.5 to 5 cm each) in a pan with 2-inch (5-cm) sides and place the pan on the floor of the oven near the front. You are going to pour about 1 cup (237 ml) of boiling water over the rocks before you put the bread in the oven. You want a good steam-filled oven for the bread to go in. This steam will condense on the dough to keep it moist and allow a good oven rise. For the boiling water, place a saucepan with about 1¼ cups (296 ml) of water on a back burner and bring to a low simmer. When the bread is risen, turn the heat up under the water and bring to a boil. *Very carefully*, with oven mitts on, making sure your arms and face are out of the way of the steam that will burst up, pour the boiling water into the pan of hot rocks. Close the oven door to allow it to fill with steam.

7. I do not have a baker's peel, so I use a thin, flat baking sheet with no raised edges on three sides under the fougasse on the foil, and then slide the foil and fougasse onto the hot stone. It will take only 13 to 16 minutes to bake each fougasse. Be sure to brown well. This magnificent, crunchy crust is wonderful. Place on a rack to cool.

Focaccia Farcita

MAKES 1 LARGE CHEESE-FILLED FOCACCIA

Served with a salad, this delicious cheese-filled bread is a meal in itself.

1 recipe Basic Dough Made with Biga (page 456)

1 tablespoon (15 ml) olive oil

Filling

3 ounces (85 g) Gorgonzola
3 tablespoons (45 ml) heavy cream

12 fresh basil leaves, cut into slivers
2 cups (8 oz/227 g) grated mozzarella

Topping

¼ cup (59 ml) olive oil
3 large cloves garlic, sliced

3 tablespoons fresh rosemary leaves, fairly finely chopped

1. After the last hour of bulk fermentation, lift the biga dough out and place on the lightly oiled counter, smooth top up. Divide the dough into two equal pieces. With both hands in a cupping

motion, tuck the sides slightly under each piece, creating a smooth top. By tucking the dough into a tight smooth round you create a covering to better hold gases. Cover each oval with plastic wrap and leave on the counter for about 20 minutes. The relaxed dough is now much easier to shape.

2. Oil a rectangular baking sheet about 11 x 17 inches (28 x 43 cm). Stretch one piece of dough to make a 10 x 14-inch (25 x 36-cm) rectangle.

3. To make the filling, crumble the Gorgonzola into the heavy cream. Beat lightly to blend a little and then spread out over the dough leaving about 1 inch (2.5 cm) around the edges bare. Sprinkle the basil over the Gorgonzola and top with the mozzarella.

4. To make the topping, heat the olive oil in a medium skillet over medium heat. Sauté the garlic and rosemary for 1 minute. Strain and save the oil. Sprinkle the garlic and rosemary around over the cheese.

5. On a clean countertop, stretch the remaining piece of dough until it is the same size as the piece in the pan. Lift it across a rolling pin and place it to cover the filling. Press this top piece down well around the edges to seal. Press dimples over the dough with your fingertips. Brush the dough with about half of the strained olive oil. Cover the dough with plastic wrap and allow to rise about 45 minutes.

6. As soon as you have shaped the dough for its final rise, arrange a shelf in the lower third of the oven, place a baking stone on it, and preheat the oven to 460°F/238°C.

7. Place a few clean small rocks (about 1 to 2 inches/2.5 to 5 cm each) in a pan with 2-inch (5-cm) sides and place the pan on the floor of the oven, near the front. You are going to pour about 1 cup (237 ml) of boiling water over the rocks before you put the bread in the oven. You want a good steam-filled oven for the bread to go in. This steam will condense on the dough to keep it moist and allow a good oven rise. For the boiling water, place a saucepan with about $1\frac{1}{4}$ cups (296 ml) of water on a back burner and bring to a low simmer. When the bread has risen, turn up the heat under the water and bring to a boil. With oven mitts on your hands, *very carefully*—making sure your face and arms are out of the way of the steam that will burst up—pour the boiling water into the pan of hot rocks. Close the oven door to allow it to fill with steam.

8. Press the dough around the edges to seal well and drizzle the saved olive oil over the top. Place the pan onto the hot stone in the oven. Bake until lightly browned, about 30 minutes. Make yourself wait until it won't burn your hands to cut and eat.

NOTE: This magnificent loaf can be made ahead, very lightly browned, cooled, wrapped well, and then reheated and browned when you want to serve.

Wild Yeast (Sourdough Starters) Levain

One of the first challenges in making a sourdough starter is the temperature. For three days, you need to maintain the starter at an even temperature of 81°F/27°C (Professor Calvel's preferred temperature), while Andrew Whitley says 28 to 30°C (82 to 86°F).

So how am I going to keep a starter at this exact temperature for three days? I followed Whitley's suggestion to get an inexpensive electric plant propagator mat. It is a waterproof heating pad that you can put under a tray of baby plants to keep them at an even warm temperature. I found one for about $30 at a local garden supply store.

Shirley's Adaptation of Whitley's Rye Sourdough Starter

Whole-grain (dark) rye has a good population of yeast and lactobacilli and is easier than nearly any grain to get a vigorous wild yeast starter going. You may be able to get this at local health food stores or Whole Foods Markets. King Arthur (see Sources, flour, page 510) does not advertise a "dark rye flour," but they say that their Organic Pumpernickel Flour is the rye equivalent of whole-wheat flour. Bob's Red Mill's dark rye flour is 100% stone ground from organic U.S. #1 dark, plump rye berries.

Two big factors in growing yeast—warm, really warm (80°F/27°C) temperatures, and oxygen—mean stirring your starter frequently. My electric plant propagator, see above, has no settings, so I put a cup of water on it and plugged it in to find out what temperature it maintained. It is supposed to be 10 to 20°F/6 to 11°C higher than ambient temperature. You can go up as high as 86°F/30°C, but you absolutely need to stay in this 80 to 86°F/27 to 30°C range.

I like to use a glass wide-mouth quart (liter) jar you can buy at a grocery or hardware store. I use bottled spring water to avoid fluoride or other additives in a city water supply. Do not use distilled water since you need some minerals. To avoid late-night feedings, and being up in the middle of the night, start Day 1 at about 9 or 10 p.m.

DAY 1

3 tablespoons plus ½ teaspoon (0.9 oz/25 g) whole-grain dark rye flour	¼ cup (59 ml, 2 oz/56 g) spring water (about 104°F/40°C)
	Total weight 2.9 oz/81 g

Stir the flour and water together in a jar and cover tightly with plastic wrap. Place in a warm spot—80°F/27°C. Stir the starter frequently, at least four times during the next 24 hours.

DAY 2 (24 HOURS AFTER DAY 1 MIXING)

Starter from Day 1 (2.9 oz/81 g)	¼ cup (59 ml, 2 oz/56 g) spring water (about 104°F/40°C)
3 tablespoons plus ½ teaspoon (0.9 oz/25 g) whole-grain dark rye flour	Total weight 5.8 oz/162 g

Stir the flour and water into the starter and replace the lid. Place back in the warm spot—80°F/27°C. Stir the starter frequently, at least four times during the next 20 hours.

DAY 3 (20 HOURS AFTER DAY 2 FEEDING)

Starter from Day 2 (5.8 oz/162 g)
3 tablespoons plus ½ teaspoon (0.9 oz/25 g) whole-grain dark rye flour

¼ cup (59 ml, 2 oz/56 g) spring water (about 104°F/40°C)
Total weight 8.7 oz/247 g

There may be a gray liquid on top. This is normal, just stir it in. Stir the flour and water into the starter. Place it back in the warm spot—80°F/27°C. Stir the starter frequently, at least four times during the next 20 hours.

DAY 4 (20 HOURS AFTER DAY 3 FEEDING)

Starter from Day 3 (8.7 oz/243 g)
3 tablespoons plus ½ teaspoon (0.9 oz/25 g) whole-grain dark rye flour

¼ cup (59 ml, 2 oz/56 g) spring water (about 104°F/40°C)
Total weight 11.4 oz/324 g

Stir the flour and water into the starter. Place it back in the warm spot—80°F/27°C. Stir the starter frequently, at least four times during the next 20 hours. At the end of this time period, your starter should have bubbled up and should smell fruity. It will taste mildly acidic.

You can convert this to a wheat starter simply by feeding Days 3 and 4 with King Arthur Unbleached All-Purpose or Gold Medal Harvest King Unbleached flour, instead of the whole-grain dark rye flour.

Working Rye or Wheat Starter

MAKES ABOUT 2½ CUPS (591 ML)

1 recipe Shirley's Adaptation of Whitley's Rye Sourdough Starter, page 460
1¼ cups (5.6 oz/159 g) spooned and leveled whole-grain dark rye flour or King

Arthur Unbleached All-Purpose or Gold Medal Harvest King flour
1⅓ cups (316 ml, 10.6 oz/300 g) spring water (about 104°F/40°C)

Stir Whitley's Rye Sourdough Starter well and take out about ¼ cup (59 ml). Freeze the remaining starter. In a clean wide-mouth quart (liter) jar, stir together the starter, flour, and water. Cover with Press'n Seal plastic wrap or plastic wrap held in place with a rubber band, and place in a warm place for 12 to 24 hours. This is now a ready-to-use starter.

Rye with Pumpkin and Sunflower Seeds

MAKES ONE 8½ x 4¼ x 3-INCH (22 x 11 x 8-CM) LOAF

The crunch of the seeds is a wonderful complement to rye bread. This recipe is adapted from Andrew Whitley's Seeded Rye. Be sure to stir the starter well before measuring.

What This Recipe Shows

A sourdough rye starter can produce risen bread—slowly, but it does rise.

¾ cup (177 ml) Working Rye or Wheat Starter (page 461), made with whole-grain dark rye flour, stirred before measuring

1¾ cup plus 2 tablespoons (8.5 oz/240 g) spooned and leveled light or dark rye flour

1 teaspoon (6 g) salt, divided

½ cup plus 2 tablespoons (148 ml, 4.9 oz/139 g) spring water

¼ cup (about 1.3 oz/38 g) pumpkin seeds

½ cup (0.8 oz/23 g) sunflower seeds

3 tablespoons (1.5 oz/43 g) butter, divided

Nonstick cooking spray

1. In a medium mixing bowl, gently stir together the Working Rye or Wheat Starter, rye flour, ¾ teaspoon (4.5 g) of the salt, and water to barely mix.

2. In a large skillet, sauté the pumpkin seeds in 1 tablespoon (0.5 oz/14 g) of the butter, stirring constantly for several minutes until very lightly browned. Remove from the pan.

3. Wipe out the skillet and sauté sunflower seeds in the remaining butter, stirring constantly until lightly roasted. When seeds have cooled, pour half of the sunflower seeds in a pie pan. Sprinkle lightly with a little of the remaining salt. Combine the other half of the sunflower seeds in a bowl with the pumpkin seeds and toss with the rest of the salt.

4. Spray an 8½ x 4¼ x 3-inch (22 x 11 x 8-cm) loaf pan generously with nonstick cooking spray.

5. Wet your hands and gently work the sunflower-pumpkin seed mixture into the dough. Roughly shape the dough into a loaf that will fit your pan. Place it in the pan of sunflower seeds and roll it gently to coat the loaf all over with seeds. Carefully drop the loaf into the pan.

6. Spray a piece of plastic wrap with nonstick cooking spray and loosely cover the pan. Allow to rise in a warm place (about 80°F/27°C). This can take 2 to 6 hours, depending on the strength of the starter. It will not double in size, but it will rise a little.

7. When the loaf has risen a little, arrange a baking stone on a rack in the lower third of the oven and preheat the oven to 425°F/218°C.

8. When loaf has risen, place it in the oven on the stone. After 15 minutes, reduce the heat to 375°F/190°C. Bake for 30 minutes more. Check the internal temperature by inserting an instant-read thermometer in the center of the loaf. It is done when it registers 200 to 210°F/93 to 99°C. Remove from the pan and place on a rack to cool.

Rye and Wheat Starter

This is my adaptation of a recipe by Calvel. Again, I used an electric plant propagator that I purchased from a nursery. Mine has no settings, so I put a cup of water on it and plugged it in to find out what temperature it maintained. It is supposed to be 10 to 20°F/6 to 11°C higher than ambient temperature. You can go up as high as 86°F/30°C, but you absolutely need to stay in the 80 to 86°F/27 to 30°C range.

I like to use a plastic container with a snap-on lid like the plastic storage containers that you can buy in packages of three to five in the grocery store. The snap-on lid works well because it is tight enough to prevent the starter from drying out and yet, if the starter gets vigorous, it will simply pop off rather than explode.

Calvel calls for a small amount of malt extract. Fortunately, both King Arthur Unbleached All-Purpose and Gold Medal Harvest King Unbleached flour already have a small amount of malted barley flour added. I find this really convenient. I can forget about malt extract.

These hours to tend the starter are tough—like feeding a new baby. But this is an outstanding starter and will give you great flavored breads.

MIX AT 9 A.M.

2⅓ cups (10.5 oz/298 g) spooned and leveled King Arthur Unbleached All-Purpose or Gold Medal Harvest King flour

2⅓ cups (10.5 oz/298 g) spooned and leveled whole-grain dark rye flour

1⅔ cups (393 ml, 13.4 oz/379 g) spring water

½ teaspoon (3 g) salt

2 teaspoons (3 g) malt extract (only if you are not using either Gold Medal Harvest King or King Arthur Unbleached flour)

In a large (8-cup, 1.9-L) plastic container with a snap-on lid, stir together both flours, the spring water, salt, and malt extract, if using. Snap on the lid. Place in a warm spot—80°F/27°C. Stir the starter frequently, at least four times during the next 22 hours.

AT 7 A.M. THE NEXT DAY (AFTER 22 HOURS)

About 1¼ cups (10.6 oz/300 g) starter from above

2⅓ cups (10.5 oz/298 g) spooned and leveled King Arthur Unbleached All-Purpose or Gold Medal Harvest King flour

¾ cup plus 1 tablespoon (192 ml, 6.5 oz/187 g) spring water

⅛ teaspoon (pinch) salt

Stir your starter and remove the amount you need for this step. Discard or freeze the rest. Stir together the starter, flour, water, and salt, and replace the lid. Place back in the warm spot—80°F/27°C. Stir the starter frequently, at least three times during the next 7 hours.

AT 2 P.M. (AFTER 7 HOURS)

About 1¼ cups (10.6 oz/300 g) starter from above

2⅓ cups (10.5 oz/298 g) spooned and leveled King Arthur Unbleached All-Purpose or Gold Medal Harvest King flour

¾ cup plus 1 tablespoon (192 ml, 6.5 oz/187 g) spring water

⅛ teaspoon (pinch) salt

Stir your starter and remove the amount you need for this step. Discard or freeze the rest. Stir together the starter, flour, water, and salt, and replace the lid. Place back in the warm spot—80°F/27°C. Stir the starter frequently, at least three times during the next 7 hours.

AT 9 P.M. (AFTER ANOTHER 7 HOURS)

About 1¼ cups (10.6 oz/300 g) starter from
  above
2⅓ cups (10.5 oz/298 g) spooned and leveled
  King Arthur Unbleached All-Purpose or
  Gold Medal Harvest King flour

¾ cup plus 1 tablespoon (192 ml,
  6.5 oz/187 g) spring water
⅛ teaspoon (pinch) salt

Stir your starter and remove the amount you need for this step. Discard or freeze the rest. Stir together the starter, flour, water, and salt, and replace the lid. Place back in the warm spot—80°F/27°C. Stir the starter frequently, at least three times during the next 6 hours.

AT 3 A.M. THE THIRD DAY (AFTER ANOTHER 6 HOURS)

About 1¼ cups (10.6 oz/300 g) starter from
  above
2⅓ cups (10.5 oz/298 g) spooned and leveled
  King Arthur Unbleached All-Purpose or
  Gold Medal Harvest King flour

¾ cup plus 1 tablespoon (192 ml,
  6.5 oz/187 g) spring water
⅛ teaspoon (pinch) salt

Stir together the starter, flour, water, and salt, and replace the lid. Place back in the warm spot—80°F/27°C. Stir the starter frequently, at least once during the next 6 hours.

AT 9 A.M. (AFTER ANOTHER 6 HOURS)

About 1¼ cups (10.6 oz/300 g) starter from
  above
2⅓ cups (10.5 oz/298 g) spooned and leveled
  King Arthur Unbleached All-Purpose or
  Gold Medal Harvest King flour

¾ cup plus 1 tablespoon (192 ml,
  6.5 oz/187 g) spring water
⅛ teaspoon (pinch) salt

Stir together the starter, flour, water, and salt, and replace the lid. Place back in the warm spot—80°F/27°C. Stir the starter frequently, at least once during the next 6 hours.

AT 3 P.M. (AFTER 6 HOURS)

The starter is ready to use.

BUILDING A STARTER

To use a sourdough starter, you need to build it up to good activity. This is done by taking a small portion of the starter and combining it with flour and water and allowing it to stand at 70°F/21°C for 12 to 16 hours. You can see exactly how this is done in the following recipe.

Sourdough Rustic Boules

MAKES 2 LARGE ROUNDS

This is essentially the same as the Rustic Boules on page 450, but made with a sourdough starter instead of the poolish.

STARTER BUILD

¼ cup (59 ml) Rye and Wheat Starter, page 463

1½ cups (355 ml) spring water (about 68°F/20°C)

2 cups (9 oz/255 g) spooned and leveled Gold Medal Harvest King or King Arthur Unbleached All-Purpose flour

Make this 12 to 16 hours before making the final dough. Stir the starter well, spoon it into a bowl, and stir in the water and the flour. Cover and allow to stand at about 70°F/21°C.

FINAL DOUGH

¾ cup (177 ml, 6.1 oz/173 g) water

3½ cups (15.8 oz/447 g) spooned and leveled Gold Medal Harvest King or King Arthur Unbleached All-Purpose flour

2 tablespoons (21 g) semolina flour

1 teaspoon (4 g) instant yeast, such as RapidRise or Quick-Rise

1 tablespoon (19 g) fine sea salt

Nonstick cooking spray

1 tablespoon (15 ml) canola oil, divided

1. In a mixer with the dough hook, beat together the water, both flours, and 2 cups (473 ml) of the built starter on low speed for about 1 minute. Cover with plastic wrap and allow to stand for about 40 minutes.

2. Sprinkle the yeast over the dough and mix for about 30 seconds. Sprinkle the salt over the dough and mix on the second speed about 1½ minutes until the dough has come together. The dough should not be firm, but not totally soft—a medium consistency. Add water or flour and mix as needed. Cover the dough with plastic wrap lightly sprayed with nonstick cooking spray and allow to ferment, ideally at about 76°F/24°C.

3. After 25 minutes, with an oiled paper towel, lightly oil an area on a clean countertop. Dump out the dough onto the counter. Lift one-third of the dough on the right and pull across to the other side. Lift one-third of the dough on the left and pull across to the other side. Lift bottom one-third of the dough up and across the dough. Lift top one-third of the dough and pull it down across the dough. Lightly oil a bowl and place the dough in the bowl with the side that was on the counter turned up. After 25 minutes, dump the dough on the lightly oiled counter with the top of the dough on the counter. Fold the dough again as before. Place the dough back in the bowl, counter side up. Cover with plastic wrap lightly sprayed with nonstick cooking spray and allow to stand 20 minutes more.

4. Place the dough on the counter and gently divide into two equal pieces. With both hands in a cupping motion, tuck the sides slightly under each piece, creating a smooth top. By tucking the dough into a tight smooth round you create a covering to better hold gases. Cover each oval with plastic wrap sprayed with nonstick cooking spray and leave on the counter for about 20 minutes. The relaxed dough is now much easier to shape.

5. Arrange a shelf in the lower third of the oven, place a baking stone on it, and preheat the oven to 460°F/238°C.

6. Put about 1¼ cups (296 ml) of water in a saucepan and heat to a very low boil for a steam bath.

7. Using your left hand as a backstop, with your right hand, press gently against the dough round and "massage" with a stroke away from you, massaging the side of the round. Rotate the round and again gently "knead" the side of the dough. Repeat with the other round. Place the rounds on a piece of Release foil, nonstick side up, or a piece of parchment sprayed with nonstick cooking spray. Cover with plastic wrap sprayed with nonstick cooking spray. Allow to rise about 25 minutes at about 76°F/24°C.

8. Place a few clean small rocks (about 1 to 2 inches/2.5 to 5 cm each) in a pan with 2-inch (5-cm) sides and place the pan on the floor of the oven. You are going to pour about 1 cup (237 ml) of boiling water over the rocks before you put the bread in the oven. You want a good steam-filled oven for the bread to go in. This steam will condense on the dough to keep it moist and allow a good oven rise. When the bread has risen, turn the heat up under the water and bring to a boil. *Very carefully,* with oven mitts on, making sure your arms and face are out of the way of the steam that will burst up, pour the boiling water into the pan of hot rocks. Close the oven door to allow it to fill with steam.

9. Slash the rounds at an angle, using several quick slashes only about ⅛ inch (3 cm) deep. Place the loaves side by side on the foil. I do not have a baker's peel, so I slide a thin, flat baking sheet with no raised edges on three sides under the foil and then slide the foil with the dough on top onto the hot stone. Bake for 34 to 38 minutes, until well browned. Remove the loaves to a rack to cool.

Basic Bread Ingredients

FLOUR BASICS

Gluten

When the cook adds water to flour and stirs, two proteins in the flour (glutenin and gliadin) grab water and each other to form elastic sheets of gluten. Different flours have different amounts of these two gluten-forming proteins and, accordingly, absorb different amounts of water and form different amounts of gluten.

Differences in Water Absorption

How many of these two proteins a flour contains determines how much water it absorbs and how much gluten it forms. Some cooks have blamed this difference in absorption on humidity, which actually makes only a minute difference compared to protein content.

> How many of the two gluten-forming proteins (glutenin and gliadin) a flour contains determines how much water it absorbs and how much gluten it forms.

This difference in water absorption can be major. For example, 2 cups (9 oz/255 g) of high-protein bread flour absorb 1 cup (237 ml) of water to form a soft, sticky dough. However, 2 cups (8.2 oz/232 g) of low-protein Southern flour or cake flour and 1 cup (237 ml) water make a dough that is between a thick soup and cottage cheese consistency. It can take almost ½ cup (2.1 oz/58 g) more low-protein flour to get the same consistency dough as with the high-protein flour. This means that even a small recipe with 2 cups (8.8 oz/249 g) of flour can be off by ½ cup (2.2 oz/62 g)! This is a difference of 25%; commercial recipes with 20 pounds (9 kg) of flour could be off by 5 pounds (2.3 kg).

> Many times in baking, a cook has to adjust—add more flour or more water to get a dough to the right consistency.

Cooks are constantly faced with this problem. The person writing the recipe uses one kind of flour and the person following the recipe uses another. You need to realize that even though you follow a recipe exactly, your dough may be very different from the dough that you are supposed to get with that recipe.

Many times in baking, a cook has to adjust—add more flour or more water to get a dough to the right consistency.

Difference in the Amount of Gluten Formed

Different flours have different amounts of the two gluten-forming proteins and thus form different amounts of gluten.

Which Flours Have More or Less Gluten-Forming Proteins?

Hard spring wheats grown in colder climates are usually high in protein and make high-protein flour, outstanding for yeast breads. Soft winter wheats, grown in moderate climates where the ground never freezes to a depth greater than about 10 inches (25.4 cm), have much less glutenin and gliadin. A few brands of flour are labeled with the kind of wheat, but most are not.

Not only are different strains of wheat different, but flour from the same strain of wheat can vary. Many things—soil, temperature, rainfall, maturity at harvest—influence protein content.

The milling process is a major determinant of the protein content of flour. When flour is milled, wheat kernels are cleaned and tempered (soaked in water), then crushed and the germ and bran removed. The endosperm (main central portion of the kernel) goes through one set of rollers and sifters after another, and these grind, sift, and separate flour into fractions called *streams*. There may be as many as eighty streams in this separation process. Just as winemakers blend juices from different vineyards to make fine wines, millers blend flour from different streams to make flours for different purposes. For a bread flour, a miller includes a lot of flour from the high-protein streams; for a low-protein, he uses the high-starch streams.

All-Purpose!

Millers in Northern states, which have an abundance of high-protein flour, blend their all-purpose—particularly their unbleached all-purpose—high in protein (13 grams per cup) for their customers who have made fine yeast breads with these flours for many years. The customers of millers in Southern states specialize in biscuits, cakes, and pie crusts and are accustomed to low-protein flour (8 to 9 grams per cup) from soft winter wheat. So Southern millers blend a low-protein flour. Actually, all-purpose flour can range from more than 13 grams protein per cup down to about 8 grams per cup. Essentially, flour labeled "all-purpose" can be anything!

> All-purpose flour can range from more than 13 grams protein per cup down to about 8 grams per cup. Essentially, flour labeled "all-purpose" can be anything!

High-Protein/Low Protein: How Can You Tell?

The Food and Drug Administration requires that flour be within 1 gram of the protein content stated on the bag. Previously, flour was labeled by 1-cup portions. Bread flour was labeled 14 grams per cup, unbleached 12 to 13 grams per cup, national brand all-purpose 12 grams per cup, Southern all-purpose 9 grams per cup, and cake flour 8 grams per cup. It was easy to tell those labeled 13 to 14 grams were high protein; those labeled below 10 grams per cup were low protein.

Unfortunately, the portion amount for the new regulations is ¼ cup and nearly every flour on the market is labeled 3 grams per ¼ cup. This means the flour can be from about 2 to 4 grams of protein per ¼ cup. The flour in the bag labeled 3 grams per ¼ cup can really have from about 8 grams per cup to 16 grams per cup. Low-protein Southern flour is now labeled 3 grams per ¼ cup, and high-protein bread flour also may be labeled 3 grams per ¼ cup. With the new regulations, you can tell absolutely nothing from the label about the specific protein content of the flour that is important for cooking.

You know that bread flour is excellent for breads. You know that cake flour is excellent for cakes. And millers have traditionally always made unbleached flour high in protein, so you know that most unbleached flours will make light yeast breads. Self-rising flour is low in protein, but if you need a low-protein flour without leavening, you will need to use a Southern low-protein flour, a pastry flour, or to mix one-third cake flour with two-thirds national brand bleached all-purpose.

Best Flour for Yeast Breads?

Knowing that the higher the protein in plain white flour, the more gluten is formed, I wanted nothing but hard spring wheat—the highest-protein flour to make breads.

I had to completely drop everything that I thought that I knew about flour and start all over. In the class that I took, Didier knew his students would believe in the very high-protein hard spring wheats. And he knew the only way that he could get us to change our minds was to show us side by side that his lower-protein flour milled from hard red winter wheat made a better baguette than our higher-protein hard spring wheat flour.

We made baguettes side by side, the same techniques, same times, same temperature. I had great confidence in my very high-protein hard spring wheat. I did not think Didier's lower-protein hard red winter wheat could possibly make loaves with as great a volume as my higher protein flour.

I would never have believed it if I had not made the breads myself. The loaves with the lower-protein winter wheat were actually as high as or a breath higher than my beloved spring wheat! And then there was the taste. I could not believe how much more flavorful the winter wheat loaves were—an amazing difference in taste.

I knew that when you add water to flour and stir, two proteins (glutenin and gliadin) in the flour grab the water and each other to form elastic sheets of gluten. And I vaguely knew that glutenin was responsible for gluten's elasticity—its ability to spring back, and that gliadin influenced gluten's extensibility—its ability to stretch. What I didn't realize was how important this extensibility is for well-risen doughs.

Having a dough that will stretch is really important. If the gluten can stretch more and more without tearing and letting the gases produced by yeast escape, you will be able to produce well-risen bread. I just needed to realize that the plastic properties of gluten consist of three parts: strength, extensibility, and elasticity.

This extensibility is dependent on the variety and origin of the wheat, on other ingredients in the dough, and on techniques.

There Is Gluten and There Is Gluten

I was a research chemist for the Vanderbilt Medical School. As a chemist, years ago when I was studying bread, I had a hard time understanding gluten. I wanted a formula—like x number of molecules of glutenin plus x number of molecules of gliadin plus x number of molecules of water equal x number of molecules of gluten. Gluten doesn't work that way—no orderly formula. It is just a mess of stuff linked together.

Gluten can have totally different amounts of glutenin and gliadin depending on the variety and growing conditions of the wheat that the flour is made from. So gluten can have more gliadin and be more extensible or it can have more glutenin and be more elastic. This is why flour from hard red winter wheat makes wonderful breads. This flour, with the proper techniques, is wonderfully extensible and can make loaves that are as high as or higher than very high-protein flours. And properly handled breads made with this flour can have wonderful flavors.

Types of Wheat

Types of wheat—winter wheat, spring wheat, hard wheat, soft wheat, durum, spelt, kamut, einkorn, emmer, and on and on. In general, hard wheats have more protein than soft wheats, and spring wheats have more protein than winter wheats. The hard red winter wheat that I have used so much in this section is a medium-high protein, about 11.7% protein.

My other favorite wheat is durum (semolina). I just love the taste of durum flour or its slightly coarser grind, semolina. You do not get as much gluten development as you would with hard red winter wheats or spring wheats, but you can make a wonderful loaf with a mix of semolina and unbleached flours, as in the recipe below.

Semolina Bread

MAKES ONE 10-INCH (25-CM) ROUND LOAF

I love the taste of semolina in bread. You may have noticed that I just can't help adding a little for flavor in many of my breads. This big round loaf is wonderful with the semolina taste and a pale yellow crumb.

What This Recipe Shows

Use unbleached flour for both good gluten and flavor, and vitamin C contributes to better gluten development.

Semolina forms some gluten but not as much as some other hard varieties of wheat.

Olive oil in the loaf imparts flavor and slightly enhances volume.

---

2 cups (9 oz/254 g) spooned and leveled King Arthur Unbleached All-Purpose or Gold Medal Harvest King flour

2 cups (11.8 oz/334 g) semolina flour

$\frac{1}{10}$ of a crushed quarter of a 500-mg vitamin C (ascorbic acid) tablet (about 10 mg)

$1\frac{1}{2}$ teaspoons (9 g) salt, divided

$1\frac{1}{2}$ cups (355 ml, 12 oz/340 g) water (about 68°F/20°C)

1 package ($2\frac{1}{4}$ teaspoons/7 g) instant yeast, such as RapidRise or Quick-Rise

3 tablespoons (45 ml) warm water (about 110°F/43°C)

$\frac{1}{4}$ cup (59 ml) good-quality olive oil, divided

Nonstick cooking spray

3 to 4 tablespoons (0.5 to 0.8 oz/15 to 22 g) coarse cornmeal

1. Place the unbleached flour and semolina flour in a mixer with the paddle attachment. Run the mixer about 30 seconds to blend well. Add $1\frac{1}{2}$ cups water (355 ml) at 68°F/20°C and mix on the lowest speed for 1 minute. Cover with plastic wrap and allow to stand 30 minutes.

2. Add the vitamin C and $1\frac{1}{4}$ teaspoons (7.5 g) of the salt. Sprinkle the yeast over the warm (about 110°F/43°C) water. Stir and allow to stand for 30 seconds only, then sprinkle over the dough. Mix on low speed for 1 minute. Add 1 tablespoon (15 ml) of the olive oil. Switch to the dough hook. Turn the mixer up to the second speed and run for 2 minutes. The dough should be soft. Add a little flour or water as needed. Mix on the second speed a few seconds to incorporate.

3. With about 1 tablespoon (15 ml) of the oil, coat a bowl and your hands. Scrape the dough into the oiled bowl, turn the dough in the bowl to lightly coat, and cover with plastic wrap. Allow the dough to rise 45 minutes.

4. Wipe a clean counter with a lightly oiled paper towel. Dump out the dough onto the counter so that the smooth top of the dough is now on the bottom. Allow it to spread out as much as it will. Pick up the dough on the left side, lift up about one-third of the dough, and gently fold it across to the right. Allow it to spread a few seconds, then lift up about one-third of the right side of the dough and bring it across to the left. Again, allow the dough a few seconds to spread. Pick up the bottom edge of the dough and bring about one-third of it up and across to the top. After it settles, pick up the top edge, lift about one-third of it up, and bring it across toward you.

5. Place the dough back in the bowl, turning it over so that the top is back on top. Cover and allow to rise for another 45 minutes.

6. After the bulk fermentation, lift out the dough and place it on the lightly oiled counter. Turn the dough over so that the top is back on top. Using both hands with a gently cupping and tucking action, shape the dough into a smooth round. Cover with a piece of plastic wrap that has been lightly sprayed with nonstick cooking spray and allow to stand for 20 minutes.

7. Arrange a shelf in the lower third of the oven, place a baking stone on it, and preheat the oven to 450°F/232°C.

8. Sprinkle a medium baking sheet or 16-inch (41-cm) round pizza pan heavily with cornmeal. If you are right-handed, prop the dough ball against your left hand and press down and forward on the opposite side of the ball with the palm of your right hand to lightly knead the side of the ball. Let the dough ball rotate slightly forward with the stroke and continue to knead the sides of the round until you have gone completely around. Pinch the bottom to seal and place on the cornmeal on the baking sheet. Stir together the remaining 2 tablespoons (30 ml) olive oil and ¼ teaspoon (1.5 g) salt and brush on the loaf. Let the dough rise until doubled, about 1 hour.

9. Place a few clean small rocks (about 1 to 2 inches/2.5 to 5 cm each) in a pan with 2-inch (5-cm) sides and place the pan on the floor of the oven near the front. You are going to pour about 1 cup (237 ml) of boiling water over the rocks just before you place the dough in the oven. The moisture will condense on the relatively cool dough and keep it a little moister, allowing the dough to rise well before it crusts. For the boiling water, place a saucepan with about 1¼ cups (296 ml) of water on a burner and bring to a low boil.

10. With a razor, quickly cut slits straight down into the dough, ⅛ to ¼ inch (0.3 to 0.6 cm) deep. I usually cut three or four slashes parallel, but you can cut a rustic square or other decorative slashes. Just be careful not to deflate the bread.

11. With oven mitts on, *very carefully* pour the boiling water into the pan with the stones. Keep your head and arms out of the way of the great billow of steam that comes up. Close the oven briefly.

12. Place the baking sheet with the loaf on the stone in the oven. Bake until well browned, 45 to 55 minutes total baking time. The loaf should sound hollow when thumped on the bottom. You can also check for doneness by inserting an instant-read thermometer in the bottom center of loaf and pushing it to the center. The loaf is done when the center is over 200°F/93°C. Place the loaf on a rack to cool.

Grains Other Than Wheat

Wheat flour is a necessity for the bubblegum-like sheets of gluten. Corn, rye, oats, barley, rice, millet, and other grains can be ground into flour to make light baking powder–leavened products like pancakes, muffins, or quick breads. But only wheat flour contains enough of the two proteins glutenin and gliadin to make good sheets of gluten. Rye contains a small amount, and triticale, a rye-wheat crossbreed, has some of these proteins too, but not enough to make a light bread.

A yeast bread made with any grain that does not contain these two proteins will not rise, no matter how much yeast is used. The yeast can produce millions of bubbles of gas, but without gluten to hold them, the bubbles float off into the air.

You can mix flours—for example, Anadama Bread is a mixture of cornmeal and wheat flour. Molasses is usually added so you have great flavors, and with enough wheat flour for gluten, you can get a successful bread. See recipe next page.

Anadama Bread

MAKES ONE 9-INCH (23-CM) ROUND LOAF

This beautiful, deeply browned bread with cornmeal and molasses has a colorful history. It is said that in the town of Rockport, Massachusetts, a local fisherman's lazy wife, Anna, always served him cornmeal mush and molasses and never bread. He was so frustrated that he took the cornmeal mush and molasses, added flour and yeast and baked it, muttering, "Anna damn her." The bread was delicious and soon everyone in the neighborhood was making Anadama Bread.

When I was in Venice, Italy, I fell in love with something that they called *polenta bianco*—white polenta. It looked like mashed potatoes but it tasted like corn. They explained that it was made from finely ground polenta. I tried finely grinding the cornmeal for this recipe and loved it. It absorbs liquid more easily and has more flavor.

What This Recipe Shows

Processing cornmeal enhances flavor and the fine grind makes it easier to absorb liquid.

Soaking the cornmeal and cooking it first prevents it from robbing the dough of its moisture.

Molasses supplies sugars and minerals for yeast.

½ cup (2 oz/61 g) yellow cornmeal

1½ cups (355 ml) water (room temperature), divided

3 cups (13.5 oz/383 g) spooned and leveled King Arthur Unbleached All-Purpose or Gold Medal Harvest King flour, divided

1 package (2¼ teaspoons/7 g) instant yeast, such as RapidRise or Quick-Rise

¼ cup (59 ml) unsulfured molasses, such as Grandma's

¼ cup (59 ml) heavy cream

½ teaspoon (1 g) freshly grated nutmeg

1 teaspoon (6 g) salt

1 tablespoon (15 ml) canola oil

Nonstick cooking spray

3 tablespoons (1.5 oz/43 g) butter, melted

1. Place the cornmeal in a food processor with the steel blade and run about 1 minute, allow the processor to cool for 1 minute, then process 1 minute more. The cornmeal should be very fine. (You can also do this in a coffee grinder in two batches.)

2. Stir the cornmeal into ¾ cup (177 ml) of the water. Allow to stand for 1 hour. In a heavy saucepan, bring ½ cup (118 ml) of the water to a boil. Stir in the cornmeal mixture and cook with steady stirring until the mixture thickens. Set aside and allow to cool.

3. When the cornmeal mixture is cool, place it in a mixer fitted with a dough hook. Add 1 cup (4.5 oz/127 g) of the flour and mix on low speed for a few seconds. Add 1 more cup (4.5 oz/127 g) of the flour and mix on low speed for about 1 minute. Cover with plastic wrap and allow to stand for 20 minutes.

4. Stir the yeast into the remaining ¼ cup (60 ml) water and mix into the dough on low speed for several seconds. Mix in the molasses for several seconds, and then mix in the cream. Add the nutmeg and the remaining cup (4.5 oz/127 g) of flour. Mix for several seconds. Sprinkle the salt across the dough and mix on the second speed for 2 minutes. Oil a bowl and place the dough into the bowl and turn to coat, cover with plastic wrap, and allow to rise until doubled, about 1 hour.

5. Turn the dough out on the counter, top side down. Pick up the dough on the left side, lift up about one-third of the dough, and gently fold it across to the right, trapping some air as you make the fold. Allow it to spread a few seconds, then lift up about one-third of the right side of the dough and bring it across to the left. Again, allow the dough a few seconds to spread. Pick up the bottom edge of the dough and bring about one-third of it up and across to the top. After it settles, lift about one-third of the top edge and bring it across toward you. With both hands in a cupping motion, tuck the sides slightly under, creating a smooth top.

6. Arrange a shelf in the lower third of the oven, place a baking stone on it, and preheat the oven to 375°F/190°C.

7. Spray a 9-inch (23-cm) round baking dish or casserole with nonstick cooking spray. Place the dough in the casserole so that the smooth top is on top. Cover with plastic wrap sprayed lightly with nonstick cooking spray and allow to rise until doubled, about 30 minutes.

8. Place the casserole on the stone and bake about 45 minutes, until the bread is deeply browned. Leave in the casserole for 5 minutes to cool, and then remove the bread to a cooling rack. Brush with the melted butter. Serve warm. This bread is great toasted.

Whole-Grain Breads

Using whole-grain flours can present challenges. For example, in a cup of whole-wheat flour you are going to have a smaller amount of the gluten-forming proteins than you have in regular white flour just because you have germ and bran taking up volume. This means that breads made with whole-wheat flour will not be as light as breads made with regular unbleached all-purpose flour.

Frequently, high-protein bread flour or even vital wheat gluten (see page 476) is combined with whole-wheat flour to produce a lighter loaf. The Land of Milk and Honey Whole Wheat (page 483) is just such a recipe.

There are actually many differences in whole-grain flour and regular processed white flours. Peter Reinhart, baker, famous cookbook author, and outstanding teacher, points out that whole-grain flour contains a wealth of enzymes that not only aid in the breaking down of starch into sugars to feed yeast but also aid in many reactions that produce flavorful products in a dough.

In his book *Whole Grain Breads,* Peter has developed techniques to take advantage of this enzyme activity to produce flavorful whole-grain breads. In addition to preparing pre-ferments, he makes "soakers." Instead of allowing the flour and liquid to stand for 20 to 30 minutes as you do in the autolysis, he soaks the flour overnight with the liquid and a little salt to limit yeast activity. He wants the enzymes to be able to be super active and have all night to produce sugars and flavorful breakdown products. If you are interested in whole-grain breads, by all means, you need to get Peter's book.

Vital Wheat Gluten

Vital wheat gluten, which is available in health food stores, is gluten that has been extracted from flour. It contains 45 to 60 grams of protein per cup, or has approximately three to five times the gluten-forming potential of bread flour. Gluten flour technically is flour blended by a miller (not extracted) that contains high concentrations of the gluten-forming proteins; however, some flour labelers do not acknowledge this distinction. You will find that some products labeled "gluten flour" are actually extracted vital wheat gluten.

Ash

Here in the United States, the first thing a baker usually wants to know about a flour is its protein content. Not so in Europe: they are concerned with the ash content. So much so that the flour is named according to its ash content. Type 55 flour in France has 0.55% ash content. In Germany the same flour is called Type 550.

What is ash? Why do European bakers consider it so important? The ash content is the percentage of minerals in a flour sample. A weighed sample of the flour is incinerated in a high-temperature furnace so that everything is burned except the minerals. This weight, divided by the weight of the sample and multiplied by one hundred, gives the percentage of minerals in the flour.

What do minerals do in baking? Why are bakers interested in the amount of minerals in the flour? Actually, minerals are a nutrient for yeast and aid in fermentation. A dough from flour with a very low ash content may rise poorly. But, the major reason bakers are interested in ash content is that it indicates exactly what part of the grain the flour is from. Minerals are concentrated in the wheat's aleurone, the layer between the bran and the endosperm. This is also the high-protein part of the wheat kernel. High ash indicates high protein.

New wheat varieties like semi-dwarf wheats contain more minerals in their endosperm. And improved farming practices producing richer soils have made higher ash levels the norm. Previously, low ash indicated a more refined or "purer flour," but now a flour can be very pure and still have an ash count that previously would have been considered high.

Today in artisan baking, higher-ash flours have many advantages. The minerals produce stronger doughs, provide better food for yeast, improve dough's tolerance, and may even enhance flavor.

DIASTATIC MALT, MALTED BARLEY FLOUR, BARLEY MALT SYRUP

Malt extract can be diastatic or nondiastatic. Nondiastatic is simply added as a sweetener; diastatic malt contains live enzymes to break starch into sugars that feed yeast. A small amount is ideal for doughs that ferment a long time, but too much can give you a slack, gooey dough. Barley malt syrup does not have live enzymes (it is nondiastatic). So, it doesn't aid in breaking down starch and only contributes a little flavor and a little sugar. Malted barley flour does contain live enzymes and is ideal to use in doughs. Both King Arthur Unbleached All-Purpose and Gold Medal Harvest King Unbleached flour have a small amount of malted barley flour added. I find this really convenient. Using these flours, I can forget about having to add any diastatic malt extract.

YEAST

Yeast is a single-celled organism that needs simple sugars and oxygen to thrive. In bread doughs, active yeast exudes a liquid that, when it touches an air bubble in the dough, releases carbon dioxide gas and alcohol. The carbon dioxide gently inflates the dough. The alcohol remains in the dough until it evaporates in a great burst in the hot oven—this is oven spring.

Yeast Types

Fresh Yeast (Cake Yeast)

Fresh yeast is difficult if not impossible to find in our local stores. You probably can buy a block of fresh yeast (it looks like a pound of butter) from one of your local bakeries. The refrigerated life is not long. Maybe you can share some with a friend or freeze some in small portions, but realize that freezing will reduce its activity considerably.

Active Dry Yeast

This is the yeast that we have had in packages and jars in grocery stores for years. You need to stir it into warm water (110°F/43°C) to plump up its cells and get it active. Cold water can damage or destroy this yeast. So be careful to allow this yeast to stand in warm water for about 10 minutes, until its cells hydrate and it becomes creamy looking.

Instant Yeast (RapidRise, Quick-Rise)

Instant yeast is typically sold dry and can be added directly to the flour and mixed in with the dough. Each company has its own line of instant yeast, and you can expect differences among different brands. They do, however, share certain qualities. All are fine, open, porous textured small particles. They are air dried instead of oven dried like active dry yeast. This texture makes it possible for the instant yeast to soak in water and become alive and active instantly.

Wild Yeast

On pages 460 and 461, there are two excellent recipes for sourdough starters. If you have tried to make a starter before and had limited success, do make one of these starters. You will be surprised at the wonderful, active starter that you get. Part of the secret is using whole-grain rye flour and keeping the starter very warm.

Yeast Food

To keep yeast well fed and growing, you need to keep it supplied with sugar and oxygen. One way to do this is with malted barley. Malted barley flour has been added to both of the basic hard red winter wheat flours that I use, King Arthur Unbleached All-Purpose and Gold Medal Harvest King Unbleached. This added malted barley flour contains live enzymes to break up starch into sugars and supply yeast with a constant food supply throughout long fermentations.

Yeast Care

When yeast is active, one way that it reproduces is by dividing—one cell divides into two, then each of those divides. Soon you have a clump of yeast. Yeast can produce carbon dioxide and alcohol as long as it gets sugar; however, it cannot reproduce without oxygen. The yeast in the center of these clumps can no longer get this necessary oxygen and food.

If you move the dough around, you break up these clumps and spread out the yeast, giving it a fresh supply of food and oxygen. When you are growing yeast in a sourdough starter, it is important to stir the starter to get more oxygen to the yeast.

In a dough, after it sits for a while, you need to break up these clumps, too. Instead of the violent punching down of the dough, simple stretching and folding does several things. It spreads out the yeast beautifully and it develops gluten.

Temperature

Yeast has optimum activity between 86°F/30°C and 95°F/35°C but needs a lower temperature for flavor development. Wild yeast prefers slightly lower temperatures.

Yeast has very little activity between 32°F/0°C and 50°F/10°C and between 116°F/47°C and 131°F/55°C, and yeast cells are killed between 138°F/59°C and 140°F/60°C.

Bacteria

In addition to yeast, bacteria cells are the other live organisms in doughs. Temperature controls which of the two is the more active at any given time. Warmer temperatures (above 70°F/21°C) give yeast an advantage, while colder temperatures limit yeast activity and give the advantage to bacteria. Bacterial activity produces many flavorful compounds, but also increases acidity, making it more difficult for baker's yeast to thrive.

Both yeast and bacteria are single-celled organisms that need oxygen to reproduce. Whenever you stir or knead the dough, you are incorporating oxygen. When dough rises, it exposes a little more of the dough to oxygen; when you knead, fold, or "punch down" the dough, you introduce more

Effect of Spices on Yeast Activity

Spice	Amount (grams of spice with 2 grams sugar and 1 gram yeast in 30 ml water)	Change in Yeast Activity (ml of gas increase or decrease in 3 hours)
Cardamom	0.1	+85
	0.5	+140
Cinnamon	0.05	+102
	0.1	+103
	0.5	+46
	1.0	-30
Ginger	0.1	+87
	0.75	+172
	1.0	+136
	2.0	+72
Dry mustard	0.25	-120
Nutmeg	0.1	+40
	0.5	+111
Thyme	0.1	+92
	0.5	+157
	1.0	+154

Wilma J. Wright, C. W. Bice, and J. M. Fogelberg. "The Effect of Spices on Yeast Fermentation." *Cereal Chemistry,* Vol. 31 (March 1954), pp. 100–112.

oxygen. Yeast and bacteria use oxygen to process their food (sugars in dough). Without oxygen, they are struggling to survive and cannot reproduce.

Yeast Activity and Spices

In some breads, spices are there not just for taste but to enhance yeast activity. There is an article in *Cereal Chemistry,* "The Effect of Spices on Yeast Fermentation." The old German bakers' tale that a pinch of ginger will make your bread rise better is true—certain spices *do* enhance yeast's activity. Ginger, cardamom, cinnamon, nutmeg, and thyme all improve yeast activity. Dry mustard, like salt, strongly inhibits yeast growth. The table on page 479 shows the effects of some of these spices.

Yeast and Baking Powder

There are many outstanding breads made with both yeast and baking powder. Marion Cunningham's wonderful waffles from her book *The Breakfast Book* stand overnight with yeast, then, the next day, you add baking soda and eggs. They are crisp on the outside and unbelievably light.

Angel biscuits and many hot roll recipes use both yeast and baking powder. In *CookWise,* I have a great hot roll recipe using both yeast and baking powder, and Marion Cunningham's waffle recipe.

VITAMIN C—ASCORBIC ACID

When you bake bread, the vitamin C (ascorbic acid) is destroyed. So vitamin C is not added to a bread dough for nutritional value or as a direct contributor to flavor. To quote Calvel, ascorbic acid "increases the forming and handling tolerance of unbaked dough and promotes the production of larger volume loaves since it allows them to be baked at a higher proof level." Vitamin C improves gas retention in sponges. It is recognized as an effective flour improver, and was at one time the only flour additive permitted in Germany and France.

LECITHIN

Lecithin is an outstanding emulsifier, which means it holds fat and moisture together and as such can help slow bread's staling. Doughs with lecithin have a slight increase in absorption. This permits a reduced mixing time, which can enhance flavor. It is also an antioxidant, which also means slowing of dough oxidation and bleaching, thus preserving precious flavor components. Calvel suggests usage levels of 0.1% to 0.15% on a flour-weight basis.

But, at levels of 0.25%, lecithin also can contribute to a more tender crust and a smoother, more even texture—some things that you may not want—so keeping the amount low is a good idea. According to D. E. Pratt, the optimum level is 0.25%, and that gives an increase in mixing and fermentation tolerance.

WATER

Water or a water-type liquid is vital for gluten formation. Chlorinated water can be a problem for sourdough starters. Distilled water is not a good idea either, because you need some minerals to enhance yeast growth; but if the water is too hard that can be a problem, too. Professor Calvel does warn against high calcium carbonate levels from deep wells. I have had good luck with bottled water labeled as spring water.

SALT

Salt is an amazing complex flavor enhancer. Salt suppresses bitterness so that other flavors can come out (see page 407).

Salt plays another major role in bread doughs. Salt strengthens and tightens gluten. If you knead a dough without salt, when you add the salt you can literally see the dough tighten. If you stretch the dough before and after the addition of salt, you will feel an amazing difference in the strength of the gluten.

I was in a frozen pizza manufacturing plant when they added the salt to the dough. Manufacturers do not add the salt until right at the end of kneading, in order to reduce strain on their machines. The big machine kneading the pizza dough was humming along and then the salt hit the dough. It was as if the machine gasped. And then it labored under great strain. The machine *struggled* under the strain. Finally, the kneading time was up. I felt relieved for the machine.

Salt also enhances the shelf life of bread.

Time of Addition of Salt

Some bakers like to knead the dough first, then work in the salt. The reasoning is that the dough is easier to knead, and requires less work from the mixer and a shorter kneading time without the salt. Then the salt can be mixed in to strengthen the dough just before it rises.

Some bakers worry that the salt may not be well distributed throughout the dough when added at the end. You may want to try it and see which method you prefer.

Different Forms of Salt

The type of salt can make a major difference in how well it blends in. Flakey sea salt and Diamond Crystal kosher salt blend faster and better than granular table salt. Most table salts are dense cubes, made by vacuum pan evaporation and referred to as "granular." Sea salt and salt made by Akzo Nobel's Alberger process (Diamond Crystal kosher salt) are formed from surface evaporation. A four-sided crystal forms, then grows on the sides only. This sinks, and another layer continues to grow on all four sides. A hollow, upside-down, four-sided, flakey pyramid is the resulting shape. With sea salt evaporation, wind usually sprays more water into the hollow space so the center may fill. With salt made by the Alberger process, you can actually see some fragile hollow, flakey pyramids with the aid of a magnifying glass.

Thomas Dommer, former Director of Technical Services, Akzo Nobel Salt, Inc., describes the difference between granular salt and this delicate hollow, flakey pyramid form as the difference between an ice cube and a snowflake. There truly is a dramatic difference. About 90% of granular salt dropped onto an inclined surface bounces off, while 95% of the flakey pyramid form sticks to the surface. The delicate flakey pyramid form also dissolves in half the time that granular does.

Two other types of salt are "compressed granular"—that is, granular salt pressed into flakes by rollers, like Morton's kosher—and a salt crystallized with a trace amount of prussiate of soda producing an open porous form called "dendritic," which is only available commercially.

Not only do these different forms of salt dissolve, mix, and adhere differently, a given volume, say 1 tablespoon, contains a different weight of salt for each form. To get as much salt as there is in 1 tablespoon of granular salt, one must use 1½ tablespoons of Morton's kosher salt or 2 tablespoons of Diamond Crystal kosher salt.

There also are differences in the composition of sea salt. Other salts, regardless of the manufacturer or form, are very pure sodium chloride with a trace amount of anticaking agent or, in the case of iodized salt, some form of iodate added. In addition to sodium chloride, sea salt may contain trace amounts of magnesium chloride, magnesium sulfate, calcium sulfate, potassium sulfate, magnesium bromide, calcium carbonate, and other minerals. Because of all these different salts, sea salt has a more complex taste with subtle nuances. Some chefs describe it as an almost sweet taste. Different sea salts have different composition reflecting the minerals in the land that drains into them. Mediterranean sea salt can taste different from New Zealand sea salt and from English sea salt. Sea salt is more expensive than granular salt, so beware of unscrupulous individuals or companies that pass off large-crystal, cheap granular salt as sea salt.

I love real sea salt and bring home a suitcase full every time I go to Sicily. One brand from Trapani lists its ingredients as *"mare-sole-vento"*: sea-sun-wind. It has delicate light flakes with marvelous complex flavors. For bread, the additional minerals in sea salt can be helpful in gluten development, too.

DAIRY PRODUCTS

Milk softens the bread crumb. I love milk in a honey whole-wheat bread. It gives the whole wheat a milder, gentler taste.

Land of Milk and Honey Whole Wheat

MAKES ONE 9 X 5 X 3-INCH (23 X 13 X 8-CM) LOAF

This delicious loaf is a bread to be proud of. It is heavenly toasted with really good butter such as Kerrygold or Plugra.

What This Recipe Shows

Allowing the bread flour to stand with liquid for 30 minutes hydrates the flour proteins and gives you good gluten with less kneading.

Gluten-forming bread flour is combined with the whole-wheat flour for a lighter loaf.

Milk contributes minerals providing for good yeast growth. Protein and sugar in the milk make better crust color, add flavor, and help keep the loaf moist.

Vitamin C is included for better gluten development.

Sugars from the milk and honey provide plenty of food to the yeast for better rises.

Honey adds flavor, feeds the yeast, and absorbs moisture from the air for good keeping qualities.

2$\frac{1}{2}$ cups (12 oz/340 g) spooned and leveled bread flour

1$\frac{1}{2}$ cups (355 ml, 12.9 oz/365 g) milk, scalded (see Note)

1$\frac{1}{4}$ cups (5.3 oz/150 g) spooned and leveled whole-wheat flour

Nonstick cooking spray

1 package (2$\frac{1}{4}$ teaspoons/7 g) instant yeast, such as RapidRise or Quick-Rise

$\frac{1}{10}$ of a crushed quarter of a 500-mg vitamin C (ascorbic acid) tablet (about 10 mg)

3 tablespoons (45 ml) honey

1 large egg yolk (0.65 oz/18 g)

1 teaspoon (6 g) fine sea salt

$\frac{1}{4}$ cup (59 ml) ice water

1 tablespoon (15 ml) canola oil, divided

1 large egg (1.75 oz/50 g), beaten

1. In a mixing bowl, stir the bread flour into the milk. With a dough hook, on low speed, mix in the whole-wheat flour for 1 minute. Cover with plastic wrap lightly sprayed with nonstick cooking spray and allow to stand for 30 minutes at 70°F/21°C.

2. Sprinkle the yeast over the dough. Mix on low for a few seconds. Add the vitamin C, honey, and egg yolk. Mix on low for a few seconds. Sprinkle the salt over the dough, add the ice water, and mix on the second speed for 2 minutes. The dough should be soft. Adjust with bread flour or water as needed.

3. Place the dough in an oiled bowl, turn to coat, and cover with plastic wrap sprayed with nonstick cooking spray. Let stand for 30 minutes.

4. With a paper towel, lightly oil an area on a clean countertop. Dump out the dough onto this area so that the smooth top of the dough is now on the bottom. Allow it to spread out as much as it will. Pick up the dough on the left side, lift up about one-third of the dough, and gently fold it across to the right, trapping some air as you make the fold. Allow it to spread a few seconds, then lift up about one-third of the right side of the dough and bring it across to the left. Again, allow the dough a few seconds to spread. Pick up the bottom edge of the dough and bring about one-third of it up and across to the top. After it settles, pick up the top edge, lift about one-third of it up, and bring it across toward you.

5. Place the dough back in the bowl, turning it over so that the smooth top is back on top. Cover with plastic wrap lightly sprayed with nonstick cooking spray and allow to rise until more than double, about 1 hour.

6. After the last rise, lift the dough out and place on the oiled counter, smooth top up. With both hands in a cupping motion, tuck the sides under, creating a smooth top. By tucking the dough into a tight smooth round you create a covering to better hold gases. With both hands, grab the sides of the round and stretch it sideways into an oval. Let it spring back slightly, and then pull it out again. Cover with plastic wrap sprayed with nonstick spray and allow to stand 15 minutes.

7. Cup the dough with both hands, fingers spread out behind the loaf on either side and thumbs in front of the loaf. Press your thumbs into the dough and down against the table. This pulls or tucks in part of the bottom half of the dough. At the same time, pull the top of the dough tight and forward with your fingers. Now move your thumbs down slightly and press down and in again to knead and tuck again. Repeat this motion two or three times until the loaf is stretched taut and well tucked in. Pinch the bottom seam tightly together. The ends go down to a slight taper. Tuck them tightly under, then pinch the ends and bottom seam together.

8. Spray a 9 x 5 x 3-inch (23 x 13 x 8-cm) loaf pan with nonstick cooking spray and place the loaf in it. Brush the loaf with the beaten egg. Cover with plastic wrap lightly sprayed with nonstick cooking spray and allow to rise until more than doubled, about 1 hour.

9. When the loaf has been rising about 20 minutes, arrange a shelf in the lower third of the oven, place a baking stone on it, and preheat the oven to 375°F/191°C.

10. Place a few clean small rocks (about 1 to 2 inches/2.5 to 5 cm each) in a metal pan with 2-inch (5-cm) sides and place the pan on the floor of the oven. You are going to pour about 1 cup (237 ml) of boiling water over the rocks just before you place the dough in the oven. The moisture will condense on the relatively cool dough and keep it a little moister, allowing the dough to rise well before it crusts. Place about 1¼ cups (296 ml) of water in a saucepan and bring to a low boil.

11. With oven mitts on, *very carefully* pour the boiling water into the pan with the stones. Keep your head and arms out of the way of the great billow of steam that comes up. Close the door immediately.

12. Brush the loaf again with beaten egg and place on the hot stone. Bake until well browned, 45 to 55 minutes. The loaf should sound hollow when thumped on the bottom. You can also check for doneness by inserting an instant-read thermometer in the bottom center of the loaf and pushing it to the center. The loaf is done when the center is over 200°F/93°C. Place the loaf on a rack to cool.

> NOTE: To scald milk, rinse a heavy nonstick pan with cold water. Pour in the milk and, over medium heat with regular stirring, bring milk almost to a simmer (about 185°F/85°C). Remove it from the heat and allow to cool.

SUGAR

Simple sugars feed yeast, but sugar can be bad news for gluten. If there is sugar around, glutenin combines with sugar, gliadin combines with sugar, and you don't get much gluten formed. Yeast doughs suffer major volume loss if the dough contains more than 1 tablespoon (0.4 oz/11 g) of sugar per cup (4.5 oz/127 g) of flour.

If you think about it, there are not many sweet yeast doughs out there. There are breads with sweet fillings, but not a lot of sugar in the dough itself. Breads that do contain sugar may have special techniques to enable them to handle a little more sugar. Some Portuguese sweet breads are kneaded for a long time to make a reasonable loaf with that amount of sugar.

FAT: RICH DOUGHS

A small amount of fat, especially fat that is solid at room temperature, slightly improves bread volume. The big problem with adding fat is that the fat can coat flour proteins and prevent their being able to combine with water, thus preventing gluten formation.

If you add the fat to the flour, you grease the gluten-forming proteins and no gluten is formed. But you can add the dissolved yeast and liquid to the flour first, work the dough to form gluten, and then add the fat.

The two brioche recipes that follow show this clearly. In the Bread-Like Brioche, I add the dissolved yeast to the flour and mix well to develop some gluten, then allow the dough to rise to further develop gluten. I chill the dough and then work in the butter. Because I develop the gluten first, the fat cannot interfere with gluten development and I have a light, airy, but very rich bread.

In the second brioche, the Cake-Like Brioche, I mix the butter into the flour well and then I add the dissolved yeast and liquid. Very little gluten is formed, and the brioche is tender and buttery like a cake.

The Ultimate Brioche I:
Light, Airy, Bread-Like Brioche

MAKES TWO 4½ x 8½-INCH (11 X 22-CM) LOAVES

I have this recipe in *CookWise,* but so many people love this bread that I consider it a classic and I had to include it here too. This is a golden, incredibly buttery bread with a deep brown crust. I considered it a great compliment when a noted professor from Paris and an expert on fine food loved this bread so much that when we met three years later he offered to help me if I would bake another loaf. English food expert Alan Davidson also loved this bread. He said he had a delightful dinner of several slices of this brioche. Try it with a little Cherry-Chambord Butter (page 154).

What This Recipe Shows

Mixing and kneading liquid and flour produces elastic sheets of gluten that remain intact when butter is added later, producing a light, well-leavened loaf.

Chilling a very rich dough before punching down makes it possible to work with the dough without losing the butter.

---

1 cup (237 ml) warm water (110°F/43°C)
1 teaspoon (4 g) and ¼ cup (1.8 oz/51 g)
    sugar, divided
1 tablespoon (1⅓ packages, 0.3 oz/9 g) active
    dry yeast
3 large egg whites (3 oz/85 g)
4 cups (19.2 oz/544 g) bread flour, divided

¼ cup (59 ml) crushed ice
5 large egg yolks (3.25 oz/92 g)
1¾ teaspoons (10.5 g) salt
Water as needed
2 cups (16 oz/454 g) butter, softened
Nonstick cooking spray
1 large egg (1.75 oz/50 g), beaten, for glaze

1. Stir together the warm water, 1 teaspoon (4 g) of the sugar, and the yeast in the bowl of a heavy-duty mixer. Let stand 2 minutes until gray foam appears, indicating yeast is alive and well. Add the egg whites and 2 cups (9.6 oz/272 g) of the flour. Beat with the paddle attachment for 2 minutes to incorporate air. Let stand for 30 minutes to 2½ hours for improved flavor and texture.

2. Add the crushed ice, egg yolks, the remaining ¼ cup (1.8 oz/51 g) sugar, the remaining 2 cups (9.6 oz/272 g) flour, and the salt. Remove the paddle, insert the dough hook, and knead for 3 minutes on medium to medium-high speed until you have a very elastic, sticky dough. The dough should be wet enough to stick to the bowl. Add more water if necessary and mix in well.

3. Let the dough rise for 10 minutes, then mix in the softened butter on low speed. Scrape down the sides and incorporate as much butter as possible. Mix again on low. There is so much butter that the dough will be a stringy mess.

4. Cover and let the dough rise at room temperature for 30 minutes, then refrigerate for 1 hour. (The dough must be cold before you punch it down.) Punch down the dough. The dough can be refrigerated overnight at this point if desired. When ready to shape, divide the dough in half and with both hands gently cup and tuck each piece into a smooth round. Cover with plastic wrap and leave on the counter for 10 minutes.

5. Spray two $4\frac{1}{2}$ x $8\frac{1}{2}$ x $2\frac{1}{2}$-inch (11 x 22 x 6.4-cm) loaf pans with nonstick cooking spray. Divide each dough half into 8 pieces and shape into cylinders $3\frac{1}{2}$ to 4 inches (9 to 10 cm) long, about the width of the pan. Arrange 8 cylinders in a row down each pan, pressing one against the other. Repeat with the other pan. Brush the dough with some of the beaten egg (try not to get egg on the pan) and let bread rise in a warm room until slightly above the pan. This will take about 2 hours, depending on how cold the dough was.

6. About 30 minutes before the dough is fully risen, place a baking stone on the lowest oven shelf and preheat the oven to 450°F/232°C. About 5 minutes before the bread is fully risen, turn the oven down to 375°F/191°C.

7. Place a few clean small rocks (about 1 to 2 inches/2.5 to 5 cm each) in a pan with 2-inch (5-cm) sides and place the pan on the floor of the oven. You are going to pour about 1 cup (237 ml) of boiling water over the rocks before you put the bread in the oven. You want a good steam-filled oven for the bread to go in. This steam will condense on the dough to keep it moist and allow a good oven rise. Place about $1\frac{1}{4}$ cups (296 ml) of water in a saucepan and bring to a low boil. When the bread has risen, turn the heat up under the water and bring to a boil. *Very carefully,* with oven mitts on, making sure your arms and face are out of the way of the steam that will burst up, pour the boiling water into the pan of hot rocks. Close the oven door to allow it to fill with steam.

8. Brush the loaves again with the remaining beaten egg and place the pans directly on the hot stone. Bake until very brown, about 50 minutes total baking time. The loaves get a deep brown because of their egg and sugar content. Remove a loaf from the pan and check for doneness by inserting an instant-read thermometer in the bottom center of the loaf to the estimated middle. The loaf is done when the center is about 200°F/93°C. Let the loaves cool in the pans for 5 minutes, then turn out on a rack to finish cooling.

The Ultimate Brioche II:
Buttery, Cake-Like Brioche

MAKES TWO 4½ X 8½-INCH (11 X 22-CM) LOAVES

This loaf is so moist and tender that it almost dissolves in your mouth. The knife falls through it when you slice. The taste is extra buttery.

What This Recipe Shows

Mixing butter directly with the flour coats the gluten-forming proteins and very little gluten is formed. The dough is like a batter and the bread is very tender.

This dough absorbs much less water than the bread-like brioche, since little gluten is being formed.

Chilling a very rich dough before punching down makes it possible to work with the dough without losing the butter.

This dough rises poorly during both rises, but amazingly well in the oven because steam is formed from the water that is not tied up in gluten.

This dough is shaped immediately after punching down (there is a minimum of gluten to relax) and the dough must be very cold to handle and shape.

¾ cup (177 ml) warm water (110°F/43°C)
1 teaspoon (4 g) and ¼ cup (1.8 oz/51 g)
     sugar, divided
1 tablespoon (1⅓ packages/9 g) active dry
     yeast
4 cups (19.2 oz/272 g) spooned and leveled
     bread flour

2 cups (16 oz/454 g) butter, softened
5 large egg yolks (3.25 oz/92 g)
3 large egg whites (3 oz/85 g)
1¾ teaspoons (10.5 g) salt
Water as needed
Nonstick cooking spray
1 large egg (1.75 oz/50 g), beaten, for glaze

1. Stir together the water, 1 teaspoon (4 g) of the sugar, and the yeast in a small bowl. Let stand 2 minutes until gray foam appears, indicating yeast is alive and well.

2. Place the remaining ¼ cup (1.8 oz/51 g) sugar, the flour, and butter in the bowl of a heavy-duty mixer. Mix with the paddle attachment until the butter and flour are completely blended. Add the egg yolks and mix for 30 seconds. Add the egg whites, salt, and dissolved yeast, and mix just to combine. The dough should not form a ball but should be a wet and sticky batter. Add a little water if necessary.

3. Cover with plastic wrap and let the dough rise at room temperature for 30 minutes, then refrigerate for 1 hour. The dough can be refrigerated overnight, if desired. The dough must be cold before you punch it down.

4. Spray two 4½ x 8½ x 2½-inch (11 x 22 x 6.4-cm) loaf pans with nonstick cooking spray. Punch down, divide in half, divide each half into 8 pieces, and shape each into a cylinder 3½ to 4 inches (9 to 10 cm) long, about the width of the pan. Arrange 8 cylinders in a row down each pan, pressing one against the other. Repeat with the other pan. Brush the dough with some of the beaten egg (try not to get egg on the pan) and let rise in a warm room until slightly above the pan. This will take about 2 hours, depending on how cold the dough was.

5. About 30 minutes before the dough is fully risen, place a baking stone on the lowest shelf of the oven and preheat the oven to 450°F/232°C. About 5 minutes before the bread is fully risen, turn the oven down to 375°F/191°C.

6. Place a few clean small rocks (about 1 to 2 inches/2.5 to 5 cm each) in a pan with 2-inch (5-cm) sides and place the pan on the floor of the oven. You are going to pour about 1 cup (237 ml) of boiling water over the rocks before you put the bread in the oven. You want a good steam-filled oven for the bread to go in. This steam will condense on the dough to keep it moist and allow a good oven rise. Place about 1¼ cups (296 ml) of water in a saucepan and bring to a low boil. When the bread has risen, turn the heat up under the water and bring to a boil. *Very carefully,* with oven mitts on, making sure your arms and face are out of the way of the steam that will burst up, pour the boiling water into the pan of hot rocks. Close the oven door to allow it to fill with steam.

7. Brush the loaves again with the remaining beaten egg and place the pans directly on the hot stone. Bake until very brown, about 50 minutes total baking time. The loaves get a deep brown because of their egg and sugar content. Remove a loaf from the pan and check for doneness by inserting an instant-read thermometer in the bottom center of the loaf to the estimated middle. The loaf is done when the center is about 200°F/93°C. Let the loaves cool in the pan for 5 minutes, then turn out on a rack to finish cooling.

Layered Doughs

Just as thin layers of fat between thin layers of dough create magnificent flakey puff pastry, thin layers of fat between yeast-leavened doughs create wonderful layered flakey breads such as croissants and leavened pastries such as Danish pastry. Think back to what creates flakiness in pastry: a flat piece of cold fat acts as a spacer in the hot oven long enough for the dough on top and dough underneath it to get partially done. Then, when the dough is hot enough to produce steam, the fat melts and the steam puffs the dough apart where the fat was.

Cold

For flakey pastry, you need large, flat, cold pieces of fat that will hold up long enough in the hot oven to act as a spacer. If the fat gets warm and melts into the dough, there goes your spacer and there goes your flake.

This means that you can't let this yeast dough with layers of cold fat get too warm or the fat will soak into the dough and you can lose your flakiness. I know that sometimes restaurant chefs get away with warmer rises, but I prefer no warmer than 70°F/21°C. This may require two to three hours to get a good rise.

Flakey, Buttery Croissants

MAKES 14 CROISSANTS AND 4 BABY CROISSANTS

I have tried a number of croissant recipes and a lot of different ratios of flour and fat, and I like Sherry Yard's croissants the best. I use less butter in the dough than she does, but I have my brush-it-with-ice-water technique (page 357) to keep the dough soft and very easy to roll so I do not need it as tender. The techniques that I use may not ordinarily be applied to croissants, but they make a wonderfully soft dough that is easy to roll and produces well-risen croissants. They are so flakey and buttery, I just love them.

I like to bake the croissants one pan at a time. Usually there is no trouble with the last pan over-rising with cool temperature rises.

What This Recipe Shows

Allowing the flour and liquid to stand for 30 minutes (autolysis) fully hydrates the flour and enhances the extensibility of the dough.

Using a lightly oiled counter instead of a floured counter avoids excess flour in the dough.

I keep the dough very soft and easy to roll by brushing it with ice water when folding if it is starting to get firm.

Keeping the dough cold at all times and keeping the rising temperature at about 70°F/21°C prevents the butter from melting and preserves maximum flakiness.

Using milk instead of water in the dough gives a little more color to make beautifully browned croissants.

The little bit of malted barley flour in either King Arthur Unbleached All-Purpose or Gold Medal Harvest King Unbleached flour contains live enzymes to provide food for the yeast during the many folding and cooling periods.

Dough

3 cups (13.5 oz/383 g) spooned and leveled King Arthur Unbleached All-Purpose or Gold Medal Harvest King Unbleached flour, divided

1 cup (8.6 oz/244 g) milk

1 package (2¼ teaspoons/7g) instant yeast, such as RapidRise or Quick-Rise

2 tablespoons (0.9 oz/25 g) sugar

2¼ teaspoons (13.5 g) fine sea salt

2 tablespoons (30 ml) water

4 tablespoons (2 oz/57 g) unsalted butter, cut in 1-tablespoon (0.5-oz/14-g) pieces

Nonstick cooking spray

1 large egg (1.75 oz/50 g)

1 tablespoon (15 ml) canola oil

Ice water, as needed

1 large egg yolk (0.65 oz/18 g)

Butter Block

3 sticks (12 oz/340 g) unsalted butter

¼ cup (1.1 oz/32 g) spooned and leveled King Arthur Unbleached All-Purpose or Gold Medal Harvest King Unbleached flour

1. For the dough: In a mixing bowl, stir 2½ cups (11.2 oz/319 g) of the flour into the milk just to mix well. Cover with plastic wrap and allow to stand for 30 minutes.

2. Remove the plastic and sprinkle the yeast over the dough. Insert the dough hook in the mixer and run 30 seconds on low to blend the yeast in. Stir the sugar and salt into the water. Sprinkle over the dough and mix a few seconds to blend. Add the butter. Mix a few seconds to distribute.

3. The dough is probably sticky and wet. You want to add flour from the remaining ½ cup (2.3 oz/64 g) until the dough is together and is no longer sticky. Add ¼ cup (1.1 oz/32 g) flour or less at a time and mix several seconds to incorporate. You may need to add all of the flour. Knead the dough for 2 minutes. It should be very soft but not sticky. If needed, adjust with a little more flour or water and knead for about 30 seconds longer. Cover with plastic wrap and refrigerate for at least 4 hours or overnight.

4. For the butter block: Cut each stick of butter lengthwise into four long sticks.

5. On a clean counter, sprinkle some flour over the butter sticks. Roll each stick to coat on all sides with flour. Flour a rolling pin and roll over the butter to soften. With your hands and the rolling pin as needed, work the butter and flour into a 6-inch (15-cm) square about 1 inch (2.5 cm) thick. Wrap with plastic wrap. Leave out on the counter.

6. With a lightly oiled paper towel, wipe a clean counter to have a very lightly oiled surface. Place the cold dough on the counter and press it out into a rough square. Cover with plastic wrap sprayed with nonstick cooking spray and allow to stand for about 5 minutes. Roll the dough into a 12-inch (30-cm) square.

7. Place the butter block on top of the dough like a diamond so that each corner of the butter block is pointed to the middle of a side of the dough. A triangle of dough should extend from each side of the butter block. Pull each of these triangles over the butter to completely wrap it. With your fingers, press the seams together well. Press across the center with a rolling pin. Roll forward. Place the rolling pin back in the center and roll back toward you. Make sure that you do not roll off the edge. Loosen the dough from the counter and rotate it a quarter turn. Wipe the counter with the oiled towel to make sure the dough is not sticking.

8. Roll the dough into a 10 x 18-inch (25 x 46-cm) rectangle with 10-inch (25-cm) side parallel to the edge of the counter. Take care not to roll off the ends. Brush the dough very lightly with ice water. Fold the bottom third up and the top third down over it as if you were folding a letter to put in an envelope. You have completed your first turn. You have three open sides and one fold. You want to press these open sides together well. Take the rolling pin and place across the middle of one of the open sides, and push down to press this side together well. Repeat with the other two open sides. Wrap the dough well with plastic wrap and refrigerate for at least 1 hour.

9. Wipe the counter with your oiled towel and place the dough from the refrigerator on the counter. Place the dough in front of you like a book with one of the shorter sides toward you. Roll the dough

out again into a 10 x 18-inch (25 x 46-cm) rectangle, taking care not to roll off the ends. If the dough is soft and easy to roll, you do not need to brush with ice water. If the dough is firm, hard to roll, and springs back, brush lightly with ice water again. Fold the bottom third up and the top third down over it as if you were folding a letter to put in an envelope. Seal the three open sides again by pressing the rolling pin down across each as you did before. You have completed two turns. Wrap the dough well and place in the refrigerator for 1 hour.

10. Make four more turns just as before in Steps 8 and 9, with 1 hour in the refrigerator between each turn. If the dough is soft and easy to roll, you do not need to brush it with ice water. After you have completed all six turns, refrigerate for 1 hour. The dough is now ready to cut and shape. If you are not using the dough within 24 hours, you should freeze it. To freeze, divide the dough into quarters and roll each quarter out into a rectangle about $\frac{1}{2}$ inch (1.25 cm) thick. Wrap well with plastic wrap, place in a heavy zip-top bag, and freeze. Thaw overnight in the refrigerator when using.

11. Wipe the counter with the oiled paper towel. Place the dough out on the counter and roll with the long side parallel to the edge of the counter into a 20 x 18-inch (50 x 46-cm) rectangle about $\frac{1}{4}$ inch (0.6 cm) thick. If the dough is very elastic, cover it with plastic wrap and allow it to stand for 5 minutes.

12. (Use the drawing described in the Note at the end of this recipe to help with the pattern of cuts to make the dough triangles.) Along the top and bottom of the 20-inch (50-cm) sides, mark a tiny notch every 5 inches (13 cm). With a ruler and a large pizza wheel or sharp knife, cut the dough in half horizontally parallel to the 20-inch (50-cm) sides. Cut from the upper left corner across the dough at an angle down to the first 5-inch (13-cm) bottom notch. Move the ruler over to the first 5-inch (13-cm) notch on the top and cut a line from that notch to the second notch on the bottom. This will be parallel to the line that you just cut. Continue cutting two more lines from the second and third top notches from the left parallel to these first two.

13. Cut a line starting at the top right corner and running down to the first 5-inch (13-cm) notch from the right side on the bottom. Move the ruler to the first 5-inch (13-cm) notch from the right side on the top and cut down to the second 5-inch notch from the right on the bottom. Continue cutting two more lines from the second and third top notches from the right parallel to these two. You now have fourteen big triangles and four small triangles of dough.

14. Cover three baking sheets with Release foil, nonstick side up, or parchment lightly sprayed with nonstick cooking spray. To shape each croissant, cut a $\frac{1}{2}$-inch (1.25-cm) slit in the middle of the short edge of a triangle. Gently pull on the corners to stretch this short edge a little and loosely roll toward the tip. I like to roll loosely to make expansion easier as the croissant rises. Place the croissants on the baking sheet with the tip of the triangle tucked under the croissant and curve each croissant just a little to form a crescent. Continue shaping and placing croissants on baking sheets about 2 inches (5 cm) apart. Cover with plastic wrap lightly sprayed with nonstick cooking spray. Place trays at cool room temperature (about 70°F/ 21°C) to rise. This will take $1\frac{1}{2}$ to 2 hours.

15. After the croissants have risen a little over 1 hour, arrange a shelf in the lower third of the oven, place a baking stone on it, and preheat the oven to 400°F/204°C.

16. Beat together the egg yolk and the egg for the egg wash. Brush each croissant with the egg wash.

17. Bake one sheet at a time. Place the baking sheet on the hot stone and bake for 12 minutes. Turn the oven down to 350°F/177°C and bake for 12 minutes more. Croissants should be well browned.

> NOTE: To get a "picture" of how the dough will be cut, take a piece of plain notebook paper and cut it into a rectangle about 9 x 10 inches (23 x 25 cm) in size. Take the longer dimension and fold it in half and then in half again, making four layers. Crease the folds firmly. Unfold and fold once across the shorter dimension, again creasing firmly before unfolding.
>
> Place before you with the long side from left to right and number the left edge number 1 at the top and bottom. Number the right edge number 5 at top and bottom, and the creases in between numbers 2, 3, and 4, respectively. Now draw a line down the long center crease.
>
> Draw lines diagonally from one numbered edge to the other as follows: from lower 1 to upper 2, from lower 2 to upper 3, from lower 3 to upper 4, and from lower 4 to upper 5. Now draw lines from the upper edge in similar manner (upper 1 to lower 2, and so on).
>
> You will now have marked off fourteen large triangles and four small triangles (at the ends). This is the pattern in which you will cut the dough for the croissants.

Ingredients

The recipes in this book were developed and tested using standard American volume quantities, such as cups, tablespoons, and fluid ounces. Many bakers use weights, and these also have been given for each recipe's list of ingredients.

In this section basic weights (ounces and grams) are listed for a variety of baking ingredients. These values were scaled to obtain the quantities listed in the individual recipes. The metric values have been obtained by scaling the American quantities and do not mean that the baker must measure to three-digit accuracy. Metric users should round off and follow their customary measurement.

Weights for most ingredients listed here are from the USDA National Nutrient Database for Standard Reference (online at www.nal.usda.gov/fnic/foodcomp/search). Weights of flours measured by volume can vary greatly, depending on how a cup is filled—spooned and leveled (used here), dipped, sifted, or packed. The author made multiple measurements for each type of flour and averaged them for the values given here. A few other ingredients that are not in the USDA database were measured by the author, or the values obtained from packages.

Ingredient	How to Measure	Quantity	Ounces	Grams
FLOURS				
All-purpose, bleached	spooned and leveled	1 cup	4.4	125
All-purpose, unbleached	spooned and leveled	1 cup	4.4	125
Almond	spooned and leveled	1 cup	3	86
Bread	spooned and leveled	1 cup	4.8	136
Cake	spooned and leveled	1 cup	4.1	116
Cornmeal, whole-grain yellow	spooned and leveled	1 cup	4.3	122
Harvest King, unbleached	spooned and leveled	1 cup	4.5	127
Instant	poured and leveled	1 cup	4.6	130
Self-rising, White Lily	spooned and leveled	1 cup	4.5	128
Semolina	spooned and leveled	1 cup	5.9	167
Rye, dark	spooned and leveled	1 cup	4.4	125
SUGARS				
Brown, dark	packed	1 cup	8.4	238
Brown, light	packed	1 cup	7.7	218

Ingredient (sugars, cont.)	How to Measure	Quantity	Ounces	Grams
Confectioners'		1 cup	4	120
Granulated, white		1 cup	7	198
EGGS (OUT OF SHELL)				
Whole		1 U.S. large	1.75	50
Whites		1 U.S. large	1	28
Yolks		1 U.S. large	0.65	18
FATS				
Butter, unsalted		1 cup	8	227
Lard		½ cup	3.6	102
Shortening		1 cup	6.7	190
DAIRY PRODUCTS				
Cheese, cream			8	227
Cheese, Parmesan	grated	1 cup	3	85
Cheese, Swiss	grated	1 cup	4	113
Sour cream		1 cup	8.5	241
FRUIT				
Apples		1 cup	3.9	110
Apples, dried		1 cup	3	86
Blueberries		1 cup	4.9	140
Dates, chopped		1 cup	5.2	147
Raisins		1 cup	5.1	145
LEAVENERS				
Baking powder		1 teaspoon	0.2	5
Baking soda		1 teaspoon	0.2	5
Yeast, active dry or instant		1 package (2¼ teaspoons)	0.25	7
Yeast, active dry or instant		1 tablespoon	0.4	12
NUTS				
Almonds, whole		1 cup	4.8	138
Hazelnuts, whole		1 cup	4.8	138
Macadamia, whole		1 cup	4.7	132
Pecans, halves		1 cup	3.5	99
Pistachios, shelled		1 cup	4.3	123
Walnuts, halves		1 cup	3.5	100

Ingredient	How to Measure	Quantity	Ounces	Grams
SPICES				
Allspice, ground		1 teaspoon		2
Cinnamon, ground		1 teaspoon		2
Cloves, ground		1 teaspoon		2
Ginger, ground		1 teaspoon		2
Mustard, dry powder		1 teaspoon		3
Nutmeg, ground		1 teaspoon		2
Pepper, black		1 teaspoon		2
Pepper, cayenne		1 teaspoon		2
Pepper, white		1 teaspoon		2
Salt		1 teaspoon	0.2	6
STARCHES				
Cornstarch		1 tablespoon	0.25	7
Potato starch		1 tablespoon	0.4	11
Tapioca starch		1 tablespoon	0.3	9
CHOCOLATE				
Cocoa, Dutch process		1 cup	2.9	82
Cocoa, natural		1 cup	2.9	82
Semisweet chips		1 cup	6	170
MISCELLANEOUS				
Carrots	grated	1 cup	3.9	110
Cream of tartar		1 teaspoon	0.1	3
Gelatin		1 envelope ($2\frac{1}{4}$ teaspoons)	0.25	7
Instant coffee powder		1 teaspoon		1
Oats, quick		1 cup	3	85
Peanut butter, crunchy		1 cup	9.1	258
Toffee bits		$1\frac{1}{3}$ cups	8	227

LIQUIDS

Quantity	Milliliters
1 teaspoon	5
1 tablespoon	15
$\frac{1}{4}$ cup	59
$\frac{1}{3}$ cup	79
$\frac{1}{2}$ cup	118
$\frac{2}{3}$ cup	156
$\frac{3}{4}$ cup	177
1 cup	237

References and Bibliography

Following are some of the most frequently used specific sources for information in *BakeWise*. The General section lists books that were valuable as background for many parts of the book.

Each chapter has a list of books and articles that pertain specifically to the topics covered in that chapter. Food-related technical and specialized books are listed first, followed by articles in similar areas from technical journals and other sources. The same source is listed in more than one chapter if material from that source was used in several chapters.

GENERAL

Belitz, Hans-Dieter, and Werner Grosch. *Food Chemistry,* trans. D. Hadziyev from second German ed. Berlin: Springer-Verlag, 1986.

Charley, Helen. *Food Science,* 1st ed. New York: The Ronald Press Company, 1971.

———. *Food Science,* 2nd ed. New York: John Wiley & Sons, 1982.

Child, Julia. *The French Chef Cookbook.* New York: Knopf, 1968.

———. *From Julia Child's Kitchen.* New York: Knopf, 1975.

———. *Julia Child & Company.* New York: Knopf, 1978.

———. *Julia Child & More Company.* New York: Knopf, 1979.

———. *The Way to Cook.* New York: Knopf, 1989.

———. *Cooking with Master Chefs.* New York: Knopf, 1993.

Child, Julia, Louisette Bertholle, and Simone Beck. *Mastering the Art of French Cooking, Vol. I.* New York: Knopf, 1961.

Child, Julia, and Simone Beck. *Mastering the Art of French Cooking, Vol. II.* New York: Knopf, 1970.

Coultate, Tom P. *Food: The Chemistry of Its Components,* 2nd ed. London: Royal Society of Chemistry, 1989.

DeMan, John M. *Principles of Food Chemistry,* rev. 3rd printing. Westport, CT: AVI Publishing, 1980.

Dupree, Nathalie. *New Southern Cooking.* New York: Knopf, 1986.

Eskin, N. A. Michael, ed. *Biochemistry of Foods,* 2nd ed. San Diego: Academic Press, 1990.

Fennema, Owen R., ed. *Principles of Food Science, Part I: Food Chemistry.* New York: Marcel Dekker, 1976.

———. *Food Chemistry,* rev. and expanded 2nd ed. New York: Marcel Dekker, 1985.

———. *Food Chemistry,* 3rd ed. New York: Marcel Dekker, 1996.

FitzGibbon, Theodora. *The Food of the Western World: An Encyclopedia of Food from North America and Europe.* New York: Quadrangle/The New York Times Book Co., 1976.

Fulton, Margaret. *Encyclopedia of Food and Cookery.* New York: W. H. Smith Publishers, 1986.

Gisslen, Wayne. *Professional Baking,* 4th ed. Hoboken, NJ: John Wiley & Sons, 2005.

Herbst, Sharon Tyler, and Ron Herbst. *The New Food Lover's Companion: More Than 6,700 A-to-Z Entries,* 4th ed. Hauppauge, NY: Barron's Educational Services, 2007.

Hughes, Osee, and Marion Bennion. *Introductory Foods,* 5th ed. New York: Macmillan, 1970.

Kamman, Madeleine. *The Making of a Cook.* New York: Weathervane Books, 1971.

Koplin, Doris. *The Quick Cook.* Atlanta: Doris Koplin, 2002.

Lang, Jennifer Harvey, ed. *Larousse Gastronomique.* New American Edition. New York: Crown Publishers, 1988.

McGee, Harold. *On Food and Cooking: The Science and Lore of the Kitchen.* New York: Scribner, 1984.

———. *The Curious Cook: More Kitchen Science and Lore.* San Francisco: North Point Press, 1990.

———. *On Food and Cooking: The Science and Lore of the Kitchen,* Completely Revised and Updated. New York: Scribner, 2004.

Mesnier, Roland, with Lauren Chattman. *Dessert University: More Than 300 Spectacular Recipes and Essential Lessons from White House Pastry Chef Roland Mesnier.* New York: Simon & Schuster, 2004.

Meyer, Lillian Hoagland. *Food Chemistry.* Westport, CT: AVI Publishing, 1960.

Montagné, Prosper. *Larousse Gastronomique,* 1st American Edition. (Charlotte Turgeon and Nina Froud, eds.) New York: Crown Publishers, 1961.

Morris, Christopher, ed. *Academic Press Dictionary of Science and Technology.* San Diego: Academic Press, 1992.

Peck, Paula. *The Art of Fine Baking.* New York: Simon & Schuster, 1961.

Penfield, Marjorie P., and Ada Marie Campbell. *Experimental Food Science,* 3rd ed. San Diego: Academic Press, 1990.

Pennington, Jean A. T. *Bowes & Church's Food Values of Portions Commonly Used.* 16th Edition. Philadelphia: J. B. Lippincott, 1994.

Pomeranz, Yeshajahu. *Functional Properties of Food Components.* Orlando, FL: Academic Press, 1985.

Pyler, Ernst John. *Baking Science and Technology.* 2 vols. Chicago: Siebel Publishing, 1952.

———. *Baking Science and Technology, Volume II,* 3rd ed. Merriam, KS: Sosland Publishing, 1988.

Rombauer, Irma S., and Marion Rombauer Becker. *The Joy of Cooking.* Indianapolis: Bobbs-Merrill, 1953.

———. *The Joy of Cooking.* Indianapolis: Bobbs-Merrill, 1975.

Rombauer, Irma S., Marion Rombauer Becker, and Ethan Becker. *Joy of Cooking: 75th Anniversary Edition.* New York: Scribner, 2006.

Smith, Andrew F., ed. in chief. *The Oxford Encyclopedia of Food and Drink in America.* New York: Oxford University Press, 2004.

Sokol, Gail. *About Professional Baking.* Clifton Park, NY: Thomson Delmar Learning, 2006.

Sultan, William J. *Practical Baking,* 5th ed. New York: Van Nostrand Reinhold, 1990.

CHAPTER 1. CAKES, LUSCIOUS CAKES! MUFFINS, QUICK BREADS, AND MORE

Books

Bennion, E. B., and G. S. T. Bamford (A. J. Bent and M. Whieldon, eds.). *The Technology of Cake Making,* 6th ed. London: Blackie Academic and Professional, 1997.

Beranbaum, Rose Levy. *The Cake Bible.* New York: William Morrow, 1988.

Berolzheimer, Ruth, ed. *250 Classic Cake Recipes.* Chicago: Consolidated Book Publishers, 1949.

Braker, Flo. *The Simple Art of Perfect Baking.* New York: William Morrow, 1985.

———. *The Simple Art of Perfect Baking,* updated and revised. San Francisco: Chronicle Books, 2003.

Brody, Lora. *Basic Baking: Everything You Need to Know to Get You Started Plus 101 Luscious Desserts That You Can Make.* New York: William Morrow, 2000.

Brown, Alton. *I'm Just Here for More Food: food x mixing + heat = baking.* New York: Stewart, Tabori & Chang, 2004.

Charley, Helen. *Food Science,* 1st ed. New York: The Ronald Press Company, 1970.

———. *Food Science,* 2nd ed. New York: John Wiley & Sons, 1982.

Corn, Elaine. *Gooey Desserts: The Joy of Decadence.* Rocklin, CA: Prima Publishing, 1993.

Corran, J. W. "Some Observations on a Typical Food Emulsion," in *Emulsion Technology: Theoretical and Applied,* 2nd ed. Brooklyn, NY: Chemical Publishing Company, 1946, pp. 176–192.

The Culinary Institute of America and Darra Goldstein. *Baking Boot Camp: Five Days of Basic Training at The Culinary Institute of America.* Hoboken, NJ: John Wiley & Sons, 2007.

Dannenberg, Linda. *Paris Boulangerie-Patisserie: Recipes from Thirteen Outstanding French Bakeries.* New York: Clarkson Potter, 1994.

Desaulniers, Marcel. *Death by Chocolate: The Last Word on a Consuming Passion.* New York: Rizzoli, 1992.

———. *Death by Chocolate Cakes: An Astonishing Array of Chocolate Enchantments.* New York: HarperCollins, 2000.

Dodge, Jim, with Elaine Ratner. *Baking with Jim Dodge.* New York: Simon & Schuster, 1991.

Dupree, Nathalie. *New Southern Cooking.* New York: Knopf, 1986.

The Editors of Family Circle, *1988 Family Circle Cookbook.* New York: The Family Circle, 1987.

Egerton, John. *Southern Food: At Home, on the Road, in History.* New York: Knopf, 1987.

Floyd County Homemaker Council. *Floyd's Finest Food.* Floyd County Homemakers Council, 1972.

Fowler, Damon Lee. *Damon Lee Fowler's New Southern Baking: Classic Flavors for Today's Cook.* New York: Simon & Schuster, 2005.

Friberg, S. "Emulsion Stability," in *Food Emulsions,* S. Friberg, ed. New York: Marcel Dekker, 1976, pp. 1–37.

González, Elaine. *The Art of Chocolate: Techniques & Recipes for Simply Spectacular Desserts and Confections.* San Francisco: Chronicle Books, 1998.

———. *Chocolate Artistry: Techniques for Molding, Decorating, and Designing with Chocolate.* Chicago: Contemporary Books, 1983.

Grausman, Richard. *At Home with the French Classics.* New York: Workman Publishing, 1988.

Healy, Bruce. *The French Cookie Book: Classic Contemporary Recipes for Easy and Elegant Cookies.* New York: William Morrow, 1994.

Healy, Bruce, and Paul Bugat. *The Art of the Cake.* New York: William Morrow, 1999.

Heatter, Maida. *Maida Heatter's Book of Great Chocolate Desserts.* New York: Knopf, 1984.

———. *Maida Heatter's Cakes.* New York: Cader Books, 1997.

Hocking, Sylvia Adams. *Sylvia's Cakes & Breads: Famous Recipes from a Small Maine Kitchen.* Camden, ME: Down East Books, 1998.

Krog, N., and J. B. Lauridsen. "Food Emulsifiers and Their Association with Water," in *Food Emulsions,* S. Friberg, ed. New York: Marcel Dekker, 1976, pp. 67–139.

Levine, Ellen, ed. *The Good Housekeeping Illustrated Book of Desserts.* New York: Hearst Books, 1991.

Lirio, Jack. *Cooking with Jack Lirio.* New York: William Morrow, 1982.

Malgieri, Nick. *Nick Malgieri's Perfect Pastry.* New York: Macmillan, 1989.

Maher, Barbara. *Ultimate Cake.* New York: Dorling Kindersley, 1996.

McGee, Harold. *The Curious Cook: More Kitchen Science and Lore.* San Francisco: North Point Press, 1990.

Medrich, Alice. *Cocolat: Extraordinary Chocolate Desserts.* New York: Warner Books, 1990.

———. *Chocolate and the Art of Low-Fat Desserts.* New York: Warner Books, 1994.

———. *BitterSweet: Recipes and Tales from a Life in Chocolate.* New York: Artisan, 2003.

———. *Pure Dessert: True Flavors, Inspiring Ingredients, and Simple Recipes.* New York: Artisan, 2007.

Mesnier, Roland, and Lauren Chattman. *Roland Mesnier's Basic to Beautiful Cakes.* New York: Simon & Schuster, 2007.

Minifie, Bernard W. *Chocolate, Cocoa, and Confectionery: Science and Technology,* 2nd ed. Westport, CT: AVI Publishing, 1980.

Paul, Pauline C., and Helen H. Palmer. "Colloidal Systems and Emulsions," in *Food Theory and Applications,* P. C. Paul and H. H. Palmer, eds. New York: John Wiley & Sons, 1972, pp. 77–114.

Peters, Colette. *Colette's Cakes: The Art of Cake Decorating.* Boston: Little, Brown and Company, 1991.

Phillips, Sarah. *Baking 9-1-1: Rescue from Recipe Disasters.* New York: Simon & Schuster, 2003.

Poses, Steven, Anne Clark, and Becky Roller. *The Frog Commissary Cookbook: Hundreds of Unique Recipes and Home Entertaining Ideas from America's Most Innovative Restaurant Group.* Garden City, NY: Doubleday & Co, 1985.

Purdy, Susan G. *Have Your Cake and Eat It, Too.* New York: William Morrow, 1993.

———. *The Family Baker: 150 Never-Let-You-Down Basic Recipes.* New York: Random House, 1999.

———. *Pie in the Sky: Successful Baking at High Altitudes.* New York: William Morrow, 2005.

Rydhag, Lisbeth. "The Effect of Temperature and Time on Emulsion Stability," in *Physical, Chemical and Biological Changes in Food Caused by Thermal Processing,* Tore Høyem and Oskar Kvåle, eds. Proceedings, International Union of Food Science and Technology. London: Applied Science Publishers, 1977, pp. 224–238.

Scharffenberger, John, and Robert Steinberg. *The Essence of Chocolate: Recipes for Baking and Cooking with Fine Chocolate.* New York: Hyperion, 2006.

Scicolone, Michele. *La Dolce Vita.* New York: William Morrow, 1993.

Wolter, Annette, and Christian Teubner. *Best of Baking.* Tuscon, AZ: HP Books, 1980. (First published as *Backvernügen wie noch nie.* Gräfe und Unzer, München, 1978.)

Yard, Sherry. *The Secrets of Baking: Simple Techniques for Sophisticated Desserts.* Boston: Houghton Mifflin, 2003.

Articles

Ash, David J., and John C. Colmey. "The Role of pH in Cake Baking." *Bakers Digest* (February 1973), pp. 36–39, 42, 68.

Bell, A. V., et al. "A Study of the Micro-Baking of Sponges and Cakes Using Cine and Television Microscopy." *J. Food Technology,* Vol. 10, No. 2 (1975), pp. 147–156.

Charley, Helen. "Effects of the Size and Shape of the Baking Pan on the Quality of Shortened Cakes." *J. Home Economics,* Vol. 44, No. 2 (February 1952), pp. 115–118.

Howard, N. B. "The Role of Some Essential Ingredients in the Formation of Layer Cake Structures." *Bakers Digest* (October 1972), pp. 28–30, 32, 34, 36–37, 64.

Howard, N. B., D. H. Hughes, and R. G. K. Strobel. "Function of the Starch Granule in the Formation of Layer Cake Structure." *Cereal Chemistry,* Vol. 45 (July 1968), pp. 329–338.

Jooste, Martha E., and Andrea Overman Mackey. "Cake Structure and Palatability as Affected by Emulsifying Agents and Baking Temperatures." *Food Research,* Vol. 17 (1952), pp. 185–196.

Kissell, L. T., J. R. Donelson, and R. L. Clements. "Functionality in White Layer Cake of Lipids from Untreated and Chlorinated Patent Flours. I. Effects of Free Lipids." *Cereal Chemistry,* Vol. 56, No. 1 (1979), pp. 11–14.

Miller, Byron S., and Henry B. Trimbo. "Gelatinization of Starch and White Layer Cake Quality." *Food Technology* (April 1965), pp. 208–216.

Trimbo, Henry B., and Byron S. Miller. "The Development of Tunnels in Cakes." *Bakers Digest* (August 1973), pp. 24–26, 71.

Wilson, J. T., and D. H. Donelson. "Studies on the Dynamics of Cake-Baking. I. The Role of Water in Formation of Cake Layer Structure." *Cereal Chemistry,* Vol. 40 (September 1963), pp. 466–481.

CHAPTER 2: PUFF, THE MAGIC LEAVENER—STEAM

Books

Beranbaum, Rose Levy. *The Pie and Pastry Bible.* New York: Scribner, 1998.

The Culinary Institute of America and Darra Goldstein. *Baking Boot Camp: Five Days of Basic Training at The Culinary Institute of America.* Hoboken, NJ: John Wiley & Sons, 2007.

Farmer, Fannie Merritt. *The Boston Cooking-School Cook Book,* 6th ed. Boston: Little, Brown and Company, 1936.

Greenspan, Dorie. *Paris Sweets: Great Desserts from the City's Best Pastry Shops.* New York: Broadway Books, 2002.

Healy, Bruce, and Paul Bugat. *Mastering the Art of French Pastry: An Illustrated Course.* Woodbury, NY: Barron's Educational Series, 1984.

Lang, Jennifer Harvey, ed. *Larousse Gastronomique, New American Edition.* New York: Crown Publishers, 1988.

Lenôtre, Gaston, revised and adapted by Philip and Mary Hyman. *Lenôtre's Desserts and Pastries.* Woodbury, NY: Barron's Educational Series, 1977. (First published as *Faites votre pâtisserie comme Lenôtre.* Paris: Flammarion, 1974.)

Medrich, Alice. *Cocolat: Extraordinary Chocolate Desserts.* New York: Warner Books, 1990.

———. *Chocolate and the Art of Low-Fat Desserts.* New York: Warner Books, 1994.

Mesnier, Roland, with Lauren Chattam. *Dessert University: More Than 300 Spectacular Recipes and Essential Lessons from White House Pastry Chef Roland Mesnier.* New York: Simon & Schuster, 2004.

Roux, Albert, and Michel Roux. *New Classic Cuisine.* Woodbury, NY: Barron's Educational Series, 1984.

Stadelman, William J., and Owen J. Cotterill, eds. *Egg Science and Technology,* 3rd ed. Westport, CT: AVI Publishing, 1986.

Wolfert, Paula. *The Cooking of South-West France.* Garden City, NY: The Dial Press/ Doubleday, 1983.

Yard, Sherry. *The Secrets of Baking: Simple Techniques for Sophisticated Desserts.* Boston: Houghton Mifflin, 2003.

Articles

Bailey, M. Irene. "Foaming of Egg White." *Industrial and Engineering Chemistry,* Vol. 27, No. 8 (August 1935), pp. 973–976.

Barmore, Mark A. "The Influence of Chemical and Physical Factors on Egg-White Foams." Colorado Agricultural College, *Colorado [Agricultural] Experiment Station, Technical Bulletin No. 9,* 1934, pp. 3–57.

———. "Baking Angel Food Cake at Any Altitude." Colorado Agricultural College, *Colorado [Agricultural] Experiment Station, Technical Bulletin No. 13,* ca. 1935, pp. 4–15.

Gillis, Jean Neill, and Natalie K. Fitch. "Leakage of Baked Soft-Meringue Topping." *J. Home Economics,* Vol. 48, No. 9 (November 1956), pp. 703–707.

Grosser, Arthur E. "The Culinary Alchemy of Eggs." *The Exploratorium,* Vol. 7, Issue 4 (Winter 1983/1984), pp. 11–14.

Handleman, Avrom R., James F. Conn, and John W. Lyons. "Bubble Mechanics in Thick Cake Foams and Their Effects on Cake Quality." *Cereal Chemistry,* Vol. 38 (May 1961), pp. 294–305.

Hester, E. Elizabeth, and Catherine J. Personius. "Factors Affecting the Beading and Leakage of Soft Meringues." *Food Technology,* Vol. 3 (July 1949), pp. 236–240.

MacDonnell, L. R., et al. "The Functional Properties of the Egg White Proteins." *Food Technology,* Vol. 9 (February 1955), pp. 49–53.

Pyler, E. J. "Basic Factors in the Production of Angel Food Cake." *Bakers Digest,* Vol. 25 (April 1951), pp. 35–37, 39.

Seidman, W. E., O. J. Cotterill, and E. M. Funk. "Factors Affecting Heat Coagulation of Egg White." *Poultry Science,* Vol. 42 (1963), pp. 406–417.

CHAPTER 3: PIE MARCHES ON AND ON

Books

Amendola, Joseph. *The Bakers' Manual for Quantity Baking and Pastry Making,* rev. 3rd ed. Rochelle Park, NJ: Hayden Book Company, 1972.

Beranbaum, Rose Levy. *The Pie and Pastry Bible.* New York: Scribner, 1998.

Berl, Christine. *The Classic Art of Viennese Pastry.* New York: John Wiley & Sons, 1998.

Bilheux, Roland, and Alain Escoffier. *Professional French Pastry Series. Vol. I: Doughs, Batters, and Meringues.* (Translated by Rhona Poritsky-Lauvand and James Peteson.) New York: Van Nostrand Reinhold, 1988.

Cherkasky, Lisa, and Renée Comet. *The Artful Pie: Unforgettable Recipes for Creative Cooks.* Shelbourne, VT: Chapters Publishing, 1993.

Child, Julia, and Simone Beck. *Mastering the Art of French Cooking, Vol. II.* New York: Knopf, 1970.

Dodge, Jim, with Elaine Ratner. *Baking with Jim Dodge: Simple and Tempting Delights from the American Baker.* New York: Simon & Schuster, 1991.

Fletcher, Helen S. *The New Pastry Cook.* New York: William Morrow, 1986.

Goode, John, and Carol Willson. *Fruit and Vegetables of the World.* Melbourne: Lothian Publishing Company, 1987.

Healy, Bruce, and Paul Bugat. *Mastering the Art of French Pastry: An Illustrated Course.* Woodbury, NY: Barron's Educational Series, 1984.

Hermé, Pierre, and Dorie Greenspan. *Chocolate Desserts by Pierre Hermé.* Boston: Little, Brown and Company, 2001.

Le Draoulec, Pascale. *American Pie: Slices of Life (and Pie) from America's Back Roads.* New York: HarperCollins, 2002.

Malgieri, Nick. *Nick Malgieri's Perfect Pastry.* New York: Macmillan, 1989.

McNair, James. *James McNair's Pie Cookbook.* New York: Chronicle, 1992.

Mesnier, Roland, with Christian Malard (Louise Rogers Lalaurie, trans.). *All the Presidents' Pastries: Twenty-Five Years in the White House: A Memoir.* Paris: Flammarion, 2007.

Patent, Greg. *A Baker's Odyssey: Celebrating Time-honored Recipes from America's Rich Immigrant Heritage.* Hoboken, NJ: John Wiley & Sons, 2007.

Rankin, Jane Lee. *Cookin' Up A Storm: The Life and Recipes of Annie Johnson.* Louisville, KY: Grace Publishers, 2003.

Robbins, Maria Polushkin, ed. *Blue-Ribbon Pies.* New York: St. Martin's Press, 1987.

Roux, Michel, and Albert Roux. *The Roux Brothers on Patisserie.* London: Little, Brown and Company, 1986.

Rubin, Maury. *Book of Tarts: Form, Function, and Flavor at the City Bakery.* New York: Morrow, 1995.

Schneider, Elizabeth. *Uncommon Fruits and Vegetables: A Commonsense Guide.* New York: Harper & Row, 1986.

Shewfelt, Robert L. "Flavor and Color of Fruits as Affected by Processing," in *Commercial Fruit Processing,* 2nd ed., J. G. Woodroof and B. S. Luh, eds. Westport, CT: AVI Publishing, 1986.

———. "Food Crops: Postharvest Deterioration," in *Encyclopedia of Food Science and Technology,* 4 vols., Y. H. Hui, editor in chief, pp. 1019–1023. New York: John Wiley & Sons, 1992.

Strause, Monroe Boston. *Pie Marches On,* 2nd ed. New York: Ahrens Publishing Company, 1951.

Walter, Carole. *Great Pies & Tarts: Over 150 Recipes to Bake, Share, and Enjoy.* New York: Clarkson Potter, 1998.

Wills, R. B. H., et al. *Postharvest: An Introduction to the Physiology and Handling of Fruit and Vegetables,* 3rd ed. New York: Van Nostrand Reinhold, 1989.

Zipes, Bruce. *Bruce's Bakery Cookbook: Recipes from the Famed New York Eatery.* New York: Clarkson Potter, 2000.

Articles

Campbell, Ada Marie, and Alice M. Briant. "Wheat Starch Pastes and Gels Containing Citric Acid and Sucrose." *Food Research,* Vol. 22 (1957), pp. 358–366.

Leach, Harry W., and Thomas J. Schoch. "Structure of the Starch Granule: II. Action of Various Amylases on Granular Starches." *Cereal Chemistry,* Vol. 38 (January 1961), pp. 34–46.

Murthy, G. K. "Thermal Inactivation of Alpha-Amylase in Various Liquid Egg Products." *J. Food Science,* Vol. 35, No. 4 (July/August 1970), pp. 352–356.

Nielson, Hester J., Jean D. Hewitt, and Natalie K. Fitch. "Factors Influencing Consistency of a Lemon-Pie Filling." *J. Home Economics,* Vol. 44, No. 10 (December 1952), pp. 782–785.

Steingarten, Jeffrey. "Ripe Now [fruits]." *Vogue* (August 1992), pp. 164, 166, 168, 196.

Wang, Anne C., Kaye Funk, and Mary E. Zabik. "Effect of Sucrose on the Quality Characteristics of Baked Custards." *Poultry Science,* Vol. 53, No. 2 (March 1974), pp. 807–813.

CHAPTER 4: AS THE COOKIE CRUMBLES

Books

Beranbaum, Rose Levy. *Rose's Christmas Cookies.* Morrow, 1990.

Betty Crocker Editors. *Betty Crocker's Cooky Book.* Hoboken, NJ: John Wiley & Sons, 2002.

Casella, Dolores. *A World of Baking.* New York: D. White, 1968.

Desaulniers, Marcel. *Death by Chocolate Cookies.* New York: Simon & Schuster, 1997.

Farmer, Fannie Merritt. *The Boston Cooking-School Cook Book.* Boston: Little, Brown and Company, 1906.

Gillespie, Gregg R. *1001 Cookie Recipes.* New York: Black Dog & Leventhal Publishers, 1995.

Healy, Bruce, with Paul Bugat. *The French Cookie Book: Classic and Contemporary Recipes for Easy and Elegant Cookies.* New York: William Morrow, 1994.

Heatter, Maida. *Maida Heatter's Book of Great Cookies.* New York: Knopf, 1977.

———. *Maida Heatter's Book of Great Desserts.* Kansas City, MO: Andrews McMeel Publishing, 1999.

Malgieri, Nick. *Chocolate: From Simple Cookies to Extravagant Showstoppers.* New York: HarperCollins, 1998.

Martha Stewart Living Omnimedia. *Martha Stewart Living Annual Recipes 2005.* Des Moines, IA: Oxmoor House, 2004.

Pendleton, Leslie Glover. *One Dough, Fifty Cookies: Baking Favorite and Festive Cookies in a Snap.* New York: Morrow, 1998.

Purdy, Susan G. *The Family Baker: 150 Never-Let-You-Down Basic Recipes.* New York: Random House, 1999.

Rombauer, Irma S., Marion Rombauer Becker, and Ethan Becker. *Joy of Cooking: 75th Anniversary Edition.* New York: Scribner, 2006.

Scharffenberger, John, and Robert Steinberg. *The Essence of Chocolate: Recipes for Baking and Cooking with Fine Chocolate.* New York: Hyperion, 2006.

Smith, Andrew F., editor in chief. *The Oxford Encyclopedia of Food and Drink in America.* New York: Oxford University Press, 2004.

CHAPTER 5: GREAT BREADS—GREAT FLAVORS

Books

Amendola, Joseph, and Donald E. Lundberg. *Understanding Baking.* Boston: CBI Publishing Company, 1970.

Beranbaum, Rose Levy. *The Bread Bible.* New York: W.W. Norton, 2003.

Bertinet, Richard. *Dough: Simple Contemporary Bread.* London: Kyle Cathie, 2005.

Bilheux, Roland, et al. *Special and Decorative Breads,* trans. Rhona Poritzky-Lauvand and James Peterson. New York: Van Nostrand Reinhold, 1989.

Blanshard, J. M. V., P. J. Frazier, and T. Galliard, eds. *Chemistry and Physics of Baking: Materials, Processes, and Products.* London: Royal Society of Chemistry, 1986.

Buehler, Emily. *Bread Science: The Chemistry and Craft of Making Bread.* Carrboro, NC: Two Blue Books, 2006.

Calvel, Raymond. *The Taste of Bread.* Ronald L. Wirtz, trans., James J. MacGuire, technical ed. Gaithersburg, MD: Aspen Publishers, 2001. (In French, *Le Goût du Pain.* France: Editions Jérôme Villette, 1990.)

Campbell, Ada Marie. "Flour," in *Food Theory and Applications,* P. C. Paul and H. H. Palmer, eds. Chapter 11. New York: John Wiley & Sons, 1972.

———. "Flour Mixtures," in *Food Theory and Applications,* P. C. Paul and H. H. Palmer, eds. New York: John Wiley & Sons, 1972.

Clayton, Bernard, Jr. *The Complete Book of Breads.* New York: Simon & Schuster, 1973.

———. *The Breads of France: And How to Bake Them in Your Own Kitchen.* Indianapolis: Bobbs-Merrill Company, 1978.

Crane, Eva, ed. *Honey: A Comprehensive Survey.* New York: Crane, Russak & Company, 1975.

Cunningham, Marion. *The Breakfast Book.* New York: Knopf, 1988.

David, Elizabeth. *English Bread and Yeast Cookery,* American Edition. New York: Viking Press, 1980.

Editors of Time-Life Books. *Breads: The Good Cook Techniques & Recipes Series.* Alexandria, VA: Time-Life Books, 1981.

Field, Carol. *The Italian Baker.* New York: Harper & Row, 1985.

Figoni, Paula. *How Baking Works: Exploring the Fundamentals of Baking Science.* Hoboken, NJ: John Wiley & Sons, 2004.

Fletcher, Helen S. *The New Pastry Cook.* New York: William Morrow, 1986.

German, Donna Rathmell, and Ed Wood. *Worldwide Sourdoughs from Your Bread Machine.* San Leandro, CA: Bristol Publishing Enterprises, 1994.

Gisslen, Wayne. *Professional Baking,* 4th ed. Hoboken, NJ: John Wiley & Sons, 2005.

Greenstein, George. *Secrets of a Jewish Baker: Authentic Jewish Rye and Other Breads.* Freedom, CA: Crossing Press, 1993.

Guinard, J. Y., and P. Lesjean. *Le Pain Retrouvé: 30 Pains et Leurs Recettes.* Paris: Editions Jacques Lanore, 1982.

Hamelman, Jeffrey. *Bread: A Baker's Book of Techniques and Recipes.* Hoboken, NJ: John Wiley & Sons, 2004.

Helou, Anissa. *Savory Baking from the Mediterranean.* New York: William Morrow, 2007.

Hollywood, Paul. *100 Great Breads.* New York: Barnes & Noble, 2004.

Kamman, Madeleine. *The Making of a Cook.* New York: Weathervane Books, 1971.

Leader, Daniel, with Lauren Chattman. *Local Breads: Sourdough and Whole-Grain Recipes from Europe's Best Artisan Bakers.* New York: W. W. Norton, 2007.

MacRitchie, F. "Baking Quality of Wheat Flours," in *Advances in Food Research,* C. O. Chichester, E. M. Mrak, and B. S. Schweigert, eds., Vol. 29, pp. 201–277. New York: Academic Press, 1984.

McGee, Harold. *On Food and Cooking: The Science and Lore of the Kitchen.* New York: Scribner, 1984.

Ortiz, Joe. *The Village Baker: Classic Regional Breads from Europe and America.* Berkeley, CA: Ten Speed Press, 1993.

Patent, Greg. *A Baker's Odyssey: Celebrating Time-Honored Recipes from America's Rich Immigrant Heritage.* Hoboken, NJ: John Wiley & Sons, 2007.

Pomeranz, Yeshajahu, ed. *Wheat: Chemistry and Technology,* 2nd ed. St. Paul, MN: American Association of Cereal Chemists, 1971.

———. *Wheat: Chemistry and Technology,* 3rd ed., 2 vols. St. Paul, MN: American Association of Cereal Chemists, 1988.

Pomeranz, Yeshajahu, and J. A. Shellenberger. *Bread Science and Technology.* Westport, CT: AVI Publishing, 1971.

Pyler, Ernst John. *Baking Science and Technology.* 2 vols. Chicago: Siebel Publishing, 1952.

Reinhart, Peter. *Brother Juniper's Bread Book: Slow Rise as Method and Metaphor.* Reading, MA: Addison-Wesley, 1991.

———. *Crust & Crumb: Master Formulas for Serious Bread Bakers.* Berkeley, CA: Ten Speed Press, 1998.

———. *Peter Reinhart's Whole Grain Breads: New Techniques, Extraordinary Flavor.* Berkeley, CA: Ten Speed Press, 2007.

Silverton, Nancy, in collaboration with Laurie Ochoa. *Nancy Silverton's Breads from the La Brea Bakery.* New York: Villard Books, 1996.

Sultan, William J. *Practical Baking,* 4th ed. New York: Van Nostrand Reinhold, 1986.

Wechsberg, Joseph. *The Cooking of Vienna's Empire. Time-Life Foods of the World Series.* Alexandria, VA: Time-Life Books, 1974.

Whitley, Andrew. *Bread Matters: The State of Modern Bread and a Definitive Guide to Baking Your Own.* London: Fourth Estate, 2006.

Wood, Ed. *World Sourdoughs from Antiquity,* revised ed. Berkeley, CA: Ten Speed Press, 1996.

Articles

Bruinsma, B. L., and K. F. Finney. "Functional (Bread-Making) Properties of a New Dry Yeast." *Cereal Chemistry,* Vol. 58, No. 5 (1981), pp. 477–480.

Cooper, Elmer J., and Gerald Reed. "Yeast Fermentation: Effects of Temperature, pH, Ethanol, Sugars, Salt, and Osmotic Pressure." *Bakers Digest,* Vol. 42, No. 6 (December 1968), pp. 22–24, 26, 28–29, 63.

Elkassabany, M., and R. C. Hoseney. "Ascorbic Acid as an Oxidant in Wheat Flour Dough. II. Rheological Effects." *Cereal Chemistry,* Vol. 57, No. 2 (1980), pp. 88–91.

Elkassabany, M., R. C. Hoseney, and P. A. Seib. "Ascorbic Acid as an Oxidant in Wheat Flour Dough. I. Conversion to Dehydroascorbic Acid." *Cereal Chemistry,* Vol. 57, No. 2 (1980), pp. 85–87.

MacRitchie, F. "Differences in Baking Quality Between Wheat Flours." *J. Food Technology,* Vol. 13 (1978), pp. 187–194.

Volpe, T., and M. E. Zabik. "A Whey Protein Contributing to Loaf Volume Depression." *Cereal Chemistry,* Vol. 52, (March–April 1975), pp. 188–197.

Wright, Wilma J., C. W. Bice, and J. M. Fogelberg. "The Effect of Spices on Yeast Fermentation." *Cereal Chemistry,* Vol. 31 (March 1954), pp. 100–112.

Sources

Listed below is contact information for equipment and ingredients marked in the text as "see Sources." I have not personally bought from all of these sources and cannot recommend specific ones from personal experience. However, most companies are well known nationally and provide name-brand supplies. You can also find many, if not most, of the equipment and ingredients at national or local cookware shops or grocery suppliers. These sources are listed as reasonable starting points for finding the less-common supplies needed for a few of the recipes in *BakeWise*.

EQUIPMENT

Baking Sheet Liners, Nonstick

Materials for liners include Teflon, Silpat, and Exopat. Hint: Search Google for: "nonstick baking sheet" and for: "nonstick baking liner"

Amazon.com, scroll to Home & Garden, then search for: "nonstick baking sheet" and for: "nonstick baking liner"

Baking Stones

Hint: Search Google for: "baking stone"

Amazon.com, scroll to Home & Garden, then search for: "baking stone"

AWMCO, Inc. (FibraMent-D stones)
11560 West 184th Place
Orland Park, IL 60467
708-478-6032
www.bakingstone.com

The Pampered Chef
One Pampered Chef Lane
Addison, IL 60101
888-687-2433
www.pamperedchef.com
(search for: "rectangle stone")

Sur La Table
800-243-0852
www.surlatable.com
(search for: "baking stone")

Williams-Sonoma
877-812-6235
www.williams-sonoma.com
(search for: "baking stone")

Cake Levelers

Hint: Search Google for: "cake leveler"

Wilton Industries
2240 West 75th Street
Woodridge, IL 60517
800-794-5866
www.wilton.com/store

Agbay Products, Inc. (heavy-duty design)
25 Browning Pond Road
Spencer, MA 01562
508-753-5169
www.agbayproducts.com/products.html

Sweet Celebrations, Inc. (formerly Maid
of Scandinavia)
7009 Washington Avenue S
Edina, MN 55439
800-328-6722
www.esweetc.com/servlet/StoreFront

Cake Strips

Hint: Search Google for: "bake even" OR "magic
cake" OR "magi cake" strips

Sugarcraft, Inc. (Magic Cake strips)
2715 Dixie Highway
Hamilton, OH 45015
513-896-7089
www.sugarcraft.com

Sweet Celebrations, Inc. (formerly Maid
of Scandinavia)
7009 Washington Avenue S
Edina, MN 55439
800-328-6722
www.esweetc.com/servlet/StoreFront
(search for: "magi-cake strips")

Wilton Industries
2240 West 75th Street
Woodridge, IL 60517
800-794-5866
www.wilton.com/store
(search for: "Bake-Even strips")

Cookie Cutters (particularly snowflake cutters)

Hint: Search Google for: "cookie cutter snowflake"

Amazon.com, scroll to Home & Garden, then
search for: "snowflake cookie cutter"

The Cookie Cutter Shop (especially, set of 8
snowflake cutters)
3021 140th Street NW
Marysville, WA 98271
360-652-3295
www.thecookiecuttershop.com/
snowflakecookiecutters.shtml

CopperGifts.com (over 1,000 designs)
900 North 32nd Street
Parsons, KS 67357
866-898-3965
www.coppergifts.com

Digital Scales

Hint: Search Google for: "portable scales"

H & C Weighing Systems (many brands)
9515 Gerwig Lane, Suite 109
Columbia, MD 21046
800-638-8582
www.affordablescales.com

Digital Thermometers (Instant-Read)

Hint: Search Google for: "digital thermometer"

King Arthur Flour—The Baker's Catalogue
58 Billings Farm Road
White River Junction, VT 05055
800-827-6836
800-777-4434 (to request catalogue)
www.kingarthurflour.com

Lame

Hint: Search Google for: "bread lame"

King Arthur Flour—The Baker's Catalogue
58 Billings Farm Road
White River Junction, VT 05055
800-827-6836
800-777-4434 (to request catalogue)
www.kingarthurflour.com
(search for: "lame bread")

Pie Crust Shields

Hint: Search Google for: "pie crust" shield

Amazon.com, scroll to Home & Garden, then
search for: "pie shield"

King Arthur Flour—The Baker's Catalogue
58 Billings Farm Road
White River Junction, VT 05055

800-827-6836
800-777-4434 (to request catalogue)
www.kingarthurflour.com

Kitchen Krafts, Inc.
P. O. Box 442
Waukon, IA 52172
800-298-5389 or 800-776-0575
www.kitchenkrafts.com

The Pampered Chef
One Pampered Chef Lane
Addison, IL 60101
888-687-2433
www.pamperedchef.com

Pie Pans with Perforated Bottoms

Hint: Search Google for: "pie pan," perforated

Amazon.com, scroll to Home & Garden, then search: "pie pan," perforated (sells Chicago Metallic brand)

Cheftools.com
300 S. Cloverdale Street, C35
Seattle, WA 98108
966-716-2433
www.cheftools.com
(search for: "perforated pie pan")

Rolling Pin Rings

(These come in sets of three or four thicknesses.)

Amazon.com search for: "rolling pin ring" (use singular)

King Arthur Flour—The Baker's Catalogue
58 Billings Farm Road
White River Junction, VT 05055
800-827-6836
800-777-4434 (to request catalogue)
Search for: "rolling pin ring" (use singular)

Cooking.com
2850 Ocean Park Blvd., Suite 310
Santa Monica, CA 90405
800-663-8810 (to order)
877-999-2433 (customer service)
www.cooking.com
Search for: "rolling pin ring" (use singular)

INGREDIENTS

Almond Flour

Bob's Red Mill
13521 SE Pheasant Court
Milwaukie, OR 97222
800-349-2173
www.bobsredmill.com/catalog

King Arthur Flour—The Baker's Catalogue
58 Billings Farm Road
White River Junction, VT 05055
800-827-6836
800-777-4434 (to request catalogue)
www.kingarthurflour.com

B-V "The Beefer-Upper"

Major Products Company
66 Industrial Avenue
Little Ferry, NJ 07643
800-222-1296
www.majorproducts.com/bv.htm

Coarse Sugar

Hint: Search Google for: "coarse sugar" OR "crystal sugar"

The Baker's Kitchen
3326 Glanzman Road
Toledo, OH 43614
419-382-2000
www.thebakerskitchen.net

CopperGifts.com
900 North 32nd Street
Parsons, KS 67357
866-898-3965
www.coppergifts.com

Diastatic Malt Powder

Hint: Search Google for: "diastatic malt"

Amazon.com, scroll to Gourmet Food, then search for: "diastatic malt"

King Arthur Flour—The Baker's Catalogue
58 Billings Farm Road
White River Junction, VT 05055
800-827-6836
800-777-4434 (to request catalogue)
www.kingarthurflour.com

Flour, Regular and Specialty

Bob's Red Mill
13521 SE Pheasant Court
Milwaukie, OR 97222
800-349-2173
www.bobsredmill.com/catalog

King Arthur Flour—The Baker's Catalogue
58 Billings Farm Road
White River Junction, VT 05055
800-827-6836
800-777-4434 (to request catalogue)
www.kingarthurflour.com
(Note: Percent protein is listed for most King Arthur flours.)

J. M. Smucker (White Lily)
800-742-6729
(800-258-1928 customer service)
onlinestore.smucker.com
(select Shop by Brand)
You can request a catalogue by mail or download an online version in PDF format.

Meringue Powder

Amazon.com, search for: "meringue powder"

Wilton Industries
2240 West 75th Street
Woodridge, IL 60517
800-794-5866
www.wilton.com/store

Sourdough Starters

Hint: Search Google for: "sourdough starter"

King Arthur Flour—The Baker's Catalogue
58 Billings Farm Road
White River Junction, VT 05055
800-827-6836
800-777-4434 (to request catalogue)
www.kingarthurflour.com

Sourdoughs International
P.O. Box 670
Cascade, ID 83611
208-382-4828
www.sourdo.com
(Note: This is the company of Dr. Ed Wood, author of *Sourdough Breads from Antiquity* and *Classic Sourdoughs*. They offer 14 different cultures.)

Vanilla Flavoring, Clear (all are imitation vanilla)

Watkins Incorporated
150 Liberty Street
P.O. Box 5570
Winona, MN 55987
507-457-3300
www.watkinsonline.com

Wilton Industries
2240 West 75th Street
Woodridge, IL 60517
800-794-5866
www.wilton.com/store

INFORMATION

U. S. Department of Agriculture
Agricultural Research Service
Nutrient Data Laboratory

The USDA National Nutrient Database for Standard Reference is online at:
www.nal.usda.gov/fnic/foodcomp/search
This database contains nutrient information on foods, and also their weights.

Index

Healy, Bruce
chocolate fan-making procedure of, 106
on creaming cake mixing method, 122
on creaming of butter and sugar, 121
flour preferred by, 60, 62, 63
on génoise, 220
lightened French buttercream of, 215
on liquid for pâte à choux, 242
nut meringue recipes of, 177
on overheating chocolate, 92
on pound cake, 13
on temperature of foam for génoise, 222
heatproof glass, precautions with, 5
heavy cream
substituting for milk in cakes, 16–19
whipped. See whipped cream
Hermé, Pierre, puff pastry technique of, 358
Hershey's Special Dark Cocoa, 111
high-altitude baking, 50
cocoa powder and, 110
high-percentage chocolate, 87, 94, 101
high-protein flour, 468
for cookies, browning and, 423
gluten formation in, 372
liquid absorption by, 372
for pâte à choux, 242
for puff pastry, 357
high-ratio cakes, 30–31, 69, 124
Hocking, Sylvia, 13
homogenized cream, whipping, 319
honey, 76
in cookies, 397
Honey Mascarpone Cream, 270–271
hygroscopic nature of, 76, 393, 397, 423
hot-oil crusts, 346
hot syrup, pouring, 187, 209
Hurlbert, Heather, 19
on buttercreams, 209
chocolate sculptures made by, 87–88
hydration of cookie dough, 374–375
hydrogenated starch, 77

I

icings and frostings, 141–150. *See also* toppings
Betty McCool's Coconut Icing, 41
buttercream. *See* buttercream icings
Carrot Cake Cream Cheese Icing, 72
Cherry-Chambord Butter Icing, 145
chocolate, 143–144. *See also* ganache
cream cheese, 144–145
double-icing technique for, 141–142
ganaches. *See* ganache
goal of, 141
Icing for Pound Cake, 18
Luscious, Creamy Chocolate Icing, 143–144
meringue, 145
Pound Cake Icing, 24
Scone Icing, 156
Serious Rum Cake Icing, 29
Simple Cream Cheese Icing, 84
soft chocolate, 142–143
whipped cream, 142
White Chocolate Cream Cheese Icing, 144–145
ingredients, 6–7. *See also specific ingredients*
acidity of, 68
baker's formulas for, 29–31, 32, 33, 34–36, 238
baker's percentages, 32, 34–35, 432
balance of, for cakes, 13–14, 29–31, 33
improvements in, 30
quantity and weight measures of, 495–497
sifting for even distribution of leaveners, 58
sources for, 88, 146, 509–510
instant coffee powder, quantity and weight measures of, 497
instant flour
in cookies, 385
Lard Crust, 349–350
for pastry crust, 343–345
protein content of, 343, 372

quantity and weight measures of, 495
Shirley's Adaptation of Strause's Special Crust for Pumpkin Pie, 298–299
Simple Very Flakey Crust, 302–304
instant-read thermometers to test cakes for doneness, 136
instant yeast, 477, 478
quantity and weight measures of, 496
insulated cookie sheets, 420
isomalt, 77
Italian buttercreams, 209–211, 212–213
Italian Buttercream, 212–213
Italian meringues, 186–188
Italian Meringue (Magnificent Pie Meringue), 187–188
in lightened French buttercream, 215

K

King Arthur flour, 385
all-purpose, 82
protein content of, 377
rye, 460
unbleached all-purpose, 461, 477, 478
kiwi
Turkey Filling, 258
kneading bread, 433, 479–480
knives for slicing cakes into layers, 39
kosher salt
in bread dough, 481
production process for, 481–482
substituting for table salt, 7
Kummer, Corby, 63

L

lactitol, 77
lame, 442
lane cake
Shirley's Not-the-Traditional Lane Cake, 44–45
lard
fat content of, 346
flakiness of pastry crust made with, 346, 349, 350
flavor of, 349